The Gender of Science

The Gender of Science

Janet A. Kourany
University of Notre Dame

Prentice
Hall

Upper Saddle River, New Jersey 07458

Library of Congress Cataloging-in-Publication Data

KOURANY, JANET A.
    The gender of science / JANET A. KOURANY.
        p. cm.
    ISBN 0-13-347972-2
    1. Women in science. 2. Sexism in science. 3. Science—Philosophy. 4. Feminism and
    science. I. Title.
    Q130.K68 2002
    500'.82—dc21   00-140052

VP, Editorial Director: *Charlyce Jones Owen*
Acquisitions Editor: *Ross Miller*
Assistant Editor: *Katie Janssen*
Editorial Assistant: *Carla Worner*
Editorial/Production Supervision: *Joanne Riker*
Prepress and Manufacturing Buyer: *Sherry Lewis*
Director of Marketing: *Beth Gillett Mejia*
Marketing Manager: *Chris Ruel*
Cover Art Director: *Jayne Conte*

This book was set in 10/11 New Baskerville by East End Publishing Services, Inc.
and was printed and bound by RR Donnelly & Sons Company. The cover was
printed by Phoenix Color Corp.

Acknowledgments appear on pages xiii–xvi, which constitute a continuation
of the copyright page.

© 2002 by Pearson Education, Inc.
Upper Saddle River, New Jersey 07458

Printed in the United States of America

10 9 8 7 6 5 4 3 2 1

ISBN 0-13-347972-2

Prentice-Hall International (UK) Limited, *London*
Prentice-Hall of Australia Pty. Limited, *Sydney*
Prentice-Hall Canada Inc., *Toronto*
Prentice-Hall Hispanoamericana, S.A., *Mexico*
Prentice-Hall of India Private Limited, *New Delhi*
Prentice-Hall of Japan, Inc., *Tokyo*
Pearson Education Asia Pte. Ltd., *Singapore*
Editora Prentice-Hall do Brasil, Ltda., *Rio de Janeiro*

To my daughter Sonya

CONTENTS

PART II
What Kind of Enterprise Is Science?   87

PART III
What Kind of Enterprise Ought Science to Be?   303

PREFACE

During the last two decades there has been a near avalanche of work in the area of gender and science—scores of books and collections of essays by historians and philosophers of science as well as scientists themselves, special issues of journals and newsletters, lectures, symposia, conferences, journal articles, bibliographies, and of course media exposés and analyses. But there have been few if any anthologies or textbooks designed specifically to structure courses on gender and science so as to introduce students to the area in a clear and systematic way, though there has been much interest in teaching such courses (to judge from the syllabi and requests for syllabi informally circulating around the country). This anthology is intended to rectify the situation. In it I have included articles that are accessible, eye-opening, and challenging to a wide range of students—students of philosophy, the sciences, gender studies/women's studies, as well as students in interdisciplinary science studies programs such as science, technology, and values. I have organized the articles so as to bring out very clearly the interrelations among them and their relevance to the students. And I have tested in the classroom over a number of years now both the anthology's format and its articles, with great success.

Work on this anthology has been made much easier as a result of the efforts of a number of people. Sue Rosser of the University of South Carolina, Helen Longino of the University of Minnesota, James Maffie of Colorado State University, and especially Alison Wylie of Washington University gave me many useful suggestions and much encouragement. Students in my Gender and Science classes over the years have been unfailingly helpful in pruning out the lemons (both readings and topics) of each new syllabus, and their suggestions for organizing or reorganizing their coursework were always well considered. I owe them a special debt of gratitude both for their generous feedback and for the sheer enjoyment of our interactions. Prentice Hall philosophy editor Ross Miller and production editor

Joanne Riker have been wonderfully resourceful and accommodating on a whole slew of thorny issues, and wonderfully pleasant to work with as well. Notre Dame history and philosophy of science graduate student Elizabeth Hayes did a stellar and truly memorable job trying to extract every last error from the proofs. My partner and fellow philosopher Jim Sterba as usual provided the necessary support, humor, love, and distractions to see the project through. Finally, our daughter Sonya, now a twenty-year-old psychology major, has helped me envision a more hopeful future for science. To her, energetic and absorbed and socially concerned scientist-to-be, I dedicate this book.

J. A. K.

ACKNOWLEDGMENTS

page 8:   "Women in the Origins of Modern Science" by Londa Schiebinger. Reprinted with permission of the publisher from *The Mind Has No Sex* by Londa Schiebinger, pp.10-11, 20-32, 44-47, 66-67, 79-82, 84-101, 260-264. Cambridge, MA: Harvard University Press. Copyright © 1989, by Londa Schiebinger.

page 34:   "Women of Third World Descent in the Sciences" by Sandra Harding. Reprinted with permission of the publisher from *Whose Science? Whose Knowledge* by Sandra Harding, pp 195-202. Ithaca, NY: Cornell University Press. Copyright © 1991 by Cornell University.

page 39:   "Women in Science: Half In Half Out" by Vivian Gornick. Reprinted with permission of the author from *Women in Science* by Vivian Gornick, pp. 69-71, 73-116. New York: Simon & Schuster. Copyright © 1983, 1990 by Vivian Gornick.

page 60:   "'How can a little girl like you teach a great big class of men?' the Chairman Said, and Other Adventures of a Woman in Science" by Naomi Weisstein. Reprinted with permission from *Working It Out*, by Sara Ruddick and Pamela Daniels, eds., pp. 242-250. New York: Pantheon Books. Copyright © 1977 by Sara Ruddick and Pamela Daniels.

page 66:   "The Anomaly of a Woman in Physics" by Evelyn Fox Keller. Reprinted with permission from *Working It Out*, by Sara Ruddick and Pamela Daniels, eds., pp. 78-91. New York: Pantheon Books. Copyright © 1977 by Sara Ruddick and Pamela Daniels.

page 75: "Women Join the Ranks of Science but Remain Invisible at the Top" by Natalie Angier, *The New York Times*, May 21, 1991. Reprinted with permission of *The New York Times*. Copyright © 1991 The New York Times Company.

page 79: "Creeping Toward Inclusivity in Science" by Phyllis Goldberg. Reprinted with permission of the author and the New York Academy of Sciences from *Women in Science and Engineering* by Cecily Selby, ed., pp. 7-15. Copyright © 1999 by the New York Academy of Sciences.

page 98: "Patriarchy, Scientists, and Nuclear Warriors" by Brian Easlea. Reprinted with permission of the author from *Beyond Patriarchy* by Michael Kaufman, ed. Toronto: Oxford University Press. Copyright © 1987 by Oxford University Press.

page 112: "Culturally Inclusive Chemistry" by Catherine Hurt Middlecamp. Reprinted with permission from *Teaching the Majority* by Sue Rosser, ed. pp 79-97. New York: Teachers College Press. Copyright © 1995 by Teachers College, Columbia University. All rights reserved.

page 125: "A World of Difference" by Evelyn Fox Keller. Reprinted with permission of Yale University Press from *Reflections on Gender and Science* by Evelyn Fox Keller, pp. 158-176. New Haven: Yale University Press. Copyright © 1985 by Yale University.

page 136: "Interviewing Women: A Contradiction in Terms" by Ann Oakley. Reprinted with permission of Routledge, Inc. from *Doing Feminist Research*, by Helen Roberts, ed. pp. 31-61. New York: Routledge. Copyright © 1981 by Routledge.

page 153: "Have Only Men Evolved?" by Ruth Hubbard. Reprinted with permission of Schenkman Publishing Co. from *Women Look at Biology Looking at Women* by Ruth Hubbard, Mary Sue Henifin, and Barbara Fried, eds. Cambridge Mass.: Schenkman. Copyright © 1979 by Schenkman Publishing Co.

page 171: "Empathy, Polyandry, and the Myth of the Coy Female" by Sarah Blaffer Hrdy. Reprinted with permission of the publisher from *Feminist Approaches to Science*, by Ruth Bleier, ed., pp. 119-146. New York: Teachers College Press. Copyright © 1986 by Teachers College, Columbia University. All rights reserved.

page 192: The Importance of Feminist Critique for Contemporary Cell Biology by The Biology and Gender Study Group: Athena Beldecos, Sarah Bailey, Scott Gilbert, Karen Hicks, Lori Kenschaft, Nancy Niemczyk, Rebecca

Rosenberg Stephanie Schaertel, and Andrew Wedel. Reprinted with permission of Indiana University Press from *Hypatia* vol 3, no. 1 (Spring 1988), pp. 61-76. Copyright © by Scott Gilbert.

page 203: The Engendering of Archaeology: Refiguring Feminist Science Studies by Alison Wylie. Reprinted with permission of University of Chicago Press from *Osiris* vol. 12 (1997), pp. 80-99. Copyright © 1997 by The History of Science Society.

page 218: "Still Seeking Transformation: Feminist Challenges to Psychology" by Sue Wilkinson. Reprinted with permission of Sage Publications, Inc. from *Knowing Feminisms* by Liz Stanley, ed., pp. 97-106. London: Sage Publications. Copyright © 1997 by Sue Wilkinson.

page 228: "Androcentric Bias in Clinical Research" by Sue Rosser. Reprinted with permission of Indiana University Press from *Women's Health—Missing from U.S. Medicine* by Sue Rosser, pp. 3-15. Booomington: Indiana University Press. Copyright © 1994 by Sue Rosser.

page 237: Man-Made Medicine and Women's Health: The Biopolitics of Sex/Gender and Race/Ethnicity by Nancy Krieger and Elizabeth Fee. Reprinted by permission of Baywood Publishing Company, Inc., Amityville, NY from *International Journal of Health Services* vol. 24, no 2, (1994) pp. 265-283).

page 250: "The New Procreative Technologies" by Ruth Hubbard. Reprinted with permission of Rutgers University Press from *The Politics of Women's Biology* by Ruth Hubbard, pp. 141-143, 147, 156, 161-178. New Brunswick, N.J.: Rutgers University Press. Copyright © 1990 by Rutgers, The State University.

page 267: "A Question of Genius: Are Men Really Smarter than Women?" by Anne Fausto-Sterling. Reprinted by permission of Basic Books, a member of Perseus Books, L.L.C. from *Myths of Gender* by Anne Fausto-Sterling, pp. 13-60. New York: Basic Books. Copyright © 1986 by Basic Books, Inc.

page 310: "Subjects, Power, and Knowledge: Description and Prescription in Feminist Philosophies of Science" by Helen E. Longino. Reprinted from *Feminist Epistemologies* by Linda Alcoff and Elizabeth Potter, eds., pp. 101, 103-120, with permission of Taylor & Francis/Routledge, Inc., http://www.routledge-ny.com. New York: Routledge. Copyright © 1993 by Routledge, Chapman, and Hall, Inc.

page 322: "Epistemological Communities" by Lynn Hankinson Nelson. Reprinted from *Feminist Epistemologies* by Linda Alcoff and Elizabeth Potter, eds.

with permission of Taylor & Francis/Routledge, Inc., http://www.routledge-ny.com. New York: Routledge. Copyright © 1993 by Routledge, Chapman and Hall, Inc.

page 340: "Strong Objectivity": A Response to the New Objectivity Question by Sandra Harding. Reprinted with permission of Kluwer Academic Publishers from *Synthese* vol. 104, no. 3 (1995), pp. 332-349.

page 353: "Introduction to *Tomorrow's Tomorrow: The Black Woman*" by Joyce A. Ladner. Reprinted with permission of the author from *Tomorrow's Tomorrow* by Joyce A. Ladner, pp. 1-14. Garden City, NY: Doubleday and Co., Inc. Copyright © 1971 by Joyce A. Ladner.

page 361: Situated Knowledges: The Science Question in Feminism and the Privilege of Partial Perspective by Donna Haraway. Reprinted with permission of the publisher from *Feminist Studies* vol. 14, no. 3 (Fall 1988), pp. 575-587, 589-596. Copyright © 1988 by Feminist Studies, Inc., c/o Department of Women's Studies, University of Maryland, College Park, MD 20742.

page 371: "Though This Be Method, Yet There Is Madness in It: Paranoia and Liberal Epistemology" by Naomi Scheman. Reprinted with permission of Westview Press, a member of Perseus Books, L.L.C. from *A Mind of One's Own* by Louise Anthony and Charlotte Witt, eds., pp. 145-166. Boulder, CO: Westview Press. Copyright © 1993 by Westview Press., Inc.

The Gender
of Science

INTRODUCTION

Science, it would seem, is not sexless; she is a man, a father, and infected too.
—Virginia Woolf, *Three Guineas*

This book is entitled *The Gender of Science*, and this immediately raises a host of questions. Does science have a gender—indeed, *can* science have a gender? If it does, what is its gender? And why should that gender be of any interest to us?

Feminist historians, sociologists, and philosophers of science, as well as feminist scientists themselves, have provided unsettling answers to these questions. The science with which we are most familiar, they have said, modern Western science, is a distinctly masculine enterprise. What's more, the masculinity of the enterprise helps to perpetuate a society biased in favor of men. Why have so many feminists taken this position? What have they offered in their defense? First, they have claimed that men control modern Western science and always have, and that women in many and various ways have been excluded from that enterprise. Second, they have claimed that the scientific enterprise men control aims to dominate a nature historically conceived of as feminine, with methodological norms (such as disinterestedness and emotional detachment, aggression and competitiveness) that mirror the norms of ideal masculinity. Third, they have claimed that the subject matter of that enterprise are research assumptions and questions and answers in which women and things feminine are left largely invisible, or else portrayed as inferior to men and the masculine. And fourth, they have claimed that the results of that research socially advantage men and disadvantage women (witness the effects of women's invisibility in medical research on men's and women's health care, for example, or the effects of women's portrayal as intellectually and physically inferior to men on the educational establishment and the workplace).

1

Such have been feminists' claims regarding science, at least the claims of many feminists in fields as diverse as the history and philosophy and sociology of science as well as science itself. Are these claims justified, and if so, what action should be taken in response? These are the issues with which we shall be concerned in this book. In Part I ("Who Are the Scientists?") we shall consider how men and women have been situated in modern Western science both in its beginnings and in more recent times, and in Part II ("What Kind of Enterprise Is Science?") we shall consider such features of this science as its aims, methods, and norms of behavior, its subject matter, and its social effects. Then in Part III ("What Kind of Enterprise Ought Science To Be?") we shall consider the main philosophical responses our results have evoked. These enquiries will put us in a position to begin the assessment of the feminists' overall stand ... but only to *begin* the assessment. Since the feminists' stand is exceedingly broad—concerned with modern Western science in general, rather than some particular branch of that science (for example, psychology, or some subfield of psychology) at some particular time (say, the end of the twentieth century)—we cannot hope to consider all the cases that have been or could be marshalled in its defense. Nevertheless, we shall consider a diverse array of cases from a diverse array of scientific fields and leave it to you, the reader, to enquire into still other cases. If you are thereby enabled and encouraged to raise questions and seek out new information about your own scientific field of study, or a field of special interest to you, and if you are enabled and encouraged to trace out the social consequences of your findings and frame modes of response to those findings, the aim of this book will have been richly fulfilled.

PART I

WHO ARE THE SCIENTISTS?

HISTORICALLY

Men, of course. We all know that. But surprisingly, given what our science text-books and histories of science have prepared us to believe, women have always been scientists as well. Indeed, we have historical evidence of women's scientific activities dating back six thousand years. Perhaps the earliest woman scientist whose name has come down to us is Merit Ptah, a physician who worked in Egypt around 2700 B.C. and whose picture is in a tomb in the Valley of the Kings. But we know that many women worked as doctors and surgeons in ancient Egypt, and we know of ancient women who worked in other scientific fields as well—for example, as chemist/chemical engineers in the perfume industry in Babylon (Tapputi-Be-latekallim), as botanists (Artemisia of Caria), as physicist/philosophers (Arete of Crete), and marine zoologists (Pythias of Assos). Even ancient mythology, which some claim mirrors the societies in which it originated, celebrated scientific women. Goddesses from Mesopotamia, Sumeria, India, Egypt, Greece, and Rome—for example, Egypt's Isis, Greece's Athena, and Rome's Minerva and Ceres—were worshipped as sources of wisdom, learning, and technical innovation in the ancient world.

The fortunes of women scientists through the ages have waxed and waned, however. The Pythagorean and Platonic schools of ancient Greece, for example, encouraged the participation of women in science and treated women and men equally, and the convents of the Middle Ages allowed some women (such as Hilde-gard of Bingen, who produced some of the greatest scientific works of the Middle Ages) to achieve great prominence and influence. The rise of universities in the twelfth through fifteenth centuries, on the other hand, most of which excluded women, brought a decline in educational opportunities for women, and the witch hunts that swept across Europe between 1300 and 1700 formed a major deterrent to women's scientific pursuits (some estimates of the number of women tortured or killed range into the millions). Modern science emerged from a variety of social locations, however—from universities and royal academies, which excluded women, but also from royal courts, the salons of the well-to-do, and the workshops of artisans, all of which allowed women considerable power and prestige. What's more, modern science has spanned the last four centuries, centuries during which it is commonly assumed women have made great and continuous progress toward equality of opportunity with men. What has been the situation of women within modern science?

In "Women in the Origins of Modern Science," historian of science Londa Schiebinger focuses on European science in the seventeenth and eighteenth centuries, more specifically on the academy system, the correspondence networks, and the Parisian salons that formed much of its heart, as well as on the craft traditions that made steady contributions to its empirical base. As Schiebinger shows, science was in many ways a new enterprise at this time, struggling for recognition, and its relation to other institutions (such as Church and State) and its role in the larger society were in a state of flux. Important questions about the nature of this new enterprise and who should have a place in it remained to be answered. One of the most important ways women found a place in the new enterprise was via the power and prestige that came with noble birth. In a world organized on the basis of birth, noble women simply outranked scholars and could trade social prestige for access to scientific knowledge. Over the course of the seventeenth and eighteenth centuries, however, the power and prestige of the nobility gradually diminished, and with it this mode of entry into science for women.

Another way women found a place in early modern science was via their acceptance in and contributions to the crafts. The crafts, with their tradition of practical experiment and application, were important for the development of modern science, Schiebinger tells us. And this was no less true of enterprises organized like the crafts—astronomy, for example, which included activities such as calendar making. Here women were frequently trained as apprentices to their fathers; but because they were prohibited from continuing their studies at the university level, almost the only route to astronomical careers open to them was to marry university-trained astronomers and become their assistants. However, as astronomy moved more and more out of the private observatories of these men and into the public world of the academy and the university, women lost their foothold in the science.

Far from moving toward equality of opportunity with men scientists during the course of the seventeenth and eighteenth centuries, Schiebinger thus suggests, European women scientists moved farther and farther from it. The African American women scientists philosopher of science Sandra Harding describes in "Women of Third World Descent in the Sciences" did not do much better in the nineteenth and early twentieth centuries. Here again the women in question tended to be relatively privileged—drawn from the upper echelons of black society—and they tended to be disproportionately in medicine. No longer excluded from universities, these women were nonetheless restricted as to the universities they could attend—

for example, women's medical schools and black universities—and they were further restricted as to the positions for which they would be considered—for example, staff positions within black hospitals, not white. Though history books say even less about these women than they do about the European scientific women who went before, these African American women of science played an undeniably important role in the survival and flourishing of the black community. Even so, by the 1920s renewed forces of racism, sexism, and professionalization acted to significantly reduce their numbers.

RECENTLY

The essays by Schiebinger and Harding portray the situations of some of the women who contributed to science in the past. What of women scientists in our own time? What have been their experiences? Vivian Gornick, a noted journalist, interviewed more than 100 women scientists in the early 1980s to find out. Her subjects were basic researchers in biology, chemistry, physics, physiology, and experimental psychology, and they were drawn from research sites across the United States—industry and government research institutes as well as colleges and universities. Gornick's subjects, moreover, ranged in age from 24 to 78, and they occupied every professional level from graduate student to senior investigator. Despite their diversity, however, their stories were remarkably similar. The women scientists had been "allowed" into science, to be sure, but had then been "held back, put off, discouraged and demoralized, frozen in position" and rendered invisible, all in an atmosphere of "defensive denial" that what was happening was happening (Gornick p. 39). Marriage to other scientists did not open the door of opportunity to these women to do science, as it had for many of the women scientists of the seventeenth century Schiebinger described, but typically locked the women into dead-end research associate positions in whatever universities their husbands accepted positions. And the research associate positions over time served to drain the women's confidence that they could do anything else more creatively demanding. What's more, marriage brought the women added home and family responsibilities, while it brought their husbands more freedom and energy to devote to science. But marriage and unenlightened spousal hiring practices and their attendent problems were not the only problems the women faced. Women scientists, for example, were considered sexual distractions (or worse) in a line of work that demanded long hours of intense and uninterrupted concentration, and they were considered less intelligent than men scientists, and also less creative and motivated. Gornick's subjects had to deal with these attitudes on a day-to-day basis. And there were other problems besides. Gornick sets out the stories of the women scientists she interviewed in "Women in Science: Half In Half Out" (scientists' names and places of work and residence as well as their fields of research are changed to preserve anonymity, but all other details of their stories are true).

Naomi Weisstein and Evelyn Fox Keller are both distinguished in their fields—Weisstein in psychology and Keller in biology as well as history and philosophy of science. But they both had experiences early in their careers similar to the ones reported by Gornick's interviewees. Their stories—reported in "'How can a little girl like you teach a great big class of men?' the Chairman said, and Other Adventures of a Woman in Science" and "The Anomaly of a Woman in Physics," respectively—give a more in-depth understanding of the kinds of problems described by Gornick. Weisstein, for example, details the importance to a successful research career of minimal research supports—access to the informal information networks that provide the latest reports of what is going on, access to necessary but expensive equipment, and the like—and how women have been denied these. She also details how women, all women, have been categorized as sexual objects and then treated accordingly. Keller, for her part, vividly portrays how the problems women have faced in science have regularly been conceptualized by them and others as personal problems rather than as the political problems that they are, and how this wrong conceptualization has made it nearly impossible to deal effectively with them. She also conveys the enormous isolation and pain women have experienced in science, and the sometimes strong resistance—in order to be "taken seriously" as scientists—women have shown to identifying, and forming alliances, with other women in science. Finally, she shows how traditional gender stereotypes—stereotypes that still hold sway—underlie the problems she discusses, and how these stereotypes must be transcended if the problems are to be solved.

CURRENTLY

By the beginning of the 1990s science writer and journalist Natalie Angier could report in her *New York Times* article "Women Join the Ranks of Science but Remain Invisible at the Top" that progress had been great for women in science since the beginnings of modern science, but that equality of opportunity with men was still far from achieved. Indeed, Angier said, women still find themselves in the lower ranks of the scientific establishment, with lower salaries and fellowship and grant opportunities. They still find themselves largely excluded from prestigious scientific academies and the most important scientific meetings and collaborations and information networks. And they still find themselves limited by family responsibilities and gender stereotypes.

By the end of the 1990s and the beginning of the twenty-first century the story is still much the same. At the forefront of science, the elite colleges and research universities have proven virtually impervious to change, and the situation is made worse by a tight job market and funding situation. At the 1998 New York Academy of Sciences conference, "Choices and Successes: Women in Science and Engineering," Nobel Laureate and Harvard Professor of Chemistry Dudley Herschbach noted that we are "creeping toward inclusivity in science." The focus of the New York conference, therefore, was not only on the progress that has already taken place, but also on ways to accelerate it. In "Creeping Toward Inclusivity in Science," sociologist Phyllis Goldberg summarizes the results of that conference. What we must work toward in science, participants suggested, are new systems for monitoring entry-level and junior women scientists' needs and progress relative to their male peers; new measures of success in science and new kinds of rewards and benefits to respond to them; a system for ranking colleges, universities, and departments on their policies regarding the retention and career development of women students and faculty; and, of course, a critical mass of women in science. Concludes conference organizer and chair, biophysicist Cecily Selby:

> We've progressed to the point where we recognize that it's not simply a matter of figuring out how women, and others who have been excluded, can be made to "adjust" to an alien environment. We're daring to dream of making the environment in which science and engineering are done inviting to every person who has the talent and the desire to participate in the scientific enterprise. The effort to realize that dream is likely to benefit women *and* men and, in the opinion of conference participants, science, engineering, and society. (Goldberg p. 84)

Women in the Origins of Modern Science

Londa Schiebinger

Institutional Landscapes

It would be a pleasant thing indeed to see a lady serve as a professor, teaching rhetoric or medicine; or to see her marching in the streets, followed by officers and sergeants; or playing the part of an attorney, pleading before judges; or seated on a bench to administer justice in the supreme court; or leading an army, serving in battle; or speaking before states and princes as the head of an embassy.

—François Poullain de la Barre, 1673

In 1910 the physicist Marie Curie was recommended for election to the prestigious Académie des Sciences in Paris. The following year Curie would become the first person ever—man or woman—to win a second Nobel prize. The fact that Curie was a woman provoked animated discussion in the Comité Secret and throughout the Académie. Some members felt that the question of whether to admit women to France's academy system was of sufficient import that it should be raised at a plenary session of the five academies constituting the Institut de France. Such a meeting was held, and there they read to the president of the institute a petition against Curie's election, reminding him that this was not the first time that a woman had presented herself for election to an academy: George Sand was not admitted to the Académie Française, nor Rosa Bonheur to the Académie des Beaux Arts, nor Sophie Germain to the Académie des Sciences. Curie's opponents urged that tradition be respected, despite the brilliance of the name advanced.

When Curie's name was finally put to a vote within the Académie des Sciences, she lost to Edouard Branly, a pioneer in wireless communication, by a narrow margin of two votes. But Curie's case raised the more general question whether women should be admitted to any of the great academies of France. This issue was settled by a greater margin; by a vote of 90 to 52, members of the Institut de France decided that no woman should ever be elected to its membership. Jacques Bétolaud (a lawyer and member of the Institut's Académie des Sciences Morales et Politiques) and his *confrères* had carried the day: by their vote members of the Institut held it "eminently wise to respect the immutable tradition against the election of women." Though some agreed with Henri Poincaré that merit should be rewarded wherever it may be found, others preferred not "to break the unity of this elite body."[1]

But was the tradition to which members of the institute appealed in fact immutable? Today we tend to assume that the exclusion of women from science was not an issue of debate until the late nineteenth or even the twentieth century. Women were not scientists, so what was there to debate? Evidence from the seventeenth and eighteenth centuries, however, suggests that at least some considered women's participation in science an open question. Not long after the founding of the Académie Française in 1635 (an important precursor to the Académie des Sciences), academy critic Gilles Ménage submitted the names of three celebrated women for consideration—Mademoiselle de Scudéry, Madame des Houlières, and Madame Dacier. None of these women were ever admitted, yet they were not excluded without serious challenge.

Indeed, it would be a mistake to see the exclusion of women from subsequent institutions of science as a foregone conclusion. The landscape was a varied one, rolling with peaks of opportunity and valleys of disappointment. Traditions that to some twentieth-century academicians seemed inevitable had, in fact, been crafted through a process of conflict and negotiation in previous centuries.

Scientific Academies

Historians of science have focused on the founding of scientific academies as a key step in the emergence of modern science. The major European academies of science were founded in the seventeenth century—the Royal Society of London in 1662, the Parisian Académie Royale des Sciences in 1666 (after 1816, the Académie des Sciences), the Societas Regia Scientiarum in Berlin in 1700 (later called the Akademie der Wissenschaften). By the end of the eighteenth century, a network of academies stretching from Saint Petersburg to Dublin, Stockholm to Palermo had consolidated Europe's intelligentsia in what one historian has called a "unified Republic of Letters." As the scepter of learning passed from courtly circles to learned academies, science took a first step toward losing its amateur status and ultimately becoming a profession. These state institutions, founded or protected by kings, provided social prestige and political protection for the fledgling science.

This first legitimation of the new science also coincides with the formal exclusion of women from science. With the founding of the academy system in Europe, a general pattern for women's place in science begins to emerge: as the prestige of an activity increases, the participation of women in that activity decreases. The exclusion of women from these academies was not a foregone conclusion, however. Women had been active participants in the aristocratic learned circles which these academies recognized as their forbears. There were, in fact, a significant number of women trained in the arts and sciences....

The exclusion of women at this particular juncture in the history of science, then, needs explanation. The seventeenth-century scientific academy had its roots in two distinct traditions—the medieval university and the Renaissance court. Insofar as academies were rooted in universities, the exclusion of women is easily explained: women were unlikely candidates for admission to institutions deriving their membership largely from the universities, which since their founding had generally proscribed women. It is also possible, however, to argue that scientific societies arose more directly from courtly traditions. Frances Yates has identified the Platonic academy founded in mid-fifteenth-century Florence under the auspices of the great prince Lorenzo de'Medici as the root of the whole academy movement.[2] If we emphasize the continuities between scientific academies and Renaissance courtly culture—where women were active participants in intellectual circles—it becomes more difficult to explain the exclusion of women from the academies.

The founding of the Académie Française—an academy devoted generally to the promotion of the French language and literature—initiated the academy system in France. Incorporated by the king in 1635, the Académie Française was the first of the modern state academies to be founded outside Italy, predating the Royal Society of London by some twenty-five years and the more specialized Académie Royale des Sciences in Paris by some thirty years. The founding of the Académie Française is a particularly important moment for our analysis of women's place in intellectual culture, for although this was not an academy devoted to science—it was here that women were first excluded from the modern institutions of learning.

In its early years, it was not clear that women would be excluded from membership in the Académie Française. Noblewomen had been active *académiciennes* at several of the courtly academies out of which the Académie Française developed. Take the case of Henri III's Palace Academy, an important precursor of the Académie Française. Established in the 1570s to enhance his own education, Henri's academy cultivated an encyclopedic learning devoted to every kind of philosophy, science, music, poetry, geography, mathematics, and painting. The assembly, meeting twice a week in the king's cabinet, was attended by the "most learned men" and "even some ladies," all of whom spoke on problems which they had studied beforehand. From contemporary accounts we know these ladies included Claude-Catherine de Clermont, marquise de Retz and Madame de Lignerolles.[3] The presence of these ladies was not purely ornamental. They took an active part in the discussions at hand. One academy member, Seigneur de Brantôme, reported that after six months' absence from Paris he was surprised to meet a lady of rank going to the academy (which he thought had been disbanded) where she was studying philosophy and discussing the principle of perpetual motion.

Women were also active in the less formal salons that sprang up between the demise of the royal Palace Academy in the 1580s and the founding of the state-financed Académie Française in 1635. Scholars today continue to debate which literary salon should be considered the one to which Richelieu offered his official protection—that of Valentin Conrart, Marie de Gournay, or Guillaume Collelet. Whichever among these is ultimately judged the true forerunner of the Académie Française, it is important to recognize that Marie le Jars, demoiselle de Gournay and a central figure in the private circles from which the academy emerged, would not become a member. Already in her seventieth year when the Académie was founded, perhaps she was considered too old for membership. Yet she was not the only prominent literary woman who deserved consideration for membership in the king's academy. Indeed, several women's names were put forward for membership in the early years of the academy, proposals that, we are told, were received with some favor.[4] Little is known about these discussions. Gilles Ménage, who included women in his own Wednesday receptions

(and for unclear reasons refused academy membership), left the following note:

> A short while ago in the Académie were nominated several women (Mademoiselle de Scudéry, Madame des Houlières, Madame Dacier, and several others) who, illustrious for their intelligence and their knowledge, are perfectly capable of enriching our language with handsome works and who have already produced marvelous ones. Monsieur Charpentier supported this proposal with the example of the academies of Padua, where erudite women are admitted. My treatise, *Mulierum Philosopharum,* furnished [to those involved in this debate] ancient examples of marks of distinction granted erudite women. Nevertheless, the proposal made to the Académie produced no results.[5]

In his *Historia mulierum philosopharum,* Ménage had documented the great numbers of philosophical women of the past to support his argument that women (like Madame Dacier, the classicist to whom he dedicated the book) merited admission to learned bodies.

The literary merit of the women proposed for membership was never in doubt: Madeleine de Scudéry won the academy's first prize for eloquence in 1671; Madame des Houlières won the prize for poetry in 1687. What was in question was their sex. Although the statutes of the academy did not specifically exclude women, some say it was originally Richelieu who refused to admit them, others say it was the poet Jean Chapelain who refused. Reflecting upon this situation, academy member Jean de la Bruyère wrote:

> I have not forgotten, gentlemen, that one of the principal statutes of that illustrious body advocates admitting only those whom one judges the most distinguished. You will not find it therefore strange that I give my vote to Monsieur Dacier, though all the same I prefer Madame, his wife, if you would admit among you persons of her sex.[6]

Thus, though women were respected members of French literary circles, they did not become salaried members of the academy.

Women faced similar problems in the early Académie Royale des Sciences. As was the case with the Académie Française, women were an integral part of the informal *réunions*, salons, and scientific circles that grew up in opposition to the tyranny of old methods in the French university system. Women gathered among the curious every Monday at Théophraste Renaudot's Bureau d'Adresse to watch his experiments. Women were especially strong among the Cartesians, who sought refuge from hostile academics in the salons of Paris. Every Wednesday persons of "all ages, both sexes, and all professions" gathered at the home of Jacques Rohault to watch him attempt to give an experimental base to Descartes's physics.[7] In the years preceding the founding of the Académie Royale des Sciences, the number of women attending informal academies and salons proliferated: women attended the Palais Précieux pour les Beaux Esprits des Deux Sexes in the 1650s; Cartesians flocked to the salons of the marquise de Sévigné and the duchess of Maine. Louis de Lesclache's lessons in philosophy were so overwhelmed by women that he was later reproached as a *professeur pour dames*. The numbers of women attending informal academies grew at such a rate that the renowned grammarian Pierre Richelet added the word *académicienne* to his dictionary in the 1680s, explaining that this was a new word signifying a person of the fair sex belonging to an academy of *gens de lettres*, coined on the occasion of the election of Madame des Houlières to the Académie Royale d'Arles.[8]

Despite their prominence in informal scientific circles, women were not to become members of the Académie Royale des Sciences. Why not? Certain aspects of the French academic system could have encouraged the election of gentlewomen. Seventeenth-century academies perpetuated Renaissance traditions of mixing learning with elegance, adding grace to life and beauty to the soul. The Académie Royale des Sciences retained a conviviality in its program, with rules of etiquette and a routine of dinners and musical entertainment, all of which tended to blur the boundaries that would later separate the scientific academy from the salon. This was an atmosphere in which the *salonnière* would have been at home. At the same time, the Académie was monarchical and hierarchical. At the head of the Académie sat twelve honorary nobles whose presence was largely ornamental; working scientists—the new aristocracy of talent—found themselves on a lowlier rung. Yet noble birth was not enough to secure women a place in the academic system. The closed and formal character of the academy discouraged the election of women. Membership in the academy was a public, salaried position with royal protection and privileges.[9] A salaried position in itself would not preclude the admission of women (Marie de Gournay, for example, received a modest *pension* from Richelieu until her death in 1645); with membership of the Académie limited to forty, however, the election of a woman would have displaced a man.

The exclusion of women from the Royal Society of London is also difficult to explain but for different reasons. At least ideologically, the Royal Society was supposed to be open to a wide range of people. Thomas Sprat, the first historian of the society, emphasized that its philosophy was not to be a parochial one restricted to the tenets of a particular religion, nation, or profession, but rather was to be "a Philosophy of *Mankind*." According to Sprat, valuable contributions were to come from both learned and vulgar hands: "from the Shops of *Mechanicks;* from the Voyages of *Merchants;* from the Ploughs of *Husbandmen;* from the Sports, the Fishponds, the Parks, the Gardens of *Gentlemen*." In addition, no special study or extraordinary preparations of learning were required: "Here is enough business for *Minds* of all sizes: And so boundless is the variety of these *Studies*, that here is also enough delight to recompence the Labors of them all, from the most ordinary capacities, to the highest and most searching *Wits*."[10]

In fact the Royal Society never made good its claim to welcome men of all classes. Merchants and tradesmen comprised only 4 percent of the society's membership; the vast majority of the members (at least 50 percent in the 1660s) came from the ranks of gentlemen *virtuosi*, or wellborn connoisseurs of the new science.[11] Considering that the society relied for its monies on dues paid by members, the absence of noblewomen from the ranks of enthusiastic patrons is puzzling.

One woman in particular—Margaret Cavendish, duchess of Newcastle—was a qualified candidate, having written some six books about natural philosophy, along with several other plays and books of poetry.... She had long been a generous patron of Cambridge University and would have been a financial asset to the impoverished society. One should recall that fellows of noble birth bestowed prestige upon the new society; men above the ranks of baron could become members without the scrutiny given other applicants. When the duchess asked for nothing more than to be allowed to visit a working session of the society, however, her request aroused a flood of controversy. Although never invited to join the Royal Society, Cavendish was allowed to attend one session after some discussion among society fellows. The famous visit took place in 1667.[12] Robert Boyle prepared his "experiments of … weighing of air in an exhausted receiver; [and] … dissolving of flesh with a certain liquor." The duchess, accompanied by her ladies, was much impressed by the demonstrations and left (according to one observer) "full of admiration."[13]

Although no official record of the discussion of Cavendish's visit remains, Samuel Pepys tells us that there was "much debate, *pro* and *con*, it seems many being against it, and we do believe the town will be full of ballads of it." When no other ballads appeared, Royal Society member John Evelyn was moved to write one of his own.[14] From Pepys's report it seems many fellows felt that Cavendish's membership would bring ridicule rather than honor. Evelyn's wife, probably reflecting the attitudes of many in the society, described the duchess's writings as "airy, empty, whimsical and rambling … aiming at science, difficulties, high notions, terminating commonly in nonsense, oaths, and obscenity."[15]

Margaret Cavendish's visit indeed appears to have set a precedent—a negative one. No woman was elected to full membership in the Royal Society until 1945. For nearly three hundred years, the only permanent female presence at the Royal Society was a skeleton preserved in the society's anatomical collection.

Women at the Periphery

Though none of Europe's academies had formal statutes barring women, no woman was elected to full membership in either the Royal Society of London, the Académie Royale des Sciences in Paris, or the Societas Regia Scientiarum in Berlin until the middle of the twentieth century. Only the Italian academies—at Bologna, Padua, and Rome—regularly admitted women. Two French women, Madeleine de Scudéry, in the seventeenth century and Emilie du Châtelet in the eighteenth, denied admission to learned societies in their own countries, were honored with membership in the Italian academies, but French academies did not reciprocate. The Italian mathematician, Maria Agnesi, who had been elected to membership in the Academy of Science at Bologna in 1747 and whose work was translated into French under the auspices of the Académie Royale des Sciences, was not invited to join the academy in Paris. Academy Secretary Bernard de Fontenelle sadly noted that, despite her academic achievements and mathematical acclaim, it was impossible for Agnesi to become a member.

That women were not allowed to become members of scientific academies does not mean that they were barred from scientific work at these institutions. In France, Madeleine Basseporte served as illustrator at the Jardin Royal des Herbes Médicinales, where she sketched on vellum the rare plants grown in the garden from 1735 until her death in 1780. She followed the famous Claude Aubriet in this post and was paid a small salary of 1,000 livres yearly.[16] Bernard de Jussieu judged Basseporte's work of great value and deposited her sketches in the archives of the Bibliothèque Royale. Only a historian of the nineteenth century judged that her reputation far outstripped her merit. Basseporte's official position at Paris's botanical garden can be explained in part by perceptions that work in medicine or botany was appropriate for a woman, for women had long been active in these fields. Basseporte also owed her position at the Jardin du Roy to the strength of women in the visual arts. The fine arts were considered (then as now) a more appropriate field for women than any science; we need only recall that seven women were elected to membership in the Académie Royale de la Peinture et de la Sculpture between 1663 and 1682 (though in 1706 this academy reversed its policy and ruled that no more women could be admitted, at a time when more and more women were applying for membership).[17] Scientific academies of the same period, by contrast, did not even flirt with the election of female members.

Also on the periphery of academic life was anatomist Marie-Catherine Biheron, who studied the art of illustration with Madeleine Basseporte. This pair provides a rare example (outside of midwifery) of a woman training a young woman who was not her daughter for a career in science. Because these women left no private papers, our knowledge of their collaboration is hazy. From Basseporte's hand we have only her drawings; from Biheron's only a four-page advertisement of her anatomical collection. What little we do know concerning their collaboration comes from the memoirs of contemporaries—Diderot, Baron Melchior von Grimm, the comtesse de Genlis—who knew them only at a distance.

Marie Biheron was born in 1719 the daughter of an apothecary. Like her teacher Basseporte, she never married. It was Basseporte who counseled Biheron to turn her skill to preparing anatomical models; Biheron was

eventually to become one of the leading wax modelers of her day. Wax, a particularly popular medium in this period, was used to model everything from scenes in Turkish baths to the figures of European royalty on display at Madame Tussaud's famous museum. The art of modeling the human body in wax was developed in the sixteenth and seventeenth centuries for use in teaching because of the shortage of cadavers for dissecting. Anatomical wax modeling—practiced by men and women alike—reached its peak in Italy and France during the eighteenth century. Many of these wax models were gynecological, showing all parts of the uterus in every state and the fetus in various states of development, for the use of students—male and female, as we are told—in midwifery and anatomy.

Though men, too, worked in wax, women were particularly prominent in modeling the female body because, until the eighteenth century, knowledge and care of the female body was a woman's domain. Anna Morandi-Manzolini (1716–1774) became particularly well known for her models displayed in the anatomical museum of the Institute of Bologna (showing how the fetus is nourished in the womb). Biheron's own work was praised for its precise and delicate replication of nature. A prestigious visitor to her collection (Sir John Pringle, physician general of Britain and later president of the Royal Society) found her models so lifelike that he reportedly exclaimed: "They want nothing but the smell." Grimm was so beguiled by her work that he refused to believe that the modeling substance was wax because it did not melt in fire.

Biheron presented her work on several occasions to the French king's academicians. The first such occasion came in 1759 at the invitation of the anatomist Jean Morand. In the record of the meeting, her renderings were praised for surpassing those of William Desnoues, the leading wax modeler of previous decades: "Where Desnoues showed only the position and color of the different parts of the human body, Biheron has reproduced exactly the consistency, suppleness, and weight of the brain, kidneys, intestine, and other parts of the human body." Here too her renderings fooled the onlooker into believing they were real: Biheron "imitated nature … with a precision and truth which no person has yet achieved."[18]

How did a woman who was not a member of the established medical community procure bodies for her studies? Though we do not have Biheron's words describing her procedures, we are told by Louis Prudhomme, writing in the 1830s, that she hired people to steal cadavers for her from the military. The business was far from pleasant. Already putrefying when she received them, she kept the cadavers in a glass cabinet in the middle of her garden. In this manner Biheron was able to make a close study of the human body and achieve astonishing perfection in her models.

In 1770 Biheron returned to Paris to demonstrate to the Académie Royale des Sciences her elaborate and lifelike model of a pregnant woman. The model reproduced exactly all the stages and mechanisms of birthing, complete with a moveable coccyx, a cervix that dilated or closed on demand, and removable infants. The device was particularly useful for demonstrating to students how to cope with dangerous deliveries without doing harm to a living subject. Models like Biheron's were used by the celebrated midwife Anne Le Boursier du Coudray, hired in the 1770s by the French government to teach as many as 4,000 women throughout the provinces the art of midwifery.[19] Biheron's models were cited in academy proceedings as late as 1830 as the best example of this kind of work.

In 1771 Biheron demonstrated her wax anatomy once again at the Académie Royale des Sciences, this time for the pleasure of the crown prince of Sweden. Accompanying her were men such as Lavoisier, Macquer, and Morand. Women of the court were also allowed to attend this special session. Biheron's greatest honor was the acquisition of her anatomical models by Catherine the Great for the Academy of Sciences in Saint Petersburg. Biheron's artificial anatomy accompanied a collection of medical instruments sent from the Parisian Académie Royale des Sciences by Morand.

These successes at the academy did not, however, translate into an academy seat, nor a *pension* from the king. For thirty years Biheron made her living by opening her collection to the curious every Wednesday for the small fee of three *livres*. She also taught lessons in her home: Diderot and Genlis, for example, were among her students. Diderot later wrote that her classes were especially valuable for young women. Prudhomme reported, however, that she was censured by the doctors and surgeons of Paris for infringing upon their monopoly. (Established surgeons presumably objected because Biheron had been attracting significant numbers of male students from their classes.) Biheron also visited London twice looking for work and met with little success, though her wax models did influence doctors William and John Hunter to open their own museum of comparative anatomy in the 1770s.

There are other examples of women scientists who were active on the periphery of the major academies. At the Académie Royale des Sciences in Paris, Emilie du Châtelet's essay on the propagation of fire was published in the proceedings of 1738. Marie Thiroux d'Arconville's anatomical illustrations were published by the academy in 1759, under the name and protection of academy member Jean J. Sue. In London the Royal Society published Caroline Herschel's discoveries of comets (in 1787, 1789, 1792, 1794, and 1796), and her revision of Flamsteed's catalog of stars was published by the society in 1787. Women also won prizes for their contributions to science. Sophie Germain won the *grand prix* of the Parisian academy in 1816 for her work on elasticity. In 1888 Sofia Kovalevskaia won the prestigious *Prix Bordin* of the Académie des Sciences for her work in mathematics.

Women were also to be found in academics on the periphery—in provincial academies or less prestigious academies in European capital cities. Madame des Houlières was elected member of the Académie Royale d'Arles in 1680. In 1788 Nicole Lepaute became a member of the Académie des Sciences of Béziers. Caroline Herschel became a member of the Royal Irish Academy in 1838.

Parisian Salons

The focus of historians on academies in the rise of modern science has drawn attention away from the other heir of the courtly circle—the salon—as an institution of science. Discussion of science was fashionable at the salons of Madame Geoffrin, Madame Helvétius, and Madame Rochefoucauld; Madame Lavoisier received academicians at her home. French salons of the seventeenth and eighteenth century competed with academies for the attention of the learned. While the academies had a salon character in their early years, combining conviviality with scientific investigation, later years saw the separation of the sciences from the humanities. It was only in the salon that the *savant* continued to be gracious as well as learned. ...

The grand salons of Paris offer unique examples of intellectual institutions run exclusively by women. These informal gatherings played a crucial role in restructuring French elites. Neither strictly aristocratic nor bourgeois, salons celebrated the superiority of acquired nobility over inherited nobility, emphasizing the virtues of talent and refinement over noble birth, and in this way opening polite society to the rich and talented. Like the academies, salons served as a major channel of communication among newly consolidated elites.[20] There was significant overlap in (male) membership among salons, academies, and writers for the *Journal des Savants*, the major French journal of scientific and cultural news. ... Bernard de Fontenelle, for example, longtime secretary of the Académie Royale des Sciences, became

président of Madame Lambert's salon. There was also overlap in membership from salon to salon. Members of Madame Lambert's salon (Fontenelle, the physicist and mathematician Jean-Jacques Dortous de Mairan, the medical doctor Jean Astruc, and others) joined the gatherings at Madame Tencin's salon after Lambert's death. After Madame Tencin's death, Madame Geoffrin's salon moved to center stage; regular members included Fontenelle, Mairan, and Montesquieu. It is hard to know exactly what went on in salons; like many other women's arts, salon discourse was not made to last. Unlike academies, salons had no journals, proceedings, or permanent secretaries.

Socially prominent women dominated the intellectual gatherings held in the magnificent salons, or sitting rooms, of their private homes. Despite their informal and private character, salons wielded substantial influence in public matters: Madame Lambert was said to have "made" academicians; Julie de Lespinasse's salon has been called "the laboratory of the *Encyclopédie*."[21] Well-placed women served as patrons to young men anxious to make careers in science. Women served effectively as intellectual power brokers because science at this time was organized as much through highly personalized patronage systems as through formal institutions.[22] Salons acted as social filters, identifying young men of talent and turning them into protégés.

The power of salon women to make or break public careers should not be underestimated. At the same time, it is important to recognize that *salonnières* (women of the salons) experienced the same limits to their power as the most royal women of the land: they served as powers behind the throne but could not themselves sit on the throne. While women maneuvered to ensure the election of their candidate to the Académie Royale des Sciences, they were powerless to bring about their own election. Throughout the seventeenth and eighteenth centuries, *salonnières* served as patrons to young men, not to young women....

Noblewomen in Scientific Networks

Historians tend to take the case of women as authors of and audience for popular science as the paradigmatic example of women's participation in modern science. Yet, as we shall see, relegating women to the status of amateur diminishes the contributions that women like Margaret Cavendish or Emilie du Châtelet made to science. Popular science was not sharply divided from professional science as it is today. Though today it would be difficult for anyone barred from university education to work in science, this was not the case in the seventeenth or eighteenth centuries, when few men or women were full-time or salaried scientists. Some, like Galileo, were resident astronomers at a princely court; Bacon and Leibniz were government ministers, as well as men of letters. At the end of his life Descartes was in the pay of Christina, queen of Sweden, as tutor in natural philosophy and mathematics. Emilie du Châtelet was a person of private means. This looser organization of science was one factor allowing those barred from universities and academies to find their way into scientific circles.

In the absence of clearly established prerequisites of education or certification, participation in science was regulated by informal networks. Entree into the scientific network rested on birth and/or talent. The leisure and resources which came with noble birth gave access to learning, while the added prestige of erudition served to bolster a declining aristocracy. In Paris, the title *membre de l'Académie* was prized as if it were a title of nobility; in England, it was said that he who is both nobly born and a scholar is doubly honored. This worked to the advantage of noblewomen, whose high social standing gave them access to science as it did to other forms of social power and influence. In informal scientific networks, noblewomen were often able to exchange social prestige for access to scientific knowledge.

Before the advent of the scientific journal, scholars and enthusiasts exchanged news of discoveries and observations through informal networks—meetings in private homes, writing letters, working for a common patron. Marin Mersenne conducted an international correspondence with intimate friends, such as Descartes, and organized a clearinghouse of information for the learned and *grand amateur* alike, passing on ideas and putting scholars in touch with one another. His home was a kind of informal academy where friends dropped in for philosophical discussion.[23]

Royal women formed crucial links in these noble networks. With family alliances connecting European courts, queens served as ambassadors preparing the way for both cultural and philosophical exchange. A prime example of this was the famed Leibniz-Clarke debate, sparked by the ascent of a German princess to the English throne. Although the controversy between Newton and Leibniz had been under way for some time, the written debate began when Princess Caroline of Ansbach, one of Leibniz's pupils, moved to England upon the succession of her father-in-law (George I) to the throne. An ardent Leibnizian, Caroline's views were challenged when she entered Newtonian England. The first letter of what was to become the Leibniz-Clarke debate was written to her. In this letter, Leibniz strongly criticized Newton's philosophical views. Caroline passed the letter on to Clarke, whom she had met while looking for a translator for Leibniz's *Theodicy*. Caroline herself debated the question of the nature of the soul with Clarke (whom she considered too much of a Newtonian); such debates lasted on occasion from six until ten o'clock in the evening.

As Princess of Wales Caroline appointed herself mediator of the debate. In 1715 she wrote to Leibniz, "I should like [Sir Isaac Newton] to be reconciled with you ... it would be a great pity if two such great men as you and he were to be estranged by misunderstandings." In a subsequent letter Caroline chided Leibniz for his dispute with Newton: "the public would profit immensely if this [reconciliation] could be brought about, but great men are like women, who never give up their lovers except with the utmost chagrin and mortal anger. And that, gentlemen, is where your opinions have got you."[24]

Women of lesser rank were also a part of these noble networks. The privileges of rank allowed Elizabeth of Bohemia to attract the attention of Descartes. Elizabeth was introduced to the French philosopher sometime after 1640 by the marquis de Dohna. The lengthy correspondence between Elizabeth and Descartes shows Elizabeth to have been a woman of serious intellectual talent. In approaching Descartes she was searching for more than learned refinements; she was looking for, as she put it, "a physician of the soul."[25] She did not hesitate, however, to voice objections to his philosophical views. Descartes's central conception of the relation between mind and matter, for example, was simply unacceptable to her. "I hope," she wrote, "you can excuse my stupidity of not being able to comprehend the idea of how the soul (without extension and immaterial) can move the body ... it seems easier to me to concede material extension to the soul than the ability of an immaterial soul to move the body."[26] Descartes took Elizabeth's objections seriously. Her questions and objections led him to elaborate his views in his 1644 *Principles of Philosophy*, where he publicly acknowledged his regard for Elizabeth's talents.

Noblewomen thus exploited their social standing to gain access to learned circles. Yet the dynamic of the exchange between Elizabeth and Descartes is noteworthy for what it reveals about rank and gender. Despite her high social standing, Elizabeth assumed the subordinate posture of a pupil, playing the role of a modest, self-effacing woman. For his part, Descartes—who was not unhappy to make his way into the world of royalty—played the role of a courtier, responding with the praise due to one of her rank. He acknowledged his lower social standing, while she affected intellectual subordination. In matters of the intellect, the privileges of rank did not outweigh the liabilities of gender.

Even the highest rank could not entirely insulate women from ridicule. In 1650

Descartes was commissioned by the audacious Queen Christina of Sweden to draw up regulations for her scientific academy. Many blamed Christina and the rigors of her philosophical schedule for Descartes's death. For her philosophical prowess the queen was often called a hermaphrodite.

Noblewomen continued to participate in these informal scientific networks until late in the eighteenth century.[27] Nobility won for certain women the attention of men of lower social rank but of significant intellectual standing. This was true across Europe....

Scientific Women in the Craft Tradition

If one considers the reputations of Madame Kirch [Maria Winkelmann] and Mlle Cunitz, one must admit that there is no branch of science ... in which women are not capable of achievement, and that in astronomy, in particular, Germany takes the prize above all other states in Europe.
—Alphonse des Vignoles, 1721

It may be surprising that between 1650 and 1710 a significant proportion—some 14 percent—of all German astronomers were women. These women came not from the aristocracy but from the workaday world of the artisanal workshop, where women as well as men were active in family businesses. Craft traditions, central to working life in early modern Europe, also contributed, to the development of modern science. This route to science was more open for women in Germany, where craft traditions remained especially strong. To be sure, Germany had its outstanding royal women—Caroline of Ansbach, Princess Elizabeth, and Sophie Charlotte, the founder of the Academy of Sciences in Berlin—but it was working women who made steady contributions to the empirical base of science. As Alphonse des Vignoles, vice-president of the Berlin academy, observed, there were more women astronomers in Germany at the turn of the eighteenth century than in any other European country

Edgar Zilsel was among the first historians to point to the importance of craft skills for the development of modern science in the West.[28] Zilsel located the origin of modern science in the fusion of three traditions: the tradition of letters provided by the literary humanists; the tradition of logic and mathematics provided by the Aristotelian scholastics; and the tradition of practical experiment and application provided by the artist-engineers.

What Zilsel does not point out, however, is that the new value attached to the traditional skills of the artisan also allowed for the participation of women in the sciences. Of the various institutional homes of the sciences, only the artisanal workshop welcomed women. Women were not newcomers to the workshop: it was in craft traditions that the fifteenth-century writer, Christine de Pizan, had located women's greatest innovations in the arts and sciences—the spinning of wool, silk, linen, and "creating the general means of civilized existence." In the workshop, women's (like men's) contributions depended less on book learning and more on practical innovations in illustrating, calculating, or observing.

Women's position in the crafts was stronger than has generally been appreciated. In fifteenth-century Nuremberg and Cologne, for example, craftswomen were active in nearly all areas of production: of the thirty-eight guilds that Margret Wensky has described in her study of working women in Cologne (a city where women's economic position was especially strong), women were full members of more than twenty of those guilds.[29] Women's membership in these guilds conferred on them limited civic rights—they could buy and sell and be represented in a court of law, for example, but they could not hold city office.

Astronomers and entomologists were never, of course, officially organized into guilds. Yet craft traditions were very much alive in the practice of these sciences. This was especially true in Germany, where stirrings of industrialization came late. Whereas

in England and Holland guilds declined after the midseventeenth century, in Germany they remained an important economic and cultural force well into the nineteenth century.[30]

Women's work in household workshops differed widely from trade to trade, from town to town. Yet it is possible to sketch general patterns. Women participated in craft production as: (1) daughters and apprentices; (2) wives who assisted their husbands as paid or unpaid artisans; (3) independent artisans; or (4) widows who inherited the family business. As we shall see, these categories were also important for defining women's place in scientific production....

Women Astronomers in Germany

The late sixteenth and early seventeenth centuries saw the birth of modern astronomy. Copernicus published his *De revolutionibus orbium coelestium* in 1543; Galileo first turned his telescope to the sky in 1609. Astronomers in this period served in a variety of social roles—that of academician, servant of the court, or amateur enthusiast. It is also possible to argue that the German astronomer of the late seventeenth century bore a close resemblance to the guild master or apprentice, and that the craft organization of astronomy gave women a prominence in the field. Between 1650 and 1710 a surprisingly large number of women—Maria Cunitz, Elisabetha Hevelius, Maria Eimmart, Maria Winkelmann and her daughters Christine Kirch and Margaretha—worked in German astronomy. All these women worked in family observatories—Johannes Hevelius built his private observatory across the roofs of three adjoining houses in 1640; Georg Christoph Eimmart built his on the Nuremberg city wall in 1678. Of this group only Maria Cunitz was not the daughter or wife of an astronomer who, in guildlike fashion, assisted a master in his trade.

It is perhaps unfair to include the example of Maria Cunitz (1610-1664) among women working within the crafts tradition, for her father was a landowner. Nonetheless, her education too depended on training given her by her father, the medical doctor Heinrich Cunitz, who owned several estates in Silesia. Sometimes called the "second Hypatia," Maria learned from her father six languages—Hebrew, Greek, Latin, Italian, French, and Polish—as well as history, medicine, mathematics, painting, poetry, and music. Her principal occupation, however, was astronomy. In 1630 she married Eliae von Lowen, a medical doctor and amateur astronomer. During the Thirty Years' War her family took refuge in Poland, where she prepared astronomical tables published in 1650 as *Urania propitia*. The main purpose of this work was to simplify Kepler's Rudolphine Tables, used for calculating the position of the planets. Maria Cunitz was not merely a calculator. Her book also treated the art and theory of astronomy.

Though Cunitz published *Urania propitia* under her maiden name, few believed that the work was her own. Her husband found it necessary to add a preface to later editions asserting that he had taken no part in the work. In the preface Cunitz assured her readers that her astronomy was reliable, though done by "a person of the female sex." Cunitz emphasized that her diligence in spending both "days and nights gathering knowledge from one or the other sciences or arts" had sharpened her understanding or—as she wrote—"at least what understanding is possible in a woman's body."[31] But Cunitz's diligence was not rewarded. In 1706, just forty years after her death, Johann Eberti judged that Cunitz had sacrificed her womanly duties to her astronomy:

> She was so deeply engaged in astronomical speculation that she neglected her household. The daylight hours she spent, for the most part, in bed (concerning which all manner of ridiculous events have been reported) because she had tired herself from watching the stars at night.[32]

This story was repeated throughout the eighteenth century in an effort to discredit her.

Maria Eimmart (1676–1707), though less well known, also practiced astronomy. From her father, Georg Christoph Eimmart, astronomer and director of the Nuremberg Academy of Art from 1699 to 1704, Maria Eimmart learned French, Latin, drawing, and mathematics. As a young girl she also learned the art of astronomy at her father's observatory, where she worked alongside his other students. ... Maria Eimmart owed her place in astronomy largely to the strong position of women in the arts. Much of Eimmart's scientific achievement derived from her ability to make exact sketches of the sun and moon. Between 1693 and 1698 she prepared 250 drawings of phases of the moon in a continuous series that laid the groundwork for a new lunar map. She also made two drawings of the total eclipse of 1706. A few sources claim that in 1701 Eimmart published a work on the sun, *Ichnographia nova contemplationum de sole*, under her father's name, but there is no evidence that this was her work. Apart from her astronomical sketches, Maria Eimmart was known for her many drawings of flowers, birds, ancient statues, and, interestingly, of ancient women. These drawings have all been lost.

After training as an apprentice to her father, the scientifically minded Eimmart secured her position at the observatory by marrying Johann Heinrich Müller in 1706. Müller was a physics teacher at a Nuremberg Gymnasium and since 1705 director of her father's observatory. Müller also benefited from the marriage. Through the principle of daughter's rights, the Eimmart observatory became part of the daughter's inheritance, passing through the daughter to her husband.[33] Maria Eimmart-Müller's astronomical career was cut short when she died in childbirth in 1707.

Elisabetha Koopman (later Hevelius, 1647–1693) of Danzig also took care to ensure her career in astronomy. In 1663 she married a leading astronomer, Johannes Hevelius, a man thirty-six years her senior. Hevelius, a brewer by trade, took over the lucrative family beer business in 1641. His first wife, Catherina Rebeschke had managed the household brewery, leaving Hevelius free to serve in city government and to pursue his avocation, astronomy. When Elisabetha Koopman, who had been interested in astronomy for many years, married the widowed Hevelius, she served, in appropriate guild fashion, as chief assistant to her husband, both in the family business and in the family observatory.

Margaret Rossiter has described "women's work" in nineteenth- and twentieth-century science (and especially in astronomy) as typically involving tedious computation, lifelong service as an assistant, and the like—all of which are a legacy of the guild wife.[34] The role of the guild wife, however, cannot be collapsed into that of a mere assistant; wives were of such import to production that every guild master was required by law to have one. The very different structure of the workplace—in the seventeenth century the observatory was in the home, not part of a university—allowed the wife a more comprehensive role. For twenty-seven years Elisabetha Hevelius collaborated with her husband, observing the heavens in the cold of night by his side…. After his death she edited and published their joint work, *Prodromus astronomiae*, a catalogue of 1,888 stars and their positions.

Maria Winkelmann at the Berlin Academy of Sciences

Of all the women astronomers in Germany, Maria Winkelmann was the most outstanding. In 1710 Winkelmann petitioned one of the newly founded learned societies, the Academy of Sciences in Berlin, for an appointment as assistant astronomer. Already a respected astronomer when her husband, Gottfried Kirch, died, Winkelmann asked to be appointed in her husband's stead. In so doing, she invoked a principle well established in the organized crafts that recognized the right of a widow to carry on the family business after her husband's death. The perpetuation of craft traditions had allowed women of the seven-teenth century access to the secrets and tools of the astronomical trade, but were these traditions—part and parcel as they were of an older order—to secure a place for women in the new institutions of science?

Maria Margaretha Winkelmann was born in 1670 at Panitzsch (near Leipzig), the daughter of a Lutheran minister. She was educated privately by her father and, after his death, by her uncle. The young Winkelmann made great progress in the arts and letters, and from an early age she received advanced training in astronomy from the farmer and self-taught astronomer Christoph Arnold, who lived in the neighboring town of Sommerfeld. Had Maria Winkelmann been male, she would probably have continued her studies at the nearby universities of Leipzig or Jena. Though women's exclusion from universities set limits to their participation in astronomy, it did not exclude them entirely. Debates over the nature of the universe filled university halls, yet the practice of astronomy—the actual work of observing the heavens—took place largely outside the universities. In the seventeenth century the art of observation was commonly learned under the watchful eye of a master. Gottfried Kirch, for example, studied at Hevelius's private observatory in Danzig; this was as important for his astronomical career as his study of mathematics with Erhard Weigal at the University of Jena.

It was at the astronomer Christoph Arnold's house that Maria Winkelmann met Kirch, Germany's leading astronomer. Though Winkelmann's uncle wanted her to marry a young Lutheran minister, he consented to her marriage to Kirch, a man some thirty years older than Winkelmann. Knowing she would have no opportunity to practice astronomy as an independent woman, Winkelmann moved, through her marriage, from being an assistant to Arnold to being an assistant to Kirch. And Kirch found in Winkelmann a much-needed second wife who could care for his domestic affairs, as well as a much-needed astronomical assistant who could help with calculations, observations, and the making of calendars.

In 1700 Kirch and Winkelmann took up residence in Berlin, the newly expanding cultural center of Brandenburg. The move represented an advance in social standing for both husband and wife. A university education at Jena and apprenticeship to the well-known astronomer Hevelius afforded Kirch the opportunity to move from the household of a tailor in the small town of Guben to the position of astronomer at the Societas Regia Scientiarum.[35] Maria Winkelmann's mobility, by contrast, came not through education but through marriage. Though coming via different routes, both served at the Berlin academy: Gottfried as astronomer, Maria as an unofficial but recognized assistant to her husband.

During her first decade at the Berlin academy, Maria Winkelmann's scientific accomplishments were many and varied. Every evening, as was her habit, she observed the heavens beginning at nine o'clock. During the course of an evening's observations in 1702, she discovered a previously unknown comet—a discovery that should have secured her position in the astronomical community. (Her husband's position at the academy rested partly on his discovery of the comet of 1680.) There is no question about Winkelmann's priority in the discovery. In the 1930s F. H. Weiss published her original report of the sighting of the comet.... Kirch also recorded in his notes from that night that his wife found the comet while he slept:

> Early in the morning (about 2:00 A.M.) the sky was clear and starry. Some nights before, I had observed a variable star, and my wife (as I slept) wanted to find and see it for herself. In so doing, she found a comet in the sky. At which time she woke me, and I found that it was indeed a comet ... I was surprised that I had not seen it the night before.[36]

News of the comet, the first "scientific" achievement of the young academy, was sent immediately to the king. The report, however, bore Kirch's, not Winkelmann's, name. Published accounts of the comet also bore Kirch's

name, which unfortunately led many historians to attribute the discovery to him alone.

Why did Winkelmann let this happen? Surely she knew that recognition for her achievements could be important to her future career. Nor was she hesitant about publishing; she was to publish three tracts under her own name between 1709 and 1711. Her inability to claim recognition for her discovery hinged, in part, on her lack of training in Latin—the shared scientific language in early eighteenth-century Germany—which made it difficult for her to publish in the *Acta eruditorum*, then Germany's only scientific journal. Her own publications were all in German.

More important to the problem of credit for the initial sighting of the comet, however, was the fact that Maria and Gottfried worked closely together. The labor of husband and wife did not divide along modern lines: he was not fully professional, working in an observatory outside the home; she was not fully a housewife, confined to hearth and home. Nor were they independent professionals, each holding a chair of astronomy. Instead, they worked very much as a team and on common problems. As Vignoles put it, they took turns observing so that their observations followed night after night without interruption. At other times they observed together, dividing the work (he observing to the north, she to the south) so that they could make observations that a single person could not make accurately. After Winkelmann's sighting of the comet on the twenty-first of April, both Kirch and Winkelmann followed its course until the fifth of May.

Though Gottfried Kirch published the report under his own name and as if he alone had made the discovery, it would be an oversimplification to fault him for "expropriating" his wife's achievement. According to Vignoles, a family friend, Kirch was timid about acknowledging his wife's contributions to their common work and so published the first report of the comet without mentioning her. Later, however, someone (we do not know who) told him "that he could feel free to acknowledge her contributions." Thus when the report of the comet was reprinted eight years later, in the first volume of the journal of the Berlin academy, *Miscellanea Berolinensia*, Kirch mentioned Winkelmann's part in the discovery. This report, published in 1710, opens with the words: "my wife ... beheld an unexpected comet."[37]

In addition to their scientific work, Kirch and Winkelmann took an active interest in the development of astronomical facilities at the academy. The Academy of Sciences in Berlin had been founded primarily to promote astronomy. In 1696 Sophie Charlotte, electress of Brandenburg, later queen of Prussia, had directed her minister, Johann Theodor Jablonski, to build an observatory, a project that took a decade to complete. The Kirch family struggled long and hard, squeezing money from academy and royal purses, to create the conditions necessary for good astronomical observations. Winkelmann took an active part in these efforts. On November 4, 1707, she wrote to Leibniz (adviser to Sophie Charlotte and president of the academy), describing her reported sighting of the northern lights ("the likes of which my husband has never seen"), yet her real motive in writing was to secure housing for the astronomers more convenient to the observatory. She asked Leibniz's intervention.

During the years of their acquaintance at the Berlin academy Leibniz had expressed a high regard for Winkelmann's scientific abilities. Though his letters to her have not been preserved, her letters to him reveal his interest in her scientific observations. In 1709 Leibniz presented her to the Prussian court, where Winkelmann was to explain her sighting of sunspots. In a letter of introduction Leibniz wrote:

> There is [in Berlin] a most learned woman who could pass as a rarity. Her achievement is not in literature or rhetoric but in the most profound doctrines of astronomy . . . I do not believe that this woman easily finds her equal in the science in which she excells... She favors the Copernican

system (the idea that the sun is at rest) like all the learned astronomers of our time. And it is a pleasure to hear her defend that system through the Holy Scripture in which she is also very learned. She observes with the best observers, she knows how to handle marvelously the quadrant and the telescope [*grandes lunettes d'approche*].[38]

He added that if only she had been sent to the Cape of Good Hope instead of Peter Kolb, the apprentice given the job, the academy would have received more reliable observations.[39]

Maria Winkelmann apparently made a good impression at the court of Frederick I. The ambassador of Denmark, on a visit to the Royal Observatory, praised her for the aid and assistance she offered her husband in his astronomical work. While at court Winkelmann distributed copies of her astrological pamphlet, *Vorstellung des Himmels bey der Zusammenkunfft dreyer Grossmächtigsten Könige*. Leibniz remarked that Winkelmann's tract was "an astrological note that on the second of that month the sun, Saturn and Venus would be in a straight line. One supposes that there is significance in this."[40]

Maria Winkelmann's three pamphlets published between 1709 and 1711 were all astrological. In his 1721 eulogy to Winkelmann, Vignoles tried to explain away her interest in astrology. "Madame Kirch," as he called her, "prepared horoscopes at the request of her friends, but always against her will and in order not to be unkind to her patrons."[41] Perhaps Winkelmann's interest in astrology was purely financial, as Vignoles suggested, but her correspondence with Leibniz reveals a belief in nature as something more than matter in motion. In her description of the extraordinary northern lights of November 4, 1707, she wrote to Leibniz, "I am not sure what nature was trying to tell us."[42] Another of Winkelmann's pamphlets, *Die Vorbereitung zur grossen Opposition*, predicting the appearance of a new comet, was reviewed favorably in the *Acta eruditorum* in 1712. The reviewer praised her talents, ranking her skill in observation and astronomical calculation as equal to that of her husband. Even though Winkelmann made "concessions" to the art of astrology, the reviewer judged her work valuable. The review closed with a lavish tribute to this woman who understood matters incomprehensible without "the force of intelligence and the zeal of hard work." Several months after the pamphlet appeared in 1711, Jablonski reported favorably that Winkelmann was becoming famous. Nowhere is there a hint that the Berlin academy objected to her astrological work.

Winkelmann mixed astrology and astronomy in calendar making, a project of both scientific and monetary interest for her and the academy. Unlike many major European courts, the Prussian court did not yet have its own calendar. In 1700 the Reichstag at Regensburg ruled that an improved calendar similar to the Gregorian calendar was to be used in German lands.[43] Thus the production of an astronomically accurate calendar became a major project for the Berlin Academy of Sciences, founded in the same year. In addition to fixing the days and months, each calendar predicted the position of the sun, moon, and planets (calculated on the basis of the Rudolphine tables); the phases of the moon; eclipses of the sun or moon to the hour; and the rising and setting of the sun within a quarter of an hour for each day of the year.

The monopoly of the sale of calendars was one of two monopolies granted to the academy by the king (the other was silk). Throughout the eighteenth century, the Berlin Academy of Sciences derived a large part of its revenues from the sale of various forms of calendars. This income (some 2,500 talers per year in the early 1700s) made the position of astronomer particularly important. Calendars—which Leibniz called "libraries for the common man"—had been issued since at least the fourteenth century and drew much of their popular appeal from astrology. Until 1768 there was little distinction between academy calendars and farmer's almanacs; each predicted the best times for haircutting, bloodletting, conceiving children, planting seeds, and felling timber.

Weather prediction, another valuable function of the academy calendars, was an important part of the duties of the academy astronomer. Between 1697 and 1774 different members of the Kirch family kept a daily record of weather. Winkelmann's observations, as was common at that time, were made with the aid of a "weatherglass," a term used for both the barometer and thermometer. Daily observation, she noted, sharpens prediction and can be of great usefulness in many areas of life, especially in agriculture and navigation. It was Winkelmann's hope that "weather can be more accurately forecast, if more diligence is applied."[44]

The Attempt to Become Academy Astronomer

Gottfried Kirch died in 1710. It fell to the executive council of the academy—President Leibniz, Secretary Jablonski, his brother and court pastor, D. E. Jablonski, and the librarian—to appoint a new astronomer. The council needed to make the appointment quickly, as the academy depended on the yearly revenues from the calendar; but apart from one in-house candidate, Jablonski could think of no one qualified for the position. Ten years earlier the council had settled on Gottfried Kirch, who despite his advanced age (sixty-one) was the best in the field. Though there were few candidates, Maria Winkelmann's name was not even considered in 1710. This is even more surprising when one considers that her qualifications were not that different from her husband's when he was appointed. They both had long years of experience preparing calendars (before coming to the Berlin Academy of Sciences, Kirch had earned his living by selling Christian, Jewish, and Turkish calendars); they had both discovered comets—Kirch in 1680, Winkelmann in 1702; and both had prepared ephemerides and recorded numerous observations. What Winkelmann did not have, which nearly every member of the academy did, was a university degree.

Kirch died in July; Winkelmann made her move in August. Since her name had not come up in discussions about the appointment, Winkelmann submitted it herself, along with her credentials. In a letter to Secretary Jablonski, she asked that she and her son be appointed assistant astronomers in charge of preparing the academy calendar.... Winkelmann made it clear that she was asking only for a position as *assistant* calendar maker. "I would not," she wrote, be so "bold as to suggest that I take over completely the office [of astronomer]." Her argument for her candidacy was twofold. First, she argued, she was well qualified, since she had been instructed in astronomical calculation and observation by her husband. Second, and more important, she had been engaged in astronomical work since her marriage and had, de facto, been working for the academy since her husband's appointment ten years earlier. Indeed, she reported, "for some time, while my dear departed husband was weak and ill, I prepared the calendar from his calculations and published it under his name." She also reminded Jablonski that he himself had remarked on how she lent a helping hand to her husband's astronomical work—work for which she was paid a wage—and asked to be allowed to stay in the astronomer's quarters. For Winkelmann, a position at the Berlin academy was not just an honor, it was a way to support herself and her four children. Her husband, she reported, had left her with no means of support.

Jablonski was aware that the academy's handling of the Winkelmann case would set important precedents for the place of women in Germany's leading scientific body. In September 1710 he cautioned Leibniz: "You should be aware that this approaching decision could serve as a precedent. We are tentatively of the opinion that this case must be judged not only on its present merits but also as it could be judged for all time, for what we concede to her could serve as an example in the future."[45] The effect on the academy's reputation of hiring a woman was a matter of some concern. Again Jablonski wrote to Leibniz:

That she be kept on in an official capacity to work on the calendar or to continue with observations simply will not do. Already during her husband's lifetime the society was burdened with ridicule because its calendar was prepared by a woman. If she were now to be kept on in such a capacity, mouths would gape even wider.[46]

By rejecting Winkelmann's candidacy, the academy ensured that the stigma attached to women would not further tarnish its already dull reputation.

Leibniz was one of the few at the academy who supported Winkelmann. In the council meeting of March 18, 1711 (one of the last meetings at which he presided before leaving Berlin), Leibniz argued that the academy, considered as either a religious or an academic body, should provide a widow with housing and salary for six months as was customary. At Leibniz's urging the academy granted Winkelmann the right to stay in its housing a while longer; the proposal that she be paid a salary, however, was defeated. Instead the council paid her forty talers for her husband's observation notebooks. Later that year the academy showed some goodwill toward Winkelmann by presenting her with a medal.

After Leibniz left Berlin Winkelmann took her case to the king. With Leibniz gone, however, the council became even more adamant in denying her requests. In 1712, after one and a half years of active petitioning, Winkelmann received a final rejection. The council found her request unseemly, (*ungereimt*) and inadmissible (*unzulässig*). "We must," the minutes read, "try and persuade her to be content and to withdraw of her own accord; otherwise we must definitely say no."

The academy never spelled out its reasons for refusing to appoint her to an official position, but Winkelman traced her misfortunes to her sex. In a poignant passage she recounted her husband's assurance that God would show his grace through influential patrons. This, she wrote, does not hold true for the "female sex." Her disappointment was deep: "Now I go through a severe desert, and because … water is scarce … the taste is bitter." It was about this time that Winkelmann felt compelled to defend women's intellectual abilities in the preface to one of her scientific works. Citing biblical authority, she argued that the "female sex as well as the male possesses talents of mind and spirit." With experience and diligent study, she wrote, a woman could become "as skilled as a man at observing and understanding the skies."[47]

Although Winkelmann had been involved in preparing the calendar for ten years and knew the work well, the position of academy astronomer was awarded to Johann Heinrich Hoffmann. Hoffmann had been a member of the academy since its founding in 1700 and had long hoped to be appointed academy astronomer. Yet his tenure as astronomer was not a happy one. By December 1711 he was already behind in his work. Jablonski wrote to Leibniz complaining that Hoffmann was guilty of neglecting his work. Jablonski suggested that perhaps Hoffmann needed an assistant; ironically he suggested "Frau Kirchin, for example, who would spur him on a bit." In 1712 Jablonski again had occasion to complain to Leibniz about Hoffmann's performance. Hoffmann had not completed the yearly observations as he should have, and his work for the calendar was incomplete. Hoffmann was officially censured by the academy for his poor performance. While Hoffmann was being reprimanded, Winkelmann was becoming, as Jablonski reported, "rather well known" for her pamphlet on the conjunction of Saturn and Jupiter.

During this period, conflict arose between Winkelmann and Hoffmann, each of whom considered the other a competitor at the observatory. Jablonski reported to Leibniz that Winkelmann had complained that "Hoffmann uses her help secretly, yet denounces her publicly and never lets her use the observatory." Unemployed and unappreciated for her scientific skills, Winkelmann moved across Berlin in October 1712 to the private observatory of Baron Bernhard Frederick von Krosigk. This did not end Hoffmann's problems with the academy. In 1715 Jablonski complained once

again to Leibniz that Hoffmann was neglecting his duties.

The Clash between Guild Traditions and Professional Science

Did Winkelmann have a legitimate claim to the post of assistant astronomer? How was it possible in 1700 for a woman to hold a semi-official position (as Winkelmann did) as assistant astronomer to her husband at the Berlin academy? Winkelmann owed her position at the academy to the perpetuation of guild traditions. Wolfram Fischer has argued that the relation of apprentice-journeyman-master provided a model for many German institutions. Fischer gives the example of the masons; W. V. Farrar has developed the example of the universities. According to Farrar, the guild character of the university system survived longer in Germany than elsewhere.[48]

But while retaining vestiges of the guild system, the Berlin academy incorporated other traditions. We should distinguish two levels of participation in the academy. At the top was a tier of university-educated, internationally renowned scientists and philosophers. This part of the organization had nothing in common with the guilds; rather, class standing and scientific distinction were important for membership at this level. Like members of the Royal Society in London and the Académie Royale des Sciences in Paris, many "gentlemen" members of the Berlin academy were of high social standing. It was its financial structure that set the Berlin academy apart from its counterparts in Paris or London and nearer craft traditions. Members of the Académie Royale des Sciences in Paris drew pensions directly from the king's purse in order to distance themselves from traditional trades and professions, considered "mere occupations." The Berlin academy, in contrast, drew much of its revenues from two trades—calendar making and silk making—and hired artisans, the second tier of participants in its activities, to carry out the tasks required.

The academy astronomer was caught between the two tiers of the hierarchy: as a university-educated mathematician, he was a distinguished gentleman; as calendar maker, he was an artisan engaged for the services he could provide. The "gentlemen" of the academy (except the president and secretary) were not paid, nor did they pay for their membership. The astronomer, however, like the other artisans of the academy, was paid a living (500 talers per year) from its coffers. It should be noted that though Maria Winkelmann asked to continue as calendar maker, she never asked to become a member of the academy (nor was she granted membership).

As the wife of an artisan-astronomer Winkelmann enjoyed a modest measure of respect at the Academy. When she petitioned the council to continue as assistant calendar maker, she was invoking (although not explicitly) principles well established in the organized crafts. In most cases guild regulations gave a widow the right to run the family business after the death of her husband. In her study of thirty-eight Cologne guilds in the late Middle Ages, Margret Wensky found that eighteen of those guilds allowed a widow to continue the family business after her husband's death.[49] The rights of widows followed three general patterns. In some guilds the widow was allowed to serve as an independent master as long as she lived. In others she was allowed to continue the family business but only with the help of journeymen or apprentices. In still others she filled in for one or two years to provide continuity until her eldest son came of age. Within lower echelons of the academy, widows were allowed to continue in their husband's position. A woman whom we know only by the name of "Pont," widow of the keeper of the academy's mulberry trees, was allowed to complete the last four years of her husband's six-year contract. This is what Maria Winkelmann tried to do. After the death of her husband she tried to carry on the "family" business of calendar making as an independent master. Yet, as we have seen, she found that traditions that had once secured women a (limited) role in science were not to apply in the new institutions.

Though the academy retained vestiges of an older order, it also contained the seeds of a new. The founding of the academy in 1700 was a first step in the professionalization of astronomy in Germany. Earlier observatories—those of Hevelius in Danzig and Eimmart in Nuremberg—had been private. The academy's observatory, however, was a public ornament of the Prussian state. Astronomers were no longer owners and directors of their own observatories but employees of the academy, selected by a patron on the basis of personal merit rather than family tradition. This shift of the character of scientific institutions from private to public had dramatic implications for women's work in science. As astronomy moved more and more out of private observatories and into the public world, women lost their toehold in modern science.

A Brief Return to the Academy

Although Winkelmann could not remain at the Berlin academy, she did continue her astronomical work. At Baron von Krosigk's private observatory in Berlin, where she and Gottfried Kirch had worked while the academy observatory was under construction, Winkelmann reached the height of her career. With her husband dead and her son away at university, she enjoyed the rank of a "master" astronomer. She continued her daily observations and—now the master—had two students to assist her. The published reports of their joint observations bear her name. During this period she also supported herself and her daughters by preparing calendars for Breslau and Nuremberg. When Krosigk died in 1714, Maria Winkelmann left his observatory for a position in Danzig as an assistant to a professor of mathematics. This part of her life remains sketchy. When this position fell through, Winkelmann again found a patron. The family of Johannes Hevelius (Gottfried Kirch's teacher) invited her and her son, Christfried, now a student in Leipzig, to reorganize the deceased astronomer's observatory and to use it to continue their own observations.

In 1716 the Winkelmann-Kirch family received an invitation from Peter the Great of Russia to become astronomers in Moscow. The family decided instead to return to Berlin when Christfried was appointed observer for the academy following the death of Hoffmann. Academy officials expressed grave reservations about the abilities of their newly appointed astronomers—Christfried Kirch was not well grounded in astronomical theory and could not express himself decently in Latin or his native German; J. W. Wagner was weak in astronomical calculation. Academy funds, however, were insufficient to support the appointment of a "celebrated" astronomer, who would require a higher salary, better housing, and a number of assistants. Under these circumstances a factor weighing in Kirch's favor was that, along with him, the academy received an extra astronomical hand—Winkelmann—with skills very similar to those of the two astronomers under consideration. Thus, Winkelmann returned once again to the work of observation and calendar making for the academy, this time as assistant to her son.

But all was not well. The opinion was still afoot that women should not do astronomy, at least not in a public capacity. In 1717 Winkelmann was reprimanded by the academy council for talking too much to visitors at the observatory. The council cautioned her to "retire to the background and leave the talking to Wagner and her son." A month later the academy again reported that "Frau Kirch meddles too much with Society matters and is too visible at the observatory when strangers visit." Again the council warned Winkelmann "to let herself be seen at the observatory as little as possible especially on *public* occasions."[50] Maria Winkelmann was forced to make a choice. She could either continue to badger the academy for a position of her own, or, in the interest of her son's reputation, she could retire, as the academy requested, to the background. Vignoles reports that she chose the latter option. Academy records show, however, that the choice was not hers. On October 21, 1717, the academy resolved to remove Winkelmann—who apparently had paid little heed to their warnings—from academy grounds. She was forced to leave her house and the observatory. The academy did not, however, seem to want her to give up her duties as mother; officials expressed the hope that Winkelmann "could find a house nearby so that Herr Kirch could continue to eat at her table."[51]

In 1717 Winkelmann quit the academy's observatory and continued her observations only at home, as was thought appropriate, "behind closed doors"—a move which Vignoles judged detrimental to the progress she might have made in astronomy. With few scientific instruments at her disposal, she was forced to quit astronomical science. Maria Winkelmann died of fever in 1720. In Vignoles's opinion "she merited a fate better than the one she received."[52]

Invisible Assistants

Maria Winkelmann was not the only woman present at the founding of the Berlin Academy of Sciences. Sophie Charlotte, queen of Prussia, was important as an ambassador of scientific ideas at the court in Berlin. Working closely with Leibniz and her ministers, Sophie Charlotte carried forth plans and negotiations for the founding of the Berlin academy with such vigor that, as we have seen, Leibniz claimed that women of elevated mind should be the ones to cultivate knowledge. Frederick II, her grandson, credited her with establishing the Academy of Sciences. He wrote that "she founded the royal Academy and brought Leibniz and many other learned men to Berlin. She wanted always to know the first principle of things." Since she died shortly after its founding, it remains unclear whether Sophie Charlotte intended to take an active part in the academy or to serve merely as patron.

The founding statutes of the Berlin Academy of Sciences did not bar women from membership. In fact, Leibniz thought women should benefit from participation. In his sketch of academy regulations of 1700, he wrote that a scientific academy would foster good taste, solid understanding, and an appreciation of God's handiwork, not only among German nobility, "but among other people of high standing (as well as among women)."[53] Yet despite his intentions women were not admitted. Perhaps the decision to use the scientific societies of London and Paris as models for the academy in Berlin reinforced the exclusion of women. Although neither the London nor the Paris society had regulations excluding women, neither society admitted them.

The fate of Winkelmann's daughters—Christine and Margaretha—reveals a process of privatization of women within the academy. Trained in astronomy from the age of ten, both Kirch daughters worked for the academy as assistants to their brother Christfried. According to Vignoles, "Margaretha, the younger sister, usually took a telescope; Christine, the older, most often took the pendulum in order to mark exactly the time of each individual observation." Christine also did calculations for her brother; she and Christfried checked each other's calculations for accuracy. Yet having witnessed the lost battles of their mother, Christine and Margaretha did not ask (as Winkelmann had) for official positions. Nor did they exude the fire of their mother, badgering the academy for housing or greeting foreign (male) visitors. Rather they molded their behavior to fit academy prescriptions, becoming "invisible helpers" to their brother. Again, Vignoles described the sisters' situation: "They helped their brother carry out his professional duties; ... nonetheless they remained very private and spoke with no one but their close friends. By the same modesty, they avoided going to the observatory when there was to be an eclipse or other observation that might attract strangers."[54]

When Christfried died in 1740, the Kirch sisters lost their male protector and were forced to observe more often at home. Although they watched the heavens daily, their situation made serious work almost impossible. When Christine sent their observations of the comets of 1742 and 1743 to Joseph-Nicolas

Delisle, director of the Paris Observatory, she complained that "we observed daily [the course of the comet] as well as we could ... but our observations were done under very bad conditions and with inferior instruments, namely with a two foot [*zwei Schühe*] telescope.... We could not use a larger telescope because our house had no window large enough to accommodate it."[55] Though Christine and Margaretha Kirch had little opportunity to go to the observatory after their brother's death, Christine continued to prepare the academy calendar—silently and behind the scenes—from at least 1720 until her death in 1782. This is not surprising; by the 1740s calendar making was no longer on the cutting edge of astronomical science but tedious and time-consuming work. Never married, Christine supported herself through her calendar work, for which she received a small pension of 400 talers per year.

After Christine Kirch retired, there were no other women doing scientific work for the Berlin Academy of Sciences until well into the twentieth century. During the eighteenth century the academy did, however, grant honorary membership to some women of the noble classes. The first to be granted honorary membership at the (then) Académie Royale des Sciences et Belles-Lettres was one of the most powerful persons in Europe at the time, Catherine the Great of Russia. Rank still spoke loudly in Prussia, and the prestige of rank outweighed the liabilities of sex. Catherine's position in the academy was wholly honorary.[56] After Frederick the Great's tenure as president, few women were elected. One exception was poet and writer Duchess Juliane Giovane, who was awarded honorary membership in 1794. No other woman was elected for 106 years, and even then it was for purely nonscientific reasons: In 1900 Maria Wentzel was awarded honorary membership for her gift of 1,500,000 marks.

It is clear that before 1949 only women of the very highest social standing were admitted to the Berlin Academy of Sciences. Though Catherine the Great and Juliane Giovane were women of intellectual stature, they were also women of social rank. Maria Winkelmann, however, was a tradeswoman who dirtied her hands in the actual work of astronomy (she was referred to by academy officials as a *Weib*, not a *Frauenzimmer*). The election of a woman purely on scientific merit had to wait until 1949, when the physicist Lise Meitner was elected—but only as a corresponding member. Meitner was followed by the chemist Irène Joliot-Curie, daughter of Marie Curie, and then by the medical doctor Cécilie Vogt in 1950. The first woman to be awarded full membership was the historian Liselotte Welskopf, in 1964. Since the founding of the Academy of Sciences in Berlin in 1700, only fourteen of its 2,900 members have been women. Of those fourteen, only four have enjoyed full membership. As of 1983 no woman had ever served in a position of leadership as academy president, vice-president, general secretary, or head of any of the various scientific sections.

In seventeenth- and eighteenth-century Europe, craft traditions gave women limited access to the tools of science. Science at this time was a new enterprise forging new ideals and institutions. With respect to the problem of women, science may be seen as standing at a fork in the road: it could either affirm and broaden practices inherited from craft traditions and welcome women as full participants, or it could reaffirm university traditions and continue to exclude them. As the case of Maria Winkelmann demonstrates, the Berlin Academy of Sciences chose to follow the latter path.

The poor representation of women in the Berlin Academy of Sciences cannot be traced simply to an absence of women qualified in science. Instead, the exclusion of women resulted from policies consciously implemented at an early period in the academy's history. These decisions, made in the early eighteenth century, held serious consequences for women's later participation....

Family Assistants: Caroline Herschel

Women were not to travel a public road in pursuit of science. With their exclusion from university..., women had few options but to pursue science privately. In the nineteenth century, the normal pattern for women in science was that of the private assistant, usually a wife, sometimes a sister or niece, who devoted her life to a man as a loyal assistant and indefatigable aide. The wifely assistant is somewhat difficult to distinguish from the guild's unpaid artisan wife, for she is the legacy of that tradition. Yet changes both in the structure of science and in the family served to distance female assistants from the world of science. A scientific wife became an increasingly private assistant, hidden from view within the domestic sanctuary....

Caroline Herschel was one of those women who fit this mold. Though better known than Maria Winkelmann..., Herschel did not display [her] independence of mind. Caroline wrote that she considered herself a "tool" for her brother, William; when he needed a soprano for his musical ventures she learned to sing, when he needed an astronomical assistant she learned to observe the heavens. Caroline Herschel did not even choose to become an astronomer. As she wrote of herself, "I found I was to be trained for an assistant-astronomer, and by way of encouragement a telescope adapted for 'sweeping' ... was given to me."[57] For most of the rest of her life, she swept the skies for comets according to her brother's instructions. It is impossible to say whether with more initiative she could have achieved greater independence in the astronomical world.

Caroline Herschel's obeisance (she once described herself as a "well-trained puppy-dog") resulted, in part, from the restrictions on women in intellectual culture. Without her family connections it is doubtful that she could have become an astronomer. She had few options. As a girl in Hanover she received an elementary education along with her brothers, learning to read and write at the garrison school. Although her father wished to give her the same lessons in music and philosophy that he gave William, her mother determined that Caroline's education would be rough and useful. She was taught to knit and to sew in order to supply the family with socks and linen. When by the age of twenty-two she had not yet married, Caroline was delighted to join her brother William in England and become his housekeeper and general assistant, first as a music copyist and performer, then as an astronomical observer and recorder. William Herschel, astronomer to King George III, was a skilled telescope maker and constructed what were for that time the most powerful reflecting telescopes. Caroline learned all she knew about astronomy from William and, throughout the many years of their collaboration, remained his faithful assistant, rarely feeling it her place to set her own projects and tasks.

Caroline Herschel's work in astronomy was limited both by her position as assistant and by the instruments at her disposal. "The employment of writing down the observations, when my brother uses the 20-feet reflector," she wrote, "does not often allow me time to look at the heavens; but as he is now on a visit to Germany, I have taken the opportunity of his absence to sweep in the neighborhood of the sun, in search of comets."[58] Only with William away and using his telescope did Caroline discover her first comet. Her remark highlights a more general problem for women working in science in this period. For one thing, women seldom had access to the best scientific equipment, and their science suffered as a result. As Caroline once remarked, she did not discover her first comet with the "seven-foot" Newtonian telescope provided for her use but with her brother's more powerful device. Furthermore, working as assistants, women were kept busy recording observations and producing calculations and rarely had opportunities to undertake their own projects. Only in her brother's absence was Caroline able to follow her own inclinations.

If Caroline stood in William's shadow, she also shared in his glory. Within a period of about ten years (1786–1797) she discovered eight comets (having a claim to priority on

five); in addition, she discovered three nebulae and published her *Catalogue of Stars* with the Royal Society. She was commended by the Royal Society, and her discoveries were announced through the Society by letter to astronomers in Paris and Munich. After the discovery of her third comet, the French astronomer Jérôme de Lalande wrote her a letter of congratulations. She also won the attention of royalty. When William Prince of Orange stopped at the Herschel house at Slough to ask some questions about planets he was well aware of her astronomical expertise. In 1787, King George III awarded her a pension of fifty pounds per year for her work as William's assistant (William received two hundred pounds as a royal astronomer).

Caroline Herschel became the first woman to publish scientific findings in the *Philosophical Transactions* of the Royal Society. Although she was never honored with membership in the Society (no woman was until 1945), she was awarded the Gold Medal of the Royal Astronomical Society, and elected ("God knows what for," she writes in her memoirs) an honorary member in 1835. As she was then eighty-five and living once again in Hanover, the election meant little.

Caroline Herschel's temperament was such that, under other circumstances, she might have acted no different. But she was hardly an exception. Women had few options in the nineteenth century. With universities closed to them, they had to continue to rely on family members for ties to the scientific world. Though women may have served science well in their positions as invisible assistants, the growth of an increasingly public world of science distanced them from centers of scientific innovation. A wife like Maria Winkelmann-Kirch could no longer become assistant astronomer to a scientific academy through marriage. Such positions became reserved for those with public certification of their qualifications.

Notes

1. Archives of the Académie des Sciences, Comité Secret, 27 December 1910.
2. Frances Yates, *The French Academies of the Sixteenth Century* (London, 1947), p. 1.
3. Ibid., p. 32.
4. D. Maclaren Robertson, *A History of the French Academy, 1635–1910* (New York, 1910), p. 61. It is doubtful that these discussions were recorded. My search of academy archives in the spring of 1986 turned up nothing.
5. *Supplément manuscrit au Menagiana*, ed. Pierre Le Gouz, Bibliothèque Nationale, MF 23254, no. 184.... See also Gilles Ménage, *Historia mulierum philosopharum* (Lyon, 1690), also translated as *The History of Women Philosophers* by Beatrice Zedler (Lanham, 1984)....
6. *Les Registres de l'Académie française, 1672–1793* (Paris, 1895),vol. l, p. 332.
7. Claude Clerselier, ed., *Lettres de M. Descartes* (1659; Paris, 1724), vol. 2, preface.
8. Pierre Richelet, *Dictionnaire de la langue françoise, ancienne et moderne* (Lyon, 1759), vol. 1, p. 21. Compare the 1719 (Rouen, vol. 1, p. 12) and 1759 editions of Richelet's dictionary. In the 1719 edition, the editors have left Richelet's remark that the academy at Arles should be praised for its "glorious conduct" with respect to women. The editors of the 1759 edition removed this sentence, noting only that "one no longer speaks of that academy."
9. The salary of only 2,000 livres per year was not enough to maintain a bourgeois lifestyle at this time in France. Members had to supplement their income from the academy with private funds.
10. Thomas Sprat, *History of the Royal Society of London* (London, 1667), pp. 62–63, 72, 435.
11. Michael Hunter reports the distribution by occupation of the Royal Society for the years 1660–1664: aristocrats 14 percent; courtiers and politicians 24 percent; gentlemen 12 percent; lawyers 6 percent; divines 8 percent; doctors 16 percent; scholars and writers 7 percent; civil servants 5 percent; merchants and tradesmen 4 percent (*The Royal Society and Its Fellows, 1660–1700: The Morphology of an Early Scientific Institution* [Chalfont St. Giles, Bucks, 1982], table 6, p. 116).
12. See Samuel Mintz, "The Duchess of Newcastle's Visit to the Royal Society," *Journal of English and Germanic Philology*, 51 (1952): 168–176.
13. Thomas Birch, *History of the Royal Society* (London, 1756–57), vol. 2, p. 175; and Samuel Pepys, *The Diary of Samuel Pepys*, ed. Robert Latham and William Matthews (London, 1970–1983), vol. 8, p. 243.
14. Pepys, *Diary*, vol. 8, p. 243....
15. Mrs. Evelyn quoted in John Evelyn, *The Diary of John Evelyn*, ed. Austin Dobson (London, 1906), vol. 2, p. 271.
16. Archives Nationales, AJ XV 510, no. 331. Basseporte received 800 livres pension plus 300 livres living expenses. Compare this to the 1,200 to 3,000 livres paid to the anatomical demonstrators.
17. Ann Sutherland Harris and Linda Nochlin, *Women Artists: 1550–1950* (Los Angeles, 1976), pp. 34–37. Despite this ruling, several women were elected to the academy of painting in the eighteenth century, but their numbers were never allowed to exceed four.
18. *Histoire de l'Académie royale des sciences. Année 1759* (Paris, 1765), p. 94.
19. Mireille Laget, "Childbirth in Seventeenth- and Eighteenth-Century France: Obstetrical Practices and Collective Attitudes," *Medicine and Society in France*, ed. Robert Forster and Orest Ranum (Baltimore, 1980), p. 169.
20. Carolyn Lougee, *Le Paradis des Femmes: Women, Salons, and Social Stratification in Seventeenth Century France* (Princeton, 1976), pp. 41–53 and 117–118. Seventeenth-century salon women came overwhelmingly from the nobility: of the women for whom such information is available 74 percent were noble (48 percent coming from old noble families and 26 percent from newly noble families). Lougee finds significant, however, the proportion of women who were newly noble (26 percent) or nonnoble (14 percent); the status of the remaining 12 percent is unknown. In a society that equated elite with noble status, Lougee points to the inclusion of such a large proportion of non- and new nobility as evidence of the extent to which salons were forging new alliances within French society. See also Joan Landes, *Women and the Public Sphere in the Age of the French Revolution* (Ithaca, 1988), pp. 23–31; Alan Kors, *D'Holboch's Coterie* (Princeton,

1976); and Evelyn Bodek, "Salonières and Bluestockings: Educated Obsolescence and Germinating Feminism," *Feminist Studies*, 3 (1976): 186. A full study of the eighteenth-century salons and their role in eighteenth-century intellectual culture remains to be written.

21. See Sara Malueg, "Women and the *Encyclopédie*," in *French Women and the Age of Enlightenment*, ed. Samia Spencer (Bloomington, 1984), p. 260; and Terry Dock, "Women in the *Encyclopédie*," (Ph.D. diss., Vanderbilt University, 1979).

22. Dorinda Outram, "Before Objectivity: Wives, Patronage, and Cultural Reproduction in Early Nineteenth-Century French Science" in *Uneasy Careers and Intimate Lives*, ed. Pnina Abir-Am and Dorinda Outram (New Brunswick, 1987) p. 19.

23. Yates, *The French Academies*, p. 285.

24. Caroline to Leibniz, in *Die Werke von Leibniz*, vol. 11, pp. 52, 71, and 90.

25. Letter from Elizabeth to Descartes, 12 June 1645, in A. Foucher de Careil, *Descartes, la Princesse Elisabeth, et la Reine Christine* (Paris, 1909), pp. 65–66.

26. Letter from Elizabeth to Descartes, 10 June 1643, in ibid., p. 50.

27. In the 1750s, Marie Ardinghelli of Tuscany charged the Abbé Nollet with the task of keeping her in touch with all recent discoveries in physics. In 1757, Nollet read part of Ardinghelli's description of an erupting volcano before a session of the Académie Royale des Sciences (*Procès-verbaux*, 76 [1757]: 335).

28. See Edgar Zilsel, "The Sociological Roots of Science," *American Journal of Sociology*, 47 (1942): 545–546; and Arthur Clegg, "Craftsmen and the Origin of Science," *Science and Society*, 43 (1979): 186–201.

29. Margret Wensky, *Die Stellung der Frau in der stadtkölnischen Wirtschaft im Spätmittelalter* (Cologne, 1981), pp. 7, 318–319. Wensky traces women's strength in Cologne's economic life to the fact that textile manufacture predominated, and this was a type of manufacture in which women were strong.

30. Jean Quataert has warned against conflating important distinctions between guilds and households (see her "Shaping of Women's Work in Manufacturing: Guilds, Households, and the State in Central Europe, 1648–1870," *American Historical Review*, 90 [1985]: 1122–1148). For the case of astronomy or entomology, however, the larger danger has been to ignore almost entirely both of these forms of production. Here I use the term *craft* to refer to household production and *guild* to refer to regulated crafts. See also Antony Black, *Guilds and Civil Society in European Political Thought from the Twelfth Century to the Present* (Ithaca, 1984). There were, of course, women artisans in France who fit the patterns I discuss below.

31. See Maria Cunitz, *Urania propitia* (Oels, 1650), p. 147.

32. Johann Eberti, *Eröffnetes Cabinet des gelehrten Frauenzimmers* (Frankfurt and Leipzig, 1706).

33. According to Peter Ketsch, family trades often passed to the daughter (see his *Frauen im Mittelalter* [Düsseldorf, 1983], vol. 1, p. 29).

34. See Margaret Rossiter, "'Women's Work' in Science, 1880–1910" *Isis*, 71 (1980): 381–398. See also her *Women Scientists in America: Struggles and Strategies to 1940* (Baltimore 1982), pp. 51–72.

35. The Berlin Academy first bore a Latin name, the Societas Regia Scientiarum. From its founding, it was known as the Brandenburgische or Berlin Societät der Wissenschaften. In the 1740s, it took a French name, Académie Royale des Sciences et Belles-Lettres. In the 1780s it became the Königlich Preussische Akademie der Wissenschaften, which it remained until its reorganization after World War II, when it took its present name, the Akademie der Wissenschaften der Deutschen Demokratischen Republik.

36. Kirch papers, Paris Observatory, MS A.B. 3.5, no. 81 B, p. 33.

37. See Gottfried Kirch, "Observationes cometae novi," *Acta eruditorum*, 21 April 1702, pp. 256–258; Vignoles, "Eloge de Madame Kirch à l'occasion de laquelle on parle de quelques autres femmes et d'un paisan astronomes," *Bibliothèque germanique*, 3 (1721), pp. 175–176; and Gottfried Kirch, "De cometa anno 1702: Berolini observato," *Miscellanea Berolinensia*, 1 (1710): 213–214.

38. Leibniz to Sophie Charlotte, January 1709, *Die Werke von Leibniz*, vol. 9, pp. 295–296.

39. Leibniz is referring to the attempt to get an exact measurement of the lunar parallax, which failed because Baron von Krosigk's apprentice, Peter Kolb, was irresponsible and only occasionally made observations.

40. Leibniz's note in the margin of Winkelmann's letter to him, 17 July 1709, Leibniz Archiv, reprinted in Harnack, "Berichte des Secretars Jablonski an den Präsidenten Leibniz," no. 87.

41. Vignoles, "Eloge de Madame Kirch," p. 182.

42. Winkelmann to Leibniz, 4 November 1707, Leibniz Archiv, Kirch, no. 472, pp. 11–12. Though astrology had begun losing ground in Germany in the sixteenth century, it continued to exercise considerable influence even within scientific circles....

43. Since the Gregorian calendar reform of 1582, Catholics and Protestants had used calendars that differed by ten days (Dietrich Wattenberg, "Zur Geschichte der Astronomie in Berlin im 16. bis 18. Jahrhundert I," *Die Sterne*, 48 [1972]: 165). The "improved" Protestant calendar was similar to the Georgian calendar except that Easter was calculated differently.

44. Gottfried Kirch and Winkelmann, *Das älteste Berliner Wetter-Buch: 1700–1701*, ed. G. Hellmann (Berlin, 1893), pp. 12 and 20–21.

45. Harnack, "Berichte des Secretars Jablonski an den Präsidenten Leibniz," no. 115. Leibniz's response to Jablonski has not been preserved.

46. Ibid., no. 116.

47. Winkelmann to the council of the Berlin Academy, 3 March 1711, DDR Academy Archives, Kirch papers, I, III, 1, p. 50; and Winkelmann, *Vorbe-reitung*, pp. 3–4.

48. Wolfram Fischer, *Handwerksrecht und Handwerkswirtschaft um 1800* (Berlin, 1955), p. 18; and W. V. Farrar, "Science and the German University System: 1790–1850," in *The Emergence of Science in Western Europe*, ed. Maurice Crosland (London, 1975), p. 181.

49. Wensky, *Die Stellung der Frau*, pp. 58–59.

50. "Protokollum Concilii, Societatis Scientiarum," 18 August 1717, DDR Academy Archives, I, IV, 6, pt. 2, p. 269, 272–273 (emphasis added).

51. Vignoles, "Eloge de Madame Kirch," p. 181; "Protokollum Concilii, Societatis Scientiarum," 21 October 1717, DDR Academy Archives, 1, IV, 6, pt. 2, pp. 275–276.

52. Vignoles, "Eloge de Madame Kirch," pp. 181–182.

53. "Leibnizens Denkschrift in Bezug auf die Einrichtung einer Societas Scientiarum et Artium in Berlin vom 26 März 1700, bestimmt für den Kurfürsten," in Harnack, *Geschichte der Akademie zu Berlin*, vol. 2, p. 80. I thank Gerda Utermöhlen of the Leibniz Archiv, Hanover, for calling this passage to my attention.

54. Alphonse des Vignoles, "Eloge de M. Kirch le Fils, Astronome de Berlin," *Journal littéraire d'Allemagne de Suisse et du Nord*, 1 (1741): 349.

55. Christine Kirch to Delisle, 24 July 1744, Paris Observatory, Delisle papers, MS A.B. 1. IV, no. 12a; and 28 April 1745, no. 42.

56. It should be pointed out that Catherine was elected in 1767, when Frederick the Great, as president of the academy, personally oversaw all academy appointments. The following year Frederick decreed that Catherine's membership in the academy should be elevated from honorary status to that of a regular foreign member....

57. Caroline Herschel, *Memoir and Correspondence of Caroline Herschel*, ed. Mrs. John Herschel (New York, 1876), p. 52....

58. "An Account of a New Comet," by Miss Caroline Herschel, read at the Royal Society, November 9, 1786, London, printed in the *Philosophical Transactions of the Royal Society of London*, 77 (1787): 1–3.

Women of Third World Descent in the Sciences

Sandra Harding

In the United States the opportunities in the sciences for women of color have been even more vigorously restricted than for white women. Specific information is difficult to come by. It is frequently absent from accounts of the experiences of "women," which tend to focus on white women; it is absent from the discussions of "minorities," which usually focus on men's lives. Quantitative data about women of color is often aggregated within the data about "women" or "minorities," or sometimes even "women and minorities." Nevertheless, some intriguing glimpses of African American women's lives in the sciences and technology are available.

A very few black women have managed to gain the education and credentialing for careers in the natural sciences, and these have been disproportionately in medicine. Darlene Clark Hine has written about the 115 black women who received M.D. degrees in the United States in the quarter-century after the end of slavery, degrees granted by the New England Female Medical College in Boston, the Women's Medical College of Philadelphia, the New York Medical College for Women, and others. Hine points out that these women led lives different from those of other physicians—men or white women—in several ways. Most obviously, "they were an integral part of the black communities in which they practiced," working at black colleges and in community clinics and hospitals, becoming clubwomen, and successfully combining their lives as wives and mothers with their careers as physicians—thereby challenging the prevailing belief that higher education and professional training made a woman less feminine (though femininity clearly had a different meaning in African American communities than it did among whites, as Sojourner Truth pointed out). Moreover, they also founded an array of health-care institutions: "They established hos-pitals and clinics, trained nurses, taught elementary health rules to students and patients, and founded homes and service agencies for poor women and unwed girls of both races." Though this small group of professionals came primarily from the upper echelons of black society, each one used her education and skills for the benefit of black people: "These early black professional women played an undeniably significant role in the overall survival struggle of all black people."[1]

By the 1920s there was a notable reduction in the number of black women physicians. Hine suggests two reasons: the convergence of renewed forces of racism, sexism, and professionalization no doubt was responsible in part; moreover, "instead of entering the medical profession, the aspiring, career-oriented black women began focusing on nursing as a more viable alternative for a professionally rewarding place in the American health care system."[2] From other sources, it becomes clear that foundations put pressure on educational institutions to limit the career aspirations of blacks in the sciences and medicine.[3] Hine's recent study of black nurses from 1890 to 1950 shows the immense struggles it took for black women to gain access to nursing education, just as black physicians were being denied access to staff positions in white hospitals and black patients were being denied access to medical treatment. Because of this discrimination and exclusion, black communities developed a parallel system of training schools and hospitals.[4]

When the topic is American scientists of African descent, the discussion of "why so few" women or men requires a more comprehensive context than when scientists of European descent are the primary population under consideration. It is amazing that any African Americans achieved scientific careers in fields other than medicine prior to World War II when one considers how severely limited graduate science education was for them.[5] Indeed, even public high school education was unavailable for some urban African Americans until as late as the mid-1960s. In the early 1960s, some cities and states in the South still provided no public education at all for blacks past the eighth grade. A recent lecturer on my campus described the Tallahassee, Florida, "Negro High School" that he had attended: segregated elementary schools asked African American parents to permit their children to be "left back" in eighth grade for four years so that their teachers could provide them with the knowledge and skills equivalent to those that European American citizens of Tallahassee could get from the four-year high school curriculum. Then they encouraged at least some of these eighth grade "graduates" to apply to the most rigorous colleges. The speaker, a college dean, had undergraduate and graduate degrees from Harvard, which he had entered straight from his segregated eighth grade in the late 1950s.

The situation in engineering and technological innovation, which have always been closely related to scientific practice, was almost as dismal. Free African Americans were legally able to patent the important technological innovations they made from the time of the first U.S. Patent Act (1790), but few received patents before the Civil War. Slaves, women as well as men, devised many inventions, but until the end of the Civil War, neither slaves nor their owners—who frequently tried—were permitted to receive patents for slaves' inventions.

Other factors also contributed to the scarcity of scientists of African descent in the United States. In both the natural and social sciences, if one divided the whole history of Western scientific projects into those that appear to have little to do with improving African American lives, those that have the consequence (intended or not) of deteriorating the quality of those lives, and all the rest, one would find very little scientific work in the first and third categories. The sciences have not in general had good effects on African American lives.[6] Why should African Americans want their young people to enter such fields as physics, chemistry, biology, mathematics and engineering in light of the resources that the sciences have provided for racist policies and practices? Until recently, there has been no push in educational institutions at any level—either primarily black or integrated ones—to encourage African American youth to pursue science careers. African American communities have insisted that their children be educated in ways that had direct benefits to African Americans.[7]

Is it fair for African Americans today to have to think that they should enter science and technology only if doing so will improve the conditions of black lives? After all, one might think, European Americans are not expected to calculate whether their work will benefit white communities before they are permitted to feel good about entering physics, chemistry, or engineering. The community service ethic has often appeared to be an unjust burden, especially when European Americans use this kind of argument to direct talented African Americans out of predominantly white institutions and fields and into black ones. "You have a duty to your people," white educators and foundations said to the "Black Apollo of Science," Edward Everett Just. "Go teach undergraduates at Howard University, instead of pursuing a research career in physics."[8]

It is no more appropriate for me, a European American, than it was for those to whom Just had to listen to pronounce on which careers African Americans should pursue. Nevertheless, we can note that while the argument against requiring a community service ethic for African Americans can appear compelling, the situation is not quite as parallel to the situation for European Americans as the argument implies. Not only have Western science and technology been complicitous with overt racist social agendas, but they also encode racial messages in the very definition of their most abstract projects. European Americans too enter science as a "calling," inspired by the heroic tales of the Great Men whose accomplishments supposedly demonstrate the highest intellectual achievements of the "human" race, whose work has purportedly brought such great benefits to "humankind." Among these benefits, they are told, are powerful rational defenses against irrational superstition, "primitive" ways of thought, and oppressive and exploitative politics that are so often supported by "the masses." Decoding the racial messages (as well as the gender and class ones) in these conventional justifications for entering the arduous training that careers in the sciences require reveals that European Americans are indeed enticed to enter science in order to improve conditions for *their* race. Not only is a "white service ethic" apparently supposed to be part of the implicit appeal of a career in science for European Americans, but— unlike the black service ethic—it contains not-so-hidden racist messages.

In spite of the Western sciences' racist agendas and coding of their mission, I think we can see why it is important that there be more African American women and men in the sciences. All the arguments … for increasing the numbers of women in the sciences are also arguments for increasing the numbers of African Americans and other persons of color. Social justice mandates making available to African Americans too the social benefits that come from careers in the sciences. Moreover, scientific literacy is crucial for anyone to function effectively in society today. Furthermore, African American young people need the mentoring and role modeling in the sciences that all scientists should provide for them but—given the racial stratification of U.S. society and the negative messages most European Americans send out about African Americans' intellectual abilities—cannot be depended upon to provide. African Americans and other people of color should also have access to the resources for designing sciences and technologies that will benefit their communities. And the sciences stand a far better chance of losing their racist agendas and codes if there is a significant African American presence among scientists. Last but not least, it is hard to imagine advancing democratic tendencies in Western societies without the prominent participation of African Americans and other persons of

color—women and men—in directing scientific and technological policy.

This is just one area where it is important to look carefully at the differences in the situations of women of color in different societies. In a few Third World countries (for example, in South America and the Caribbean), just as in the West, social stratification has sometimes permitted women in the upper classes to gain education and careers little different from those of their brothers.[9] Consequently, the women already in the sciences in these countries are frequently members of an economic and political elite that is far less likely to challenge the West's ideas about how the sciences and technologies should function than would less economically and politically advantaged members of those societies. Nevertheless, the new histories show again and again that women in privileged classes have frequently been a powerful force for progressive social change, contrary to the conventional opinion of some men on the left that they are always a conservative force in history. Even in the dominant groups, women's relatively marginal status as women, coupled with the ethic of caring for others that is expected of these women too, often makes possible their sympathetic identification with the needs and interests of people more marginal than they. Many activists who have worked to improve the conditions of racially and economically marginalized women in the United States and Europe have come from the upper classes.

How are the cautions raised in the conventional feminist literatures about women's experiences in the social structure of science pertinent here? First, focusing on a few African American women "worthies" who have managed to gain access to European American science institutions does not tell us much about the vast majority of such women who work in the sciences or may have aspired to scientific and technological careers. Even more than the lives of Great European American Men and the few Great European American Women who have achieved recognition in the sciences, these lives are by definition extraordinary. Furthermore, the histories of women in the sciences have tended to focus disproportionately on elites, as did their "prefeminist" counterparts. This has the effect of making almost invisible any presence of women of color in the sciences. A search for Great African American Women in the sciences would suffer from the fact that it tried to establish the individuality of a few women at the expense of the masses whose efforts made those achievements possible. Such an approach would advance Eurocentric preoccupations with individualism and meritocracy at the expense of understanding and supporting the collective and community-focused ways in which science and technology have in fact been practiced in our own and other cultures.

Another challenge is to resist the temptation to assess the contributions of African American women to science and technology only from the perspective of what European American elite men or women count as scientifically and technologically interesting and valuable. Hine's studies of black women physicians' educational and social work to benefit their communities' activities and of black women's later focus on nursing rather than doctoring highlight the importance of kinds of scientific activities that are devalued in dominant white, Western men's science circles. It is also important to discover what their achievements and participation in science and technology mean to women of African descent.

I have been discussing primarily African American *women*, but it sounds odd to talk of African American women as if their situation has not been fundamentally shaped by conditions they have shared with the men of their communities. The discussions of the participation by women of European descent in the history of science and technology gained their point primarily through contrasts between the opportunities and experiences of such women and those of the men of their race, class, and culture. But even though comparison of the situation of women of African descent with their brothers' situations can be illuminating, focusing only or even primarily on that gender

contrast distorts the account. In order to understand the participation of African American women in the sciences and technologies, it is necessary to set that story within the general patterns of African American history—not just of European American history. Black women are not "like white women, only different"; they are created through and creators of a broader history of race relations. The histories of women in the sciences tend to be embedded largely in European American history, which is understandable if one's focus is on what the dominant culture is willing to count as science. But if science is part of the larger society ... we need to understand how patterns of race relations in the larger society have had consequences for African Americans' experiences of and interactions with the sciences.

Finally, we can wonder whether the entrance of large numbers of African American women and men into positions of authority in the sciences and their technologies would leave the content of scientific claims and the logic of research and explanation unchanged....

Notes

1. Darlene Clark Hine, "Co-Laborers in the Work of the Lord: Nineteenth Century Black Women Physicians," in *"Send Us a Lady Physician": Women Doctors in America, 1835–1920,* ed. Ruth J. Abram (New York: Norton, 1985), 117.

2. Ibid.

3. E.g., Kenneth Manning, *Black Apollo of Science: The Life of Edward Everett Just* (New York: Oxford University Press, 1983).

4. Hine, *Black Women in White: Racial Conflict and Cooperation in the Nursing Profession, 1890–1950* (Bloomington: Indiana Press, 1989)

5. Accounts of these past and present struggles are becoming available. See, e.g., Sara Lawrence Lightfoot, *Balm in Gilead: Journey of a Healer* (New York: Addison-Wesley, 1989); Manning, *Black Apollo;* Aimee Sands, "Never Meant to Survive: A Black Woman's Journey" (interview with Evelynn Hammonds), *Radical*

Teacher 30 (1986); Ivan Van Sertima, ed., *Blacks in Science: Ancient and Modern* (New Brunswick, N.J.: Transaction Books, 1986); and others listed in Anne Fausto-Sterling, "Women and Minorities in Science: Course Materials Guide," (available from Fausto-Sterling, Division of Biology and Medicine, Brown University, Providence, R.I. 02912)

6. For the social sciences, see, e.g., Robert V. Guthrie, *Even the Rat Was White: A Historical View of Psychology* (New York: Harper & Row, 1976); Joyce Ladner, ed., *The Death of White Sociology* (New York: Random House, 1973).

7. I am indebted to Evelynn Hammonds for emphasizing the importance of this issue.

8. See Manning, *Black Apollo.*

9. Nancie L. Gonzalez, "Professional Women in Developing Nations: The United States and the Third World Compared," in *Women in Scientific and Engineering Professions,* ed. Violet B. Haas and Carolyn C. Perrucci (Ann Arbor: University of Michigan Press, 1989).

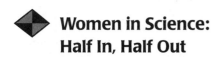

Women in Science: Half In, Half Out

Vivian Gornick

Imagine then: To have had science in you. To have known yourself gifted with the means of achieving such articulation of mind and spirit, and to have had the thing almost within your grasp. Almost, but not quite.

George Eliot once wrote a friend that he could not imagine what it was like "to have a man's genius locked up inside you and yet have to suffer the slavery of being a girl." What if you have been a woman, and you have had science locked up inside of you? What then? What, until now, has that been like?

A forty-six-year-old physicist had worked for sixteen years at an industrial research laboratory at the level of Senior Scientist (the equivalent of professor at a university). She had always thought The Lab an eminently fair and decent place. "You did your work, you were treated with respect, that was it." True, from time to time, the question of why there were so few women at her level did come up, but each time her colleagues quite reasonably assured her that The Lab wanted to hire women, it was just that so few women went into science, hardly anyone qualified came their way. If ever one did show up (here a hand inevitably waved in her direction), they were quick to take her.

When the women's movement began making trouble, this physicist was asked to look more closely at The Lab's system of employment and advance. To her surprise, she saw that: "There did seem to be built-in discriminations that weren't so apparent if you didn't know what to look for. For instance, the scientific supporting staff were of two classes, each of which required only a B.S. for employment. One class was that of Senior Technical Assistant—straight technician, a decent enough job from which there was no place to go, but one in which you could remain for the rest of your life if you wanted to. The other class—the Graduate Studies Program—was a job in which people could go on for an M.S., and then take a place somewhere on the ladder leading to Senior Scientist. When we looked closely, we saw that the first class was all women, the second class all men.

"I didn't feel angry at this discovery. It was, I thought, an understandable, unconscious discriminatory practice, one that would be easy to correct. The thing that I couldn't understand, and that did make me angry, was this: My colleagues were all very intelligent men, men whose grasp of scientific complexity was enormous. And yet, here we came and showed them a rather simple social reality, and they didn't seem to know what we were talking about. They remained puzzled and defensive. They went on saying that if women didn't enter science it wasn't their fault, they took whoever came their way who was qualified. When we showed them it wasn't that simple, they continued to balk. Then I began to think the feminists had something, after all."

Science has a vested interest in the idea of the intellectual meritocracy. It is important to scientists to believe that they act rationally, that they do not distort or ignore evidence, that neither their work nor their profession is seriously influenced by politics, ambition, or prejudice.

Such, clearly, cannot be the case. Scientists, like all other people, make decisions on the basis of a shared social reality, are pulled about by convictions rooted in emotional prejudice, act on inherited ideas of what is natural, and are certainly influenced by politics, ambition, and issues of class, sex, and race. But, as they have a strong need to believe they are guided by intellectual objectivity, they have a more difficult time than other kinds of workers do in perceiving themselves as discriminatory.

Thus, the atmosphere in which women in science have been held back, put off, discouraged and demoralized, frozen in position is particularly disturbing because of its defensive denial that what is happening is happening. In business, a woman looks into the eyes of a corporation executive who says openly to her, "We know what you're all about, we've held you off as long as we could, and now you'll have to take us to court to get what you want." In science, a woman looks into the eyes of a man who thinks of himself as decent, fairminded, above all reasonable, and who says to her, "I really don't know what you're talking about. Surely you're not saying we've discriminated against you."...

It has been said of women in science that they select themselves out. Those words do not sufficiently indicate the experience behind the moment of attrition—the conditions of work under which women in science have felt invisible and discounted, left out and whittled down. Such experience is both subtle and gross; it accumulates from more than one point of origin; is felt as an institutional assault, a psychological infliction, choice forced on one rather than choice freely made. Consider the following:

- An eighty-year-old biologist now being honored for discoveries made in her forties worked for years as a research associate. Another scientist—a man who has known the biologist more than twenty years—was astonished to learn this and said recently, "You mean to tell me she never had a proper job? I didn't know that." It is inconceivable that if the biologist had been a man the scientist would not have known he did not have a proper job.

- A sixty-eight-year-old physiologist active all her life in university research said, "I worked for years among men who never walked into my office to talk to me, who nodded to me in the hall as they nodded to the maintenance men or the cleaning women, never invited me to their conferences or their seminars or their research programs. I was the invisible woman in science."

- A twenty-two-year-old woman who graduated from Harvard in the summer of 1980 with a BS in psychology had entered the university as a chemistry major (she had been an A student in chemistry in high school), but dropped out at the end of the first year: "Freshman chem is taught at Harvard by a famous chemist, a man in his sixties who would put an equation on the board and in a room of five hundred people turn and say, 'Get that, girls?' The first time I heard him say this I laughed. The second time I became angry. The third time I was scared. Something began grinding at my insides every time I walked into that lecture hall. I started thinking, *Do* you get it? *Can* you get it? And then I thought, You *don't* get it. You *can't* get it. I couldn't go on with it. The percentage of boys dropping out of science is high but, believe me, it's a thousand times higher for girls, and I know it's for the same reason I dropped out."

This is the kind of experience that becomes lodged in the psyche: both the individual one and the collective one. It may go unrecorded in the intellect but it is being registered in the nerve and in the spirit. It means sustaining a faint but continuous humiliation that, like low-grade infection, is cumulative in its power and disintegrating in its ultimate effect.

The Research Associate

Ellen Smithing; thirty-seven years old; biophysicist at a Midwestern institute of technology. Born and raised in Iowa, the daughter of schoolteachers one generation removed from farmers, she liked science in high school, graduated from a small women's college as a chemistry major, and went quietly on to graduate school. After she had received her degree, she became a post-doctoral fellow at a medical school in Chicago, and two years later was asked to stay on in the lab as a research associate.

She had never thought of being anything other than a research associate, and was grateful for the offer. "I loved doing science. I loved the systematic nature of lab work, loved physically designing and executing the experiments, even loved washing test tubes and beakers. And I loved thinking about scientific problems, even if the problems were someone else's. Being a research associate seemed perfect. It let me do what I most loved doing.

"I had worked at this lab seven years, and one day I realized I had done the major work on a problem, and I wanted my name first on the paper. The next day I started looking for a job. If not for the women's movement I don't think I'd have realized that my ego needed gratification and that I could get a real job if I tried. I'd still be a research associate."

Sarah Griswold; fifty-six years old; the only tenured woman in the chemistry department of an Ivy League university. She spent twenty-three years as a research associate in this university; eight years ago the feminists on the campus demanded she be tenured; fearful of scandal, the university acceded. Griswold herself has since become an ardent feminist; tenure now is an irony; in the deepest sense she's through with science:

"I came to this university as a graduate student during World War II. When I received my degree there was not the slightest possibility of a woman getting a decent job at a university with research facilities. The only question was, Do you go out to teach at East Jesus Tech, or do you stay on here at this great and benevolent institution as a research associate? For me, the answer was a given.

"To be a research associate was, I thought, marvelous, and I thought so for many, many

years. It left me free from meetings, from administrative responsibilities, from having to raise money, or teach classes. I was beyond all that, I could really do research. And the university, I thought, was wonderful. After all, it let me work here, didn't it? It was paying me to do what I loved doing. How could I bitch? What did *I* have to complain about?

"The other side of being a research associate, of course, is that you can never control the laboratory, never set the terms of the work, never be privy to the inner exchanges of the real scientists, never expand, grow, have respect or responsibility.

"I worked here twenty-three years, alongside many men who knew my work was certainly as good as theirs and often superior to theirs. And research associate was all that was ever permitted me. I hate the bastards. They've taken the heart out of science for me."

Margie Clarkson; forty-one years old; a biochemist now working on a trial basis at a research institute in Washington where tenure is dependent on hard work and the publication of research papers. Permanently depressed, her ability to work is severely hampered, and her future as a scientist imperiled.

Clarkson married the most brilliant student in biochemistry at her university when she was nineteen years old, and became a scientist to achieve the comradeship of a working marriage. She had the brains and the motivation; she ploughed through her bachelor's degree and then she ploughed through graduate school. When she received her degree she and her husband went out into academic science as a team—he as professor, she as his research associate. He moved from one excellent job to another, receiving tenure in a series of universities, each one more and more to his liking—better pay, better space, better teaching conditions, better climate, better everything—and Margie, of course, went along with him, his right-hand woman, always beside him in the lab.

Two years ago her husband announced that he had fallen in love with a graduate student and he wanted a divorce. Clarkson's eyes glaze over, her face petrifies, her voice wanders as she recalls this time: "I never knew what hit me. One day I had everything anyone needed for a decent life, the next day I was wandering around in a state of total disaster. It wasn't just that I'd lost my husband and my home and my job, it was as though I'd lost my place in the world. Not only had I been a research associate all these years—and suddenly I saw it for the dead-end job that it is—but I'd been *his* research associate. I looked around and saw that people I'd worked with for years didn't really believe I could do the work. They thought I'd been riding on his coattails all these years, that I couldn't pull my weight in a lab at all. It was unbelievable. They were making excuses not to give me a recommendation for another job. How I landed this job I'll never know. And to tell you the truth I don't think I'll be able to keep it … I'm so depressed … I can't shake it … I feel like I'm staring into space half the time."

Glenda Pennell; thirty-four years old; a plant biologist who has just been offered tenure at three first-rank universities. She has not yet decided which one she will grace with her political currency as well as her brains. A self-conscious feminist, Glenda feels she must take this factor into consideration when making her choice.

"Yale made me a feminist. Yale and the question of being a research associate. I was always very good at science, very smart, very serious. It's true, like most women, I don't remember thinking too much about my career, about what it meant, or what it took, to be a scientist. I just enjoyed doing science, that's all, I didn't really think beyond that. As an undergraduate at MIT I was the student of a Famous Man. He was my mentor, and he wanted me to do well, and I sort of knew I'd gained entrée to the elite in science through him.

"So I get to Yale and I'm all set, I think. That's day one. On day two I'm shot down. At a separate meeting for women graduate students, the graduate adviser said to us, actually *said* to us: 'You are being trained to become research associates, and to become the wives of the men you are now going to school with.' Mind you, this is 1968. It was devastating. After that not one woman in that class thought of actually going out to get a job.

"I worked in a lab at Yale; we were fourteen women on that floor, grad students, post-docs, research associates. We all knew we had more in common as women working in science than we did as either post-docs or associates or students. Then something crazy happened.

"You know, most scientists have in mind three categories of people when they think of scientists: idea people, technique people, and people who work hard. They think women fall into the last category most frequently, if not always. No one expects a brilliant new idea or technique to come from a woman. Well, one of the women on our floor, a research associate, did something fantastic. She invented a new technique. She'd been doing fine work for years as an associate but now, overnight, she got twelve job offers. Imagine, one day nothing, the next day twelve job offers. That was it. The day after that we were all organizing ourselves to get jobs. For me, of course, it was fairly easy. The minute I had my degree the Famous Man at MIT joined the Famous Man at Yale who now had a vested interest in my future, and I was on my way.

"But that memory of Yale and the research associates has never left me, and I'm not sure where we'd all be today if it weren't for the women's movement. As it is, many of those fourteen women are still either research associates, or they've left science altogether. One of them, Louise Anderson, was a research associate for her husband for sixteen years. She thought hers was the perfect working life. Then another associate, a woman much older than herself, said to her, 'There'll come a time, you'll want to do certain things, and you won't be able to, and then you'll start going backward, there's no way to stop it,' and suddenly Louise realized how restless she was. From there to resentful was one short step.

She left Yale, her husband, and science within a year."

Patricia Moran; sixty-one years old; biochemist; tenured professor at the teaching hospital of a large and prestigious medical school in the Midwest. Married thirty years to a professor of surgical medicine, she came to work at the school because they wanted her husband, and they promised him they'd "do something for Patty."

She received a Ph.D. from Yale in 1943 and, "Well, the boys in my class (in those days we were all boys and girls) got twenty-five interviews, I got three. Two of the three were lousy, the third was at Cornell Medical School. It was lousy, too, but it was Cornell. Good people all around, exciting atmosphere, a chance for research. They wouldn't give me a job in the biochemistry department. No woman had ever gotten a job in that department in any medical school. The men just wouldn't have them. You were always used in the departments of medicine where a Ph.D. is inferior to an M.D. They needed biochemists in medicine, of course, but no man would take the job, only women. I worked there as an assistant professor for five years with no hope at all of getting tenure.

"Then I got married and went to Philadelphia with my husband. That's what you did in those days: he went, I went. We came here when he got his job at this school. I became an associate in biochemistry attached to medicine. I remained just that for seventeen years. No money, no sabbaticals, no security, no recognition, and of course no hope of ever getting on a tenured track line. My boss, who was a sweet kindly guy, said to me when I grumbled, 'Patty, you shouldn't be ambitious for yourself. You should be interested in furthering Bob's career.' And when I realized I *was* ambitious for myself I felt guilty.

"My husband left this school for another one in the city twelve years ago. Suddenly, I felt free to act as I wanted to. I went to the biochemistry department and demanded a tenure track position. It was the late sixties. I got it. They made me assistant professor. So

there I was, seventeen years after I'd left Cornell, right back where I started.

"I continued working here, getting a renewal of my contract each year, working in my lab. In 1976 I didn't get a renewal in the mail. I called the secretary of the university. It had always been a man. Now the name read L. Cheney. I asked to speak to Mr. Cheney. I was told Cheney was a woman. I said what was on my mind. They said, 'Ms. Cheney will call you back later.' That was at nine in the morning. She called at three in the afternoon. I thought I'd been fired. She apologized for taking so long. I said, 'Don't apologize, just tell me what's happening.' 'You've got tenure,' she said. 'What?' I said. 'That's right,' she said. She said she remembered my saying at some meeting where I was shooting off my damn fool mouth that I was the oldest nontenured professor at the school. She looked into it. It seemed they couldn't keep me this long without giving me tenure. I had it. 'They'll never believe me,' I said. 'Oh yes they will,' she said, 'because I'm the one who tells them when someone's got tenure and when someone doesn't.'

"So, finally, I had it. Not because they gave it to me but because a strong-minded woman discovered it was mine by default."

Academic science is the model for professional science. To rise in this system, one must climb an extraordinarily narrow ladder: from graduate student to post-doctoral fellow to research associate to assistant professor (or principal investigator). The majority of women in science have never completed that rise. They have remained research associates attached to the principal investigator for most or all of their working lives. The cause of arrest is multiple and it has a history.

In an article called "Women's Work in Science, 1880–1910" (adapted from her larger work, *Women Scientists in America*) Margaret Rossiter describes how women began to be employed in the 1880s as assistants in astronomy labs by such liberal academics as Edward Pickering, director of the Harvard College Observatory. Rossiter goes on to observe that "If Pickering and some other observatory directors were progressive in greatly expanding women's employment in astronomy in the 1880s and 1890s, they were not so far ahead of their time as to promote them for important or even outstanding work. Not only did the women have no chance for advancement, they rarely received a raise—at least at Harvard—even after years of devoted service. Because they were not promoted … when their scientific work was good, as happened to the more talented men, the female assistants were forced (or expected) to make a whole career out of a job that should have been just a stepping stone to more challenging and prestigious roles."

Here we have a precise truth about women in science—that they've been "allowed" into science for a hundred years now, but for the most part under severely circumscribed conditions, doing segregated work known in the subtext as "women's work." These are the historic beginnings of the woman scientist as permanent research associate.

Women like Patricia Moran or Sarah Griswold (that is, women now in their late fifties or sixties or seventies) could do no other than become and remain research associates, women so hungry to work in science they would accept whatever was permitted them because it was either that or nothing, either here or nowhere, either this sort of today or absolutely no tomorrow. That so many of them did excellent, even brilliant, work is an astonishment.

The male scientist equipped with an ordinary degree of intellectual competence and emotional drive accepts as a given that he is expected to do independent work, not that he will be greeted with amazement should independence surface in his work. Women in science have always had to face the amazement. That amazement is crippling. A forty-eight-year-old research associate explains why:

"The men in science who confide in you, 'The women really don't want the responsibility. I told my associate, do this piece of work with me, we'll put your name on the paper first, and you'll go out and get a job, and she refused, said she liked it just fine where she was.' The stupid sonofabitch. Ask him if *he*

lived surrounded by the expectation of failure if he wouldn't be scared to go out there. It's a matter of nerve, and the way I see it, nerve is gathered up in a man no matter how terrified he is, and dissipated in a woman no matter how hungry she is."

It took a scientist of extraordinary, rather than ordinary, drive to do good work as a research associate—someone who could abstract mightily, turn inward, concentrate with a self-sustaining force rare in men and women alike. But there have been associates—starting with those astronomy assistants of the 1880s—who did just that. They were people, these women now in their sixties and seventies, made in a different psychological proportion—the brilliant exceptions in whom the fear of freakishness became a badge of wounded honor, the mind a secret weapon: "The world be damned, I'll occupy a society of one, and I'll think." These were the research associates of forty years ago and more.

Generations of women scientists have been and continue to be made into permanent research associates through marriage to other scientists. Typically, a pair of scientists meet in graduate school, fall in love, and marry. What a romantic couple! Love *and* science. Marriage *and* work. Together in the lab all day, discussing the work at home in the evening. What could be better?

Even if they should get their degrees at the same university and complete comparable post-docs, it has been most usual that he has been offered a job as assistant professor, and she has then "looked around for something in science." That something in science is inevitably a research associateship in or near the university he will be working at; sometimes it is as *his* research associate. It is not at all rare that twenty years pass like a ball moving fast through the air, and suddenly there they are, immobilized in middle life, he full professor and respected scientist, she still research associate.

And then there is the research associate in thrall to the Ivy League, to that conviction bred into all of us, as empire is bred into colonials, that the Ivy League is incomparable, that to be within its walls is to reside inside the Kingdom of Intellectual Heaven, to be outside is to be thrust from Paradise, hurled into an outer darkness where all knowledge and all experience is of an inferior cast.

Sarah Griswold cannot articulate it even now, but one can feel in her that configuration of awe and soul-belief in the superiority of the Ivy League; that in the life and thought interlaced inside these Jude-denying stone walls, was to be found the Kingdom of Transcendent Truth and Beauty—the Great, the True, the Real Science—and that it would be agony for her to tear herself from it. She could not bear to leave The University— where no woman, whatever the level of her accomplishment, would ever, on the longest day of her life, be made professor.

This historic relation between women, associateships, and the Ivy League is now, prophetically, beginning to alter. In this matter at least the future cannot repeat the past.

A forty-two-year-old physiobiologist, now tenured at a Midwestern state university but with past experience of the Ivy League, says: "When I left a research associateship at the University of Pennsylvania for a professorship in the Midwest everyone in Philly said to me, 'Are you crazy? You're leaving Penn for the Midwest?' I said, 'No, I'm leaving an associateship for a real job.' They didn't get it."

A thirty-six-year-old biophysicist at a Southwestern state university says, "I'd rather be a professor out in the boondocks than a research associate at Harvard. For god's sake, isn't it obvious? To occupy a place on the margin, no matter how great the university, is to give up your life. Now that women are refusing to do that, you'll see how many 'brilliant' women scientists will 'suddenly' emerge in the next generation. You just watch. Because, at the very least, that's what it takes to be 'brilliant,' you know. Not accepting their terms. Risking loss, defeat, and obscurity as they define it."

Five generations of women were willing to occupy peripheral, often humiliating positions in order to do science, and because they were, thousands of young women are now walking through the doors of professional science on the strength of the intellectual legacy the research associates have accumulated. The men who denied many of these women, who would not acknowledge them until they were forced to, nevertheless *knew* the quality of their work, their scientific intelligence, their devotion and their tenacity; knew, as Margaret Rossiter says, that "science benefited from this practice, since the women, having no alternatives, remained on the job for decades and completed many major projects."

Still, the sex-linked connection to the research associate is far from broken. In the late spring of 1980 I walked one evening along the lakefront in Chicago with a twenty-nine-year-old cell biologist. Tall, handsome, with the rangy self-confidence of the American golden girl, Linda Dolan had studied biology under a scientist who had himself not taken the conventional route, suffered for it, not risen in academic science, and proceeded to push her forward because she had become his daughter-surrogate in science. He was convinced that if she made all the right decisions she would be a fine scientist.

A few years ago Linda met another biologist at Woods Hole, married him, and moved to Chicago to be with her husband. Her mentor had urged her to get a university job of her own, but Linda could not find one and "still be married to Ronald." So she had done the next best thing: gotten a fellowship and gone to work in someone else's lab in Chicago. Now, two years later, her husband was unhappy at his job, and they decided to leave Chicago and find a place in the world suitable for them both.

I saw Linda Dolan again in the late summer of that year. She and her husband were leaving Chicago within the month. Ronald had been offered three tenured jobs. At two of the three universities, Linda had been offered research associateships. They had decided on one.

It was a filthy hot afternoon when we walked again on the lakefront. Linda did not look like the golden girl she had seemed in the spring; her good looks seemed abruptly, prematurely faded, without the high color of our previous meeting, her lustrous brown hair dull and lank, her arms white and too fleshy. She knew that I understood the meaning of the historic road she and her husband were about to travel. "Don't worry, she pleaded with me. "I won't do it for long. If something doesn't give, if I don't get a decent job there, I'll leave. I know the danger I'm in."

The Professional Marriage: Four Physicists

Science is strongly marked by professional marriages. Many of these marriages originate in graduate school—either a pair of students fall in love or a graduate student and her professor fall in love—and many of them come out of having worked together—men and women spend long hours in the lab, the intensity of the work is eroticizing, sexual affairs explode easily, and often people fall in love and marry.

Women in science who are married are most often married to other scientists and consider themselves one half of a professional marriage. The professional marriage does not, cannot mean to the husband-scientist what it must mean to the wife-scientist. He may not even consider himself a partner in a professional marriage; she must. It is possible that neither his intellectual life nor his career will be affected by his attachment to his wife; hers is always affected by her attachment to her husband.

If a husband and wife work together in science, it is almost invariably assumed that he does the "real" work (that is, the thinking), and she the subordinate work (execution of the experiments). Concomitantly, the woman scientist has social access, and obligation, to scientists who mainly associate with her because she is her husband's wife. Thus, she is often in the dreadful position of being scorned intellectually for seeming to receive

unearned privilege—a bind from which she cannot readily extricate herself.

If a husband and wife pair of scientists do not work together, then they are faced with the monumental problem of how to live equitably without the sacrifice of either one of their working lives. If husband and wife are friends the worldly circumstance in which these people find themselves is at best difficult, at worst defeating; either way solace and comradeship is required. If they are *not* friends the circumstance of their lives can be brutalizing and may leave one or both with the taste of ashes.

Nina and Leon Braverman are both fifty-three years old: two small, compact people whose faces appear fragile and luminous—as though an intelligence of the spirit is shared between them; they seem to have the same voice as well—gentle, sadly civilized. These two have known each other since childhood. They grew up in the same orthodox Jewish neighborhood in Detroit, discovered their love of science and each other in high school, got married in college, became physics majors, and went on to graduate school together. Leon studied general relativity, Nina high energy physics.

Nina and Leon are Talmudists of physics. Although they have raised three children and live a life apparently indistinguishable from that of most academics, their mutual love of physics is the binding material in a shared inner life that is remarkable for its rigor, its endurance, its primacy. They have spent years meshing their separate intellectual talents for the exquisite pleasure of contemplating physics problems together. For them, physics remained visionary, an exploration to which one gave oneself with a sense of privilege. These are two who recoil from their younger fellow scientists. Nina says of physics today: "There's not a whole person in sight. These people are all careerists manufacturing data."

Nina never cared much about the career, she says, but "Deprive me of doing physics and I start to die." She has had to be more reflective about the matter of b ig deprived of physics than has Leon. Thinking back on her life in science she says: "In graduate school I had entrée to a good study group because I was 'one of the boys.' We would get together, a bunch of us, and we'd do the problems. If you weren't able to do that you'd get slaughtered in class. I'd never have survived without that study group. Only years later did I realize that no girls were permitted into the group, and that if I hadn't been Leon's wife I'd never have been in. But being his wife sort of de-sexed me, made me kosher."

Nina's was the fashionable field of physics when they graduated, but it was Leon who got hired at a university three hundred and fifty miles from home. She got a research associateship. After that it was one associateship, or fellowship, or off-the-line grant after another for her. And then, of course, she gave birth to and cared for two children.

Nina sits talking quietly at the wooden table in the kitchen of a shabby frame house in the small Western university town where they have finally come to rest with tenure for each of them: "Leon had one very important insight very early on. He said to me, 'Nina, if you want to be a person like everybody else, you've got to have a regular job.' He was no feminist. Who was in those days? But he saw *that.*

"But we couldn't swing it. For years we tried. Twenty years at least. Leon would keep leaving one job after another in the hope that we'd get me a job also. Impossible. Nepotism rules were fierce, we never seemed to have the pull, or the luck, or whatever it took. But we never stopped doing physics together. Sometimes we worked openly—I'd get a grant and I could apply it to Leon's work, or he'd make his work match the demands of my grant. Something, anything. If not, we'd work on our own, at home, late at night, after we'd done everything else we had to do. The important thing was that I never stopped doing physics. I couldn't. I really felt I couldn't live without doing physics. For years I felt that way.

"Now I can't say that's so true anymore. I'm tired these days. It's odd, but I think my becoming a conscious feminist had something to do with my getting so tired I couldn't work so well anymore.

"We used to go to Aspen every summer. It was an exciting community of people who gathered there, purely for the love of doing science. One summer in the early seventies I was teased about women's lib. I laughed. I'd never thought of women's lib. But I found myself defensive, which surprised me. And in trying to form my argument to defend the women's movement position, I found myself thinking about a lot of things I'd never consciously thought of before. I guess I was becoming a feminist right then and there. Well, we had all been this intimate community of scientists. Now, men I had known a long time suddenly turned ugly. One physicist became exasperated and said to me, 'Listen, women are good for only one thing, having their behinds pinched.' I was stunned. This from a man who'd known me for years.

"After that Leon and I decided we were going to get me a job or go to court. And that's what finally happened. We got these jobs here, with tenure for him when we came, and the firm promise of tenure for me in five years. When the five years were up they denied me tenure, and we sued. It was such a long fight. And it wasn't the physicists who got me tenure, it was the feminists. As I said, I'm tired now."

Forty-nine years old; strong-featured face, brooding eyes, a mass of sexy dark hair she tosses about like a forties movie vamp, the walk seductive and knowing, the mouth sullen and grievance-collecting in repose, then surprisingly girlish in laughter when the eyes fill with a sudden shimmering light. Alma Norovsky is a theoretical physicist at a university renowned for its devotion to the life of the mind. Of her colleagues Alma says drily: "They're very theoretical. People are always asking me how women are treated here. 'Women?, I answer. 'They're a theoretical concept.'

Divorced four years from the physicist husband she married in graduate school, on her own for the first time in her life, in love with her new independence and happy to be working here, Alma nevertheless sighs. "How do you work in physics, or live among academic liberal men, and not explode all day long every day? Once in a while I'm able to control myself.... Last year at a conference I was standing with a group of physicists, all men, and I was introduced to a new member of the group. He said, 'You're the first good-looking physicist I've ever met.' I casually indicated the man standing beside me and said, 'Oh, that's not true. You know Richard here. He's good-looking, and he's a physicist.' They all looked startled, and then some of them nodded their heads appreciatively. I was proud of myself then, but usually it's awful. Still. Always. At every dinner table, in the office, the constant little indications that you don't really exist. You've got to remind them that you're a thinking, working being just like themselves all the time. It's wearing."

She was a pretty girl, bold and flirtatious, loved exercising her power to attract, she'd be damned if she'd give that up ("Why? What for? It was so much fun"). So nobody took her seriously although she was a fine physics student from high school on. Her father, a frustrated scientist, adored and encouraged her, but he floundered. She went to a small women's college where the science courses were bad and the teachers worse, but sexual success made her stubborn and determined on her own seriousness. She bulled her way through into an Ivy League education.

In her second year in graduate school she met and married Lawrence Norovsky, a strongly ambitious fellow student in physics. She says of this time: "I enjoyed being one of the few women in physics, but I certainly did not enjoy it when I realized women in physics were considered ugly, undesirable, clumsy eccentrics. I wanted to be sexually lovely and desirable, and still be a fine physicist." What she doesn't say—although it's apparent—is that she also wanted to attract the attention of a

man of power, the kind of man whose interest in her would always be mixed: compelled and antagonistic, attracted by her brains but enjoying her subordinate status as his wife, his relationship to her over the years intermittently eroticized by her professional intelligence, but his sense of her life as equal to his own never maturing.

When Lawrence accepted a job at a university in northern Massachusetts, Alma had had a baby and had not yet finished her degree. She remembers that everyone seemed to be patting her on the head, as though indulging a child's whimsical insistence, when she said she would finish her degree in Massachusetts. But "There were four women in science at the university in Massachusetts. When I think back on it, how those women influenced my life! They arrived one day, sat down in my living room and began giving me full instructions in how to organize myself, my time, my babysitter problem, my shopping and laundry problems. They never for a moment assumed that I wouldn't finish the degree. They had come as compatriots, in a situation they knew nobody but themselves understood, to give me the benefit of their experience. And I did as they said, and finally I finished. But not with any help from my husband, I can assure you.

"When I was just beginning to write the dissertation, and it was in its earliest stages, Lawrence suddenly decided to go to the Physics Institute in Paris for two years. He said to me, 'You can finish in two years. What's the difference?' Then I put my foot down. I don't know why it was, but I suddenly said no, absolutely no, this I will not do. He sent all his friends to see me, to persuade me to go with him. They said I was ruining his career, how could I be so selfish, so I'd finish in a year or two, what was the big deal? I didn't answer any of them, but I stayed where I was. He went to Paris, I sent the children to my parents, and I worked furiously at finishing my degree. Which I did in one year. Then I collected the children and followed him to Paris. Where I was immediately given an office, lab space, treated like a scientist. And the first thing my husband announced was that I was not welcome to join his group for lunch, or anything else for that matter. That was the first time he told me that under no circumstances would we ever work together, that physics was competitive, and he wouldn't have his marriage disfigured by a competitive relationship forming between us. Hah! His idea of avoiding competition between us was for me never to become anything.

"We came back home. Lawrence went to work at Brookhaven. I had three children. I didn't really want to work as a full-time physicist. I got an associateship at Stony Brook. I never was an equal of my husband's physics friends, but I never thought there was anything wrong with that. After all, they worked hard and long, and what was I doing? Why should they treat me as an equal?

"In 1971 I lost my job at Stony Brook, and I couldn't find another one. Suddenly, I was walking around in a daze. What had happened? I'd been a good physicist. I had wanted to do important work. What was I? Nothing. How had I ended up here? What had gone wrong with my career?

"That summer I talked with Nina Braverman at Aspen. We compared notes. It was astonishing how similar the pattern of our lives had been! For the first time it hit me that my life had developed as it had because I was a woman, and I'd made women's choices, and ended up where women in science end up. It hit me like a ton of bricks. All at once, I saw everything. From that moment on I became a rabid feminist. And I mean rabid. Shortly after that my marriage fell apart.

"I remember thinking back to one incident. After I'd lost my job at Stony Brook I was going crazy sitting home, not doing any science at all. One day I was visiting my husband at the lab. Another scientist there, a friend of ours, suddenly said to me, 'Alma, I've got an extra desk in my office. Why don't you come and use it as a guest worker?' That meant no pay but the privilege of working in the lab, using its facilities, and talking with the scientists. I responded gratefully and went to work there. Afterward, I thought, Why is it Lawrence never thought of this for me? How come a friend saved me but my husband never thought of doing so?

"Lawrence was insecure and that insecurity always made him more aware of protecting himself than of seeing his behavior toward me as unjust. And then there was the related, deeper truth that he never took me seriously as a physicist. Why should he when it was so much more convenient not to? He wasn't like Leon Braverman, and if I didn't do it for myself he certainly wasn't going to do it for me.

"I'm sure I'm being unfair to him, and if he were here he'd put a whole different construction on these same events. But that's the reality, isn't it? It's not a matter of fair, it's what we all did to each other, and no amount of looking at it fairly will make me feel any better about my marriage or my husband or the lost working years of my life."

"What Makes You Think You're Worth Educating?"

Margie Clarkson said that two conversations from her school years, placed back to back, were memorable. When she was graduated from college a teacher told her that the most significant thing she had done was to marry her husband. Then, when she entered graduate school in 1962, the graduate adviser said to her: "What makes you think you're worth educating? You're a woman, and you're already married."

She remembers: "The first time I wasn't insulted. The second time I was. My parents had always acted as though every person was worth educating. Now I was being told I wasn't a person."

Claire Morrissey, a forty-year-old tenured molecular biologist at the N.I.H. had been the first woman graduate student of a Nobel Prize winner famous for his womanizing as well as for his sex-blind encouragement of anyone he feels has scientific fire in the belly. This is how she came to work for him:

"I grew up and went to school in the Midwest. I was good at science in high school and I enjoyed the attention it brought me. It was fun being good at something girls weren't supposed to be good at, but I had no scientific ambition to speak of.

"My college was run on a work-study program and in my second year I went to work in a genetics lab at M.I.T. The structure of DNA had recently been discovered and the lab was filled with the excitement of making scientific history. Everyone knew what they were doing there would fill the textbooks in twenty years. I worked as a technician. The head of the lab thought I was good and told me so. I went back a second summer to that lab. Then the third summer I went to work in the lab of the Nobel laureate. He insisted I come back and take a Ph.D. in his department.

"I didn't know what I wanted to do. I went home and actually it was that summer in a lab in my home city that I devised an experiment, it worked, and suddenly I saw the difference between being the researcher and being the technician. I called the laureate and asked if I could be admitted to his department in September.

"He arranged immediately for me to become the student of another biologist in the department. But on my first interview with him this biologist said, 'And what are you going to do with your education when you get married and have three children?' I was amazed to find myself offended to the core. In that moment I realized I was serious about science. I turned and walked out the door. And that's how I became the laureate's first, but certainly not his last, woman graduate student."

Millie Warnickey is a forty-two-year-old physiological psychologist working at a research foundation attached to an Ivy League university. A large, bouncy woman, Millie's style is madcap, buoyant, shrewdly self-know-

ing, carefully reckless. The most highly rewarded, promoted, and fully granted scientist at her foundation, she's all cheerful cunning and good-hearted calculation. Political to the bone, Millie says, "The worst thing about discrimination is having to be cheerful about it." A typically successful Ivy League feminist, she is a master strategist always working hard to get what she wants without alienation or revolution.

Millie grew up in the West, the daughter of a pair of working-class descendants of the pioneers, who taught her to value her own independence. She went to a small college in the Midwest where her untutored love of science was cultivated and nourished. Her favorite teacher had himself been the student of a famous scientist, and spoke often of the Great Man. Millie determined to become the student of this scientist, and when the time came she applied for admission to the university where he taught, was admitted, and presented herself at his laboratory door. The Great Man told her that under no condition would he ever take her as his student because a woman is inherently an inferior scientist.

"I went back to the dorm, lay down on my bed, and to my everlasting shame cried my eyes out. Another grad student—a man, older than me—passed my door and asked what I was crying about. I told him. He said, 'Come with me.' He took me down to the Great Man's lab and taught me the technique he was famous for. The next morning when The Man came in I was doing an experiment using his technique. He was impressed, and agreed to take me on.

"But what has he learned about women as scientists? Nothing. He considers me a freak, an extraordinary exception, and to this day he will tell everyone he knows that there is only one woman who works like a man in the lab. That is, only one woman who is a real scientist."

Sharlene George, the thirty-five-year-old geneticist at the Philadelphia medical school, is a woman in whom a rage to prevail cohered early. Sharlene had thought she would like to become a doctor. Her college adviser said, "Miss George, in order to get into medical school you'll have to be holier than God." Sharlene's response: "I'll be holier than God." But she found the company of pre-med students distasteful, thought them crude and philistine, bent on money and prestige. In her third year she went to work in a biology lab and decided on research.

By the time she was graduating Sharlene knew that being a woman was a definite disadvantage in science. Wherever she turned at school people seemed continually to be asking, with sharpness and suspicion, if she planned to marry—in which case she clearly would not be fitted for the life of a research scientist. "It seemed as though the only way I could become a scientist was to take a vow of lifetime celibacy."

She had done exceptionally well in school—straight *A*s, all 99th percentiles on her Graduate Record Exam, and had published research as an undergraduate. She applied to a number of fine schools for admission as a graduate student, among them Stanford.

There is a famous Harvard-M.I.T.-Stanford "shunt." It is *the* elite graduate education in science—the assurance of a brilliant career. Students are carefully chosen, and then teachers have a very special interest in educating, grooming, and placing these students during the crucial formative period in their careers. They will become part of an invaluable "old boy network" that has to do with being privy to important work done before publication, special conferences and symposia attended and participated in, elite jobs offered and received.

You must be invited to apply to some of these schools. Sharlene submitted her records and was then invited to apply. She was flown to the interview at the school's expense and underwent eight hours of interviewing with every person of importance in the biology department. She remembers that although many questions were asked about science and her special interests, there were also an incredible number of questions about her plans as a woman. Did she intend to marry? Or to

have children? Was she engaged? What was that ring on her finger?

At the culminating session she was interviewed by the head of the department who was, at the moment, a star: "he had recently reported a breakthrough in cancer research, TV cameras everywhere, the phones ringing; he's playing the political, ambitious scientist, hardly speaking to me at all during the interview." When he did speak to her it was to say, "Miss George, do you know why I'm interviewing you?" Sharlene replied that she presumed it was because her records were superlative and she was so clearly a fine candidate for graduate school. "No," the star said. "That's not why at all. It's because this year (it was 1967, the height of the Vietnam War) I'm reduced to the lame, the halt, the blind, and the women."

Sharlene was accepted at this school. She chose to go elsewhere.

Maureen Shaw, a forty-three-year-old M.D. and biophysicist, sits on the admissions committee of the medical school where she teaches. The men on this committee always asked of a woman applicant, "Why should we give you this precious space when everyone knows you're going to take ten years off to raise children?" Shaw says: "I told them, just two years ago, they had to stop asking this question. That it was unfair, irrelevant, illegal, and cruel. But they wouldn't stop. Finally, I told them if they did not stop asking this question of women applicants, I was going to start asking male applicants why they should be considered when everyone knew they were going to die ten years earlier."

Women in Chemistry: Like Jews in Czarist Russia

When I would ask if there was a woman in the chemistry department the answer would often be: "Yes, of course. Haven't you met our Mrs. Godbless? Wonderful woman. She's been with us for years." Mrs. Godbless invariably proved to be a faculty wife who was employed by the year as an associate or a fellow or a visiting professor, and had been teaching freshman chemistry for twenty years.

After I had met the fourth or fifth Mrs. Godbless, it struck me that many physics and chemistry departments had these women hanging around the edges of the department, haunting the premises like maiden aunts hidden away in back bedrooms who come shyly into the kitchen or the living room for a family meal or when there are guests, not certain of their welcome, knowing they do not pay their way. This circumstance seemed most typical in departments where there was not a single woman either tenured or in a tenure track position.

Margaret Darnell is a sixty-three-year-old physiologist who received her Ph.D. in chemistry in 1935, and taught her subject for the next six years at a small college in her hometown. "The school was new, I worked as an associate, I was a bright little thing, they treated me like a mascot. No trouble at all. Then I went out into the real world. My husband, he's a lawyer, decided to join a firm in the Midwest. When we got where we were going—which was the state university's hometown—I went to the school and asked for a job. The head of the chemistry department looked at me in amazement. He said to me, 'Mrs. Darnell, we don't hire *women* here. Go home and take care of your husband.'

"A few months later the Japanese attacked Pearl Harbor and the United States was at war. The chemistry head calls up and says, 'Mrs. Darnell, it's your patriotic duty to report to work.' 'Dr. Buller,' I say, 'I took your advice. I went home and took care of my husband. I'm pregnant.' 'Mrs. Darnell,' he says, 'we need you.' One day I was a flower of American womanhood, the next I was a peasant told to drop her baby in the fields and report for work. I taught chemistry throughout the war. Of course, I got the sack the day after the armistice was signed."

Annie Morris is a forty-seven-year-old physical chemist who recently lost a five-year battle for tenure. For Annie the struggle for tenure was a recapitulation of her lifelong sense of herself as an outsider in chemistry, one who barely holds on, knows her hold to be precarious, and knows further that one day she must slip and fall.

Annie is overweight and moon-faced. She wears round glasses, has a slightly fixed stare, a soft southern blur in her speech, a headful of flat, wiglike curls, and a manner altogether awkward and socially maladept. But when she starts talking science the awkwardness disappears, the face takes on definition, the body pulls itself together, the voice is altered by the unmistakable sound of intellectual authority.

I once heard two scientists discussing Annie's denial of tenure. One said, "Well, you've got to admit, she *is* odd, and it is understandable that people might not want to have an eccentric around for twenty years." The other one replied, "Come off it. There are guys in that department who are social basket cases. They wheel them in in the morning, close the lab door behind them, then take them home quick, they shouldn't scare the students. She's a brilliant chemist. If she's a crazy lady now, you'd better believe they *made* her one. She never knew what hit her from the first day she entered academic science."

She was raised in a family of coal miners. She played near the fields and wanted to know why there were rainbows in the coal. Her grandfather, who adored her, brought home a chemistry book. By the time she was in high school she had a chemistry lab, which she had built by herself in the cellar, and all the freedom she could handle in a high school where there were not too many like her. She went to a Midwestern state university, did very well in chemistry, and was admitted to CalTech. The only woman in the class, she blundered her way through social and intellectual ostracism ("You know, scientists are the most socially unskilled people in the world, and if you're a woman, and a chemist besides, you *really* don't know what's happening"), and accomplished two acts of some importance: She married Jim Morris, a fellow student, and she graduated first in her class.

The year was 1959. Jim Morris, who had graduated a third of the way down in the class, received fourteen job offers. Annie could not get a job. She was offered work as a technician, she was offered research associateships, she was offered fellowships on Jim's grant. At CalTech no one lifted a finger to help her.

Recalling that time, her voice takes on the slow-witted disbelief of a Jew in Czarist Russia wandering about, bleating, "But they *said* if I won the gold medal I'd be all right." And indeed, she does look half mad as she says, very softly: "You know? They lie. I mean, they just lie. They say if you do good you'll be rewarded. And they're *lying*. They're lying, and it never occurs to you that that can be the case."

I asked Annie if she had considered taking any of the fellowships or associateships? The crazy lady disappeared, and the grownup woman hardened. "Hell, no," she said curtly. "I was first in my class at CalTech."

At last an offer came from a chemical research foundation in the Midwest. Jim got a job in industry in the same city and off they went, relieved and happy. When she arrived at the foundation Annie discovered the job was really that of technician in the lab of a pharmacologist. Twenty years after the fact her voice becomes dazed. "I couldn't believe they were doing this to me. Not only was it a technician's job, it was technician to an *incompetent.* This guy wanted me to run experiments to prove something two equations on a piece of paper could disprove in the time it took to write them down. That was one of the lowest points in my life, when I realized why they had brought me out here.

"But I knew I had to stay. There was no place for me to go. So then I had to work my way, with guile and a political savvy I had to learn, into a real job at the foundation where supposedly a job was mine by right. I worked there in total isolation. The place was openly sexist, and I was a permanent oddity. The men ate in a dining room that permitted only men.

I was not allowed in the dining room. Once a chemist from Scotland came especially to see me. The others at the foundation wanted to have lunch with him, too. They *still* wouldn't let me into the dining room. My colleagues had to run around and find an outside place to eat so I could join them. Most of these men were decent enough sorts. But nobody could even *imagine* challenging the system.

"It was the pits. Working like that. They had said to me, 'If you become pregnant you'll get fired.'" Annie's eyes get her crazy-lady glint in them, and she says softly, so softly: "Can you imagine what it means to hear something like that? I mean, that says something *deep* to you. About what you *are*.

"So I got pregnant, and they never knew it. I just wore a lab coat one size larger. Who ever really looked at me? I came back two days after the baby was born, and I never told a soul there that I had had a child."

It went on like this for years. At last she was offered a job at the state university in the city where they lived. She thought that was the end of her troubles in chemistry. She had grants, publications, citations, and her research had gained her an international reputation—but tenure was denied her. She took the university to court. Later, in the heaps of trial papers, there was a copy of a letter sent by her department chairman to three eminent chemists. The letter said, in effect: "We don't like her, and we don't want her; what would you do?" Each of the chemists had replied: "Give her tenure." But they did not. She could not find another job. Although she had a grant, she had nowhere to take it. Research chemistry was over for her.

In 1960 chemistry department heads said as openly as they had in 1940: "We don't hire women." In 1980, of course, no one would dare say this. Yet, at one of the great research universities one of the Mrs. Godblesses told me: "The chemistry department here doesn't advertise. It's illegal now, but they still do it that way. Somehow, they consider it a 'shame' to advertise. They write to their friends. And of course their friends are men who have only male graduate students. But even so, some awfully good young women get through the system and come up here for interviews. It's always the same. They look at these excellent young women and they say, 'She's very good but she lacks seasoning. Let her go off somewhere else for the year and then we'll consider her again.' Of the young men just like her they say, 'We'd better grab him before someone else does.'"

"My mother said, 'Be a scientist,' but she didn't really mean it"

Anne Polsky, thirty-eight-year-old molecular biologist, daughter of a lawyer and a music teacher: "My mother said, 'Be a scientist,' but she didn't really mean it. What she really meant was, 'Get married and teach high school biology so you can be a help and a pride to your husband.' When I took science seriously she felt betrayed."

Lillian Delgado, thirty-six-year-old chemist, daughter of working class immigrants: "My mother was an unhappy woman who lived through her three daughters. When we were young she said to us, 'In this world there are somebodies and there are nobodies. You've got to be a somebody.' Oddly enough, to her that meant becoming a doctor or a lawyer. But it was pure fantasy, something she'd picked up from forties movies; she didn't have the vaguest idea of what it was all about. She thought we should *get* the medical or law degree, but she didn't think we should really *use* it. She thought we'd be these classy mothers and wives who did a little law or medicine on the side. When I became serious about chemistry she was against it, and gave me a hard time. But it was too late. She'd already instilled drive and will in me. She didn't understand when she did it that she wouldn't be able to control it."

Alice Albright Williams, forty-three-year-old neuroanatomist, descended from a distinguished New England family: "My father was a scientist, my mother was his technician. I was sent to Radcliffe in the expectation that I would become a doctor. I was miserable in Cambridge and when I read Henry Adams who told me it was men's deepest need to achieve and women's to nurture, I said, 'Aha!' and went looking for a husband. When I called home to say I was getting married my father was devastated. 'Darling,' he said. 'I thought you'd get your degree first and *then* marry.' You see, all the wives in our family are accomplished. Years later, when I got divorced and became a serious scientist, my father demurred, 'Darling, what about the children?'"

Every woman receives a mixed message about love and work in her youth. For most, the contradiction is paralyzing. The control required to work well becomes diluted and evaporates.

Self-disciplining of a highly individual nature was required of women drawn to the arts or the humanities, but the structure of science was powerful, and forced upon women who were potential scientists a rigor of working habits that ultimately (even against the childish and anarchic will) made them into productive and disciplined workers; among the scientists the mixed message most often backfired.

Still, the message was given and it was often sufficiently received to prove immensely retarding. Among the scientists, as well as among all other women, thousands experienced an unraveling of nerve over the question of work and love—or, more accurately, career and marriage. Some of the most forlorn women in science are now those in their forties who received Ph.D.s in the sixties, then got married and tried to build a working life around their marriages. They are the lost women scientists.

But this is indeed a "time of struggle," and many now are being admirably "timely."

Jessie Snyder is a forty-year-old botanist/ecologist whose office walls on the top floor of the natural history building of a Southwestern university are covered with huge photographs of a tropical cactus plant the size of a tree. This plant grows for two hundred years, blooms for one or two years, then dies. Jessie—her hair the color and texture of straw, her eyes ice blue, her body lanky and muscular, her face prematurely weathered—stares lovingly at the photographs. She jams her white cotton blouse back inside the belt of her blue jeans, picks up a pencil to gesture with and begins talking. "The questions we ask are: What evolutionary pressures gathered to create this in nature? What in the surround contributes to the life of this organism? What is the nature of the development of the reproductive system of such plants? These are questions that interest us. We are whole-organism biologists, looking at everything around the organism as well as everything in it.

"These, of course, are ultimate questions. There are other questions to ask in ecology, and some of them interest me, and I cultivate those interests because they're the ones that will get me funding. For instance, the questions asked in population plant biology." Jessie turns to another photograph on the wall, one that shows groups of trees growing together in thick clumps in small spaces in the forest. She explains that because of the low wind dispersal of seeds, most of these are baby trees that grew very close to the mother tree. It also appeared that most of these trees were dying and no one could figure out why. Jessie discovered that a massive fungal infection emanating from the mother tree was killing off the ones growing close beside her; the ones whose seeds the winds had thrown farther away were surviving. This is the kind of information valued and supported in Jessie's field, and so she does some of this sort of work. "But these questions are not the ones that interest the most, it's the evolutionary questions that grab you."

A tropical plant specialist who spends half the year in the tropical rain forests of South America, Jessie Snyder is so entirely the hard-working scientist whose interior life is wrapped around "these questions" that it comes as something of a jolt when she casually announces: "It's only in the last two years that I am able to say to myself, I'm a scientist. Whatever it is that scientists do, that's what I do. It's only just now that I have the courage to be what I am."

She was born and raised in a small town in Minnesota and sent to a second-rate college in the middle of the state where that famous twin message—you can't be smart and still be a woman—went out strongly and was strongly received. She decided to become a high school science teacher because she had always been good at observing nature, went off to a nearby state university to receive a Master of Arts and Education in Science ("A silly degree that doesn't make you either a teacher or a scientist"), and went out into the world to teach. She hated it—hated the kids, hated the high school, hated teaching. Inside herself, aimlessness amounted nearly to desolation.

She met a man she liked who was living in Washington. She went West ostensibly to try teaching there but really to be with him. Through this man she came to live with a group of *National Geographic* types on a farm outside of Seattle, and it was here, at this time—she was thirty—that her fine sense of natural history suddenly took a swift and developing leap forward. With these people she began to watch plants and animals like a nineteenth-century "describer"; or like an agriculturist; or like a veterinarian; or like a plant biologist collecting specimens—all of whom coexist in her. The relationship with the man dissolved, but Jessie was newly put together. She entered the University of Washington as a Ph.D. candidate in ecology; within the year her life fell into place:

"All those false starts I made. I didn't know how to become a serious worker. Somewhere in my psyche I was hovering all those years, in limbo, expecting to become a wife and mother who also worked, but not too seriously, one who might perhaps go back to work after the children were grown as my mother had done. I just couldn't get it together, I'm sure, because I think (although I wasn't conscious of it) I was waiting for the right man to come along and make my future cohere."

She has had a number of love attachments over the years, and marriage proposals as well, but she has always felt, she says, with every man she's known that she couldn't really be herself: She was never completely there, some vital part was always missing. "Thank heaven, that always stopped me from marrying." She has a lover now, an ecologist at another university who shares her work. Deep into the green heart of Peru and Panama, Jessie and her ecologist-lover go to collect and to classify the largest rain forests in the world. Only here does he know who she is and, more important, does she know who she is.

Marilyn Ames is a forty-one-year-old endocrinologist who runs a lab in a cancer research center in Boston. One of her great skills as a scientist lies in knowing everyone in her field (who is doing what and where), reading everything that is written, and remembering everything she reads. She knows, for instance, that there is a scientist in Los Angeles who has a particularly excellent strain of cell culture that she needs, and that there is a man at Bell Labs whose technique for purifying the cell culture is extremely reliable. She will remember this when they are doing a particular series of experiments in her lab, and will get on the phone and arrange for these two elements to be brought to her aid.

At the same time that the cell culture in Los Angeles and the technique at Bell Labs is on her mind, it is also on her mind that she must make herself available to her four-to-seven workers, raise grant money, oversee experiments, replace lost or broken equipment, know what is going on in her lab eighteen hours a day. And she does so gladly, eagerly, with the pleasure of one for whom the all-encompassing business of doing science is only recently arrived at.

Marilyn Ames is a classic scientist delayed by the mixed message a woman receives in early life. She was raised in a suburb of Hartford. Both her parents were doctors, but her mother was devoted to her husband ("She practiced medicine on the side"). From the time she was a little child Marilyn knew she wanted to be a scientist; her absorption with

observing nature systematically, and through experimentation, was fully developed by the time she was ten. At home her parents enjoyed their pretty little girl "being scientific" as though she possessed a clever trait that might make her a more interesting wife, just as mother's being a doctor had made *her* a more interesting wife. In high school Marilyn won the national science medal. Her father answered the phone when the news came and kept saying into it, "What is this, some sort of joke?" while Marilyn, almost in tears, pulled at his sleeve and kept shaking her head no, it wasn't a joke.

She wanted to go to Radcliffe where she knew she would get a good education. Her parents said no, they wanted her to be a lady. They insisted on Smith. "I guess from that moment on I was lost. When I didn't oppose them on the Radcliffe issue the die was cast." She married directly upon graduation and went out to California with her husband. "Luckily" he agreed that Marilyn might enter graduate school. She worked hard, but always around her marriage, and eventually got her degree. They came back east to New Haven because of her husband's work. "Luckily" she landed a good job at a medical research institute. Her marriage fell apart and she remarried, this time a Boston businessman. She moved to Boston and "luckily" went to work at the cancer research center. Her point with all these "luckily"s is that at any given moment she was prepared to move, or to stop working, or to accept the inability to advance in her work, if it meant imperiling relations with her husband.

Some years into her second marriage she and her husband went to Europe together. At a scientific conference in Paris Marilyn heard an American scientist speak, and she fell in love with his mind. She turned to look at her businessman husband and thought, Why am I married to him? She left her husband, took a leave of absence from the research center, and went out West to live with the scientist she had heard speak in Paris: "Even though I knew it was detrimental to my work, and certainly to my career, I felt I had to do this. I had to see if I could make a life with this man. That seemed infinitely more important to me than my work."

Within a year—she was now in her late thirties—she was wandering about in a daze, repeating to herself, What am I doing? What am I doing? "I had suddenly realized that the scientist was an arrogant bastard, a self-involved man who enjoyed the status of having a scientist for a mistress, but certainly did not take her work and her career as seriously as he took his own. When I was invited to give my first paper in Europe, and I was delirious with joy, he said to me, 'Ah, what do you want to go for? It's all show, anyway.' I said to him, 'For you it's nothing. You've been through it a hundred times. For me it's a lot, it's prestige and recognition and fun.' He said he wasn't going, and he didn't want me to go either. I went, but he wouldn't come. Not even to keep me company when I wanted him to."

She left him then and came back to Boston to the research center where she has been a hard-driving scientist ever since. She is now a woman of affairs—"I cannot and will not live without a man"—but they are conducted around her work, or they are not conducted at all. "It's not an ideal life"—she shrugs—"but it's a helluva lot better this way than the other way."

Julia Waxman is a thirty-eight-year-old biophysicist, originally trained as a high-energy physicist, who this past year was tenured in the physics department of a Northeastern university where she had worked for years as a research associate. It is almost a certainty that Julia was tenured because the university feared she was about to leave and take her highly prized physicist husband with her. Julia is very tired, and doesn't really *give* a damn anymore why the university gave her tenure.

She was born into a family of enlightened orthodox Jews. The atmosphere at home was gentle, loving, intelligent, timid. Both parents adored education and expected the girls as well as the boys to become professional workers. The children were all stamped to one degree or another with this expectation.

In her second year in college Julia discovered the beauty of physics, felt compelled by it, and decided on physics as her life's work. She was admitted to graduate study at Brown where she was the only girl in the class. Which did not bother her at all; like so many others, Julia says she never noticed it; she is the kind of guarded, inexpressive woman who makes a perfect candidate for the "I never noticed" school.

At Brown she met and married Barry Waxman, her male counterpart: smart, gentle, religious. Barry had just completed his dissertation when they met. Halfway through her degree, he received a post-doctoral fellowship at Harvard. Julia was admitted to Harvard as a grad student and followed him to Cambridge. After one year at Harvard Barry received his job at this university. Julia, of course, came along with him. Here she had their first child and slowly finished her degree at Harvard through the mail.

There was, of course, no job for her. She went to work at the university as research associate to a biophysicist. In time she left high-energy physics and became a biophysicist herself. The years passed. She had another child. By all accounts her work was superior but no job could or would be found for her. Barry felt for her, but neither one of them was in the habit of making demands. They simply didn't see anything for it but to accept as a given the position in which they found themselves.

More years passed. Then, she says mildly, she fell into depression. "What form did your depression take?" I ask. Very quietly she says: "I began not to want to go out. I didn't want to meet people who were visiting the university. I was always explaining why I was where I was, always in these peripheral positions. I began to feel bad about myself. I didn't want to have to explain myself anymore. If I was good, people's eyes seemed to be saying to me, why didn't I have a job? And I agreed with them. It began to eat at me.

"Finally, Barry and I agreed that I would look for a job, and that he would get one where I got one. As soon as I went looking I found a job. NIH made me a fantastic offer, one that made everyone here sit up and take notice. I came to the department and I told them if they didn't give me a job I'd be leaving. They didn't say yes and they didn't say no. After all these years here. They waited until the last possible minute. I had three days to tell NIH whether or not I'd come. And then the department said okay, they'd give me tenure.

"Sometimes I'm a bit sorry they capitulated. It would have been easier to start all over some place fresh. Here, I suddenly became the head of a research group of which I had simply been a part. The grad students—who looked on me as one of them!—resented it. And then there's been the difficulty of learning how to carry a full teaching load—as well as learning how to organize and run a lab. I didn't know how to do any of it. It's best to learn those things when you're younger. I have difficulty, great difficulty with it. I'm exhausted all the time."

Julia Waxman smooths her good wool skirt of an unfashionable length across her knees. Beneath her thick unshaped hair, neat, unadorned features announce: Take no notice of me. Pretend I'm not here. I want no trouble. I'd rather die than seem aggressive or unladylike, say or do anything anyone might interpret as rude or offensive. Yet, at the end of our time together, when I ask this timid, unadventurous woman, "If you had it to do all over again would you do it the same?" she shakes her head without hesitation. "Absolutely not. If I had it to do all over again I'd certainly not do what I did. I wouldn't follow Barry. I'd have had a job of my own from the start. It's been very bad for me. Bad for me as a person. Bad for me as a scientist."

Janet Moran, twenty-eight years old, a botanist/ecologist in training, is Jessie Snyder's graduate student. Tall, skinny, goofy; blue-jeaned, frizzy-haired, wearing tinted granny eyeglasses. A child of her generation, Janet has moved from small-town Republicanism to membership in a farming commune to activism in a university town collective to leadership of encounter groups to graduate studies in science. She's all smart-ass cool; her two favorite words are "neat" and "nerd"; they apparently account for all things good and all things bad.

Born and raised in Iowa, Janet was the smartest kid in town. She loved goofing off, being sassy and popular, and always able to talk her way out of trouble. She also loved plants and the outdoors, loved watching the way things grew, was more systematic in her observations than she consciously knew.

Went to Iowa State; science courses were for fun; was going to take engineering and "make bucks"; left engineering three days after she started; got disoriented; dropped out; started living with a boy from high school; left him; went back to school, this time to the university at Ames; was drawn repeatedly to botany and ecology courses for the healing fun of it; took chemistry and physics because you couldn't learn more biology, ecology, and plant life without them; never saw herself as a scientist, was just fooling around "in science"; dropped out again; went West to join friends living in a collective in Oregon, learned fast about "groups"; was fascinated by power (still is), how it worked among people; drifted back to Ames after a year; lived in a group house; started baking bread in a collective; was soon managing the collective; after a while went back to school (it just seemed more interesting); graduated finally with a double major in botany and biology; drifted again; again lived in a group house, got involved in running encounter groups, suddenly saw it was "either groups or science." For the first time she said to herself, I'm not fooling around in science. I am a scientist. She came to the Southwest to become Jessie Snyder's student.

Still addicted to group houses, Janet leans back in a painted kitchen chair on a Saturday morning, while five other grad students are in varying stages of making breakfast, and has no trouble reflecting on her recent years:

"For a long time I thought I didn't want to be a scientist because I couldn't stand other scientists. They all seemed like such nerds. They were so humorless, so narrow, most of them had such tiny sights set for themselves. They seemed to say no to so much in order to say yes to so little. They don't know anything about anything. They don't know life is sex and power. They don't know biology is sex and power. They're scared of sex so they don't know.

"I still think all this is true. But I realize now that's not why I didn't want to be a scientist. I didn't want to become a scientist because I was scared myself. I could never imagine myself a college professor. Who, me? Become an adult? Nah. What're ya kidding? Not me. I'm too nearsighted. Or too short. Or too something. Maybe too much of a girl. Yeah. Maybe that's it. Somebody's gonna come along someday and take care of me. I don't really *have* to do this stuff. I'm just killing time, having fun, goofing off."

Her chair comes crashing down on the kitchen floor. "But god, I think I see it coming." She pushes her granny glasses back into place, flashes a huge grin, and says brashly: "This past year I realized I'm gonna be a star. I went on a field trip with other ecologists, and I saw. I'm brighter than most of them, and my scope is wider. Much wider. I'm interested in ultimate questions, not approximate ones. Not why does a plant grow in this much daylight, today in this place, under these conditions, but rather, what happens to the whole system if you kill this plant or grow that organism? What are the historic reasons, the evolutionary pressures that make this or stop that? Why has it been growing like this, and not like that? What's the history, the ecological history, of this condition or that?" She grins again. "Science became so much more fun once I stopped thinking someone was gonna come along and take care of me."

Recognition at Last: The National Academy of Sciences

Vivian Davidson is a fifty-nine-year-old geneticist who as a graduate student in the 1940s had already earned an international reputation for the research she was then doing, and would continue to do for the next twenty years and more. Two years ago she was elected to the National Academy of Sciences. The Academy has a membership of thirteen hundred. Of that thirteen hundred perhaps twenty-nine or thirty are women. Of that twenty-nine or thirty almost all were elected within the past six or seven years.

The scroll that Vivian received from the Academy had her name engraved on it, and then went on to announce that Vivian Davidson was being honored for "his" accomplishments, and that "he" was now entitled, and "he" could, and "he" should. She was so amazed by all the "he"s that she sent a letter to the Academy inquiring whether the source of the problem might be that the engraver was British and had taken Vivian for a man's name, or was it perhaps that the printing process was lagging behind the process of election of women to the Academy. The letter she received back from the Academy secretary (a man) was an angry one informing her that she was the first person ever to complain, the scroll was an honor, its plate had been struck in 1868 by Abraham Lincoln, and it had a historic value the Academy was not about to tamper with.

At the next Academy meeting in Washington, Vivian raised the matter of the scroll's wording with some of the other women scientists. Each one said she had never noticed the use of "he" instead of "she" on the scroll. "That's probably true," Vivian said sadly. "They're so grateful to be allowed into the club, they wouldn't dream of making waves. In all likelihood they *haven't* noticed."

I told the story of Vivian Davidson and the Academy scroll to a group of scientists at a party in Woods Hole in the summer of 1980. One woman in the group was a member of the Academy. When I reached the end of the story, and everyone was either gaping or laughing, this woman—thin, whitehaired, chain-smoking—said coldly: "That is absolutely untrue. I have a scroll and I'm quite sure it doesn't say 'he.'" The party fell silent. The woman stared at me, I stared at her. There was nothing for me to say. The following October I received a postcard from her. In a scrupulously neat small hand she had written: "I want to apologize to you. I looked at my scroll when I got home. You were right. It *does* say 'he.'"

As of this writing the scroll still reads "he," there are still only thirty-odd women in the Academy, and most of them are still grateful to have been allowed into the club.

 ## "How can a little girl like you teach a great big class of men?" the Chairman Said, and Other Adventures of a Woman in Science

Naomi Weisstein

I am an experimental psychologist. I do research in vision. The profession has for a long time considered this activity, on the part of one of my sex, to be an outrageous violation of the social order and against all the laws of nature. Yet at the time I entered graduate school in the early sixties, I was unaware of this. I was remarkably naive. Stupid, you might say. Anybody can be president, no? So, anybody can be a scientist. Weisstein in Wonderland. I had to discover that what I wanted to do constituted unseemly social deviance. It was a discovery I was not prepared for: Weisstein is dragged, kicking and screaming, out of Wonderland and into Plunderland. Or Blunderland, at the very least.

What made me want to become a scientist in the first place? The trouble may have started with *Microbe Hunters*,[1] de Kruif's book about the early bacteriologists. I remember reading, about Leeuwenhoek's discovery of organisms too small to be seen with the naked eye. When he told the Royal Society about this, most of them thought he was crazy. He told them he wasn't. The "wretched beasties" were there, he insisted; one could see them unmistakably through the lenses he had so carefully made. It was very important to me

that he could reply that he had his evidence: evidence became a hero of mine.

It may have been then that *I* decided that I was going to become a scientist, too. I was going to explore the world and discover its wonders. I was going to understand the brain in a better and more complete way than it had been understood before. If anyone questioned me, I would have my evidence. Evidence and reason: my heroes and my guides. I might add that my sense of ecstatic exploration when reading *Microbe Hunters* has never left me through all the years I have struggled to be a scientist.

As I mentioned, I was not prepared for the discovery that women were not welcome in science, primarily because nobody had told me. In fact, I was supported in thinking—even encouraged to think—that my aspirations were perfectly legitimate. I graduated from the Bronx High School of Science in New York City where gender did not enter very much into intellectual pursuits; the place was a nightmare for everybody. We were all, boys and girls alike, equal contestants; all of us were competing for that thousandth of a percentage point in our grade average that would allow entry into one of those high-class out-of-town schools, where we could go, get smart, and lose our New York accents.

I ended up at Wellesley, and this further retarded my discovery that women were supposed to be stupid and incompetent: the women faculty at Wellesley were brilliant. (I learned later on that they were at Wellesley because the schools that had graduated them,—the "very best" schools where you were taught to do the very best research—couldn't, or didn't care to, place them in similar schools, where they could continue their research.) So they are our brilliant unknowns, unable to do research because they labor under enormous teaching loads, unable to obtain the minimal support necessary for scholarship—graduate students, facilities, communication with colleagues. Whereas I was ignorant then about the lot of women in the academy, others at Wellesley knew what it was like. Deans from an earlier, more conscious feminist era would tell me that I was lucky to be at a women's college where I could discover what I was good at and do it. They told me that women in a man's world were in for a rough time. They told me to watch out when I went on to graduate school. They said that men would not like my competing with them. I did not listen to the deans, however; or, when I did listen, I thought what they were telling me might have been true in the nineteenth century, but not then, in the late fifties.

So my discovery that women were not welcome in psychology began when I got to Harvard, on the first day of class. That day, the entering graduate students had been invited to lunch with one of the star professors in the department. After lunch, he leaned back in his chair, lit his pipe, began to puff, and announced: "Women don't belong in graduate school."

The male graduate students, as if by pre-arranged signal, then leaned back in their chairs, puffed on their newly bought pipes, nodded, and assented: "Yeah."

"Yeah," said the male graduate students. "No man is going to want you. No man wants a woman who is more intelligent than he is. Of course, that's not a real possibility, but just in case. You are out of your *natural* roles; you are no longer feminine."

My mouth dropped open, and my big blue eyes (they have since changed back to brown) went wide as saucers. An initiation ceremony, I thought. Very funny. Tomorrow, for sure, the male graduate students will get it.

But the male graduate students never were told that they didn't belong. They rapidly became trusted junior partners in the great research firms at Harvard. They were carefully nurtured, groomed, and run. Before long, they would take up the white man's burden and expand the empire. But for me and for the other women in my class, it was different. We were shut out of these plans; we were *shown* we didn't belong. For instance, even though I was first in my class, when I wanted to do my dissertation research, I couldn't get access to the necessary equipment. The excuse was that I might break the equipment. This was certainly true. The equipment was eminently breakable. The male graduate students working with it broke it every week; I didn't expect to be any different.

I was determined to collect my data. I had to see how the experiment I proposed would turn out. If Harvard wouldn't let me use its equipment, maybe Yale would. I moved to New Haven, collected my data at Yale, returned to Harvard, and was awarded my Ph.D. in 1964, and afterward could not get an academic job. I had graduated Phi Beta Kappa from Wellesley, had obtained my Ph.D. in psychology at Harvard in two and one half years, ranked first in my graduate class, and I couldn't get a job. Yet most universities were expanding in 1964, and jobs were everywhere. But at the places where I was being considered for jobs they were asking me questions like—"How can a little girl like you teach a great big class of men?" At that time, still unaware of how serious the situation was, I replied, "Beats me. I guess I must have a talent."

and

"Who did your research for you?" This last was from a famous faculty liberal at another school, who then put what I assume was a fatherly hand on my knee and said in a tone of deep concern, "You ought to get married."

Meanwhile, I was hanging on by means of a National Science Foundation postdoctoral fellowship in mathematical biology, at the University of Chicago, and attempting to do some research. Prior to my second postdoctoral year, the University of Chicago began negotiations with me for something like a real job: an instructorship jointly in the undergraduate college and the psychology department. The negotiations appeared to be proceeding in good faith, so I wrote to Washington and informed them that I would not be taking my second postdoctoral year. Then, ten days before classes began, when that option as well as any others I might have taken had been closed, the person responsible for the negotiations called to tell me that, because of a nepotism rule—my husband taught history at the University of Chicago—I would not be hired as a regular faculty member. If I wanted to, I could be appointed lecturer, teaching general education courses in the college; there was no possibility of an appointment in psychology. The lectureship paid very little for a lot of work, and I would be teaching material unconnected with my research. Furthermore, a university rule stipulated that lecturers (because their position in the university was so insecure) could not apply for research grants. He concluded by asking me whether I was willing to take the job; ten days before the beginning of classes, he asked me whether I was willing to take the only option still available to me.

I took the job, and "sat in," so to speak, in the office of another dean, until he waived the restriction on applying for research grants. Acknowledging my presence, he told a colleague: "This is Naomi Weisstein. She hates men."

I had simply been telling him that women are considered unproductive precisely because universities do their best to keep women unproductive through such procedures as the selective application of the nepotism rule. I had also asked this dean whether I could read through the provisions of the

rule. He replied that the nepotism rule was informal, not a written statute—flexibility being necessary in its application. Later, a nepotism committee set up partly in response to my protest agreed that the rule should stay precisely as it was: that it was a good idea, should not be written out, and should be applied selectively.

Lecturers at major universities are generally women. They are generally married to men who teach at these major universities. And they generally labor under conditions which seem almost designed to show them that they don't belong. In many places, they are not granted faculty library privileges; in my case, I had to get a note from the secretary each time I wanted to take a book out for an extended period. Lecturers' classrooms are continually changed; at least once a month, I would go to my assigned classroom only to find a note pinned to the door instructing me and my class to go elsewhere: down the hall, across the campus, out to Gary, Indiana.

In the winter of my first year, notices were distributed to all those teaching the courses I was teaching, announcing a meeting to discuss the next year's syllabus. I didn't receive the notice. As I was to learn shortly, this is the customary way a profession that prides itself on its civility and genteel traditions indicates to lecturers and other "nuisance personnel" that they're fired: they simply don't inform them about what's going on. I inquired further. Yes, my research and teaching had been "evaluated" (after five months: surely enough time), and they had decided to "let me go" (a brilliant euphemism). Of course, the decision had nothing to do with my questioning the nepotism rules and explaining to deans why women are thought unproductive.

I convinced them to "let me stay" another year. I don't know to this day why they changed their minds. Perhaps they changed their minds because it looked like I was going to receive the research grant for which I had applied, bringing in money not only for me, but for the university as well. A little while later, Loyola University in Chicago offered me a job.

So I left the University of Chicago. I was awarded the research grant and found the Psychology Department at Loyola at first very supportive. The chairman, Ron Walker, was especially helpful and especially enlightened about women at a time when few academic men were. I was on my way, right? Not exactly. There is a big difference between a place like Loyola and a place with a heavy commitment to research—any large state university, for example—a difference that no amount of good will on the part of an individual chairman could cancel out. The Psychology Department was one of the few active departments at Loyola. The other kinds of support one needs to do experimental psychology— machine and electrical shops, physics and electrical engineering departments, technicians, a large computer—were either not available or were available at that time only in primitive form.

When you are a woman at an "unknown" place, you are considered out of the running. It was hard for me to keep my career from "shriveling like a raisin" (as an erstwhile colleague predicted it would). I was completely isolated. I did not have access to the normal channels of communication, debate, and exchange in the profession—those informal networks where you get the news, the comment and the criticism, the latest reports of what is going on. I sent my manuscripts to various people for comment and criticism before sending them off to journals; few replied. I asked others working in my field to send me their prepublication drafts; even fewer responded. Nobody outside Loyola informed me about special meetings in my area of psychology, and few inside Loyola knew about them. Given the snobbery rife in academic circles (which has eased lately since jobs are much harder to find and thus even "outstanding" young male graduates from the "best" schools may now be found at places formerly beneath their condescension), my being at Loyola almost automatically disqualified me from the serious attention of professional colleagues.

The "inner reaches" of the profession, from which I had been exiled, are not just metaphorical and intangible. For instance, I am aware of two secret societies of experimental psychologists in which fifty or so of the "really excellent" young scientists get together regularly to make themselves better scientists. The ostensible purpose of these societies is to allow these "best and brightest" young psychologists to get together to discuss and criticize each other's work; they also function, of course, to define who is excellent and who is not, and to help those defined as excellent to remain so, by providing them with information to which "outsiders" in the profession will not have access until much later (if at all).

But the intangibles are there as well. Women are treated in ways men hardly ever experience. Let me give you one stunning example. I wrote up an experiment I thought was really good and its results, which were fascinating, and sent the paper to a journal editor whose interests I knew to be close to what was reported in my paper. The editor replied that there were some control conditions that should be run, and some methodological loose ends, so they couldn't publish the paper. Fair enough. He went on to say that they had much better equipment over there, and they would like to test my ideas themselves. Would I mind? I wrote them back, told them I thought it was a bit unusual, asked if they were suggesting a collaboration, and concluded by saying that I would be most happy to visit with them and collaborate on my experiment. The editor replied with a nasty letter explaining to me that by suggesting that they test my ideas themselves, they had merely been trying to help me. If I didn't want their help in this way, they certainly didn't want mine, that is, they had had no intention of suggesting a collaboration.

In other words, what they meant by "did I mind" was: Did I mind if they took my idea and did the experiment themselves? As we know, instances of taking someone else's idea and pretending it's your own are not at all uncommon in science. The striking thing about this exchange, however, was that the editor was arrogant enough, and assumed that I would be submissive enough, so that he could openly ask me whether I would agree to this arrangement. Would I mind? No, of course not. Women are joyful altruists. We are happy to give of ourselves. After all, how many good ideas do you get in your lifetime? One? Two? Why not give them away?

Generally, the justification for treating women in such disgraceful ways is simply that they are women. Let me give another spectacular example. I was promised the use of a small digital laboratory computer, which was to be purchased on a grant. The funds from the grant would become available if a certain job position entailing administration of this grant could be filled. I was part of the group which considered the candidates and which recommended appointing a particular individual. During the discussions of future directions of this individual's work, it was agreed that he would of course share the computer with me. He was hired, bought the computer, and refused me access to it. I offered to put in money for peripherals which would make the system faster and easier for both of us to work with, but this didn't sway him. As justification for his conduct, the man confessed to the chairman that he simply couldn't share the computer with me: he has difficulty working with women. To back this up, he indicated that he'd been "burned twice." Although the chairman had previously been very helpful and not bothered in the least about women, he accepted that statement as an explanation. Difficulty in working with women was not a problem this man should work out. It was *my* problem. Colleagues thought no worse of him for this problem; it might even have raised him in their estimation. He obtained tenure quickly, and retains an influential voice in the department. Yet if a woman comes to *any* chairman of *any* department and confesses that she has difficulty working with men, she is thought pathological.

What this meant for me at the time was that my research was in jeopardy. There were experimental conditions I needed to run that

simply could not be done without a computer. So there I was, doing research with stone-age equipment, trying to get by with wonderwoman reflexes and a flashlight, while a few floors below, my colleague was happily operating "his" computer. It's as if we women are in a totally rigged race. A lot of men are driving souped-up, low-slung racing cars, and we're running as fast as we can in tennis shoes we managed to salvage from a local garage sale.

Perhaps the most painful of the appalling working conditions for women in science is the peculiar kind of social-sexual assault women sustain. Let me illustrate with a letter to *Chemical and Engineering News* from a research chemist named McGauley:

> There are differences between men and women ... just one of these differences is a decided gap in leadership potential and ability ... this is no reflection upon intelligence, experience, or sincerity. Evolution made it that way. ... Then consider the problems that can arise if the potential employee, Dr. Y (a woman) [*sic:* he could at least get his chromosomes straight] will be expected to take an occasional business trip with Dr. X. ... Could it be that the guys in shipping and receiving will not take too kindly to the lone Miss Y?[2]

Now what is being said here, very simply, and to paraphrase the Bible, is that women are trouble. And by trouble, McGauley means sexual trouble. Moreover, somehow, someway, it is our fault. *We* are provoking the guys in shipping and receiving. Women are universally assigned by men, first—no matter who the women are or what they have in mind—to sexual categories. Then, we are accused by men of taking their minds away from work. When feminists say that women are treated as sex objects, we are compressing into a single, perhaps rhetorical phrase, an enormous area of discomfort, pain, harassment, and humiliation.

This harassment is especially clear at conventions. Scientific meetings, conferences, and conventions are harassing and humiliating for women because women, by and large, cannot have male colleagues. Conversations, social relations, invitations to lunch, and the like are generally viewed as sexual, not professional, encounters if a woman participates in them. It does not cross many men's minds that a woman's motivation may be entirely professional.

I have been at too many professional meetings where the "joke" slide was a woman's body, dressed or undressed. A woman in a bikini is a favorite with past and perhaps present presidents of psychological associations. Hake showed such a slide in his presidential address to the Midwestern Psychological Association, and Harlow, past president of the American Psychological Association, has a whole set of such slides, which he shows at the various colloquia to which he is invited. This business of making jokes at women's bodies constitutes a primary social-sexual assault. The ensuing raucous laughter expresses the shared understanding of what is assumed to be women's primary function—to which we can always be reduced. Showing pictures of nude and sexy women insults us: it puts us in our place. You may think you are a scientist, it is saying, but what you really are is an object for our pleasure and amusement. Don't forget it.

I could continue recounting the horrors, as could almost any woman who is in science or who has ever been in science, but I want to stop now and ask: What conclusions can we draw from my experience? What does it all add up to?

Perhaps we should conclude that persistence will finally win out. Or that life is hard, but cheerful struggle and a "sense of humor" may make it bearable. Or perhaps we should search back through my family, and find my domineering mother and passive father or my domineering father and passive mother, to explain my persistence. Perhaps, but all these conclusions are beside the point. The point is that none of us should have to face this kind of offense. The point is that we must change this man's world and this man's science.

How will other women do better? One of the dangers of this kind of narrative is that it may validate the punishment as it singles out the few survivors. The lesson appears to be that those (and only those) with extraordinary strength will survive. This is not the way I see it. Many have had extraordinary strength and have *not* survived.

Much of the explanation for my professional survival has to do with the emergence and growth of the women's movement. I am an experimental psychologist, a scientist. I am also a feminist. I am a feminist because I have seen my life and the lives of women I know harassed, dismissed, damaged, destroyed. I am a feminist because without others I can do little to stop the outrage. Without a political and social movement of which I am a part— without feminism—my determination and persistence, my clever retorts, my hours of patient explanation, my years of exhortation amount to little. If the scientific world has changed since I entered it, it is not because I managed to become an established psychologist within it. Rather, it is because a women's movement came along to change its character. It is true that as a member of that movement, I have acted to change the character of the scientific world. But without the movement, none of my actions would have brought about change. And now, as the strength of the women's movement ebbs, the old horrors are returning. This must not happen.

Science, knowledge, the search for fundamental understanding is part of our humanity. It is an endeavor that seems to give us some glimpse of what we might be and what we might do in a better world. To deny us the right to do science is to deny us our humanity. We shall not have our humanity denied.

Notes

1. Paul de Kruif, *Microbe Hunters* (New York: Harcourt, Brace & World, 1926).
2. T. J. McGauley, letter to *Chemical and Engineering News*, December 7, 1970, pp. 8–9.

The Anomaly of a Woman in Physics

Evelyn Fox Keller

A couple of months ago I was invited to give a series of lectures at a major university as one of a "series of distinguished guest lecturers" on mathematical aspects of biology. Having just finished teaching a course on women at my own college, I somehow felt obliged to violate the implicit protocol and address the anomalous fact of my being an apparently successful woman scientist. Though I had experienced similar vague impulses before, for a variety of reasons arising from a mix of anger, confusion, and timidity, it had never seemed to me either appropriate or possible to yield to such an impulse. Now, however, it seemed decidedly inappropriate, somewhat dishonest, and perhaps even politically unconscionable to deliver five lectures on my work without once making reference to the multitude of contradictions and conflicts I had experienced in arriving at the professional position presumed on this occasion. Therefore, in a gesture that felt wonderfully bold and unprofessional, I devoted the last lecture to a discussion of the various reasons for the relative absence of women in science, particularly in the higher ranks. The talk formed itself—with an ease, clarity, and lack of rancor that amazed me. I felt an enormous sense of personal triumph. Somehow, in the transformation of what had always appeared to me an essentially personal problem into a political problem, my anger had become depersonalized, even defused, and a remarkable sense of clarity emerged. It suggested to me that I might, now, be able to write about my own rather painful and chaotic history as a woman in science.

Origins are difficult to determine and obscure in their relation to final consequences. Suffice it to say that in my senior year of college I decided I would be a scientist. After several years of essentially undirected intellectual ambition, I majored in physics partly for the sake of discipline and partly out of the absence of any clear sense of vocation; and in my last year I fell in love with theoretical physics.

I invoke the romantic image not as a metaphor, but as an authentic, literal description of my experience. I fell in love, simultaneously and inextricably, with my professors, with a discipline of pure, precise, definitive thought, and with what I conceived of as its ambitions. I fell in love with the life of the mind. I also fell in love, I might add, with the image of myself striving and succeeding in an area where women had rarely ventured. It was a heady experience. In my adviser's fantasies, I was to rise, unhampered, right to the top. In my private fantasies, I was to be heralded all the way.

It was 1957. Politics conspired with our fantasies. Graduate schools, newly wealthy with National Science Foundation money, competed vigorously for promising students, and a promising female student was a phenomenon sufficiently unique to engage the interest and curiosity of recruiters from Stanford to Harvard. Only Cal Tech and Princeton were closed to me—they were not yet admitting women—and I felt buoyant enough to challenge them. I particularly wanted to go to Cal Tech to study with Richard Feynman—a guru of theoretical physics—on whose work I had done my senior thesis. In lieu of my being accepted at Cal Tech, an influential friend of mine volunteered to offer Feynman a university chair at MIT, where I would be admitted. Heady indeed.

Even then I was aware that the extreme intoxication of that time was transitory—that it had primarily to do with feeling "on the brink." Everything that excited me lay ahead. I had fantasies of graduate school and becoming a physicist; what awaited me, I thought, was the fulfillment of those fantasies. Even the idea of "doing physics" was fantasylike. I could form no clear picture of myself in that role, had no clear idea of what it involved. My conception of a community of scholars had the airiness of a dream. I was intoxicated by a vision that existed primarily in my head.

Well, Feynman was not interested in leaving Cal Tech, and so I went to Harvard. More accurately, I was pressured, and eventually persuaded, by both a would-be mentor at Harvard and my adviser, to go to Harvard. At Harvard I was promised the moon and the sun—I could do anything I wanted. Why I was given this extraordinary sales pitch seems, in retrospect, all but inexplicable. At the time, it seemed quite natural. I dwell on the headiness of this period in order to convey the severity of the blow that graduate school at Harvard actually was.

The story of my graduate school experience is a difficult one to tell. It is difficult in part because it is a story of behavior so crude and so extreme as to seem implausible.

Moreover, it is difficult to tell because it is painful. In the past, the telling of this story always left me so badly shaken, feeling so exposed, that I became reluctant to tell it. Many years have passed, and I might well bury those painful recollections. I do not because they represent a piece of reality—an ongoing reality that affects others, particularly women. Even though my experiences may have been unique—no one else will share exactly these experiences—the motives underlying the behavior I am going to describe are, I believe, much more prevalent than one might think, and detectable in fact in behavior much less extreme.

I tell the story now, therefore, because it may somehow be useful to others. I *can* tell the story now because it no longer leaves me feeling quite so exposed. Let me try to explain this sense of exposure.

Once, several months into my first year in graduate school, a postdoctoral student in an unusual gesture of friendliness offered me a ride home from a seminar and asked how I was doing. Moved by his gesture, I started to tell him. As I verged on tears, I noticed the look of acute discomfort on his face. Somehow, I had committed a serious indiscretion.

It was as if I had publicly disrobed. Whatever I said, then and always after, it somehow seemed I had said too much. Some of this feeling remains with me even now as I write this article. It is a consequence of the assumption in the minds of others that what I am describing must have been a very personal, private experience—that is, that it was produced somehow by forces within myself. It was not. Although I clearly participated in and necessarily contributed to these events, they were *essentially* external in origin. That vital recognition has taken a long time. With it, my shame began to dissolve, to be replaced by a sense of personal rage and, finally, a transformation of that rage into something less personal—something akin to a political conscience.

That transformation, crucial in permitting me to write this, has not, however, entirely removed the pain from the process of recollecting a story that retains for me considerable horror. If I falter at this point, it is because I realize that in order for this story to be meaningful, even credible, to others, I must tell it objectively—I must somehow remove myself from the pain of which I write. The actual events were complex. Many strands weave in and out. I will describe them, one by one, as simply and as fairly as I can.

My first day at Harvard I was informed, by the very man who had urged me to come, that my expectations were unrealistic. For example, I could not take the course with Schwinger (Harvard's answer to Feynman) that had lured me to Harvard, and I ought not concern myself with the foundations of quantum mechanics (the only thing that did concern me) because, very simply, I was not, could not be, good enough. Surely my ambition was based on delusion—it referred to a pinnacle only the very few, and certainly not I, could achieve. Brandeis, I was told bluntly, was not Harvard, and although my training there might have earned me a place at Harvard, distinction at Brandeis had no meaning here. Both I and they had better assume I knew nothing. Hence I ought to start at the beginning. The students they really worried about, I was informed, were those who were so ignorant and naive that they could not apprehend the supreme difficulty of success at Harvard.

These remarks were notable for their blatant class bias and arrogance, as well as for their insistent definition of me on the basis of that bias—a gratuitous dismissal of my own account that I experienced recurrently throughout graduate school. The professor's remarks were all the more remarkable in that I had expressed exactly the same intentions in our conversation the previous spring and had then been encouraged. What could account for this extraordinary reversal? There had been no intervening assessment of my qualifications. Perhaps it can be explained simply by the fact that the earlier response was one of someone in the position of selling Harvard, while now it seemed there was an obligation to defend her. (It is ironic that universities should be associated with the feminine gender.) Nor was it coincidental, I suspect, that this man was shortly to assign to one of the senior graduate students (male, of course) the task of teaching me how to dress.*

Thus began two years of almost unmitigated provocation, insult, and denial. Lacking any adequate framework—political or psychological—for comprehending what was happening to me, I could only respond with personal rage: I felt increasingly provoked, insulted, and denied. Where political rage would have been constructive, personal rage served only to increase my vulnerability. Having come to Harvard expecting to be petted and fussed over (as I had been before) and expecting, most of all, validation and approval, I was entirely unprepared for the treatment I received. I could neither account for nor respond appropriately to the enormous discrepancy between what I expected and what I found. I had so successfully internalized the cultural identification between

male and intellect that I was totally dependent on my (male) teachers for affirmation—dependency made treacherous by the chronic confusion of sexuality and intellect in relationships between male teachers and female students. In seeking intellectual affirmation, I sought male affirmation, and thereby became exquisitely vulnerable to the male aggression surrounding me.

I had in fact been warned about the extreme alienation of the first year as a graduate student at Harvard, but both my vanity and my naiveté permitted me to ignore these warnings. I was confident that things would be different for me. That confidence did not last long. Coming from everywhere, from students and faculty alike, were three messages. First, physics at Harvard was the most difficult enterprise in the world; second, I could not possibly understand the things I thought I understood; and third, my lack of fear was proof of my ignorance. At first, I adopted a wait-and-see attitude and agreed to take the conventional curriculum, though I privately resolved to audit Schwinger's course. Doing so, as it turned out, seemed such an act of bravado that, daily, all eyes turned on me as I entered the class and, daily, I was asked by half a dozen people with amusement if I still thought I understood. Mysteriously, my regular courses seemed manageable, even easy, and as I became increasingly nervous about my failure to fear properly, I spent more and more evenings at the movies. In time, the frequent and widespread iteration of the message that I could not understand what I thought I understood began to take its toll. As part of a general retreat, I stopped attending Schwinger's course. I had begun to lose all sense of what I did or did not understand, there and elsewhere. That I did well in my exams at the end of the semester seemed to make no difference whatever.

Meanwhile, it was clear that I was becoming the subject—or object—of a good deal of attention in the Physics Department. My seriousness, intensity, and ambition seemed to cause my elders considerable amusement, and a certain amount of curiosity as well. I

---

*My attire, I should perhaps say, was respectable. It consisted mainly of skirts and sweaters, selected casually, with what might have been called a bohemian edge. I wore little or no makeup.

was watched constantly, and occasionally addressed. Sometimes I was queried about my peculiar ambition to be a theoretical physicist—didn't I know that no woman at Harvard had ever so succeeded (at least not in becoming a *pure* theoretical physicist)? When would I too despair, fail, or go elsewhere (the equivalent of failing)? The possibility that I might succeed seemed to be a source of titillation; I was leered at by some, invited now and then to a faculty party by others. The open and unbelievably rude laughter with which I was often received at such events was only one of many indications that I was on display—for purposes I could either not perceive or not believe. My fantasy was turning into nightmare.

In lieu of support I began to long for anonymity, but the anomaly of my position had made it so public that there was no hiding. My real world began to resemble a paranoid delusion. Many people in Cambridge knew who I was and speculated about me. None of them offered friendship. Once, feeling particularly lonely on a Saturday night, I went for a walk by the Charles River. I was sitting on a bench, deep in thought, when a young man, a stranger, appeared out of the dark, sat down, and began to recite a detailed knowledge of me—what I was doing, who my friends were, where I had come from, and other particulars. Finishing his recitation, he got up and walked away. When real events so take on the qualities of delusion, it becomes difficult indeed to expect the credulity of others. Yet I remained frighteningly sane and had no difficulty in recognizing the reality—only in understanding it.

It is sometimes hard to separate affront to oneself as a person from affront to one's sensibilities. Not only do they tend to generate the same response—one feels simply affronted—but it is also possible (as I believe was true here) that the motives for both affronts are not unrelated. I went to graduate school with a vision of theoretical physics as a vehicle for the deepest inquiry into nature—a vision perhaps best personified, in recent times, by Einstein. The use of mathematics to further one's understanding of the nature of space, time, and matter represented a pinnacle of human endeavor. I went to graduate school to learn about foundations. I was taught, instead, how to do physics. In place of wisdom, I was offered skills. Furthermore, this substitution was made with moralistic fervor. It was wrong, foolhardy, indeed foolish, to squander precious time asking why. Proper humility was to bend to the grindstone and learn techniques. Contemporary physics, under the sway of operationalism, had, it seemed, dispensed with the tradition of Einstein—almost, indeed, with Einstein himself. General relativity, the most intellectually ambitious venture of the century, seemed then (wrongly) a dead subject. Philosophical considerations of any sort in the physical sciences were at an all-time low. Instead, techniques designed to calculate nth-order corrections to a theory grievously flawed at its base were the order of the day.

Physics had become a major industry. Huge investments poured into experiments, the results of which needed subsequently to be matched by theoretical calculations. Paralleling the influx of money was an influx of manpower. They couldn't all be creative innovators. The Baconian vision of an army of scientific foot soldiers was imminent; and Harvard physicists, whatever they were doing, were, by definition, the best—they were the generals. The status of the elite had to be protected even though the very conception of elite was uncertain. While there was general agreement about what the student rank and file should (or rather, should not) be doing, the generals seemed considerably confused about what they should be doing. The work of Harvard's most distinguished theoretician conveyed a sense of grand sweep. While he was roundly faulted and criticized for the abstract formality of his approach, his status as the best went unchallenged. Even among the elite, then, there was a lack of clarity about the nature and rules of progress and excellence, and a certain amount of scrambling. Somehow the notion of different but equally valid postures did not seem tenable—the preoccupation with ranking was overriding.

My naiveté and idealism were perfect targets. Not only did I not know my place in the scheme of things as a woman, but by a curious coincidence, I was apparently equally ingenuous concerning my place as a thinker. I needed to be humbled. Though I writhed over the banality of the assignments I was given, I did them, acknowledging that I needed in any case to learn the skills. I made frequent arithmetic errors—reflecting a tension that endures within me even today between the expansiveness of conception and the precision of execution, my personal variation perhaps of the more general polar tension in physics as a whole. When my papers were returned with the accuracy of the conception ignored and the arithmetic errors streaked with red—as if with a vengeance—I wondered whether I was studying physics or plumbing. Who has not experienced such a wrenching conflict between idealism and reality? Yet my fellow students seemed oddly untroubled. From the nature of their responses when I tried to press them for deeper understanding of the subject, I thought perhaps I had come from Mars. Why, they wondered, did I want to know? That they were evidently content with the operational success of the formulas mystified me. Even more mystifying was the absence of any appearance of the humility of demeanor that one would expect to accompany the acceptance of more limited goals. I didn't fully understand then that in addition to the techniques of physics, they were also studying the techniques of arrogance. This peculiar inversion in the meaning of humility was simply part of the process of learning how to be a physicist. It was intrinsic to the professionalization, and what I might even call the masculinization, of an intellectual discipline.

To some extent the things I describe here are in the nature of the academic subculture. They reflect the perversion of academic style—familiar in universities everywhere—a perversion that has become more extensive as graduate schools have tended to become increasingly preoccupied with professional training. My experiences resemble those of many graduate students—male and female alike. What I experienced as a rather brutal assault on my intellectual interests and abilities was I think no accident, but rather the inevitable result of the pervasive attempt of a profession to make itself more powerful by weeding out those sensibilities, emotional and intellectual, that it considers inappropriate. Not unrelated is a similar attempt to maintain the standards and image of a discipline by discouraging the participation of women—a strategy experienced and recounted by many other women. Viewed in this way, it is perhaps not surprising that the assault would be most blatant in a subject as successful as contemporary physics, and in a school as prestigious as Harvard.

Perhaps the most curious, undoubtedly the most painful, part of my experience was the total isolation in which I found myself. In retrospect, I am certain that there must have been like-minded souls somewhere who shared at least some of my disappointments. But if there were, I did not know them. In part, I attribute this to the general atmosphere of fear that permeated the graduate student body. One did not voice misgivings because they were invariably interpreted to mean that one must not be doing well.* The primary goal was to survive, and, better yet, to *appear* to be surviving, even prospering. So few complaints were heard from anyone. Furthermore, determined not to expose the slightest shred of ignorance, few students were willing to discuss their work with any but (possibly) their closest friends. I was, clearly, a serious threat to my fellow students' conception of physics as not only a male stronghold but a male *retreat*, and so I was least likely to be sought out as a colleague. I must admit that my own arrogance and ambition

---

*Indeed, most people then and later assumed I had done badly—particularly after hearing my story. Any claims I made to the contrary met with disbelief.

did little to allay their anxieties or temper their resistances. To make matters even worse, I shared with my fellow classmates the idea that a social or sexual relationship could only exist between male and female students if the man was "better" or "smarter" than the woman—or at the very least, comparable. Since both my self-definition and my performance labeled me as a superior student, the field of sociability and companionship was considerably narrowed.

There was one quite small group of students whom I did view as like-minded and longed to be part of. They too were concerned with foundations; they too wanted to know why. One of them (the only one in my class) had in fact become a close friend during my first semester. Though he preached to me about the necessity of humility, the importance of learning through the tips of one's fingers, the virtue of precision—he also listened with some sympathy. Formerly a Harvard undergraduate, he explained to me the workings of Harvard and I explained to him how to do the problems. With his assistance, I acquired the patience to carry out the calculations. We worked together, talked together, frequently ate together. Unfortunately, as the relationship threatened to become more intimate, it also became more difficult—in ways that are all too familiar—until, finally, he decided that he could no longer afford the risk of a close association with me. Out of sympathy for his feelings, I respected his request that I steer clear of him and his friends—with the consequence that I was, thereafter, totally alone. The extent of my isolation was almost as difficult for *me* to believe as for those to whom I've attempted to describe it since. Only once, years later in a conversation with another woman physicist, did I find any recognition. She called it the "sea of seats": you walk into a classroom early, and the classroom fills up, leaving a sea of empty seats around you.

Were there no other women students? There were two, who shared neither my ambition, my conception of physics, nor my interests. For these reasons, I am ashamed to say, I had no interest in them. I am even more ashamed to admit that out of my desire to be taken seriously as a physicist I was eager to avoid identification with other women students who I felt could not be taken seriously. Like most women with so-called male aspirations, I had very little sense of sisterhood.

Why did I stay? The Harvard Physics Department is not the world. Surely my tenacity appears as the least comprehensible component of my situation. At the very least, I had an extraordinary tolerance for pain. Indeed, one of my lifelong failings has been my inability to know when to give up. The very passion of my investment ruled out alternatives.

I had, however, made some effort to leave. At the very beginning, a deep sense of panic led me to ask to be taken back at Brandeis. Partly out of disbelief, partly out of the conviction that success at Harvard was an invaluable career asset, not to be abandoned, I was refused, and persuaded to continue. Although I had the vivid perception that rather than succeed I would be undone by Harvard, I submitted to the convention that others know better; I agreed to suspend judgment and to persevere through this stinging "initiation rite." In part, then, I believed that I was undergoing some sort of trial that would terminate when I had proven myself, certainly by the time I completed my orals. I need be stoic only for one year. Unfortunately, that hope turned out to be futile. The courses were not hard, never became hard in spite of the warnings and I generally got A's. But so did many other students. Exams in fact were extremely easy.

When I turned in particularly good work, it was suspected, indeed sometimes assumed, that I had plagiarized it. On one such occasion, I had written a paper the thesis of which had provoked much argument and contention in the department. This I learned, by chance, several weeks after the debate was well underway. In an effort to resolve the paradox created by my results, I went to see the professor for whom I had written the paper.

After an interesting discussion, which incidentally resolved the difficulty, I was asked, innocently and kindly, from what article(s) I had copied my argument.

The oral exams, which I had viewed as a forbidding, milestone, proved to be a debacle. My committee chairman simply failed to appear. The result was that I was examined by an impromptu committee of experimentalists on mathematical physics. Months later, I was offered the following explanation: "Oh, Evelyn, I guess I owe you an apology. You see, I had just taken two sleeping pills and overslept." The exam was at 2:00 P.M. Nevertheless, I passed. Finally, I could begin serious work. I chose as a thesis adviser the sanest and kindliest member of the department. I knocked on his door daily for a month, only to be told to come back another time. Finally I gained admittance, to be advised that I'd better go home and learn to calculate.

My second year was even more harrowing than the first. I had few courses and a great deal of time that I could not use without guidance. I had no community of scholars. Completing the orals had not served in any way to alleviate my isolation. I was more alone than ever. The community outside the physics department, at least that part to which I had access, offered neither solace nor support. The late fifties were the peak of what might be called home-brewed psychoanalysis. I was unhappy, single, and stubbornly pursuing an obviously male discipline. What was wrong with me? In one way or another, this question was put to me at virtually every party I attended. I was becoming quite desperate with loneliness. And as I became increasingly lonely I am sure I became increasingly defensive, making it even more difficult for those who might have been sympathetic to me or my plight to approach me to commiserate. Such support might have made a big difference. As it was, I had neither colleagues nor lovers, and not very many friends. The few friends I did have viewed my situation as totally alien. They gave sympathy out of love, though without belief. And I wept

because I had no friend whose ambition I could identify with. Was there no woman who was doing, had done, what I was trying to do? I knew of none. My position was becoming increasingly untenable.

Had I been married, would I have fared differently? I came to believe not only that marriage offered the only support possible, but even more, that my failure to marry was somehow the root of all my difficulties. But, it seemed, my career choice, and my attitude toward it, discouraged all suitors. Where was the way out? Ideally, I had thought they would come together—physics and love. But they seemed to cancel each other out. My most frequent fantasy was that I would return to the Physics Department one day, victoriously, a physicist with a baby in my arms. My impoverished imagination could conceive of no better vindication. Even my fantasies conformed to stereotype.

What had happened to my dreams? Although I had, shortly after my orals, arranged to transfer out of Harvard at the end of the second year, when that time came, my hopes and plans (not to speak of momentum) were too thoroughly shattered for me to consider going elsewhere. After two years of virtually continuous denial of my perceptions, my values, and my ambitions— an experience that might then have been described as brainwashing, and ought now be called schizophrenogenic—my demoralization was complete. Feeling pushed to the wall, I decided, midyear, to give up physics and return to a world I realized must still exist, somewhere outside. Though I remained officially enrolled in graduate school in order to collect my monthly stipend, my commitment to physics was over. Even before I stopped attending classes formally, this change of heart was visible enough to trigger a remarkable change in my fellow students, who became, overnight, friendly and sympathetic. Clearly, I was no longer a threat. Ironically, at the end of my second year, during which I had done virtually no work and attended few classes, I still got A's. I include this as a comment on the grading system at Harvard.

I recognize that this account reads in so many ways like that of a bad marriage—the passionate intensity of the initial commitment, the fantasies on which such a commitment (in part) is based, the exclusivity of the attachment, the apparent disappearance of alternative options, the unwillingness and inability to let go, and finally, the inclination to blame oneself for all difficulties. Although I can now tell this story as a series of concrete, objective events that involved and affected me, at the time I eventually came to accept the prevalent view that what happened to me at Harvard simply manifested my own confusion, failure, neurosis—in short that *I* had somehow "made" it happen. The implications of such internalization were—as they always are—very serious.

Now I had to ask *how* I had "made" it happen—what in me required purging? It seemed that my very ambition and seriousness were at fault, and that these qualities—qualities I had always admired in others—had to be given up. Giving up physics, then, seemed to mean giving up parts of me so central to my sense of myself that a meaningful extrication was next to impossible. I stayed on at Harvard, allowing myself to be convinced once again that I must finish my degree, and sought a dissertation project outside the Physics Department.

After drifting for a year, I took advantage of an opportunity to do a thesis in molecular biology while still nominally remaining in the Physics Department. That this rather unusual course was permitted indicated at least a recognition, on the part of the then chairman, of some of the difficulties I faced in physics. Molecular biology was a field in which I could find respect, and even more important, congeniality. I completed my degree, came to New York to teach (physics!), married, bore children, and ultimately began to work in theoretical biology, where I could make use of my training and talents. This proved to be a rewarding professional area that sustained me for a number of critical years. If my work now begins to take me outside this professional sphere, into more political and philosophical concerns, this reflects the growing confidence and freedom I have felt in recent years.

Inner conflict, however, was not to disappear with a shift in scientific specialization. While it is true that I was never again to suffer the same acute—perhaps bizarre—discomfort that I did as a graduate student in physics, much of the underlying conflict was to surface in other forms as I assumed the more conventional roles of wife, mother, and teacher. The fundamental conflict—between my sense of myself as a woman and my identity as a scientist—could only be resolved by transcending all stereotypical definitions of self and success. This took a long time, a personal analysis, and the women's movement. It meant establishing a personal identity secure enough to allow me to begin to liberate myself from everyone's labels—including my own. The tension between "woman" and "scientist" is not now so much a source of personal struggle as a profound concern.

After many years, I have carved out a professional identity very different from the one I had originally envisioned, but one that I cherish dearly. It is, in many important ways, extraprofessional. It has led me to teach in a small liberal arts college that grants me the leeway to pursue my interests on my own terms and to combine the teaching I have come to love with those interests, and that respects me for doing so. It has meant acquiring the courage to seek both the motives and rewards for my intellectual efforts more within myself. Which is not to say that I no longer need affirmation from others; but I find that I am now willing to seek and accept support from different sources—from friends rather than from institutions, from a community defined by common interests rather than by status.

As I finished writing this essay, I came across an issue of the annals of the *New York Academy of Sciences* (March 15, 1973) devoted to "Successful Women in the Sciences." The volume included brief autobiographical accounts of a dozen or so women, two of whom were trained in physics and one in mathematics. Because material of this kind is almost nonexistent, these first-person reports are an important contribution "to the literature." I read them avidly. More than avidly, for the remarks of these women, in their directness and honesty, represent virtually the only instance of professional circumstances with which to compare my own experience.

It may be difficult for those removed from the mores of the scientific community to understand the enormous reticence with which anyone, especially a woman, would make public his or her personal impressions and experiences, particularly if they reflect negatively on the community. To do so is not only considered unprofessional, it jeopardizes one's professional image of disinterest and objectivity. Women, who must work so hard to establish that image, are not likely to take such risks. Furthermore, our membership in this community has inculcated in us the strict habit of minimizing any differences due to our sex. I wish therefore to congratulate women in the mainstreams of science who demonstrate such courage.

Their stories, however, are very different from mine. Although a few of these women describe discrete experiences similar to some of mine, they were able to transcend their isolation and discomfort, and in their perseverance and success, to vindicate their sex. I am in awe of such fortitude. In their stories I am confirmed in my sense that with more inner strength I would have respond-ed very differently to the experiences I've recorded here. The difficulty, however, with success stories is that they tend to obscure the impact of oppression, while focusing on individual strengths. It used to be said by most of the successful women that women have no complaint precisely because it has been demonstrated that with sufficient determination, anything can be accomplished. If the women's movement has achieved anything, it has taught us the folly of such a view. If I was demolished by my graduate school experiences, it was primarily because I failed to define myself as a rebel against norms in which society has heavily invested. In the late fifties, "rebel" was not a meaningful word. Conflicts and obstacles were seen to be internal. My insistence on maintaining a romantic image of myself in physics, on holding to the view that I would be rewarded and blessed for doing what others had failed to do, presupposed a sense of myself as special, and therefore left me particularly vulnerable. An awareness of the political and social realties might have saved me from persisting in a search for affirmation where it could not and would not be given. Such a political consciousness would have been a source of great strength. I hope that the political awareness generated by the women's movement can and will support young women who today attempt to challenge the dogma, still very much alive, that certain kinds of thought are the prerogative of men.

Women Join the Ranks of Science but Remain Invisible at the Top

Natalie Angier

The National Academy of Sciences announced its annual roll of new members this month, bestowing a highly coveted honor on a small group of American researchers. But of the 60 American scientists elected to the academy this year, only 6 are women. Some women in science take little satisfaction in the academy's election results.

"I think it's a disgusting percentage," said Dr. Susan E. Leeman, a neuroscientist at the University of Massachusetts Medical School in Worcester who was one of the newly chosen members. "I'm very proud and pleased to have been elected, but 6 out of 60? Isn't that amazing."

Since 1970, only a trickle of women—at most half a dozen in any one year—have won election to the academy, even though the number of eligible candidates would seem to have steadily increased.

According to the National Research Council, the percentage of Ph.D. scientists who are women doubled from 10 percent in 1973 to 20 percent in 1989, the last year for which figures are available. And if scientists with all types of degrees, from master's to medical, are taken into account, women today make up almost one-third of the total.

Dr. Peter Raven, the academy's home secretary and the official in charge of conducting elections, said that the academy was trying hard to recruit younger members and hence more who are women. But the continuing scarcity of female academy members is one facet of a larger issue: women have been swelling the lower and middle ranks of science for years, yet still have not managed to pierce the upper scientific strata in anything beyond token numbers.

The problem is hardly limited to science, of course, but if science is a profession where advancement depends solely on the merit of an individual's ideas, the barriers to women might be expected to be lower than in other walks of life.

But in extensive interviews with women at all stages of their scientific careers and in a broad variety of disciplines, the researchers insisted that in fact some of the difficulties they encountered were peculiar to their trade, and that certain characteristics of the scientific culture were likelier to impede women's progress than to propel it.

Among those characteristics is the extreme insularity of science, and the need to be at the center of the rumor mill if one is to hear of vital new results before competitors do.

Women said that because they were often excluded from the most important scientific meetings and collaborations, they were frequently left out of the gossip loop. They also said they were given far fewer chances to present their findings and ideas to powerful audiences of their peers, a key method for winning converts and scientific influence.

Other women objected to the raw fisticuffs style that so many researchers adopt in their dissections of one another's results, intelligence, and all-round scientific and personal worthiness.

"The legal barriers to progress have been removed," said Dr. Londa Schiebinger, a history professor at Pennsylvania State University in University Park and the author of "The Mind has No Sex?" about the history of women in science. "The most visible barriers are gone. So what we're left with are the things that aren't very well perceived. And these are things that can be hard to talk about, not only because they're unquantifiable, but because they evoke a lot of hostility when you mention them to men."

To be sure, many women pointed out that progress had been great since the days when women were forbidden to serve at telescopes or to accompany male researchers on field studies, and some expressed great optimism that the changes would continue to proceed smartly.

"If you go back 20 years, it was hard then for women to get a job at entry levels" said Dr. Mildred Dresselhaus, an engineer and solid state physicist who has been on the faculty of Massachusetts Institute of Technology since 1960. "I think that's turned around recently very significantly. I think we're in an era now where men are sensitized and they want to give women an equal shot." Yet Dr. Dresselhaus admitted that "when push comes to shove, what people say and what they do don't always agree."

Despite the greater opportunities in the lower ranks, women remain poorly represented in the upper echelons.

Far fewer women than men hold tenured professorships in science, and fewer still are heads of their departments. Women make up only 3 percent of the physics faculty members in the United States, and about 2 percent of the engineering faculty.

The record in the life sciences like biology and biomedicine is somewhat better, with 22 percent of all faculty members in biology being women. But even here a quarter of them fall into categories, like "research associate" or "staff scientist," that offer no chance of tenure. By comparison, fewer than 10 percent of male biologists are in positions that are not on a tenure track.

Even as full professors, women almost never run the sort of large laboratories that earn multimillion-dollar Federal grants and give them visibility.

"When women get tenure, they're often secluded in their little cubbyhole, doing their own little thing," said Dr. Leeman. "As they age, they're not put on committees of power,

they don't participate in allocation of resources, the division of space or the direction an institution is going in."

Women's salaries reflect the age-related discrepancies in power. The National Science Foundation has found that although women and men command roughly the same salaries at entry-level positions in science, differences in annual raises soon have an impact. After a decade of laboring full time in science, men earn 25 percent to 35 percent more than women do. And while male scientists' salaries continue to rise until retirement, women's peak before age 50, and then either stagnate, or even drop.

The reasons for the failure of women to break through science's traditional glass ceiling, or even to touch it with upstretched arms, are a complex mix of the obvious and the elusive. Many said it was partly a result of their being the ones who bear and care for children. Combining motherhood and science is particularly hard, they said, because the mechanics of research experiments often require all-night vigils that cannot be interrupted. And several studies have shown that a majority of married female scientists are married to other scientists, who themselves are tethered to the laboratory for days upon nights and thus may have trouble contributing much to child care.

But others argued that far subtler factors than maternity come into play in keeping women from the scientific forefront. Some of the researchers said that beliefs about women's innate inferiority to men in mathematics and abstract reasoning still held strong sway over some male scientists, even when the particular women have, through their achievements, proved themselves to be extremely skilled in math.

Dr. Vera C. Rubin, a scientist at the department of terrestrial magnetism at the Carnegie Institution in Washington, recently reviewed figures showing how, for several years in a row, male mathematicians received a proportionately higher number of fellowships to support their graduate work relative to the pool of men and women who applied.

In 1990, for example, 134 men applied for the fellowships, and 21 got them. But of the 56 women who applied, only 1 received the support.

From her own long-term experience as a professor and administrator, Dr. Rubin knew that by the time they were in graduate school all but the most talented female mathematicians had been weeded out, and she was dismayed by the differences in grant awards. Her distress only mounted when she discussed her findings with a few men.

"I went up to several male mathematicians, including my son, Carl, who's quite eminent in his field," she said. "I presented them with the numbers and asked 'Can you believe this?' They all said, 'Well, the men must be better than the women.' That was all there was to it. And my son is married to a mathematician!"

Others attributed the barriers facing women to the singular dynamics of the scientific subculture, and the differences between the myth of the scientist and the reality.

Politics and business may demand a certain conformity in appearance, behavior and mindset from their participants, making it particularly difficult for women to blend into the male backdrop. But science is supposedly a haven for the misfits and the eccentrics of society. By the old stereotype, scientists are eggheaded loners who stare into microscopes or telescopes with such single-mindedness that they could not be expected to notice another person's presence, let alone the person's sex.

But as women and men quickly learn during their training, science in fact is one of the most gregarious of trades. Many scientific enterprises require extensive collaborations between teams of researchers. And men still seem to feel more comfortable collaborating with men than with women.

"There is a lot of friendship and social interactions that go on at the scientific level, and a lot of important information is exchanged in those interactions," said Dr. Elaine Fuchs, professor of molecular and cell biology at the University of Chicago. "You may be at a complete disadvantage in your ability to do good science if you can't get inside information. And though in an ideal world it would be otherwise, men usually feel more chummy with other men."

The difficulties of collaborating are multiplied by the extraordinarily international texture of science. Foreign scientists flock here in huge numbers, and when male researchers come from conservative nations like Japan, Middle Eastern countries and India, they may be even more reluctant to collaborate with women than are American scientists.

Many women complained that they were often excluded from the all-important conference circuit, a crucial route to scientific prominence. Meetings are where researchers exchange their latest findings long before the information is disseminated in scientific journals. But many female scientists believe that when conference organizers put together their roster of speakers, deciding who are the most respected elders, or the hottest young turks, or the most amusing raconteurs, women seem to come to mind rarely.

"Women appear invisible to men," said Dr. Margaret Davis, a professor of ecology at the University of Minnesota in Minneapolis who herself often organizes conferences. "If you ask men for the names of seminar or symposium speakers, the names you get back from them are almost invariably male. If you ask women, you get both male and female names."

At the biggest skin cancer meeting of the year, held last month in New York, all but 1 of the 47 researchers on the program were men, even though the field of dermatology research is known to have a number of outstanding female investigators.

When asked why he thought women were largely … omitted from the program, Dr. Darrell S. Rigel of the New York School of Medicine, a conference participant, said he thought it was an act of benign neglect on the part of the conference coordinators. He then hastened to add that the ratio would be different at a skin cancer meeting that he and his colleagues had organized.

"We've got lots of women on our panel," he said. But on checking the exact number, he laughed nervously. "Oh, wait a minute," he said. "Only 2 out of 28. Hmm. It never occurred to me. I just don't choose people on basis of gender. But this does raise my consciousness."

Women who are invited to speak encounter other difficulties. Many complain that they are subjected to a level of scrutiny not accorded their male peers, and that withering scrutiny does not come from the men alone.

"When I listen to somebody talk, I tend to find fault with the way a woman speaks more than with a man," said Dr. Marjorie Oettinger, who recently got her doctorate at the Whitehead Institute for Biomedical Research and is already becoming quite well known for her successes in the field of immunology. "If she sounds aggressive, or whiny, or ditzy or schoolmarmish, I notice. I always feel bad about that, but I know I'm more sensitized to how a woman is presenting herself."

Their fear of being unduly criticized may prompt many women to forgo the podium altogether, although it is on the stage where scientists often do the best job of wooing others to believe in their genius and their vision.

"Young women won't talk on a subject unless they really know it and are totally prepared," said Dr. Florence Haseltine of the National Institute for Child Health and Development in Bethseda, Md., who frequently organizes seminars. "They'll say, 'I don't know, I don't feel qualified to do that.' Men will talk about anything. If you ask a man to speak, he'll almost never turn you down."

Another aspect of the scientific culture that can alienate women is its brutality. Scientists often engage in scathing intellectual brawls where they try to demolish the other's results with little regard for the niceties of social etiquette. Women often feel uncomfortable with the demand that they up the insult ante if their research is to be believed.

"Scientists can be like schoolyard toughs," said Dr. Caroline Porco, a planetary scientist at the University of Arizona in Tucson who has been appointed head of NASA's Cassini spacecraft mission, scheduled to fly past Saturn in the early 21st century. "I grew up as the only girl with four brothers, but still I wasn't prepared for what I encountered at Stanford when I went there in 1974, as a graduate student. You'd present your results and somebody would say, 'How did you get here? Why are you wasting my time? If you had half a brain you could have done that calculation.'"

What is more, said Dr. Porco, if she had had the inclination to respond in kind, "the guys would probably say, 'She's a pushy bitch.'"

Many researchers, men and women alike, said that the greatest changes would probably come with the efforts of women themselves—women like Dr. Christiane Nüsslein-Volhard, a renowned fruit-fly geneticist at the Max Planck Institute in Tubingen and a woman of boundless verve and intelligence. For the past 15 years, Dr. Nüsslein-Volhard has attracted young women from around the world to her laboratory, and those women have in turn become powerhouses in fruit-fly genetics at the great universities, both here and abroad.

As a result, the study of how the tiny insect develops from fertilization to completion is now dominated by women. "Oh, there are plenty of guys around like me," said Dr. Claude Desplan, a fruit-fly expert at Rockefeller University in New York. "It's a big field, and one of the most exciting fields, and a lot of people are jumping on it. But many, many of the best people are women, and nearly all of them have trained with Christiane."

Creeping Toward Inclusivity in Science

Phyllis Goldberg

Our field absolutely needs women. My field of computer science is 50 years old, and I have been with it 40 years. You all know the progress that has been made in this field, but in some ways we have not progressed. Computers are not very user friendly. Many of the systems we have—DOS, C, etc.—are monuments to the egos, mostly male, that created them. The computing field is just the beginning of this extraordinarily exciting time in science, and women are going to play a great part in it.

—Frances Allen, IBM Fellow,
TJ Watson Research Center

My conclusion is that when bright people have a multitude of choices of careers, for many—not all, but for many—it's not enough for the work to be exciting and challenging. They must also feel that they are valued members of the community. Being recognized as a valued member of the scientific community has in the past been much more readily obtainable for men, and it continues to be that way. So things have changed, but not enough and way too slowly.

—Judy Franz, Executive Officer,
American Physical Society

The composition of what the science and engineering and the nation's workforce will look like in the 21st century is very much in the hands of the way the federal agencies award monies in the name of research and development. Public money defines the public interest, so that if it is in the public interest to develop all the talents of our population, then either federal money is helping solve the problem or it is supporting the system as it is. ... We are undercutting our ability to compete globally. ... [T]his is not an issue of

women in science, or ethnic or racial minorities, or persons with disabilities. This is an issue of the health of science. The federal government has got to act in a more responsible way. And universities have got to recognize that they are not just replenishing their workforces. They are contributing to the workforce of the entire nation.

—Daryl E. Chubin, Directorate for
Education and Human Resources,
National Science Foundation

Leaders in American science threw down the gauntlet of inclusion at the New York Academy of Sciences conference, "Choices and Successes: Women in Science and Engineering," that took place in New York City on March 12-13, 1998. Organized and chaired by biophysicist Cecily C. Selby, the conference brought together a diverse group of 250 scientists and engineers to consider why and how—to retain talented and interested women in science and engineering.

The occasion marked the 25th anniversary of the Academy's landmark 1972 conference, "Women in Science: Determinants of Success." The specific goal of the 1998 gathering was to assess whether, where, and how progress has taken place in the intervening quarter of a century, and to recommend ways of accelerating it based on research and the "best practices" to be found in corporate, government, and academic institutions.

Those who participated in the 1998 conference work in a variety of settings: large and small industries, colleges and universities, government agencies. From student to Nobel laureate, they stand on every rung of the professional ladder. They brought a wide range of life experiences and points of view to the dialogue. Yet for all their diversity, they agreed that definite progress has been made—and that it has not gone far or fast enough. As

Dudley Herschbach, a Nobel Laureate and Professor of Chemistry at Harvard University, put it: We are "creeping toward inclusivity in science."

Although more women are enrolling in science and engineering studies, for example, they drop out at rates proportionately higher than men do. In a study conducted by conference participant Elaine Seymour, the Director of Ethnography and Evaluation Research at the University of Colorado at Boulder, it was found that women switched from science majors to non-science majors at a rate of 70% (national samples) and 54% (highly selective institutions) compared to 61% and 39%, respectively, for men. This "leaky pipeline" continues to leak throughout graduate school and postdoctoral work.

A major concern expressed at the conference was that—unlike the private sector and government, where self-interest (dictated by a combination of competition for talented women and civil rights legislation enacted over the last two decades) has compelled measurable progress in policies and practices—the elite colleges and research universities have proven virtually impervious to change. The pool of female candidates for tenured professorships at such institutions, for example, is shallow. Who, then, will serve as role models for a new generation of women scientists? And where will industry recruit the women scientists and engineers of the caliber needed in positions of top management to lead the transformation of the workplace where science and engineering are practiced?

The shared perspective of the conference seemed to be that science, and society *require* the broad talent and wisdom that can only be assured by increasing diversity in the workforce and the workplace. How do we bring it about? Through substantive changes in the attitudes, policies, and practices that inform how we (1) educate, and evaluate, the workforce and (2) manage the workplace. In other words, diversity doesn't just happen—it must be aided and abetted.

Changes: What Difference Has the Last Twenty-Five Years Made?

"I had no idea what lay ahead of me," Nobel Laureate Gertrude B. Elion, Scientist Emeritus at Glaxo Wellcome, Inc., recalled. "Women in chemistry? What was I thinking of? After an entire summer of job hunting, I had to face reality.… I had been given every excuse for not hiring me, even when there was an opening.… I often wonder why I didn't give up then and there. I almost did. I actually went to secretarial school for six weeks. However, when I was offered a three-month job as a laboratory assistant in Biochemistry at the New York Hospital School of Nursing, I left secretarial school and never looked back.…

"What advice can I give young women today? I have no mysterious secrets to impart. The most important advice is to choose the field that makes you happiest. There is nothing better than loving your work.…"

Dr. Elion's recollections of what one colleague referred to as the "Heroic Past" had its counterpart in the cautionary statement made by Dr. Herschbach. "In contrast to the many recent trends that offer encouragement to young women pursuing careers in science, particularly academic careers he noted, "there are now at least two major factors that have become increasingly daunting. One is the tight job market and funding situation. The other, perhaps more recalcitrant, is the expansion of time [it takes] to complete a Ph.D. degree.… What should have been an invigorating, adventurous jaunt on the way to an independent position has, for far too many, stretched into a grueling marathon.…"

"The problem and the solution may lie in the institution of science itself," Paula M. Rayman, the Director of the Radcliffe Public Policy Institute, suggested. "Given that science, like most elements of our culture, is socially constructed, the current dilemmas regarding women in science may well be the result of the inability of science, as currently constructed, to accomplish [certain] goals. Perhaps it is time to ask, as Yentsch and Sinderman do, 'Is it time to change the rules by which the games of science are played?' A key issue in women's participation in science is whether the scientific community of which we are all members can nurture and develop a sense of cooperation and collaboration in a culture of competition."

Choices: What Keeps Women in Science and Engineering?

The future of science and engineering depends on which human beings choose to pursue them. A broad array of evidence was cited indicating that many prevalent practices and attitudes in those fields are leftovers from an era when women were either overtly excluded from them or were allowed in only as "second-class citizens" with access neither to power nor to recognition. Although more women are currently becoming scientists and engineers than in the past (there is considerable variation by discipline as well as by specialty within particular disciplines), a significant number drop out after a relatively short time because they perceive that (1) conditions in the workplace are frequently incompatible with their needs and priorities and (2) the work itself is based on a model that implicitly or explicitly identifies characteristically male ways of doing things (thinking, speaking, creating) with *the scientific way* to do those activities while simultaneously denigrating other styles as *unscientific*. Meanwhile, there are still too many talented women who are "turned off" by science and engineering in the first place because of such (by and large accurate) perceptions.

Such perceptions extend to the meaning and value women assign to the traditional reward system. The rewards typically offered by organizations—higher salary, increased prestige, elevated status, more challenge—do not necessarily reflect what many women deem most necessary and important to them. Conversely, what many women tend to regard as rewarding—collaborative effort, supportive workplace, quality of life, better "fit" between professional and personal life—is rarely included in the traditional package of rewards and benefits. To support the values and interests of a diverse workforce, rewards are needed that honor different ways of doing things, as well as different perceptions of success. Personnel policies would benefit from designing rewards that relate to different parameters for defining success and that relate to "what women want."

Some of the participants in the conference devised an equation to say, "what women want":

$$\text{Success} = \int_0^\infty \left[\sum \text{Satisfaction}\,(I,\, t,\, p) \right] dt$$

where I = individual, t = time (life span), p = parameters like contribution to society, joy of living, peer recognition, family, money, and power.

Shenda Baker, a professor of chemistry at Harvey Mudd College and a Clare Boothe Luce Professor, put it this way: "The general consensus from the 1998 meeting was that peer recognition is now expected, and a measure of success comes from assessing all aspects of life. We thus defined success as 'the sum over a lifetime of our satisfaction in career, family and personal life, indicating that balance has become much more of an issue."

In other words, women are different from men. But although Professor Higgins in *My Fair Lady* could demand, "Why can't a woman be more like a man?" the conference participants agreed that it is not acceptable for professors, employers, or anyone else to ask that question in real life.

"Through our lengthy interviews with 200 [male and female scientists], and also some comparative peer review of their work, it turned out that on average there *were* differences between men and women in what they meant by 'good science.'" Gerald Holton, Professor Emeritus of Physics and History of Science at Harvard University, said in reporting some of the results from Project Access, the study he conducted with Gerhard Sonnert. "Can such differences in beliefs and resulting research strategies help explain the differences in their career outcomes? Women scientists in our sample on the whole tended to uphold, to a statistically significant degree, more consciously what might be called the traditional standards of good science—the pursuit of fundamentals, with care, with objectivity, with replicability."

According to Mary Frank Fox, Professor of Sociology in the School of History, Technology, and Society at the Georgia Institute of Technology who was a discussant in the "work" session, "Gender differences reported [in the Project Access study] are not so much in ways of thinking or in methods of inquiry; rather they represent differences in ways of behaving and of organizing scientific work. These patterns of women and men are *social modes;* and because science is a *social system*, such gendered modes or styles are important, potentially, in understanding the participation and performance of women (and other underrepresented groups) in science. Science can ultimately be advantaged not by marginalizing, but by examining and ultimately responding to, behavioral modes of its increasingly diverse participants."

Sue V. Rosser, the Director of the Center for Women's Studies and Gender Research at the University of Florida (Gainesville), has applied a five-stage model for examining the effects of laboratory climate on the careers of women scientists based on data obtained from a survey of 1997 NSF POWRE (Professional Opportunities for Women in Research and Education) awardees. At the first stage, women are not present, and no notice is taken of their absence. At the second, women scientists are superfluous, virtually invisible "add-ons." At the third stage, women scientists in the laboratory are viewed as "a problem, an anomaly, or deviant." By the next stage, there is a focus on attracting and retaining women scientists. At the fifth (and highest) stage, the laboratory climate is "redefined and reconsidered [so as] to include us all." Dr. Rosser noted that this "is where we would all like to be because it would allow the most creative, productive work from all scien-

tists, regardless of their gender, to make a better science."

How can we get from here to there? Diane Hoffman-Kim, an assistant professor at Brown University and a discussant of Dr. Rosser's paper, said: "Often styles of discourse, created, maintained, and dominated by men, function to exclude women, to impede their confidence, communication, and access to information essential for their careers. A number of women are also put off by a reverence for exclusive individualism and a scorn for collaboration in science. I find that to work toward a critical mass [of women scientists] is essential for women's success. Otherwise, with one established and dominant norm of what a scientist does and is, who in the male-dominated lab group will be chosen for a project, nominated for a fellowship, sent to a meeting?"

Successes: Which Policies and Practices Work?

"The matter of inclusion has to do with economics:" said Roberta W. Gutman, the Vice President and Director of Global Diversity at Motorola. "That's why I believe that we are going to crack the code first in industry.... We are seeing the consequences of *not* cracking it before the rest of the institutions.... Women have been tremendous contributors to corporate America when we allowed them to do so. Until very recently—I'd say in the last ten years—corporate America allowed only enough women in management to avoid problems with the government."

Ms. Gutman noted that the number of women vice presidents at Motorola has risen from two in 1989 to 43 today. Meanwhile, the Chemistry Department at Harvard can boast only one tenured woman on its faculty. Nor is Harvard an anomaly. A survey of the 25 top-ranked university chemistry departments in the country revealed that only 7% of their professors are women. Industry hires and promotes women scientists and engineers, it was generally agreed, because doing so is good for business. Yet while the private sector is visibly out in front of academia, it cannot afford to rest on its laurels. Women continue to be underrepresented in senior management positions throughout corporate America.

The biotechnology industry is a case in point. Susan Eaton reported that 50% of the research scientists in this relatively new field are women. This may be a result of the opportunity for flexibility in scheduling and part-time work. Additionally, the drawing power of women already in an industry for those at an earlier point in their careers may be a factor. Yet the majority of biotech company founders, directors, and CEOs are men, and men are more likely than women to be able to advance to senior management positions without a doctorate.

"Recruiting women is not enough," Mary C. Mattis, Vice President of Research and Advisory Services at Catalyst, Inc., pointed out. "It's what you do with them when you get them.... Successful companies pay attention to women scientists early in their careers to see that their assignments are challenging and their supervisors are committed to seeing women succeed. Concomitantly, companies need to monitor the mobility of entry-level and junior women scientists relative to their male peers. The individual side of the success equation is all about exceeding expectations, personal flexibility, and working hard to make male supervisors feel comfortable around you ... refusing to give in to despair, cynicism, or bitterness." Success requires knowing how to pick battles carefully, Dr. Mattis pointed out, "since battles take a lot of energy."

From the government front, Beverly K. Hartline, the Assistant Director for Physical Sciences and Engineering in the Office of Science and Technology Policy (Executive Office of the President), reported that the Department of Energy's contractual performance goals for its Thomas Jefferson National Accelerator Facility include staff diversity and the participation in research of students from groups that are traditionally underrepresented in physical science and engineering. "In the spirit that one gets what one measures," she said, "it is seemingly little steps like this one that will inexorably drive the opportunities for and participation of women in science and engineering to higher levels." Dr. Hartline suggested that collegiality; opportunities for advancement, visibility, and leadership; credit for contributions; and supportive mentoring by more senior colleagues (regardless of gender) and by peers "can make a big difference ... for the retention of female and minority professionals."

"We don't have enough women to form an old girls' network—or a middle-aged, or a young women's network," Cynthia M. Friend, a professor of chemistry at Harvard, observed. In its absence, she noted, "The old boys' network is very effective. I think many of the women here are beneficiaries of it. I know I am. I had absolutely no woman advisors and no woman professors. Male colleagues helped me learn what I needed to know."

Dr. Friend noted that women often delay publishing their research until they have the "whole picture." Consequently, they tend to publish less frequently than men do, which in turn adversely affects their chances for promotion and tenure. She urged women to publish data that is "interesting," and provokes questions instead of waiting until they have all the answers.

"The newest generation of women scientists has a sense of entitlement to a place in academic science," Mary S. Erskine observed. Clare Boothe Luce Professor of Biology at Boston University, Dr. Erskine was referring to "the women of the Title IX generation who have, in a sense, grown up with the assumption that they will be significant players now and in the future." She noted that "the women's movement has had an impact in some visible ways on hiring and promotion of women in some areas of science, but certainly we all know that the less visible issues which stigmatize women scientists are extremely powerful influences on women of all generations, still."

Although progress for women scientists and engineers seems to be slowest in academia—a critical issue for the future of science, as many participants noted—the picture is not altogether bleak. The Clare Boothe Luce Professorship Program, established in 1986, is in outstanding example of a support system for early-career women scientists and engineers. Sponsored by the Henry Luce Foundation, the program funds approximately 60 tenure-track positions at colleges and universities throughout the country. These positions are earmarked for early-career women scientists and engineers. CBL professors receive an additional 20% of their salaries for professional expenses (travel, student research assistance, manuscript preparation, teaching relief, journals and books, and childcare). Funding includes start-up costs for laboratories and scholarships for women students at the institution where the CBL professor is appointed. In addition to the much-appreciated financial security, the awards carry considerable prestige and enhance the stature of the early-career professors.

The Future: What Have We Learned and How Can it Help?

"It's very. very tough to be a successful scientist or engineer," Eleanor Baum, Dean of Engineering at the Cooper Union and Chair-Elect of the New York Academy of Sciences Board of Governors, said. "It's also hard to be a woman, especially a working woman where you are torn, no matter what your profession is, by demands of work, family life, relationships…. We also have to contend with continued learning in our fields because the fields change." Dean Baum pointed out. "As an academic, I am appalled to hear of the really oppressive environment in universities. Universities are very slow to change, and they are dominated by systems which are very slow and very difficult to affect. And it is very clear that we have got to do something about that."

One tactic for fostering change, suggested Lilian Shiao-Yen Wu, a research scientist at

IBM Thomas J. Watson Research Center, might be to devise a system for ranking academic institutions and departments analogous to the one created by *US News and World Report* to rank companies "in order of climates and policies promoting the retention and career development of women students and professors." The suggestion was well received.

"Whether we realize it or not, we've all contributed in some way to the problem," said James Preston, the Chairman and CEO of Avon. "And now we have a special responsibility to find the solutions. I believe that if we are to make real progress in reversing the structural deficiencies that are holding women back from these professions, everyone has to work together in forging a solution—business, academia, government, the media, and individuals. If women regard the business and academic arenas as less than ideal environments in which to build their careers, then we in industry and higher education have to take the steps that are necessary to create an atmosphere in which women can contribute and succeed."

"When teaching and mentoring objectives reflect beliefs that science education should exclude those who do not fit the mold defined by decades of male dominance, women more than men are repelled," Dr. Selby said in summing up the sense and sensibility of the conference. "When the ethics, values, styles, and behaviors of a department, or a university, are not congruent with theirs, women more than men will opt out. When funding and job constraints prolong the time it takes to complete a doctorate or relegate young scientists to underpaid and powerless postdoctoral positions, women more than men choose to work outside the academy. When these same constraints prompt non-collegial competitive practices, women more than men are likely to lose their commitment to science and engineering. When work is directed toward narrow rather than comprehensive goals, women more than men reject it. When the rewards available reflect models of success that do not include family, community, and quality of life, women are more apt than men to seek alternative work which is rewarding on their terms. When the systems in which science and engineering are practiced do not meet their needs and interests, women are more ready than men to conclude that the system should change. And if it cannot, or will not, change, they are prepared to reject the system."

This situation is not so much a "woman problem" as it is a problem for science and engineering; as long as women's talents and abilities are not fully used, our scientific and technical enterprises lose. Our economy is, in turn, diminished. In other words, the question now is not what universities and corporations may be willing or compelled to concede to women. It is, rather, what sort of work environments encourage "the best and the brightest" human beings in our society, regardless of their gender (or any other extraneous-to-science characteristic), to contribute to the advancement of science.

"Ultimately, this is a cultural question and economic—or rather, it is a complex set of questions having to do with societal goals, values, and aesthetics," Dr. Selby points out. "We've progressed to the point where we recognize that it is not simply a matter of figuring out how women, and others who have been excluded, can be made to 'adjust' to an alien environment. We're daring to dream of making the environment in which science and engineering are done inviting to every person who has the talent and the desire to participate in the scientific enterprise. The effort to realize that dream is likely to benefit women *and* men and, in the opinion of conference participants, science, engineering, and society."

PART II

WHAT KIND OF ENTERPRISE IS SCIENCE?

From the beginnings of modern science right up to the present day women have been excluded from science's most central institutions and activities in a variety of ways. That much was suggested in Part I. So what? Certainly, whether women enjoy equality of opportunity with men in science is an important justice issue. But is it any more than that? Might men's control of science also have important consequences regarding the kind of enterprise science is? And conversely, might the kind of enterprise science is have important consequences regarding who controls or continues to control science and who is excluded from it? One way to answer these questions is to look for traces of masculinity in science as we know it, especially the science most dominated by men. Another way is to look at the work of women scientists to see if gender-related differences from mainstream science can be found in it. In the readings that follow both modes of analysis will be in evidence.

SCIENCE'S AIMS, METHODS, AND NORMS OF BEHAVIOR

Consider, to begin with, physics, generally considered the foremost exemplar of modern science. Consider, in particular, such features of physics as its aims, methods, and the norms of behavior applied to its practitioners. "Indisputably," physicist Brian Easlea maintains in "Patriarchy, Scientists, and Nuclear Warriors," physics is dominated by men, a result not of chance, but of strenuous attempts since its beginnings to keep women out. But, adds Easlea, physics is masculine in other ways as well. First, its ideological aim as well as its aim in practice is the conquest of nature, a nature conceptualized as having no moral claim on us; this nature, moreover, is regularly portrayed as female in physicists' informal prose, lectures, and talks. Second, the method of physics, as of science in general, is said to revolve around hard experimental facts and mathematical rigor, uncontaminated by "feminine" emotionality or intuitiveness or subjectivity. Third, its practitioners, particularly the most successful ones, behave in culturally masculine ways, displaying what one anthropologist of physics (Sharon Traweek) has characterized as "aggressive individualism, haughty self-confidence, and a sharp competitive edge." And fourth, the research projects of physics are regularly tied to the military, a bailiwick of masculinity. Given this masculinity of physics, "it isn't altogether surprising if girls, whose gender socialization is quite different from that of boys, are reluctant to study physics at school. What's more, it is in no way irrational, as British science teacher Hazel Grice points out, for girls to reject a subject that appears to offer 'as the apex of its achievement a weapon of mass annihilation'" (Easlea p. 102).

Of course, adds chemist Catherine Hurt Middlecamp in "Culturally Inclusive Chemistry," the "culture" of physics and the physical sciences extends to more than just the arrogance and competitiveness of physical scientists and their ties to the military. It includes, as well, many other features of the scientific scene. The culture of the physical sciences also includes, for example, an insistence on speed: Chemists, for one, typically talk fast, in their classrooms they call on the students who put their hands up first, they give quizzes and tests under the pressure of time, they measure professional success by who is able to publish first. The culture of chemistry, moreover, includes a detachment from the world being investigated: "We noted that the chemistry building had few connections to the natural world. The building hummed with technical sounds. The windows did not open to the world outside; only a few potted plants dotted the interior landscape. There were, however, plenty of liquids and solids stored carefully in bottles and jars, all presumably once of natural origin…. Given the isolation, it was easy to understand how scientists might come to believe that their work was objective and value-free. Anything that connected the research to social, industrial, or military applications was simply not visible" (Middlecamp pp. 118–19). And this culture includes great optimism about the prospects of mastering what must therefore be a rather simple world: "We cataloged some of the truths that chemists were likely to teach: The universe is logical and ordered. Chemicals are made up of atoms. They react in predictable, reproducible ways. In essence, a 'truth' exists, and chemists believe that they have figured out a good part of it" (Middlecamp, p. 119). According to Middlecamp, these and other observations offered by the participants in the graduate seminar "Culturally Inclusive Chemistry" bespeak the fact that chemistry and other physical sciences are not only a "men's game" … played by men's rules" (Middlecamp, p. 118), but a Western game as well, and she explores ways in which the teaching of chemistry, and ultimately chemistry itself, can be made more "culturally inclusive."

In contrast to the Western masculine scientific enterprise Easlea and Middlecamp describe is the "different" way of doing science of Nobel Prize-winning biologist Barbara McClintock, described by Evelyn Fox Keller in "A World of Difference." Indeed, according to Keller, McClintock did not aim, in her conceptualizations of the objects of her research, to reduce nature to simplicity in an effort to *master* it, to predict and control its behavior.

> Her recurrent remark, "Anything you can think of you will find," is a statement about the capacities not of mind but of nature. It is meant not as a

description of our own ingenuity as discoverers but as a comment on the resourcefulness of natural order; in the sense not so much of adaptability as of largesse and prodigality. Organisms have a life and an order of their own that scientists can only begin to fathom. "Misrepresented, not appreciated, ... [they] are beyond our wildest expectations.... They do everything we [can think of], they do it better, more efficiently, more marvelously." In comparison with the ingenuity of nature, our scientific intelligence seems pallid. (Keller, p. 127)

McClintock aimed not to master nature but to "listen to" it, to know its living forms in minute detail so as to understand and appreciate their complexity and diversity. Accordingly, McClintock chose maize for her research, a far more complex, slower-reproducing, and more environment-responsive organism than the bacteria studied by most of her colleagues in molecular genetics; she focused on the peculiarities of individual organisms, while her colleagues focused on repeatable properties of large groups; and she proceeded by a kind of global, integrative intuition, while her colleagues worked, step by step, trying to establish simple, linear chains of cause and effect on the molecular level, and trying to explain everything else in their terms. Of course, all this "listening to" nature, this concern with complexity and diversity, this desire to know in detail and firsthand, took time. No thought of competition here, no race to a common goal, no rush to publish, to "scoop" opponents, to convince others. And far from taking a detached, unemotional, disinterested stance toward the objects of her research, McClintock identified with them, merged with them; "her vocabulary is consistently a vocabulary of affection, of kinship, of empathy." Thus, McClintock reported: "No two plants are exactly alike. They're all different, and as a consequence, you have to know that difference. I start with the seedling, and I don't want to leave it. I don't feel I really know the story if I don't watch the plant all the way along. So I know every plant in the field. I know them intimately, and I find it a great pleasure to know them" (Keller p. 128). And again: "I found that the more I worked with [the chromosomes], the bigger and bigger [they] got, and when I was really working with them I wasn't outside, I was down there. I was part of the system. I was right down there with them, and everything got big. I even was able to see the internal parts of the chromosomes—actually everything was there. It surprised me because I actually felt as if I was right down there and these were my friends.... As you look at these things, they become part of you. And you forget yourself" (Keller, p. 129). Indeed, it was McClintock's intimate personal relationship with the objects of her research, according to Keller, that enabled her to make her revolutionary scientific discoveries, discoveries that were different in kind from those made using more traditional methods:

To a large degree, both the kinds of questions one asks and the explanations that one finds satisfying depend on one's a priori relation to the objects of study. In particular, I am suggesting that questions asked about objects with which one feels kinship are likely to differ from questions asked about objects one sees as unalterably alien. Similarly, explanations that satisfy us about a natural world that is seen as "blind, simple and dumb," ontologically inferior, may seem less self-evidently satisfying for a natural world seen as complex and, itself, resourceful. I suggest that individual and communal conceptions of nature need to be examined for their role in the history of science, not as causal determinants but as frameworks upon which all scientific programs are developed. (Keller, p. 130)

Consider another example of a "different" way of doing science, sociologist Ann Oakley's research with new mothers described in "Interviewing Women: A Contradiction in Terms." According to Oakley, the traditional aim of interviewing, as of other survey methods in social research, is to gather data about people, data that are both amenable to statistical treatment and relevant to social theory. As a consequence, the interviews that are part of a research project are supposed to be conducted in such a way that the personalities, beliefs, and values of the various interviewers, as well as other "local features" of the interview situations, do not affect—do not "bias"—the data obtained. To be sure, interviewers are supposed to show no reactions to interviewees' comments, are supposed to dodge interviewees' questions about themselves (the interviewers) and their views, are supposed to refrain from emotional involvement with interviewees and their problems—are supposed to be, in short, detached, unemotional, disinterested, and objective. Indeed, Oakley suggests that a power hierarchy is set up as an essential part of such a research process: "It is important to note that while the interviewer must treat the interviewee as an object or data-producing machine which, when handled correctly will function properly, the interviewer herself/himself has the same status from the point of view of the person/people, institution or corporation conducting the research. Both interviewer and interviewee are thus depersonalized participants in the research process," and both are used to achieve the personal goals of researchers (Oakley, p. 139).

As a feminist woman sociologist interviewing women during their transition to motherhood, however, Oakley found herself unable to engage in this objectifying, exploitative—this "masculine"—mode of research. Indeed, as a feminist woman sociologist Oakley aimed to document women's own accounts of their lives in an effort to give the subjective situation of women greater visibility both in sociology and in society. This meant that Oakley had to become, in her interviews, a data-gathering instrument for those whose lives were being researched, women, rather than a data-gathering instrument for the theoretical concerns of herself and other researchers. And it meant that she had to gather her data not in a hierarchical way but in a way that engaged her subjects and herself in a joint and mutually beneficial enterprise. Thus, Oakley followed such nonstandard procedures as answering her subjects' questions as honestly and fully as she could. And she refrained from exploiting either her subjects or the information they gave her ["For instance, if the interview clashed with the demands of housework and motherhood I offered to, and often did, help with the work that had to be done" (Oakley, p. 145)]. As a result, nearly three-quarters of the women interviewed felt that being interviewed had affected them in a positive way—had led them to reflect on their experiences more than they would otherwise have done, for example, or had reduced the level of their anxiety or reassured them of their normality—and no one felt that being interviewed had affected her in a negative way. And, adds Oakley, far from her feminist mode of interviewing yielding biased data, it yielded better results, in terms of the quality and depth of information gathered, than the traditional "masculine" mode of interviewing. Indeed, interviewees showed a sincere interest in Oakley and her research, just as Oakley, in her research, showed a sincere interest in them and their experiences. " . . . In most cases, the goal of finding out about people through interviewing is best achieved when the relationship of interviewer and interviewee is non-hierarchical and when the interviewer is prepared to invest his or her own personal identity in the relationship" (Oakley, p. 141).

SCIENCE'S SUBJECT MATTER

If the differing experiences and interests and attitudes of men and women have an effect on the way they do science, their aims and methods and the like—and this is the view suggested by the readings of the previous section—might such differences have an effect on men's and women's scientific *output* as well—the kinds of questions they pursue and observational data they collect, and even the kinds of theories they accept? Consider the case of Darwin's theory of evolution, discussed by biologist Ruth Hubbard in "Have Only Men Evolved?" As Hubbard would have it, it is far from clear that this theory was especially impressive in its handling of the available evidence when it was first proposed. In fact, "given the looseness of many of his arguments—he credited himself with being an expert wriggler" (Hubbard, p. 157), Hubbard finds it "surprising" that Darwin's theory found such wide acceptance. What *was* crucial to its acceptance, she suggests, was the social outlook it expressed. The three main ideas of Darwin's theory, after all, were endless variation, natural selection from among the variants, and the resulting survival of the fittest. The intrinsic optimism of the theory, the picture of progressive development of species one from another, fit well with the liberal, laissez-faire capitalistic outlook of Darwin's scientific contemporaries. And Darwin's theory fit well with those contemporaries' Victorian ideas of sex roles as well: Its notion of natural selection via the mechanism of sex ("sexual selection") typecast males—including human males—as the active, mentally and physically superior sex ever out to win the attention of passive females. Of course ["we should remember that Darwin's theory of sexual selection was put forward in the midst of the first wave of feminism" (Hubbard, p. 164)] Darwin's theory did not fit well with the feminist views of women such as Antoinette Brown Blackwell and Eliza Burt Gamble. "But these women did not have Darwin's . . . professional status or scientific experience; nor indeed could they, given their limited opportunities for education, travel and participation in the affairs of the world. Their books were hardly acknowledged or discussed by professionals, and they have been, till now, merely ignored and excluded from the record" (Hubbard, p. 158). As a result, the critique of Darwin's theory made by women such as Blackwell and Gamble did not have any significant effect on its reception by Darwin's colleagues.

But if Darwinian reflections of the social outlook of Darwin's contemporaries were central to the reasons these men accepted Darwinian theory, then what grounds are there for believing that Darwinian theory—or, in fact, any other scientific theory for which comparable claims can be made—represents an objective account of the world?

> The mythology of science asserts that with many different scientists all asking their own questions and evaluating the answers independently, whatever personal bias creeps into their individual answers is cancelled out when the large picture is put together. This might conceivably be so if scientists were women and men from all sorts of different cultural and social backgrounds who came to science with very different ideologies and interests. But since, in fact, they have been predominantly university-trained white males from privileged social backgrounds, the bias has been narrow and the product often reveals more about the investigator than about the subject being researched. (Hubbard, p. 167)

The solution, suggests Hubbard, is to expose and analyse and consider alternatives to the values and attitudes that scientists have, consciously or not, introduced into their theories about the world—as Hubbard herself has attempted to do in her essay.

If Victorian ideas of sex roles pervaded only Darwin's original theory, the result might not be so worrisome. But, as Hubbard emphasizes, the same Victorian ideas have pervaded what Darwin's theory has helped to create—contemporary sociobiology, ethology, and evolutionary biology, among other fields. Indeed, in "Empathy, Polyandry, and the Myth of the Coy Female," biological anthropologist Sarah Blaffer Hrdy traces the modern development of sexual selection theory and shows the impact women in the field of primatology in the 1970s and 1980s have had on it. In the face of abundant, generally available evidence to the contrary, Hrdy tells us, modern sexual selection theory up to the mid-1970s still featured sexually aggressive, promiscuous males actively courting sexually "coy," passive females. More precisely, sexual selection theory featured sexually aggressive males. Since it was assumed that variance in female reproductive success was small compared to the very great variance among males, it was thought that selection operated primarily on males. Hence, males were the focus of investigation, and such topics as female promiscuity and the effect of female social status and female expertise in child rearing on female reproductive success were ignored. Starting in the 1970s, however, Hrdy suggests, increasing numbers of women researchers became active in primatology and—just as men primatologists had done before them—identified with primates of their own sex and allowed this identification to influence their research focus. But because feminism was then changing the self-perception of these women, their identification with female primates was simultaneously leading them to new (nonandrocentric, nonsexist) perceptions and questions and hypotheses about female primates. The result for primatology, says Hrdy, has been a new focus on female reproductive strategies, and with it, a fundamental rethinking of sexual selection theory.

But primatology is not the only area in which traditional ideas of sex roles have been both historically dominant and recently undercut with the help of women researchers. In "The Importance of Feminist Critique for Contemporary Cell Biology," the Biology and Gender Study Group tells of the active male/passive female narratives used to portray fertilization throughout most of the twentieth century and before. In these narratives, for example, sperm are typecast as suitors actively courting the passive egg (which then chooses the best one with which to mate), or they are typecast as heroic warriors in an epic struggle against the hostile vaginal and uterine environment for the passive egg as prize, or they are typecast as active, would-be princes vying to awaken the passive, slumbering egg. The Biology and Gender Study Group also tells of the active male/passive female narratives used to portray mammalian sex determination in biological theory until 1986—for example, that the induction of testicular tissue is an active (gene-directed, dominant) event while the induction of ovarian tissue is a passive (automatic) event. During the 1980s these narratives were reevaluated and ultimately replaced. Gerald and Heide Schatten, for example, discovered using electron microscopy that egg and sperm are mutually active partners in fertilization—for example, that when the sperm contacts the egg, it does not burrow through but is rather clasped and drawn in by small fingerlike projections emanating from the egg's surface. And Eva Eicher and Linda Washburn proposed a new model of sex determination based on extensive genetic evidence (including data that could not be explained by previous accounts), a model according to which the induction of ovarian tissue is as much an active, genetically directed developmental process as the induction of testicular tissue. Concludes the Biology and Gender Study Group: "The studies of Eicher and Washburn on sex determination and those of the Schattens on fertilization can be viewed as feminist-influenced critiques of cell and molecular biology. They have controlled for gender biases rather than let the ancient myth run uncontrolled through their interpretations" (The Biology and Gender Study Group, p. 196). As a consequence,

> We have come to look at feminist critique as we would any other experimental control. Whenever one performs an experiment, one sets up all the controls one can think of in order to make as certain as possible that the result obtained does not come from any other source. One asks oneself what asumptions one is making. Have I assumed the temperature to be constant? Have I assumed that the pH doesn't change over the time of the reaction? Feminist critique asks if there may be some assumptions that we haven't checked concerning gender bias. In this way feminist critique should be part of normative science. Like any control, it seeks to provide critical rigor, and to ignore this critique is to ignore a possible source of error. (The Biology and Gender Study Group p. 192.)

In "The Engendering of Archaeology: Refiguring Feminist Science Studies" philosopher of science Alison Wylie tells of some of the recent developments in archaeology that can similarly be viewed as feminist-influenced critiques of science. These include work showing that women and gender have been omitted from the archaeology of the past even when they are a crucial part of the story to be told, and work showing that women and gender have been conceptualized in the archaeology of the past in twentieth-century, white, androcentric, middle-class, North American ways. This work began to appear in the late 1980s as a result of the doubling of women in North American archaeology that occurred in the late 1970s and early 1980s. Interestingly, however, Wylie reports, only about half of the women who initially pursued this new work identified themselves as feminists, and many of these reported reservations about what that label means. As a result Wylie prefers to explain this new work in terms of the women's different "standpoint" from the men who preceded them rather than in terms of the influence of feminism:

> ... The expanded cohort of women entering the field at the turn of the 1980s brought to their work in archaeology a standpoint of sensitivity to gender issues—no doubt in some sense a gendered standpoint—but not an explicitly feminist standpoint.... It was a distinctive self-consciousness about gender relations that put these new participants in a position to think differently about their discipline and their subject matter, to identify gaps in analysis, to question taken-for-granted assumptions about women and gender, and to envision a range of alternatives for inquiry and interpretation that simply had not occurred to their older, largely male colleagues—colleagues whose gender privilege (as men working in a highly masculinized disciplinary culture) includes an unquestioning fit between their gendered experience and the androcentrism that partially frames the research traditions in which they work. (Wylie, p. 210)

All this new work of the women archaeologists, adds Wylie, has occurred against a backdrop of controversy in archaeology between "objectivists" and "relativists," that is, between those who think that archaeology, when properly shielded from sociopolitical influences, can produce genuine (i.e., objective) knowledge of the cultural past, and those who think it cannot. But the new work of the women archeologists, Wylie suggests, is both objective (or at least more objective than previous work) and sociopolitically influenced, and hence, exemplifies a promising way to resolve this twenty-year-old controversy.

Women have not been as successful in psychology. "The discipline remains resolutely misogynist" (Wilkinson, p. 218), reports psychologist Sue Wilkinson in "Still Seeking Transformation: Feminist Challenges to Psychology." It has not been for want of trying. Indeed, historically, psychology's central assertion, according to Wilkinson, has been that women are inferior to men, and feminist women in psychology have pursued five different theoretical research traditions in response. According to the first tradition, psychology cannot say that women are inferior simply because psychology does not *know* what women are like—psychology has in the past omitted women from research samples, used insufficiently sensitive measures, failed to use control groups, and so on. According to the second tradition, women *are* inferior to men—are less assertive, have lower self-esteem, less self-confidence, and the like, and hence, are less successful in professional life—but only because we are *socialized* to be this way. According to the third tradition, women *are* different from men—have different ways of knowing, different modes of moral evaluation, and so forth—but our characteristics are *superior* rather than inferior. According to the fourth response, women are neither inferior nor superior to men. Indeed, there are elements of masculinity and femininity in both women and men, and mental health and well-being depend on the ability to deploy these flexibly according to the situation. And finally, according to the fifth and most recent research tradition, sex/gender "difference" has to do with power relations between the sexes rather than relatively fixed sets of attributes, and is highly contingent historically, culturally, and socially. "These five competing feminist traditions offer different, and often incompatible, theoretical and/or political tools for challenging and transforming psychology" (Wilkinson, p. 222). Nonetheless, they have all been marginalized, albeit to different degrees, by the psychological profession. "In psychology, we are still seeking transformation" (Wilkinson, p. 225).

SCIENCE'S SOCIAL EFFECTS

If women's past exclusion from science's most central institutions and activities has left its mark on the knowledge that science has produced—knowledge that only now is being transformed by women scientists—has this had any larger consequences? Take the practice of medicine. According to biologist and health researcher Sue Rosser in "Androcentric Bias in Clinical Research," "health care practitioners must treat the majority of the population, which is female, based on information gathered from clinical research in which drugs may not have been tested on females, in which the etiology of the disease in women has not been studied, and in which women's experience has been ignored" (Rosser, p. 231). Just consider the research scene. Since it is predominantly white, middle/upper-class men who have determined medicine's agenda in general and its funding priorities in particular, it is not surprising that the focus of contemporary medicine has been on men's diseases, disabilities, and dysfunctions. Indeed, research on specifically female conditions—for example, dysmenorrhea, incontinency in older women, and nutrition in postmenopausal women—has received low priority, funding, and prestige, and suggestions for fruitful research questions based on the personal experience of women have also been largely ignored. Moreover, diseases like heart disease that affect both sexes have been defined as "male" diseases, and most of the funding for heart-disease research has been channeled into studies focusing on how the disease progresses and manifests itself in white, middle-aged, middle-class males. Very little funding has been appropriated for studying heart disease in women, despite the fact that it is the Number 1 killer of U.S. women (especially older women and poor black women who have had several children). Finally, the scientific community has often failed to include females in animal studies in basic research as well as in clinical research unless the research has centered on controlling reproduction. And when women have been used as experimental subjects, they have often been treated as less than fully human (as in investigations of the side effects of oral contraceptives on women, in which poor Mexican-American women were not told they were participating in research, or receiving placebos rather than the oral contraceptives they had requested). As a consequence, the medical care that women receive is far inferior to that received by men.

But adding gender as a variable in medical research is not enough, according to health researchers Nancy Krieger and Elizabeth Fee. In "Man-Made Medicine and Women's Health," they point out that not only do men and women show different patterns of disease, diverse groups of women (as well as men) show different patterns of disease. Take hypertension, for example. Working-class and poor women are at greater risk than affluent women, black women within each income level are at greater risk than white women, and the rates of hypertension among Hispanic women vary by national origin (e.g., Mexican women have the lowest rates while Puerto Rican and Cuban women have the highest). And while men in each racial/ethnic group have higher rates of hypertension than women, women in some racial/ethnic groups have higher rates than men in other groups. Thus, Krieger and Fee suggest, standard categories of race and sex cannot explain patterns of disease. Only sensitivity to social categories can. For instance, racism "structures living and working conditions, affects daily interactions, and takes its toll on people's dignity and pride. All of this must be considered when we examine the connection between race/ethnicity and health.... A recent study of hypertension, for example, found that black women who responded actively to unfair treatment were less likely to report high blood pressure than women who internalized their responses. Interestingly, the black women at highest risk were those who reported *no* experiences of racial discrimination" (Krieger and Fee, p.242). We need a new kind of medical research and practice, in short, one that takes into account the complex patterns of sex/gender, race/ethnicity, and social class. Krieger and Fee explore some of what this would involve.

Of course, reproduction is one area of women's lives that *has* been investigated by scientists. It is far from clear, argues Ruth Hubbard in "The New Procreative Technologies," that this investigation has always yielded benefits for women, however. Consider the new reproductive technologies that have resulted—prenatal diagnosis and screening and fetal therapy, for example, or in vitro fertilization or the other methods to help infertile couples have children. If these technologies have extended women's reproductive choices, Hubbard points out, they have done so only for the middle- and upper-class women who can afford them. But Hubbard is not even clear that the choices of middle-and-upper class women have been extended by the new technologies. For one thing these new technologies, and the increasing medicalization of birth that they entail, make women dependent on "experts" and thereby rob women of control over their reproductive processes. For another they put women under social and even legal pressure to use the new technologies, in some cases curtailing the legal rights of women to refuse diagnostic or therapeutic procedures intended to improve the health of fetuses. And these are procedures that might for all we know now turn out to bring more harm than good. "Most therapies become established on the basis of custom and professional consensus and are not preceded by rigorous, scientific evaluation of their outcomes" (Hubbard, p. 254). Thus, the current sometimes indiscriminate use of ultrasound or the surgical treatments of fetuses in utero might have the unfortunate outcomes that the indiscriminate use of X-rays or forceps or artificial induction of labor had in the past. And finally, the new reproductive technologies have high emotional costs as well as financial ones. They make women

> look on every fetus as potentially disabled and in need of on-going medical surveillance. But the reality is that only the rare fetus is at risk for serious genetic or developmental problems as long as pregnant women have access to adequate nutrition and the necessary economic and social supports, and can live in a relatively healthful environment. Poverty, malnutrition, and urban decay place a fetus at far greater risk than do the inherited disabilities for which prenatal tests are being developed. (*The Politics of Women's Biology*, pp. 144–45)

But it is with just these conditions that poor women, women whose reproductive choices are assuredly not extended by the new reproductive technologies, have still to deal.

Medical care is not the only area in which women are at a disadvantage because of the nature of past scientific research. The educational establishment, says biologist Anne Fausto-Sterling, is another, the employment scene still another—because of the nature of past research on the comparative intelligence of men and women. "JOBS AND EDUCATION—that's what it's really all about. At the crux of the question 'Who's smarter, men or women?' lie decisions about how to teach reading and mathematics, about whether boys and girls should attend separate schools, about job and career choices, and, as always, about money—how much employers will have to pay to whom and what salaries employees, both male and female, can command" (Fausto-Sterling, p. 267). In "A Question of Genius: Are Men Really Smarter Than Women?" Fausto-Sterling analyzes the nineteenth -and twentieth-century biological and psychological investigations of the intellectual abilities of men and women. In essence, she suggests, these investigations have been attempts to show that men are smarter than women—because men are less variable, or more variable, or have larger and more developed frontal lobes, or smaller frontal lobes and larger parietal lobes, or particular genes, or particular modes of brain functioning, or the like. These attempts have all ultimately failed, of course, through lack of evidence, or contrary evidence, or lack of methodological rigor, or analytical problems of one kind or another. Nevertheless, they have had the effect—for example, through press coverage of preliminary findings of girls' lesser abilities in mathematics that are never followed up with coverage of the critiques made of those findings—of keeping men in the better jobs with the better salaries and the better educational and job-related opportunities, especially in the sciences. And the battle still "rages with as much heat and as little light as ever" (Fausto-Sterling p. 267).

Patriarchy, Scientists, and Nuclear Warriors

Brian Easlea

In a lecture at the University of California in 1980, the Oxford historian Michael Howard accused the world's scientific community, and particularly the Western scientific community, of an inventiveness in the creation and design of weapons that has made, he believes, the pursuit of a "stable nuclear balance" between the superpowers virtually impossible. At the very least, he found it curious that a scientific community that had expressed great anguish over its moral responsibility for the development of the first crude fission weapons "should have ceased to trouble itself over its continuous involvement with weapons-systems whose lethality and effectiveness make the weapons that destroyed Hiroshima and Nagasaki look like clumsy toys."[1] On the other hand, in the compelling pamphlet *It'll Make a Man of You: A Feminist View of the Arms Race*, Penny Strange expresses no surprise at the militarization of science that has occurred since the Second World War. While acknowledging that individual scientists have been people of integrity with a genuine desire for peace, she tersely states that "weapons research is consistent with the attitudes underlying the whole scientific worldview" and that she looks forward to "an escape from the patriarchal science in which the conquest of nature is a projection of sexual dominance."[2] My aim in this article is to explore the psychological attributes of patriarchal science, particularly physics, that contribute so greatly to the apparent readiness of scientists to maintain the inventive momentum of the nuclear arms race.

My own experiences as a physicist were symptomatic of the problems of modern science. So I begin with a brief account of these experiences followed by a look at various aspects of the masculinity of science, particularly physics, paying special attention to the ideology surrounding the concept of a scientific method and to the kinds of sexual rhetoric used by physicists to describe both their "pure" research and their contributions to weapons design. I conclude with some thoughts on the potential human integrity of a life in science—once patriarchy and its various subsystems have become relics of history.

A Personal Experience of Physics

Growing up in the heart of rural England, I wanted in my early teens to become a professional bird-watcher. However, at the local grammar school I was persuaded that boys who are good at mathematics become scientists: people just don't become bird-watchers. I did in fact have a deep, if romantic, interest in physics, believing that somehow those "great men" like Einstein and Bohr truly understood a world whose secrets I longed to share. So I went to University College London in 1954 to study physics and found it excruciatingly boring. But I studied hard and convinced myself that at the postgraduate level it would be different if only I could "do research"—whatever that mysterious activity really was. It didn't seem remarkable to me at the time that our class consisted of some forty men and only three or four women. At that time, I was both politically conservative and politically naive, a situation not helped by the complete absence of any lectures in the physics curriculum on "science and society" issues.

In my final year it was necessary to think of future employment. Not wanting to make nuclear weapons and preferring to leave such "dirty" work to other people, I considered a career in the "clean and beautiful" simplicity of the electronics industry. I came very close to entering the industry but in the end, to my great happiness, was accepted back at University College to "do research" in mathematical physics. It was while doing this research that I was to begin my drift away from a career in physics.

One event in my graduate years stands out. As an undergraduate I had only twice ever asked about the nature of reality as presented by modern physics, and both times the presiding lecturer had ridiculed my question. However, one day a notice appeared announcing that a famous physicist, David Bohm, together with a philosopher of science were inviting physics students to spend a weekend in a large country house to discuss fundamental questions of physics. That weekend was an enlightening experience that gave me the confidence to believe that physics was not solely a means for manipulating nature or a path to professional mundane achievement through the publication of numerous, uninteresting papers, but ideally was an essential part of human wisdom.

In the early 1960s, while I was on a two-year NATO Fellowship at the Institute of Theoretical Physics in Copenhagen, the first cracks and dents began to appear in my worldview. I met scientists from around the world, including the Soviet Union, who engaged me in animated political discussions. With a group of physicists I went on a ten-day tour of Leningrad and Moscow and, equipped with a smattering of Russian, I left the group to wander about on my own and kept meeting people who, at this high point of the Cold War, implored me to believe that Russia wanted peace. I couldn't square this image of Russia and the Russian people with what I had become accustomed to in Britain and would soon be exposed to while teaching at the University of Pittsburgh.

It seemed to be a world gone mad: my new university in Pittsburgh awarded honorary degrees to Werner von Braun, the former Nazi missile expert, and to Edward Teller, the father of the H-bomb. The Cuban blockade followed; Kennedy, Khrushchev, and physics were going to bring about the end of the world. I kept asking myself how the seemingly beautiful, breathtaking physics of Rutherford, Einstein, Heisenberg, and Niels Bohr had come to this.

New experiences followed which deepened my frustration with physics and increased my social and philosophic interests. University appointments in Brazil gave me a first-hand experience with the type of military regime that the United States so liked to support to save the world from communism. In the end I returned to the University of Sussex, where I taught "about science" courses to non-science students and "science and society" courses to science majors.

The more I learned, the more I became convinced that the reason physics was so misused and the reason the nuclear arms race existed was the existence of capitalist societies, principally the United States, that are based on profit making, permanent war economies, and the subjugation of the Third World. My pat conclusion was that if capitalism could be replaced by socialism, human behavior would change dramatically. But I felt uneasy with this belief since oppression and violence had not first appeared in the world in the sixteenth century. As the years went by and the feminist movement developed, I came to explore the profound psychological connections between the discipline of physics and the world of the warriors—connections that are ultimately rooted in the social institutions of patriarchy. That is the focus of this paper.

The Masculinity of Physics

Indisputably, British and American physics is male-dominated. In Britain in the early 1980s, women made up only 4 percent of the membership of the Institute of Physics, and in the United States women made up only 2 percent of the faculty of the 171 doctorate-awarding physics departments.[3] This male domination of physics has obviously not come about by chance; not until recently have physicists made serious attempts to encourage women to study the discipline and enter the profession. Indeed, in the first decades of the twentieth century strenuous attempts by physicists to keep women out of their male preserve were not unknown. Symbolic of such attempts in the 1930s was that of no less a man than the Nobel laureate Robert Millikan, who in 1936 wrote to the President of Duke University questioning the wisdom of the University's appointment of a woman to a full physics professorship.[4] As the statistics amply demonstrate, the male domination of physics continues despite publicized attempts by physicists to eliminate whatever prejudice still exists against the entry of women into the profession.

A second aspect of the masculinity of physics is that the men who inhabit this scientific world—particularly those who are successful in it—behave in culturally masculine ways. Indeed, as in other hierarchical male-dominated activities, getting to the top invariably entails aggressive, competitive behavior. Scientists themselves recognize that such masculine behavior, though it is considered unseemly to dwell upon it, is a prominent feature of science. The biologist Richard Lewontin even goes so far as to affirm that "science is a form of competitive and aggressive activity, a contest of man against man that provides knowledge as a side-product."[5] Although I wouldn't agree with Lewontin that knowledge is a mere "side-product" of such competition, I would, for example, agree with the anthropologist Sharon Traweek, who writes that those most prestigious of physicists—the members of the high-energy physics "community"—display the highly masculine behavioral traits of "aggressive individualism, haughty self-confidence, and a sharp competitive edge."[6] Moreover, Traweek's verdict is supported by

the remarks of the high-energy physicist Heinz Pagels, who justifies such masculine behavior by explaining that a predominant feature in the conduct of scientific research has to be intellectual aggression, since, as he puts it, "no great science was discovered in the spirit of humility."[7] Scientists, then, physicists included, behave socially in a masculine manner.

A third aspect of the masculinity of physics is the pervasiveness of the ideology and practice of the conquest of nature rather than a human goal of respectful interaction and use. Although, of course, many attitudes (including the most gentle) have informed and continue to inform the practice of science, nevertheless a frequently stated masculine objective of science is the conquest of nature. This was expressed prominently by two of the principal promoters and would-be practitioners of the "new science" in the seventeenth century, Francis Bacon and René Descartes, the former even claiming that successful institutionalization of his method would inaugurate the "truly masculine birth of time." Although modern scientists usually attempt to draw a distinction between "pure" and "applied" science, claiming that pure science is the attempt to discover the fundamental (and beautiful) laws of nature without regard to possible application, it is nevertheless widely recognized that it is causal knowledge of nature that is sought, that is, knowledge that in principle gives its possessors power to intervene successfully in natural processes. In any case, most "pure" scientists know very well that their work, if successful, will generally find application in the "conquest of nature." We may recall how the first investigators of nuclear energy wrote enthusiastically in the early years of the twentieth century that their work, if successful, would provide mankind with an almost limitless source of energy. Both the "pure" and the technological challenges posed by the nucleus proved irresistible: the nucleus was there to be conquered and conquest was always incredibly exciting. Even in today's beleaguered domain of nuclear power for "peaceful" purposes, the ideology and practice of the conquest of nature has not disappeared. Thus, rallying the troops in 1979 at the twenty-fifth anniversary of the formation of the UK Atomic Energy Authority, the physicist chairman of the Authority, Sir John Hill, said that we will be judged "upon our achievements and not upon the plaintive cries of the faint-hearted who have lost the courage and ambitions of our forefathers, which made mankind the master of the earth."[8]

The masculine goal of conquest undoubtedly makes its presence felt in our images of nature and beliefs about the nature of reality; this constitutes a fourth aspect of the masculinity of physics and of science in general. That which is to be conquered does not usually emerge in the conqueror's view as possessing intrinsically admirable properties that need to be respected and preserved. Much, of course, could be written on specific images of nature, particularly with respect to "pure" and "applied" research objectives, and the subject does not lend itself to obvious generalizations. Nevertheless, it is clear that from the seventeenth century onwards, natural philosophers, men of science, and scientists tended to see the "matter" of nature as having no initiating, creative powers of its own (a point of view maintained only with some difficulty after the development of evolutionary theory in the nineteenth century). The historian of science, R. S. Westfall, is certainly not wrong when he writes that "whatever the crudities of the seventeenth century's conception of nature, the rigid exclusion of the psychic from physical nature has remained as its permanent legacy."[9] No matter what the cognitive arguments in favor of science's generally reductionist conception of "matter" and nature, it is clear that a nature that is seen as "the mere scurrying of matter to and fro" is a nature not only amenable to conquest but also one that requires no moral self-examination on the part of its would-be conqueror. "Man's place in the physical universe," declared the Nobel laureate physical chemist (and impeccable Cold-War warrior) Willard Libby, "is to be its master ... to be its king through the power he alone possesses—the Principle of Intelligence."[10]

A fifth aspect of the masculinity of physics lies in the militarization the discipline has undergone in the twentieth century. Optimistically, Francis Bacon had expressed the hope in the seventeenth century that men would cease making war on each other in order to make collective warfare on nature. That hope has not been realized, nor is it likely to be. We may, after all, recall C. S. Lewis's opinion that "what we call Man's power over nature turns out to be a power exercised by some men over other men [and women] with nature as its instrument."[11] In the overall militarization of science that has occurred largely in this century and that was institutionalized during and after the Second World War, physics and its associated disciplines have indeed been in the forefront. For example, in a courageous paper to the *American Journal of Physics,* the physicist E. L. Woollett reported that at the end of the 1970s some 55 percent of physicists and astronomers carrying out research and development in the United States worked on projects of direct military value and he complained bitterly that physics had become a largely silent partner in the nuclear arms race.[12] It is estimated that throughout the world some half million physical scientists work on weapons design and improvement. As the physicist Freeman Dyson has reported, not only is the world of the scientific warriors overwhelmingly male-dominated but he sees the competition between physicists in weapons creation, allied to the (surely masculine) thrill of creating almost limitless destructive power, as being in large part responsible for the continuing qualitative escalation of the nuclear arms race.[13] Moreover, competition between weapons physicists is still a powerful motivating force in the nuclear arms race. Commenting on the rivalry at the Livermore Weapons Laboratory between two physical scientists, Peter Hagelstein and

George Chapline, as to who would be the first to achieve a breakthrough in the design of a nuclear-bomb-powered X-ray laser, the head of the Livermore "Star Wars" Group, Lowell Wood, alleged: "It was raw, unabashed competitiveness. It was amazing—even though I had seen it happen before … two relatively young men … slugging it out for dominance in this particular technical arena."[14] And he then went on to agree with Richard Lewontin's unflattering description of motivation throughout the world of science:

> I would be very surprised if very many major scientific endeavors, maybe even minor ones, happen because a disinterested scientist coolly and dispassionately grinds away in his lab, devoid of thoughts about what this means in terms of competition, peer esteem, his wife and finally, prizes and recognition. I'm afraid I'm sufficiently cynical to think that in excess of 90 percent of all science is done with these considerations in mind. Pushing back the frontiers of knowledge and advancing truth are distinctly secondary considerations.[15]

One might, no doubt naively, like to believe that male scientists do not compete among themselves for the privilege of being the first to create a devastating new weapon. That belief would certainly be quite wrong.

Given such a sobering description of the masculine world of physics in Britain and North America, it isn't altogether surprising if girls, whose gender socialization is quite different from that of boys, are reluctant to study physics at school. What's more, it is in no way irrational, as British science teacher Hazel Grice points out, for girls to reject a subject that appears to offer "as the apex of its achievement a weapon of mass annihilation."[16]

Scientific Method for Scientists and Warriors

One common description of physics is that it is a "hard," intellectually difficult discipline, as opposed to "soft" ones, such as English or history. The hard-soft spectrum spanning the academic disciplines is, of course, well-known, and within the sciences themselves there is also a notorious hard-soft spectrum, with physics situated at the hard end, chemistry somewhere toward the middle, biology toward the soft end, and psychology beyond. Insofar as mind, reason, and intellect are (in a patriarchy) culturally seen as masculine attributes, the hard-soft spectrum serves to define a spectrum of diminishing masculinity from hard to soft.

But what is held to constitute intellectual difficulty? It seems that the more mathematical a scientific discipline, the more intellectually difficult it is believed to be and hence the "harder" it is. Mathematics not only makes a discipline difficult, it seems: it also makes it rigorous; and the discipline is thus seen to be "hard" in the two connecting senses of difficult and rigorous. The fact that physics, and especially theoretical physics, makes prodigious use of sophisticated mathematics no doubt contributes to their enviable position at the masculine end of the hard-soft spectrum. It is perhaps of more relevance, however, that mathematics and logical rigor are usually seen as essential components of the "scientific method" and it is the extent to which a discipline is able to practice the "scientific method" that determines its ultimate "hardness" in the sense of intellectual difficulty, the rigor of its reasoning, and the reliability and profundity of its findings. Physics, it is widely believed, is not only able to but does make excellent use of the "scientific method," which thus accounts for its spectacular successes both in the understanding of physical processes and in their mastery. While, of course, all the scientific disciplines aspire to practice the "scientific method," it is physics and related disciplines that are held to have succeeded best.

But does such a procedure as the "scientific method" really exist? If it does, it is deemed to enjoy masculine rather than feminine status insofar as it rigorously and inexorably arrives at truth about the natural world and not mere opinion or wishful thinking. Such a method must therefore, it seems, be ideally characterized by logically rigorous thinking aided by mathematics and determined by experimental, that is, "hard" evidence with no contamination by feminine emotion, intuition, and subjective desires. "The scientific attitude of mind," explained Bertrand Russell in 1913, "involves a sweeping away of all other desires in the interests of the desire to know— it involves the suppression of hopes and fears, loves and hates, and the whole subjective emotional life, until we become subdued to the material, able to see it frankly, without preconceptions, without biases, without any wish except to see it as it is."[17] Such a view of the scientific method remains incredibly influential. In 1974 the sociologist Robert Bierstedt could confirm that "the scientist, *as such*, has no ethical, religious, political, literary, philosophical, moral, or marital preferences. ... As a scientist he is interested not in what is right or wrong, or good and evil, but only in what is true or false."[18] Numerous examples could be given. Emotion, wishful thinking, intuition, and other such apparent pollutants of cognition are held to betray and subvert the objectivity of the scientific method, which is the hard, ruthless application of logic and experimental evidence to the quest to understand and master the world. Thus while the philosopher of science Hans Reichenbach could tell the world in 1951 that "the scientific philosopher does not want to belittle the value of emotions, nor would he like to live without them" and that the philosopher's own life could be as passionate and sentimental as that of any literary man, nevertheless the truly scientific philosopher "refuses to muddle emotion and cognition, and likes to breathe the pure air of logical insight and penetration."[19] Perhaps that is why the Nobel laureate physicist, Isidor Rabi, then eighty-four years of age, could confide in the early 1980s to Vivian Gornick that women were temperamentally unsuited to science, that the female nervous system was "simply different." "It makes it impossible for them to stay with the thing," he explained. "I'm afraid there's no use quarrelling with it, that's the way it is."[20]

Now the view of successful "scientific method" as masculine logic, rigor, and experimentation necessarily untainted and uncontaminated with feminine emotion, intuition, and wishful thinking is completely and hopelessly wrong. Such a scientific method is as elusive as "pure" masculinity. If nothing else, the invention of theories demands considerable intuition and creative imagination, as every innovative scientist knows and often has proclaimed. Does this therefore mean that the masculine "objectivity" of scientific method is intrinsically compromised? The philosopher of science, Carl Hempel, explains that it doesn't, since "scientific objectivity is safeguarded by the principle that while hypotheses and theories may be freely invented and *proposed* in science [the so-called context of discovery], they can be *accepted* into the body of scientific knowledge only if they pass critical scrutiny [the context of justification], which includes in particular the checking of suitable test implications by careful observation and experiment."[21] Alas for this typical defense of scientific objectivity, for ever since the work of Thomas Kuhn in his 1962 essay *The Structure of Scientific Revolutions*, it is generally accepted that no hard and fast distinction can be readily drawn between such a feminine context of discovery and a masculine context of justification.[22]

For this is what seems to be at issue. Not only does the notion of scientific objectivity appear to entail a clear-cut distinction between the masculine investigator and the world of "feminine" or "female" matter, within the psyche of the masculine investigator there also appears to be a pressing need to establish an inviolable distinction between a masculine mode of "hard," rigorous reasoning determined by logic and experimental evidence and, should it operate at all, a feminine mode characterized by creative imagination, intuition, and emotion-linked preferences. However, such clear-cut distinctions neither exist nor are possible in scientific practice, no matter how much the masculine mode appears paramount in normal research. What certainly does exist (although not uniformly so) is a very impassioned commitment to deny an evaluative subjective component to scientific practice; we may see such a masculine commitment as stemming from an emotional rejection and repudiation of the feminine within masculine inquiry. In other words, the impassioned claim that there exists an unemotional, value-free scientific method (or context of justification) may be interpreted as an emotional rejection and repudiation of the feminine and, if this is so, it would mean that scientific practice carried out (supposedly) in an "objective," value-free, unemotional way is in fact deeply and emotionally repressive of the feminine. This is a hornets' nest with all kinds of implications, but it may help to explain why much of modern science has, I shall argue, been embraced so uncritically by a society that is misogynistic and, in the case of the war industries, misanthropic as well. It is partly because patriarchal science is fundamentally antifeminine that its practitioners are psychologically vulnerable to the attractions of the "defense" industry.

We learn from Freeman Dyson that the world of the warriors, which comprises military strategists, scientists, and Pentagon officials, is ostentatiously defined by a "deliberately cool," quantitative style that explicitly excludes "overt emotion and rhetoric"—it is a style modelled on "scientific method" and directly opposed to, for example, the "emotional," "anecdotal" style of the anti-nuclear campaigner Helen Caldicott, whose arguments, according to Dyson, the warriors find unacceptable even when they manage to take them seriously.[23] For her part, Helen Caldicott believes that great rage and hatred lie suppressed behind the seemingly imperturbable, "rational" mask of scientific military analysis.[24] The military historian Sue Mansfield has posed the problem at its starkest: the stress placed in the scientific world on "objectivity" and a quantitative approach as a guarantee of truth, together with the relegation of emotions to a peripheral and unconscious existence, has,

she maintains, carried "from its beginnings in the seventeenth century the burden of an essential hostility to the body, the feminine, and the natural environment."[25]

Sexual Rhetoric by Scientists and Warriors

The stereotype of the sober male scientist dispassionately investigating the properties of matter with, obviously, not a single sexual thought in mind is singularly undermined by the extent to which scientists portray nature as female in their informal prose, lectures, and talks. Indeed, according to the historian of science, Carolyn Merchant, the most powerful image in Western science is "the identification of nature with the female, especially a female harbouring secrets."[26] Physicists often refer to their "pure" research as a kind of sexual exploration of the secrets of nature—a female nature that not only possesses great subtlety and beauty to be revealed only to her most skilfull and determined admirers and lovers, but that is truly fearsome in her awesome powers.

"Nature," wrote the high-energy physicist Frank Close in the *Guardian*, "hides her secrets in subtle ways." By "probing" the deep, mysterious, unexpectedly beautiful submicroscopic world, "we have our eyes opened to her greater glory."[27] The impression is given of a non-violent, male exploration of the sexual secrets of a mysterious, profoundly wonderful female nature. From the end of the nineteenth century to the middle 1980s, such sentiments have frequently been expressed by famous physicists. Thus, addressing the annual meeting of the British Association in 1898, the physicist Sir William Crookes announced to his audience, "Steadily, unflinchingly, we strive to pierce the inmost heart of nature, from what she is to reconstruct what she has been, and to prophesy what she yet shall be. Veil after veil we have lifted, and her face grows more beautiful, august, and wonderful, with every barrier that is withdrawn."[28]

But no matter how many veils are lifted, ultimately the fearsome and untameable "femaleness" of the universe will remain.[29] Even if female nature is ultimately untameable, scientific research and application can reveal and make usable many of nature's comparatively lesser secrets. It is striking how successful scientific research is frequently described in the language of sexual intercourse, birth, and claims to paternity in which science or the mind of man is ascribed the phallic role of penetrating or probing into the secrets of nature—with the supposed hardness of successful scientific method now acquiring an obvious phallic connotation. Accounts of the origins of quantum mechanics and nuclear physics in the first decades of the twentieth century illustrate this well. In 1966 the physicist, historian, and philosopher of science, Max Jammer, admiringly announced that those early achievements of physicists in quantum mechanics clearly showed "how far man's intellect can penetrate into the secrets of nature on the basis of comparatively inconspicuous evidence"; indeed, Victor Weisskopf, Nobel laureate, remembers how the physicists at Niels Bohr's institute were held together "by a common urge to penetrate into the secrets of nature."[30] While Frederick Soddy was already proudly convinced by 1908 that "in the discovery of radioactivity … we had penetrated one of nature's innermost secrets,"[31] it was Soddy's collaborator in those early years, Sir Ernest Rutherford, who has been adjudged by later physicists and historians to have been the truly masculine man behind nuclear physics' spectacular advances in this period. Referring to Rutherford's triumphant hypothesis in 1911 that the atom consisted of an extremely concentrated nucleus of positively charged matter surrounded by a planetary system of orbiting electrons, one of Rutherford's assistants at the time, C. G. Darwin, later wrote that it was one of the "great occurrences" of his life that he was "actually present half-an-hour after the nucleus was born."[32] Successful and deep penetration, birth, and ensuing paternity: these are the hallmarks of great scientific advance.

At first sight it might seem that there is little untoward in such use of sexual, birth, and paternity metaphors, their use merely demonstrating that nuclear research, like scientific research in general, can be unproblematically described by its practitioners as a kind of surrogate sexual activity carried out by male physicists on female nature. However, not only did all the early nuclear pioneers (Rutherford included) realize that enormous quantities of energy lay waiting, as it were, to be exploited by physicists—"it would be rash to predict," wrote Rutherford's collaborator, W. C. D. Whetham, "that our impotence will last forever"[33]—but, ominously, some of the sexual metaphors were extremely aggressive, reminding one forcibly of the ideology of (masculine) conquest of (female) nature. Indeed, since Rutherford's favorite word appears to have been "attack" it does not seem startling when one of the most distinguished physicists in the United States, George Ellery Hale, who was convinced that "nature has hidden her secrets in an almost impregnable stronghold," wrote admiringly to Rutherford in astonishingly military-sexual language. "The rush of your advance is overpowering," he congratulated him, "and I do not wonder that nature has retreated from trench to trench, and from height to height, until she is now capitulating in her inmost citadel."[34]

The implications of all this were not lost on everyone. Well before the discovery of uranium fission in 1939, the poet and Cambridge historian Thomas Thornely expressed his great apprehension at the consequences of a successful scientific assault on nature's remaining nuclear secrets:

> Well may she start and desperate strain,
> To thrust the bold besiegers back;
> If they that citadel should gain,
> What grisly shapes of death and pain
> May rise and follow in their track![35]

Not surprisingly, just as military scientists and strategists have adopted the formal "scientific style" of unemotional, quantitative argument, so they also frequently make informal use of sexual, birth, and paternity metaphors in their research and testing. Now, however, these metaphors become frighteningly aggressive, indeed obscene: military sexual penetration into nature's nuclear secrets will, the metaphors suggest, not only shake nature to her very foundations but at the same time demonstrate indisputable masculine status and military paternity. We learn that the first fission bomb developed at the Los Alamos laboratory was often referred to as a "baby"—a baby boy if a successful explosion, a baby girl if a failure. Secretary of War Henry Stimson received a message at Potsdam after the successful Trinity test of an implosion fission weapon which (after decoding) read:

> Doctor has just returned most enthusiastic and confident that the little boy [the uranium bomb] is as husky as his big brother [the tested plutonium bomb]. The light in his eyes discernible from here to Highhold and I could have heard his screams from here to my farm.[36]

Examples are abundant: the two bombs (one uranium and one plutonium) exploded over Japanese cities were given the code names "Little Boy" and "Fat Man"; a third bomb being made ready was given the name "Big Boy." Oppenheimer became known as the Father of the A-Bomb and indeed the National Baby Institution of America made Oppenheimer its Father of the Year. Edward Teller, publicly seen as the principal physicist behind the successful design of the first fusion weapon or H-bomb, seemingly takes pains in his memoirs to draw readers' attention to the fact that it was a "phallic" triumph on his part.[37] After the enormous blast of the first H-bomb obliterated a Pacific island and all its life, Teller sent a triumphant telegram to his Los Alamos colleagues, "It's a boy."[38] Unfortunately for Teller, his paternity status of "Father of the H-Bomb" has been challenged by some physicists who claim that the mathematician Stanislaw Ulam produced the original idea and that all Teller did was to gestate the bomb after Ulam had inseminated

him with his idea, thus, they say, making him the mere Mother.

Following the creation of this superbomb, a dispute over two competing plans for a nuclear attack against the Soviet Union occurred between strategists in the RAND think tank and the leading generals of the Strategic Air Command (SAC) of the U.S. Air Force. In a circulated memorandum the famous strategist Bernard Brodie likened his own RAND plan of a limited nuclear strike against military targets while keeping the major part of the nuclear arsenal in reserve to the act of sexual penetration but with withdrawal before ejaculation; he likened the alternative SAC plan to leave the Soviet Union a "smoking radiating ruin at the end of two hours" to sexual intercourse that "goes all the way."[39] His colleague Herman Kahn coined the term "wargasm" to describe the all-out "orgastic spasm of destruction" that the SAC generals supposedly favored.[40] Kahn's book *On Escalation* attempts, like an elaborate scientific sex manual, a precise identification of forty-four (!) stages of increasing tension culminating in the final stage of "spasm war."[41] Such sexual metaphors for nuclear explosions and warfare appear to be still in common use. In 1980 General William Odom, then a military adviser to Zbigniew Brzesinski on the National Security Council, told a Harvard seminar of a strategic plan to release 70 to 80 percent of America's nuclear megatonnage "in one orgasmic whump,"[42] while at a London meeting in 1984, General Daniel Graham, a former head of the Defense Intelligence Agency and a prominent person behind President Reagan's Strategic Defense Initiative, brought some appreciative chuckles from his nearly all-male audience in referring to all-out nuclear "exchange" as the "wargasm."[43]

What is one to make of such metaphors and in particular of an analogy that likens ejaculation of semen during sexual intercourse (an act, one hopes, of mutual pleasure and possibly the first stage in the creation of new life) with a nuclear bombardment intended to render a huge country virtually lifeless, perhaps for millennia to come? And what conception of pleasure was foremost in Kahn's mind when he coined the term "wargasm"—surely the most obscene word in the English language—to describe what he sees as the union between Eros and Thanatos that is nuclear holocaust? I find such comparisons and terminology almost beyond rational comment. Simone de Beauvoir's accurate observation that "the erotic vocabulary of males" has always been drawn from military terminology becomes totally inadequate.[44] Brodie's and Kahn's inventiveness has surely eclipsed Suzanne Lowry's observation in the *Guardian* that "'fuck' is the prime hate word" in the English language.[45] Indeed, given the sexual metaphors used by some of the nuclear warriors, one can understand Susan Griffin's anguished agreement with Norman Mailer's (surprising) description of Western culture as "drawing a rifle sight on an open vagina"—a culture, Griffin continues, "that even within its worship of the female sex goddess hates female sexuality."[46] We may indeed wonder why a picture of Rita Hayworth, "the ubiquitous pinup girl of World War II," was stenciled on the first atomic bomb exploded in the Bikini tests of 1946.[47]

Unconscious Objectives of Patriarchy and Patriarchal Physics

There has been much analysis of the Catholic Church's dichotomization of women into two stereotypes: the unattainable, asexual, morally pure virgin to which the Christian woman could aspire but never reach and the carnal whore-witch representing uncontrollable sexuality, depravity, wickedness, and the threat of universal chaos and disorder. During the sixteenth and seventeenth centuries such a fear and loathing of women's apparent wickedness came to a head in the European witch craze that was responsible for the inquisition and execution of scores of thousands of victims, over 80 percent of them female. A major historian of the witch craze, H. C. E. Midelfort, has noted that "one cannot begin to understand the European witch craze with-

out recognizing that it displayed a burst of misogyny without parallel in Western history."[48]

Whatever the causes of the European witch craze, what may be particularly significant is that it coincided with the first phase of the scientific revolution, the peak of the witch craze occurring during the decades in which Francis Bacon, René Descartes, Johannes Kepler, and Galileo Galilei made their revolutionary contributions. In *one* of its aspects, I believe that the scientific revolution may be seen as a secularized version of the witch craze in which sophisticated men either, like Francis Bacon, projected powerful and dangerous "femaleness" onto nature or, like René Descartes, declared nature to be feminine and thus totally amenable to manipulation and control by (the mind of) man. We recall how Simone de Beauvoir declared that woman is seemingly "represented, at one time, as pure passivity, available, open, a utensil"—which is surely Descartes's view of "feminine" matter—while "at another time she is regarded as if possessed by alien forces: there is a devil raging in her womb, a serpent lurks in her vagina, eager to devour the male's sperm"—which has more affinity to Francis Bacon's view of "female" matter.[49] Indeed, Bacon likened the experimental investigation of the secrets of "female" nature to the inquisition of witches on the rack and looked forward to the time when masculine science would shake "female" nature to her very foundations. It is, I believe, the purified natural magical tradition advocated by Bacon (with considerable use of very aggressive sexual imagery) that contributed in a major way to the rise of modern science. Believing firmly in the existence of the secrets of nature that could be penetrated by the mind of man, Bacon predicted that eventually the new science would be able to perform near miracles. And indeed the momentous significance of the scientific revolution surely lies in the fact that, unlike the rituals of preliterate societies which in general failed to give their practitioners power over nature (if this is what they sought), the male practitioners of modern science have been rewarded with truly breathtaking powers to intervene successfully in natural phenomena (we have become blasé about the spectacular triumphs of modern science, but what a near miracle is, for example, a television picture). Bacon's prediction that the new science he so passionately advocated would inaugurate the "truly masculine birth of time" and eventually shake nature to her very foundations has been triumphantly borne out by the achievements of modern physics and the sad possibility of devastating nature with environmental destruction, nuclear holocaust, and nuclear winter.

Clearly modern science possesses what might be called a rational component. In this article I am taking for granted the fact that modern science produces knowledge of nature that "works" relative to masculine (and other) expectations and objectives and that the intrinsic interest and fascination of scientific inquiry would render a non-patriarchal science a worthy and central feature of a truly human society. What I am here concerned with is the "truly masculine" nature of scientific inquiry involving the discipline's would-be rigid separation between masculine science and "female" nature and the possibility of an underlying, if for the most part unconscious, hostility to "dangerous femaleness" in the minds of some, or many, of its practitioners—a hostility presumably endemic to patriarchal society. A case can be made—and has been both by Carolyn Merchant and myself—that a powerful motivating force, but not the only one, behind the rise of modern science was a kind of displaced misogyny.[50] In addition a case can be made that a powerful motivating force behind some (or much) modern science and particularly weapons science is a continuation of the displaced misogyny that helped generate the scientific revolution.

Certainly a counterclaim is possible that modern science might have had some misogynistic origins, but that this has no relevance today. In disagreement with such a counterclaim, however, it can be plausibly argued that

the industrialized countries have remained virulently misogynistic, as seen in the prevalence of violence practiced and depicted by men against women. If there is indeed a link between misogyny, insecure masculinity, and our conceptions of science, particularly weapons science, then we are given a way to understand why nuclear violence can be associated in warriors' minds with sexual intercourse and ejaculation. Moreover, not only does Sue Mansfield suggest that at a deep level the scientific mentality has carried from its inception in the seventeenth century "the burden of an essential hostility to the body, the feminine, and the natural environment," but she also points out that, if human life survives at all after a nuclear holocaust, then it will mean the total restoration of the power of arm-bearing men over women. This leads her to make a significant comment that "though the reenslavement of women and the destruction of nature are not conscious goals of our nuclear stance, the language of our bodies, our postures, and our acts is a critical clue to our unexamined motives and desires."[51]

Of course, at the conscious level the scientific warrior today can, and does, offer a "rational" explanation for his behavior: his creation of fission and fusion weapons, he maintains, has made the deliberate starting of world war unthinkable and certainly has preserved peace in Europe for the last forty years. Whatever financial gain comes his way is not unappreciated but is secondary to the necessity of maintaining his country's security; likewise whatever scientific interest he experiences in the technological challenge of his work is again secondary to the all-important objective of preserving the balance of terror until world statesmen achieve multilateral disarmament. While well-known arguments can be made against the coherence of such a typical rationalization, what I am suggesting is that at a partly conscious, partly unconscious, level the scientific warrior experiences not only an almost irresistible need to separate his (insecure) masculinity from what he conceives as femininity but also a compulsive desire to create the weapons that unmistakably affirm his masculinity and by means of which what is "female" can, if necessary and as a last resort, be annihilated. (And it must be noted that scientific warriors can be supported by women or even joined by female warriors in their largely unconscious quest to affirm masculine triumph over the feminine and female.)

Conclusion

Looking over the history of humanity—the "slaughter-bench of history" as Hegel called it—I feel compelled to identify a factor—beyond economic and territorial rationales—that could help explain this sorry escalation of weaponry oppression, and bloodshed. It seems to me of paramount importance to try to understand why men are generally the direct oppressors, oppressing other men and women, why in general men allow neither themselves nor women the opportunity to realize full humanity.

While the political scientist Jean Bethke Elshtain may well be correct when she writes skeptically that no great movement will ever be fought under the banner of "androgyny," I suggest that it could well be fought under the banner of "a truly human future for everyone."[52] And that would entail the abolition of the *institutionalized* sexual division of labor. Men and women must be allowed the right to become complete human beings and not mutilated into their separate masculine and feminine gender roles. At the same time, I agree with Cynthia Cockburn when she writes in her book *Machinery of Dominance* that "men need more urgently to learn women's skills than women need to learn men's" and that "the revolutionary step will be to bring men down to earth, to domesticate technology and reforge the link between making and nurturing."[53]

In such a world "education" could not remain as it is now in Britain and the United States (and elsewhere). Certainly there would be no "physics" degree as it exists today, although there would be studies that would eventually take "students" to the frontiers of research in "physics." Needless to say, such an educational system would not be male-dominated (or female-dominated), it would not institutionalize and reward socially competitive aggressive behavior, and there would be no objective in "physics" education of the "conquest of nature," although it would certainly recognize the need to find respectful, ecologically sound ways of making use of nature. Moreover, images of nature would, I suspect, undergo some profound changes (with probably major changes to some theories as well), and clearly in a truly human world there would be no militarization of physics. As for the "scientific method," this would be recognized to be a somewhat mysterious activity, perhaps never completely specifiable, certainly an activity making use of the full range of *human* capacities from creative intuition to the most rigorous logical reasoning.

As for sexual imagery, that would surely thrive in the new truly human activity of scientific research, given that sexual relations—deprived of the hatred that now so greatly distorts sexuality—would continue to provide not only much of the motivation but also the metaphors for describing scientific activity (and much else). Consider, for example, the language of a woman who was awarded just about every honor the discipline of astrophysics could bestow (but only after she spent years challenging blatant sexism and discrimination). The images invoked by Cecilia Payne-Gaposchkin are more directly erotic than the "equivalent" sexual imagery used by male scientists and physicists (not to mention their frequent aggressive imagery); her language was of her friendship, her love, her delight, her ecstasy with the world of "male" stars and galaxies. Writing of nature as female, Payne-Gaposchkin advises her fellow researchers: "Nature has always had a trick of surprising us, and she will continue to surprise us. But she has never let us down yet. We can go forward with confidence,

Knowing that nature never did betray
The heart that loved her."[54]

But it was an embrace of relatedness that Payne-Gaposchkin had sought and which had given her great satisfaction throughout her life, the satisfaction arising, in the words of Peggy Kidwell, from a sustained impassioned, loving endeavor "to unravel the mysteries of the stars."[55] In a truly human world, the principal purpose and result of science, as Erwin Schrödinger once said, will surely be to enhance "the general joy of living."[56]

Notes

I am most grateful to Michael Kaufman for his extremely skillful pruning of a very long manuscript.

1. Michael Howard, "On Fighting a Nuclear War," in Michael Howard, *The Causes of War and Other Essays* (London: Temple Smith, 1983), 136.

2. Penny Strange, *It'll Make a Man of You* (Nottingham, England: Mushroom Books with Peace News, 1983), 24–5.

3. These statistics are taken from *Girls and Physics: A Report by the Joint Physics Education Committee of the Royal Society and the Institute of Physics* (London, 1982), 8, and Lilli S. Hornig, "Women in Science and Engineering: Why So Few?" *Technology Review* 87 (November/ December, 1984), 41.

4. See Margaret W. Rossiter, *Women Scientists in America: Struggles and Strategies to 1940* (Baltimore: Johns Hopkins University Press, 1982),190–1.

5. Richard Lewontin, "Honest Jim' Watson's Big Thriller, about DNA," Chicago *Sun Times*, 25 Feb. 1968, 1–2, reprinted in James D. Watson, *The Double Helix ... A New Critical Edition*, edited by Gunther S. Stent (London: Weidenfeld, 1981),186.

6. Sharon Traweek, "High-Energy Physics: A Male Preserve," *Technology Review* (November/December, 1984), 42–3; see also her *Beamtimes and Lifetimes: The World of High-Energy Physicists* (Boston: Harvard University Press, 1988).

7. Heinz Pagels, *The Cosmic Code: Quantum Physics as the Language of Nature* (London: Michael Joseph, 1982), 338.

8. Sir John Hill, "The Quest for Public Acceptance of Nuclear Power," *Atom*, no. 273 (1979): 166–72.

9. Richard S. Westfall, *The Construction of Modern Science* (1971; Cambridge: Cambridge University Press, 1977), 41. It should be noted, however, that quantum mechanics is essentially an antireductionist theory; see, for example, the (controversial) book by Fritjof Capra, *The Tao of Physics* (London: Fontana, 1976).

10. Willard Libby, "Man's Place in the Physical Universe," in John R. Platt, ed., *New Views of the Nature of Man* (Chicago: University of Chicago Press, 1965), 14–15.

11. C. S. Lewis, *The Abolition of Man* (1943; London: Geoffrey Bles, 1946), 40.

12. E. L. Woollett, "Physics and Modern Warfare: The Awkward Silence," *American Journal of Physics* 48 (1980): 104–11.

13. Freeman Dyson, *Weapons and Hope* (New York: Harper and Row, 1984), 41–2.

14. William J. Broad, *Star Warriors: A Penetrating Look into the Lives of the Young Scientists Behind Our Space Age Weaponry* (New York: Simon and Schuster, 1985), 204.

15. Ibid.

16. Hazel Grice, letter to the *Guardian,* 9 Oct. 1984, 20.

17. Bertrand Russell, "Science in a Liberal Education," the *New Statesman* (1913) reprinted in *Mysticism and Logic and Other Essays* (Harmondsworth: Penguin, 1953), 47–8.

18. Robert Bierstedt, *The Social Order* (1957; New York: McGraw-Hill, 1974), 26.

19. Hans Reichenbach, *The Rise of Scientific Philosophy* (1951; Berkeley and Los Angeles: California University Press, 1966), 312.

20. Vivian Gornick, *Women in Science: Portraits from a World in Transition* (New York: Simon and Schuster, 1984), 36.

21. Carl Hempel, *Philosophy of Natural Science* (Englewood Cliffs, N.J.: Prentice-Hall, 1966), 16.

22. See, for example, Imre Lakatos and Alan Musgrave, eds., *Criticism and the Growth of Knowledge* (Cambridge: Cambridge University Press,

1970): Sandra Harding, "Is Gender a Variable in Conceptions of Rationality? A Survey of Issues," *Dialectica: International Journal of Philosophy of Knowledge* 36 (1982): 225–42: and Harry M. Collins, ed., special issue of *Social Studies of Science* 11 (1981): 3–158, "Knowledge and Controversy: Studies of Modern Natural Science."

23. Freeman Dyson, *Weapons and Hope*, 4–6.

24. Helen Caldicott, "Etiology: Missile Envy and Other Psychopathology," in her *Missile Envy: The Arms Race and Nuclear War* (New York: William Morrow, 1984).

25. Sue Mansfield, *The Gestalts of War: An Inquiry into Its Origins and Meaning as a Social Institution* (New York: Dial Press, 1982), 224.

26. Carolyn Merchant, "Isis' Consciousness Raised," *Isis* 73 (1982): 398–409.

27. Frank Close, "And now at last, the quark to top them all," the *Guardian*, 19 July 1984, 13, and "A shining example of what ought to be impossible," the *Guardian*, 8 Aug. 1985, 13.

28. Sir William Crookes, quoted in E. E. Fournier d'Albe, *The Life of Sir William Crookes* (London: Fisher Unwin, 1923), 365.

29. See, for example, the physicist Paul Davies's account of "black holes," "naked singularities," and "cosmic anarchy" in his *The Edge of Infinity: Naked Singularities and the Destruction of Space-time* (London: Dent, 1981), especially 92–3, 114, 145.

30. Max Jammer, *The Conceptual Development of Quantum Mechanics* (New York: McGraw-Hill, 1966), 61, and Victor Weisskopf, "Niels Bohr and International Scientific Collaboration," in S. Rozenthal, ed., *Niels Bohr: His Life and Work as Seen by His Friends and Colleagues* (Amsterdam: North Holland, 1967), 262.

31. Frederick Soddy, *The Interpretation of Radium* (London, 1909), 234.

32. C. G. Darwin quoted in A. S. Eve, *Rutherford* (Cambridge: Cambridge University Press, 1939), 199, 434.

33. W. C. D. Whetham, *The Recent Development of Physical Science* (London: Murray, 1904) 242.

34. G. E. Hale quoted in Helen Wright, *Explorer of the Universe: A Biography of George Ellery Hale* (New York: Dutton, 1966), 283, and in A. S. Eve, *Rutherford*, 231.

35. "The Atom" from *The Collected Verse of Thomas Thornely* (Cambridge: W. Heffer, 1939), 70–1, reprinted in John Heath-Stubbes and Phillips Salmon, eds., *Poems of Science* (Harmondsworth: Penguin, 1984), 245.

36. Richard G. Hewlett and Oscar E. Anderson, *A History of the United States Atomic Energy Commission* (Pennsylvania State University Press, 1962), vol. 1, *The New World, 1939–1946*, 386.

37. Edward Teller with Allen Brown, *The Legacy of Hiroshima* (London: Macmillan, 1962), 51–3.

38. Edward Teller, *Energy from Heaven and Earth* (San Francisco: W. H. Freeman, 1979), 151. See also Norman Moss, *Men Who Play God* (Harmondsworth: Penguin, 1970), 78. For general detail see my *Fathering the Unthinkable: Masculinity, Scientists and the Nuclear Arms Race* (London: Pluto Press 1983), ch. 3.

39. Bernard Brodie's memorandum is referred to by Fred Kaplan in *The Wizards of Armageddon* (New York: Simon and Schuster, 1983), 222. I have not seen the text of Brodie's memorandum. The chilling phrase "smoking, radiating ruin at the end of two hours" comes from a declassified Navy memorandum on a SAC briefing held in March 1954; see David Alan Rosenberg, "A Smoking Radiating Ruin at the End of Two Hours: Documents on American Plans for Nuclear War with the Soviet Union 1954–55," *International Security* 6 (1981/82), 3–38.

40. Herman Kahn, *On Escalation: Metaphors and Scenarios* (London: Pall Mall, 1965),194.

41. Note that Gregg Herken in *Counsels of War* (New York: Knopf, 1985), 206, writes that Bernard Brodie objected to Herman Kahn's "levity" in coining the term "wargasm."

42. Quoted in Thomas Powers, "How Nuclear War Could Start," *New York Review of Books*, 17 Jan. 1985, 34.

43. Roger Hutton, (personal communication), who attended the meeting when researching the Star Wars project.

44. Simone de Beauvoir, *The Second Sex* (1949; Harmondsworth: Penguin, 1972), 396.

45. Suzanne Lowry, "O Tempora, O Mores," the *Guardian*, 24 May 1984, 17.

46. Susan Griffin, *Pornography and Silence: Culture's Revenge Against Nature* (London: Women's Press, 1981), 217.

47. Paul Boyer, *By the Bomb's Early Light: American Thought and Culture at the Dawn of the Atomic Age* (New York: Pantheon, 1985), 83.

48. H. C. E. Midelfort, "Heartland of the Witch-craze: Central and Northern Europe," *History Today* 31 (February 1981): 28.

49. Simone de Beauvoir, *The Second Sex*, 699.

50. See, for example, Carolyn Merchant, *The Death of Nature: Women, Ecology and the Scientific Revolution* (San Francisco: Harper and Row, 1980), and my *Science and Sexual Oppression: Patriarchy's Confrontation with Women and Nature* (London: Weidenfeld, 1981), ch. 3 and *Fathering the Unthinkable*, ch. 1.

51. Sue Mansfield, *The Gestalts of War*, 223.

52. Jean Bethke Elshtain, "Against Androgyny," Telos 47 (1981), 5–22.

53. Cynthia Cockburn, *Machinery of Dominance* (London: Pluto Press, 1985), 256–7.

54. Katherine Haramundanis, ed., *Cecilia Payne-Gaposchkin: An Autobiography and Other Recollections* (Cambridge: Cambridge University Press, 1984), 237.

55. Ibid., 28.

56. "Science, Art and Play," reprinted in E. C. Schrödinger, *Science, Theory and Man* (New York: Dover, 1957), 29; see, for example, Euan Squires, *To Acknowledge the Wonder: The Story of Fundamental Physics* (Bristol: Adam Hilger, 1985).

 # Culturally Inclusive Chemistry

Catherine Hurt Middlecamp

It was the first day of class. Sixteen of us had gathered for a new seminar course entitled Culturally Inclusive Chemistry[1] (Middlecamp & Moore, 1994). As we moved our chairs into a semicircle facing the chalkboard, I began with the usual words of welcome. However, when it came time to introduce ourselves, I headed off in a new direction.

"As we start off the course," I announced, "we probably should find out some things about each other." I walked over to the board and began writing at the far left edge:

credit	*undergrad*
no credit	*grad*
	postdoc

"Here are some things that I would like to know about you," I explained. "In a minute, I'd like each of you to come up and put a mark under whether you are taking the course for credit or not, and whether you are an undergrad, graduate student, or postdoc. But first, let's work together to put up more questions. Then we come up and mark off our answers." The idea seemed reasonable enough.

I continued, "I'm curious about one more thing. How many chemists are here?" With a mischievous twinkle in my eye, I added two new categories:

chemist
nonchemist

At this point, a few eyebrows rose. I was well aware that a number of people from fields other than chemistry were present.

"That's right," I said, acknowledging the frown from a physicist. "Not everyone would classify people as chemists or nonchemists. Questions sometimes reveal as much about their authors as about anything else, but we'll get to that in a minute." I pressed them to continue. "I've put up three of my questions. What would you like to know about each other?"

There was plenty that they wanted to know. Some of their questions could be easily framed in terms of categories:

teaching	*parent*
not teaching	*nonparent*

Other questions required that we negotiate which categories to use. For example, somebody wanted to know how many Republicans and Democrats there were. We decided to add the category "other" as well. Another person wanted to know who in the group was Christian. Which categories for religion should we list? Did it matter and, if so, to whom? We ended up listing the categories of Christian, agnostic, atheist, and other.

We also negotiated the rules for answering the questions. Optimist. Pessimist. Cynic. Is it all right to check more than one category? Could we leave a question blank? We decided that both of these were fine and later found that our group included nine optimists, no pessimists, and three cynics, one of whom was also an optimist.

"I'd like to know," stated one of the participants, "who believes all this stuff about cultural inclusiveness in chemistry." This was a tough question to pin down in the format I had given. After considerable discussion, we framed his question in terms of whether we believed that the course content would "probably be useful" or "probably not be useful," or if we were "undecided."

I cut short the discussion that was brewing and urged, "Let's move to answering our questions." We left our seats and converged on the chalkboard, each of us checking off the categories that suited us. Who were we? Who weren't we? What would our responses tell us, and what wouldn't they? How were our questions limiting what we would be able to find out?

Our discussion highlighted several aspects of the data. In some ways, we were quite a diverse group. The class contained undergraduates, graduate students, postdocs, faculty, and academic staff members. We represented the fields of chemistry, physics, science education, and veterinary science, with all but the last having at least two members. We had members from different cultural and ethnic groups as well.

In other ways, we appeared to be a relatively homogeneous group. We held many interests and affiliations in common. Each category, however, had a minority of at least one person. The visibility of those in the minority varied. In some cases, people readily claimed membership in the minority group and tried to locate their colleagues ("Who are the other two cynics out there?"). In other cases, those in the minority didn't choose to reveal their identities and nobody asked them to do so. Certain tallies on the board (such as for religion and political party) stood silently and unquestioned.

We also discussed the process itself. Most of us were familiar with other ways of introducing ourselves, such as speaking to the group one at a time. The experience of having the answers to several questions simultaneously (and anonymously) gave us different information.

Focusing the Issues

As an entry point into "culturally inclusive science," this exercise did a better job of laying the groundwork for the course than I had anticipated. Together we had an experience of seeing the limitations of our questions and our answers. It helped us focus on a number of ideas, ones that I suspected would emerge time and again throughout the semester:

1. The consequences of our categories
2. The role of our questions
3. The missing pieces of information
4. The freedom to experiment

Our class discussions are summarized in the sections that follow.

The Consequences of Our Categories

The tendency to put things in categories runs deep on college campuses, if not in our society. Many lines are drawn. Our classes contain majors and nonmajors. Our students are from minority or majority groups. Our faculty are tenured or untenured. We have separate departments of English, biology, and music. We also may have colleges of engineering, medicine, or agriculture.

Scientists contribute their own lines of division. The world is made up of animals and plants; elements and compounds. The world of science includes biology, chemistry, and physics. Each of these fields has further divisions such as zoology, organic chemistry, or astrophysics. There are "hard" sciences and "soft" sciences. There are scientific and non-scientific approaches to solving problems.

Our categories reveal more about our *conceptions* of the world than they do about the actual nature of the world. Furthermore, the divisions that we create take on meaning and value depending on the structures that support them. For example, it may be more prestigious to teach the majors than the nonmajors. Some areas of medicine may be more likely to receive funding than others. Faculty salaries may be higher in the physical sciences than in the social sciences.

Finally, our categories rarely serve to connect that which they divide. Faculty and students may be more aware of their differences than what they share in common. It is a rare event that brings people together as learners regardless of their field. A variety of connections will be needed, however, for those of us working to create culturally inclusive classrooms.

The Role of Our Questions

Chemistry courses, as well as other science courses, require that students answer questions and solve problems. A quick survey of our texts and exams would reveal the importance we place on answering questions correctly. What often is lost is the significance of *asking* questions, and the expertise required to do so.

The right to ask questions is connected to power. Some people may have the right to ask questions; others may not. Some people's questions are attended to; the concerns of others may be left unanswered. How do these dynamics play out in the classroom?

Predictably, the issue of power will arise throughout the semester.

Many of us could use coaching in how to ask better questions. One question that we might learn to add to our repertoire is, What are two other explanations that fit the same facts? Similarly, the question What is it good for? may be worth exploring. For the research chemist, this latter question is useful when there is something that cannot be gotten rid of, such as a side product in a chemical reaction. This question is equally useful for the teacher who is confronted with an "undesirable" classroom behavior that is unlikely to go away but perhaps could be constructively channeled elsewhere.

Questions of how best to promote change and educational reform are bound to arise in a seminar course like ours. Students repeatedly ask, How can we change this? Along with this question, I believe that they also need to learn to ask, What enables the current situation to persist? Persistence and change need to be explored together (Watzlawick, Weakland, & Fisch, 1974).

Finally, in an "objective" field such as chemistry, the subjective nature of questions needs to be explored. For example, my earlier question that involved classifying people as chemists or nonchemists revealed something about my worldview (and is reminiscent of census forms that asked if you were white or nonwhite). What does it mean to categorize something by what it is *not*? Who has the right to set the categories? Because it is people who raise questions, all questions, including scientific ones, have a subjective nature.

The Missing Pieces of Information

A colleague once expressed to me his surprise that scientists collected such little information on their students. For example, did we know how many students were reenrolling after previously dropping or failing the course? Did we know who our "satisfied customers" were? What might both these groups teach us? What he viewed as a lack of data stood in sharp contrast to the wealth of information he saw being collected in the laboratory. I think he's right. The trouble is, we don't always know what we need to know about our students. Fortunately, if given the opportunity, our students can usually teach us both what to ask and where to look for possible answers. Furthermore, we need not only to understand our students better but also to know more about ourselves and our discipline.

The data we collect need to be ongoing and timely rather than a snapshot from a single questionnaire. During the semester, we speak with a variety of students who are currently taking chemistry. We also gather demographic data to reveal trends in the years to come.

Finally, we need to take responsibility for the outcomes revealed by the data. For example, continuing students may outperform transfer students. Asian students may experience difficulties rather than being the "model minority" (Suzuki, 1989). Documentation of such outcomes can make possible a level of accountability that is missing from some of our classrooms. A director at the National Science Foundation commented: "The only way I know to ensure we make progress is to emphasize accountability. We have to go into a goals-oriented, no-nonsense mode" (Sims, 1992, p. 1185).

The Freedom to Experiment

Chemists know how to set up and run experiments in the laboratory. We need experiments in the classroom as well. In either locale, a single experiment is unlikely to suffice. Just as it is necessary to persist with an idea in the lab, we need to persist in finding different and improved ways to teach. In the process, we need to allow ourselves (and our colleagues) the opportunity to make mistakes.

I began this course by running an "experiment," that is, I attempted to have us introduce ourselves by checking off boxes on the chalkboard. This idea was actually one in a series of experiments. I tried the idea of taking a class survey by putting a line up on the board and labeling its ends as *Strongly Agree* and *Strongly Disagree*. I then asked each student to put an X on the line representing his or her view on a particular issue, and we discussed the resulting picture. Another time, I asked one group of students to think up soluble salts and list them on the board and another to do the same for insoluble salts. Again, the composite picture gave us plenty to discuss. It was only on the third round that I asked students to design and answer their own questions.

Looking ahead, I'm wondering how to put this idea to use with larger numbers of students. Over the course of the semester, we may come up with some ideas. In any case, we need to work together to build our repertoire of different ways of asking and answering questions.

These four ideas are by no means a complete set of those relevant to the course. They are, however, a useful subset with which to begin. All relate to each other as well as to the topic of cultural inclusivity in our teaching. These ideas will also be relevant when more controversial topics such as sexism and racism arise later in our discussions.

Cultural Inclusiveness

The next time we met, I asked the members of the class what they wanted to accomplish over the course of the semester. I suggested that we divide into small groups to work out some ideas.

Many of the group discussions centered around the term *cultural inclusiveness*. People wanted to clarify what it meant both to them and to their students. Each group kept a written record that I collated and distributed. The comments included:

"I would like to understand how science is culturally determined, and what needs to be done to make it more *culturally inclusive*—is it just a change in teaching approach or is it a more fundamental problem with science as a paradigm?"

"Am I culturally inclusive right now? Why or why not?"

"Which culture are we including: a race culture or a nonscience culture?"

"First, I would like to discuss how race and ethnicity issues relate to science teaching and to the science research climate. Second, I would like to use this knowledge to analyze ways to appropriately change teaching methods and the science climate."

As we looked through these and other responses, we saw the different ways in which we had expressed the same sentiments: the hope that we would better reach *all* our students, and the fear that we would somehow turn away those who were different from us.

At this point in the course, I offered three questions as possible yardsticks to measure the skills that we might want to develop:

1. How much do you know about the cultural backgrounds of your students?
2. How much do you know about the culture of your own discipline, especially its norms for teaching and learning?
3. How well are you able to teach and learn in ways that are different from those commonly used in your discipline?

Over the next few weeks, we explored each of these questions in turn. In the sections that follow, I summarize our classroom discussions and activities.

How Much Do You Know About the Cultural Backgrounds of Your Students?

Teachers need both an appreciation of and a comfort level with the cultures represented by their students. How do we become knowledgeable about their different cultural norms and values? Most of us already know how. In fact, we have been doing this all our lives as we have come to know a variety of people and places. However, for each one of us there are

groups of people who are not in our cultural repertoire, so to speak. When the students in our classrooms match those missing from our repertoire, both we and our students may experience difficulties.

There is no single way to learn "culture." As a class, we explored a number of different avenues. For example, we discussed material taken from the books and journals listed in the Appendix. Conferences and workshops also provided us with resources, and a group of us attended a national conference on Asian Americans.[2] We returned with many stories, including one from a Hmong refugee who was now attending the university:

Let us imagine for a moment what life would be like for you after having lived for generations in a city in America, and all of a sudden being forced to migrate to the mountains of northern Laos, where there are no televisions or radios, no stoves or refrigerators, no hot water or electricity. Again let us imagine that in leaving your city, you can only bring half of your family with you. ... Well, for my family, what you are now imagining is a reality, but with the scenario in reverse. (Roop & Roop, 1991, p. 57)

We recognized the strengths of the Hmong people, such as fluency in several languages and an ability to recall the spoken word. We also talked about what it would be like to be from an oral culture where literacy was a relatively new concept. From a colleague who worked in the Hmong community, we learned how using media such as video and film played to the strengths of her students. Later in the semester, at a class "film fest," we watched an educational video produced by Hmong university students.[3]

To get at issues related to cultural stereotypes, we adapted an exercise from another national conference (Kean & Tate, 1991). The goal of our exercise (at least as stated) was to design interview questions that could help us learn about a particular type of student, such as a 45-year-old nurse returning to earn a degree in pharmacy, or a new student coming to the university after 18 years on the reservation. We broke into small groups, each one with a different type of student. As we wrote interview questions, we noted any differences between what we were curious to know and what we thought it appropriate to ask. After sharing our questions with the larger group, we discussed what such an exercise might teach us. We discussed how interviews could set a person up as being able to speak for an entire group rather than as an individual. We discussed the implications of asking students to come in for an interview rather than going to them. Later in the semester, after a lengthy discussion about these and other issues, we invited a group of undergraduates to join us for class. Figure 1 lists the discussion questions that we offered them beforehand. We also gave them the opportunity to create their own questions and agenda.

Finally, we acknowledged the time commitment required to extend our cultural knowledge. Small investments, however, can have large payoffs. As a case in point, I told the story of my investing a few hours in locating a map of Puerto Rico, framing it, and putting it up in my office. The reward has been substantial. Students have been pleased to point out their hometowns for me. Through their stories, I have become knowledgeable about different urban and rural areas in Puerto Rico and more aware of the cultural differences on the island.

How Much Do You Know About the Culture of Your Own Discipline, Especially Its Norms for Teaching and Learning?

Chemistry has its own culture, or perhaps what might better be termed its own set of minicultures. Chemists share a number of things, including a core of scientific knowledge ("truth"), a system of symbolic representations, a technical language, professional behaviors and values, preferences about how the discipline should be organized, and strategies for adapting and surviving (Bullivant, 1993). Chemists may even share a dress code, as they have been hailed as the "loose cannons on the frigate of fashion" (Ganem, 1993, p. 10).

It is difficult to perceive the "givens" in one's own culture. Academic disciplines are no exception: "Too often, academics cannot see the profound intellectual or "cultural" values inherent in their particular disciplines. If we could recognize how culture-bound our disciplines have made us, ... perhaps integrating multicultural content into our curricula might make more sense to us" (Rodrigues,

Figure 1   Questions for Student Panel Invited to Chemistry 901.

1. What would you like to know about those of us here in Chemistry 901?
2. What would you like us to know about your experiences in chemistry? You might include: why you are taking chemistry, what you like about chemistry, what you thought your chemistry course would be like, or what it actually was like.
3. How do you choose where to sit in a classroom or lecture hall? When you are already seated, do you notice anything about how people seat themselves around you?
4. When you need to find a lab partner, what is this like for you? Is there anything you might want to comment about?
5. What advice would you like to give to those of us who teach chemistry?
6. If somebody (instructor, student) does or says something that offends you, in what ways might you respond?
7. Do you go to your professor for help?

1992, p. B1). One of the "givens" to which scientists seem particularly blind is the fact that science is influenced by culture: "We tend to forget that many of the core propositions upon which the sciences rest, such as objectivity, positivism, and empiricism, are cultural products and thus may be culture-bound" (Gordon, Miller, & Rollock, 1990, p. 14). All scientific inquiry requires a perspective, for research is not only investigation but also interpretation. Scientists' perspectives condition what they perceive as important for the advancement of science as well as the design of research and the weight given to conclusions (Frankel, 1993, p. B1).

Well aware that we would have our blind spots, we began an investigation of the culture of chemistry. Our methodology was simple: We would "study" the chemistry building and its occupants. I suggested that people choose their own methods of study and that they feel free to be creative. For example, they might want to read the graffiti on the desktops or eavesdrop at the vending machines. To comply with safety regulations, I provided eye protection to those not already wearing it.

Armed with our ideas of what we would "study," we left the classroom and headed off in different directions. Some checked out the seven floors of research labs. Others went to the library and classrooms. Some interviewed people, some tallied behaviors; others observed the scientific apparatus and the cartoons posted on office doors. Once our tasks were complete, we returned to discuss our experiences:

"I saw a lot of *stuff,* but not very many people."

"The culture of science has certain smells."

"The older looking people were men, but in the classrooms there seemed to be an even male-female split."

"Chemists speak in a lot of jargon."

"There are an awful lot of locked doors."

We examined the results of our demographic surveys. There were more young faces than older ones. The younger people were more ethnically diverse and included more women. Although there were some older women, presumably secretaries by their context, most of the older people were white and male. A seminar room displayed 18 photographs of white, mostly elderly gentlemen. Nothing that we observed contradicted the generalization: "The culture of science evolved in a period when it was being practiced exclusively by men, and that has greatly influenced the outcome. It is a men's game and it continues to be played by men's rules" (Tilghman, 1993, p. A23).

We recalled snatches of conversations that we had heard in the hallways:

"What are you majoring in?"

"Chemistry."

"Oh [dead silence]. You must be *smart.*"

We wondered who had decided that scientists were any smarter than other people. We also discussed who might benefit from the idea that chemistry is hard. Chemistry has its mythologies (Bowen, 1992), as does any discipline.

We discussed the classroom practices that some of us had observed. Professors talked fast. Students who put their hands up first were called on. Quizzes and tests were given under the pressure of time. Speed was apparently the norm, if not a virtue. There seemed to be little time to contemplate anything.

We noted that the chemistry building had few connections to the natural world. The building hummed with technical sounds. The windows did not open to the world outside; only a few potted plants dotted the interior landscape. There were, however, plenty of liquids and solids stored carefully in bottles and jars, all presumably once of natural origin. We saw complex apparatus that could manipulate and measure these chemicals, often at arm's length.

We talked ecology. Chemical facts and concepts were presented sequentially in the lecture hall. It seemed easy to miss how the bits of information were interrelated and how they fit into a broader context. The laboratories seemed equally remote from the real world. Given the isolation, it was easy to understand how scientists might come to believe that their work was objective and value-free. Anything that connected the research to social, industrial, or military applications was simply not visible.

At times, we sounded like philosophers. What was scientific "truth"? We cataloged some of the truths that chemists were likely to teach: The universe is logical and ordered. Chemicals are made up of atoms. They react in predictable, reproducible ways. In essence, a "truth" exists, and chemists believe that they have figured out a good part of it. As far as the students are concerned: "Science is taught—or at least it is heard by students in most introductory courses—as a series of sibylline statements. The professor is not indulging in conjecture; he is telling the truth" (Belenky, Clinchy, Goldberger, & Tarule, 1986, p. 215).

Thus, our explorations of the miniculture of the chemistry department brought forth a number of useful ideas. These were useful as we explored the last of my three questions.

How Well Are You Able to Teach and Learn in Ways That Are Different From Those Commonly Used in Your Discipline?

This was a hard one. Those of us who came together for Chemistry 901 were reasonably expert in the usual ways of teaching and learning chemistry. We all had succeeded (more or less) in the current teaching system. And yet, almost to a person, we believed that there were other ways in which to proceed. We were willing to entertain, even push, the questions of how to change the customary ways of doing things.

To reveal how we might frame chemical knowledge in other ways, I asked the group to return to the question of "researching" the culture of chemistry (see the previous section). Perhaps those from other cultures or learning traditions would approach and carry out this same task very differently. As models, I presented the writings of a Native American woman who contrasted Western with Native science (Spencer, 1990) and of a Japanese man who contrasted Western and Eastern science (Motokawa, 1989).

In her writing, the Native American woman explained first her tribal descent and how she had become responsible for passing along an ancient tradition. She had learned the tradition from her father and explained how, in order to keep things in balance, a man should receive the teachings from a woman, and a woman from a man. She then engaged us with a tale of Hawk and Eagle: "When hunting, Hawk sees Mouse ... and dives directly for it. When hunting, Eagle sees the whole pattern ... sees movement in the general pattern and dives for the movement, learning only later that it is Mouse" (Spencer, 1990, p. 17). Hawk represented the tendency to look at the specific (Western science), and Eagle represented the tendency to look at the whole (indigenous science). Each complemented the other. She presented to us a personal practice called "go-and-be-Eagle." When doing this, she *became* Eagle in her heart and mind and looked at the world from Eagle's perspective. As Eagle, she was able to learn about the world and conceptualize it in new ways.

The Japanese man offered his reflections after having completed a research appointment in the United States. He commented about how he had come to this country believing science to be universal but had left realizing that people from different cultures think in different ways. He engaged us by recounting a tale of "hamburger science" and "sushi science." Hamburger is cooked and seasoned, and the skills of the chef are evident. Sushi is raw fish and seems to require no cooking skill at all. However, real skills are employed on the part of the sushi chef: "Sushi is also great: we taste the materials themselves. Chefs' skills are hidden. They are devoted to keeping the fresh and natural flavor of the materials. These are two different attitudes toward cooking" (Motokawa, 1989, p. 490). Similar to the differences in cooking philosophies, he saw that there were different types of sciences in the world. Western and Eastern science differed in some fundamental premises. He contrasted scientists who advertised "I" and "my something" to those who preferred to keep silent and let nature speak for itself. He contrasted a science of giants and heroes to one that was more modest in scale:

> In the East, mind and body should walk hand in hand. The size of rules and ideas, and thus the size of mind, should match that of body.... The strength of the West and also the problem of the West lie in a habit that people let mind walk far ahead of body. The oversized rules, which are created by oversized minds, are deepening the gap between mind and body. (Motokawa, 1989, p. 499)

From these different perspectives on Western science, Native science, and Eastern science, we approached the "culture of chemistry" for a second time. We began by proposing *how* we might investigate the culture of the chemistry building and its occupants using a different cultural approach. Not unexpectedly, this time our ideas were quite different:

> "I would remove myself from my usual work surroundings in order to more honestly listen to my thoughts and feelings about the culture of science."

> "The observations would be nonintrusive."

> "[I would] observe all night and day to see how the lateness of the day changed things."

> " [I would] sit in on a lecture and 'become' that teacher and those students, ... 'be-

come' that researcher or technician.... I don't feel Westerners have the skills to 'become one' with people, things, or abstractions very effectively. Our intuitive skills have not been honed."

In the process of trying out our ideas, we came to new and sometimes unexpected insights:

> "It's impossible to tell in advance what you will learn, since that depends on what you observe at each stage.... What's different is the placing of the specific phenomena back into the whole rather than saying, 'OK, we understand that now. Let's move on to something else.'"

> "I sensed the need to reclaim space for people in the building. It has little color, texture, light, fresh air. There is a need for space that doesn't belong to something or to someone. I think that we could all teach, learn, and do research better in such an environment."

> "It turned out that I noticed things that I wouldn't have thought of beforehand."

Again, the exercise provided us with a starting point. After engaging ourselves in it, we were better able to see the norms practiced by science as we knew it and to contrast these with the norms more common to indigenous and Eastern science.

Changes in our norms for teaching and learning are not necessarily large or dramatic. As a case in point, I offered a story about a friend of mine who had spent time in Indonesia. She had presented a lecture, after which her host asked the audience if there were any questions. To her surprise, a lengthy silence followed—upwards of 15 minutes— during which time tea was served. Those gathered knew that it took time (and a cup of tea) for people to assimilate the material and come up with good questions.

The period of time allowed for students to come up with questions reflects both how we conceive the questioning process and our social norms for using time. Our teaching repertoire could be increased simply by making changes in how we structure time for generating questions or for a number of other activities. As we make these changes, we might find that our classroom habits change as well, such as any tendencies to favor those who are the quickest to raise their hands or to call on one group of people more than another.

Chemistry, Race, Ethnicity, and Gender

Our class discussions thus far had sought to raise issues and provide us with new information. Together we had examined some of our current practices in teaching and learning, with an eye for how we might change our goals or accomplish them in different ways.

Some of the tasks in being culturally inclusive seemed overwhelming. For example, we noted that we could spend the rest of the semester (if not the rest of our lives) in increasing our cultural knowledge of the students we teach. However, among those gathered for Chemistry 901, I sensed an urgency to move on. *What* were we going to do in the classroom, and *how* were we going to do it?

I shared in their desire to do something. I don't think they realized, however, that I didn't know just what to do. There was no book that I could pull off the shelf to provide step-by-step directions. There was no consensus in the scientific community regarding cultural inclusiveness. It would require all our resources to move ahead.

Although our path was new, there were many who had gone before us. The pioneers had come from a number of disciplines, including women's studies, ethnic studies, mathematics, history of science, curriculum and instruction, sociology, and counseling psychology. The Appendix contains a partial reading list. A number of people in the class commented that some of our texts were "hard

to get through" because of their style or language. In addition, we read several dozen articles and essays.

At this point in the semester, we paused to map out the topics that we wanted to discuss in the coming months. Our list was ambitious: the curriculum, textbooks, laboratory, evaluation, grading, and teaching and learning styles. Three of our discussions are summarized in the sections that follow.

Curriculum

We began with the concept of metaphor, that is, the idea that something is like something else. We noted the metaphors in our language. For example a person might come through the academic "pipeline" and "climb a career ladder," only to hit a "glass ceiling." Metaphor is more than just a part of our language; it is part of our very thoughts and lives. Metaphor affects "how we perceive, how we think and what we do" (Lakoff & Johnson, 1980, p. 4). Thus, in a real sense, the metaphor becomes the reality.

The metaphors that we hold as educators affect the curriculum, its outcomes, and our role as teachers. We worked in groups to expose some of our underlying metaphors. For example, were schools like factories? Was teaching like a mother robin feeding her young? Was learning like being the captain of the starship *Enterprise*, exploring new worlds and going where no person had gone before?

For the sake of discussion, we picked two metaphors: chemistry as "a terrain to be covered," and the chemistry curriculum as a "bus tour"—specifically, a six-day, 30-country bus tour of Europe. We asked what we might like to change about these metaphors. In the case of "chemistry as a terrain," our answers included filling in some of the potholes, removing some of the land mines, teaching the skill of map reading, setting up a first-aid station, and bringing along a geologist. For the curriculum as a "bus tour," we suggested passing through only one time zone in a day, having breaks for recreation, taking turns driving, traveling on some unplanned routes, and even getting off the bus.

Our metaphors also helped us raise questions. For example, what if we journeyed only as fast as the slowest person? What were the responsibilities of the passengers? Were there other ways to travel? Who was the driver? Which metaphors involved groups and which were individual? Depending on our metaphors, we could see that we would teach differently and would expect different outcomes.

Textbooks

We began by posing a number of questions: Could we teach without a textbook? What kind of textbook (and process of using a textbook) would be ideal for culturally inclusive chemistry? What if the students chose the textbook? How much does the textbook matter? What do the students really do with their textbooks anyway?

We discussed how novels and biographies can add "the human element" to topics in the course. Each of us brought to class a title for possible inclusion in a general chemistry course. Included in our list were *Hiroshima* by John Hersey (human chronicle of the days before and after the bomb dropped), *What Do You Care What Other People Think?* by Richard Feynman (includes a description of the *Challenger* investigation), *Clan of the Cave Bear* by Jean Auel (primitive technologies and natural products chemistry), and *The Mysterious Affair at Styles* by Agatha Christie (a strychnine whodunit) (Southward, Hollis, & Thompson, 1992).

We looked at a preprint of an undergraduate textbook that will use case studies of current issues (in their social, economic, and political context) to introduce topics in general chemistry (Schwartz et al., 1993), and some of us attended a seminar by a member of its editorial board. We wondered whether the textbooks available were driving the courses we would teach, or vice versa. Just after our discussion, a science editor from the publishing industry stopped by my office. She will participate in our discussion next year.

Evaluation

Predictably, questions came up about tests and grading. One of the avenues we explored for evaluation was take-home test questions. We raised issues such as who would write the questions and what types of questions would be useful. We also wanted to know how to easily generate take-home questions, since after the first year, the answers would be at large on campus.

As mentioned earlier, we thought it important that students generate (and answer) their own questions. This would serve many purposes: It would provide practice in posing questions, involve students in their own learning, generate ideas for course content, and, for us instructors, provide a window into the world of our students.

I shared with the class a recent experience. I had come across the statistic that the rainfall on some mountain slopes in Hawaii may exceed 50 feet annually. *Fifty feet of rain a year?* This was inconceivable to me. How many inches was this in a month? In a day? As I was making meaning for myself out of the numbers, I realized that I was doing "conversion factor problems," as we call them in chemistry. More important, these were my problems. I was conceiving and answering them on the spot. I came up with other questions that were harder to answer. Where did all the rain go? What was it like to live there? Was agriculture possible? I found myself wondering what questions our students would ask, given the opportunities.

In Chemistry 901, we tried to find materials that would spark questions from a wide variety of students. Intriguing facts and figures (such as the 50 feet of rain a year) could be taken from different kinds of almanacs. As a class, we worked for a while on a geographer's map that showed the countries from which we imported strategic materials. Using this map, we were able to frame some generic questions: What if we could no longer import element X from country Y? How do we use element Z, and how might we recycle it? What if we ran out of element Q on our planet? Questions such as these could be used year after year, each time substituting a different geographic region or chemical element. Such choices could be made by individual students, the class as a whole, or the instructor.

Conclusion

Sixteen weeks later, summer was upon us. The semester was ending far before we were ready to: We had no definitive answers, and we had no finished product in our hands. The final word had not been written. Nor should it have been.

What we had learned and experienced in our weeks together was a *process*. We had drawn upon the resources of each individual. We had utilized the strengths of large and small groups. We had raised questions and then refined them. We had noticed some things that were missing. We had argued and discussed and changed our minds and sometimes changed them again. We had allowed for differences and sought commonalities. We had both invited others to come to us and gone to them. We had crossed disciplinary and cultural lines. In short, we had been willing to experiment in a number of different ways.

Rather than finding answers, I believe that we ended up with a better set of questions. I also believe that we shared among ourselves and with others a common hope: "By listening more diligently to what non-traditional voices can tell them, scientists may discover new ways of thinking about, looking at, or solving old problems" (Frankel, 1993, p. B1).

Notes

1. This graduate course was first offered in 1992 as Race and Ethnicity in the Teaching of Chemistry (1 credit) and was jointly taught with John Moore and Brenda Pfaehler. This chapter presents a composite version of the first two years of the course.

2. Asian Americans: Probing the Past, Living the Present, Shaping the Future, University of Wisconsin–LaCrosse, March 25–27, 1993.

3. *After the war: A family album* [Videotape]. Newist, CESA #7 Telecommunications, IS 1110, University of Wisconsin–Green Bay, Green Bay, WI 54301.

Appendix: Selected Readings from Chemistry 901

Adams, M. (Ed.). *Promoting diversity in college classrooms.* (1992). New Directions for Teaching and Learning, No. 52. San Francisco: Jossey-Bass.

Banks, J. A., & Banks, C. A. (1993). *Multicultural education: Issues and perspectives.* Boston: Allyn and Bacon.

Border, L. L., & Van Notechism, N. (Eds.). *Teaching for diversity.* (1992). New Directions for Teaching and Learning, No. 49. San Francisco: Jossey-Bass.

Bowers, C. A. (1988). *The cultural dimensions of educational computing.* New York: Teachers College Press.

D'Souza, D. (1991). *Illiberal education: The politics of race and sex on campus.* New York: Vintage Books.

Harding, S. (1991). *Whose science? whose knowledge?* Ithaca, NY: Cornell University Press.

Koshland, D. E., Jr. Minorities in science, science: The pipeline problem. (1992). *Science, 258,* 1057–1276.

Lemke, J. L. (1990). *Talking science: Language, learning and values.* Norwood, NJ: Ablex.

Rosser, S. V. (1990). *Female-friendly science.* Elmsford, NY: Pergamon Press.

Scarcella, R. (1990). *Teaching language minority students in the multicultural class*room. Englewood Cliffs, NJ: Prentice-Hall.

Tobias, S. (1990). *They're not dumb, they're different.* Tucson, AZ: Research Corporation.

Watzlawick, P., Weakland, J., & Fisch, R. (1974). *Change: Principles of problem formation and problem resolution.* New York: W. W. Norton.

Women in science '93: Gender & culture. (1993). *Science, 260,* 265–460.

References

Belenky, Mary, Clinchy, Blythe, Goldberger, Nancy, & Tarule, Jill. (1986). *Women's ways of knowing.* New York: Basic Books.

Bowen, Craig W. (1992). Myths and metaphors: Their influence on chemistry instruction. *Journal of Chemical Education, 69(6)*, 479–482.

Bullivant, Brian M. (1993). Culture: Its nature and meaning for educators. In James A. Banks & Cherry A. Banks (Eds.), *Multicultural education* (pp. 29-47). Boston: Allyn & Bacon.

Frankel, Mark. (1993, November 10). Multicultural science. *Chronicle of Higher Education, 40* (12), B1–2.

Ganem, Bruce. (1993, February). Yipes, stripes, scientists got 'em. *Cornell Alumni News*, 10.

Gordon, Edmund, Miller, Fayneese, & Rollock, David. (1990). Coping with communicentric bias in knowledge production in the social sciences. *Educational Researcher, 19(3)*, 14–16.

Kean, Elizabeth, & Tate, Maurice. (1991). Enhancing teachers' abilities to teach multiculturally. Fourth National Conference on Race & Ethnicity in American Higher Education, San Antonio, TX, May 31–June 4.

Lakoff, George, & Johnson, Mark. (1980). *Metaphors we live by*. Chicago: University of Chicago Press.

Middlecamp, Catherine H., & Moore, John. (1994). Race and ethnicity in the teaching of chemistry: A new graduate seminar. *Journal of Chemical Education, 71*, 288–291.

Motokawa, Tatsuo. (1989). Sushi science and hamburger science. *Perspectives in Biology and Medicine, 12*(4), 489–504.

Rodrigues, Richard. (1992, April 29). Rethinking the cultures of disciplines. *Chronicle of Higher Education, 38*(33), B1.

Roop, Peter, & Roop, Connie. (1991). *The Hmong in America: We sought refuge here*, Appleton, WI: Appleton Area School District.

Schwartz, A. Truman, Bunce, Diane, Silberman, Robert, Stanitski, Conrad, Stratton, Wilmer, & Zipp, Arden. (1993). *Chemistry in context*. Dubuque, IA: Wm. C. Brown.

Sims, C. (1992). What went wrong: Why programs failed. *Science, 258*, 1185–1187.

Southward, Robin, Hollis, W. Gary, & Thompson, David. (1992). Precipitation of a murder. *Journal of Chemical Education, 69*, 536–537.

Spencer, Paula. (1990). A Native American worldview. *Noetic Sciences Review, 15*, 14–20.

Suzuki, B. H. (1989). Asian Americans as the "model minority." *Change, 21*, 13-15.

Tilghman, Shirley. (1993, January 26). Science vs. women—a radical solution. *New York Times*, A23.

Watzlawick, Paul, Weakland, John H., & Fisch, Richard. (1974). *Change: Principles of problem formation and problem resolution*. New York: W. W. Norton.

A World of Difference

Evelyn Fox Keller

O Lady! We receive but what we give,
And in our life alone does Nature live:
Ours is her wedding garment, ours her
shroud!

Samuel Taylor Coleridge,
"Dejection: An Ode"

If we want to think about the ways in which science might be different, we could hardly find a more appropriate guide than Barbara McClintock. Known to her colleagues as a maverick and a visionary, McClintock occupies a place in the history of genetics at one and the same time central and peripheral—a place that, for all its eminence, is marked by difference at every turn.

Born in 1902, McClintock began in her twenties to make contributions to classical genetics and cytology that earned her a level of recognition few women of her generation could imagine. Encouraged and supported by many of the great men of classical genetics (including T. H. Morgan, R. A. Emerson, and Lewis Stadler), McClintock was given the laboratory space and fellowship stipends she needed to pursue what had quickly become the central goal of her life: understanding the secrets of plant genetics. She rejected the more conventional opportunities then available to women in science (such as a research assistantship or a teaching post at a woman's college)* and devoted herself to the life of pure research. By the mid 1930s, she had already made an indelible mark on the history of genetics. But the fellowships inevitably ran out. With no job on the horizon, McClintock thought she would have to leave science. Morgan and Emerson, arguing that "it would be a scientific tragedy if her work did not go forward" (quoted in Keller 1983, p. 74), prevailed

*For an excellent overview of the opportunities available to women scientists in the 1920's and 1930's, see Rossiter 1982.

upon the Rockefeller Foundation to provide two years interim support. Morgan described her as "the best person in the world" in her field but deplored her "personality difficulties": "She is sore at the world because of her conviction that she would have a much freer scientific opportunity if she were a man" (p. 73). Not until 1942 was McClintock's professional survival secured: at that time, a haven was provided for her at the Carnegie Institution of Washington at Cold Spring Harbor, where she has remained ever since. Two years later she was elected to the National Academy of Science; in 1945 she became president of the Genetics Society of America.

This dual theme of success and marginality that poignantly describes the first stage of McClintock's career continues as the leitmotif of her entire professional life. Despite the ungrudging respect and admiration of her colleagues, her most important work has, until recently, gone largely unappreciated, uncomprehended, and almost entirely unintegrated into the growing corpus of biological thought. This was the work, begun in her forties, that led to her discovery that genetic elements can move, in an apparently coordinated way from one chromosomal site to another—in short, her discovery of genetic transposition. Even today, as a Nobel laureate and deluged with other awards and prizes for this same work, McClintock regards herself as, in crucial respects, an outsider to the world of modern biology—not because she is a woman but because she is a philosophical and methodological deviant.

No doubt, McClintock's marginality and deviance is more visible—and seems more dramatic—to her than to others. During the many years when McClintock's professional survival seemed so precarious, even her most devoted colleagues seemed unaware that she had no proper job, "What do you mean?," many of them asked me. "She was so good!

How could she not have had a job?" Indeed, as Morgan himself suggested, her expectation that she would be rewarded on the basis of merit, on the same footing as her male colleagues, was itself read as a mark of her ingratitude—of what he called her "personality difficulties."

When discussing the second stage of her career, during which her revolutionary work on genetic transposition earned her the reputation more of eccentricity than of greatness, her colleagues are likely to focus on the enduring admiration many of them continued to feel. She, of course, is more conscious of their lack of comprehension and of the dismissal of her work by other, less admiring, colleagues. She is conscious, above all, of the growing isolation that ensued.

Today, genetic transposition is no longer a dubious or isolated phenomenon. As one prominent biologist describes it, "[Transposable elements] are everywhere, in bacteria, yeast, *Drosophila*, and plants. Perhaps even in mice and men," (Marx 1981, quoted in Keller 1983, p. 193). But the significance of transposition remains in considerable dispute. McClintock saw transposable elements as a key to developmental regulation; molecular biologists today, although much more sympathetic to this possibility than they were twenty, or even ten, years ago, are still unsure. And in evolutionary terms, McClintock's view of transposition as a survival mechanism available to the organism in times of stress seems to most (although not to all) pure heresy.

My interest here, as it has been from the beginning, is less on who was "right" than on the differences in perceptions that underlay such a discordance of views. The vicissitudes of McClintock's career give those differences not only special poignancy but special importance. In *A Feeling for the Organism: The Life and Work of Barbara McClintock* (Keller 1983), I argued that it is precisely the duality of success and marginality that lends her career its significance to the history and philosophy of science. Her success indisputably affirms her legitimacy as a scientist, while her marginality provides an opportunity to examine the role and fate of dissent in the growth of scientific knowledge. This duality illustrates the diversity of values, methodological styles, and goals that, to varying degrees, always exists in science; at the same time, it illustrates the pressures that, to equally varying degrees, operate to contain that diversity.

In the preface to that book (p. xii), I wrote:

The story of Barbara McClintock allows us to explore the condition under which dissent in science arises, the function it serves, and the plurality of values and goals it reflects. It makes us ask: What role do interests, individual and collective, play in the evolution of scientific knowledge? Do all scientists seek the same kinds of explanations? Are the kinds of questions they ask the same? Do differences in methodology between different subdisciplines even permit the same kinds of answers? And when significant differences do arise in questions asked, explanations sought, methodologies employed, how do they affect communication between scientists? In short, why could McClintock's discovery of transposition not be absorbed by her contemporaries? We can say that her vision of biological organization was too remote from the kinds of explanations her colleagues were seeking, but we need to understand what that distance is composed of, and how such divergences develop.

I chose, in effect, not to read the story of McClintock's career as a romance—neither as "a tale of dedication rewarded after years of neglect—of prejudice or indifference eventually routed by courage and truth" (p. xii), nor as a heroic story of the scientist, years "ahead of her time," stumbling on something approximating what we now know as "the truth." Instead, I read it as a story about the languages of science—about the process by which worlds of common scientific discourse become established, effectively bounded, and yet at the same time remain sufficiently permeable to allow a given piece of work to pass from incomprehensibility in one era to acceptance (if not full comprehensibility) in another.

In this essay, my focus is even more explicitly on difference itself. I want to isolate McClintock's views of nature, of science, and of the relation between mind and nature, in order to exhibit not only their departure from more conventional views but also their own internal coherence. If we can stand inside this world view, the questions she asks, the explanations she seeks, and the methods she employs in her pursuit of scientific knowledge will take on a degree of clarity and comprehensibility they lack from outside. And at the heart of this world view lies the same respect for difference that motivates us to examine it in the first place. I begin therefore with a discussion of the implications of respect for difference (and complexity) in the general philosophy expressed in McClintock's testimony, and continue by discussing its implications for cognition and perception, for her interests as a geneticist, and for the relation between her work and molecular biology. I conclude the essay with a brief analysis of the relevance of gender to any philosophy of difference, and to McClintock's in particular.

Complexity and Difference

To McClintock, nature is characterized by an a priori complexity that vastly exceeds the capacities of the human imagination. Her recurrent remark, "Anything you can think of you will find,"* is a statement about the capacities not of mind but of nature. It is meant not as a description of our own ingenuity as discoverers but as a comment on the resourcefulness of natural order; in the sense not so much of adaptability as of largesse and prodigality. Organisms have a life and an order of their own that scientists

*All quotations from Barbara McClintock are taken from private interviews conducted between September 24, 1978, and February 25, 1979; most of them appear in Keller 1983.

can only begin to fathom. "Misrepresented, not appreciated, ... [they] are beyond our wildest expectations.... They do everything we [can think of], they do it better, more efficiently, more marvelously." In comparison with the ingenuity of nature, our scientific intelligence seems pallid. It follows as a matter of course that "trying to make everything fit into set dogma won't work.... There's no such thing as a central dogma into which everything will fit."

In the context of McClintock's views of nature, attitudes about research that would otherwise sound romantic fall into logical place. The need to "listen to the material" follows from her sense of the order of things. Precisely because the complexity of nature exceeds our own imaginative possibilities, it becomes essential to "let the experiment tell you what to do." Her major criticism of contemporary research is based on what she sees as inadequate humility. She feels that "much of the work done is done because one wants to impose an answer on it—they have the answer ready, and they [know what] they want the material to tell them, so anything it doesn't tell them, they don't really recognize as there, or they think it's a mistake and throw it out.... If you'd only just let the material tell you."

Respect for complexity thus demands from observers of nature the same special attention to the exceptional case that McClintock's own example as a scientist demands from observers of science: "If the material tells you, 'It may be this,' allow that. Don't turn it aside and call it an exception, an aberration, a contaminant.... That's what's happened all the way along the line with so many good clues."

Indeed, respect for individual difference lies at the very heart of McClintock's scientific passion. "The important thing is to develop the capacity to see one kernel [of maize] that is different, and make that understandable," she says. "If [something] doesn't fit, there's a reason, and you find out what it is." The prevailing focus on classes and numbers, McClintock believes, encourages researchers to overlook difference, to "call it an exception, an aberration, a contaminant." The consequences of this seem to her very costly. "Right and left," she says, they miss "what is going on."

She is, in fact, here describing the history of her own research. Her work on transposition in fact began with the observation of an aberrant pattern of pigmentation on a few kernels of a single corn plant. And her commitment to the significance of this singular pattern sustained her through six years of solitary and arduous investigation—all aimed at making the difference she saw understandable.

Making difference understandable does not mean making it disappear. In McClintock's world view, an understanding of nature can come to rest with difference. "Exceptions" are not there to "prove the rule"; they have meaning in and of themselves. In this respect, difference constitutes a principle for ordering the world radically unlike the principle of division of dichotomization (subject-object, mind-matter, feeling-reason, disorder-law). Whereas these oppositions are directed toward a cosmic unity typically excluding or devouring one of the pair, toward a unified, all-encompassing law, respect for difference remains content with multiplicity as an end in itself.

And just as the terminus of knowledge implied by difference can be distinguished from that implied by division, so the starting point of knowledge can also be distinguished. Above all, difference, in this world view, does not posit division as an epistemological prerequisite—it does not imply the necessity of hard and fast divisions in nature, or in mind, or in the relation between mind and nature. Division severs connection and imposes distance; the recognition of difference provides a starting point for relatedness. It serves both as a clue to new modes of connectedness in nature, and as an invitation to engagement with nature. For McClintock, certainly, respect for difference serves both these functions. Seeing something that does not appear to fit is, to her, a challenge to find the larger

multidimensional pattern into which it does fit. Anomalous kernels of corn were evidence not of disorder or lawlessness, but of a larger system of order, one that cannot be reduced to a single law.

Difference thus invites a form of engagement and understanding that allows for the preservation of the individual. The integrity of each kernel (or chromosome or plant) survives all our own pattern-making attempts; the order of nature transcends our capacities for ordering. And this transcendence is manifested in the enduring uniqueness of each organism: "No two plants are exactly alike. They're all different, and as a consequence, you have to know that difference," she explains. "I start with the seedling, and I don't want to leave it. I don't feel I really know the story if I don't watch the plant all the way along. So I know every plant in the field. I know them intimately and I find it a great pleasure to know them." From days, weeks, and years of patient observation comes what looks like privileged insight: "When I see things, I can interpret them right away." As one colleague described it, the result is an apparent ability to write the "autobiography" of every plant she works with.

McClintock is not here speaking of relations to other humans, but the parallels are nonetheless compelling. In the relationship she describes with plants, as in human relations, respect for difference constitutes a claim not only on our interest but on our capacity for empathy—in short on the highest form of love: love that allows for intimacy without the annihilation of difference. I use the word *love* neither loosely nor sentimentally, but out of fidelity to the language McClintock herself uses to describe a form of attention, indeed a form of thought. Her vocabulary is consistently a vocabulary of affection, of kinship, of empathy. Even with puzzles, she explains, "The thing was dear to you for a period of time, you really had an affection for it. Then after a while, it disappears and it doesn't bother you. But for a short time you feel strongly attached to that little toy." The crucial point for us is that McClintock can risk the suspension of boundaries between subject and object without jeopardy to science precisely because, to her, science is not premised on that division. Indeed, the intimacy she experiences with the objects she studies—intimacy born of a lifetime of cultivated attentiveness—is a wellspring of her powers as a scientist.

The most vivid illustration of this process comes from her own account of a breakthrough in one particularly recalcitrant piece of cytological analysis. She describes the state of mind accompanying the crucial shift in orientation that enabled her to identify chromosomes she had earlier not been able to distinguish: "I found that the more I worked with them, the bigger and bigger [the chromosomes] got, and when I was really working with them I wasn't outside, I was down there. I was part of the system. I was right down there with them, and everything got big. I even was able to see the internal parts of the chromosomes—actually everything was there. It surprised me because I actually felt as if I was right down there and these were my friends. ... As you look at these things, they become part of you. And you forget yourself."

Cognition and Perception

In this world of difference, division is relinquished without generating chaos. Self and other, mind and nature survive not in mutual alienation, or in symbiotic fusion, but in structural integrity. The "feeling for the organism" that McClintock upholds as the sine qua non of good research need not be read as "participation mystique"; it is a mode of access—honored by time and human experience if not by prevailing conventions in science—to the reliable knowledge of the world around us that all scientists seek. It is a form of attention strongly reminiscent of the concept of "focal attention" developed by Ernest Schachtel to designate "man's [*sic*] capacity to *center* his attention on an object fully, so that he can perceive or understand it from *many sides*, as fully as possible" (p. 251). In Schachtel's language, "focal attention" is the principal tool that, in conjunction with our natural interest in objects per se, enables us to progress from mere wishing and wanting to thinking and knowing—that equips us for the fullest possible knowledge of reality in its own terms. Such "object-centered" perception ... presupposes "a temporary eclipse of all the perceiver's egocentric thoughts and strivings, of all preoccupation with self and self-esteem, and a full turning towards the object, ... [which, in turn] leads not to a *loss* of self, but to a heightened feeling of aliveness" (p. 181). Object-centered perception, Schachtel goes on to argue, is in the service of a love "which wants to affirm others in their total and unique being ... [which affirms objects as] "part of the same world of which man is a part" (p. 226). It requires

> an experiential realization of the kinship between oneself and the other ... a realization [that] is made difficult by fear and by arrogance—by fear because then the need to protect oneself by flight, appeasement, or attack gets in the way; by arrogance because then the other is no longer experienced as akin, but as inferior to oneself. (p. 227)

The difference between Schachtel and McClintock is that what Schachtel grants to the poet's perceptual style in contrast to that of the scientist, McClintock claims equally for science. She enlists a "feeling for the organism"—not only for living organisms but for any object that fully claims our attention—in pursuit of the goal shared by all scientists: reliable (that is, shareable and reproducible) knowledge of natural order.

This difference is a direct reflection of the limitations of Schachtel's picture of science. It is drawn not from observation of scientists like McClintock but only from the more stereotypic scientist, who "looks at the object with one or more hypotheses ... in mind and thus 'uses' the object to corroborate or disprove a hypothesis, but does not encounter the object as such, in its own fullness," For Schachtel,

> modern natural science has as its main goal prediction, i.e. the power to manipulate objects in such a way that certain predicted events will happen.... Hence, the scientist usually will tend to perceive the object merely from the perspective of [this] power.... That is to say that his view of the object will be determined by the ends which he pursues in his experimentation.... He may achieve a great deal in this way and add important data to our knowledge, but to the extent to which he remains within the framework of this perspective he will not perceive the object in its own right. (1959, p. 171)

To McClintock, science has a different goal; not prediction per se, but understanding; not the power to manipulate, but empowerment—the kind of power that results from an understanding of the world around us, that simultaneously reflects and affirms our connection to that world.

What Counts as Knowledge

At the root of this difference between McClintock and the stereotypic scientist lies that unexamined starting point of science: the naming of nature. Underlying every discussion of science, as well as every scientific discussion, there exists a larger assumption about the nature of the universe in which that discussion takes place. The power of this unseen ground is to be found not in its influence on any particular argument in science but in its framing of the very terms of argument—in its definition of the tacit aims and goals of science. As I noted in the introduction to this section, scientists may spend fruitful careers, building theories of nature that are astonishingly successful in their predictive power, without ever feeling the need to reflect

on these fundamental philosophical issues. Yet if we want to ask questions about that success, about the value of alternative scientific descriptions of nature, even about the possibility of alternative criteria of success, we can do so only by examining those most basic assumptions that are normally not addressed.

We have to remind ourselves that, although all scientists share a common ambition for knowledge, it does not follow that what counts as knowledge is commonly agreed upon: The history of science reveals a wide diversity of questions asked, explanations sought, and methodologies employed in this common quest for knowledge of the natural world; this diversity is in turn reflected in the kinds of knowledge acquired, and indeed in what counts as knowledge. To a large degree, both the kinds of questions one asks and the explanations that one finds satisfying depend on one's a priori relation to the objects of study. In particular, I am suggesting that questions asked about objects with which one feels kinship are likely to differ from questions asked about objects one sees as unalterably alien. Similarly, explanations that satisfy us about a natural world that is seen as "blind, simple and dumb," ontologically inferior, may seem less self-evidently satisfying for a natural world seen as complex and, itself, resourceful. I suggest that individual and communal conceptions of nature need to be examined for their role in the history of science, not as causal determinants but as frameworks upon which all scientific programs are developed. More specifically, I am claiming that the difference between McClintock's conception of nature and that prevailing in the community around her is an essential key to our understanding of the history of her life and work.

It provides, for example, the context for examining the differences between McClintock's interests *as a geneticist* and what has historically been the defining focus of both classical and molecular genetics—differences crucial to the particular route her research took. To most geneticists, the problem of inheritance is solved by knowing the mechanism and structure of genes. To McClintock, however, as to many other biologists, mechanism and structure have never been adequate answers to the question "How do genes work?" Her focus was elsewhere: on function and organization. To her, an adequate understanding would, by definition, have to include an account of how they function in relation to the rest of the cell, and, of course, to the organism as a whole.

In her language, the cell itself is an organism. Indeed, "Every component of the organism is as much an organism as every other part." When she says, therefore, that "one cannot consider the [gene] as such as being all important—more important is the overall organism," she means the genome as a whole, the cell, the ensemble of cells, the organism itself. Genes are neither "beads on a string" nor functionally disjoint pieces of DNA. They are organized functional units, whose very function is defined by their position in the organization as a whole. As she says, genes function "only with respect to the environment in which [they are] found."

Interests in function and in organization are historically and conceptually related to each other. By tradition, both are primary preoccupations of developmental biology, and McClintock's own interest in development followed from and supported these interests. By the same tradition, genetics and developmental biology have been two separate subjects. But for a geneticist for whom the answer to the question of how genes work must include function and organization, the problem of heredity becomes inseparable from the problem of development. The division that most geneticists felt they had to live with (happily or not) McClintock could not accept. To her, development, as the coordination of function, was an integral part of genetics.

McClintock's views today are clearly fed by her work on transposition. But her work on transposition was itself fed by these interests. Her own account (see Keller 1983, pp. 115–17) of how she came to this work and of how she followed the clues she saw

vividly illustrates the ways in which her interests in function and organization—and in development—focused her attention on the patterns she saw and framed the questions she asked about the significance of these patterns. I suggest that they also defined the terms that a satisfying explanation had to meet.

Such an explanation had to account not so much for how transposition occurred, as for why it occurred. The patterns she saw indicated a programmatic disruption in normal developmental function. When she succeeded in linking this disruption to the location (and change in location) of particular genetic elements, that very link was what captured her interest. (She knew she was "on to something important.") The fact that transposition occurred—the fact that genetic sequences are not fixed—was of course interesting too, but only secondarily so. To her, the paramount interest lay in the meaning of its occurrence, in the clue that transposition provided for the relation between genetics and development. Necessarily, a satisfying account of this relation would have to take due note of the complexity of the regulation process.

Transposition and the Central Dogma

Just two years after McClintock's first public presentation of her work on transposition came the culminating event in the long search for the mechanism of inheritance. Watson and Crick's discovery of the structure of DNA enabled them to provide a compelling account of the essential genetic functions of replication and instruction. According to their account, the vital information of the cell is encoded in the DNA. From there it is copied onto the RNA, which, in turn, is used as a blueprint for the production of the proteins responsible for genetic traits. In the picture that emerged—DNA to RNA to protein (which Crick himself dubbed the "central dogma")—the DNA is posited as the central actor in the cell, the executive governor of cellular organization, itself remaining impervious to influence from the subordinate agents to which it dictates. Several years later, Watson and Crick's original model was emended by Jacques Monod and François Jacob) to allow for environmental control of the rates of protein synthesis. But even with this modification, the essential autonomy of DNA remained unchallenged: information flowed one way, always from, and never to, the DNA.

Throughout the 1950s and 1960s, the successes of molecular genetics were dramatic. By the end of the 1960s, it was possible to say (as Jacques Monod did say), "The Secret of Life? But this is in large part known—in principle, if not in details" (quoted in Judson 1979, p. 216). A set of values and interests wholly different from McClintock's seemed to have been vindicated. The intricacies, and difficulties, of corn genetics held little fascination in comparison with the quick returns from research on the vastly simpler and seemingly more straightforward bacterium and bacteriophage. As a result, communication between McClintock and her colleagues grew steadily more difficult; fewer and fewer biologists had the expertise required even to begin to understand her results.

McClintock of course shared in the general excitement of this period, but she did not share in the general enthusiasm for the central dogma. The same model that seemed so immediately and overwhelmingly satisfying to so many of her colleagues did not satisfy her. Although duly impressed by its explanatory power, she remained at the same time acutely aware of what it did not explain. It neither addressed the questions that were of primary interest to her—bearing on the relation between genetics and development—nor began to take into account the complexity of genetic organization that she had always assumed, and that was now revealed to her by her work on transposition.

McClintock locates the critical flaw of the central dogma in its presumption: it claimed to explain too much. Baldly put, what was true of *E. coli* (the bacterium most commonly studied) was not true of the elephant, as Monod (and others) would have had it (Judson 1979. p. 613). Precisely because higher organisms are multicellular, she argued, they necessarily require a different kind of economy. The central dogma was without question inordinately successful as well as scientifically productive. Yet the fact that it ultimately proved inadequate even to the dynamics of *E. coli* suggests that its trouble lay deeper than just a too hasty generalization from the simple to the complex; its presumptuousness, I suggest, was built into its form of explanation.

The central dogma is a good example of what I have earlier called (following Nanney 1957) master-molecule theories (Keller 1982). In locating the seat of genetic control in a single molecule, it posits a structure of genetic organization that is essentially hierarchical, often illustrated in textbooks by organizational charts like those of corporate structures. In this model, genetic stability is ensured by the unidirectionality of information flow, much as political and social stability is assumed in many quarters to require the unidirectional exercise of authority.

To McClintock, transposition provided evidence that genetic organization is necessarily more complex, and in fact more globally interdependent, than such a model assumes. It showed that the DNA itself is subject to rearrangement and, by implication, to reprogramming. Although she did not make the suggestion explicit, the hidden heresy of her argument lay in the inference that such reorganization could be induced by signals external to the DNA—from the cell, the organism, even from the environment.

For more than fifty years, modern biologists had labored heroically to purge biological thought of the last vestiges of teleology, particularly as they surfaced in Lamarckian notions of adaptive evolution. But even though McClintock is not a Lamarckian, she sees in transposition a mechanism enabling genetic structures to respond to the needs of the organism. Since needs are relative to the environmental context and hence subject to change, transposition, by implication, indirectly allows for the possibility of environmentally induced and genetically transmitted change. To her, such a possibility is not heresy—it is not even surprising. On the contrary, it is in direct accord with her belief in the resourcefulness of the natural order. Because she has no investment in the passivity of nature, the possibility of internally generated order does not, to her, threaten the foundations of science. The capacity of organisms to reprogram their own DNA implies neither vitalism, magic, nor a countermanding will. It merely confirms the existence of forms of order more complex than we have, at least thus far, been able to account for.

The renewed interest in McClintock's work today is a direct consequence of developments (beginning in the early 1970s) in the very research programs that had seemed so philosophically opposed to her position; genetic mobility was rediscovered within molecular biology itself. That this was so was crucial, perhaps even necessary, to establishing the legitimacy of McClintock's early work, precisely because the weight of scientific authority has now come to reside in molecular biology. As a by-product, this legitimization also lends McClintock's views of science and attitudes toward research somewhat more credibility among professional biologists. To observers of science, this same historical sequence serves as a sharp reminder that the languages of science, however self-contained they seem, are not closed. McClintock's

> eventual vindication demonstrates the capacity of science to overcome its own characteristic kinds of myopia, reminding us that its limitations do not reinforce themselves indefinitely. Their own methodology, allows, even obliges, scientists to continually reencounter phenomena even their best theories cannot accommodate. Or—to look at it from the other side—however severely communication between science and nature may be impeded by the preconceptions of a particular time, some

channels always remain open; and, through them, nature finds ways of reasserting itself. (Keller 1983, p. 197)

In this sense, the McClintock story is a happy one.

It is important, however, not to overestimate the degree of rapprochement that has taken place. McClintock has been abundantly vindicated: transposition is acknowledged, higher organisms and development have once again captured the interest of biologists, and almost everyone agrees that genetic organization is manifestly more complex than had previously been thought. But not everyone shares her conviction that we are in the midst of a revolution that "will reorganize the way we look at things, the way we do research." Many researchers remain confident that the phenomenon of transposition can somehow be incorporated, even if they do not yet see how, into an improved version of the central dogma. Their attachment to this faith is telling. Behind the continuing skepticism about McClintock's interpretation of the role of transposition in development and evolution, there remains a major gap between her underlying interests and commitments and those of most of her colleagues.

The Issue of Gender

How much of this enduring difference reflects the fact that McClintock is a woman in a field still dominated by men? To what extent are her views indicative of a vision of "what will happen to science," as Erik Erikson asked in 1964 (1965, p. 243), "if and when women are truly represented in it—not by a few glorious exceptions, but in the rank and file of the scientific elite?"

On the face of it, it would be tempting indeed to call McClintock's vision of science "a feminist science." Its emphasis on intuition, on feeling, on connection and relatedness, all seem to confirm our most familiar stereotypes of women. And to the extent that they do, we might expect that the sheer presence of more women in science would shift the balance of community sentiment and lead to the endorsement of that vision. However, there are both general and particular reasons that argue strongly against this simple view.

The general argument is essentially the same as that which I [have] made against the notion of "a different science."... To the extent that science is defined by its past and present practitioners, anyone who aspires to membership in that community must conform to its existing code. As a consequence, the inclusion of new members, even from a radically different culture, cannot induce immediate or direct change. To be a successful scientist, one must first be adequately socialized. For this reason, it is unreasonable to expect a sharp differentiation between women scientists and their male colleagues, and indeed, most women scientists would be appalled by such a suggestion.

McClintock is in this sense no exception. She would disclaim any analysis of her work as a woman's work, as well as any suggestion that her views represent a woman's perspective. To her, science is not a matter of gender, either male or female; it is, on the contrary, a place where (ideally at least) "the matter of gender drops away." Furthermore, her very commitment to science is of a piece with her lifelong wish to transcend gender altogether. Indeed, her adamant rejection of female stereotypes seems to have been a prerequisite for her becoming a scientist at all. (See Keller 1983, chaps. 2 and 3.) In her own image of herself, she is a maverick in all respects—as a woman, as a scientist, even as a woman scientist.

Finally, I want to reemphasize that it would be not only misleading but actually contradictory to suggest that McClintock's views of science were shared by none of her colleagues. Had that been so, she could not have had even marginal status as a scientist. It is essential to understand that, in practice, the scientific tradition is far more pluralistic than any particular description of it suggests, and certainly more pluralistic than its dominant ideology.

For McClintock to be recognized as a scientist, the positions that she represents, however unrepresentative, had to be, and were, identifiable as belonging somewhere within that tradition.

But although McClintock is not a total outsider to science, she is equally clearly not an insider. And however atypical she is as a woman, what she is *not* is a man. Between these two facts lies a crucial connection—a connection signaled by the recognition that, as McClintock herself admits, the matter of gender never does drop away.

I suggest that the radical core of McClintock's stance can be located right here: Because she is not a man, in a world of men, her commitment to a gender-free science has been binding; because concepts of gender have so deeply influenced the basic categories of science, that commitment has been transformative. In short, the relevance of McClintock's gender in this story is to be found not in its role in her personal socialization but precisely in the role of gender in the construction of science.

Of course, not all scientists have embraced the conception of science as one of "putting nature on the rack and torturing the answers out of her." Nor have all men embraced a conception of masculinity that demands cool detachment and domination. Nor even have all scientists been men. But most have. And however variable the attitudes of individual male scientists toward science and toward masculinity the metaphor of a marriage between mind and nature necessarily does not look the same to them as it does to women. And this is the point.

In a science constructed around the naming of object (nature) as female and the parallel naming of subject (mind) as male, any scientist who happens to be a woman is confronted with an a priori contradiction in terms. This poses a critical problem of identity: any scientist who is not a man walks a path bounded on one side by inauthenticity and on the other by subversion. Just as surely as inauthenticity is the cost a woman suffers by joining men in misogynist jokes, so it is, equally, the cost suffered by a woman who identifies with an image of the scientist modeled on the patriarchal husband. Only if she undergoes a radical disidentification from self can she share masculine pleasure in mastering a nature cast in the image of woman as passive, inert, and blind. Her alternative is to attempt a radical redefinition of terms. Nature must be renamed as not female, or, at least, as not an alienated object. By the same token, the mind, if the female scientist is to have one, must be renamed as not necessarily male, and accordingly recast with a more inclusive subjectivity. This is not to say that the male scientist cannot claim similar redefinition (certainly many have done so) but, by contrast to the woman scientist, his identity does not require it.

For McClintock, given her particular commitments to personal integrity, to be a scientist, and not a man, with a nonetheless intact identity, meant that she had to insist on a different meaning of mind, of nature, and of the relation between them. Her need to define for herself the relation between subject and object, even the very terms themselves, came not from a feminist consciousness, or even from a female consciousness. It came from her insistence on her right to be a scientist—from her determination to claim science as a human rather than a male endeavor. For such a claim, difference makes sense of the world in ways that division cannot. It allows for the kinship that she feels with other scientists, without at the same time obligating her to share all their assumptions.

Looked at in this way McClintock's stance is, finally, a far more radical one than that implied in Erikson's question. It implies that what could happen to science "when women are truly represented in it" is not simply or even, "the addition, to the male kind of creative vision, of women's vision" (p. 243) but, I suggest, a thoroughgoing transformation of the very possibilities of creative vision, for everyone. It implies that the kind of change we might hope for is not a direct or readily apparent one but rather an indirect and subterranean one. A first step toward such a transformation would be the undermining of the commitment of scientists to the masculinity of their profession that would be an inevitable concomitant of the participation of large numbers of women.

However, we need to remember that, as long as success in science does not require self-reflection, the undermining of masculinist or other ideological commitments is not a sufficient guarantee of change. But nature itself is an ally that can be relied upon to provide the impetus for real change: nature's responses recurrently invite reexamination of the terms in which our understanding of science is constructed. Paying attention to those responses—"listening to the material"—may help us to reconstruct our understanding of science in terms born out of the diverse spectrum of human experience rather than out of the narrow spectrum that our culture has labeled masculine.

References

Erikson, Erik H. 1965. Concluding Remarks. In *Women in the Scientific Professions*, ed. J. Mattfeld and C. van Aiken, Cambridge: MIT Press.

Judson, Horace 1979. *The Eighth Day of Creation: Makers of the Revolution in Biology*. New York: Simon & Schuster.

Keller, Evelyn Fox 1982. Feminism and Science. *Signs: Journal of Women in Culture and Society* 7, no. 3, pp. 589–602.

Keller, Evelyn Fox 1983. *A Feeling for the Organism: The Life and Work of Barbara McClintock*. New York: Freeman.

Marx, Jean L. 1981. A Movable Feast in the Eukaryotic Genome. *Science* 211, p. 153.

Nanney, David L. 1957. The Role of the Cytoplasm in Heredity. In *The Chemical Basis of Heredity*, ed. W. D. McElroy and H. B. Glass, Baltimore: Johns Hopkins University Press.

Rossiter, Margaret W. 1982. *Women Scientists in America*. Baltimore: Johns Hopkins University Press.

Schachtel, Ernest 1959. *Metamorphosis*. New York: Basic Books.

Interviewing Women: A Contradiction in Terms

Ann Oakley

Interviewing is rather like marriage: everybody knows what it is, an awful lot of people do it, and yet behind each closed front door there is a world of secrets. Despite the fact that much of modern sociology could justifiably be considered "the science of the interview" (Benney and Hughes, 1970, p. 190), very few sociologists who employ interview data actually bother to describe in detail the process of interviewing itself. The conventions of research reporting require them to offer such information as how many interviews were done and how many were not done; the length of time the interviews lasted; whether the questions were asked following some standardized format or not; and how the information was recorded. Some issues on which research reports do not usually comment are: social/personal characteristics of those doing the interviewing; interviewees' feelings about being interviewed and about the interview; interviewers' feelings about interviewees; and quality of interviewer-interviewee interaction; hospitality offered by interviewees to interviewers; attempts by interviewees to use interviewers as sources of information; and the extension of interviewer-interviewee encounters into more broadly-based social relationships.

I shall argue in this chapter that social science researchers' awareness of those aspects of interviewing which are "legitimate" and "illegitimate" from the viewpoint of inclusion in research reports reflect their embeddedness in a particular research protocol. This protocol assumes a predominantly masculine model of sociology and society. The relative undervaluation of women's models has led to an unreal theoretical characterization of the interview as a means of gathering sociological data which cannot and does not work in practice. This lack of fit between the theory and practice of interviewing is especially likely to come to the fore when a feminist interviewer is interviewing women (who may or may not be feminists).

Interviewing: A Masculine Paradigm?

Let us consider first what the methodology textbooks say about interviewing. First, and most obviously, an interview is a way of finding out about people. "If you want an answer, ask a question.... The asking of questions is the main source of social scientific information about everyday behaviour" (Shipman, 1972, p. 76). According to Johan Galtung (1967, p. 149):

The survey method ... has been indispensable in gaining information about the human condition and new insights in social theory.

The reasons for the success of the survey method seem to be two:

(1) *theoretically relevant* data are obtained (2) they are amenable to *statistical treatment*, which means (a) the use of the powerful tools of correlation analysis and multi-variate analysis to test substantive relationships, and (b) the tools of statistical tests of hypotheses about generalizability from samples to universes.

Interviewing, which is one[1] means of conducting a survey is essentially a conversation, "merely one of the many ways in which two people talk to one another"(Benney and Hughes, 1970, p. 191), but it is also, significantly, an *instrument* of data collection: "the interviewer is really a tool or an instrument"[2]

(Goode and Hatt, 1952, p. 185). As Benny and Hughes express it, (1970, pp. 196–7):

> Regarded as an information-gathering tool, the interview is designed to minimize the local, concrete, immediate circumstances of the particular encounter—including the respective personalities of the participants—and to emphasize only those aspects that can be kept general enough and demonstrable enough to be counted. As an encounter between these two particular people the typical interview has no meaning; it is conceived in a framework of other, comparable meetings between other couples, each recorded in such fashion that elements of communication in common can be easily isolated from more idiosyncratic qualities.

Thus an interview is "not simply a conversation. It is, rather, a pseudo-conversation. In order to be successful, it must have all the warmth and personality exchange of a conversation with the clarity and guidelines of scientific searching" (Goode and Hatt, 1952, p. 191). This requirement means that the interview must be seen as "a specialized pattern of verbal interaction—initiated for a specific purpose, and focussed on some specific content areas, with consequent elimination of extraneous material" (Kahn and Cannell, 1957, p. 16).

The motif of successful interviewing is "be friendly but not too friendly". For the contradiction at the heart of the textbook paradigm is that interviewing necessitates the manipulation of interviewees as objects of study/sources of data, but this can only be achieved via a certain amount of humane treatment. If the interviewee doesn't believe he/she is being kindly and sympathetically treated by the interviewer, then he/she will not consent to be studied and will not come up with the desired information. A balance must then be struck between the warmth required to generate "rapport" and the detachment necessary to see the interviewee as an object under surveillance; walking this tight-

rope means, not surprisingly, that "interviewing is not easy" (Denzin, 1970, p. 186), although mostly the textbooks do support the idea that it *is* possible to be a perfect interviewer and both to get reliable and valid data and make interviewees believe they are not simple statistics-to-be. It is just a matter of following the rules.

A major preoccupation in the spelling out of the rules is to counsel potential interviewers about where necessary friendliness ends and unwarranted involvement begins. Goode and Hatt's statement on this topic quoted earlier, for example, continues (1952, p. 191):

> Consequently, the interviewer cannot merely lose himself[3] in being friendly. He must introduce himself as though beginning a conversation but from the beginning the additional element of respect, of professional competence, should be maintained. Even the beginning student will make this attempt, else he will find himself merely "maintaining rapport", while failing to penetrate the clichés of contradictions of the respondent. Further he will find that his own confidence is lessened, if his only goal is to maintain friendliness. He is a professional researcher in this situation and he must demand and obtain respect for the task he is trying to perform.

Claire Selltiz and her colleagues give a more explicit recipe. They say (1965, p. 576):

> The interviewer's manner should be friendly, courteous, conversational and unbiased. He should be neither too grim nor too effusive; neither too talkative nor too timid. The idea should be to put the respondent at ease, so that he[4] will talk freely and fully.... [Hence,] A brief remark about the weather, the family pets, flowers or children will often serve to break the ice. Above all, an informal, conversational interview is dependent upon a thorough mastery by the interviewer of the actual questions in his schedule. He should be familiar enough with them to ask them con-

versationally, rather than read them stiffly; and he should know what questions are coming next, so there will be no awkward pauses while he studies the questionnaire.

C.A. Moser, in an earlier text, (1958, pp. 187–8, 195) advises of the dangers of "over-rapport".

Some interviewers are no doubt better than others at establishing what the psychologists call "rapport" and some may even be too good at it—the National Opinion Research Centre Studies[5] "found slightly less satisfactory results from the ... sociable interviewers who are "fascinated by people" ... there is something to be said for the interviewer who, while friendly and interested does not get too emotionally involved with the respondent and his problems. Interviewing on most surveys is a fairly straightforward job, not one calling for exceptional industry, charm or tact. What one asks is that the interviewer's personality should be neither over-aggressive nor over-sociable. Pleasantness and a business-like nature is the ideal combination.

"Rapport", a commonly used but ill-defined term, does not mean in this context what the dictionary says it does ("a sympathetic relationship", *O.E.D.*) but the acceptance by the interviewee of the interviewer's research goals and the interviewee's active search to help the interviewer in providing the relevant information. The person who is interviewed has a passive role in adapting to the definition of the situation offered by the person doing the interviewing. The person doing the interviewing must actively and continually construct the "respondent" (a telling name) as passive. Another way to phrase this is to say that both interviewer and interviewee must be "socialised" into the correct interviewing behaviour (Sjoberg and Nett, 1968, p. 210):

it is essential not only to train scientists to construct carefully worded questions and draw representative samples but also to educate the public to respond to questions on matters of interest to scientists and to do so in a manner advantageous for scientific analysis. To the extent that such is achieved, a common bond is established between interviewer and interviewee. [However,] It is not enough for the scientist to understand the world of meaning of his informants; if he is to secure valid data via the structured interview, respondents must be socialized into answering questions in proper fashion.

One piece of behaviour that properly socialized respondents do not engage in is asking questions back. Although the textbooks do not present any evidence about the extent to which interviewers do find in practice that this happens, they warn of its dangers and in the process suggest some possible strategies of avoidance: "Never provide the interviewee with any formal indication of the interviewer's beliefs and values. If the informant[6], poses a question ... parry it" (Sjoberg and Nett, 1968, p. 212). "When asked what you mean and think, tell them you are here to learn, not to pass any judgement, that the situation is very complex" (Galtung 1967, p. 161). "If he (the interviewer) should be asked for his views, he should laugh off the request with the remark that his job at the moment is to get opinions, not to have them" (Selltiz *et al.*, 1965, p. 576), and so on. Goode and Hatt (1952, p. 198) offer the most detailed advice on this issue:

What is the interviewer to do, however, if the respondent really wants information? Suppose the interviewee does answer the question but then asks for the opinions of the interviewer. Should he give his honest opinion, or an opinion which he thinks the interviewee wants? In most cases, the rule remains that he is there to obtain information and to focus on the respondent, not himself. Usually, a few simple phrases will shift the emphasis back to the respondent. Some which have been fairly successful are "I guess I haven't thought enough about it to give a good answer right now", "Well, right now, your opinions are more important than mine", and "If you really want to know what I think, I'll be honest and tell you in a moment, after we've finished the interview." Sometimes the diversion can be accomplished by a head-shaking gesture which suggests "That's a hard one!" while continuing with the interview. In short, the interviewer must avoid the temptation to express his own views, even if given the opportunity.

Of course the reason why the interviewer must pretend not to have opinions (or to be possessed of information the interviewee wants) is because behaving otherwise might "bias" the interview. "Bias" occurs when there are systematic differences between interviewers in the way interviews are conducted, with resulting differences in the data produced. Such bias clearly invalidates the scientific claims of the research, since the question of which information might be coloured by interviewees' responses to interviewers' attitudinal stances and which is independent of this "contamination" cannot be settled in any decisive way.

The paradigm of the social research interview prompted in the methodology textbooks does, then, emphasize (a) its status as a mechanical instrument of data-collection; (b) its function as a specialized form of conversation in which one person asks the questions and another gives the answers; (c) its characterization of interviewees as essentially passive individuals, and (d) its reduction of interviewers to a question asking and rapport-promoting role. Actually, two separate typifications of the interviewer are prominent in the literature, though the disjunction between the two is never commented on. In one the interviewer is "a combined phonograph and recording system" (Rose, 1945, p. 143); the job of the interviewer "is fundamentally that of a reporter, not an evangelist, a curiosity-seeker, or a debater" (Selltiz *et al.*, 1965, p. 576). It is important to note that while the interviewer must treat the interviewee as an ob-

ject or data-producing machine which, when handled correctly will function properly, the interviewer herself/himself has the same status from the point of view of the person/people, institution or corporation conducting the research. Both interviewer and interviewee are thus depersonalized participants in the research process.

The second typification of interviewers in the methodology literature is that of the interviewer as psychoanalyst. The interviewer's relationship to the interviewee is hierarchical and it is the body of expertise possessed by the interviewer that allows the interview to be successfully conducted. Most crucial in this exercise is the interviewer's use of non-directive comments and probes to encourage a free association of ideas which reveals whatever truth the research has been set up to uncover. Indeed, the term "nondirective interview" is derived directly from the language of psychotherapy and carries the logic of interviewer-impersonality to its extreme (Selltiz *et al.*, 1965, p. 268):

Perhaps the most typical remarks made by the interviewer in a nondirective interview are: "You feel that ..." or "Tell me more" or "Why?" or "Isn't that interesting?" or simply "Uh huh." The nondirective interviewer's function is primarily to serve as a catalyst to a comprehensive expression of the subject's feelings and beliefs and of the frame of reference within which his feelings and beliefs take on personal significance. To achieve this result, the interviewer must create a completely permissive atmosphere, in which the subject is free to express himself without fear of disapproval, admonition or dispute and without advice from the interviewer.

Sjoberg and Nett spell out the premises of the free association method (1968, p. 211):

the actor's (interviewee's) mental condition (is) ... confused and difficult to grasp. Frequently the actor himself does not know what he believes; he may be so "immature" that he cannot perceive or cope with his own subconscious thought patterns ... the interviewer must be prepared to follow the interviewee through a jungle of meandering thought ways if he is to arrive at the person's true self.

It seems clear that both psychoanalytic and mechanical typifications of the interviewer and, indeed, the entire paradigmatic representation of "proper" interviews in the methodology textbooks, owe a great deal more to a masculine social and sociological vantage point than to a feminine one. For example, the paradigm of the "proper" interview appeals to such values as objectivity, detachment, hierarchy and "science" as an important cultural activity which takes priority over people's more individualized concerns. Thus the errors of poor interviewing comprise subjectivity, involvement, the "fiction"[7] of equality and an undue concern with the ways in which people are not statistically comparable. This polarity of "proper" and "improper" interviewing is an almost classical representation of the widespread gender stereotyping which has been shown, in countless studies, to occur in modem industrial civilizations (see for example Bernard, 1975, part I; Fransella and Frost, 1977; Griffiths and Saraga, 1979; Oakley, 1972; Sayers, 1979). Women are characterized as sensitive, intuitive, incapable of objectivity and emotional detachment and as immersed in the business of making and sustaining personal relationships. Men are thought superior through their capacity for rationality and scientific objectivity and are thus seen to be possessed of an instrumental orientation in their relationships with others. Women are the exploited, the abused; they are unable to exploit others through the "natural" weakness of altruism—a quality which is also their strength as wives, mothers and housewives. Conversely, men find it easy to exploit, although it is most important that any exploitation be justified in the name of some broad political or economic ideology ("the end justifies the means").

Feminine and masculine psychology in pa-triarchal societies is the psychology of subordinate and dominant social groups. The tie between women's irrationality and heightened sensibility on the one hand and their materially disadvantaged position on the other is, for example, also to be found in the case of ethnic minorities. The psychological characteristics of subordinates "form a certain familiar cluster: submissiveness, passivity, docility, dependency, lack of initiative, inability to act, to decide, to think and the like. In general, this cluster includes qualities more characteristic of children than adults—immaturity, weakness and helplessness. If subordinates adopt these characteristics, they are considered well adjusted" (Miller, 1976, p. 7). It is no accident that the methodology textbooks (with one notable exception) (Moser, 1958)[8] refer to the interviewer as male. Although not all interviewees are referred to as female, there are a number of references to "housewives" as the kind of people interviewers are most likely to meet in the course of their work (for example Goode and Hatt, 1952, p. 189). Some of what Jean Baker Miller has to say about the relationship between dominant and subordinate groups would appear to be relevant to this paradigmatic interviewer-interviewee relationship (Miller, 1976, pp. 6–8):

A dominant group, inevitably, has the greatest influence in determining a culture's overall outlook—its philosophy, morality, social theory, and even its science. The dominant group, thus, legitimizes the unequal relationship and incorporates it into society's guiding concepts....

Inevitably the dominant group is the model for "normal human relationships." It then becomes "normal" to treat others destructively and to derogate them, to obscure the truth of what you are doing by creating false explanations and to oppose actions toward equality. In short, if one's identification is with the dominant group, it is "normal" to continue in this pattern....

It follows from this that dominant groups generally do not like to be told about or even quietly reminded of the existence of inequality. "Normally" they can avoid awareness because their explanation of the relationship becomes so well integrated in *other terms;* they can even believe that both they and the subordinate group share the same interests and, to some extent, a common experience....

Clearly, inequality has created a state of conflict. Yet dominant groups will tend to suppress conflict. They will see any questioning of the "normal" situation as threatening; activities by subordinates in this direction will be perceived with alarm. Dominants are usually convinced that the way things are is right and good, not only for them but especially for the subordinates. All morality confirms this view and all social structure sustains it.

To paraphrase the relevance of this to the interviewer-interviewee relationship we could say that: interviewers define the role of interviewees as subordinates; extracting information is more to be valued than yielding it; the convention of interviewer-interviewee hierarchy is a rationalization of inequality; what is good for interviewers is not necessarily good for interviewees.

Another way to approach this question of the masculinity of the "proper" interview is to observe that a sociology of feelings and emotion does not exist. Sociology mirrors society in not looking at social interaction from the viewpoint of women (Smith, 1979; Oakley, 1974, Chapter 1). While everyone has feelings, "Our society defines being cognitive, intellectual or rational dimensions of experience as superior to being emotional or sentimental. (Significantly, the terms 'emotional' and 'sentimental' have come to connote excessive or degenerate forms of feeling). Through the prism of our technological and rationalistic culture, we are led to perceive and feel emotions as some irrelevancy or impediment to getting things done." Hence their role in interviewing. But "Another reason for sociologists' neglect of emotions may be the discipline's attempt to be recognized as a 'real science' and the consequent need to focus on the most objective and measurable features of social life. This coincides with the values of the traditional 'male culture'" (Hochschild, 1975, p. 281).

Getting involved with the people you interview is doubly bad: it jeopardizes the hardwon status of sociology as a science and is indicative of a form of personal degeneracy.

Women Interviewing Women: Or Objectifying Your Sister

Before I became an interviewer I had read what the textbooks said interviewing ought to be. However, I found it very difficult to realize the prescription in practice, in a number of ways which I describe below. It was these practical difficulties which led me to take a new look at the textbook paradigm. In the rest of this chapter the case I want to make is that when a feminist interviews women: (1) use of prescribed interviewing practice is morally indefensible; (2) general and irreconcilable contradictions at the heart of the textbook paradigm are exposed; and (3) it becomes clear that, in most cases, the goal of finding out about people through interviewing is best achieved when the relationship of interviewer and interviewee is non-hierarchical and when the interviewer is prepared to invest his or her own personal identity in the relationship.

Before arguing the general case I will briefly mention some relevant aspects of my own interviewing experience. I have interviewed several hundred women over a period of some ten years, but it was the most recent research project, one concerned with the transition to motherhood, that particularly highlighted problems in the conventional interviewing recipe. Salient features of this research were that it involved repeated interviewing of a sample of women during a critical phase in their lives (in fact 55 women were interviewed four times; twice in pregnancy and twice afterwards and the average total period of interviewing was 9.4 hours.) It included for some[9] my attendance at the most critical point in this phase: the birth of the baby. The research was preceded by nine months of participant observation chiefly in the hospital setting of interactions between mothers or mothers-to-be and medical people. Although I had a research assistant to help me, I myself did the bulk of the interviewing—178 interviews over a period of some 12 months.[10] The project was my idea[11] and the analysis and writing up of the data was entirely my responsibility.

My difficulties in interviewing women were of two main kinds. First, they asked me a great many questions. Second, repeated interviewing over this kind of period and involving the intensely personal experiences of pregnancy, birth and motherhood, established a rationale of personal involvement I found it problematic and ultimately unhelpful to avoid.

Asking Questions Back

Analyzing[12] the tape-recorded interviews I had conducted, I listed 878 questions that interviewees had asked me at some point in the interviewing process. Three-quarters of these (see Table 1) were requests for information (e.g. "Who will deliver my baby?" "How do you cook an egg for a baby?") Fifteen per cent were questions about me, my experiences or attitudes in the area of reproduction ("Have you got any children?" "Did you breast feed?"); 6 per cent were questions about the research ("Are you going to write a book?" "Who pays you for doing this?"), and 4 per cent were more directly requests for advice on a particular matter ("How long should you wait for sex after childbirth?" "Do you think my baby's got too many clothes on?"). Table

2 goes into more detail about the topics on which interviewees wanted information. The largest category of questions concerned medical procedures: for example, how induction of labour is done, and whether all women attending a particular hospital[13] are given episiotomies. The second-largest category related to infant care or development: for example, "How do you clean a baby's nails?" "When do babies sleep through the night?" Third, there were questions about organizational procedures in the institutional settings where antenatal or delivery care was done; typical questions were concerned with who exactly would be doing antenatal care and what the rules are for husbands' attendance at delivery. Last, there were questions about the physiology of reproduction; for example "Why do some women need caesareans?" and (from one very frightened mother-to-be) "Is it right that the baby doesn't come out of the same hole you pass water out of?"

It would be the understatement of all time to say that I found it very difficult to avoid answering these questions as honestly and fully as I could. I was faced, typically, with a woman who was quite anxious about the fate of herself and her baby, who found it either impossible or extremely difficult to ask questions and receive satisfactory answers from the medical staff with whom she came into contact, and who saw me as someone who could not only reassure but inform.[14] I felt that I was asking a great deal from these women in the way of time, co-operation and hospitality at a stage in their lives when they had every reason to exclude strangers altogether in order to concentrate on the momentous character of the experiences being lived through. Indeed, I *was* asking a great deal—not only 9.4

Table 1   Questions Interviewees Asked (total 878), Transition to Motherhood Project (percentages)

Information requests	76
Personal questions	15
Questions about the research	6
Advice questions	4

hours of interviewing time but confidences on highly personal matters such as sex and money and "real" (i.e. possibly negative or ambivalent) feelings about babies, husbands, etc. I was, in addition, asking some of the women to allow me to witness them in the highly personal act of giving birth. Although the pregnancy interviews did not have to compete with the demands of motherhood for time, 90 per cent of the women were employed when first interviewed and 76 per cent of the first interviews had to take place in the evenings. Although I had timed the first postnatal interview (at about five weeks postpartum) to occur after the disturbances of very early motherhood, for many women it was nevertheless a stressful and busy time. And all this in the interests of "science" or for some book that might possibly materialise out of the research—a book which many of the women interviewed would not read and none would profit from directly (though they hoped that they would not lose too much).

The Transition to Friendship?

In a paper on "Collaborative Interviewing and Interactive Research", Laslett and Rapoport (1975) discuss the advantages and disadvantages of repeated interviewing. They say (p. 968) that the gain in terms of collecting more information in greater depth than would otherwise be possible is partly made by "being responsive to, rather than seeking to avoid, respondent reactions to the interview situation and experience." This sort of research is deemed by them "interactive." The principle of a hierarchical relationship

between interviewer and interviewee is not adhered to and "an attempt is made to generate a collaborative approach to the research which engages both the interviewer and respondent in a joint enterprise." Such an approach explicitly does not seek to minimize the personal involvement of the interviewer but as Rapoport and Rapoport (1976, p. 31) put it, relies "very much on the formulation of a relationship between interviewer and interviewee as an important element in achieving the quality of the information... required."[15]

As Laslett and Rapoport note, repeated interviewing is not much discussed in the methodological literature: the paradigm is of an interview as a "one-off" affair. Common sense would suggest that an ethic of detachment on the interviewer's part is much easier to maintain where there is only one meeting with the interviewee (and the idea of a "one-off" affair rather than a long-term relationship is undoubtedly closer to the traditional masculine world view I discussed earlier).

In terms of my experience in the childbirth project, I found that interviewees very often took the initiative in defining the interviewer-interviewee relationship as something which existed beyond the limits of question-asking and answering. For example, they did not only offer the minimum hospitality of accommodating me in their homes for the duration of the interview: at 92 per cent of the interviews I was offered tea, coffee or some other drink; 14 percent of the women also offered me a meal on at least one occasion. As Table 1 suggests, there was also a certain amount of interest in my own situation. What

Table 2 Interviewees' Requests for Information (total 664), Transition to Motherhood Project (percentages)

Medical procedures	31
Organisational procedures	19
Physiology of reproduction	15
Baby care/development/feeding	21
Other	15

sort of person was I and how did I come to be interested in this subject?

In some cases these kind of "respondent" reactions were evident at the first interview. More often they were generated after the second interview and an important factor here was probably the timing of the interviews. There was an average of 20 weeks between interviews 1 and 2, an average of 11 weeks between interviews 2 and 3 and an average of 15 weeks between interviews 3 and 4. Between the first two interviews most of the women were very busy. Most were still employed and had the extra work of preparing equipment/clothes/a room for the baby—which sometimes meant moving house. Between interviews 2 and 3 most were not out at work and, sensitized by the questions I had asked in the first two interviews to my interest in their birth experiences, probably began to associate me in a more direct way with their experiences of the transition to motherhood. At interview 2 I gave them all a stamped addressed postcard on which I asked them to write the date of their baby's birth so I would know when to re-contact them for the first postnatal interview. I noticed that this was usually placed in a prominent position (for example on the mantlepiece), to remind the woman or her husband to complete it and it probably served in this way as a reminder of my intrusion into their lives. One illustration of this awareness comes from the third interview with Mary Rosen, a 25-year-old exhibition organizer: "I thought of you after he was born, I thought she'll *never* believe it—a six-hour labour, a 9 lb 6 oz baby and *no* forceps—and all without an epidural, although I had said to you that I wanted one." Sixty two per cent of the women expressed a sustained and quite detailed interest in the research; they wanted to know its goals, any proposed methods for disseminating its findings, how I had come to think of it in the first place, what the attitudes of doctors I had met or collaborated with were to it and so forth. Some of the women took the initiative in contacting me to arrange the second or a subsequent interview, although I had made it clear that I would get

in touch with them. Several rang up to report particularly important pieces of information about their antenatal care—in one case a distressing encounter with a doctor who told a woman keen on natural childbirth that this was "for animals: in this hospital we give epidurals"; in another case to tell me of an ultrasound result that changed the expected date of delivery. Several also got in touch to correct or add to things they had said during an interview—for instance, one contacted me several weeks after the fourth interview to explain that she had had an emergency appendicectomy five days after my visit and that her physical symptoms at the time could have affected some of her responses to the questions I asked.

Arguably, these signs of interviewees' involvement indicated their acceptance of the goals of the research project rather than any desire to feel themselves participating in a personal relationship with me. Yet the research was presented to them as *my* research in which I had a personal interest, so it is not likely that a hard and fast dividing line between the two was drawn. One index of their and my reactions to our joint participation in the repeated interviewing situation is that some four years after the final interview I am still in touch with more than a third of the women I interviewed. Four have become close friends, several others I visit occasionally, and the rest write or telephone when they have something salient to report such as the birth of another child.

A Feminist Interviews Women

Such responses as I have described on the part of the interviewees to participation in research, particularly that involving repeated interviewing, are not unknown, although they are almost certainly under-reported. It could be suggested that the reasons why they were so pronounced in the research project discussed here is because of the attitudes of the interviewer—i.e. the women were reacting to my own evident wish for a relatively intimate and non-hierarchical relationship. While I was careful not to take direct initiatives in this direction, I certainly set out to convey to the people whose cooperation I was seeking the fact that I did not intend to exploit either them or the information they gave me. For instance, if the interview clashed with the demands of housework and motherhood I offered to, and often did, help with the work that had to be done. When asking the women's permission to record the interview, I said that no one but me would ever listen to the tapes; in mentioning the possibility of publications arising out of the research I told them that their names and personal details would be changed and I would, if they wished, send them details of any such publications, and so forth. The attitude I conveyed could have had some influence in encouraging the women to regard me as a friend rather than purely as a data-gatherer.

The pilot interviews, together with my previous experience of interviewing women, led me to decide that when I was asked questions I would answer them. The practice I followed was to answer all personal questions and questions about the research as fully as was required. For example, when two women asked if I had read their hospital case notes I said I had, and when one of them went on to ask what reason was given in these notes for her forceps delivery, I told her what the notes said. On the emotive issue of whether I experienced childbirth as painful (a common topic of conversation) I told them that I did find it so but that in my view it was worth it to get a baby at the end. Advice questions I also answered fully but made it clear when I was using my own experiences of motherhood as the basis for advice. I also referred women requesting advice to the antenatal and childbearing advice literature or to health visitors, GPs, etc. when appropriate—though the women usually made it clear that it was my opinion in particular they were soliciting. When asked for information I gave it if I could or, again, referred the questioner to an appropriate medical or non-medical authority. Again, the way I responded to interviewee's questions probably encouraged them

to regard me as more than an instrument of data-collection.

Dissecting my practice of interviewing further, there were three principal reasons why I decided not to follow the textbook code of ethics with regard to interviewing women. First, I did not regard it as reasonable to adopt a purely exploitative attitude to interviewees as sources of data. My involvement in the women's movement in the early 1970s and the rebirth of feminism in an academic context had led me, along with many others, to re-assess society and sociology as masculine paradigms and to want to bring about change in the traditional cultural and academic treatment of women. "Sisterhood", a somewhat nebulous and problematic, but nevertheless important, concept,[16] certainly demanded that women re-evaluate the basis of their relationships with one another.

The dilemma of a feminist interviewer interviewing women could be summarized by considering the practical application of some of the strategies recommended in the textbooks for meeting interviewee's questions. For example, these advise that such questions as "Which hole does the baby come out of?" "Does an epidural ever paralyze women?" and "Why is it dangerous to leave a small baby alone in the house?" should be met with such responses from the interviewer as "I guess I haven't thought enough about it to give a good answer right now," or "a head-shaking gesture which suggests 'that's a hard one'" (Goode and Hatt, quoted above). Also recommended is laughing off the request with the remark that "my job at the moment is to get opinions, not to have them" (Selltiz *et al.*, quoted above).

A second reason for departing from conventional interviewing ethics was that I regarded sociological research as an essential way of giving the subjective situation of women greater visibility not only in sociology, but, more importantly, in society, than it has traditionally had. Interviewing women was, then, a strategy for documenting women's own accounts of their lives. What *was* important was not taken-for-granted sociological assumptions about the role of the interviewer but a new awareness of the interviewer as an instrument for promoting a sociology for women[17]—that is, as a tool for making possible the articulated and recorded commentary of women on a very personal business of being female in a patriarchal capitalist society. Note that the formulation of the interviewer role has changed dramatically from being a data-collecting instrument for researchers to being a data-collecting instrument for those whose lives are being researched. Such a reformulation is enhanced where the interviewer is also the researcher. It is not coincidental that in the methodological literature the paradigm of the research process is essentially disjunctive, i.e. researcher and interviewer functions are typically performed by different individuals.

A third reason why I undertook the childbirth research with a degree of scepticism about how far traditional percepts of interviewing could, or should, be applied in practice was because I had found, in my previous interviewing experiences, that an attitude of refusing to answer questions or offer any kind of personal feedback was not helpful in terms of the traditional goal of promoting "rapport." A different role, that could be termed "no intimacy without reciprocity", seemed especially important in longitudinal in-depth interviewing. Without feeling that the interviewing process offered some personal satisfaction to them, interviewees would not be prepared to continue after the first interview. This involves being sensitive not only to those questions that are asked (by either party) but to those that are not asked. The interviewee's definition of the interview is important.

The success of this method cannot, of course, be judged from the evidence I have given so far. On the question of the rapport established in the Transition to Motherhood research I offer the following cameo:

A.O.: "Did you have any questions you wanted to ask but didn't when you last went to the hospital?"

M.C.: "Er, I don't know how to put this really. After sexual intercourse I had some bleeding, three times, only a few drops and I didn't tell the hospital because I didn't know how to put it to them. It worried me first off, as soon as I saw it I cried. I don't know if I'd be able to tell them. You see, I've also got a sore down there and a discharge and you know I wash there lots of times a day. You think I should tell the hospital; I could never speak to my own doctor about it. You see I feel like this but I can talk to you about it and I can talk to my sister about it."

More generally the quality and depth of the information given to me by the women I interviewed can be assessed in *Becoming A Mother* (Oakley, 1979), the book arising out of the research which is based almost exclusively on interviewee accounts.

So far as interviewees' reactions to being interviewed are concerned, I asked them at the end of the last interview the question, "Do you feel that being involved in this research— my coming to see you—has affected your experience of becoming a mother in any way?" Table 3 shows the answers.

Nearly three-quarters of the women said that being interviewed had affected them and the three most common forms this influence took were in leading them to reflect on their experiences more than they would otherwise have done; in reducing the level of their anxiety and/or in reassuring them of their normality; and in giving a valuable outlet for the verbalization of feelings. None of those who thought being interviewed had affected them regarded this affect as negative. There were many references to the "therapeutic" effect of talking: "getting it out of your system." (It was generally felt that husbands, mothers, friends, etc., did not provide a sufficiently sympathetic or interested audience for a detailed recounting of experiences and difficulties of becoming a mother.) It is perhaps important to note here that one of the main conclusions of the research was that there is a considerable discrepancy between the expectations and the reality of the different aspects of motherhood—pregnancy, childbirth, the emotional relationship of mother and child, the work of childrearing. A dominant metaphor used by interviewees to describe their reactions to this hiatus was "shock." In this sense, a process of emotional recovery is endemic in the normal transition to motherhood and there is a general need for some kind of "therapeutic listener" that is not met within the usual circle of family and friends.

On the issue of co-operation, only 2 out of 82 women contacted initially about the research actually refused to take part in it,[18] making a refusal rate of 2 per cent which is extremely low. Once the interviewing was under way only one woman voluntarily dropped out (because of marital problems); an attrition from 66 at interview 1 to 55 at interview 4 was otherwise accounted for by miscarriage, moves, etc. All the women who were asked if they would mind me attending the birth said they didn't mind and all got in touch either directly or indirectly through their husbands when they started labour. The postcards left after interview 2 for interviewees to return after the birth were all completed and returned.

Is a "Proper" Interview Ever Possible?

Hidden amongst the admonitions on how to be a perfect interviewer in the social research methods manuals is the covert recognition

that the goal of perfection is actually unattainable: the contradiction between the need for "rapport" and the requirement of between-interview comparability cannot be solved. For example, Dexter (1956, p. 156) following Paul (1954), observes that the pretence of neutrality on the interviewer's part is counterproductive: participation demands alignment. Selltiz *et al.* (1965, p. 583) says that

> Much of what we call interviewer bias can more correctly be described as interviewer *differences*, which are inherent in the fact that interviewers are human beings and not machines and that they do not work identically.

Richardson and his colleagues in their popular textbook on interviewing (1965, p. 129) note that

> Although gaining and maintaining satisfactory participation is never the primary objective of the interviewer, it is so intimately related to the quality and quantity of the information sought that the interviewer must always maintain a dual concern: for the quality of his respondent's participation and for the quality of the information being sought. Often ... these qualities are independent of each other and occasionally they may be mutually exclusive.

It is not hard to find echoes of this point of view in the few accounts of the actual process of interviewing that do exist. For example,

Table 3   "Has the Research Affected Your Experience of Becoming a Mother?" (percentages)

No	27
Yes:	73
Thought about it more	30
Found it reassuring	25
A relief to talk	25
Changed attitudes/behaviour	7

Percentages do not add up to 100% because some women gave more than one answer.

Zweig, in his study of *Labour, Life and Poverty,* (1949, pp. 1–2)

> dropped the idea of a questionnaire or formal verbal questions ... instead I had casual talks with working class men on an absolutely equal footing ...
>
> I made many friends and some of them paid me a visit afterwards or expressed a wish to keep in touch with me. Some of them confided their troubles to me and I often heard the remark: "Strangely enough, I have never talked about that to anybody else". They regarded my interest in their way of life as a sign of sympathy and understanding rarely shown to them even in the inner circle of their family. I never posed as somebody superior to them, or as a judge of their actions but as one of them.

Zweig defended his method on the grounds that telling people they were objects of study met with "an icy reception" and that finding out about other peoples' lives is much more readily done on a basis of friendship than in a formal interview.

More typically and recently, Marie Corbin, the interviewer for the Pahls' study of *Managers and Their Wives,* commented in an Appendix to the book of that name (Corbin, 1971, pp. 303–5):

> Obviously the exact type of relationship that is formed between an interviewer and the people being interviewed is something that the interviewer cannot control entirely, even though the nature of this relationship and how the interviewees classify the interviewer will affect the kinds of information given ... simply because I am a woman and a wife I shared interests with the other wives and this helped to make the relationship a relaxed one.

Corbin goes on:

> In these particular interviews I was conscious of the need to establish some kind of confidence with the couples if the sorts of information required were to be forthcoming. ... In theory it should be possible to establish confidence simply by courtesy towards and interest in the interviewees. In practice it can be difficult to spend eight hours in a person's home, share their meals and listen to their problems and at the same time remain polite, detached and largely uncommunicative. I found the balance between prejudicing the answers to questions which covered almost every aspect of the couples' lives, establishing a relationship that would allow the interviews to be successful and holding a civilized conversation over dinner to be a very precarious one.

Discussing research on copper mining on Bougainville Island, Papua New Guinea, Alexander Mamak describes his growing consciousness of the political context in which research is done (1978, p. 176):

> as I became increasingly aware of the unequal relationship existing between management and the union, I found myself becoming more and more emotionally involved in the proceedings. I do not believe this reaction is unusual since, in the words of the well known black sociologist Nathan Hare, "If one is truly cognizant of adverse circumstances, he would be expected, through the process of reason, to experience some emotional response".

And, a third illustration of this point, Dorothy Hobson's account of her research on housewives' experiences of social isolation contains the following remarks (1978, pp. 80–1):

> The method of interviewing in a one-to-one situation requires some comment. What I find most difficult is to resist commenting in a way which may direct the answers which the women give to my questions. However, when the taped interview ends we usually talk and then the women ask me questions about my life and family. These questions often reflect areas where they have experienced ambivalent feelings in their own replies. For example, one

woman who said during the interview that she did not like being married, asked me how long I had been married and if I liked it. When I told her how long I had been married she said, "Well I suppose you get used to it in time, I suppose I will". In fact the informal talk after the interview often continues what the women have said during the interview.

It is impossible to tell exactly how the women perceive me but I do not think they see me as too far removed from themselves. This may partly be because I have to arrange the interviews when my own son is at school and leave in time to collect him.[19]

As Bell and Newby (1977, pp. 9–10) note "accounts of doing sociological research are at least as valuable, both to students of sociology and its practitioners, as the exhortations to be found in the much more common textbooks on methodology". All research is political, "from the micropolitics of interpersonal relationships, through the politics of research units, institutions and universities, to those of government departments and finally to the state"—which is one reason why social research is not "like it is presented and prescribed in those texts. It is infinitely more complex, messy, various and much more interesting" (Bell and Encel, 1978, p. 4). The "cookbooks" of research methods largely ignore the political context of research, although some make asides about its "ethical dilemmas": "Since we are all human we are all involved in what we are studying when we try to study any aspect of social relations" (Stacey, 1969, p. 2); "frequently researchers, in the course of their interviewing, establish rapport not as scientists but as human beings; yet they proceed to use this humanistically gained knowledge for scientific ends, usually without the informants' knowledge" (Sjoberg and Nett, 1968, pp. 215–16). These ethical dilemmas are generic to all research involving interviewing for reasons I have already discussed. But they are greatest where there is least social distance between the interviewer and interviewee. Where both

share the same gender socialisation and critical life-experiences, social distance can be minimal. Where both interviewer and interviewee share membership of the same minority group, the basis for equality may impress itself even more urgently on the interviewer's consciousness. Mamak's comments apply equally to a feminist interviewing women (1978, p. 168):

> I found that my academic training in the methodological views of Western social science and its emphasis on "scientific objectivity" conflicted with the experiences of my colonial past. The traditional way in which social science research is conducted proved inadequate for an understanding of the reality, needs and desires of the people I was researching.

Some of the reasons why a "proper" interview is a masculine fiction are illustrated by observations from another field in which individuals try to find out about other individuals—anthropology. Evans-Pritchard reported this conversation during his early research with the Nuers of East Africa (1940, pp. 12–13):

I: "Who are you?"

Cuol: "A man."

I: "What is your name?"

Cuol: "Do you want to know my *name?*"

I: "Yes."

Cuol: "You want to know *my* name?"

I: "Yes, you have come to visit me in my tent and I would like to know who you are."

Cuol: "All right, I am Cuol. What is your name?"

I: "My name is Pritchard."

Cuol: "What is your father's name?"

I: "My father's name is also Pritchard."

Cuol: "No, that cannot be true, you cannot have the same name as your father."

I: "It is the name of my lineage. What is the name of your lineage?"

Cuol: "Do you want to know the name of my lineage?"

I: "Yes."

Cuol: "What will you do with it if I tell you? Will you take it to your country?"

I: "I don't want to do anything with it. I just want to know it since I am living at your camp."

Cuol: "Oh well, we are Lou."

I: "I did not ask you the name of your tribe. I know that. I am asking you the name of your lineage."

Cuol: "Why do you want to know the name of my lineage?"

I: "I don't want to know it."

Cuol: "Then why do you ask me for it? Give me some tobacco."

I defy the most patient ethnologist to make headway against this kind of opposition [concluded Evans-Pritchard].

Interviewees are people with considerable potential for sabotaging the attempt to research them. Where, as in the case of anthropology or repeated interviewing in sociology, the research cannot proceed without a relationship of mutual trust being established between interviewer and interviewee the prospects are particularly dismal. This inevitably changes the interviewer/anthropologist's attitude to the people he/she is studying. A poignant example is the incident related in Elenore Smith Bowen's[20] *Return to Laughter* when the anthropologist witnesses one of her most trusted informants dying in childbirth (1956, p. 163):

I stood over Amara. She tried to smile at me. She was very ill. I was convinced these women could not help her. She would die. She was my friend but my epitaph for her would be impersonal observations scribbled in my notebook, her memory preserved in an anthropologist's file: "Death (in childbirth)/Cause: witchcraft/Case of Amara." A lecture from the past reproached me: "The anthropologist can-

not, like the chemist or biologist, arrange controlled experiments. Like the astronomer, his mere presence produces changes in the data he is trying to observe. He himself is a disturbing influence which he must endeavour to keep to the minimum. His claim to science must therefore rest on a meticulous accuracy of observations and on a cool, objective approach to his data."

A cool, objective approach to Amara's death?

One can, perhaps, be cool when dealing with questionnaires or when interviewing strangers. But what is one to do when one can collect one's data only by forming personal friendships? It is hard enough to think of a friend as a case history. Was I to stand aloof, observing the course of events?

Professional hesitation meant that Bowen might never see the ceremonies connected with death in childbirth. But, on the other hand, she would see her friend die. Bowen's difficult decision to plead with Amara's kin and the midwives in charge of her case to allow her access to Western medicine did not pay off and Amara did eventually die.

An anthropologist has to "get inside the culture"; participant observation means "that … the observer participates in the daily life of the people under study, either openly in the role of researcher or covertly in some disguised role" (Becker and Geer, 1957, p. 28). A feminist interviewing women is by definition both "inside" the culture and participating in that which she is observing. However, in these respects the behaviour of a feminist interviewer/researcher is not extraordinary. Although (Stanley and Wise, 1979, pp. 359–61)

Descriptions of the research process in the social sciences often suggest that the motivation for carrying out substantive work lies in theoretical concerns … the research process appears a very orderly and coherent process indeed. … The personal tends to be carefully removed from public statements; these are full of rational argument [and] careful discussion of academic points. [It can equally easily be seen that] all research is "grounded", because no researcher can separate herself from personhood and thus from deriving second order constructs from experience.

A feminist methodology of social science requires that this rationale of research be described and discussed not only in feminist research but in social science research in general. It requires, further, that the mythology of "hygienic" research with its accompanying mystification of the researcher and the researched as objective instruments of data production be replaced by the recognition that personal involvement is more than dangerous bias—it is the condition under which people come to know each other and to admit others into their lives.

Notes

1. I am not dealing with others, such as self-administered questionnaires, here since not quite the same framework applies.
2. For Galtung (1967, p. 138) the appropriate metaphor is a thermometer.
3. Most interviewers are, of course, female.
4. Many "respondents" are, of course, female.
5. See Hyman *et al.* (1955).
6. This label suggests that the interviewer's role is to get the interviewee to "inform" (somewhat against his/her will) on closely guarded and dangerous secrets.
7. Benney and Hughes (1970) discuss interviewing in terms of the dual conventions or "fictions" of equality and comparability.
8. Moser (1958, p. 185) says, "since most interviewers are women I shall refer to them throughout as of the female sex."
9. I attended six of the births.
10. What I have to say about my experience of interviewing relates to my own experience and not that of my research assistant.
11. I am grateful to the Social Science Research Council for funding the research and to Bedford College, London University, for administering it.
12. The interviews were fully transcribed and the analysis then done from the transcripts.
13. The women all had their babies at the same London maternity hospital.
14. I had, of course, made it clear to the women I was interviewing that I had no medical training, but as I have argued elsewhere (Oakley, 1981b) mothers do not see medical experts as the only legitimate possessors of knowledge about motherhood.
15. It is, however, an important part of the Rapoports' definition of "interactive research" that psychoanalytic principles should be applied in analysing processes of "transference" and "countertransference" in the interviewer-interviewee relationship.
16. See Mitchell and Oakley (1976) and Oakley (1981a) on the idea of sisterhood.
17. See Smith (1979).
18. Both these were telephone contacts only. See Oakley (1980), Chapter 4, for more on the research methods used.
19. Hobson observes that her approach to interviewing women yielded no refusals to co-operate.
20. Elenore Smith Bowen is a pseudonym for a well-known anthropologist.

References

Becker, H.S. and Geer, B. (1957), "Participant Observation and Interviewing: A Comparison? *Human Organisation*, Vol. XVI, pp. 28–32.

Bell, C. and Encel, S. (eds) (1978), *Inside the Whale*, Pergamon Press, Oxford.

Bell, C. and Encel, S. (1978) "Introduction" to Bell and Encel (eds), *Inside the Whale*, Pergamon Press, Oxford.

Bell, C. and Newby, H. (1977), *Doing Sociological Research*, Allen & Unwin, London.

Benney, M. and Hughes, E.C. (1970), "Of Sociology and the Interview" in N.K. Denzin (ed.), *Sociological Methods: A Source Book*, Butterworth, London.

Bernard, J. (1975), *Women, Wives, Mothers*, Aldine, Chicago.

Bowen, E.S. (1956), *Return to Laughter*, Gollancz, London.

Corbin, M. (1971), "Appendix 3" in J.M. and R.E. Pahl, *Managers and their Wives*, Allen Lane, London.

Denzin, N.K. (1970) (ed.), *Sociological Methods: A Source Book*, Butterworth, London.

Denzin, N.K. (1970) "Introduction: Part V" in N.K. Denzin (ed.), *Sociological Methods: A Source Book*, Butterworth, London.

Dexter, L.A. (1956), "Role Relationships and Conceptions of Neutrality in Interviewing", *American Journal of Sociology*, Vol. LX14, p. 153–7.

Evans-Pritchard, E.E. (1940), *The Nuer*, Oxford University Press, London.

Fransella, F. and Frost, K. (1977), *On Being a Woman*, Tavistock, London.

Galtung, J. (1967), *Theory and Methods of Social Research*, Allen & Unwin, London.

Goode, W.J. and Hatt, P.K. (1952), *Methods in Social Research*, McGraw Hill, New York.

Griffiths, D. and Saraga, E. (1979), "Sex Differences and Cognitive Abilities: A Sterile Field of Enquiry" in O. Hartnett *et al.* (eds), *Sex Role Stereotyping*, Tavistock, London.

Hartnett, O., Boden, G. and Fuller, M. (eds) (1979) *Sex-Role Stereotyping*, Tavistock, London.

Hobson, D. (1978), "Housewives: Isolation as Oppression" in Women's Studies Group, Centre for Contemporary Cultural Studies, *Women Take Issue*, Hutchinson, London.

Hochschild, A.R. (1975), "The Sociology of Feeling and Emotion: Selected Possibilities" in M. Millman and R.M. Kanter (eds), *Another Voice: Feminist Perspectives on Social Life and Social Science*, Anchor Books, New York.

Hyman, H.H. *et al.* (1955), *Interviewing in Social Research*, University of Chicago Press.

Kahn, R.L. and Cannell, L.F. (1957), *The Dynamics of Interviewing*, John Wiley, New York.

Laslett, B. and Rapoport, R. (1975), "Collaborative Interviewing and Interactive Research," *Journal of Marriage and the Family*, November, pp. 968–77.

Mamak, A.F. (1978), Nationalism, Race-Class Consciousness and Social Research on Bougainville Island, Papua, New Guinea, in C. Bell and S. Encel (eds), *Inside the Whale*, Pergamon Press, Oxford.

Miller, J.B. (1976), *Toward a New Psychology of Women*, Beacon Press, Boston.

Mitchell, J. and Oakley A. (1976), "Introduction" in J. Mitchell and A. Oakley (eds), *The Rights and Wrongs of Women*, Penguin, Harmondsworth.

Moser, C.A.(1958), Survey *Methods in Social Investigation*, Heinemann, London.

Oakley, A. (1972), *Sex, Gender and Society*, Maurice Temple Smith, London.

Oakley. A.(1974), *The Sociology of Housework*, Martin Robertson, London.

Oakley, A. (1979), *Becoming a Mother*, Martin Robertson, Oxford.

Oakley, A. (1980), *Women Confined: Towards a Sociology of Childbirth*, Martin Robertson, Oxford.

Oakley, A. (1981a), *Subject Women*, Martin Robertson, Oxford.

Oakley, A. (1981b), "Normal Motherhood: An Exercise in Self-Control", in B. Hutter and G. Williams (eds), *Controlling Women*, Croom Helm, London.

Paul, B. (1954), "Interview Techniques and Field Relationships" in A.C. Kroeber (ed.), *Anthropology Today*, University of Chicago Press.

Rapoport, R. and Rapoport, R. (1976), *Dual Career Families Reexamined*, Martin Robertson, London.

Richardson, S.A. *et al.* (1965), *Interviewing: Its Forms and Functions*, Basic Books, New York.

Rose, A.M. (1945),"A Research Note on Experimentation in Interviewing", *American Journal of Sociology*, Vol. 51, pp. 143–4.

Sayers, J. (1979), *On the Description of Psychological Sex Differences* in 0. Hartnett *et al.* (eds), *Sex Role Stereotyping*, Tavistock, London.

Selltiz, C., Jahoda, M., Deutsch, M. and Cook, S.W. (1965), *Research Methods in Social Relations*, Methuen, London.

Shipman, M.D. (1972), *The Limitations of Social Research*, Longman, London.

Sjoberg, G. and Nett, R. (1968), *A Methodology for Social Research*, Harper & Row, New York.

Smith, D.E. (1979), "A Sociology for Women" in J.A. Sherman and E.T. Beck (eds), *The Prism of Sex*, University of Wisconsin Press, Madison.

Stacey, M. (1969), *Methods of Social Research*, Pergamon, Oxford.

Stanley, L. and Wise, S. (1979), "Feminist Research, Feminist Consciousness and Experiences of Sexism", *Women's Studies International Quarterly*, vol. 2, no. 3, pp. 359–79.

Zweig, F. (1949), *Labour, Life and Poverty*, Gollancz, London.

SCIENCE'S SUBJECT MATTER

 ## Have Only Men Evolved?

Ruth Hubbard

... with the dawn of scientific investigation it might have been hoped that the prejudices resulting from lower conditions of human society would disappear, and that in their stead would be set forth not only facts, but deductions from facts, better suited to the dawn of an intellectual age. ...

The ability, however, to collect facts, and the power to generalize and draw conclusions from them, avail little, when brought into direct opposition to deeply rooted prejudices.

Eliza Burt Gamble,
The Evolution of Woman (1894)

Science is made by people who live at a specific time in a specific place and whose thought patterns reflect the truths that are accepted by the wider society. Because scientific explanations have repeatedly run counter to the beliefs held dear by some powerful segments of the society (organized religion, for example, has its own explanations of how nature works), scientists are sometimes portrayed as lone heroes swimming against the social stream. Charles Darwin (1809–82) and his theories of evolution and human descent are frequently used to illustrate this point. But Darwinism, on the contrary, has wide areas of congruence with the social and political ideology of nineteenth-century Britain and with Victorian precepts of morality, particularly as regards the relationships between the sexes. And the same Victorian notions still dominate contemporary biological thinking about sex differences and sex roles.

Science and the Social Construction of Reality

For humans, language plays a major role in generating reality. Without words to objectify and categorize our sensations and place them in relation to one another, we cannot evolve a tradition of what is real in the world. Our past experience is organized through language into our history within which we have set up new verbal categories that allow us to assimilate present and future experiences. If every time we had a sensation we gave it a new name, the names would have no meaning: lacking consistency, they could not arrange our experience into reality. For words to work, they have to be used consistently and in a sufficient variety of situations so that their volume—what they contain and exclude—becomes clear to all their users.

If I ask a young child, "Are you hungry?", she must learn through experience that "yes" can produce a piece of bread, a banana, an egg, or an entire meal; whereas "yes" in answer to "Do you want orange juice?" always produces a tart, orange liquid.

However, all acts of naming happen against a backdrop of what is socially accepted as real. The question is *who* has social sanction to define the larger reality into which one's everyday experiences must fit in order that one be reckoned sane and responsible. In the past, the Church had this right, but it is less looked to today as a generator of new definitions of reality, though it is allowed to stick by its old ones even when they conflict with currently accepted realities (as in the case of miracles). The State also defines some aspects of reality and can generate what George Orwell called Newspeak in order to interpret the world for its own political purposes. But, for the most part, at present science is the most respectable legitimator of new realities.

However, what is often ignored is that science does more than merely define reality; by setting up first the definitions—for example, three-dimensional (Euclidian) space—and—

then specific relationships within them—for example, parallel lines never meet—it automatically renders suspect the sense experiences that contradict the definitions. If we want to be respectable inhabitants of the Euclidian world, every time we see railroad tracks meet in the distance we must "explain" how what we are seeing is consistent with the accepted definition of reality. Furthermore, through society's and our personal histories, we acquire an investment in our sense of reality that makes us eager to enlighten our children or uneducated "savages," who insist on believing that railroad tracks meet in the distance and part like curtains as they walk down them. (Here, too, we make an exception for the followers of some accepted religions, for we do not argue with equal vehemence against our fundamentalist neighbors, if they insist on believing literally that the Red Sea parted for the Israelites, or that Jesus walked on the Sea of Galilee.)

Every theory is a self-fulfilling prophecy that orders experience into the framework it provides. Therefore, it should be no surprise that almost any theory, however absurd it may seem to some, has its supporters. The mythology of science holds that scientific theories lead to the truth because they operate by consensus: they can be tested by different scientists, making their own hypotheses and designing independent experiments to test them. Thus, it is said that even if one or another scientist "misinterprets" his or her observations, the need for consensus will weed out fantasies and lead to reality. But things do not work that way. Scientists do not think and work independently. Their "own" hypotheses ordinarily are formulated within a context of theory, so that their interpretations by and large are sub-sets within the prevailing orthodoxy. Agreement therefore is built into the process and need tell us little or nothing about "truth" or "reality." Of course, scientists often disagree, but their quarrels usually are about details that do not contradict fundamental beliefs, whichever way they are resolved.[1] To overturn orthodoxy is no easier in science than in philosophy, religion, econom-

ics, or any of the other disciplines through which we try to comprehend the world and the society in which we live.

The very language that translates sense perceptions into scientific reality generates that reality by lumping certain perceptions together and sorting or highlighting others. But what we notice and how we describe it depends to a great extent on our histories, roles, and expectations as individuals and as members of our society. Therefore, as we move from the relatively impersonal observations in astronomy, physics and chemistry into biology and the social sciences, our science is increasingly affected by the ways in which our personal and social experience determine what we are able or willing to perceive as real about ourselves and the organisms around us. This is not to accuse scientists of being deluded or dishonest, but merely to point out that, like other people, they find it difficult to see the social biases that are built into the very fabric of what they deem real. That is why, by and large, only children notice that the emperor is naked. But only the rare child hangs on to that insight; most of them soon learn to see the beauty and elegance of his clothes.

In trying to construct a coherent, self-consistent picture of the world, scientists come up with questions and answers that depend on their perceptions of what has been, is, will be, and can be. There is no such thing as objective, value-free science. An era's science is part of its politics, economics and sociology: it is generated by them and in turn helps to generate them. Our personal and social histories mold what we perceive to be our biology and history as organisms, just as our biology plays its part in our social behavior and perceptions. As scientists, we learn to examine the ways in which our experimental methods can bias our answers, but we are not taught to be equally wary of the biases introduced by our implicit, unstated and often unconscious beliefs about the nature of reality. To become conscious of these is more difficult than anything else we do. But difficult as it may seem, we must try to do it if our picture of the world is to be more than a reflection of various aspects of ourselves and of our social arrangements.[2]

Darwin's Evolutionary Theory

It is interesting that the idea that Darwin was swimming against the stream of accepted social dogma has prevailed, in spite of the fact that many historians have shown his thinking fitted squarely into the historical and social perspective of his time. Darwin so clearly and admittedly was drawing together strands that had been developing over long periods of time that the questions why he was the one to produce the synthesis and why it happened just then have clamored for answers. Therefore, the social origins of the Darwinian synthesis have been probed by numerous scientists and historians.

A belief that all living forms are related and that there also are deep connections between the living and nonliving has existed through much of recorded human history. Through the animism of tribal cultures that endows everyone and everything with a common spirit; through more elaborate expressions of the unity of living forms in some Far Eastern and Native American belief systems; and through Aristotelian notions of connectedness runs the theme of one web of life that includes humans among its many strands. The Judaeo-Christian world view has been exceptional—and I would say flawed—in setting man (and I mean the male of the species) apart from the rest of nature by making him the namer and ruler of all life. The biblical myth of the creation gave rise to the separate and unchanging species which that second Adam, Linnaeus (1707–78), later named and classified. But even Linnaeus—though he began by accepting the belief that all existing species had been created by Jehovah during that one week long ago ("Nulla species nova")—had his doubts about their immutability by the time he had identified more than four thousand of them: some species ap-

peared to be closely related, others seemed clearly transitional. Yet as Eiseley has pointed out, it is important to realize that:

> Until the scientific idea of 'species' acquired form and distinctness there could be no dogma of 'special' creation in the modern sense. This form and distinctness it did not possess until the naturalists of the seventeenth century began to substitute exactness of definition for the previous vague characterizations of the objects of nature.[3]

And he continues:

> … it was Linnaeus with his proclamation that species were absolutely fixed since the beginning who intensified the theological trend…. Science, in its desire for classification and order,… found itself satisfactorily allied with a Christian dogma whose refinements it had contributed to produce.

Did species exist before they were invented by scientists with their predilection for classification and naming? And did the new science, by concentrating on differences which could be used to tell things apart, devalue the similarities that tie them together? Certainly the Linnaean system succeeded in congealing into a relatively static form what had been a more fluid and graded world that allowed for change and hence for a measure of historicity.

The hundred years that separate Linnaeus from Darwin saw the development of historical geology by Lyell (1797–1875) and an incipient effort to fit the increasing number of fossils that were being uncovered into the earth's newly discovered history. By the time Darwin came along, it was clear to many people that the earth and its creatures had histories. There were fossil series of snails; some fossils were known to be very old, yet looked for all the world like present-day forms; others had no like descendants and had become extinct. Lamarck (1744–1829), who like Linnaeus began by believing in the fixity of species, by 1800 had formulated a theory of evolution that involved a slow historical process, which he assumed to have taken a very, very long time.

Possibly one reason the theory of evolution arose in Western, rather than Eastern, science was that the descriptions of fossil and living forms showing so many close relationships made the orthodox biblical view of the special creation of each and every species untenable; and the question, how living forms merged into one another, pressed for an answer. The Eastern philosophies that accepted connectedness and relatedness as givens did not need to confront this question with the same urgency. In other words, where evidences of evolutionary change did not raise fundamental contradictions and questions, evolutionary theory did not need to be invented to reconcile and answer them. However one, and perhaps the most, important difference between Western evolutionary thinking and Eastern ideas of organismic unity lies in the materialistic and historical elements, which are the earmark of Western evolutionism as formulated by Darwin.

Though most of the elements of Darwinian evolutionary theory existed for at least a hundred years before Darwin, he knit them into a consistent theory that was in line with the mainstream thinking of his time. Irvine writes:

> The similar fortunes of liberalism and natural selection are significant. Darwin's matter was as English as his method. Terrestrial history turned out to be strangely like Victorian history writ large. Bertrand Russell and others have remarked that Darwin's theory was mainly 'an extension to the animal and vegetable world of laissez faire economics.' As a matter of fact, the economic conceptions of utility, pressure of population, marginal fertility, barriers in restraint of trade, the division of labor, progress and adjustment by competition, and the spread of technological improvements can all be paralleled in The

Origin of Species. But so, alas, can some of the doctrines of English political conservatism. In revealing the importance of time and the hereditary past, in emphasizing the persistence of vestigial structures, the minuteness of variations and the slowness of evolution, Darwin was adding Hooker and Burke to Bentham and Adam Smith. The constitution of the universe exhibited many of the virtues of the English constitution.[4]

One of the first to comment on this congruence was Karl Marx (1818–83) who wrote to Friedrich Engels (1820–95) in 1862, three years after the publication of *The Origin of Species:*

> It is remarkable how Darwin recognizes among beasts and plants his English society with its division of labor, competition, opening up of new markets, 'inventions,' and the Malthusian 'struggle for existence.' It is Hobbes's 'bellum omnium contra omnes,' [war of all against all] and one is reminded of Hegel's *Phenomenology,* where civil society is described as a 'spiritual animal kingdom,' while in Darwin the animal kingdom figures as civil society.[5]

A similar passage appears in a letter by Engels:

> The whole Darwinist teaching of the struggle for existence is simply a transference from society to living nature of Hobbes's doctrine of 'bellum omnium contra omnes' and of the bourgeois-economic doctrine of competition together with Malthus's theory of population. When this conjurer's trick has been performed ... the same theories are transferred back again from organic nature into history and now it is claimed that their validity as eternal laws of human society has been proved.[5]

The very fact that essentially the same mechanism of evolution through natural selection was postulated independently and at about the same time by two English naturalists, Darwin and Alfred Russel Wallace (1823–1913), shows that the basic ideas were in the air—which is not to deny that it took genius to give them logical and convincing form.

Darwin's theory of *The Origin of Species by Means Of Natural Selection*, published in 1859, accepted the fact of evolution and undertook to explain how it could have come about. He had amassed large quantities of data to show that historical change had taken place, both from the fossil record and from his observations as a naturalist on the Beagle. He pondered why some forms had become extinct and others had survived to generate new and different forms. The watchword of evolution seemed to be: be fruitful and modify, one that bore a striking resemblance to the ways of animal and plant breeders. Darwin corresponded with many breeders and himself began to breed pigeons. He was impressed by the way in which breeders, through careful selection, could use even minor variations to elicit major differences, and was searching for the analog in nature to the breeders' techniques of selecting favorable variants. A prepared mind therefore encountered Malthus's *Essay on the Principles of Population* (1798). In his *Autobiography*, Darwin writes:

In October 1838, that is, fifteen months after I had begun my systematic enquiry, I happened to read for amusement Malthus on *Population*, and being well prepared to appreciate the struggle for existence which everywhere goes on from long-continued observation of the habits of animals and plants, it at once struck me that under these circumstances favourable variations would tend to be preserved and unfavourable ones to be destroyed. The result of this would be the formation of new species. Here, then, I had at last got a theory by which to work.[6]

Incidentally, Wallace also acknowledged being led to his theory by reading Malthus. Wrote Wallace:

The most interesting coincidence in the matter, I think, is, that I, *as well as Darwin*, was led to the theory itself through Malthus. It suddenly flashed upon me that all animals are necessarily thus kept down—'the struggle for existence'—while *variations*, on which I was always thinking, must necessarily often be *beneficial*, and would then cause those varieties to increase while the injurious variations diminished.[7] [Wallace's italics]

Both, therefore, saw in Malthus's struggle for existence the working of a natural law which effected what Herbert Spencer had called the "survival of the fittest."

The three principal ingredients of Darwin's theory of evolution are: endless variation, natural selection from among the variants, and the resulting survival of the fittest. Given the looseness of many of his arguments—he credited himself with being an expert wriggler—it is surprising that his explanation has found such wide acceptance. One reason probably lies in the fact that Darwin's theory was historical and materialistic, characteristics that are esteemed as virtues; another, perhaps in its intrinsic optimism—its notion of progressive development of species, one from another—which fit well into the meritocratic ideology encouraged by the early successes of British mercantilism, industrial capitalism and imperialism.

But not only did Darwin's interpretation of the history of life on earth fit in well with the social doctrines of nineteenth-century liberalism and individualism. It was used in turn to support them by rendering them aspects of natural law. Herbert Spencer is usually credited with having brought Darwinism into social theory. The body of ideas came to be known as social Darwinism and gained wide acceptance in Britain and the United States in the latter part of the nineteenth and on into the twentieth century. For example, John D. Rockefeller proclaimed in a Sunday school address:

The growth of a large business is merely the survival of the fittest.... The American Beauty rose can be produced in the splendor and fragrance which bring cheer to its beholder only by sacrificing the early buds which grow up around it. This is not an evil tendency in business. It is merely the working-out of a law of nature and a law of God.[8]

The circle was therefore complete: Darwin consciously borrowed from social theorists such as Malthus and Spencer some of the basic concepts of evolutionary theory. Spencer and others promptly used Darwinism to reinforce these very social theories and in the process bestowed upon them the force of natural law.[9]

Sexual Selection

It is essential to expand the foregoing analysis of the mutual influences of Darwinism and nineteenth-century social doctrine by looking critically at the Victorian picture Darwin painted of the relations between the sexes, and of the roles that males and females play in the evolution of animals and humans. For although the ethnocentric bias of Darwinism is widely acknowledged, its blatant sexism—or more correctly, androcentrism (male-centeredness)—is rarely mentioned, presumably because it has not been noticed by Darwin scholars, who have mostly been men. Already in the nineteenth century, indeed within Darwin's life time, feminists such as Antoinette Brown Blackwell and Eliza Burt Gamble called attention to the obvious male bias pervading his arguments.[10,11] But these women did not have Darwin's or Spencer's professional status or scientific experience; nor indeed could they, given their limited opportunities for education, travel and participation in the affairs of the world. Their books were hardly acknowledged or discussed by professionals, and they have been, until now, merely ignored and excluded from the record.

However, it is important to expose Darwin's androcentrism, and not only for historical reasons, but because it remains an integral and unquestioned part of contemporary biological theories.

Early in *The Origin of Species*, Darwin defines sexual selection as one mechanism by which evolution operates. The Victorian and androcentric biases are obvious:

> This form of selection depends, not on a struggle for existence in relation to other organic beings or to external conditions, but on a struggle of individuals of one sex, generally males, for the possession of the other sex.[12]

And,

> Generally, the most vigorous males, those which are best fitted for their places in nature, will leave most progeny. But in many cases, victory depends not so much on general vigor, as on having special weapons confined to the male sex.

The Victorian picture of the active mate and the passive female becomes even more explicit later in the same paragraph:

> the males of certain hymenopterous insects [bees, wasps, ants] have been frequently seen by that inimitable observer, M. Fabre, fighting for a particular female who sits by, an apparently unconcerned beholder of the struggle, and then retires with the conqueror.

Darwin's anthropomorphizing continues, as it develops that many male birds "perform strange antics before the females, which, standing by as spectators, at last choose the most attractive partner." However, he worries that whereas this might be a reasonable way to explain the behavior of peahens and female birds of paradise whose consorts anyone can admire, "it is doubtful whether [the tuft of hair on the breast of the wild turkey-cock] can be ornamental in the eyes of the female bird." Hence Darwin ends this brief discussion by saying that he "would not wish to attribute all sexual differences to this agency."

Some might argue in defense of Darwin that bees (or birds, or what have you) do act that way. But the very language Darwin uses to describe these behaviors disqualifies him as an "objective" observer. His animals are cast into roles from a Victorian script. And whereas no one can claim to have solved the important methodological question of how to disembarrass oneself of one's anthropocentric and cultural biases when observing animal behavior, surely one must begin by trying.

After the publication of *The Origin of Species*, Darwin continued to think about sexual selection, and in 1871, he published *The Descent of Man and Selection in Relation to Sex*, a book in which he describes in much more detail how sexual selection operates in the evolution of animals and humans.

In the aftermath of the outcry *The Descent* raised among fundamentalists, much has been made of the fact that Darwin threatened the special place Man was assigned by the Bible and treated him as though he was just another kind of animal. But he did nothing of the sort. The Darwinian synthesis did not end anthropocentrism or androcentrism in biology. On the contrary, Darwin made them part of biology by presenting as "facts of nature" interpretations of animal behavior that reflect the social and moral outlook of his time.

In a sense, anthropocentrism is implicit in the fact that we humans have named, catalogued, and categorized the world around us, including ourselves. Whether we stress our upright stance, our opposable thumbs, our brain, or our language, to ourselves we are creatures apart and very different from all others. But the scientific view of ourselves is also profoundly androcentric. *The Descent of Man* is quite literally his journey. Elaine Morgan rightly says:

It's just as hard for man to break the habit of thinking of himself as central to the species as it was to break the habit of thinking of himself as central to the universe. He sees himself quite unconsciously as the main line of evolution with a female satellite revolving around him as the moon revolves around the earth. This not only causes him to overlook valuable clues to our ancestry, but sometimes leads him into making statements that are arrant and demonstrable nonsense.... Most of the books forget about [females] for most of the time. They drag her on stage rather suddenly for the obligatory chapter on Sex and Reproduction, and then say: 'All right, love, you can go now,' while they get on with the real meaty stuff about the Mighty Hunter with his lovely new weapons and his lovely new straight legs racing across the Pleistocene plains. Any modifications of her morphology are taken to be imitations of the Hunter's evolution, or else designed solely for his delectation.[13]

To expose the Victorian roots of post-Darwinian thinking about human evolution, we must start by looking at Darwin's ideas about sexual selection in *The Descent*, where he begins the chapter entitled 'Principles of Sexual Selection' by setting the stage for the active, pursuing male:

With animals which have their sexes separated, the males necessarily differ from the females in their organs of reproduction; and these are the primary sexual characters. But the sexes differ in what Hunter has called secondary sexual characters, which are not directly connected with the act of reproduction; for instance, the male possesses certain organs of sense or locomotion, of which the female is quite destitute, ors has them more highly-developed, in order that he may readily find or reach her; or again the male has special organs of prehension for holding her securely.[14]

Moreover, we soon learn:

in order that the males should seek efficiently, it would be necessary that they should be endowed with strong passions; and the acquirement of such passions would naturally follow from the more eager leaving a larger number of offspring than the less eager.[15]

Darwin is worried because among some animals, males and females do not appear to be all that different:

a double process of selection has been carried on; that the males have selected the more attractive females, and the latter the more attractive males.... But from what we know of the habits of animals, this view is hardly probable, for the male is generally eager to pair with any female.[16]

Make no mistake, wherever you look among animals, eagerly promiscuous males are pursuing females, who peer from behind languidly drooping eyelids to discern the strongest and handsomest. Does it not sound like the wish-fulfillment dream of a proper Victorian gentleman?

This is not the place to discuss Darwin's long treatise in detail. Therefore, let this brief look at animals suffice as background for his section on Sexual Selection in Relation to Man. Again we can start on the first page: "Man is more courageous, pugnacious and energetic than woman, and has more inventive genius."[17] Among "savages," fierce, bold men are constantly battling each other for the possession of women and this has affected the secondary sexual characteristics of both. Darwin grants that there is some disagreement whether there are "inherent differences" between men and women, but suggests that by analogy with lower animals it is "at least probable." In fact, "Woman seems to differ from man in mental disposition, chiefly in her greater tenderness and less selfishness," [18] for:

Man is the rival of other men; he delights in competition, and this leads to ambition

which passes too easily into selfishness. These latter qualities seem to be his natural and unfortunate birthright.

This might make it seem as though women are better than men after all, but not so:

The chief distinction in the intellectual powers of the two sexes is shown by man's attaining to a higher eminence, in whatever he takes up, than can women—whether requiring deep thought, reason, or imagination, or merely the use of the senses and hands. If two lists were made of the most eminent men and women in poetry, painting, sculpture, music (inclusive both of composition and performance), history, science, and philosophy, with half-a-dozen names under each subject, the two lists would not bear comparison. We may also infer ... that if men are capable of a decided pre-eminence over women in many subjects, the average of mental power in man must be above that of woman.... [Men have had] to defend their females, as well as their young, from enemies of all kinds, and to hunt for their joint subsistence. But to avoid enemies or to attack them with success to capture wild animals, and to fashion weapons, requires the aid of the higher mental faculties, namely, observation, reason, invention, or imagination. These various faculties will thus have been continually put to the test and selected during manhood.[19]

"Thus," the discussion ends, "man has ultimately become superior to woman" and it is a good thing that men pass on their characteristics to their daughters as well as to their sons, "otherwise it is probable that man would have become as superior in mental endowment to woman, as the peacock is in ornamental plumage to the peahen."

So here it is in a nutshell: men's mental and physical qualities were constantly improved through competition for women and hunting, while women's minds would have become vestigial if it were not for the fortunate circumstance that in each generation daughters inherit brains from their fathers.

Another example of Darwin's acceptance of the conventional mores of his time is his interpretation of the evolution of marriage and monogamy:

> ... it seems probable that the habit of marriage, in any strict sense of the word, has been gradually developed; and that almost promiscuous or very loose intercourse was once very common throughout the world. Nevertheless, from the strength of the feeling of jealousy all through the animal kingdom, as well as from the analogy of lower animals ... I cannot believe that absolutely promiscuous intercourse prevailed in times past....[20]

Note the moralistic tone; and how does Darwin know that strong feelings of jealousy exist "all through the animal kingdom?" For comparison, it is interesting to look at Engels, who working largely from the same early anthropological sources as Darwin, had this to say:

> As our whole presentation has shown, the progress which manifests itself in these successive forms [from group marriage to pairing marriage to what he refers to as "monogamy supplemented by adultery and prostitution"] is connected with the peculiarity that women, but not men, are increasingly deprived of the sexual freedom of group marriage. In fact, for men group marriage actually still exists even to this day. What for the woman is a crime entailing grave legal and social consequences is considered honorable in a man or, at the worse, a slight moral blemish which he cheerfully bears.... Monogamy arose from the concentration of considerable wealth in the hands of a single individual—a man—and from the need to bequeath this wealth to the children of that man and of no other. For this purpose, the monogamy of the woman was required, not that of the man, so this monogamy of the woman did not in any way interfere with open or concealed polygamy on the part of the man.[21]

Clearly, Engels did not accept the Victorian code of behavior as our natural biological heritage.

Sociobiology: A New Scientific Sexism

The theory of sexual selection went into a decline during the first half of this century, as efforts to verify some of Darwin's examples showed that many of the features he had thought were related to success in mating could not be legitimately regarded in that way. But it has lately regained its respectability, and contemporary discussions of reproductive fitness often cite examples of sexual selection.[22] Therefore, before we go on to discuss human evolution, it is helpful to look at contemporary views of sexual selection and sex roles among animals (and even plants).

Let us start with a lowly alga that one might think impossible to stereotype by sex. Wolfgang Wickler, an ethologist at the University of Munich, writes in his book on sexual behavior patterns (a topic which Konrad Lorenz tells us in the Introduction is crucial in deciding which sexual behaviors to consider healthy and which diseased):

> Even among very simple organisms such as algae, which have threadlike rows of cells one behind the other, one can observe that during copulation the cells of one thread act as males with regard to the cells of a second thread, but as females with regard to the cells of a third thread. The mark of male behavior is that the cell actively crawls or swims over to the other; the female cell remains passive.[23]

The circle is simple to construct: one starts with the Victorian stereotype of the active male and the passive female, then looks at animals, algae, bacteria, people, and calls all passive behavior feminine, active or goal-oriented behavior masculine. And it works! The Victorian stereotype is biologically determined: even algae behave that way.

But let us see what Wickler has to say about Rocky Mountain Bighorn sheep, in which the sexes cannot be distinguished on sight. He finds it "curious":

> that between the extremes of rams over eight years old and lambs less than a year old one finds every possible transition in age, but no other differences whatever; the bodily form, the structure of the horns, and the color of the coat are the same for both sexes.

Now note: "... the typical female behavior is absent from this pattern." Typical of what? Obviously not of Bighorn sheep. In fact we are told that "even the males often cannot recognize a female," indeed, "the females are only of interest to the males during rutting season." How does he know that the males do *not* recognize the females? Maybe these sheep are so weird that most of the time they relate to a female as though she were just another sheep, and whistle at her (my free translation of "taking an interest") only when it is a question of mating. But let us get at last to how the *females* behave. That is astonishing, for it turns out:

> that *both* sexes play two roles, either that of the male or that of the young male. Outside the rutting season the females behave like young males, during the rutting season like aggressive older males. (Wickler's italics)

In fact:

> There is a line of development leading from the lamb to the high ranking ram, and the female animals ($\female$) behave exactly as though they were in fact males ($\male$) whose development was retarded.... We can say that the only fully developed mountain sheep are the powerful rams....

At last the androcentric paradigm is out in the open: females are always measured against the standard of the male. Sometimes they are like young males, sometimes like older ones; but never do they reach what Wickler calls "the final stage of fully mature physical structure and behavior possible to this species." That, in his view, is reserved for the rams.

Wickler bases this discussion on observations by Valerius Geist, whose book, *Mountain Sheep*, contains many examples of how androcentric biases can color observations as well as interpretations and restrict the imagination to stereotypes. One of the most interesting is the following:

> Matched rams, usually strangers, begin to treat each other like females and clash until one acts like a female. This is the loser in the fight. The rams confront each other with displays, kick each other, threat jump, and clash till one turns and accepts the kicks, displays, and occasional mounts of the larger without aggressive displays. The loser is not chased away. The point of the fight is not to kill, maim, or even drive the rival off, but to treat him like a female.[24]

This description would be quite different if the interaction were interpreted as something other than a fight, say as a homosexual encounter, a game, or a ritual dance. The fact is that it contains none of the elements that we commonly associate with fighting. Yet because Geist casts it into the imagery of heterosexuality and aggression, it becomes perplexing.

There would be no reason to discuss these examples if their treatments of sex differences or of male/female behavior were exceptional. But they are in the mainstream of contemporary sociobiology, ethology, and evolutionary biology.

A book that has become a standard reference is George Williams's *Sex and Evolution*.[25] It abounds in blatantly biased statements that describe as "careful" and "enlightened" research reports that support the androcentric paradigm, and as questionable or erroneous those that contradict it. Masculinity and femininity are discussed with reference to the behavior of pipefish and seahorses; and cichlids and catfish are judged downright abnormal because both sexes guard the young. For present purposes it is sufficient to discuss a few points that are raised in the chapter entitled "Why Are Males Masculine and Females Feminine and, Occasionally, Vice-Versa?"

The very title gives one pause, for if the words masculine and feminine do not mean of, or pertaining, respectively, to males and females, what *do* they mean—particularly in a scientific context? So let us read.

On the first page we find:

Males of the more familiar higher animals take less of an interest In the young. in courtship they take a more active role, are less discriminating in choice of mates, more inclined toward promiscuity and polygamy, and more contentious among themselves.

We are back with Darwin. The data are flimsy as ever, but doesn't it sound like a description of the families on your block?

The important question is who are these "more familiar higher animals?" Is their behavior typical, or are we familiar with them because, for over a century, androcentric biologists have paid disproportionate attention to animals whose behavior resembles those human social traits that they would like to interpret as biologically determined and hence out of our control?

Williams' generalization quoted above gives rise to the paradox that becomes his chief theoretical problem:

Why, if each individual is maximizing its own genetic survival should the female be less anxious to have her eggs fertilized than a male is to fertilize them, and why should the young be of greater interest to one than to the other?

Let me translate this sentence for the benefit of those unfamiliar with current evolutionary theory. The first point is that an individual's *fitness* is measured by the number of her or his offspring that survive to reproductive age. The phrase, "the survival of the fittest," therefore signifies the fact that evolutionary history is the sum of the stories of those who leave the greatest numbers of descendants. What is meant by each individual "maximizing its own genetic survival" is that every one tries to leave as many viable offspring as possible. (Note the implication of conscious intent. Such intent is not exhibited by the increasing number of humans who intentionally *limit* the numbers of their offspring. Nor is one, of course, justified in ascribing it to other animals.)

One might therefore think that in animals in which each parent contributes half of each offspring's genes, females and males would exert themselves equally to maximize the number of offspring. However, we know that according to the patriarchal paradigm, males are active in courtship, whereas females wait passively. This is what Williams means by females being "less anxious" to procreate than males. And of course we also know that "normally" females have a disproportionate share in the care of their young.

So why these asymmetries? The explanation: "The *essential* difference between the sexes is that females produce large immobile gametes and males produce small mobile ones" (my italics). This is what determines their "different optimal strategies." So if you have wondered why men are promiscuous and women faithfully stay home and care for the babies, the reason is that males "can quickly replace wasted gametes and be ready for another mate," whereas females "can not so readily replace a mass of yolky eggs or find a substitute father for an expected litter." Therefore females must "show a much greater degree of caution" in the choice of a mate than males.

E. O. Wilson says that same thing somewhat differently:

One gamete, the egg, is relatively very large and sessile; the other, the sperm, is small and motile.... The egg possesses the yolk required to launch the embryo into an advanced state of development. Because it represents a considerable energetic investment on the part of the mother the embryo is often sequestered and protected, and sometimes its care is extended into the postnatal period. *This is the reason why* parental care is *normally* provided by the female....[26] [my italics]

Though these descriptions fit only some of the animal species that reproduce sexually, and are rapidly ceasing to fit human domestic arrangements in many portions of the globe,[27] they do fit the patriarchal model of the household. Clearly, androcentric biology is busy as ever trying to provide biological "reasons" for a particular set of human social arrangements.

The ethnocentrism of this individualistic, capitalistic model of evolutionary biology and sociobiology with its emphasis on competition and "investments," is discussed by Sahlins in his monograph, *The Use and Abuse of Biology.* He gives many examples from other cultures to show how these theories reflect a narrow bias that disqualifies them from masquerading as descriptions of universals in biology. But, like other male critics, Sahlins fails to notice the obvious androcentrism.

About thirty years ago, Ruth Herschberger wrote a delightfully funny book called *Adam's Rib,*[28] in which she spoofed the then current androcentric myths regarding sex differences. When it was reissued in 1970, the book was not out of date. In the chapter entitled "Society Writes Biology," she juxtaposes the then (and now) current patriarchal scenario of the dauntless voyage of the active, agile sperm toward the passively receptive, sessile egg to an improvised "matriarchal" account. In it the large, competent egg plays the central role and we can feel only pity for the many millions of minuscule, fragile sperm most of which are too feeble to make it to fertilization.

This brings me to a question that always puzzles me when I read about the female's larger energetic investment in her egg than the male's in his sperm: there is an enormous disproportion in the *numbers* of eggs and sperms that participate in the act of fertilization. Does it really take more "energy" to generate the one or relatively few eggs than the large excess of sperms required to achieve fertilization? In humans the disproportion is enormous. In her life time, an average woman produces about four hundred eggs, of which in present-day Western countries, she will "invest" only in about 2.2[29] Meanwhile the average man generates several billions of sperms to secure those same 2.2 investments!

Needless to say, I have no idea how much "energy" is involved in producing, equipping and ejaculating a sperm cell along with the other necessary components of the ejaculum that enable it to fertilize an egg, nor how much is involved in releasing an egg from the ovary, reabsorbing it in the oviduct if unfertilized (a partial dividend on the investment), or incubating 2.2 of them to birth. But neither do those who propound the existence and importance of women's disproportionate energetic investments. Furthermore, I attach no significance to these questions, since I do not believe that the details of our economic and social arrangements reflect our evolutionary history. I am only trying to show how feeble is the "evidence" that is being put forward to argue the evolutionary basis (hence *naturalness*) of woman's role as homemaker.

The recent resurrection of the theory of sexual selection and the ascription of asymmetry to the "parental investments" of males and females are probably not unrelated to the rebirth of the women's movement. We should remember that Darwin's theory of sexual selection was put forward in the midst of the first wave of feminism.[30] It seems that when women threaten to enter as equals into the world of affairs, androcentric scientists rally to point out that our *natural* place is in the home.

The Evolution of Man

Darwin's sexual stereotypes are doing well also in the contemporary literature on human evolution. This is a field in which facts are few and specimens are separated often by hundreds of thousands of years, so that maximum leeway exists for investigator bias. Almost all the investigators have been men; it should therefore come as no surprise that what has emerged is the familiar picture of Man the Toolmaker. This extends so far that when skull fragments estimated to be 250,000 years old turned up among the stone tools in the gravel beds of the Thames at Swanscombe and paleontologists decided that they are probably those of a female, we read that "The Swanscombe woman, or her husband, was a maker of hand axes...."[31] (Imagine the reverse: The Swanscombe man, or his wife, was a maker of axes ....) The implication is that if there were tools, the Swanscombe *woman* could not have made them. But we now know that even apes make tools. Why not women?

Actually, the idea that the making and use of tools were the main driving forces in evolution has been modified since paleontological finds and field observations have shown that apes both use and fashion tools. Now the emphasis is on the human use of tools as weapons for hunting. This brings us to the myth of Man the Hunter, who had to invent not only tools, but also the social organization that allowed him to hunt big animals. He also had to roam great distances and learn to cope with many and varied circumstances. We are told that this entire constellation of factors stimulated the astonishing and relatively rapid development of his brain that came to distinguish Man from his ape cousins. For example, Kenneth Oakley writes:

Men who made tools of the standard type...must have been capable of forming in their minds images of the ends to which they laboured. Human culture in all its diversity is the outcome of this capacity for conceptual thinking, but the leading factors in its development are tradition coupled with invention. The primitive hunter made an implement in a particular fashion largely because as a child he watched his father at work or because he copied the work of a hunter in a neighbouring tribe. The standard hand axe was not conceived by any one individual *ab initio*, but was the result of exceptional individuals in successive generations not only copying but occasionally improving on the work of their predecessors. As a result of the co-operative hunting, migrations and rudimentary forms of barter, the traditions of different groups of primitive hunters sometimes became blended.[32]

It seems a remarkable feat of clairvoyance to see in such detail what happened some 250,000 years in pre-history, complete with the little boy and his little stone chipping set just like daddy's big one.

It is hard to know what reality lurks behind the reconstructions of Man Evolving. Since the time when we and the apes diverged some fifteen million years ago, the main features of human evolution that one can read from the paleontological finds are the upright stance, reduction in the size of the teeth, and increase in brain size. But finds are few and far between both in space and in time until we reach the Neanderthals some 70,000 to 40,000 years ago—a jaw or skull, teeth, pelvic bones, and often only fragments of them.[33] From such bits of evidence as these come the pictures and statues we have all seen of that line of increasingly straight and upright, and decreasingly hairy and ape-like men marching in single file behind *Homo sapiens*, carrying their clubs, stones, or axes; or that other one of a group of beetle-browed and bearded hunters bending over the large slain animal they have brought into camp, while over on the side long-haired, broad-bottomed females nurse infants at their pendulous breasts.

Impelled, I suppose, by recent feminist critiques of the evolution of Man the Hunter, a few male anthropologists have begun to take note of Woman the Gatherer, and the stereotyping goes on as before. For example Howells, who acknowledges these criticisms as just, nonetheless assumes "the classic division of labor between the sexes" and states as fact that stone age men roamed great distances "on behalf of the whole economic group, while the women were restricted to within the radius of a fraction of a day's walk from camp." Needless to say, he does not *know* any of this.

One can equally well assume that the responsibilities of providing food and nurturing young were widely dispersed through the group that needed to cooperate and devise many and varied strategies for survival. Nor is it obvious why tasks needed to have been differentiated by sex. It makes sense that the gatherers would have known how to hunt the animals they came across; that the hunters gathered when there was nothing to catch, and that men and women did some of each, though both of them probably did a great deal more gathering than hunting. After all, the important thing was to get the day's food, not to define sex roles. Bearing and tending the young have not necessitated a sedentary way of life among nomadic peoples right to the present, and both gathering and hunting probably required movement over large areas in order to find sufficient food. Hewing close to home probably accompanied the transition to cultivation, which introduced the necessity to stay put for planting, though of course not longer than required to harvest. Without fertilizers and crop rotation, frequent moves were probably essential parts of early farming.

Being sedentary ourselves, we tend to assume that our foreparents heaved a great sigh of relief when they invented agriculture and could at last stop roaming. But there is no reason to believe this. Hunter/gatherers and other people who move with their food still exist. And what has been called the agricultural "revolution" probably took considerably longer than all of recorded history. During this time, presumably some people settled down while others remained nomadic, and some did some of each, depending on place and season.

We have developed a fantastically limited and stereotypic picture of ways of life that evolved over many tens of thousands of years, and no doubt varied in lots of ways that we do not even imagine. It is true that by historic times, which are virtually now in the scale of our evolutionary history, there were agricultural settlements, including a few towns that numbered hundreds and even thousands of inhabitants. By that time labor was to some extent divided by sex, though anthropologists have shown that right to the present, the division can be different in different places. There are economic and social reasons for the various delineations of sex roles. We presume too much when we try to read them in the scant record of our distant prehistoric past.

Nor are we going to learn them by observing our nearest living relatives among the apes and monkeys, as some biologists and anthropologists are trying to do. For one thing, different species of primates vary widely in the extent to which the sexes differ in both their anatomy and their social behavior, so that one can find examples of almost any kind of behavior one is looking for by picking the appropriate animal. For another, most scientists find it convenient to forget that present-day apes and monkeys have had as long an evolutionary history as we have had, since the time we and they went our separate ways many millions of years ago. There is no theoretical reason why their behavior should tell us more about our ancestry than our behavior tells us about theirs. It is only anthropocentrism that can lead someone to imagine that "A possible preadaptation to human ranging for food is the behavior of the large apes, whose groups move more freely and widely compared to gibbons and monkeys, and whose social units are looser."[34] But just as in the androcentric paradigm men evolved while women cheered from the bleachers, so in the anthropocentric one, humans evolved while the apes watched from the trees. This view leaves out not only the fact that the apes have been evolving away from us for as long a time as we from them, but that certain aspects of their evolution may have been a response to our own. So, for example, the evolution of human habits may have put a serious crimp into the evolution of the great apes and forced them to stay in the trees or to hurry back into them.

The current literature on human evolution says very little about the role of language, and sometimes even associates the evolution of language with tool use and hunting—two purportedly "masculine" characteristics. But this is very unlikely because the evolution of language probably went with biological changes, such as occurred in the structure of the face, larynx, and brain, all slow processes. Tool use and hunting, on the other hand, are cultural characteristics that can evolve much more quickly. It is likely that the more elaborate use of tools, and the social arrangements that go with hunting and gathering, developed in part as a consequence of the expanded human repertory of capacities and needs that derive from our ability to communicate through language.

It is likely that the evolution of speech has been one of the most powerful forces directing our biological, cultural, and social evolution, and it is surprising that its significance has largely been ignored by biologists. But, of course, it does not fit into the androcentric paradigm. No one has ever claimed that women can not talk; so if men are the vanguard of evolution, humans must have evolved through the stereotypically male behaviors of competition, tool use, and hunting.

How to Learn Our History? Some Feminist Strategies

How *did* we evolve? Most people now believe that we became who we are by a historical process, but, clearly, we do not know its course, and must use more imagination than fact to reconstruct it. The mythology of science asserts that with many different scientists all asking their own questions and evaluating the answers independently, whatever personal bias creeps into their individual answers is cancelled out when the large picture is put together. This might conceivably be so if scientists were women and men from all sorts of different cultural and social backgrounds who came to science with very different ideologies and interests. But since, in fact, they have been predominantly university-trained white males from privileged social backgrounds, the bias has been narrow and the product often reveals more about the investigator than about the subject being researched.

Since women have not figured in the paradigm of evolution, we need to rethink our evolutionary history. There are various ways to do this:

(1) We can construct one or several estrocentric (female-centered) theories. This is Elaine Morgan's approach in her account of *The Descent of Woman* and Evelyn Reed's in *Woman's Evolution*.[35] Except as a way of parodying the male myths, I find it unsatisfactory because it locks the authors into many of the same unwarranted suppositions that underlie those very myths. For example, both accept the view that our behavior is biologically determined, that what we do is a result of what we were or did millions of years ago. This assumption is unwarranted given the enormous range of human adaptability and the rapid rate of human social and cultural evolution. Of course, there is a place for myth-making and I dream of a long poem that sings women's origins and tells how we felt and what we did; but I do not think that carefully constructed "scientific" mirror images do much to counter the male myths. Present-day women do not know what prehistoric hunter/gatherer women were up to any more than a male paleontologist like Kenneth Oakley knows what the little tool-maker learned from his dad.

(2) Women can sift carefully the few available facts by paring away the mythology and

getting as close to the raw data as possible. And we can try to see what, if any, picture emerges that could lead us to questions that perhaps have *not* been asked and that should, and could, be answered. One problem with this approach is that many of the data no longer exist. Every excavation removes the objects from their locale and all we have left is the researchers' descriptions of what they saw. Since we are concerned about unconscious biases, that is worrisome.

(3) Rather than invent our own myths, we can concentrate, as a beginning, on exposing and analyzing the male myths that hide our overwhelming ignorance, "for when a subject is highly controversial—and any question about sex is that—one cannot hope to tell the truth."[36] Women anthropologists have begun to do this. New books are being written, such as *The Female of the Species*[37] and *Toward an Anthropology of Women*,[38] books that expose the Victorian stereotype that runs through the literature of human evolution, and pull together relevant anthropological studies. More important, women who recognize an androcentric myth when they see one and who are able to think beyond it, must do the necessary work in the field, in the laboratories, and in the libraries, and come up with ways of seeing the facts and of interpreting them.[39]

None of this is easy, because women scientists tend to hail from the same socially privileged families and be educated in the same elite universities as our male colleagues. But since we are marginal to the mainstream, we may find it easier than they to watch ourselves push the bus in which we are riding.

As we rethink our history, our social roles, and our options, it is important that we be ever wary of the wide areas of congruence between what are obviously ethno- and androcentric assumptions and what we have been taught are the scientifically proven facts of our biology. Darwin was right when he wrote that "False facts are highly injurious to the progress of science, for they often endure long...."[40] Androcentric science is full of "false facts" that have endured all too long

and that serve the interests of those who interpret as women's biological heritage the sexual and social stereotypes we reject. To see our alternatives is essential if we are to acquire the space in which to explore who we are, where we have come from, and where we want to go.

Notes

1. For a discussion of this process, see Thomas S. Kuhn, *The Structure of Scientific Revolutions*, 2nd ed. (University of Chicago Press, 1970).

2. Berger and Luckmann have characterized this process as "trying to push a bus in which one is riding." [Peter Berger and Thomas Luckmann, *The Social Construction of Reality* (Garden City: Doubleday & Co., 1966), p. 12.]. I would say that, worse yet, it is like trying to look out of the rear window to *watch* oneself push the bus in which one rides.

3. Loren Eiseley, *Darwin's Century* (Garden City: Doubleday & Co., Anchor Books Edition, 1961), p. 24.

4. William Irvine, *Apes, Angels, and Victorians* (New York: McGraw-Hill, 1972), p. 98.

5. Quoted in Marshall Sahlins, *The Use and Abuse of Biology* (Ann Arbor: University of Michigan Press, 1976), pp. 101–102.

6. Francis Darwin, ed., *The Autobiography of Charles Darwin* (New York: Dover Publications, 1958). pp. 42-43.

7. Ibid., pp. 200–201.

8. Richard Hofstadter, *Social Darwinism in American Thought* (Boston: Beacon Press, 1955), p. 45.

9. Though not himself a publicist for social Darwinism like Spencer, there can be no doubt that Darwin accepted its ideology. For example, near the end of *The Descent of Man* he writes: "There should be open competition for all men; and the most able should not be prevented by laws or customs from succeeding best and rearing the largest number of offspring." Marvin Harris has argued that Darwinism, in fact, should be known as biological Spencerism, rather than Spencerism as social Darwinism. For a discussion of the issue, *pro* and *con, see* Marvin Harris. *The Rise of Anthropological Theory, A History of Theories of Culture* (New York: Thomas Y. Crowell, 1968). Ch. 5: Spencerism;

and responses by Derek Freeman and others in *Current Anthropology* 15 (1974). pp. 211–237.

10. Antoinette Brown Blackwell, *The Sexes Throughout Nature* (New York: G. P. Putnam's Sons, 1975; reprinted Westport, Conn.: Hyperion Press. 1978). Excerpts in which Blackwell argues against Darwin and Spencer have been reprinted in Alice S. Rossi. ed., *The Feminist Papers* (New York: Bantam Books, 1974), pp. 356–377.

11. Eliza Burt Gamble, *The Evolution of Woman: An Inquiry into the Dogma of Her Inferiority to Man* (New York: G. P. Putnam's Sons, 1894).

12. Charles Darwin, *The Origin of Species and the Descent of Man* (New York: Modern Library Edition), p. 69.

13. Elaine Morgan. *The Descent of Woman* (New York: Bantam Books, 1973), pp. 3–4.

14. Darwin, Origin of Species. ... p. 567.

15. Ibid., p. 580.

16. Ibid., p. 582.

17. Ibid., p. 867.

18. Ibid., p. 873.

19. Ibid., pp. 873–874.

20. Ibid., p. 895.

21. Frederick Engels, *The Origin of the Family. Private Property and the State*, E.B. Leacock, ed. (New York: International Publishers, 1972), p. 138.

22. One of the most explicit contemporary examples of this literature is E. O. Wilson's *Sociobiology: The New Synthesis* (Cambridge: Harvard University Press, 1975); *see* especially Chapters 1, 14–16 and 27.

23. Wolfgang Wickler. *The Sexual Code: The Social Behavior of Animals and Men* (Garden City: Doubleday, Anchor Books, 1973), p. 23.

24. Valerius Geist, *Mountain Sheep* (Chicago: University of Chicago Press, 1971), p. 190.

25. George C. Williams, *Sex and Evolution* (Princeton: Princeton University Press, 1975).

26. Edward O. Wilson, *Sociobiology: The New Synthesis* (Cambridge: Harvard University Press, Belknap Press, 1975), pp. 316-317. Wilson and others claim that the growth of a mammalian fetus inside its mother's womb represents an energetic "investment" on her part, but it is not clear to me why they believe that. Presumably the mother eats and metabolizes, and some of the food she eats goes into building the growing embryo. Why does that represent in investment of *her* energies? I can see that the embryo of an undernourished woman perhaps requires such an investment—in which case what one would have to do is see that the mother gets enough to eat. But what "energy" does a properly nourished woman "invest" in her embryo (or indeed, in her egg)? It would seem that the notion of pregnancy as "investment" derives from the interpretation of pregnancy as a debilitating disease.

27. For example, at present in the United States, 24 percent of households are headed by women and 46 percent of women work outside the home. The fraction of women who work away from home while raising children is considerably larger in several European countries and in China.

28. Ruth Herschberger, *Adam's Rib* (1948; reprinted ed., New York: Harper and Row, 1970).

29. Furthermore, a woman's eggs are laid down while she is an embryo, hence at the expense of her mother's "metabolic investment." This raises the question whether grandmothers devote more time to grandchildren they have by their daughters than to those they have by their sons. I hope sociobiologists will look into this.

30. Nineteenth-century feminism is often dated from the publication in 1792 of Mary Wollstonecraft's (1759–1797) *A Vindication of the Rights of Woman;* it continued right through Darwin's century. Darwin was well into his work at the time of the Seneca Falls Declaration (1848), which begins with the interesting words: "When, in the course of human events, it becomes necessary for one portion of the family of man to assume among the people of the earth a position different from that which they have hitherto occupied, but one to which the *laws of nature and of nature's God* entitle them ..." (my italics). And John Stuart Mill (1806–1873) published his essay on *The Subjection of Women* in 1869, ten years after Darwin's *Origin of Species* and two years before the *Descent of Man and Selection in Relation to Sex.*

31. William Howells, *Evolution of the Genus Homo* (Reading: Addison-Wesley Publishing Co., 1973). p. 88.

32. Kenneth P. Oakley, *Man the Toolmaker* (London: British Museum, 1972), p. 81.

33. There are also occasional more perfect skeletons, such as that of *Homo erectus* at Choukoutien, commonly known as Peking Man, who was in fact a woman.

34. Howells, p. 133.

35. Evelyn Reed, *Woman's Evolution* (New York: Pathfinder Press, 1975).

36. Virginia Woolf, *A Room of One's Own* (1945; reprinted ed., Penguin Books, 1970), p. 6.

37. M. Kay Martin and Barbara Voorhis. *Female of the Species* (New York: Columbia University Press, 1975).

38. Rayna R. Reiter, ed., *Toward an Anthropology of Women* (New York: Monthly Review Press, 1975).

39. This is what Sarah Blaffer Hardy and Nancy Tanner have done. *See* Sarah Blaffer Hardy, *The Woman That Never Evolved* (Cambridge, MA: Harvard University Press, 1981); and Nancy Makepeace Tanner, *On Becoming Human* (Cambridge: Cambridge University Press, 1981).

40. Darwin, *Origin of Species.* ... p. 909.

Empathy, Polyandry, and the Myth of the Coy Female

Sarah Blaffer Hrdy

Sexual selection theory (Bateman, 1948; Darwin, 1871; Trivers, 1972; Williams, 1966) is one of the crown jewels of the Darwinian approach basic to sociobiology. Yet so scintillating were some of the revelations offered by the theory, that they tended to outshine the rest of the wreath and to impede comprehension of the total design, in this instance, the intertwined, sometimes opposing, strategies and counter strategies of both sexes which together compose the social and reproductive behavior of the species. (Hrdy & Williams, 1983, p. 7)

But why did that happen, and how? And what processes led to the current destabilization of the model and reformulation of our thinking about sexual selection?

Introduction

For over three decades, a handful of partially true assumptions were permitted to shape the construction of general evolutionary theories about sexual selection. These theories of sexual selection presupposed the existence of a highly discriminating, sexually "coy," female who was courted by sexually undiscriminating males. Assumptions underlying these stereotypes included, first, the idea that relative male contribution to offspring was small, second, that little variance exists in female reproductive success compared to the very great variance among males, and third, that fertilization was the only reason for females to mate. While appropriate in some contexts, these conditions are far from universal. Uncritical acceptance of such assumptions has greatly hampered our understanding of animal breeding systems particularly, perhaps, those of primates.

These assumptions have only begun to be revised in the last decade, as researchers began to consider the way Darwinian selection operates on females as well as males. This paper traces the shift away from the stereotype of female as sexually passive and discriminating to current models in which females are seen to play an active role in managing sexual consortships that go beyond traditional "mate choice." It is impossible to understand this history without taking into account the background, including the gender, of the researchers involved. Serious consideration is given to the possibility that the empathy for other females subjectively felt by women researchers may have been instrumental in expanding the scope of sexual selection theory.

Anisogamy and the Bateman Paradigm

In one of the more curious inconsistencies in modern evolutionary biology, a theoretical formulation about the basic nature of males and females has persisted for over three decades, from 1948 until recently, despite the accumulation of abundant openly available evidence contradicting it. This is the presumption basic to many contemporary versions of sexual selection theory that males are ardent and sexually undiscriminating while females are sexually restrained and reluctant to mate. My aims in this paper will be to examine this stereotype of "the coy female," to trace its route of entry into modern evolutionary thinking and to examine some of the processes that are only now, in the last decade, causing us to rethink this erroneous corollary to a body of theory (Darwin, 1871) that has otherwise been widely substantiated. In the course of this examination, I will speculate about the role that empathy and identification by researchers with same-sex individuals may have played in this strange saga.

Obviously, the initial dichotomy between actively courting, promiscuous males and passively choosing, monandrous females dates back to Victorian times. "The males are almost always the wooers," Darwin wrote in 1871, and he was very clear in his own writings that the main activity of females was to choose the single best suitor from among these wooers. As he wrote in *The Descent of Man and Selection in Relation to Sex* (1871), "It is shown by various facts, given hereafter, and by the results fairly attributable to sexual selection, that the female, though comparatively passive, generally exerts some choice and accepts one male in preference to the others." However the particular form in which these ideas were incorporated into modern and ostensibly more "empirical" versions of post-Darwinian evolutionary thought derived from a 1948 paper about animals by a distinguished plant geneticist, Angus John Bateman.

Like so much in genetics, Bateman's ideas about the workings of nature were based primarily on experiments with *Drosophila*, the minuscule flies that materialize in the vicinity of rotting fruit. Among the merits of fruitflies rarely appreciated by housekeepers are the myriad of small genetic differences that determine a fruitfly's looks. Bred over generations in a laboratory, distinctive strains of *Drosophila* sporting odd-colored eyes, various bristles, peculiar crenulations here and there, grotesquely shaped eyes, and so forth can be produced by scientists, and these markers are put to use in tracing genealogies.

Bateman obtained various lots of differently decorated *Drosophila* all belonging to the one species, *Drosophila melanogaster*. He housed three to five flies of each sex in glass containers and allowed them to breed. On the basis of 64 such experiments, he found (by counting the offspring bearing their parents' peculiar genetic trademarks) that while 21% of his males failed to fertilize any female, only 4% of his females failed to produce offspring.

A highly successful male, he found, could produce nearly three times as many offspring as the most successful female. Furthermore, the difference between the most successful and the least successful male, what is called the *variance* in male reproductive success, was always far greater than the variance among females. Building upon these findings, Bateman constructed the centerpiece to his paradigm: whereas a male could always gain by mating just one more time, and hence benefit from a nature that made him undiscriminatingly eager to mate, a female, already breeding near capacity after just one copulation, could gain little from multiple mating and should be quite uninterested in mating more than once or twice.

From these 64 experiments with *Drosophila*, Bateman extrapolated to nature at large: selection pressures brought about by competition among same-sexed individuals for representation in the gene pools of succeeding generations would almost always operate more strongly upon the male than upon the female. This asymmetry in breeding potential would lead to a nearly universal dichotomy in the sexual nature of the male and female:

> One would therefore expect to find in all but a few very primitive organisms ... that males would show greater intra-sexual selection than females. This would explain why ... there is nearly always a combination of an undiscriminating eagerness in the males and a discriminating passivity in the females. Even in a derived monogamous species (e.g. man) this sex difference might be expected to persist as a rule. (Bateman, 1948, p. 365)

This dichotomy was uncritically incorporated into modern thinking about sexual selection. In his classic 1972 essay on "Parental Investment and Sexual Selection," Harvard biologist Robert Trivers acknowledged Bateman's paper as "the key reference" (provided him, as it happens by one of the major evolutionary biologists of our time, and Trivers' main mentor at Harvard, Ernst Mayr). Trivers' essay on parental investment, carrying with it Bateman's model, was to become the second most widely cited paper in all of sociobiology, after Hamilton's 1964 paper on kin selection.

Expanding on Bateman's original formulation, Trivers argued that whichever sex invests least in offspring will compete to mate with the sex investing most. At the root of this generalization concerning the sexually discriminating female (apart from Victorian ideology at large) is the fact of anisogamy (gametes unequal in size) and the perceived need for a female to protect her already substantial investment in each maternal gamete; she is under selective pressure to select the best available male to fertilize it. The male, by contrast, produces myriad gametes (sperm), which are assumed to be physiologically cheap to produce (note, however, that costs to males of competing for females are rarely factored in), and he disseminates them indiscriminately.

Two central themes in contemporary sociobiology then derive directly from Bateman. The first theme is the dichotomy between the "nurturing female," who invests very much more per offspring than males, and "the competitive male," who invests little or nothing beyond sperm but who actively competes for access to any additional female (see for example Daly & Margo Wilson,* 1983, pp. 78–79; Trivers, 1985, p. 207). As Trivers noted in his summary of Bateman's experiments with *Drosophila*, "A female's reproductive success did not increase much, if any, after the first copulation and not at all after the second; most females were uninterested in copulating more than once or twice" (1972, p. 138). And so it was that "coyness" came to be the single most commonly mentioned attribute of females in the literature

*In this chapter, I designate women researchers by spelling out their first names; the point of using this admittedly odd convention will become clear in the section on "The Role of Women Researchers."

on sociobiology. Unlike the male, who, if he makes a mistake can move on to another female, the female's investment was initially considered to be so great that she was constrained from aborting a bad bet and attempting to conceive again. (Criticisms and recent revisions of the notion are discussed later in the section, "The Females Who Forgot to be Coy.") In this respect, contemporary theory remains fairly faithful to Darwin's original (1871) two-part definition of sexual selection. The first part of the theory predicts competition between males for mates; the second, female choice of the best competitor.

The second main sociobiological theme to derive from Bateman is not explicitly discussed in Darwin but is certainly implicit in much that Darwin wrote (or more precisely, did not write) about females. This is the notion that female investment is already so large that it cannot be increased and the idea that most females are already breeding close to capacity. If this were so, the variance in female reproductive success would be small, making one female virtually interchangeable with another. A logical corollary of this notion is the incorrect conclusion that selection operates primarily on males.

The conviction that intrasexual selection will weigh heavily upon males while scarcely affecting females was explicitly stated by Bateman, but also appears in implicit form in the writings of contemporary sociobiologists (Daly & Margo Wilson, 1983, Chapter 5; Wilson, 1978, p. 125). It is undeniable that males have the capacity to inseminate multiple females while females (except in species such as those squirrels, fish, insects, and cats, where several fathers can sire a single brood) are inseminated—at most—once each breeding period. But a difficulty arises when the occasionally true assumption that females are not competing among themselves to get fertilized is then interpreted to mean that there will be reduced within-sex competition among females generally (e.g., Freedman, 1979, p. 33).

Until about 1980—and even occasionally after that—some theoreticians were writing about females as though each one was relatively identical in both her reproductive potential and in her realization of that potential. This erroneous generalization lead some workers (perhaps especially those whose training was not in evolutionary biology per se) to the erroneous and patently non-Darwinian conclusion that females are not subject to selection pressure at all and the idea that competition among males is somehow more critical because "leaving offspring is at stake" (Carol Cronin, 1980, p. 302; see also Virginia Abernethy, 1978, p. 132). To make an unfortunate situation worse, the close conformity between these notions and post-Victorian popular prejudice meant that ideas about competitive, promiscuous men and choosey women were selectively picked up in popular writing about sociobiology. An article in *Playboy Magazine* celebrating "Darwin and the Double Standard" (Morris, 1979) comes most vividly to mind, but there were many others.

The Females Who Forgot to Be Coy

Field studies of a number of animal groups provide abundant examples of females who, unlike Bateman's *Drosophila*, ardently seek to mate more than once or twice. Furthermore, fertilization by the best male can scarcely be viewed as their universal goal since in many of these cases females were not ovulating or else were actually pregnant at the time they solicit males.

It has been known for years (among some circles) that female birds were less than chaste, especially since 1975 when Bray, Kennelly, and Guarino demonstrated that when the "master" of the blackbird harem was vasectomized, his females nevertheless conceived (see also Lumpkin, 1983). Evelyn Shaw and Joan Darling (1985) review some of this literature on "promiscuous" females, particularly for marine organisms. Among shiner perch, for example, a female who is not currently producing eggs will nevertheless court

and mate with numbers of males, collecting from each male sperm that are then stored in the female's ovaries till seasonal conditions promote ovulation. Female cats, including leopards, lions, and pumas are notorious for their frequency of matings. A lioness may mate 100 times a day with multiple partners over a 6–7-day period each time she is in estrus (Eaton, 1976). Best known of all, perhaps, are such primate examples as savanna baboons, where females initiate multiple brief consortships, or chimpanzees, where females alternate between prolonged consortships with one male and communal mating with all males in the vicinity (DeVore, 1965; Hausfater, 1975; Caroline Tutin, 1975). However, only since 1979 or so has female promiscuity been a subject of much theoretical interest (see for example Alatalo, Lundberg, & Stahlbrandt, 1982; Sandy Andelman, in press; Gladstone, 1979; Sarah Blaffer Hrdy, 1979; Susan Lumpkin, 1983; Meredith Small, forthcoming; R. Smith, 1984; Wirtz, 1983), largely I believe because theoretically the phenomenon should not have existed and therefore there was little theoretical infrastructure for studying it, certainly not the sort of study that could lead to a PhD (or a job).

In terms of the order Primates, evidence has been building since the 1960s that females in a variety of prosimian, monkey, and ape species were managing their own reproductive careers so as actively to solicit and mate with a number of different males, both males within their (supposed) breeding unit and those outside it. As theoretical interest increased, so has the quality of the data.

But before turning to such evidence, it is first critical to put sex in perspective. To correct the stereotype of "coyness," I emphasize female sexual activity but, as always in such debates, reality exists in a plane distinct from that predefined by the debate. In this case, reality is hours and hours, sometimes months and months, of existence where sexual behavior is not even an issue, hours where animals are walking, feeding, resting, grooming. Among baboons (as in some human societies) months pass when a pregnant or lactating mother engages in no sexual behavior at all. The same is generally true for langurs, except that females under particular conditions possess a *capacity* to solicit and copulate with males even if pregnant or lactating, and they sometimes do so. At such times, the patterning of sexual receptivity among langurs could not be easily distinguished from that of a modern woman. The same could be said for the relatively noncyclical, semicontinuous, situation-dependent receptivity of a marmoset or tamarin.

With this qualification in mind—that is the low frequencies of sexual behavior in the lives of *all* mammals, who for the most part are doing other things—let's consider the tamarins.

Tamarins are tiny South American monkeys, long thought to be monogamous. Indeed, in captivity, tamarins do breed best when a single female is paired with one mate. Add a second female and the presence of the dominant female suppresses ovulation in the subordinate. (The consequences of adding a second male to the cage are unknown, since such an addition was thought to violate good management practices.) Nevertheless, in the recent (and first) long-term study of individually marked tamarins in the wild, Anne Wilson Goldizen discovered that given the option, supposedly monogamous saddle-backed tamarins (*Saguinus fuscicollis*) will mate with several adult males, each of whom subsequently help to care for her twin offspring in an arrangement more nearly "polyandrous" than monogamous (Goldizen & Terborgh, forthcoming). Furthermore the presence of additional males, and their assistance in rearing young may be critical for offspring survival. (One of the ironies here, pointed out in another context by Janet Sayers (1982), is that females are thus presumed to commit what is known in sociobiology as a *Concorde fallacy;* that is, pouring good money after bad. Although in other contexts (e.g., Dawkins, 1976) it has been argued that creatures are selected to cut bait rather than

commit Concorde fallacies, mothers were somehow excluded from this reasoning (however, see Trivers, 1985, p. 268, for a specific acknowledgement and correction of the error). I happen to believe that the resolution to this contradiction lies in recognizing that gamete producers and mothers do indeed "cut bait" far more often than is generally realized, and that skipped ovulations, spontaneous abortion, and abandonment of young by mothers are fairly routine events in nature. That is, the reasoning about the Concorde fallacy is right enough, but our thinking about the commitment of mothers to nurture no matter what has been faulty.

Indeed, on the basis of what I believe today (cf. Hrdy, 1981, p. 59), I would argue that a polyandrous component* is at the core of the breeding systems of most troop-dwelling primates: females mate with many males, each of whom may contribute a little bit toward the survival of offspring. Barbary macaques provide the most extreme example (Taub, 1980), but the very well-studied savanna baboons also yield a similar, if more moderate, pattern. David Stein (1981) and Jeanne Altmann (1980) studied the complex

---

*For want of a better term, *polyandrous* is used here to refer to a female with more than one established mate. The term *promiscuous* will be used to refer to multiple, brief consortships, some of which may last longer. Whereas *polyandrous* is a poor term because it suggests some stable, institutionalized relationship, which is probably wrong for describing tamarins, *promiscuous* is also problematic. It implies a lack of selectivity among females, which may or may not be the case. Davies and Lundberg (1984, p. 898) have recently proposed using the term *polygnandry* to refer to "two or three males sharing access to two, three or four females." Such a term applies to Barbary macaques and might be a good one for the baboon situation except that there is not a 100% overlap in the females with which each male mates. Clearly, the terminology needs to be cleared up, but for the time being the important point is to emphasize the contrast between what we now know and the old stereotype of monandrous females selecting a single mate.

interactions between adult males and infants. They found that (as suggested years ago by Tim Ransom and Bonnie Ransom, 1971) former, or sometimes future, consorts of the mother develop special relationships with that female's infant, carrying it in times of danger and protecting it from conspecifics, possibly creating enhanced feeding opportunities for the infant. These relationships are made possible by the mother's frequent proximity to males with whom she has special relationships and by the fact that the infant itself comes to trust these males and seek them out; more is at issue than simply male predilections. Altmann aptly refers to such males as *god-fathers*. Infants, then, are often the focal-point of elaborate male-female-infant relationships, relationships that are often initiated by the females themselves (Barbara Smuts, 1985).

Even species such as Hanuman langurs, blue monkeys, or redtail monkeys, all primates traditionally thought to have "monandrous" or "uni-male" breeding systems, are far more promiscuous than that designation implies. Indeed, mating with outsiders is so common under certain circumstances as to throw the whole notion of one-male breeding units into question (Cords, 1984; Tsingalia & Thelma Rowell, 1984). My own first glimpse of a langur, the species I was to spend nearly 10 years studying intermittently, was of a female near the Great Indian Desert in Rajasthan moving rapidly through a steep granite canyon, moving away from her natal group to approach and solicit males in an all-male band. At the time, I had no context for interpreting behavior that merely seemed strange and incomprehensible to my Harvard-trained eyes. Only in time, did I come to realize that such wandering and such seemingly "wanton" behavior were recurring events in the lives of langurs.

In at least three different sets of circumstances female langurs solicit males other than their so-called *harem-leaders:* first, when males from nomadic all-male bands temporarily join a breeding troop; second, when

females leave their natal troops to travel temporarily with all-male bands and mate with males there; and third, when a female for reasons unknown to any one, simply takes a shine to the resident male of a neighboring troop (Hrdy 1977; Moore 1985; filmed in Hrdy, Hrdy, & Bishop, 1977). It may be to abet langurs in such projects that nature has provided them attributes characteristic of relatively few mammals. A female langur exhibits no visible sign when she is in estrus other than to present to a male and to shudder her head. When she encounters strange males, she has the capacity to shift from cyclical receptivity (that is, a bout of heat every 28 days) into a state of semicontinuous receptivity that can last for weeks. Monkeys with similar capacities include vervets, several of the guenons, and gelada baboons, to mention only a few (reviewed in Hrdy & Whitten, 1986).

A number of questions are raised by these examples. First, just exactly why might females bother to be other than coy, that is why should they actively seek out partners including males outside of their apparent breeding units (mate "promiscuously", seek "excess" copulations, beyond what are necessary for fertilization)? Second, why should this vast category of behaviors be, until recently, so generally ignored by evolutionary theorists? As John Maynard Smith noted, in the context of mobbing behavior by birds, "behavior so widespread, so constant, and so apparently dangerous calls for a functional explanation" (1984, p. 294).

To be fair, it should be acknowledged that mobbing behavior in birds is more stereotyped than sexual behavior in wild cats or monkeys, and it can be more systematically studied. Nevertheless, at issue here are behaviors exhibited by the majority of species in the order primates, the best studied order of animals in the world, and the order specifically included by Bateman in his, extrapolation from coyness in arthropods to coyness in anthropoids. Furthermore, females engaged in such "promiscuous matings" entail obvious risks ranging from retaliatory attacks by males, venereal disease, the energetic costs of multiple solicitations, predation risks from leaving the troop, all the way to the risk of lost investment by a male consort who has been selected to avoid investing in other males' offspring (Trivers, 1972). In retrospect, one really does have to wonder why it was nearly 1980 before promiscuity among females attracted more than cursory theoretical interest.

Once the initial conceptual block was overcome (and I will argue in the last section that the contributions of women researchers was critical to this phase, at least in primatology), once it was recognized that oh yes, females mate promiscuously and this is a most curious and fascinating phenomenon, the question began to be vigorously pursued. (Note though that the focus of this paper is on male-centered theoretical formulations, readers should be aware that there are other issues here, such as the gap between theoreticians and field-workers, which I do not discuss.)

In my opinion, no conscious effort was ever made to leave out female sides to stories. The Bateman paradigm was very useful, indeed theoretically quite powerful, in explaining such phenomena as male promiscuity. But, although the theory was useful in explaining male behavior, by definition (i.e., *sexual selection* refers to competition between one sex for *access* to the other sex) it excluded much within-sex reproductive competition among females, which was not over fertilizations per se but which also did not fall neatly into the realm of the survival-related phenomena normally considered as due to natural selection. (The evolution of sexual swellings might be an example of a phenomenon that fell between definitional cracks and hence went unexplained until recently [Clutton-Brock & Harvey, 1976; Hrdy, 1981]). To understand female promiscuity, for example, we first needed to recognize the limitations of sexual selection theory and then needed to construct a new theoretical base for explaining selection pressures on females.

The realization that male-male competition and female choice explains only a small part of the evolution of breeding systems has led to much new work (e.g., Wasser, 1983, and work reviewed therein). We now have, for example, no fewer than six different models to explain how females might benefit from mating with different males (see Smith, R., 1984, for a recent review).

These hypotheses, most of them published in 1979 or later, can be divided into two categories, first those postulating genetic benefits for the offspring of sexually assertive mothers, and second, those postulating nongenetic benefits for either the female herself or her progeny. All but one of these (the oldest, "prostitution hypothesis") was arrived at by considering the world from a female's point of view.

Whereas all the hypotheses specifying genetic benefits predict that the female should be fertile when she solicits various male partners (except in those species where females have the capacity to store sperm), this condition is not required for the nongenetic hypotheses. It should be noted, too, that only functional explanations for multiple matings are listed. The idea that females simply "enjoy" sex begs the question of why females in a genus such as *Drosophila* do not appear highly motivated to mate repeatedly, while females in other species apparently are so motivated and have evolved specific physiological apparatus making promiscuity more likely (e.g., a clitoris, a capacity for orgasm brought about by prolonged or multiple sources of stimulation, a capacity to expand receptivity beyond the period of ovulation, and so forth; see Hrdy, 1981, Chapter 7 for discussion). Nevertheless, the possibility persists that promiscuous behaviors arise as endocrinological accidents or perhaps that females have orgasms simply because males do (Symons, 1979), and it is worth remembering that an act of faith is involved in assuming that there is any function at all. (I mention this qualifier because I am not interested in arguing a point that can not currently be resolved.)

Assuming that promiscuous behaviors and the physiological paraphernalia leading to them have evolved, four hypotheses are predicated on genetic benefits for the offspring of sexually assertive mothers: (a) the "fertility backup hypothesis," which assumes that females will need sperm from a number of males to assure conception (Meredith Small, forthcoming; Smith, R., 1984); (b) "the inferior cuckold hypothesis," in which a female paired with an inferior mate surreptitiously solicits genetically superior males when conception is likely (e.g., Benshoof & Thornhill, 1979); (c) "the diverse paternity" hypothesis, whereby females confronted with unpredictable fluctuations in the environment produce clutches sired by multiple partners to diversify paternity of offspring produced over a lifetime (Parker, 1970; Williams, 1975); or (d) in a somewhat obscure twist of the preceding, females in species where litters can have more than one father alter the degree of relatedness between sibs and maternal half-sibs by collecting sperm from several fathers (Davies & Boersma, 1984).

The remaining explanations are predicated on nongenetic benefits for females and do not assume the existence of either genetic differences between males or the existence of female capacities to detect them: (e) the "prostitution" hypothesis, whereby females are thought to exchange sexual access for resources, enhanced status, etc.—the oldest of all the explanations (first proposed by Sir Solly Zuckerman 1932, recently restated by Symons, 1979; see also, Nancy Burley & Symanski, 1981, for discussion); (f) the "therapeutic hypothesis" that multiple matings and resulting orgasm are physiologically beneficial to females or make conception more likely (Mary Jane Sherfey, 1973); (g) the "keep 'em around" hypothesis whereby females (with the connivance of dominant males in the group) solicit subordinate males to discourage these disadvantaged animals from leaving the group (Stacey, 1982); and (h) the "manipulation hypothesis," suggesting that females, mate with a number of males in order to confuse information available to males about paternity and thereby extract investment in, or tolerance for, their infants from different males (Hrdy, D. B., 1979; Stacey, 1982).

It is this last hypothesis that I now want to focus on, not because that hypothesis is inherently any better than others, but because I know the most about it and about the assumptions that needed to be changed before it could be dreamed up.

The "manipulation hypothesis," first conceived in relation to monkeys, grew out of a dawning awareness that, first of all, individual females could do a great deal that would affect the survival of their offspring, and second, that males, far from mere dispensers of sperm, were critical features on the landscape where infants died or survived. That is, females were more political, males more nurturing (or at least not neutral), than some earlier versions of sexual selection theory would lead us to suppose.

A Female Is Not a Female Is Not a Female

To his credit, A. J. Bateman was a very empirical scientist. He was at pains to measure "actual" and not just "potential" genetic contribution made by parents. Not for him the practice—still prevalent in primatology several decades later—of counting up some male's copulations and calling them *reproductive success*. Bateman counted offspring actually produced. And, in a genus such as *Drosophila*, where infant mortality is probably fairly random and a stretch of bad weather accounts for far more deaths than a spate of bad parenting, the assumption that one mother is equivalent to another mother is probably not farfetched. Such factors as the social status of the mother, her body size, her expertise in child-rearing, or the protection and care elicited from other animals may indeed make little difference. But what if he had been studying monkeys or even somebody's favorite fish? Even for

Drosophila conditions exist in which females benefit from multiple copulations. In a series of experiments with *Drosophila pseudoobscura*, Turner and Anderson (1983) have shown that the number of offspring that survive to maturity was significantly higher for females allowed to mate for longer periods and with more partners than for females isolated from males after brief mating periods. This effect was most pronounced in laboratory groups that were nutritionally stressed.

The female coho salmon buries her eggs in nests, which she guards for as long as she lives. Females fight over the best nest sites, and about one out of three times, a female will usurp another female's nest and destroy her eggs. Females vary greatly in size, and their differing dimensions may be translated into different degrees of fecundity. A big female may produce more than three times as many eggs as a small one. Differences in the survival of eggs to hatching lead to even greater variance in female reproductive success; there may be as much as a 30-fold difference in number of surviving offspring (Van den Berghe, 1984).

But the mother salmon only breed once; consider an iteroparous monkey mother who, although she produces only one or two infants at a time, breeds over many years and who, like a macaque or baboon, may inherit her feeding range and troop rank from her mother at birth. These legacies will affect her reproductive output and will, in turn, pass to her own daughters. Males of course enter this system, and vary among themselves, but in most instances they are transients, breeding briefly, and indeed, possibly living shorter lives on average than females. Take the extreme example of the gelada baboon who has only one chance for controlling access to a small "harem" of females (who by the way have about as much to do with controlling the male, as he does in controlling them). The male gelada baboon breeds in his unit for several years before another male enters, pushing him into forced retirement. The former "harem-leader" lingers on in the troop,

but as a celibate watcher, possibly babysitting, but breeding no more (Dunbar, 1984). It is a tale of the tortoise and the hare. After the male hare is dismissed, the female tortoise breeds on year after year.

Although we do not yet have data on the lifetime reproductive success of males or females from any species of wild primate, I will be surprised if the variance among males exceeds the variance among females by as much as traditionally thought in species such as Japanese or rhesus macaques or gelada baboons. In the most polyandrous species, such as tamarins, variance in the reproductive success of twin-producing females may actually be greater than that for males. If we carry out our calculations over generations, remembering that every male, however wildly reproductively successful, has a mother and a grandmother (e.g., see Hartung, in press) differences in the degree of variance between the two sexes grow even smaller, though extremes of variance in reproductive success will of course crop up one generation sooner for fathers than for mothers.

The anisogamy paradigm of Bateman offered powerful insights into the selective pressures that operate on males; for many mammals, selection weighs heaviest on males in competition with other males for access to females. In addition, Bateman provided the framework that eventually led to an understanding of why males tend to compete for mates while females compete for resources. But the Bateman and the anisogamy paradigm also led us to overlook the full range of possible sources of variance in female reproductive success; not only variance arising from female-female competition over resources to translate into large gametes, but also variance arising from other factors as well. Not all females conceive. In some cases, such as marmosets, the presence of the dominant female suppresses ovulation in her subordinates. Some offspring, once conceived, are not carried to term. Among the factors leading to spontaneous abortion in baboons may be harassment by other females or the arrival of strange males (Mori & Dunbar, in press; Wasser & Barash, 1984). And of course, offspring once born need not survive. If born to a low-ranking toque macaque mother, a juvenile daughter may die of starvation, or if born to a mother chimp who for some reason is incapacitated, an offspring may be killed by a higher-ranking female. Having survived, a maturing female howler monkey may nevertheless find herself unable to join a breeding group and never have a chance to reproduce. A mother's condition, her competitive abilities, and her maternal skills are all very much at issue in the case of creatures such as primates. Yet, as amazing as it sounds, only relatively recently have primatologists begun to examine behaviors other than direct mother-infant interactions that affect the fates of infants (for elaboration see Hrdy, 1981; Small, 1984). Not the least among the variables affecting their survival is the role played by males, and the capacity of females to influence this male performance.

Male Involvement with Infants

Even for *Drosophila* it was a mistake to imagine that male investment never went further than chromosomes. Recent research makes it clear that, as in various butterflies and cockroaches, male fruitflies may sometimes transmit along with their sperm essential nutrients that otherwise would be in short supply (Markow & Ankney, 1984). When assumptions about minimal male involvement are extrapolated to species such as primates, however, far more than underestimation of male involvement is at stake. I would argue that it is not only ill-advised but impossible to understand primate breeding systems without taking into account the role of males in determining the survival or demise of infants.

There is probably no order of mammals in which male involvement with infants is more varied, more complex, or more crucial than among primates. About 10% of all mam-

malian genera exhibit some form of direct male care, that is the male carries the infant or provisions it. Among primates, however, the percentage of genera with direct, positive (if also sometimes infrequent) interactions between males and infants is roughly four times that, the highest figure reported for any order of mammals (Devra Kleiman & Malcolm, 1981; Vogt, 1984). Conversely, infanticide has been reported for over 15 different species of primates belonging to 8 genera and is probably widespread among apes and monkeys (Hausfater & Hrdy, 1984). Indeed, some male care is probably a direct outgrowth of the need by males to protect infants from other males (Busse & Hamilton, 1981). Yet, oddly, after two decades of intensive study of wild primates, we are only now beginning to scratch the surface of the rich interactions that exist between infants and adult males, which seem to have such critical repercussions for infant survival (see Hrdy, 1976; and especially, Taub, 1984a, 1984b). Effects of these relationships for infants after they grow up have rarely been investigated, although several researchers have recently suggested the possibility that fathers among gibbons and orangutans may play a role in helping their sons to set up or defend territories (MacKinnon, 1978; Tilson, 1981). These cases are of special importance because apart from intervention by brothers or by fathers in adopting an orphan (among gorillas and chimpanzees) direct, "maternal-like" care of infants by males is not typically seen among apes. But, the fact that parental investment by males does not take the same form as investment by females does not lessen its importance for offspring or its cost to the parent. My focus here is on primates, but I believe I could make many of the same points if I were a student of amphibians or fish in which male care is very common. One critical role of males is to protect immatures from distantly related conspecifics. It has long been assumed that one reason for male care among these species was the greater certainty of paternity permitted in species with external fertilization (i.e., the male can *know* which eggs he fertilized). But surely among these groups, as among primates, there has been selection on females to manipulate this situation.

The main exception to a general pattern of ignoring interactions between males and infants was of course the study of male care among monogamous primates. It has been known for over 200 years, ever since a zoologist-illustrator named George Edwards decided to watch the behavior of pet marmosets in a London garden, that among certain species of New World monkeys males contributed direct care for infants that equalled or exceeded that given by females (Edwards, 1758). Mothers among marmosets and tamarins typically give birth to twins, as often as twice a year, and to ease the female in her staggering reproductive burden the male carries the infant at all times except when the mother is actually suckling it. It was assumed that monogamy and male confidence of paternity was essential for the evolution of such care (Kleiman, 1977), and at the same time, it was assumed that monogamy among primates must be fairly rare (e.g., see Symons, 1979, or virtually any textbook on physical anthropology prior to 1981).

Recent findings, however, make it necessary to revise this picture. First of all, monogamy among primates turns out to be rather more frequent than previously believed (either obligate or facultative monogamy can be documented for some 17–20% of extant primates) and, second, male care turns out to be far more extensive than previously thought and not necessarily confined to monogamous species (Hrdy, 1981). Whereas, previously, it was assumed that monogamy and male certainty of paternity facilitated the evolution of male care, it now seems appropriate to consider the alternative possibility, whether the extraordinary capacity of male primates to look out for the fates of infants did not in some way pre-adapt members of this order for the sort of close, long-term relationships between males and

females that, under some ecological circumstances, leads to monogamy! Either scenario could be true. The point is that on the basis of present knowledge there is no reason to view male care as a restricted or specialized phenomenon. In sum, though it remains true that mothers among virtually all primates devote more time and/or energy to rearing infants than do males, males nonetheless play a more varied and critical role in infant survival than is generally realized.

Male-infant interactions are weakly developed among prosimians, and in these primitive primates, male care more or less (but not completely) coincides with monogamy (Vogt, 1984). Direct male care occurs in 7 out of 17 genera, including one of the most primitive of all lemurs, the nest-building ruffed lemur (*Lemur variegatus*), where the male diligently tends the nest while the mother forages (personal communication from Patricia Wright). Among New World monkeys, 12 of 16 genera (Vogt, 1984) or, calculated differently, 50% of all species (Wright, 1984) exhibit direct male care, often with the male as the primary caretaker. That is, shortly after birth, an adult male—often with the help of various immatures in the group or other males—will take the infant, carry it (or them, in the frequent case of twins) on his back, share food with infants, either adult males or juveniles may catch beetles to feed them, or assist them by cracking the casing of tough fruit.

The role of males as primary caretakers for single (nontwin) infants is very richly developed among the night monkeys, *Aotus trivirgatus*. These small, monogamously mated, South American monkeys are the only nocturnal higher primate. Because of the difficulty in watching them, their behavior in the wild has gone virtually undocumented until detailed behavioral studies were undertaken by Patricia Wright using an image intensifier and other gear to allow her to work at night. Combining her observations of captive *Aotus* with field observations, a picture emerges in which the male is primary caretaker (in terms of carrying the infant) from the infant's first day of life, although the mother, of course, still is providing physiologically very costly milk. Based on captive observations, the mother carried the infant 33% of the time during the first week of life, the male 51%, and a juvenile group member 15%. In the wild, the infant was still being carried by the male at 4 months of age, although "weaning" tantrums were seen, as the male would try to push the infant off his back. By 5 months, the infant was relatively independent of either parent (Patricia Wright, 1984).

There is little question that there is an association between monogamy and extensive male care. Nevertheless, this does not mean that the evolution of male care is precluded by situations in which females mate with more than one male, as discussed for the case of savannah baboons.

Recent research on male-infant relations among baboons reveals that during their first week of life infant baboons at Amboseli spend about a third of their daylight hours within 5 feet of an adult mate, often, but not always, a former sexual consort of the mother. This level of proximity was maintained throughout the first 7 weeks and then dropped sharply. At the same time, the amount of time infants spend in actual contact with an adult male, which is never much, is rising from 1% in the first week to 3% by the eighth week. During their first half-year of life, infants spend .5% of their time connected with an adult male, a low figure (Stein, 1984). Averaging together data from a number of different baboon field studies, David Taub calculates that a male-infant interaction takes place only about once every 19 hours (or, adjusting for the number of males in a multi-male troop, one interaction per male every 344 hours). However, Taub concurs with Busse and Hamilton (1981) and others, that the proximity of these males may be crucial for infant survival, particularly critical for discouraging attacks on the infant either by incoming males, unfamiliar with the infant's mother or, as suggested by

Wasser (1983) for forestalling harassment by female troop members belonging to competing matrilines. That is, when the cost of care is fairly low (the male need only remain in the vicinity of the infant but can engage in other activities) and when it is rendered nonexclusively to several infants (e.g., to the offspring of each of the male's special female friends), male care certainly does occur in nonmonogamous systems. What is offered may not be "quantity" time, but it may well be "quality" time—"quality" in a very real sense: enhancing infant survival.

Yet, even these caveats can be dispensed with in the unusual case of the polyandrous tamarin species (*Saguinus fuscicollis*) studied by Goldizen. The female mates with several males and each of them subsequently helps rear the infant. Indeed, preliminary data from Goldizen's continuing research suggests that infants with several male caretakers are more likely to survive than infants born in small groups with only one adult male. Here, then, is both quality and quantity time, combined in a nonmonogamous breeding system, a system where males have a probability but no certainty of paternity. If we pause for a moment and consider the tamarin case from the male's point of view, the system Goldizen reports almost certainly derived initially from a monogamous one in which mates were indeed caring for offspring likely to be their own. Only after such a system was established could a female have plausibly manipulated the situation to enlist the aid of two helpers.

Assuming that primate males do indeed remember the identity of past consorts and that they respond differentially to the offspring of familiar and unfamiliar females, females would derive obvious benefits from mating with more than one male. A researcher with this model in mind has quite different expectations about female behavior than one expecting females to save themselves in order to mate with the best available male. The resulting research questions will be very different.

The Role of Women Researchers

When generalizations persist for decades after evidence invalidating them is also known, can there be much doubt that some bias was involved? We were predisposed to imagine males as ardent, females as coy; males as polygynists, females monandrous. How else could the *Drosophila* to primate extrapolation have entered modern evolutionary thinking unchallenged?

Assuming, then, this bias, a preconstituted reality in which males played central roles, what factors motivated researchers to revise invalid assumptions? What changes in the last decade brought about the new focus on female reproductive strategies and, with it, the recognition that certain assumptions and corollaries of the Bateman paradigm, and especially female monandry, were seriously limited and even, if applied universally, quite wrong.

The fact that there is relatively less intrasexual selection for mates among females does not mean reduced intrasexual competition or reduced selection among females in other spheres of activity. To understand male-male competition for mates is to understand only a small part of what leads to the evolution of particular primate breeding systems. We need also consider the many sources of variance in female reproductive success, including a whole range of female behaviors not directly related to "mothering" that may have repercussions on the fates of their infants.

Polyandrous mating with multiple males, mating with males when conception is not possible—what from the males' point of view might be termed "successive" matings—can only be understood within this new framework, but it requires a whole new set of assumptions and research questions. As a result, sexual selection theory is currently in a state of flux; it is being rethought as actively as any area in evolutionary biology. What processes contributed to this destabilization of a long-held paradigm? And in particular, what led us to rethink the myth of the coy or monandrous female?

Improved methodologies and longer studies would not by themselves have led us to revise the myth of the coy female, simply because the relevant information about "female promiscuity" was already in hand long before researchers began to ask why females might be mating with more than one male. Indeed, at least one writer, working in a framework well outside of primatology and evolutionary biology, picked up on the reports of female promiscuity in baboons and chimpanzees at an early date (1966) and asked why it had evolved. This of course was the feminist psychiatrist Mary Jane Sherfey in her book, *The Evolution of Female Sexuality* (1973). Sherfey's vision of the "sexually insatiable" female primate was generally ignored by primatologists and biologists both because of her ideological perspective and because her standards of evidence were far from scientific. If her ideas were mentioned, it was typically with sarcasm and derision (Symons, 1979, pp. 76–77, 94, 262, 311). And, yet, it is important to note that however extreme her views (and scholarly balance was not Sherfey's strong point), they provided a valuable antidote to equally extreme ideas about universally coy females that were widely held by scientists within the academic mainstream of evolutionary biology. Elsewhere, I wrote about the various factors which caused us to recognize the importance of female dominance hierarchies in the lives of cercopithecine monkeys (Hrdy, 1984). Changes in methodology (e.g., focal animal sampling of all individuals in a group) and the emergence of long-term studies played critical roles in revising male-centered models of primate social organization. In that case as well, some of the relevant information was available long before we decided it was significant (e.g., the detailed Japanese studies indicating matrilineal inheritance of rank, Kawai, 1958; Kawamura, 1958). But, in the "coy female" case, I don't think that the duration of the studies or the field methods made as much difference as the particular research questions being asked. Ultimately, however, long-term studies are going to be very important for testing the various hypotheses to explain why females mate with multiple males.

New or better data alone did not change the framework in which we asked questions; rather, I believe, something motivational changed. Among the factors leading to a reevaluation of the myth of the coy female, the role of women researchers must be considered. That is, I seriously question whether it could have been just chance or just historical sequence that caused a small group of primatologists in the 1960s, who happened to be mostly male, to focus on male-male competition and on the number of matings males obtained, while a subsequent group of researchers, including many women (beginning in the 1970s), started to shift the focus to female behaviors having long-term consequences for the fates of infants (reviewed in Hrdy & Williams, 1983).

In this paper, I deliberately included first names whenever the work of a woman was cited. I did this to emphasize just how many women are currently working specifically in this area. Even a casual inspection reveals that women are disproportionately represented among primatologists compared to their representation in science generally. For example, in 1984, just over a third of the members (36%) of the American Society of Primatologists were women.* As we reconstruct the journey from Bateman (1948) to the recogni-

---

*It should be noted however that membership in the ASP signals the *motivation* of women to join, since all one has to do is sign up and pay dues. Recognition and acceptance may be quite different. Contrast, for example, the position of women on editorial boards (4 of 40 on the *International Journal of Primatology* are women; 0 of 19 on the editorial board of the journal *Behavioral Ecology and Sociobiology*). When we examine the prestigious roster of *elected* fellows of the Animal Behavior Society for 1985, 1 of 62 is a woman. All 19 autobiographical chapters in *Leaders in the Study of Animal Behavior* are by men.

tion that the adjectives *coy* and *female* are something less than synonymous, it seems clear that the insights of women are implicated at every stage along the way and that their involvement exceeds their representation in the field. Having said this, I need to remind readers that as history my account here is biased by a conscious focus on contributions by women. A broader treatment would also have to describe the pioneering research on long-term male female relations by T. M. Ransom and Robert Seyfarth and the extensive studies of male-infant relations by Mason, Mitchell, Redican, Stein, Taub, and others (see Taub, 1984a, 1984b, for reviews). I am acutely aware that my treatment here is biased both by my particular purpose (discussing the role of empathy by females for other females in causing us to revise old assumptions) and by my own involvement in the transition of primatology from the study of primate "behavior" to the study of primate "sociobiology." Hence, I leave to someone else the task of writing a balanced history of primatology in this period (e.g., see Alison Jolly, 1985).

The contributions of women researchers can be interpreted in several ways. Perhaps, women are simply better observers. As Louis Leakey used to say in an effort to justify his all-too-evident preference for women researchers, "You can send a man and a woman to church, but it is the woman who will be able to tell you what everyone had on" (personal communication, 1970). Or perhaps women are by temperament more pragmatic or more empirical, less open to theoretical bias. A difficulty with both ideas, of course, is that a few women were present in primatology in the 1960s, and both sexes participated in perpetuating myths about monkeys living in male-centered societies, where the primary activities of females had to do with mothering (e.g., Jane Goodall, 1971 or Phyllis Jay, 1963; but see Jane Lancaster, 1975; and Thelma Rowell, 1972, for exceptions). Women seemed just as vulnerable to bias as men.

If the presence of women was a constant but our ideas changed, perhaps, as Donna

Haraway (1976) likes to remind us, the interpretations of primatologists simply mirror ideological phases in the history of the Western world. Indeed, it is disconcerting to note that primatologists are beginning to find politically motivated females and nurturing males at roughly the same time that a woman runs for vice president of the United States and Gary Trudeau starts to poke fun at "caring males" in his cartoons.

Or, perhaps, as Thelma Rowell (1984) suggested it was easier "for females to empathize with females, and ... empathy is a covertly accepted aspect of primate studies" (p. 16). Perhaps, the insights were there all along but it took longer to challenge and correct male-centered paradigms because the perceptions of women fieldworkers lacked the authority of male theorists.

In *A Feeling for the Organism*, Evelyn Fox Keller (1983) hints at the possibility that women biologists may have some special sensibility concerning the creatures that they study, an ability to enter into the lives of their subjects-a suggestion that maize geneticist Barbara McClintock, the subject of her biography, would surely deny. Among other things, such a singular "gift" for women might be thought to confine women to particular areas of science or to diminish their accomplishments. That is, as primatologist Linda Fedigan wrote recently,

I do admit to some misgivings about the wider implications of female empathy. Rowell may be correct about our sense of identification with other female primates, but I well remember my dismay when, having put many hours of effort into learning to identify the individual female monkeys of a large group, my ability was dismissed as being inherent in my sex by a respected and senior male colleague. (p. 308)

To put Fedigan's concern in perspective one needs to realize that in conversations with primatologists and, indeed, among ethologists generally, it is fairly commonplace

to hear it said that women seem better able than men to learn to individually identify large numbers of animals. In a now legendary study, the seemingly incredible capacity of British ornithologist Dafila Scott to identify and remember hundreds of unmarked swans was tested by a male colleague. Indeed, it is occasionally suggested that the difficulty men have learning individuals is one reason why more men go into the ecological side of primatology.

Similarly, and I believe justifiably, women primatologists have worried about identifying too closely with the study of mothers and infants for fear that this area would become the "home economics" of primatology, a devalued women's domain within the discipline, or for fear that it would exacerbate the already common view that women study monkeys because it satisfies a deep-felt need to be around cuddly creatures.

Yet, suppose that there is some truth to the idea that women identified with same-sex subjects and allowed this identification to influence research focus? After all, isn't this what male primatologists, and many other ethologists as well, were doing throughout the 1960s and, occasionally, into the 1980s?

Even today, one can encounter lovely examples of what I call the *punch line phenomenon*, when a covert identification by researchers with same-sex individuals suddenly becomes overt in a last paragraph or emphatic comment. For example, in a seemingly impartial 1982 paper entitled, "Why Do Pied Flycatcher Females Mate with Already Mated Males?", the authors present data to show that females who mate with already mated males rear fewer offspring than female flycatchers who are the sole mates of males, regardless of the kind of territories they had to offer her. Surely, this modern, post-"coy female" paper, focused as it is upon the reproductive success of females, a paper essentially about female strategies, will not succumb to a male-centered perspective. Yet by the end of the paper, by some imperceptible process, the female has become object, the male protagonist: "Our conclusion is that polygamous pied flycatcher males deceive their secondary females" (p. 591) and the strategy works, according to the authors, because the females lack the time to check out whether the male already has a mate whose offspring he will invest in: "it pays for a pied flycatcher female to be fast rather than coy, and therefore *she* [italics mine] can be deceived...."

My own work, before I began consciously to consider such matters, provides another example. The last line of *The Langurs of Abu: Female and Male Strategies of Reproduction* (1977), a book in which I scrupulously devoted equal space to both sexes, reads, "For generations, langur females have possessed the means to control their own destinies: caught in an evolutionary trap they have never been able to use them" (p. 309). 1 might as well have said *we.*

On a conversational level, few primatologists bother to deny this phenomenon. As a colleague remarked recently when the subject came up, "Of course I identify with them. I sometimes identify with female baboons more than I do with males of my own species." But why, we still need to ask, was the process of same-sex identification by women different in the 1970s and 1980s than in the early years of primatology?

I leave the general answers to such questions to social historians, who are more qualified than I to deal with them. At this point in the chapter, I abandon scholarship and attempt briefly to trace my own experiences as I remember them, particularly as they relate to the recognition of the active roles females were playing in the evolution of primate breeding systems.

Reminiscence

In 1970, as a first-year graduate student at Harvard, I began research on infanticidal behavior by males and ended, a decade later, almost entirely focused on the reproductive strategies of females. What processes were involved?

Some months after starting my fieldwork in Rajasthan, India, I abandoned my original hypothesis (that infanticide was a response to crowding) and adopted an interpretation based on classical sexual selection theory: infanticide was an outcome of male-male competition for access to females. That is, males only killed infants when they (the males) invaded breeding units from outside; mothers whose infants were killed subsequently mated with the killer sooner than if the mothers had continued to lactate (Hrdy, 1974). By killing infants sired by other males, the usurpers increased their own opportunities to mate with fertile females.

The story was straightforward enough and in line with everything I had been taught at Harvard. But, there were loose ends, not the least of which was my growing emotional involvement with the plight of female langurs. Every 27 months, on average, some male was liable to show up and attempt to kill a female's infant, and increasingly, my identification was with the female victimized in this way, not with the male who, according to the sexual selection hypothesis, was thereby increasing his reproductive success. If infanticide really was an inherited male trait that could be elicited by particular conditions (as I believed was the case), why would females put up with this system? Why not refuse to breed with an infanticidal male and wait until a male without any genetic propensity for infanticide showed up? Consideration of this question led to many others related to the question of intrasexual competition among females generally (Hrdy, 1981).

First came an unconscious process of identification with the problems a female langur confronts followed by the formulation of conscious questions about how a female copes with them. This, in turn, led to the desire to collect data relevant to those questions. Once asked, the new questions and new observations forced reassessment of old assumptions and led to still more questions. Even events I had seen many times before (e.g., females leaving their troops to solicit extratroop males) raised questions as they never had before.

If it was really true that females did not benefit from additional matings, why were female langurs taking such risks to solicit males outside their troop? Why would already pregnant females solicit and mate with males? What influence might such behavior have for the eventual fate of the female's offspring? What were the main sources of variance in female reproductive success and what role did nonreproductive sexuality play in all this? Why is situation-dependent receptivity, as opposed to strictly defined cyclical receptivity or estrus, so richly developed in the order primates? Where did the idea of the coy female ever come from anyway? These are the questions that preoccupied me since 1977 and all of them grow out of an ability to imagine females as active strategists.

Yet, identification with same-sex individuals in another primate species may not be quite so simple as it sounds. This history of primatology suggests that the nature of this identification was changing over time as the self-image of women researchers also changed. In my own case, changes in the way I looked at female langurs were linked to a dawning awareness of male-female power relationships in my own life, though "dawning" perhaps overstates the case.

It would be difficult to explain to an audience of political activists how intelligent human beings could be as politically unaware as many field biologists and primatologists are. Almost by definition, we are people who lead isolated lives and, by and large, avoid joining groups or movements. In addition, I was the sole woman in my cohort, since I was the first woman graduate student my particular advisor had taken on and only toward the end of the 1970s did I begin to read anything by feminist scholars like Carolyn Heilbrun and Jean Baker Miller. Each step in understanding what, for example, might be meant by a term like *androcentric* was embarked upon very slowly and dimly, sometimes resentfully, as some savage on the fringe of civilization

might awkwardly rediscover the wheel. When I did encounter feminist writings, I was often put off by the poor quality of the scholarship. Sherfey's book is a case in point: highly original insights were imbedded in what seemed to me a confused and often erroneous matrix. Nevertheless, the notion of "solidarity" with other women and, indeed, the possibility that female primates generally might confront shared problems was beginning to stir and to raise explicit questions about male-female relations in the animals I studied. That is, there were two (possibly more) interconnected processes: an identification with other females among monkeys taking place at roughly the same time as a change in my definition of women and my ability to identify and articulate the problems women confront.

Such an admission raises special problems for primatologists. My discipline has the choice of either dismissing me as a particularly subjective member of the tribe or else acknowledging that the tribe has some problems with objectivity. It is almost a cliche to mention now how male-biased the early animal behavior studies were (see Wasser, 1983). But, in the course of the last decade of revision, are we simply substituting a new set of biases for the old ones?

The feminist charge that most fields, including psychology, biology, and animal behavior, have been male-centered, is, I think, by now undeniable. Yet to me, the noteworthy and encouraging thing is how little resistance researchers in my own field have exhibited when biases are pointed out. Although I still sense in Britain a reluctance to admit that male bias was ever actually a problem, among primatologists in the United States it is now widely acknowledged, and this has to be a healthy sign. Indeed, in animal behavior and primatology, there has been something more like a small stampede by members of both sexes to study female reproductive strategies, as well as perhaps a rush to substitute a new set of biases for the old. (That is, among feminist scholars it is now permissible to say that males and females are different, provided one also stipulates that females are more cooperative, more nurturing, more supportive—not to mention equipped with unique moral sensibilities; among sociobiologists *kudos* accrue to the author of the most Machiavellian scenario conceivable.)

There are of course antidotes to the all-too-human element that plagues our efforts to study the natural world. Common sense in methodology is one. No one will ever again be permitted to make pronouncements about primate breeding systems after having studied only one sex or after watching only the conspicuous animals. A recognition of the sources of bias is another. If, for example, we suspect that identification with same-sex individuals goes on or that certain researchers identify with the dominant and others with the oppressed and so forth, we would do well to encourage multiple studies, restudies, and challenges to current theories by a broad array of observers. We would also do well to distinguish explicitly between what we know and what we know is only interpretation. But really (being generous) this is science as currently practiced: inefficient, biased, frustrating, replete with false starts and red herrings, but nevertheless responsive to criticism and self-correcting, and hence better than any of the other more unabashedly ideological programs currently being advocated.*

References

Abernethy, V. (1978). Female hierarchy: An evolutionary perspective. In L. Tiger & H. Fowler (Eds.), *Female Hierarchies*. Chicago: Beresford Book Service.

Alatalo, R. V., Lundberg A., & Stahlbrandt, K. (1982). Why do pied flycatcher females mate

*Recent feminist programs advocating "conscious partiality" come to mind. If an unbiased knowledge is impossible, this argument runs, an explicitly biased, politically motivated approach is preferable to the illusion of impartial research.

with already mated males. *Animal Behaviour, 30,* pp. 585–593.

Altmann, J. (1980). *Baboon mothers and infants.* Cambridge: Harvard University Press.

Altmann, S. (Ed.). (1965). *Japanese monkeys: A collection of translations.* Edmonton, Canada: The editor.

Andelman, S. (forthcoming). Concealed ovulation and prolonged receptivity in vervet monkeys *(Cercopithecus aethiops).*

Bateman, A. J. (1948). Intra-sexual selection in drosophila. *Heredity, 2,* pp. 349–368.

Benshoof, L., & Thornhill, R. (1979). The evolution of monogamy and concealed ovulation in humans. *Journal of Biological Structures, 2,* pp. 95–106.

Bleier, R. (1984). *Science and gender.* Elmsford, NY: Pergamon.

Bray, O. E., Kennelly, J. J., & Guarino, J. L. (1975). Fertility of eggs produced on territories of vasectomized red-winged blackbirds. *Wilson Bulletin, 87,* No. 2, pp. 187–195.

Burley, N., & Symanski, R. (1981). Women without: An evolutionary perspective on prostitution. In *The immoral landscape: Female prostitution in Western societies.* Toronto: Butterworth.

Busse, C., & Hamilton, W. J., III. (1981). Infant carrying by male chacma baboons. *Science, 212,* pp. 1281–1283.

Clutton-Brock, T. H., & Harvey, P. (1976). Evolutionary rules and primate societies. In P. P. G. Bateson & R. A. Hinde (Eds.), *Growing points in ethology.* Cambridge: Cambridge University Press.

Cords, M. (1984). Mating patterns and social structure in redtail monkeys *(Cercopithecus ascanius).* *Zeitschrift für Tierpsychologie, 64,* pp. 313–329.

Cronin, C. (1980). Dominance relations and females. In D. R. Omark, F. F. Strayer, and D. G. Freeman (Eds.), *Dominance relations.* New York: Garland Press.

Daly, M., & Wilson, M. (1983). *Sex, evolution and behavior.* Boston: Willard Grant Press.

Darwin, C. (1871). *The descent of man and selection in relation to sex* (1887 edition). New York: D. Appleton and Co.

Davies, E. M., & Boersma, P. D. (1984). Why lionesses copulate with more than one male. *The American Naturalist, 123,* no. 5, pp. 594–611.

Davies, N. B., & Lundberg, A. (1984). Food distribution and a variable mating system in the dunnock, *Prunella modularis*. *Journal of Animal Ecology, 53*, pp. 895–912.

Dawkins, R. (1976). *The selfish gene*. Oxford: Oxford University Press.

DeVore, I. (Ed.). (1965). *Primate behavior*. New York: Holt, Rinehart and Winston.

Diamond, J. (1984). Theory and practice of extramarital sex. *Nature, 312*, p. 196.

Dunbar, R. (1984). *Reproductive decisions: An economic analysis of gelada baboon social strategies*. Princeton, NJ: Princeton University Press.

Eaton, R. (Ed.). (1976). *The world's cats II*. Seattle, WA: Feline Research Group, Woodland Park Zoo.

Edwards, G. (1758). *Gleanings of Natural History* (Vol. 5). London: College of Physicians.

Fedigan, L. (1984). Sex ratios and sex differences in primatology (book review of *Female primates)*. *American Journal of Primatology, 7*, pp. 305–308.

Freedman, D. (1979). *Human sociobiology: A holistic approach*. New York: The Free Press.

Fujioka, M., & Tamagishi, S. (1981). Extramarital and pair copulations in the cattle egret. *Auk, 98*, pp. 134–144.

Gladstone, D. (1979). Promiscuity in monogamous colonial birds. *The American Naturalist, 114*, no. 4, pp. 545–557.

Goldizen, A. W., & Terborgh, J. (in press). Cooperative polyandry and helping behavior in saddle-backed tamarins (*Saguinus fuscicollis*). Proceedings of the IXth Congress of the International Primatological Society. Cambridge: Cambridge University Press.

Goodall, J. (1971). *In the shadow of man*. Boston: Houghton Mifflin.

Haraway, D. (1976). The contest for primate nature: Daughters of man-the-hunter in the field. In M. Kann (Ed.), *The future of American democracy: Views from the left*. Philadelphia, PA: Temple University Press.

Hartung, J. (in press). Matrilineal inheritance: New theory and analysis. *The Behavioral and Brain Sciences*.

Hausfater, G. (1975). Dominance and reproduction in baboons (*Papio cynocephalus*). *Contributions to Primatology* (Vol. 7). Basel, Switzerland: S. Karger.

Hausfater, G., & Hrdy, S. B. (Eds.). (1984). *Infanticide: Comparative and evolutionary perspectives*. New York: Aldine.

Hrdy, D. B. (1979). Integrated field study of the behavior, genetics and diseases of the Hanuman langur in Rajasthan, India. Proposal submitted to the National Science Foundation.

Hrdy, S. B. (1974). Male-male competition and infanticide among the langurs (*Presbytis entellus*) of Abu, Rajasthan. *Folia Primatologica, 22*, pp. 19–58.

Hrdy, S. B. (1976). The care and exploitation of nonhuman primates by conspecifics other than the mother. *Advances in the Study of Behavior, VI*, pp. 101–158.

Hrdy, S. B. (1977). *The langurs of Abu: Female and male strategies of reproduction*. Cambridge: Harvard University Press.

Hrdy, S. B. (1979). Infanticide among animals: A review, classification and examination of the implications for the reproductive strategies of females. *Ethology and Sociobiology, 1*, pp. 3–40.

Hrdy, S. B. (1981). *The woman that never evolved*. Cambridge: Harvard University Press.

Hrdy, S. B. (1984). Introduction: Female reproductive strategies. In M. Small, (Ed.), *Female primates: Studies by women primatologists*. New York: Alan Liss.

Hrdy, S. B., Hrdy, D. B., & Bishop, J. (1977). *Stolen copulations*. 16 mm color film. Peabody Museum.

Hrdy, S. B., & Whitten, P. (1986). The patterning of sexual activity. In D. Cheney, R. Seyfarth, B. Smuts, R. Wrangham, & T. Struhsaker (Eds.), *Primate societies*. Chicago: University of Chicago Press.

Hrdy, S. B., & Williams, G. C. (1983). Behavioral biology and the double standard. In S. K. Wasser (Ed.), *Social behavior of female vertebrates*. New York: Academic Press.

Jay, P. (1963). The female primate. In S. Farber & R. Wilson (Eds.), *The potential of woman*. New York: McGraw-Hill.

Jolly, A. (1985). *The evolution of primate behavior*. New York: Macmillan.

Kawai, M. (1958). On the system of social ranks in a natural troop of Japanese monkeys: I. Basic rank and dependent rank. *Primates, 1–2*, pp. 111–130.

Kawamura, S. (1958). Matriarchal social ranks in the Minoo-B troop: A study of the rank system of Japanese monkeys. *Primates, 1–2,* pp. 149–156.

Keller, E. F. (1983). *A feeling for the organism: The life and work of Barbara McClintock.* New York: W. H. Freeman.

Kleiman, D. (1977). Monogamy in mammals. *Quarterly Review of Biology, 52,* pp. 39–69.

Kleiman, D., & Malcolm, J. (1981). The evolution of male parental investment in mammals. In D. J. Gubernick & P. H. Klopfer (Eds.), *Parental care in mammals.* New York: Plenum Press.

Koyama, N. (1967). On dominance rank and kinship of a wild Japanese monkey in Arashiyama. *Primates, 8,* pp. 189–216.

Lamb, M. (1984). Observational studies of father-child relationships in humans. In D. Taub (Ed.), *Primate paternalism.* New York: Van Nostrand Reinhold.

Lancaster, J. (1975). *Primate behavior and the emergence of human culture.* New York: Holt, Rinehart and Winston.

Lott, D. (1981). Sexual behavior and intersexual strategies in American Bison. *Zeitschrift für Tierpsychologie, 56,* pp. 97–114.

Lumpkin, S. (1983). Female manipulation of male avoidance of cuckoldry behavior in the ring dove. In S. C. Wasser (Ed.), *The social behavior of female vertebrates.* New York: Academic Press.

MacKinnon, J. (1978). *The ape within us.* New York: Holt, Rinehart and Winston.

Markow, T. A., & Ankney, P. F. (1984). *Drosophila* males contribute to oogenesis in a multiple mating species. *Nature, 224,* pp. 302–303.

Moore, J. (1985). Demography and sociality in primates. Doctoral dissertation, Harvard University. Cambridge.

Mori, U., & Dunbar, R.I.M. (in press). Changes in the reproductive condition of female gelada baboons following the takeover of one-male units. *Zeitschrift für Tierpsychologie.*

Morris, S. (1979, August). Darwin and the double standard. *Playboy Magazine.*

Parker, G. A. (1970). Sperm competition and its evolutionary consequences in the insects. *Biological Review, 45,* pp. 525–567.

Ransom, T., & Ransom, B. (1971). Adult-male-infant interactions among baboons (*Papio anubis*). *Folia Primatologica, 16,* pp. 179–195.

Rowell, T. (1972). *Social behaviour of monkeys.* Baltimore, MD: Penguin Book.

Rowell, T. (1984). Introduction: Mothers, infants and adolescents. In M. Small (Ed.), *Female primates.* New York: Alan Liss.

Sayers, J. (1982). *Biological politics.* London: Tavistock.

Scarr, S. (1984). *Mother care: Other care.* New York: Basic Books.

Seyfarth, R. (1978). Social relationships between adult male and female baboons, part 2: Behavior throughout the female reproductive cycle. *Behaviour, 64,* nos. 3–4, pp. 227–247.

Shaw, E., & Darling, J. (1985). *Female strategies.* New York: Walker.

Sherfey, M. J. (1973). *The evolution of female sexuality* (first published 1966). New York: Vintage Books.

Small, M. (Ed.). (1984). *Female primates.* New York: Alan Liss.

Small, M. (Forthcoming). Primate female sexual behavior and conception: Is there really sperm to spare?

Smith, J. M. (1984). Optimization theory in evolution. In E. Sober (Ed.), *Conceptual issues in evolutionary biology.* Cambridge, MA: The M.I.T. Press.

Smith, R. (1984). Sperm competition. In *Sperm competition and the evolution of animal mating systems.* New York: Academic Press.

Smuts, B. B. (1985). *Sex and friendship in baboons.* New York: Aldine Publishing Co.

Stacey, P. B. (1982). Female promiscuity and male reproductive success in social birds and mammals. *The American Naturalist, 120,* no. 1, pp. 51–64.

Stein, D. (1981). The nature and function of social interactions between infant and adult male yellow baboons (*Papio cynocephalus*). Doctoral dissertation, University of Chicago.

Stein, D. (1984). Ontogeny of infant-adult male relationships during the first year of life for yellow baboons (*Papio cynocephalus*). In D. Taub (Ed.), *Primate paternalism.* New York: Van Nostrand Reinhold.

Symons, D. (1979). *The evolution of human sexuality.* Oxford: Oxford University Press.

Taub, D. (1980). Female choice and mating strategies among wild Barbary macaques (*Macaca syl-*

vana). In D. Lindburg (Ed.), *The macaques*. New York: Van Nostrand Reinhold.

Taub, D. (1984a). Male-infant interactions in baboons and macaques: A critique and reevaluation. Paper presented at the American Zoological Society Meetings, Philadelphia, PA.

Taub, D. (1984b). *Primate paternalism*. New York: Van Nostrand Reinhold.

Tiger, L. (1977). The possible biological origins of sexual discrimination. In D. W. Brothwell (Ed.), *Biosocial man*. London: The Eugenics Society.

Tilson, R. (1981). Family formation strategies of Kloss' gibbons. *Folia Primatologica, 35,* pp. 259–287.

Trivers, R. L. (1972). Parental investment and sexual selection. In B. Campbell (Ed.), *Sexual selection and the descent of man*. Chicago: Aldine.

Trivers, R. L. (1985). *Social evolution*. Menlo Park, CA: Benjamin/Cummings.

Tsingalia, H. M., & Rowell, T. E. (1984). The behaviour of adult male blue monkeys. *Zeitschrift für Tierpsychologie, 64,* pp. 253–268.

Turner, M. E., & Anderson, W. W. (1983). Multiple mating and female fitness in *Drosophilia pseudoobscura*. *Evolution, 37,* no. 4, pp. 714–723.

Tutin, C. (1975). Sexual behaviour and mating patterns in a community of wild chimpanzees (*Pan troglodytes schweinfurthii*). Doctoral dissertation submitted to the University of Edinburgh, Edinburgh.

Van den Berghe, E. (1984). Female competition, parental care, and reproductive success in salmon. Paper presented at Animal Behavior Society Meetings, Cheney, Washington, August 13–17.

Vogt, J. (1984). Interactions between adult males and infants in prosimians and New World monkeys. In D. Taub (Ed.), *Primate paternalism*. New York: Van Nostrand Reinhold.

Wasser, S. C. (Ed.). (1983). *The social behavior of female vertebrates*. New York: Academic Press.

Wasser, S. C., & Barash, D. (1984). Reproductive suppression among female mammals. *Quarterly Review of Biology,* pp. 513–538.

Williams, G. C. (1966). *Adaptation and natural selection*. Princeton, NJ: Princeton University Press.

Williams, G. C. (1975). *Sex and evolution*. Princeton, NJ: Princeton University Press.

Wilson, E. O. (1978). *On human nature*. Cambridge: Harvard University Press.

Wirtz, P. (1983). Multiple copulations in the Waterbuck. *Zeitschrift für Tierpsychologie, 61,* pp. 78–82.

Wright, P. (1984). Biparental care in *Aotus trivirgatus* and *Callicebus molloch*. In M. Small (Ed.), *Female primates*. New York: Alan Liss.

Zuckerman, Sir S. (1932). *The social life of monkeys and apes*. London: Butler and Turner, Ltd.

The Importance of Feminist Critique for Contemporary Cell Biology

THE BIOLOGY AND GENDER STUDY GROUP

Athena Beldecos, Sarah Bailey, Scott Gilbert, Karen Hicks
Lori Kenschaft, Nancy Niemczyk, Rebecca Rosenberg
Stephanie Schaertel, and Andrew Wedel

Nancy Tuana … has traced the seed-and-soil analogy from cosmological myths through Aristotle into the biology of the 1700s. Modeling his embryology after his social ideal, Aristotle promulgated the notions of male activity versus female passivity, the female as incomplete male, and the male as the real parent of the offspring. The female merely provided passive matter to be molded by the male sperm. While there were competing views of embryology during Aristotle's time, Aristotle's principles got the support of St. Thomas and were given the sanction of both religion and scientific philosophy (Horowitz 1976, 183). In this essay, we will attempt to show that this myth ultimately found its way into the core of modern biology and that various "revisionist" theories have been proposed … to offset this myth.

We have come to look at feminist critique as we would any other experimental control. Whenever one performs an experiment, one sets up all the controls one can think of in order to make as certain as possible that the result obtained does not come from any other source. One asks oneself what assumptions one is making. Have I assumed the temperature to be constant? Have I assumed that the pH doesn't change over the time of the reaction? Feminist critique asks if there may be some assumptions that we haven't checked concerning gender bias. In this way feminist critique should be part of normative science. Like any control, it seeks to provide critical rigor, and to ignore this critique is to ignore a possible source of error.

The following essay is not an attempt to redress past injustices which biology has inflicted upon women. This task has been done by several excellent volumes that have recently been published (Sayers 1982; Bleier 1984, 1986;Fausto-Sterling 1985). Rather, this paper focuses on what feminist critique can do to strengthen biology. What emerges is that gender biases [have informed] several areas of modern biology and that these biases have been detrimental to the discipline. In other words, whereas most feminist studies of biology portray it—with some justice—as a privileged oppressor, biology has also been a victim of the cultural norms. These masculinist assumptions have impoverished biology by causing us to focus on certain problems to the exclusion of others, and they have led us to make particular interpretations when equally valid alternatives were available.

Sperm Goes A'Courtin'

If Aristotle modeled fertilization and sex determination on the social principles of his time, he had plenty of company among more contemporary biologists. The first major physiological model of sex determination was proposed in 1890 when Sir Patrick Geddes and J. Arthur Thomson published *The Evolution of Sex*, one of the first popular treatises on sexual physiology. By then, it had been established that fertilization was the result of the union of sperm and egg. But still unanswered was the mechanism by which this event constructed the embryo. One of the central problems addressed by this highly praised volume was how sex was determined. Their theory was that there were two types of metabolism: *anabolism*, the storing up of energy, and *katabolism*, the utilization of stored energy. The determination of sexual characteristics depended on which mode of metabolism prevailed. "In the determination of sex, influences favoring katabolism tend to result in the production of males, as those favoring anabolism similarly increase the production of females" (Geddes and Thomson 1890, 45, 267). This conclusion was confirmed by looking at the katabolic behavior of adult males (shorter life span, greater activity and smaller size) compared to the energy-conserving habits of females who they described as "larger, more passive, vegetative, and conservative."[1] In a later revision (1914, 205–206) they would say, "We may speak of women's constitution and temper as more conservative, of man's more unstable … We regard the woman as being more anabolic, man as relatively katabolic; and whether this biological hypothesis be a good one or not, it certainly does no social harm."

This microcosm/macrocosm relationship between female animals and their nutritive, passive eggs and between male animals and their mobile, vigorous sperm was not accidental. Geddes and Thomson viewed the sperm and egg as representing two divergent forms of metabolism established by protozoan organisms, and "what was decided among the prehistoric protozoa cannot be annulled by Act of Parliament." Furthermore, as in Aristotle, the difference between the two is nutrition. The motivating force impelling the sperm towards the egg was hunger. The yolk-laden egg was seen as being pursued by hungry sperm seeking their nourishment. The Aristotelian notion of activity and passivity is again linked with the role of female as nutrient provider. It is also linked with that most masculine of British rituals, the hunt.[2]

It is usually assumed that the discovery of the X and Y sex chromosomes put an end to these environmental theories of sex determination. This is today's interpretation and not that of their discoverer. What the genetics texts do not tell us is that C.E. McClung placed his observations of sex chromosomes directly in the context of Geddes and Thomson's environmental model. Using a courtship analogy wherein the many spermatic suitors courted the egg in its ovarian parlour, McClung (1901, 224) stated that the egg "is able to attract that form of spermatozoon which will produce an individual of the sex most desirable to the welfare of the species." He then goes on to provide an explicit gender-laden correlation of the germ cells mirroring the behavior of the sexual animals that produced them:

> The ovum determines which sort of sperm shall be allowed entrance into the egg substance. In this we see the extension, to its ultimate limit, of the well-known role of selection on the part of the female organism. The ovum is thus placed in a delicate adjustment with regard to the surrounding conditions and reacts in a way to best subserve the interests of the species. To it come two forms of spermatozoa from which selection is made in response to environmental necessities. Adverse conditions demand a preponderance of males, unusually favorable conditions induce an excess of females, while normal environments apportion an approximately equal representation of the sexes. (McClung 1902, 76)

McClung concluded this paper by quoting that Geddes and Thomson's theory of anabolism and katabolism provided the best explanation as to whether the germ cells would eventually grow into "passive yolk-laden ova or into minute mobile spermatozoa."

The Sperm Saga

Courtship is only one of the narrative structures used to describe fertilization. Indeed, "sperm tales" make a fascinating subgenre of science fiction. One of the major classes of sperm stories portrays the sperm as a heroic victor. In these narratives, the egg doesn't choose a suitor. Rather, the egg is the passive prize awarded to the victor. This epic of the heroic sperm struggling against the hostile uterus is the account of fertilization [frequently] seen in ... introductory biology texts. The following is from one of the best introductory textbooks [of the past].

> Immediately, the question of the fertile life of the sperm in the reproductive tract becomes apparent. We have said that one ejaculation releases about 100 million sperm into the vagina. Conditions in the vagina are very inhospitable to sperm, and vast numbers are killed before they have a chance to pass into the cervix. Millions of others die or become infertile in the uterus or oviducts, and millions more go up the wrong oviduct or never find their way into an oviduct at all. The journey to the upper portion of the oviducts is an extremely long and hazardous one for objects so tiny.... Only one of the millions of sperm cells released into the vagina actually penetrates the egg cell and fertilizes it. As soon as that one cell has fertilized the egg, the [egg] cell membrane becomes impenetrable to other sperm cells, which soon die. (Keeton 1976, 394)

We might end the saga by announcing, "I alone am saved." These sperm stories are variants of the heroic quest myths such as the Odyssey or the Aeneid. Like Aeneas, the spermatic hero survives challenges in his journey to a new land, defeats his rivals, marries the princess and starts a new society. The sperm tale is a myth of our origin. The founder of our body is the noble survivor of an immense struggle who deserved the egg as his reward. It is a thrilling and self-congratulatory story.

The details of these fertilization narratives fit perfectly into Campbell's archetype of such myths. Campbell (1956, 387), however,

believes that "there is no hiding place for the gods from the searching telescope or microscope. In this he has been wrong. The myth lies embedded within microscopic science".[3]

The next passage comes from a book ... given expectant mothers. It, too, starts with the heroic sperm model but then ventures off into more disturbing images.

> Spermatozoa swim with a quick vibratory motion.... In ascending the uterus and Fallopian tube they must swim against the same current that waft the ovum downward.... Although a million spermatozoa die in the vagina as a result of the acid secretions there, myriads survive, penetrate the neck of the uterus and swarm up through the uterine cavity and into the Fallopian tube. *There they lie in wait for the ovum.* As soon as the ovum comes near the *army of spermatozoa,* the latter, as if they *were tiny bits of steel drawn by a powerful magnet, fly at the ovum.* One *penetrates,* but only one.... *As soon as the one enters, the door is shut on other suitors.* Now, as if *electrified,* all the particles of the ovum (now fused with the sperm) exhibit vigorous agitation. (Russell 1977, 24, emphasis added)

In one image we see the fertilization as a kind of martial gang rape, the members of the masculine army lying in wait for the passive egg. In another image, the egg is a whore, attracting the soldiers like a magnet, the classical seduction image and rationale for rape. The egg obviously wanted it. Yet, once *penetrated,* the egg becomes the virtuous lady, closing its door to the other *suitors.* Only then is the egg, because it has fused with a sperm, rescued from dormancy and becomes active. The fertilizing sperm is a hero who survives while others perish, a soldier, a shard of steel, a successful suitor, and the cause of movement in the egg. The ovum is a passive victim, a whore and finally, a proper lady whose fulfillment is attained.

The accounts in such textbooks must seem pretty convincing to an outsider. The following is from a paper on the history of conception theories, published—by a philosopher—in 1984.

Aristotle's intuitions about the male as trigger which begins an epigenetic process is a foreshadowing of modern biological theory in which the sperm is the active agent that must move and penetrate the ovum. The egg passively awaits the sperm, which only contributes a nucleus, whereas the egg contributes all the cytoplasmic structures (along with its nucleus) to the zygote. In other words, the egg contributes the material and the form, and the sperm contributes the activating agent and the form.... Thus even modern biology recognizes the specialized and differentiated roles of male and female in an account of conception. Aristotle's move in such a direction was indeed farsighted. (Boylan 1984, 110)

Energetic Eggs and Active Anlagen

Until very recently, textbook accounts have emphasized (even idealized) the passivity of the egg. The notion of the male semen "awakening the slumbering egg" is seen as early as 1795 (Reil 1795, 79), and this idea, according to historian Tim Lenoir (1982, 37) "was to have an illustrious future." Since 1980, however, there has been a new account of sperm-egg interactions. This revisionism has been spurred on by new data (and new interpretations of old data) which has forced a re-examination of the accepted scenario. The egg appears to be less a "silent partner" and more an energetic participant in fertilization. Two of the major investigators forcing this re-evaluation are Gerald and Heide Schatten. Using scanning electron microscopy, they discovered that when the sperm contacts the egg, it does not burrow through.[4] Rather, the egg directs the growth of microvilli—small finger-like projections of the cell surface—to clasp the sperm and slowly draw it into the cell. The

mound of microvilli extending to the sperm had been known since 1895 when E. B. Wilson published the first photographs of sea urchin fertilization. But this structure has been largely ignored until the recent studies, and its role is still controversial.

In 1983, the Schattens wrote a review article for laypeople on fertilization. Entitled "The Energetic Egg," it consciously sought to change the metaphors by which fertilization is thought about and taught.

In the past years, investigations of the curious cone that Wilson recorded have led to a new view of the roles that sperm and egg play in their dramatic meeting. The classic account, current for centuries, has emphasized the sperm's performance and relegated to the egg the supporting role of Sleeping Beauty—a dormant bride awaiting her mate's magic kiss, which instills the spirit that brings her to life. The egg is central to this drama, to be sure, but it is as passive a character as the Grimm brothers' princess. Now, it is becoming clear that the egg is not merely a large yolk-filled sphere into which the sperm burrows to endow new life. Rather, recent research suggests the almost heretical view that sperm and egg are mutually active partners. (Schatten and Schatten 1983, 29)

Other studies are showing this mutual activity in other ways. In mammals, the female reproductive tract is being seen as more than a passive or even hostile conduit through which sperm are tested before they can reach the egg. Freshly ejaculated mammalian sperm are not normally able to fertilize the eggs in many species. They have to become *capacitated*. This capacitation appears to be mediated through secretions of the female genital tract. Furthermore, upon reaching the egg, mammalian sperm release enzymes which digest some of the extracellular vestments which surround the egg. These released enzymes, however, are not active. They become activated by interacting with another secretion of the female reproductive tract. Thus, neither the egg nor the female reproductive tract is a passive element in fertilization. The sperm and the egg are both active agents and passive substrates. "Ever since the invention of the light microscope, researchers have marveled at the energy and endurance of the sperm in its journey to the egg. Now, with the aid of the electron microscope, we can wonder equally at the speed and enterprise of the egg, as it clasps the sperm and guides its nucleus to the center" (Schatten and Schatten 1983, 34).

As we have seen above, the determination of maleness and femaleness has also been inscribed by concepts of active masculinity and passive femaleness. (This means that *sex*, not just *gender*, can be socially constructed!) Indeed, until 1986, all modern biological theories of mammalian sex determination have assumed that the female condition is developed passively, while the male condition is actively produced from the otherwise female state (for review, see Gilbert 1985, 643). This has been based largely on Jost's experiments where rabbits developed the female body condition when their gonadal rudiments were removed before they had differentiated into testes or ovaries. But these experiments actually dealt with the generation of secondary sexual characteristics and not the primary sex determination event—the differentiation of sexually indifferent gonadal primordia into ovaries or testes.

During [recent] years, these theories of primary sex differentiation(notably the H-Y antigen model wherein male cells synthesized a factor absent in female cells which caused the gonadal primordia to become testes) have been criticized by several scientists, and a new hypothesis has been proposed by Eva Eicher and Linda Washburn of the Jackson Laboratory. This new model is based on extensive genetic evidence and incorporates data that could not be explained by the previous accounts of sex determination. In their introductory statement, Eicher and Washburn point out the active and passive contexts that

have been ascribed to the development of the primary sexual organs. They put forth their hypotheses as a controlled corrective for traditional views.

> Some investigators have over-emphasized the hypothesis that the Y chromosome is involved in testis determination by presenting the induction of testicular tissue as an active (gene directed, dominant) event while presenting the induction of ovarian tissue as a passive (automatic) event. Certainly, the induction of ovarian tissue is as much an active, genetically directed developmental process as is the induction of testicular tissue or, for that matter, the induction of any cellular differentiation process. Almost nothing has been written about genes involved in the induction of ovarian tissue from the undifferentiated gonad. The genetics of testis determination is easier to study because human individuals with a Y chromosome and no testicular tissue or with no Y chromosome and testicular tissue, are relatively easy to identify. Nevertheless, speculation on the kind of gonadal tissue that would develop in an XX individual if ovarian tissue induction fails could provide criteria for identifying affected individuals and thus lead to the discovery of ovarian determination genes. (Eicher and Washburn 1986, 328)

Again, we see that alternative versions of long-held scientific "truths" can be generated. A feminist critique of cellular and molecular biology does not necessarily mean a more intuitivistic approach. Rather, it involves being open to different interpretations of one's data and having the ability to ask questions that would not have occurred within the traditional context. The studies of Eicher and Washburn on sex determination and those of the Schattens on fertilization can be viewed as feminist-influenced critiques of cell and molecular biology. They have controlled for gender biases rather than let the ancient myth run uncontrolled through their interpretations. Yet the techniques used in their analyses are not different than those of other scientists working in their respective fields, and the approaches used in these studies are no "softer" than those used by researchers working within the traditional paradigms.[5]

A Nuclear Family:
The Sexualization of the Cell

The sperm and egg are *gametes*; that is marriage partners. As we have seen, their interactions have been modeled on various courtship behaviors. This extrapolates, however, into a husband-wife arrangement in the zygote cell. It is again not surprising, then, to find this relationship reflected in the relationship between nucleus and cytoplasm. The sperm, after all, is viewed as a motile nucleus while the cytoplasm of the zygote and its descendants is derived entirely from the ovum (Morgan 1926, 45). One might argue that the ovum provides a nuclear component equal to that of the sperm, but this is usually overlooked (note the parentheses in the above quotation from Boylan). Even today among biologists, the term "maternal inheritance" is identical with "cytoplasmic inheritance." The nucleus came to be seen as the masculine ruler of the cell, the stable yet dynamic inheritance from former generations, the unmoved mover, the mind of the cell. The cytoplasm became the feminine body of the cell, the fluid, changeable, changing partner of the marriage.

This marriage trope was extremely prevalent during the 1930's when there were at least four competing views of the relationship between the cytoplasm and the nucleus (Gilbert, in press). What one finds is that the relationship of husband to wife becomes that of nucleus to cytoplasm. In Germany, one of the dominant theories modeled the cell after an autocratic Prussian family. The nucleus contained all the executive functions and the cytoplasm did whatever the nucleus commanded. Indeed, the cytoplasm existed only to be physically acted upon by the nuclear genes. As Harwood (1984, 3) has pointed out, defenders of this *Kernmonopol* wrote of the supremacy (*"Uberlegenheit"*) of the genes and the dominating role of the nucleus ("*die dominierende Rolle des Kernes*"). The leading American geneticist, T.H. Morgan, modeled the cell after a more American family. First, the nucleus and the cytoplasm conferred; *then*, the nucleus told the cytoplasm what to do. The nucleus, like the ideal American husband, still had the power and the final decision; but the decision was made only after discussions with the female partner. Not only was this a more American view of marriage, it was also the relationship between T.H. Morgan and his wife (G. Allen, Personal Communication). A third view came from C.H. Waddington, a British socialist. Waddington married a successful architect and viewed his marriage as a partnership. Werskey (1978, 221) has pointed out that Waddington respected women as intellectual equals, and Waddington viewed the marriage of nucleus and cytoplasm as a partnership. In *Organisers and Genes* (1940), Waddington tried to show the equality of nucleus and cytoplasm, neither dominating the other. His cell, like his notion of marriage, was a partnership between equals. The fourth view comes from the American Black embryologist E.E. Just (1939) who declared the cytoplasm to dominate over the nucleus. The nucleus was subservient to the commands given it by the cytoplasm, and only the cytoplasm was endowed with vitality. This also reflects Just's view of male/female relationships, for "Just saw himself working for Hedwig [his lover] as a slave works for his master" (Manning 1983, 265). For Just, who viewed fertilization largely as a consequence of the cytoplasmic activity of the egg, the male was subservient to the female. Thus, all four views of nuclear/ cytoplasmic interactions reflect views of male/female interactions.

Contemporary biology, although aware of the interactions of the cytoplasm and nucleus, still tends to portray the nucleus as the head of the family's hierarchy. Jacob (1976, 224) writes, "Among all the constituents of living organisms, the genetic material has a privileged position. It occupies the summit of the pyramid and decides the properties of the organism. The other constituents are charged with the execution of the decision." The term "genetic engineering" (like "reproductive technology") is a masculine metaphor appropriating the role of procreation to technology. Haraway (1984) claims that "genetic engineering ... is a science fiction expression suggesting the triumph of the phallogocentric lust to recreate the world without the intermediary of fleshy women's bodies." In genetic engineering, the assumption has been that DNA is the "master molecule," and introductory biology texts still call DNA by that name.[6] This isn't surprising given the hierarchical "central dogma" of DNA→RNA→Protein and the views of].D. Watson ("the best home for a feminist is in another person's lab"). David Nanney (1957, 136) and Evelyn Fox Keller (1985, 150) have criticized this view, and Nanney has put forth an alternative model. He argues against the "Master Molecule concept.... This is in essence the theory of the Gene, interpreted to suggest a totalitarian government." He opposed this to "The 'Steady State' concept. By this term ... we envision a dynamic self-perpetuating organization of a variety of molecular species which owes its specific properties not to the characteristic of any particular molecule, but to the functional interrelationships of these molecular species." E.E. Just, in fact, had criticized McClung's notion of chromosomal hegemony on the same grounds. McClung (1924, 634) had claimed that, "Taken together, the chromosomes represent the sum total of all the elements of control over the processes of metabolism, irritability, contractibility, reproduction, etc., that are involved in the life of the organism." Note the use of the nucleus as the repository of all the control functions of the cell. Just (1936, 305) replied that "Such statements are

absolutely without foundation in fact." Just (1936, 292) also linked nuclear hegemony with authoritarianism. It is not surprising that Nanney is one of the leading authorities on extrachromosomal inheritance and the cell cortex, and that E.E. Just attempted to popularize E.B. Wilson's observations on the eggs' activity in fertilization.

The master-molecule has become, in DNA, the unmoved mover of the changing cytoplasm. In this cellular version of the Aristotelian cosmos, the nucleus is the efficient cause (as Aristotle posited the sperm to be) while the cytoplasm (like Aristotle's conception of the female substrate) is merely the *material* cause. The nuclear DNA is the essence of domination and control. Macromolecule as machomolecule. Keller (1985) notes that on the cellular level, the hierarchical depiction of DNA in most textbooks looks like "organizational charts of corporate structures" and that genetic stability is ensured by the unidirectionality of information flow, much as political and social stability is assumed in many quarters to require the unidirectional exercise of authority." This hierarchy on the cellular level is supported by sociobiology on the organismal level. Here, bodies are merely vehicles for the propagation of genes. They are the fruit which nourishes the seeds. Similarly, the metaphors of sociobiology are drawn from the investment economics of our present society (Haraway 1979; Schwartz 1986).

The steady-state view of the cell is presently a minority opinion, but it has ... been eloquently expressed by Lynn Margulis and by Lewis Thomas (1974, 1). Here, the cell is seen as an ecologically interacting entity where process and interrelatedness are fundamental characteristics of life, not the properties of a single molecule.

The modeling of the nucleus began with a template of domination: "What controls what?" This was secondarily sexualized such that the nucleus (mate) was seen as dominating the passive (female) cytoplasm. This sexualization of the cell has had enormously important effects on how biologists view the cell and this view, now "objectified" by science, supports the social behaviors which imposed it in the first place. The sexualization of the cell has placed blinders on researchers, making certain observations (and interpretations) "normal" and others "aberrant." In this section, we have tried to show that the tendency to equate activity with masculinity and passivity with femaleness has caused the research programs of fertilization and sex determination to be directed in a way different than it might have otherwise been. But can such degenderization succeed, or are we engrained in our telling of sexual stories? There is a case where the degenderizing of the cell has succeeded to the benefit of the science. In protozoology at the turn of the century, gender distinctions had been placed on unicellular organisms (a strange situation considering these are cells and lack vaginas, penises, ovaries, or testes). M. Hartmann (1929), one of the leading protozoologists of his time held that whenever differences were found within species, these differences would be male and female. In an article opposing this view, T.M. Sonneborn (1941, 705) noted that "the characteristics by which the female is ordinarily recognized are larger size, lesser activity, greater storage of nutritive reserves, and egg-like form; and the male by the corresponding opposite characters." Sonneborn pointed out that this dichotomy had created artificial problems that had directed research into less productive areas, and that a better protozoology could emerge if the male and female distinctions were abandoned. Sonneborn's ideas prevailed, and the analysis of mating types (*plus* and *minus*: "a" and "alpha"; not male and female) has become one of the most exciting areas of the field.

Fertilization Metaphors in Organic Chemistry

The sperm-egg interaction is a metaphor in-and-of-itself. Sometimes, the metaphor is explicit and sometimes implicit, but many things appear to interact "like the sperm and egg." Implied in this analogy is an active partner and a passive partner. We see this in many introductory textbooks of organic chemistry. Collisions between two molecules which lead to the formation of new compounds are often depicted sexually or aggressively, an active, small molecule "attacking" a large, passive, heavy compound. Nucleophilic and electrophilic "attacks" are standard language in organic chemistry. "The entering group is a negative species which is attacking the nucleus of the reactive carbon. ... (Cason 1966, 66, 76). In the same book, college sophomores are also taught that "the nucleophile attempting a backside attack on the molecule is confronted with a problem that may be likened to the effort to penetrate a set of propellers spinning at high speed."

The notions of penetration and entry are often standard parts of organic chemistry lectures. It is not surprising to read that the "characteristic reaction of a carbene is insertion." Another book (Cook and Crump 1969, 71) describes the alkene bond as "being 'ripe for plucking' by an approaching electrophile." The heroic nucleophile or electrophile must be, like the sperm, tested. "The potency of a nucleophile in affecting a displacement is termed its nucleophilicity or nucleophilic strength" (Cason 1966, 363).

Who would have expected nucleophallic and electrophallic molecules? It appears that an arbitrary genderization of molecules has been made, where one of the colliding molecules is called the "attacking" group and the other is the passive recipient of this attack. In both nucleophilic and electrophilic "attack," the "attacking" molecule is not the larger, but the smaller, faster one. The large molecules, those that are "looser" in terms of their electronic configuration (more resonance, pi-bonding) are the passive attacked groups. This arbitrary imagery *is*, we believe, analogous to small, hard mobile sperm penetrating the large, soft, immobile eggs. The imagery conforms to stereotypic attributions of maleness to energetic elements and femaleness to the passive ones. These stereotypes are being propagated by the language of science which gives students a wrong idea of nature (i.e., that it is gender-biased) but which purports to be objective.

Nature as Text

> Like other sciences, biology today has lost many of its illusions. It is no longer seeking the truth. It is building its own truth.
> —Francois Jacob (1976, 16)

Science is a creative human endeavor whereby individuals and groups of individuals collect data about the natural world and try to make sense of them. Each of the basic elements of scientific research—conceptualization, execution, and interpretation—involves creativity. In fact, these three elements are the same as most any artistic, literary or musical endeavor. Two aspects of science are especially creative, namely the conceptual designing of an experiment and the interpreting of the results. Usually, the interpretation is put in the context of a narrative which includes the data but is not dependent upon them (Medawar 1963, 377; Figlio 1976, 17; Landau 1984, 262). Since science is a creative endeavor, it should be able to be criticized as such; and Lewis Thomas (1984, 155) has even suggested that schools of science criticism should exist parallel to that of literary, music and art criticism.

As a creative part of our social structure, biology should be amenable to analysis by feminist critique which has provided new insights into literature, art and the social sciences. Indeed, feminist examinations of sociobiology (Sayers 1982; Bleier 1984) primate research (Haraway 1986), and scientific methods (Keller 1985) have provided an important contribution to the literature of those fields. Researchers in those fields are aware of the feminist criticism and the result has created a better science—one in which methods of data collection and interpretation have been scrutinized for sexual biases.

Any creative enterprise undertaken by human beings is subject to the influences of society. It is not surprising, then, to see how gender becomes affixed to cells, nuclei and even chemicals. Even the interpretations of mathematical equations change with time! The interpretation that Newton gave to his Law of Gravity (i.e., that it was evidence of God's power and benevolence) differs (Dobbs 1985) from the interpretation of eighteenth century physicists (that it was evidence for a mechanical universe devoid of purpose), and from that of contemporary physicists (that it is the consequence of gravitons traversing the curvature of space around matter).

By using feminist critique to analyze some of the history of biological thought, we are able to recognize areas where gender bias has informed how we think as biologists. In controlling for this bias, we can make biology a better discipline. Moreover, it is important that biology be kept strong and as free from gender bias as possible; for it is in a unique position to do harm or good. As Heschel has remarked (albeit with masculine pronouns):

> The truth of a theory about man is either creative or irrelevant, but never merely descriptive. A theory about the stars never becomes a part of the being of the stars. A theory about man enters his consciousness, determines his self-understanding, and modifies his very existence. The image of a man affects the nature of man.... We become what we think of ourselves. (1965, 7)

A theory about life affects life. We become what biology tells us is the truth about life. Therefore, feminist critique of biology is not only good for biology but for our society as well. Biology needs it both for itself and for fulfilling its social responsibilities.

Notes

Lest anyone believe that this is strictly an academic exercise, the *New York Times* (25 March 1987, Sec. I, p. 20) reported an article wherein Adrianus Cardinal Simonis, Primate of the Netherlands, cited fertilization as evidence for the passive duties of women. In this essay, the Archbishop pointed to the egg that merely "waits" for the male's sperm, which he described as the "dynamic, active, masculine vector of new life."

1. The apparent exception of mammalian males was considered due to the extra burden *they* had when their mates were pregnant.

2. Once given "objectivity" by science, the notion that men are active because of their spermatic metabolism and women are passive because of their ovum-like ways finds its way into popular definition of masculinity and femininity. Freud (1933, 175) felt it necessary to counter this view when he lectured on "Femininity": "The male sex-cell is actively mobile and searches out the female one, and the latter, the ovum, is immobile and waits passively ... The male pursues the female for the purpose of sexual union, seizes hold of her and penetrates into her. But by this you have precisely reduced the characteristic of masculinity to the factor of aggressiveness as far as psychology is concerned." Freud recognized that "it is inadequate to make masculine behavior coincide with activity and feminine with passivity," and that "it serves no useful purpose and adds nothing to your knowledge."

3. There is ample evidence for the ovum as mythic princess. The ovum is not allowed to see sperm before it is of age, and when it travels to meet the sperm this "ripe" ovum not only has a "corona" (crown) but "vestments." It is also often said to have "attendant cells." According to Jung (1967, 171, 204), the hero is the symbol *par excellence* of the male libido and of the longing to reunite with the mother. If true, the sperm is an excellent embodiment of heroic fantasy. But this does not mean we have to follow this myth. Indeed, one could make a heroic tale about the ovum which has to take a "leap" into the unknown, though its chances of survival are less than 1%. Indeed, the human ovum, too, is a survivor of a process which has winnowed out nearly all of the original 2 million oocytes, and left it the only survivor of its cohort.

4. The "burrowing" metaphor is also commonly seen in textbooks, and it brings with it the seed-and-soil imagery. This plowing trope was, for many ancient cultures, a metaphor of necessary violence. The active/passive dichotomy is remarkably evident in the verb *to fertilize*. The traditional statement is that the "sperm fertilizes the egg." The sperm is active, the egg is passive. This inverts the original meaning of *fertilize* which involves the nourishment of the soil. The verb no longer connotes nutrition in this context, but activation.

5. Although Eicher and Washburn have emphasized that both sexes are actively created, at least two reviews on sex determination have recently proposed one or the other sex as being the "default" condition of the species. It should be noted that the views expressed in this essay may or may not be those of the scientists whose work we have reviewed. It is our contention that these research programs are inherently critical of a masculinist assumption with these respective fields. This does not mean that the research was consciously done with this in mind.

6. Metaphor and connotive language is extremely important in producing the gender-related images. Introductory biology textbooks also refer to the pituitary as "the master gland." (After all, it controls the other organs of sex and internal secretion from its privileged position in the brain. The apical, brainy organ controls the organs of lower functions; the sex glands being furthest removed.) There are other metaphors that could have been utilized. The pituitary could be called the "switchboard" gland (a female gender image) or the "integrator" gland (a dialectical image). Similarly, it is not merely a figure of speech to say that the seed analogy is at the heart of cell biology. The German word *Kern* (and Germany was where most of the pioneering work on cytology and fertilization was done) means more than the English equivalent "nucleus." It also means kernel, center, quintessence and elite position. Similarly both sperm and semen (and their German equivalents) have the same etymology, namely "seed." *Mater*, however, gives the root for maternal, material, matter and matrix.

   The seed metaphor was so real to Leeuwenhoek that he actually performed dissections of plant seeds, insisting that the embryonic human would be found in the sperm just as the embryonic plants were found in the seeds (Ruestow 1983, 204). His "spermatozoa" were precisely that: mobile, ensouled, seed-animals. To him, the uterus (and the female sex) served to nourish the seed. The father was the sole parent.

References

Bleier, R. 1984. *Science and gender: A critique of biology and its theories on women.* New York: Pergamon Press.

———. 1986. *Feminist approaches to science.* New York: Pergamon Press.

Boylan, M. 1984. The Galenic and Hippocratic challenges to Aristotle's conception theory. *Journal of the History of Biology* 17:83–112.

Campbell, J. 1956. *The hero with a thousand faces.* Cleveland: Meridian Books.

Cason, J. 1966. *Principles of modern organic chemistry.* New Jersey: Prentice Hall.

Cook, P.L. and J.W. Crump. 1969. *Organic chemistry: A contemporary view.* Lexington, MA: Heath.

Dobbs, B.J.T. 1985. Newton and stoicism. *Southern Journal of Philosophy* 23(Supp):109–123.

Eicher, E.M. and L. Washburn. 1986. Genetic control of primary sex determination in mice. *Annual Review of Genetics* 20:327–60.

Fausto-Sterling, A. 1985. *Myths and gender: Biological theories about men and women.* New York: Basic Books.

Figlio, L.M. 1976, The metaphor of organization. *Journal of the History of Science* 14:12–53.

Freud, S. [1933] 1974. Femininity. In *Women in analysis,* ed. J. Strouse. New York: Grossman.

Geddes, P. and J.A. Thomson. 1890. *Evolution and sex.* New York: Moffitt.

———. 1914. *Problems of sex.* New York: Moffitt.

Gilbert, S.F:. 1985. *Developmental biology.* Sunderland, MA: Sinauer Associates.

———. In Press. Cellular Politics: Goldschmidt, Just, and the attempt to reconcile embryology and genetics. In *The American development of biology,* ed. K. Benson, J. Maienschein and R. Rainger. University of Pennsylvania Press.

Haraway D. 1979. The biological enterprise: Sex, mind, and profit from human engineering to sociobiology. *Radical History Review* 20:206–237.

———. 1984. Lieber Kyborg als Gottin! Fur eine sozialistische-feministische Unterwanderung der Gentechnologie. In *Argument-Sonderband* 105, ed. B.P. Lange and A.M. Stuby, 66–84.

———. 1986. Primatology is politics by other means. In *Feminist approaches to science,* ed. R. Bleier, 77–119. New York: Pergamon Press.

Hartmann, M. 1929. Verteilung, Bestimmung, und Vererbung des Geschlechtes bei den Protisten und Thallophyten. *Handb. D. Verer,* II.

Harwood, J. 1984. The reception of Morgan's chromosome theory in Germany: Inter-war debate over cytoplasmic inheritance. *Medical History Journal* 19:3–32.

Heschel, A.J. 1965. *Who is man?* Stanford: Stanford University Press.

Horowitz, M.C. 1976. Aristotle and woman. *Journal of the History of Biology* 9:183–213.

Jacob, F. 1976. *The Logic of life.* New York: Vintage.

Jung, C.G. 1967. *Symbols of transformation.* Princeton: Princeton University Press.

Just, E.E. 1936. A single theory for the physiology of development and genetics. *American Naturalist* 70:267–312.

———. 1939. *The biology of the cell surface.* Philadelphia: Blakiston.

Keeton, W.C. 1976. *Biological science,* 3rd ed. New York: W.W. Norton.

Keller, E.F. 1985. *Reflections on gender and science.* New Haven: Yale University Press.

Landau, M. 1984. The narrative structure of anthropology. *American Scientist* 72:262–268.

Lenoir, T. 1982, *The strategy of life,* Dordrecht: D. Reidel.

Manning, K.R. 1983. *The black apollo of science: The life of Ernest Everett Just.* New York: Oxford University Press.

McClung, C.E. 1901. Notes on the accessory chromosome. *Anatomischer Anzeiger* 20.

———. 1902. The accessory chromosome—Sex determinant? *The Biological Bulletin* 3.

———. 1924. The chromosome theory of heredity. In *General Cytology.* Chicago: University of Chicago Press.

Medawar, P.B. 1963. Is the scientific paper a fraud? *The Listener* (12 September): 377.

Morgan, T. H. 1926. *The theory of the gene.* New Haven: Yale University Press.

Nanney, D.L. 1957. The role of the cytoplasm is heredity. In *The chemical basis of heredity*, ed W.E. McElroy and H.B. Glenn, 134–166. Baltimore: Johns Hopkins University Press.

Reil, J.C. 1795. Von der Lebenskraft, *Arch. f.d. Physiol.* 1. Quoted in *The strategy of life*. See Lenoir 1982.

Ruestow, E.G. 1983. Images and ideas: Leewuenhoek's perception of the spermatozoa. *Journal of the History of Biology* 16:185–224.

Russell, K.P. 1977. *Eastman's expectant motherhood.* 6th ed. New York: Little.

Sayers, J. 1982. *Biological politics: Feminist and anti-feminist perspectives.* New York and London: Tavistock.

Schatten, G. and H. Schatten. 1983. The energetic egg. *The Sciences* 23(5):28–34.

Schwartz, B. 1986. *The battle for human nature: Science, morality, and modern life.* New York: W.W. Norton.

Sonneborn, T.M. 1941. Sexuality in unicellular organisms. In *Protozoa in biological research*, ed. G.N. Calkins and F.M. Summers. Chicago: University of Chicago Press.

Thomas, L. 1974. *The lives of a cell.* New York: Viking.

———. 1984. *Late night thoughts on listening to Mahler's ninth symphony.* New York: Bantam.

Werskey, G. 1978. *The visible college.* New York: Holt, Reinhart and Winston.

Waddington, C.H. 1940. *Organisers and genes.* Cambridge: Cambridge University Press.

The Engendering of Archaeology

Refiguring Feminist Science Studies

Alison Wylie

Internal Critiques: The Sociopolitics of Archaeology

In the last fifteen years archaeologists have been drawn into heated debates about the objectivity of their enterprise. These are frequently provoked by critical analyses that demonstrate (with hindsight) how pervasively some of the best, most empirically sophisticated archaeological practice has reproduced nationalist, racist, classist, and, according to the most recent analyses, sexist and androcentric understandings of the cultural past. Some archaeologists conclude on this basis that however influential the rhetoric of objectivity may be among practitioners, the practice and products of archaeology must inevitably reflect the situated interests of its makers. A great many others regard such claims with suspicion, if not outright hostility.

They maintain the conviction—a central and defining tenet of North American archaeology since its founding as a profession early in this century—that archaeology is, first and foremost, a science and that, therefore, the social and political contexts of inquiry are properly external to the process of inquiry and to its products.[1]

The feminist critiques of archaeology on which I focus here are relative newcomers to this growing tradition of internal "sociopolitical" critique. Not surprisingly, they have drawn sharply critical reactions that throw into relief the polarized positions that dominate thinking about the status and aims of archaeology. And yet, I will argue, these feminist interventions do not readily fit any of the epistemic options defined in this debate.... In this essay I first characterize what I will identify provisionally as the feminist initiatives that have emerged in archaeology since the late 1980s (qualifications of this designation come later) and then consider their larger implications. My immediate concern is how, within the rubric of feminist science studies, we are to understand the late and rapid emergence of an archaeological interest in questions about women and gender. This leads, in turn, to a set of reflexive questions about how to do feminist science studies.

Feminist Critiques in Archaeology

Critiques of sexism and androcentrism in archaeology fall into two broad categories that parallel analyses of other dimensions of archaeological practice (e.g., its nationalism, classism, and racism): "content" and "equity" critiques. In addition—and in this feminist critiques are distinctive—there is emerging a move toward "integrative" analyses that combine content and equity critiques.

Content Critiques. Two types of content critique can usefully be distinguished. The first draws attention to erasure, to ways in which the choice of research problem or the determination of significant sites or periods or cultural complexes leaves out of account women and gender even when they are a crucial part of the story to be told.[2] For example, Anne Yentsch delineates previously unacknowledged patterns of change in the ceramic ware of domestic assemblages that testify to the gradual transfer of women's productive activities (specifically, domestic dairy production) from the home to commercial enterprises whenever these became capable of industrialization; she argues that this largely unexamined process of appropriation of "women's work" is crucial for understanding the transformation of the rural economy in the northeastern United States through the eighteenth and nineteenth centuries. Similarly, Donna Seifert describes the difference it makes to our understanding of the archaeology of urban centers if we take seriously the presence of prostitutes, for example, in

"Within Sight of the White House." And Cheryl Claassen draws attention to the rich insights that follow from a focus on the shellfishing activities associated primarily with women and children in the Shell Mound Archaic. To take a prehistoric example that I will discuss in more detail later in this essay, Pat Watson and Mary Kennedy argue that dominant explanations of the emergence of horticulture in the Eastern Woodlands share a common flaw: although women are presumed to have been primarily responsible for collecting plants under earlier gatherer-hunter/foraging subsistence regimes and for cultivating them when gourds and maize were domesticated, they play no role at all in accounts of how this profoundly culture-transforming shift in subsistence practice was realized.[3] Watson and Kennedy say they are "leery" of explanations that remove women from the one domain granted them as soon as an exercise of initiative is envisioned.

Often, however, straightforward erasure is not the problem; and so a second sort of critique is required, one that focuses on how women and gender are represented when they are taken into account. From the outset feminist critics have emphasized that, although questions about women and gender have never been on the archaeological research agenda, archaeological research problems and interpretations are routinely framed in gendered terms.[4] The functions ascribed to artifacts and sites are often gender specific, and models of such diverse cultural phenomena as subsistence practices among foragers, social organization in agrarian societies, and the dynamics of state formation often turn on the projection onto prehistory of a common body of presentist, ethnocentric, and overtly androcentric assumptions about sexual divisions of labor and the status and roles of women. Women in prehistoric foraging societies are presumed to be tied to "home bases" while their male counterparts quite literally "bring home the bacon," despite extensive ethnohistoric evidence that women in such contexts are highly mobile and that their foraging activities are often responsible for most of the dietary intake of their families and communities.

More subtle but equally problematic are interpretations of large-scale cultural transformations that treat gender roles and domestic relations as a stable (natural) substrate of social organization that is unchanged by the rise and fall of states and is, therefore, explanatorily irrelevant. In another case that I will consider further, Christine Hastorf argues that the domestic units encountered in the highland Andes at the time of the Spanish conquest cannot be projected back into prehistory as if their form was a given. She offers compelling archaeological evidence that households and gender roles were substantially reshaped by the extension of Inka influence into these territories. In a parallel analysis, Elizabeth Brumfiel argues not just that the Aztec system of economic and political control changed domestic relations but that, given its basis in exacting tribute in the form of locally produced cloth, it depended fundamentally on the intensified and restructured exploitation of female (domestic) labor.[5] In these cases, critical (re)analysis reveals ways in which understanding has been limited not by ignoring women and gender altogether, but by conceptualizing them in normatively middle-class, white, North American terms.

Equity Critiques. Alongside these forms of content critique, there has grown up a substantial and largely independent body of literature concerning the demography, institutional structures, funding sources, training, and employment patterns that shape archaeology. Feminist analyses of the status of women constitute some of the most fine-grained and empirically rich work of this sort.[6] These "equity critiques" document not only persistent patterns of differential support, training, and advancement for women in archaeology, but also entrenched patterns of gender segregation in the areas in which women typically work.

While such studies provide fascinating detail on ways in which women are marginalized within archaeology, rarely are they used as a basis for understanding how the content of archaeological knowledge is shaped. And although content critics provide compelling evidence that the silences and distortions they identify are systematically gendered, rarely do they make any connection between these and the gender imbalances in the training, employment, and reward structures of the discipline documented by equity critics. In general, sociopolitical critics in archaeology have tended to sidestep explanatory questions about how the silences and stereotypes they delineate are produced or why they persist.[7]

Integrative Critiques. There is one study, undertaken from an explicitly feminist perspective, that illustrates the potential fruitfulness of "integrative analyses": analyses that explore the link between workplace inequities and androcentric bias in the content of research. It is an analysis of Paleo-Indian research undertaken by Joan Gero. She begins by documenting a strong pattern of gender segregation: the predominantly male community of Paleo-Indian researchers focuses almost exclusively on stereotypically male activities—specifically, on large-scale mammoth- and bison-hunting practices, the associated kill sites and technologically sophisticated hunting tool assemblages, and the replication of these tools and of the hunting and butchering practices they are thought to have facilitated. Gero finds that the women in this field have been largely displaced from these core research areas; they work on expedient blades and flake tools and focus on edge-wear analysis. Moreover, in the field of lithics analysis generally, women are cited much less frequently than their male colleagues even when they do mainstream research, except when they coauthor with men. Not surprisingly, Gero argues, their work on expedient blades and patterns of edge wear is almost completely ignored, despite the fact that these analyses provide evidence that Paleo-Indians exploited a wide range of plant materials, presumably foraged as a complement to the diet of Pleistocene mammals. Gero's thesis is that these "social *relations* of paleo research practice" derail the Paleo-Indian research program as a whole: "women's exclusion from Pleistocene lithic and faunal analysis ... is intrinsic to, and necessary for, the bison-mammoth knowledge construct."[8] The puzzles that dominate Paleo-Indian research are quite literally created by the preoccupation with male-associated (hunting) activities. They turn on questions about what happened to the mammoth hunters when the mammoths went extinct: Did they disappear, to be replaced by small game and plant foraging groups, or did they effect a miraculous transformation as the subsistence base changed? These questions can only arise, Gero argues, if researchers ignore the evidence from female-associated tools that Paleo-Indians depended on a much more diversified set of subsistence strategies than acknowledged by standard "man the (mammoth/bison) hunter" models. This is precisely the sort of evidence produced mainly by women working on microblades and edge-wear patterns; it is reported in publications that remain largely outside the citation circles that define the dominant focus of inquiry in this area.

Archaeology as Politics By Other Means

When critiques of androcentrism and sexism appeared in archaeology in the late 1980s, debate about the implications of sociopolitical critiques was already sharply polarized. Some of the most uncompromising critics of the explicitly positivist "New Archaeology" of the 1960s and 1970s parlayed local analyses of the play of interests in archaeology into a general rejection of all concepts or ideals of objectivity. Through the early 1980s they insisted, on the basis of arguments familiar in philosophical contexts (underdetermination

of theory by evidence, theory-ladenness, and various forms of holism), that archaeologists simply "create facts," that evidential claims depend on "an edifice of auxiliary theories and assumptions" that archaeologists accept on purely conventional grounds, and that there is, therefore, no escape from the conclusion that any use of archaeological data to test reconstructive hypotheses about the past can "only result in tautology."[9] The choice between tautologies, then, must necessarily be determined by standpoint-specific interests and the sociopolitics that shape them; archaeology is quite literally politics by other means.

With these arguments, some critics within archaeology broach what Bruce Trigger has described as a nihilistic "hyperrelativism" now familiar in many of the social sciences. Given critical analyses that "shatter" pretensions to objectivity, demonstrating that there is no "view from nowhere," no immaculately conceived foundation of fact, no transcontextual or transhistorical standard of rationality, it is assumed that epistemic considerations play no significant role at all.[10] What counts as sound argument and evidence (as "good reasons" for accepting a knowledge claim) is entirely reducible to the sociopolitical realities that constitute the standpoint of practitioners, or communities of practitioners, and the conventions of their practice. For a great many archaeologists, these conclusions were grounds for summarily dismissing postprocessualism and any aligned analysis that purports to bring into view the play of politics in archaeology. A dominant counter-response has been to call for a return to basics, to the real (empirical) business of archaeology. Not surprisingly, the feminist critiques that appeared in the late 1980s met with considerable skepticism.

What distinguishes the interventions of feminist critics in these debates is their refusal, for the most part, to embrace any of the polarized responses generated by this growing crisis of confidence in objectivist ideals. In most cases feminist critics in archaeology depend on painstakingly careful empirical analysis to establish their claims about gaps or bias in content, about inequities in the role and status of women in the field, and about the links between equity and content critiques. But however pervasive the androcentrism or sexism they delineate, and however sharply they criticize pretensions to neutrality and objectivity, they are deeply reticent to embrace any position approaching the hyperrelativism described by Trigger. They are clear about the social, political nature of the archaeological enterprise, and yet they do not consider the outcomes of inquiry or the criteria of adequacy governing practice to be reducible to the sociopolitics of practice.

Two lines of argument support this stance. For one thing, it is evident that, as a matter of contingent empirical fact, "reasons"—appeals to evidence and considerations of explanatory power, as well as of internal and cross-theory consistency—do frequently play a critical role in determining the content of archaeological interpretations and the presuppositions that frame them, including those embraced or advocated by feminists. That is to say, reasons can be causes; they shape belief and the outcomes of archaeological inquiry, although their form and authority are never transparent and never innocent of the power relations that constitute the social contexts of their production. For another, close scrutiny of archaeological practice makes it clear that, as Roy Bhaskar argued years ago, one crucial and much-neglected feature of science "is that it is *work;* and hard work at that.... [It] consists ... in the transformation of given products." Most important, these "products" are built from materials that archaeologists do not construct out of whole cloth, whose properties they can be (disastrously) wrong about, and whose capacities to act or be acted upon can be exploited to powerful effect by those intent on "intervening" in the world(s) they study when these worlds are accurately understood.[11] Sociologically reductive accounts cannot make sense of these features of archaeological practice, including

the practice of feminists and other critics in and of archaeology. Perhaps feminists have been more alert to these considerations because here, as in other contexts, they are painfully aware that the world is not (just) what we make it, and the cost of systematic error or self-delusion can be very high; effective activism requires an accurate understanding of the forces we oppose, conceptually, politically, and materially.

Most recently, the critics within archaeology who raised the specter of hyper relativism have backed away from their strongest (and most untenable) claims.[12] They seem to have recognized that, insofar as they mean to expose systematic error and explain it (e.g., by appeal to the conditions that shape knowledge production), their own practice poses a dilemma: they bring social contingencies into view by exploiting precisely the evidential constraints and other epistemic considerations they mean to destabilize. They make good use of the fact that, as enigmatic and richly constructed as archaeological evidence may be, it does routinely resist appropriation in any of the terms compatible with dominant views about the past. This capacity of the world we investigate to subvert our best expectations can force us to reassess not only specific claims about the past but also background assumptions we may not have known we held, assumptions that constitute our standpoint in the present. As critics within archaeology have moved beyond reaction against the New Archaeology and have undertaken to build their own alternative research programs, they tend to embrace epistemic positions that have much in common with those occupied by feminist critics and practitioners....

Gender Research in Archaeology

Feminist initiatives appeared much later in archaeology than in such cognate fields as sociocultural anthropology and history. It was not until 1984, just over a decade ago, that the first paper appeared in Anglo-American archaeology that argued explicitly for the relevance of feminist insights and approaches to the study of gender. And it was another seven years before a book presented a substantial body of original work in the area. This took the form of a collection edited by Joan Gero and Margaret Conkey, *Engendering Archaeology: Women and Prehistory*[13] which was the outcome of a small working conference convened by the editors in 1988 specifically for the purpose of mobilizing interest in the questions about women and gender posed by Conkey and Janet Spector in 1984. ... Most participants had never considered these questions and had no special interest in feminist initiatives.

The following year, the graduate student organizers of an annual thematic conference at the University of Calgary chose "The Archaeology of Gender" as their topic for the fall 1989 "Chacmool" conference. To everyone's surprise, the open call for papers advertising this meeting drew over a hundred contributions on a wide range of topics, a substantially larger response than had been realized for any previous Chacmool conference.[14] The only previous meetings on gender had been annual colloquia at the meetings of the Society for Historical Archaeology (beginning in 1988) and several Norwegian and British conferences and conference sessions.[15] The 1989 Chacmool proceedings were published two years later, and in the meantime at least five other widely advertised public conferences, and a number of smaller-scale workshops and conference symposia, were organized in Australia, North America, and the United Kingdom; several of these have produced published proceedings or edited volumes.[16] In an annotated bibliography of papers on archaeology and gender that were presented at conferences from 1964 through 1992, the editor/compiler, Cheryl Claassen, indicates that only twenty-four of a total of 284 entries were presented before 1988 and that only two of these appeared in print; more than half the

entries are papers presented between 1988 and 1990, and fully 40 percent of those presented after 1988 have been published. So, despite the fact that little more than Conkey and Spector's 1984 paper was in print by the late 1980s, when various groups of enterprising organizers set about arranging archaeological conferences on gender, there seems to have been considerable interest in the topic that was, in a sense, just waiting for an outlet, an interest that has since taken hold across the field as a whole.[17]

The questions raised by these developments are conventional enough; they have to do with theory change, with why these initiatives should have appeared in the form they did and when they did, and with their implications for the presuppositions of entrenched traditions of research.[18] I have found these to be resolutely intractable questions, however, because the conditions shaping the emergence of gender research in archaeology are so multidimensional: a great many factors are at work, none of them separable from the others, and they operate on different scales, some highly local while others are quite general. Indeed, nothing brings home, more forcefully the need for an *integrative* program of feminist science studies than grappling with the complexities of these recent developments in archaeology. What follows is a provisional and, most important, a *syncretic* account of the conditions responsible for the "engendering" of archaeology; fully integrated categories of analysis remain to be formulated. My aim is to illustrate why none of the familiar strategies for explaining science is adequate taken on its own. This will inevitably raise more questions than I can answer but will allow me to specify, in the conclusion, some of the tasks at hand in reframing science studies....

Sociopolitical Factors

My thesis is that nothing in the theoretical content, intellectual history, methodological refinement, or evidential resources of contemporary archaeology can explain why an interest in questions about women and gender should have arisen (only) in the late 1980s. Sociopolitical features of the research community and its practice play a central role in determining the timing, the form, and the impact of the feminist critiques and research programs on gender that have begun to challenge the entrenched androcentrism of archaeology. In order better to understand these factors, I undertook a survey of everyone who participated in the 1989 Chacmool conference and did interviews with a number of those I identified as "catalysts": those who had been instrumental in organizing this and related conferences and in producing the publications that drew attention to the need for and promise of feminist initiatives in archaeology. My immediate aim was to determine what factors had converged in creating the substantial constituency of archaeologists who were ready and willing to attend a conference on gender despite the lack of visible work in the area.

At the outset I assumed that the emergence of feminist initiatives in archaeology had followed roughly the same course as in other closely affiliated disciplines (e.g., sociocultural anthropology, history, paleontology): they appeared when a critical mass of women entered the field who had been politicized in the women's movement and were therefore inclined to notice, and to be skeptical of, the taken-for-granteds about gender that had hitherto structured archaeological interpretation and the research agenda of the field. In archaeology a significant increase in the representation of women was not realized until after the mid 1970s. I expected, then, that participants in the 1989 Chacmool conference would prove to be predominantly women drawn from the first professional cohorts in which women were strongly represented and that they would have been attracted to the topic of the conference because of prior involvement in feminist activism and scholarship. This account would suggest that the 1989 Chacmool conference

afforded participants an opportunity to integrate preexisting feminist commitments with professional interests in archaeology.

In the event, 72 percent of the 1989 Chacmool participants responded to the survey, providing me with enormously detailed answers to a lengthy list of open-ended questions about their background training and research interests, their reasons for attending the conference, their involvement with feminist scholarship and activism, and their views about why gender research should be emerging in archaeology in the late 1980s. Preliminary analysis suggests that my initial hypothesis captures the experience and motivations of most of the "catalysts" but not of conference participants. The survey results do bear out my hypothesis about the demographic profile of contributors to the Chacmool program but confound my assumptions about their backgrounds and why they attended this first public conference on "The Archaeology of Gender."

Those who attended the 1989 Chacmool conference were disproportionately women, and these women, more than the men, were drawn from cohorts that entered the field in the late 1970s and early 1980s, when the representation of women in North American archaeology doubled. Altogether 80 percent of submissions to the conference were made by women; this more than inverts the ratio of women to men in North American archaeology as a whole, where women make up roughly 36 percent of practitioners.[19] And while the average age of men and women at the time of the conference was very similar (forty-three as compared to forty years), the men were more widely distributed across age grades; altogether 60 percent of the women (twice the proportion of men) were clustered in the twenty-six to forty age range. Combined with information about their education and employment status, this suggests that, as I had expected, the majority of those who attended the conference were middle-ranked professional women who would have completed their graduate training and achieved some measure of job security by the mid to late 1980s, just when the first stirrings of public interest in questions about women and gender began to appear in archaeology. Moreover, most of these women made it clear that the call for papers tapped an existing interest in questions about gender; only a fifth reported ever having attended a Chacmool conference in the past (over half of the men reported being regular or previous attendees), and virtually all said the main reason they attended the 1989 Chacmool conference was the topic.

The survey responses also make it clear, however, that an avowed interest in questions about gender does not necessarily reflect a feminist standpoint. Nearly half of the women (and more of the men) said explicitly that they do not identify themselves as feminists, and many of those who embraced the label recorded reservations about what it means. Although three-quarters of respondents (both men and women) said they had a prior interest in research on gender, altogether two-thirds described the Chacmool conference as opening up a new area of interest for them, and less than half reported any previous involvement in women's studies or familiarity with feminist research in other fields. These results are consistent with Marsha Hanen and Jane Kelley's analysis of the conference abstracts, which reveals what they describe as a "dearth" of references to feminist literature, authors, influences, or ideas.[20] Most striking, just half of the women and a quarter of the men who responded to the survey indicated any involvement in women's groups, in action on women's issues, or in "feminist activism," and most described their involvement as limited to "being on a mailing list" or "sending money," usually to women's shelters and reproductive rights groups. Very few had been involved in any direct action or frontline work with the agencies and groups they supported. No doubt this level of involvement in the women's movement (broadly construed) is substantially higher than is typical for North American

archaeologists. Even so, it does not support the hypothesis that the majority of participants in the Chacmool conference on "The Archaeology of Gender" had been independently politicized as feminists and had welcomed this conference as a first public opportunity to integrate their feminist and archaeological commitments.

The results of this preliminary analysis suggest, then, that the expanded cohort of women entering the field at the turn of the 1980s brought to their work in archaeology a standpoint of sensitivity to gender issues—no doubt in some sense a gendered standpoint—but not an explicitly feminist standpoint. Hanen and Kelley describe this orientation as a largely untheorized and apolitical "grass roots" interest in questions about gender relations and categories.[21] It would seem that the 1989 Chacmool call for papers resonated with a latent awareness of the contested and contestable nature of gender roles, considered both as a feature of daily life and as a possible topic for investigation in archaeology. Indeed, for many the conference seems to have been attractive because it provided an opportunity to engage these questions at arm's length, on the relatively safe (or at least familiar) terrain of archaeological inquiry. And for some this scholarly interest proved to be politicizing: a number of respondents noted, in their survey returns and in subsequent correspondence, that their work on the "archaeology of gender" has put them in touch with feminist scholarship in other fields and has led to an involvement in women's groups active on issues such as workplace equity, sexual harassment, reproductive rights, and violence against women. By contrast, almost all who played a role as catalysts had already been politicized as feminists and then brought this explicitly feminist angle of vision to bear on the programs of research in which they were engaged as archaeologists.

In these two rather different senses, then, the appearance of gender research in archaeology in the last few years seems to reflect a growing awareness, among relatively young professionals in the field, of the gendered dimensions of their experience, perhaps provoked by the fact that the gender composition of their own cohort disrupts the status quo. And perhaps, as amorphous and ill-defined a standpoint as this is, it was sufficient to incline (some) members of this cohort, especially the women, to greater awareness of and skepticism about the androcentrism inherent in extant research programs. Much remains to be done to determine what constitutes this "grass roots" standpoint of gender sensitivity, how it is articulated in archaeological contexts, how it relates to the gender politics of the larger society, and how it shapes archaeological practice; evaluation and refinement of this hypothesis will depend, in part, on further analysis of the survey responses and, in part, on comparative analysis (within archaeology and across fields). But if this line of argument is plausible, it was a distinctive self-consciousness about gender relations that put these new participants in a position to think differently about their discipline and their subject matter, to identify gaps in analysis, to question taken-for-granted assumptions about women and gender, and to envision a range of alternatives for inquiry and interpretation that simply had not occurred to their older, largely male colleagues—colleagues whose gender privilege (as men working in a highly masculinized disciplinary culture) includes an unquestioning fit between their gendered experience and the androcentrism that partially frames the research traditions in which they work.

Content Analysis and the Role of Evidence

If it is accepted that sociopolitical factors are centrally responsible for the emergent (archaeological) interest in women and gender as a research subject, broader questions about epistemic implications immediately arise. My thesis is that although such examples make it clear that the standpoint of practitioners affects every aspect of inquiry—the formation of questions, the (re)definition of categories of analysis, the kinds of material treated as (potential) evidence, the bodies of background knowledge engaged in interpreting archaeological data as evidence, the range of explanatory and reconstructive hypotheses considered plausible, and the array of presuppositions held open to systematic examination—they also demonstrate that standpoint does not, in any strict sense, determine the outcomes of inquiry. The results produced by those working from a gender-sensitive standpoint are not explicable, in their details, in terms of the angle of vision or social location that constitutes this standpoint. Consider, briefly, two examples that illustrate this point.[22]

In their critique of theories about the emergence of horticulture in the Eastern Woodlands, mentioned earlier, Pat Watson and Mary Kennedy begin with a conceptual analysis that draws attention to the conspicuous absence of women in accounts of how this transition was realized, even though they are accorded a central role in plant collection (before) and cultivation (after).[23] One explanatory model identifies male shamans as the catalysts for this transition; their interest in manipulating plant stocks resulted in the development of cultigens. In another, the plants effectively domesticate themselves by an "automatic" process of adaptation to conditions disrupted by human activities (in "domestilocalities"). As Watson and Kennedy point out, women passively follow plants around when they are wild and passively tend them once domesticated but play no role in the transition from one state to the other. The authors then deploy collateral evidence to show that this failure to recognize women as potential catalysts of change carries substantial costs in explanatory elegance and plausibility. The automatic domestication thesis must counter ethno- and paleobotanical evidence that the key domesticates appeared very early in environments that were by no means optimal for them, evidence suggests that some human intervention must have been involved in the process of domestication. Likewise, the shaman hypothesis must ignore the implications of presuming that women were involved full time in the exploitation of the plants that later became domesticates, as well as ethnohistorical evidence that shamanism is by no means a male preserve and that women in foraging societies often hold the primary expertise about plant and animal resources that informs group movement and other subsistence-related decision making.

Whatever standpoint-specific factors might have put Watson and Kennedy in a position to notice the common incongruity in these explanatory models (the disappearing women), what makes their analysis compelling is their identification of internal contradictions in the logic of these models and their use of collateral evidence to call into question the assumptions that underlie these contradictions. They grant their opponents the assumptions they make about sexual divisions of labor in foraging and horticultural societies but point out that the archaeological record does not, in fact, deliver any evidence that, interpreted subject to these assumptions, would indicate that men mediated the transition to horticulture. And they make use of independent paleobotanical evidence to call into question the plausibility of "automatic domestication" accounts that deny human agency any substantial role in the transition. In neither case are the presuppositions of Watson and Kennedy's (re)interpretation of the evidence dependent on the assumptions about women's capacities that they criticize or embrace.

In a project that moves beyond critique, also mentioned earlier, Christine Hastorf relies on a similar strategy, exploiting independent background knowledge and sources of evidence to reassess the way in which women's labor and domestic units are conceptualized in state-formation theories for the highland Andes.[24] She compares the sex ratios and lifetime dietary profiles of skeletal material recovered from burials in the Montaro Valley through the period when the Inka first made their imperial presence felt in this region. She found that the dietary intake of men and women was undifferentiated until the advent of Inka influence but then diverged sharply on the isotope value associated with the consumption of maize. Comparing these results with patterns of change over time in other aspects of the sites, she found independent evidence of intensified production and increasingly segregated work areas related to the processing of maize. To interpret these findings she relied on ethnohistoric sources that establish the association of women with maize processing and beer production and suggest that Inka rule involved negotiating with local men as the heads of households and communities and extracting them from their households to serve as conscript labor on Inka construction projects. These multiple lines of evidence suggest that the gendered organization of domestic units was significantly altered by Inka rule; the hierarchical, gender-differentiated divisions of labor and consumption patterns now familiar in the region were established when local communities were incorporated into a state system. This means that gender relations and household organization cannot be treated as a stable substrate that predates, and persists as a given through, the rising and falling fortunes of states; state formation in the Andes depended on a fundamental restructuring of household-based social relations of production.

As in Watson and Kennedy's case, nothing in the social and political factors that may have informed Hastorf's interest in questions about gender determines that she should have found such striking divergence in the dietary profiles of men and women or such congruence in patterns of change over time in several materially and inferentially independent aspects of the archaeological record. The presuppositions that Hastorf uses to construct data as evidence are not the same as those that define the questions she asks or to the range of hypotheses she entertains; they may be radically theory-laden, but they are not laden by the same theories that are tested against this evidence or frame her research program. To put the point more generally, feminist practitioners exploit the fact that androcentric assumptions about gender roles generally lack the resources to ensure that archaeological data will conform to androcentric, presentist expectations; these assumptions do not deliver, along with reconstructive hypotheses, the linking principles necessary to establish evidential claims about the antecedent conditions that produced the contents of a specific archaeological record.

There is nothing unique to feminist or gender-sensitive research in this respect. The limited independence of facts of the record from the background assumptions that establish their import as evidence is the primary methodological resource that archaeologists use to assess the credibility of claims about the past in most contexts of inquiry.[25] It is in this that the capacity of evidence to resist our expectations resides. We can exploit this potential in any number of standpoint-specific ways; critics of racism, sexism, nationalism, and classism in archaeology use it to bring into view taken-for-granteds that we should be questioning. That they should do so is no doubt overdetermined by a range of social, theoretical, political, and empirical factors, but exactly how they proceed and what they find out—where or, indeed, whether they locate incongruities that open a space for critical engagement—is also very much a function of the evidence they engage when they assess their own interpretive hypotheses and the background assumptions, the auxiliaries, on which they rely. It is this capacity of even quite remote subjects of inquiry to act back on us that we must keep in view when negotiating polarized debates about the implications of recognizing the limitations and partiality of our sciences.

Conclusions

I draw four forward-looking conclusions concerning the tasks that face proponents of a genuinely interdisciplinary, integrative program of feminist science studies.

1. Critiques that bring into view the pervasive ways in which social and political factors shape inquiry, including those foregrounded by feminist critics of science, should not be the *end* of discussion about such epistemological questions as what constitutes evidence and "good reasons" in a given context of scientific practice. Rather, they should be the beginning of a new kind of discussion, which feminists are especially well situated to carry forward.

2. To set discussion on a new footing, we must break the grip of the presupposition (held by objectivists and relativists alike) that objectivity is an all-or-nothing affair, that it is something we have only if the process and products of inquiry are (implausibly) free of any social or political entanglements and something we lose irrevocably if there is any evidence that science reflects the standpoint of its makers. We must also give up the view that "neutral" investigators are best fitted to maximize the cluster of (often sharply divergent) virtues we associate with "objectivity."[26] We need accounts of knowledge production, authorization, credibility, and use that recognize that the contextual features of social location (standpoint) can make a *constructive* difference in maximizing these epistemic virtues, including quite pragmatic virtues such as reliability under specific ranges of application (a capacity to "travel"[27]) and intersubjective stability. The contributions of feminist researchers (both critical and constructive) make it clear that diverse standpoints can greatly enhance the likelihood of realizing specific sorts of empirical accuracy or explanatory breadth and

may ensure that a rigorously critical perspective will be brought to bear (or, indeed, that detachment will be preserved) in the evaluation of claims or assumptions that members of a homogeneous community might never think to question.

3. These proposals have concrete implications for research practice. According to current objectivist wisdom, we can best safeguard the authority of science and of specific scientific claims by eliminating from the processes by which we evaluate knowledge claims any hint of contamination from social or political context. But from the foregoing, it follows that a commitment to objectivity may require direct consideration of the sociopolitical standpoint of inquirers in the adjudication of knowledge claims as an integral part of scientific inquiry.[28]

4. Finally, these observations have implications for feminist science studies. They suggest a need for analyses of science that are at once empirically grounded (historically, sociologically, and in the sciences themselves) and epistemically sophisticated, that work "right at the boundary" (as Pickering has put it) between the existing science studies disciplines, and that bring together equity and content critiques. They suggest, further, that feminist science studies must incorporate a normative as well as a descriptive component and that science studies practitioners, most especially feminists, should deliberately position themselves as "insider/outsiders" with respect to the sciences they study. The work of a great many feminist theorists of science already exemplifies this hybrid stance.[29] Indeed, this active engagement with the sciences may be one reason why feminist practitioners and analysts of science have resisted the categories imposed by debates between philosophers and sociologists, constructivists and objectivists in their various fields of (metascientific) practice.

Notes

1. As in many social sciences, archaeologists have set enormous store in establishing the scientific credibility and authority of their discipline and its products the last thirty years. In North America this took the form of widespread commitment to the pro-science, explicitly positivist goals of the New Archaeology, which embody objectivist ideals in an especially stringent form. Reconstructive hypotheses were to be treated as the starting point, not the end point, of research, and any investigation of the archaeological record was to be designed... as an empirical test of these hypotheses; whatever their sources, they were to be confronted with evidence from the surviving record of the pasts they purport to describe and accepted or rejected on this basis. The expectation was that a rigorously scientific methodology would preserve archaeologists from the pernicious influence of standpoint-specific interests and power relations as they either operate within the field or impinge on it from outside; they would ensure that archaeology is "self-cleansing" of intrusive bias and therefore produces genuine (i.e., objective) knowledge of the cultural past. These developments are discussed in more detail in Alison Wylie, "The Constitution of Archaeological Evidence: Gender, Politics, and Science," in *Disunity and Contextualism: New Directions in the Philosophy of Science Studies*, ed. Peter Galison and David Stump (Palo Alto, Calif.: Stanford Univ. Press, 1996), pp. 311-343.

2. These critiques closely parallel those that draw attention to the archaeological record of, for example, colonial and neocolonial domination in areas where archaeology has focused on the "eclipsed civilizations" or hominid origins of much earlier periods (e.g., in Latin America and Africa), that of slaves on plantation sites where the "great houses" and lives of landholding planters had been the primary focus of archaeological attention, and that of First Nations communities in areas long occupied by Euro-Americans that were not recognized because their patterns of settlement did not conform to the European model of nucleated villages. These examples are discussed in more detail in Alison Wylie, "Evidential Constraints: Pragmatic Empiricism in Archaeology," in *Readings in the Philosophy of Social Science*, ed. Lee McIntyre

and Michael Martin (Cambridge, Mass.: MIT Press, 1994), pp.747–766.

3. Anne Yentsch, "Engendering Visible and Invisible Ceramic Artifacts, Especially Dairy Vessels," in *Gender in Historical Archaeology,* ed. Donna Seifert, special issue of *Historical Archaeology,* 1991, 25(4):132–155; Seifert, "Within Sight of the White House: The Archaeology of Working Women," ibid., pp.82-108; Cheryl Claassen, "Gender, Shellfishing, and the Shell Mound Archaic," in *Engendering Archaeology: Women and Prehistory,* ed. Joan M. Gero and Margaret W. Conkey (Oxford: Blackwell, 1991), pp. 276–300; and Patty Jo Watson and Mary C. Kennedy, "The Development of Horticulture in the Eastern Woodlands of North America: Women's Role," ibid., pp. 255-275.

4. See, e.g., Margaret W Conkey and Janet D. Spector, "Archaeology and the Study of Gender," in *Advances in Archaeological Method and Theory,* Vol. 7, ed. Michael B. Schiffer (New York: Academic, 1984), pp. 1–38; and Spector and Mary K. Whelan, "Incorporating Gender into Archaeology Courses," in *Gender and Anthropology: Critical Reviews for Research and Teaching,* ed. Sandra Morgen (Washington, D.C.: American Anthropological Association, 1989), pp. 65–94.

5. Christine A. Hastorf, "Gender, Space, and Food in Prehistory," in. *Engendering Archaeology,* ed. Gero and Conkey (cit. n. 3), pp. 132–159; and Elizabeth M. Brumfiel, "Weaving and Cooking: Women's Production in Aztec Mexico," ibid., pp. 224–253.

6. Much of this "equity" literature appears in society or institution newsletters, in publications produced by in-house report series, or is circulated as informal reports and internal documents. Some of the more accessible and widely known of these studies and reports include Carol Kramer and Miriam Stark, "The Status of Women in Archaeology," *Anthropology Newsletter,* 1988, 29(9): 1, 11–12; Joan M. Gero, "Gender Bias in Archaeology: A Cross-Cultural Perspective," in *The Socio-Politics of Archaeology,* ed. Gero, David M. Lacy, and Michael L. Blakey (Research Reports, 23) (Amherst: Dept. Anthropology, Univ. Massachusetts, 1983); and Gero, "Socio-Politics and the Woman-at-Home Ideology," *American Antiquity,* 1985, 50:342-350. A number of related studies are collected in Dale Walde

and Noreen D. Willows, eds., *The Archaeology of Gender: Proceedings of the 22nd Annual Chacmool Conference* (Calgary: Archaeological Association, Univ. Calgary, 1991); Hilary du Cros and Laurajane Smith, eds., *Women in Archaeology: A Feminist Critique* (Canberra: Australian National Univ. Occasional Papers, 1993); Margaret C. Nelson, Sarah M. Nelson, and Alison Wylie, eds., *Equity Issues for Women in Archaeology* (Archaeological Papers, 5) (Washington, D.C.: American Anthropological Association, 1994); and Cheryl Claassen, ed., *Women in Archaeology* (Philadelphia: Univ. Pennsylvania Press, 1994). The collection edited by Nelson et al. includes reprints of a number of earlier and otherwise inaccessible reports, along with newer studies and overviews of work in a number of different national contexts and subfields of archaeology.

In discussing this literature it is important to note that women are perhaps the only traditionally excluded group (with the possible exception of men from working-class backgrounds) to gain sufficient levels of representation within archaeology to develop such critiques on their own behalf. Nevertheless, studies of the sociopolitics of archaeology document many other dimensions on which the demographic homogeneity of the discipline has been maintained. See, e.g., the discussion of recruiting and training practices in Jane H. Kelley and Marsha P. Hanen, *Archaeology and the Methodology of Science* (Albuquerque: Univ. New Mexico Press, 1988), Ch. 4. Thomas C. Patterson considers ways in which the interests of intranational elites have shaped archaeology in Patterson, "The Last Sixty Years: Toward a Social History of Americanist Archaeology in the United States," *American Anthropologist,* 1986, 88:7–22; Patterson, "Some Postwar Theoretical Trends in U.S. Archaeology," *Culture,* 1986, 11:43–54; and Patterson, *Toward a Social History of Archaeology in the United States* (Orlando, Fla.: Harcourt Brace, 1995), he offers an analysis of the GI bill's educational support on the class structure of the discipline. Bruce G. Trigger explores the alignment of archaeology with nationalist agendas of various sorts in *A History of Archaeological Thought* (Cambridge: Cambridge Univ. Press, 1989).

7. Typically these studies identify correlations, at a general level, between sociopolitical features

of the discipline and of its products, offering an implicitly functional explanation for androcentric, nationalist, racist, or classist gaps and biases in content, but rarely do they supply an account of mediating mechanisms. Some important exceptions are reported in the landmark collection of essays, *The Socio-Politics of Archaeology,* ed. Gero et al., that appeared in 1983. Working at a local, infrastructural scale, Martin H. Wobst and Arthur S. Keene argued that the fascination archaeologists have with "origins" research should be understood as, at least in part, a consequence of structural features of disciplinary practice: Wobst and Keene, "Archaeological Explanation as Political Economy," ibid., pp. 79–90. Researchers who control the understanding of originary events or cultural arc formations must be acknowledged, in various ways, by all who work on later, linked periods and developments; they established themselves as the "eye of the needle" through which all else must pass. This line of argument has recently been extended and reframed in feminist terms by Margaret Conkey, in collaboration with Sarah H. Williams, "Original Narratives: The Political Economy of Gender in Archaeology," in *Gender, Culture, and Political Economy: Feminist Anthropology in the Post-Modern Era,* ed. Micaela di Leonardo (Berkeley: Univ. California Press, 1991), pp. 102–139.

8. Joan M. Gero, "The Social World of Prehistoric Facts: Gender and Power in Prehistoric Research," in *Women in Archaeology,* ed. du Cros and Smith (cit. n. 6), pp. 31–40, on p. 37.

9. Ian Hodder, "Archaeology, Ideology, and Contemporary Society," *Royal Anthropological Institute News,* 1983, *56*:6 Hodder, "Archaeology in 1984," *Antiquity,* 1984, *58*:26; and Michael Shanks and Christopher Tilley, *Re-constructing Archaeology* (Cambridge: Cambridge Univ. Press, 1987), p. 111.

10. Bruce G. Trigger, "Hyperrelativism, Responsibility, and the Social Sciences," *Canadian Review of Sociology and Anthropology,* 1989, *26*:776–797; Thomas Nagel, *The View from Nowhere* (Oxford: Oxford Univ. Press, 1986); and Richard Berstein, *Beyond Objectivism and Relativism: Science, Hermeneutics, and Praxis* (Philadelphia: Univ. Pennsylvania Press, 1983). See also Alison Wylie, "On 'Heavily Decomposing Red Herrings': Scientific Method in Archaeology and the Ladening of Evidence with Theory," in *Metaarchaeology,* ed. Lester Embree (Boston: Reidel, 1992), pp. 269–288.

11. David Henderson, "The Principle of Charity and the Problem of Irrationality," *Synthese,* 1987, *73*:225–252 (reasons as causes); Roy Bhaskar, *A Realist Theory of Science,* 2nd ed. (Brighton, Sussex: Harvester, 1978), p. 57; and Ian Hacking, *Representing and Intervening: Introductory Topics in the Philosophy of Natural Science* (Cambridge: Cambridge Univ. Press, 1983).

12. See, e.g., Ian Hodder, "Interpretive Archaeology and Its Role," *Amer. Antiquity,* 1991, *56*:7-18; and Christopher Tilley, "Archaeology as Socio-Political Action in the Present," in *Critical Traditions in Archaeology: Essays in the Philosophy, History, and Socio-Politics of Archaeology* (Cambridge: Cambridge Univ. Press, 1989), pp. 117–135.

13. Conkey and Spector, "Archaeology and the Study of Gender," (cit. n. 4); and Gero and Conkey, eds., *Engendering Archaeology* (cit. n. 3).

14. Marsha P. Hanen and Jane Kelley undertook an analysis of the abstracts for papers presented at this conference with the aim of determining how wide ranging they were in topic and orientation. The results are published in Hanen and Kelley, "Gender and Archaeological Knowledge," in *Metaarchaeology,* ed. Embree (cit. n. 10), pp. 195-227. Chacmool conferences have been held at the University of Calgary every fall since 1966. They are sponsored by the archaeology undergraduate society of the Department of Archaeology, but graduate students and faculty are centrally involved in their organization. They have developed a strong reputation in North America and, increasingly, abroad as well-focused, congenial working conferences that have steadily increased in size and scope since their inception. The 1989 meeting represents something of a threshold, in which the number of submissions grew substantially, from the forty to sixty typical of previous years to more than a hundred, a pattern of growth that has been sustained by subsequent Chacmool conferences.

15. These include a thematic conference held in Norway in 1979, the proceedings of which appeared eight years later: Reidar Bertelsen, Arnvid Lillehammer, and Jenny-Rita Naess, eds., *Were They All Men? An Examination of Sex Roles in Prehistoric Society* (AmS-Varia, 17) (Stavanger:

Arkeologisk Museum I Stavanger, 1987). Also, several sessions on women and gender were organized for the annual meetings of the Theoretical Archaeology Group in the United Kingdom (in 1982, 1985, and 1987); see Karen Arnold, Roberta Gilchrist, Pam Graves, and Sarah Taylor, "Women in Archaeology," *Archaeology Reviews from Cambridge* (special issue), 1988, 7:2–8.

16. Walde and Willows, eds., *Archaeology of Gender* (cit. n. 6) (Chacmool proceedings); Cheryl Claassen, ed., *Exploring Gender through Archaeology* (Monographs in World Archaeology, 11) (Madison, Wis.: Prehistory Press, 1992); Claassen, ed., *Women in Archaeology* (cit. n. 6); du Cros and Smith, eds., *Women in Archaeology* (cit. n. 6); and Seifert, ed., *Gender in Historical Archaeology* (cit. n. 3).

17. Cheryl Claassen, "Bibliography of Archaeology and Gender: Papers Delivered at Archaeology Conferences, 1964–1992," *Annotated Bibliographies for Anthropologists*, 1992, *1*(2). See also the annotated bibliography compiled by Elisabeth A. Bacus et al., eds., *A Gendered Past: A Critical Bibliography of Gender in Archaeology* (Technical Reports, 25) (Ann Arbor: Univ. Michigan Museum of Anthropology, 1993). Some earlier archaeological publications on women and gender include Anne Barstow, "The Uses of Archeology for Women's History: James Mellaart's Work on the Neolithic Goddess at Catal Huyuk," *Feminist Studies*, 1978, *4*(3):7-17; Alice Kehoe, "The Shackles of Tradition," in *The Hidden Half: Studies of Plains Indian Women,* ed. Patricia Albers and Beatrice Medicine (Washington, D.C.: Univ. Press America, 1983), pp. 53–73; several important contributions by Alice Kehoe, Sarah Nelson, Patricia O'Brien, Pamela Bumstead, et al., to *Powers of Observation: Alternative Views in Archeology,* ed. Nelson and Kehoe (Archaeological Papers, 2) (Washington, D.C.: American Anthropological Association, 1990); Rayna Rapp, "Gender and Class: An Archaeology of Knowledge Concerning the Origin of the State," *Dialectical Anthropology,* 1977, 2:309-316; and Janet D. Spector, "Male/Female Task Differentiation among the Hidatsa: Toward the Development of an Archaeological Approach to the Study of Gender," in *Hidden Half,* ed. Albers and Medicine, pp. 77–99.

18. The formulation of these questions is discussed in more detail in Alison Wylie, "Feminist Critiques and Archaeological Challenges," in *Archaeology of Gender,* ed. Walde and Willows (cit. n. 6), pp. 17-23.

19. Counts of the membership lists for the Society for American Archaeology and the Archaeological Institute of America show that, before 1973, women never made up more than 13 percent of the society's members; in 1973 their representation jumped to 18 percent and by 1976 to 30 percent. Altogether 36 percent of SAA members were women in the fall of 1988, when the Chacmool call for papers was distributed, a level of representation that has been stable in the field since then. See, e.g., Kramer and Stark, "Status of Women in Archaeology" (cit. n. 6); and Patterson, *Toward a Social History of Archaeology* (cit. n. 6), pp. 81–82.

20. Hanen and Kelley, "Gender and Archaeological Knowledge" (cit. n. 14).

21. Ibid.

22. The analysis of these examples has been developed in more detail in Wylie, "Evidential Constraints" (cit. n. 2).

23. Watson and Kennedy, "Development of Horticulture" (cit. n. 3).

24. Hastorf, "Gender, Space, and Food in Prehistory" (cit. n. 5)

25. This analysis is developed in more detail in Wylie, "Evidential Constraints" (cit. n. 2); and Wylie, "Constitution of Archaeological Evidence" (cit. n. 1).

26. See, e.g., Elisabeth Lloyd, "Objectivity and the Double Standard for Feminist Epistemologies," *Synthese,* 1996, *104*:351-381.

27. Haraway, *Simians, Cyborgs, and Women: the Reinvention of Nature* (New York: Routledge, 1991).

28. Feminist researchers move in this direction when they insist on the need for rigorous reflexivity, in the sense explicated by Fonow and Cook and by Mies: Mary Margaret Fonow and Judith A. Cook, "Back to the Future: A Look at the Second Wave of Feminist Epistemology and Methodology," in *Beyond Methodology: Feminist Scholarship as Lived Research,* eds. Mary Margaret Fonow and Judith A. Cook (Bloomington: Indiana Univ. Press, 1991), pp. 1–15; and Maria Mies, "Towards a Methodology for Feminist Re-

search," in *Theories of Women's Studies*, eds. Gloria Bowles and Renate Duelli Klein (New York: Routledge & Kegan Paul, 1983), pp. 117–139

29. See, e.g., Keller, Fausto-Sterling, and Haraway, and the collaborative work of Helen Longino and Ruth Doell: "Body, Bias and Behavior: A Comparative Analysis of Reasoning in Two Areas of Biological Science," *Signs: Journal of Women in Culture and Society*, 1983, 9:206–227.

Still Seeking Transformation

Feminist Challenges to Psychology

Sue Wilkinson

Psychology as Oppressor

Feminists have always criticised psychology and have worked for change in its theories, institutions and practices—but the discipline remains resolutely misogynist (Ussher, 1991), heterosexist (Kitzinger, 1990) and racist (Sayal-Bennett, 1991). Unlike sociology, where the feminist project has been said to have "come of age" (Roseneil, 1995), feminism within psychology is still desperately struggling for autonomy and influence. Why is the development of feminism in, and against, psychology apparently so much slower? What has impeded us in our struggles to transform the discipline?

Psychology is highly institutionalised, relative to other disciplines. Its professional bodies—the British Psychological Society (BPS) in the UK, and the American Psychological Association (APA) in the USA—regulate the content and practice of the discipline. These bodies validate undergraduate and postgraduate courses, gatekeep the most prestigious academic journals, operate a professional registration scheme for psychologists ("chartering" in the UK), and determine the criteria for judgements of mental health and "illness"

(APA's *Diagnostic and Statistical Manual*). Feminist psychologists' challenges to and attempts to transform psychology are inevitably determined by, and constructed in opposition to, these institutional structures of the discipline.

Throughout the (relatively short) history of psychology, feminists working within and beyond the discipline have criticised its treatment of women, exposing both the prejudices cloaked by the mantle of "science" and the damages perpetrated in the name of "therapy". Early twentieth-century feminists such as Helen Thompson Wooley (1910: 340)—a psychologist herself—commented on research purporting to demonstrate women's mental inferiorities that: "There is perhaps no field aspiring to be scientific where flagrant personal bias, logic martyred in the cause of supporting a prejudice, unfounded assertions, and even sentimental rot and drivel, have run riot to such an extent as here." More than half a century later, as second-wave feminism gathered momentum, feminist activist and psychologist Naomi Weisstein (1968: 197) asserted that: "Psychology has nothing to say about what women are really like, what they need and what they want ... because psychology does not know." Other feminist psychologists characterised the discipline as "a psychology against women" (Nancy Henley, 1974: 20) which has "distorted facts, omitted problems, and perpetuated pseudoscientific data relevant to women" (Mary Parlee, 1975:124). The whole patriarchal mental health system was indicted by feminist psychologist Phyllis Chesler (1972) in her classic book *Women and Madness;* in 1970 Chesler had taken the platform at the annual APA conference, not to deliver the expected academic paper but to demand that the APA provide "one million dollars 'in reparations' for those women who had never been helped by the mental health professions but who had, instead, been further abused by them" (Chesler, 1989: xvii).

Feminists, especially lesbian feminists, have always been—and still are—located in the contested borderlands of the discipline. We occupy a marginal space in which definitions and practices are *not* simply taken for granted, but subjected to constant interrogation and (sometimes) reformulation. Our very existence challenges psychology's hegemonic accounts of behaviours and identities appropriate to our sex: we are not "proper" women. Our work transgresses the discipline's authoritative statements of scientific orthodoxy: we are not "proper" scientists. Our exposés of psychological theory as "rot and drivel" and of mental health practice as "abuse" threaten seriously to bring the discipline into disrepute: we are bad, mad, and very dangerous to know. So, psychology's response to such criticisms from the borderlands has not been to apologise, to pay out the million dollars, or to put its house in order. Rather, it has resorted to various forms of exclusion: in particular, physical exclusion accompanied by hostility; exclusion by definition; and exclusion based on liberal rhetorics. Together, these constitute a formidable array of armaments in establishment psychology's battery of responses to feminist challenges. And, of course, in addition to the external obstacles which have been put in our way, feminists in psychology (as in the women's liberation movement more generally) have had to confront the difficulties inherent in working together across our differences and in spite of the things that divide us.

Feminist Challenges

Historically, psychology's central assertion is that women are inferior to men. Feminist challenges are lodged within five distinctive theoretical traditions: (i) psychology is poor science—it has mismeasured women; (ii) the problem is oppression, not women; (iii) women are indeed different from men—but superior; (iv) mental health is unrelated to sex/gender; and (v) psychology is asking the wrong questions. Feminists have institutionalised these challenges via intellectual and political alliances: the USA Association for Women in Psychology (AWP), founded in the late 1960s; and the UK Women in Psychology (WIP, recently relaunched as the Alliance of Women in Psychology) and the Lesbians in Psychology Sisterhood (LIPS). These informal organisations later functioned as pressure groups for the formal representation of feminist work within the professional bodies. AWP was key to the establishment of Division 35 ("Psychology of Women") within the APA in 1973; WIP successfully campaigned for a BPS "Psychology of Women" Section in late 1987; and LIPS, having failed to get a BPS "Psychology of Lesbianism" Section, is now leading the struggle for a "Lesbian and Gay Psychology" Section.

The Mismeasure of Women

This tradition of feminist research refutes mainstream psychology's statement that women are inferior by arguing that mainstream researchers have consistently omitted women from their samples, or mismeasured us—it says that psychology as presently conducted is lousy science. Many of psychology's classic theories (e.g. Kohlberg's theory of moral reasoning, Erikson's theory of lifespan development) have been derived from all-male samples; and its empirical studies are riddled with technical flaws (e.g. experimental biases, inadequate sampling techniques, lack of control groups, insufficiently sensitive measures), which function to reinforce the ideological biases from which it suffers (e.g. sexism, heterosexism, racism, classism). Naomi Weisstein (1968: 197), castigating sex differences research as "theory without evidence", indicts the practice of sexist researchers: "[They] simply refuse to look at the evidence against their theory and practice. And they support their theory and practice with stuff so transparently biased as to have no standing as empirical evidence."

Feminist activism has also provided a spectacularly successful institutional challenge to the whole mental health system in the USA. Two particularly misogynistic diagnostic categories—"Self-Defeating Personality Disorder" (masochism) and "Late Luteal Phase Dysphoric Disorder" (premenstrual syndrome)—have now been removed from the DSM, following their exposure by feminists as "without any adequate scientific basis" (Franklin, 1987) and as "deeply flawed and dangerous"(Caplan et al., 1992).

The Problem Is Oppression

This feminist tradition *accepts* psychology's assertion of women's inferiority but contends that such "inferiority" is simply an index of our oppression, arguing that women's shortcomings arise from gender-related motives, fears or concepts which lead us to act against our own best interests. Matina Horner's (1972) concept of "fear of success" provided a classic—and very popular—explanation for women's failure to advance in professional life. Other explanations have included lack of assertiveness, low self-esteem, poor self-confidence, under-estimation and under-valuation of achievement, and failure to develop an autonomous self (Tavris, 1993).

Innovative (in psychology) in its focus on women *per se*, (rather than in relation to, or comparison with, men), this framework remains the dominant one in contemporary feminist psychology. It underpins both the therapy industry (which is seen as offering "compensatory socialization": Marecek and Hare-Mustin, 1987, cited in Crawford and Marecek, 1989) and the growth in pop-psych, self-help manuals (e.g. *The Cinderella Complex*—Dowling, 1981; *The Doormat Syndrome*—Namka, 1989). It seems to be popular because, if women's failings can be placed at the door of oppression, we do not have to blame ourselves, and because it suggests ways in which individual change wrought by therapy can improve women's lives. This tradition has been institutionalised by the growing range of feminist counselling and psychotherapy services, such as The Women's Therapy Centre, in London and New York (individual and group therapies, plus therapist training), and The Pink Practice in London (counselling and psychotherapy for lesbians and gay men).

Women are Different—and Superior

The third approach of feminist psychologists is to agree that women *are* different from men—but to argue that women's characteristics are superior, rather than inferior, to men's. These researchers *maximise*—and celebrate—sex differences. Broadly akin to what is sometimes labelled "cultural feminism", and largely in response to androcentric theories in psychology, classic work in this tradition has identified women's distinctive "ways of knowing" (Belenky et al., 1986) and women's "different (moral) voice" (Gilligan, 1982; Brown and Gilligan, 1992). Helen Haste (1994), seeking to document and explain the huge influence of Carol Gilligan's (1982) book *In a Different Voice*, suggests:

Gilligan's work touched a nerve ... For all the criticisms of the book's limitations in the academic community, the message was novel and it was important... women were being denied a voice; and philosophically, it meant there *was* an alternative voice in the culture—that there is more than one way of looking at the world. (pp. 399–400)

This kind of approach has been enthusiastically embraced in a range of applied areas, particularly youth work and secondary education. It has been institutionalised in, for example, research on young women's experiences in schools, commissioned by the American Association of University Women (1991); the development of feminist pedagogy and curriculum materials—including "retreats" for teachers to consider "what it means to be a woman teaching girls in this culture at this time" (Brown and Gilligan, 1992: 241-2); and the launch of a glossy magazine called *New Moon*, which celebrates young women's growth, development and "self-affirmation" throughout their teenage years.

Mental Health Is Unrelated to Gender

The fourth theoretical tradition of feminist psychology argues that women are neither inferior nor superior to men—in fact, these researchers refuse to compare the sexes. They *minimise*—indeed, undermine—the importance of sex differences, arguing that being male or female is not a central determinant of psychological functioning. Rather, there are elements of masculinity and femininity in everyone, and a key aspect of mental health and wellbeing is the ability to deploy these flexibly according to the situation (so we are able to be relatively confident and assertive in a job interview, say, while being relatively self-effacing and sympathetic to a friend in distress). Back in 1974, Sandra Bem first proposed such "psychological androgyny" as "a new standard of mental health, one that removes the burden of stereotype and allows people to feel free to express the best traits of men and women" (Bem, 1974: 125).

Perhaps because it removes the critical spotlight *both* from psychology *and* from women, and also offers a reframing of the familiar concept of "sex roles" in the positive context of improving mental health, this work has had surprising success in penetrating mainstream psychological theory. Detached from its feminist intent, it sits comfortably with the discipline's liberal rhetorics—and also offers the bonus of an associated measuring scale: the Bem Sex Role Inventory (BSRI). This was widely used in the 1970s and 1980s to correlate androgyny with many different indices of mental functioning, and it is still one of the most popular scales in use in (mainstream and feminist) social psychology today.

These Are the Wrong Questions

Finally—and most recently—feminist psychologists working within the framework of social constructionism (e.g. Hare-Mustin and Marecek, 1994; Hollway, 1994) have argued that sex/gender should no longer be theorised as "difference", but reconceptualised as a principle of social organisation, structuring power relations between the sexes. In this tradition of feminist psychology, as within postmodern varieties of feminism more generally, sex/gender is seen as a relatively flexible—albeit politically-driven—process, rather than as a relatively fixed set of attributes; it is also acknowledged to be highly historically, culturally and socially contingent (Bohan, 1992).

This tradition of work has gained almost no institutional toe-hold in psychology: indeed, to most psychologists it is unrecognisable as psychology. Its institutional challenge is provided by its transdisciplinary nature—and the opportunities it affords for alliances with feminists (and other critical theorists) outside psychology: both in other social science disciplines and in a transdisciplinary women's studies context. Particularly challenging work is being done where feminist psychologists are entering into dialogue with historians and sociologists of science to develop transdisciplinary analyses of psychology's particular oppressive practices (e.g. Bhavnani and Haraway, 1994; Morawski, 1994); and where feminist psychologists are orchestrating and contributing to key debates in contemporary feminist theory (e.g. "heterosexuality": Wilkinson and Kitzinger, 1993; "representing the Other": Wilkinson and Kitzinger, 1996).

These five competing feminist traditions offer different, and often incompatible, theoretical and/or political tools for challenging and transforming psychology. All five can also (in different ways) be dismissed, ridiculed or assimilated by the mainstream of the discipline. In the next section of this chapter, I will look at the ways in which psychology actively and systematically excludes feminist theoretical challenges—and the theorists who provide such challenges.

Psychology's Exclusions

Feminist incursions from the borderlands, as exemplified by the theoretical challenges outlined above, are comprehensively and systematically excluded from psychology's institutions and practices. Three kinds of exclusion are commonplace: (i) physical exclusion and hostility: (ii) exclusion by definition; and (iii) exclusion by means of liberal rhetorics.

Physical Exclusion and Hostility: Are You Normal?

The most effective means of excluding particular kinds of theory is to exclude the theorists. Historically, the exclusion of women from all higher education was justified with reference to psychology, which provided the "evidence" that women were mentally and physically unsuited to such exertions (Ehrenreich and English, 1979). Within psychology itself, there is a contemporary gender imbalance in the higher reaches: in (British) academic psychology, although women constitute

nearly 80% of undergraduate population, they constitute only about 20% of university teaching staff. In clinical psychology, while almost all trainee places are filled by women, they hold less than 25% of Top Grade posts.

Such imbalance is underpinned by a whole range of academic and professional practices which ensure that women remain marginalised within psychology. These include: the portrayal of women in negative and gender-biased ways in introductory psychology textbooks (Peterson and Kroner, 1992); minimal coverage of "psychology of women" (let alone feminist psychology) in most British undergraduate psychology degrees; limited representation of women on the major committees and in the senior membership grades of professional bodies such as the BPS (Wilkinson, 1990); citation practices which ensure feminist psychologists cite mainstream work but that the practice does not happen in reverse (Lykes and Stewart, 1986); and a rated status of "psychology of women" as lower than almost any other area of the discipline—excepting lesbian and gay psychology (Harari and Peters, 1987).

Organisational struggles within British psychology provide some vivid examples of the overt hostility which often accompanies such physical exclusion. In 1985, the proposers of the BPS "Psychology of Women" Section were told: "we would not expect to have a psychology of animals section" (BPS, October 1985: letter to section proposers, circulated to supporters). In April 1995, *The Psychologist* (the house journal of the British Psychological Society, circulated monthly to some 24,000 psychologists nationally and internationally) published the following letters under the heading "Are you normal?":

... I object to the misleading use in a publication of a scientific society of the innocent-sounding word "gay" when referring to what is the abnormal practice of anal intercourse between males. Secondly, I object to attempts to mislead readers about the epidemiological incidence and prevalence of male and female homosexuality which in statistical-mathematical terms is fortunately still tiny. (Hamilton, 1995: 151)

... at work, as elsewhere, there is, indeed, a normality of life for the vast majority of people ... It is certainly not a matter of heterosexuality being flaunted—it is simply the ordinariness of life from which homosexuals and lesbians, however much they may wish it were different, are perforce excluded. (Davis, 1995: 151–2)

Horrific as these statements may sound to non-psychologists, for those of us working within the discipline they are entirely unsurprising. They are simply the most recent manifestations of psychology's anti-feminism. The letters are responses to a review article on lesbian and gay relationships (Kitzinger and Coyle, 1995), published alongside the lesbian feminist-led initiative to establish a BPS "Psychology of Lesbianism Section"/"Lesbian and Gay Psychology Section". Such appeals to "normality" (elsewhere "the natural order of things": Davis, 1995), buttressed by the "scientific" tools of "epidemiology", "statistics" and "mathematics", are an all-too-familiar armament in establishment psychology's battery of responses to institutional challenges.

Exclusion by Definition: Politics not Science

Guillaumin (1995: 156) notes that the first texts of minority groups are always discounted as *theory*, and presented as *"political"* products. The exclusion is particularly easy to achieve in mainstream psychology, which defines "science" and "politics" as polar opposites, and legitimates psychological theory as a product of "science" alone. "[W]hen I write as a feminist," observes Celia Kitzinger (1990: 124), "I am defined out of the category of 'psychologist'. When I speak of social structure, of power and politics, when I use language rooted in my understanding of oppression, I

am told what I say does not qualify as 'psychology'".

Exclusion of feminist work on the grounds that it is "politics, not science" is a constant refrain. In commenting on the initial "Psychology of Women" Section proposal, the BPS (July, 1985) suggested that it was "loaded politically", and that a clear distinction must be made between "the scientific duty [sic] of the psychology of womanhood" and "a feminist pressure group". A recent letter to *The Psychologist* (Martin, 1995) deemed the proposal for a "Lesbian and Gay Psychology" Section "more like a self-interested political initiative than one inspired by scientific curiosity."

Exclusion by Liberal Rhetorics— We Don't Discriminate

As in other highly bureaucratic, patriarchal institutions, the BPS makes heavy use of conventional liberal rhetorics—"meritocracy", "equal opportunities", "inclusivity", "non-discrimination"—to justify its actions (see Wilkinson, 1990 for examples). Such liberal rhetorics are used, first, as a way of defusing political challenges to the organisation, and, second, as a way of assimilating dissidents and neutralising their disruptive influences. This is apparent in early arguments against the formation of a BPS "Psychology of Women" Section: "In a nutshell, the argument was put forward that to single out the psychology of women in this way could be regarded as patronising to women, or, at best, an admission of failure" (BPS, October 1985, letter to "Psychology of Women" Section proposers). A related argument favoured a "more inclusive" grouping called "Psychology of Gender". A variant of the "non-discrimination" rhetoric appears in opposition to the proposed "Lesbian and Gay Psychology" Section (along with assertions that "Psychology of Sexuality" would be "more inclusive"):

the creation of a Gay and Lesbian Section in the Society would itself [sic] be the ultimate in homophobic actions, damaging the very cause it seeks to promote.... To create such a grouping is surely to stereotype homosexual people and to exaggerate differences between them and heterosexual people beyond the sexual domain. (Seager, 1995)

This kind of "more liberal than thou" assertion has been a powerful strategy in mainstream psychology's dismissal of feminist theories which *maximise* sex differences (such as Gilligan's "different voice")—and it may also account for the relative success within the mainstream of feminist theories which *minimise* sex differences (such as Bem's "psychological androgyny"). "Reversal" strategies, such as the accusation that feminists are seeking to substitute matriarchy for patriarchy, or ignoring the oppression of men, are used to mock, trivialise, and dismiss feminist challenges. They are, of course, self-protective and self-interested ploys used by those who stand to gain by not having to engage with theoretical and institutional challenges to their power base.

Feminist Psychology's Internal Problems

A key strength of feminist psychology is the vigour and variety of debate within and between its various theoretical traditions. The greatest internal threat to feminist psychology is not debate and disagreement between different theoretical positions or empirical approaches but problems of envy and competition between women. In common with many feminist organisations, the early history of the BPS "Psychology of Women" Section was beset by power struggles between individuals, and later, there was a split over the proposed formation of a "Psychology of Lesbianism" Section (c.f. Comely et al., 1992). A second threat to the efficacy of feminist psychology is excessive preoccupation with internal affairs. Thus, internal BPS paperwork dominates the committee meetings of the "Psychology of Women" Section; and meetings are spent wallowing in the minutiae of memos from the secretariat and endlessly redrafting documents which outsiders will never read. Feminists have made little or no impact on BPS initiatives of key importance externally, such as on its recent Working Party on Recovered Memories, which addressed crucial issues around child sexual abuse and "false memory syndrome". The BPS has not contributed to key parliamentary debates on single mothers or commented on crucial legislation such as the Child Support Act. The "Psychology of Women" Section has done virtually nothing to prompt the BPS into appropriate action on such issues. Collective activism is needed to avoid the organisation being co-opted (or exhausted) by the demands of the system. The challenge for feminist psychologists in the future is to regain a sense of unity and political purpose, and to work effectively together on an agenda which reflects our own political priorities.

Toward Transformation

Despite the wealth and diversity of feminist theorising within psychology, the formidable exclusionary practices of the discipline and its institutions, some of which I have discussed here, are a substantial barrier to change and transformation. Nonetheless, there have been large and small successes both within and beyond the institutional framework imposed by professional bodies like the BPS. Within the BPS, the "Psychology of Women" Section *has* been successful in a variety of ways: as a forum for debate and development within the field of feminist psychology; as a crucial life-line for many individual women within a deeply hostile discipline; as a catalyst for raising the general awareness of women's issues and creating change within British psychology. It remains to be seen whether it can sustain and develop these roles; and what might be achieved, in theoretical and institutional terms, were the initiative for a BPS "Lesbian and Gay Psychology" Section to succeed.

Outside the BPS, and sometimes in direct opposition to it, the reconstituted pressure group, now called the Alliance of Women in Psychology, has a membership which explicitly includes users and survivors of psychology. Also independent of the BPS, the international journal *Feminism & Psychology*, now in its sixth volume, has a subscription base of around 1000 and still rising. Both the Alliance and the journal "put feminism first" as a political priority, and, by virtue of being outside the BPS, are less vulnerable to assimilation by the mainstream than is the "Psychology of Women" Section. Both also benefit from alliances with other feminist organisations, and explicit dialogue and debate within transdisciplinary contexts.

Feminist psychologists are still in the borderlands of our discipline. We do not have the luxury of deciding deliberately to "confine ourselves to the margins of the academy" (Roseneil, 1995: 196)—we are resolutely positioned there by the psychological centre. Our struggles are not yet against incorporation, but still against exclusion. There are, of course, benefits as well as disadvantages of being so positioned. Our exclusions as feminists, and as lesbians, from the mainstream of British psychology have provided the impetus to struggle for change—and arguably have provoked more radical initiatives (sometimes followed by more radical transformations) than would have been likely in a more liberal context. For example, if the BPS "Psychology of Women" Section had offered regular and explicit platforms for its lesbian members, it is unlikely that the proposal for a "Psychology of Lesbianism" Section would have been initiated; and had POWS supported this initiative from the outset, it is unlikely that it would be continuing, albeit in a different form, or that it would have had such an impact both within and beyond the BPS. Similarly, the context of exclusion has informed several recent analyses of hegemonic identities: e.g. masculinity (Griffin and Wetherell, 1992), heterosexuality (Wilkinson and Kitzinger, 1993) and whiteness (Wong, 1994).

Further, the paradoxical location of feminist psychologists—simultaneously within and against an academic discipline—offers us both "insider" and "outsider" viewpoints to inform critique and political action. From our enforced vantage-point on the margins of psychology, we are well-placed to analyse the discipline's oppressive practices and seek their transformation. As Jill Morawski writes:

> many of us have spoken and written about how our inquiry pushes against the dominant narrative of scientific change, a story whose plot is overdetermined by the myths of positivism, progress and democracy and by a politics of memory that over and over again forget the gender arrangements of science. (1994: 69)

As we have seen, feminist psychologists are making a distinctive contribution to the development of feminist theory and practice in transdisciplinary arenas: perhaps in another twenty years we will have "come of age" *within* our own discipline. In psychology, we are still seeking transformation.

References

American Association of University Women (1991) *Shortchanging Girls, Shortchanging America*. Washington, DC: AAUW

Belenky, Mary, Clinchy, Blythe, Goldberger, Nancy and Tarule, Jill (1986) *Women's Ways of Knowing*. New York: Basic Books.

Bem, Sandra L. (1974) "The measurement of psychological androgyny", *Journal of Consulting and Clinical Psychology*, 42: 155–62.

Bhavnani, Kum-Kum and Haraway, Donna (1994) "Shifting the subject: A conversation between Kum-Kum Bhavnani and Donna Haraway", *Feminism & Psychology: An International Journal*, 4(1): 19–39.

Bohan, Janis S. (ed.) (1992) *Seldom Seen, Rarely Heard: Women's Place in Psychology*. Boulder, CO: Westview Press.

Brown, Lyn Mikel and Gilligan, Carol (1992) *Meeting at the Crossroads: Women's Psychology And Girls'*

Development. Cambridge, MA: Harvard University Press.

Caplan, Paula J., McCurdy-Myers, Joan and Gans, Maureen (1992) "Should 'Premenstrual Syndrome' be called a psychiatric abnormality?", *Feminism & Psychology: An International Journal,* 2(1): 27–44.

Chesler, Phyllis (1972) *Women and Madness.* Garden City, NY: Doubleday.

Chesler, Phyllis (1989) Preface to 2nd edn of *Women and Madness.* San Diego, CA: Harcourt Brace Jovanovich.

Comely, Louise, Kitzinger, Celia, Perkins, Rachel and Wilkinson, Sue (1992) "Lesbian psychology in Britain: Back into the closet?", *Feminism & Psychology: An International Journal,* 2(2): 265–8.

Crawford, Mary and Marecek, Jeanne (1989) "Psychology reconstructs the female 1968–1988", *Psychology of Women Quarterly,* 13: 147–65.

Davis, Michael (1995) "Are you normal?" (Letter), *The Psychologist,* 8(4): 151–2.

Dowling, Colette (1981) *The Cinderella Complex: Women's Hidden Fear of Independence.* London: Fontana.

Ehrenreich, Barbara and English, Deidre (1979) *For Her Own Good: 150 Years of the Experts' Advice to Women.* London: Pluto.

Franklin, Deborah (1987) "The politics of masochism", *Psychology Today,* January: 57–9.

Gilligan, Carol (1982) *In a Different Voice: Psychological Theory and Women's Development.* Cambridge, MA: Harvard University Press.

Griffin, Christine and Wetherell, Margaret (eds) (1992) "Open Forum: Feminist psychology and the study of men and masculinity", *Feminism & Psychology: An International Journal,* 2(2): 133–68.

Guillaumin, Colette (1995) *Racism, Sexism, Power and Ideology.* London: Routledge.

Hamilton, Vernon (1995) "Are you normal?" (Letter), *The Psychologist,* 8(4): 151.

Harari, H. and Peters, J. (1987) "The fragmentation of psychology: Are APA divisions symptomatic?", *American Psychologist,* 42: 822–4.

Hare-Mustin, Rachel T. and Marecek, Jeanne (1994) "Asking the right questions: Feminist psychology and sex differences", *Feminism & Psychology: An International Journal,* 4(4): 531–7.

Haste, Helen (1994) "'You've come a long way, babe': A catalyst of feminist conflicts", *Feminism & Psychology: An International Journal,* 4(3): 399–403.

Henley, Nancy (1974) "Resources for the study of psychology and women", *R. T: Journal of Radical Therapy,* 4: 20–1.

Hollway, Wendy (1994) "Beyond sex differences: A project for feminist psychology", *Feminism & Psychology: An International Journal,* 4(4): 538–46.

Horner, Matina S. (1972) "Toward an understanding of achievement-related conflicts in women", *Journal of Social Issues,* 28: 157–76.

Kitzinger, Celia (1990) "Heterosexism in psychology", *The Psychologist,* 3(9): 391–2.

Kitzinger, Celia and Coyle, Adrian (1995) "Lesbian and gay couples: Speaking of difference", *The Psychologist,* 8(2): 64–9.

Lykes, M. Brinton and Stewart, Abigail (1986) "Evaluating the feminist challenge to research in personality and social psychology: 1963-1983", *Psychology of Women Quarterly,* 10: 393–412.

Martin, Brian H. (1995) "Sectional misapprehensions" (Letter), *The Psychologist,* 8(9): 392.

Miner, Valerie and Longino, Helen E. (1987) *Competition: A Feminist Taboo?* New York: The Feminist Press.

Morawski, Jill G. (1994) *Practicing Feminisms, Reconstructing Psychology: Notes on a Liminal Science.* Ann Arbor, MI: University of Michigan Press.

Namka, Lynn (1989) *The Doormat Syndrome.* Deerfield Beach, FL: Health Communications Inc.

Parlee, Mary Brown (1975) "Review essay: Psychology", *Signs,* 1:119–38.

Peterson, Sharyl Bender and Kroner, Traci (1992) "Gender biases in textbooks for introductory psychology and human development", *Psychology of Women Quarterly,* 16: 17–36.

Roseneil, Sasha (1995) "The coming of age of feminist sociology: Some issues of practice and theory for the next twenty years", *British Journal of Sociology,* 46(2): 191–205.

Sayal-Bennett, Anuradha (1991) "Equal opportunities—Empty rhetoric?", *Feminism & Psychology: An International Journal,* 1(1): 74–7.

Seager, Martin (1995) "Sectioned off?" (Letter), *The Psychologist,* 8(7): 295.

Tavris, Carol (1993) "The mismeasure of woman", *Feminism & Psychology: An International Journal,* 3(2): 149–68.

Ussher, Jane M. (1991) *Women's Madness: Misogyny or Mental Illness?* Hemel Hempstead: Harvester Wheatsheaf.

Weisstein, Naomi (1968, reprinted 1993) "Psychology constructs the female; or, the fantasy life of the male psychologist (with some attention to the fantasies of his friends, the male biologist and the male anthropologist)", *Feminism & Psychology: An International Journal*, 3(2): 195–210.

Wilkinson, Sue (1990) "Women's organisations in psychology: Institutional constraints on disciplinary change", *Australian Psychologist*, 25(3): 256–69.

Wilkinson, Sue and Kitzinger, Celia (eds) (1993) *Heterosexuality: A "Feminism & Psychology" Reader*. London: Sage.

Wilkinson, Sue and Kitzinger, Celia (eds) (1996) *Representing the Other: A "Feminism & Psychology" Reader*. London: Sage.

Wong, L. Mun (1994) "Di(s)-secting and dis(s)-closing 'whiteness': Two tales about psychology", *Feminism & Psychology: An International Journal*, 4(1): 133–53.

Wooley, Helen Thompson (1910) "Psychological literature: A review of the recent literature on the psychology of sex", *Psychological Bulletin*, 7:335–42.

SCIENCE'S SOCIAL EFFECTS

 ## Androcentric Bias in Clinical Research

Sue Rosser

In scientific research, whether it be in the behavioral, biomedical, or physical sciences, researchers rarely admit that data have been gathered and interpreted from a particular perspective. Since research in biology, chemistry, and physics centers on the physical and natural world, it is presumed to be "objective"; therefore, the term "perspective" does not apply to it. The reliability and repeatability of data gathered and hypotheses tested using the scientific method convince researchers that they are obtaining unbiased information about the physical, natural world.

Most researchers in the behavioral, biomedical, and physical sciences are trained in the scientific method and believe in its power. Few, however, are aware of its historical and philosophical roots in logical positivism and objectivity. Positivism implies that "all knowledge is constructed by inference from immediate sensory experiences" (Jaggar, 1983, pp. 355–356). It is premised on the assumption that human beings are highly individualistic and obtain knowledge in a rational manner that may be separated from their social conditions. This leads to the belief in the possibilities of obtaining knowledge that is both objective and value-free, the cornerstone of the scientific method.

Scientists, like all scholars, hold, either explicitly or implicitly, certain beliefs about their enterprise. Most believe, for example, that the laws and facts gathered by scientists are constant, providing that experiments have been done correctly. Historians of science posit that, quite to the contrary, the individuals who make observations and create theories are people who live in a particular country during a certain time in a definable

socioeconomic condition, and thus their situations and mentalities inevitably impinge on their discoveries. Even their "facts" are contingent. Aristotle "counted" fewer teeth in the mouths of women than in those of men— adding this dentitional inferiority to all the others (Arditti, 1980). Galen, having read the book of Genesis, "discovered" that men had one less rib on one side than women did (Webster and Webster, 1974). Clearly, observation of what would appear by today's standards to be easily verifiable facts can vary depending upon the theory or paradigm by which the scientist is influenced.

Although every scientist strives to remain as neutral and value-free as possible, most scientists, feminists, and philosophers of science recognize that no individual can be completely objective. Instead "objectivity is defined to mean independence from the value judgments of any particular individual" (Jaggar, 1983, p. 357). The paradigms themselves, however, also are far from value-free. The present values of the culture and its history heavily influence the ordering of observable phenomena into theory. The world view of a particular society, time, and person limits the questions that can be asked and thereby the answers that can be given. Kuhn (1970) has demonstrated that the very acceptance of a particular paradigm that may appear to cause a "scientific revolution" within a society depends in fact upon the congruence of that theory with the institutions and beliefs of the society.

Longino (1990) has explored the extent to which methods employed by scientists can be objective and lead to repeatable, verifiable results while contributing to hypotheses or theories that are congruent with nonobjective institutions and ideologies of the society. "Background assumptions are the means by which contextual values and ideology are incorporated into scientific inquiry" (1990, p. 216). The institutions and beliefs of our society reflect the fact that the society is patriarchal. Even female scientists have only recently become aware of the influence of patriarchal bias in the paradigms of science.

In the past two decades, feminist historians and philosophers of science (Fee, 1981, 1982; Harding, 1986; Haraway, 1978, 1989; Longino, 1990) and feminist scientists (Bleier, 1984, 1986; Fausto-Sterling, 1985; Birke, 1986; Keller, 1983, l985; and Rosser, 1988) have pointed out the bias and absence of value neutrality in science, particularly biology. By excluding females as experimental subjects, focusing on problems of primary interest to males, utilizing faulty experimental designs, and interpreting data based in language or ideas constricted by patriarchal parameters, scientists have introduced bias or flaws into their experimental results in several areas of biology. These flaws and biases were permitted to become part of the mainstream of scientific thought and were perpetuated in the scientific literature for decades. Because most scientists were men, values held by them as males were not distinguished as biasing; rather they were congruent with the values of all scientists and thus became synonymous with the "objective" view of the world (Keller, 1982, 1985).

A first step for feminist scientists was recognizing the possibility that androcentric bias would result from having virtually all theoretical and decision-making positions in science held by men (Keller, 1982). Not until a substantial number of women had entered the profession (Rosser, 1986) could this androcentrism be exposed. As long as only a few women were scientists, they had to demonstrate or conform to the male view of the world in order to be successful and have their research meet the criteria for "objectivity."

Once the possibility of androcentric bias was discovered, scientists set out to explore the extent to which it had distorted science. They recognized potential distortion on a variety of levels of research and theory: the choice and definition of problems to be studied, the exclusion of females as experimental subjects, bias in the methodology used to collect and interpret data, and bias in theories and conclusions drawn from the data. They also began to realize that since the practice of modern medicine depends heavily on clinical research, any flaws and ethical problems in this research are likely to result in poorer health care and inequity in the medical treatment of disadvantaged groups. Recent evidence suggests that gender bias may have flawed some medical research.

Choice and Definition of Problems for Study

With the expense of sophisticated equipment, maintenance of laboratory animals and facilities, and salaries for qualified technicians and researchers, virtually no medical research is undertaken today without federal or foundation support. Gone are the days when individuals had laboratories in their homes or made significant discoveries working in isolation using homemade equipment. In fiscal year 1989, the National Institutes of Health (NIH) funded approximately $7.1 billion in research (*Science and Government Report,* 1990). Private foundations and state governments funded a smaller portion (*National Science Foundation,* 1987).

The choice of problems for study in medical research is substantially determined by a national agenda that defines what is worthy of study, i.e., funding. As Marxist (Zimmerman et al., 1980), African-American (McLeod, 1987), and feminist (Hubbard, 1990) critics of scientific research have pointed out, the research that is undertaken reflects the societal bias toward the powerful, who are overwhelmingly white, middle- to upper-class, and male in the United States. Obviously, the majority of the members of Congress, who appropriate the funds for NIH and other federal agencies, fit this description; they are more likely to vote funds for health research which they view as beneficial as defined from their perspective.

It may be argued that actual priorities for medical research and allocations of funds are set not by members of Congress but by the leaders in medical research who are employees of NIH or other federal agencies or who are brought in as consultants. Unfortunately the same descriptors—white, middle- to upper-class, and male—tend to characterize the it individuals in the theoretical and decision-making positions within the medical hierarchy and scientific establishment.

Having a preponderance of male leaders setting the priorities for medical research results in definite effects on the choice and definition of problems for research: Hypotheses have not been formulated to focus on gender bias as a crucial part of the question being asked. Because it is clear that many diseases have different frequencies (heart disease, lupus), symptoms (gonorrhea), or complications (most sexually transmitted diseases) in the two sexes, scientists should routinely consider and test for differences or lack thereof based on gender in any hypothesis being tested. For example, when exploring the metabolism of a particular drug, tests should routinely be run in both males and females.

Five dramatic, widely publicized recent examples demonstrate that sex differences have *not* routinely been considered as part of the question asked. In a longitudinal study of the effects of a cholesterol-lowering drug, gender differences were not tested; the drug was tested on 3,806 men and no women (Hamilton, 1985). The Multiple Risk Factor Intervention Trial (1990) examined mortality from coronary heart disease in 12,866 men only. The Health Professionals Follow-Up Study (Grobbee et al., 1990) looked at the association between coffee consumption and heart disease in 45,589 men. The Physician's Health Study (Steering Committee of the Physician's Health Study Group, 1989) found that low-

dose aspirin therapy reduced the risk of myocardial infarction in 22,071 men. A study published in September 1992 in the *Journal of the American Medical Association* surveyed the literature from 1960 to 1991 on studies of clinical trials of medications used to treat acute myocardial infarction. Women were included in only about 20 percent of those studies; elderly people (over seventy-five years) were included in only 40 percent (Gurwitz, Nananda, and Avorn, 1992).

Some diseases which affect both sexes are defined as male diseases. Heart disease has been so designated because at younger ages it occurs more frequently in men than in women. Therefore, most of the funding for heart disease has been appropriated for research on predisposing factors (such as cholesterol level, lack of exercise, stress, smoking, and weight) using white, middle-aged, middle-class males.

This "male disease" designation has resulted in very little research being directed toward high-risk groups of women. Heart disease is a leading cause of death in older women (Kirschstein, 1985; Healy, 1991), who live an average of eight years longer than men (Boston Women's Health Book Collective, 1984). It is also frequent in poor African-American women who have had several children (Manley et al., 1985). Virtually no research has explored predisposing factors for these groups who fall outside the disease definition established from an androcentric perspective.

Recent data indicate that the designation of AIDS as a disease of male homosexuals and IV drug users has led to a failure among researchers and health care practitioners to understand the etiology and diagnosis of AIDS in women (Norwood, 1988). AIDS is currently increasing more rapidly among women than in any other group, and women appear to manifest different symptoms of AIDS than men. However, it was not until October 1992 that the Centers for Disease Control (CDC) announced a case definition that includes gynecologic conditions and other symptoms of

AIDS in women; this case definition was enacted in January 1993 (Bell, 1993).

Research on conditions specific to females has been accorded low priority, funding, and prestige, despite the fact that women make up half of the population and receive more than half of the health care. In 1988, the NIH allocated only 13.5 percent of its total budget to research on illnesses of major consequence to women (Narrigan, 1991). The Women's Health Initiative, launched by NIH in 1991 to study cardiovascular diseases, cancers, and osteoporosis, is attempting to raise the priority of women's health and provide baseline data on previously understudied causes of death in women (Pinn and LaRosa, 1992). Additional examples that might be targeted include dysmenorrhea, incontinence in older women, nutrition in postmenopausal women, and effects of exercise level and duration upon alleviation of menstrual discomfort. The issue of exposure to VDTs, which has resulted in "clusters" of women in certain industries giving birth to deformed babies, has also received low priority. In contrast, significant amounts of time and money are expended upon clinical research on women's bodies in connection with other aspects of reproduction. In this century up until the 1970s, considerable attention was devoted to the development of contraceptive devices for females rather than for males (Cowan, 1980; Dreifus, 1978). Furthermore, substantial clinical research has resulted in increasing medicalization and control of pregnancy, labor, and childbirth. Feminists have critiqued (Ehrenreich and English, 1978; Holmes, 1981) the conversion of a normal, natural process controlled by women into a clinical, and often surgical, procedure controlled by men. More recently, the new reproductive technologies such as amniocentesis, in vitro fertilization and artificial insemination have become a major focus as means are sought to overcome infertility. Feminists (Arditti, Duelli Klein, and Minden, 1984; Corea and Ince, 1987; Corea et al., 1987; Klein, 1989) have warned of the extent to which these technologies place pressure on women to produce a "perfect" child while placing control in the hands of the male medical establishment.

These examples suggest that considerable resources and attention are devoted to women's health issues when those issues are directly related to men's interest in controlling the production of children. Contraceptive research may permit men to have sexual pleasure without the worry of producing children. Research on infertility, pregnancy, and childbirth has allowed men to assert more control over the production of more "perfect" children and over an aspect of women's lives over which they previously held less power.

Suggestions of fruitful questions for research based on the personal experience of women have also been ignored. In the health care area, women have often reported (and accepted among themselves) experiences that could not be documented by scientific experiments or were not accepted as valid by the researchers of the day. For decades, dysmenorrhea was attributed by most health care researchers and practitioners to psychological or social factors despite reports from an overwhelming number of women that these were monthly experiences in their lives. Only after prostaglandins were "discovered" was there widespread acceptance among the male medical establishment that this experience reported by women had a biological component (Kirschstein, 1985).

These four types of bias raise ethical issues. Health care practitioners must treat the majority of the population, which is female, based on information gathered from clinical research in which drugs may not have been tested on females, in which the etiology of the disease in women has not been studied, and in which women's experience has been ignored.

Approaches and Methods

The scientific community has often failed to include females in animal studies in both basic and clinical research unless the research centered on controlling the production of children. While the reasons for this exclusion (cleaner data from males due to lack of interference from estrous or menstrual cycles, fear of inducing fetal deformities in pregnant subjects, and higher incidence of some diseases in males) may be viewed as practical from a financial standpoint, it results in drugs that have not been adequately tested in women subjects before being marketed and a lack of information about the etiology of some diseases in women.

Using males as experimental subjects not only ignores the fact that females may respond differently to the variable tested, it may also lead to less accurate models even in the male. Models which more accurately simulate functioning of complex biological systems may be derived by using female rats or primates as subjects in experiments. With the exception of insulin and the hormones of the female reproductive cycle, traditional endocrinological theory assumed that most of the twenty-odd human hormones are maintained at a constant level in both males and females. Thus, the male of the species was chosen as the experimental subject because of his noncyclicity. However, new techniques of measuring blood hormone levels have demonstrated episodic, rather than steady, patterns of secretion of virtually all hormones in both males and females. As Joan Hoffman (1982) points out, the rhythmic cycle of hormone secretion as also portrayed in the cycling female rat appears to be a more accurate model for the secretion of most hormones.

When females have been used as experimental subjects, often they have been treated as not fully human. In his attempts to investigate the side effects (Goldzieher et al., 1971a) of nervousness and depression (Goldzieher et al., 197lb) attributable to oral contraceptives, Goldzieher gave dummy pills to seventy-six women who sought treatment at a San Antonio clinic to prevent further pregnancies. None of the women was told that she was participating in research or receiving place-

bos (Veatch, 1971; Cowan, 1980). The women in Goldzieher's study were primarily poor, multiparous Mexican-Americans. Research that raises similar questions about the ethics of informed consent was carried out on poor Puerto Rican women during the initial phases of testing the effectiveness of the birth control pill as a contraceptive (Zimmerman et al., 1980). Recent data have revealed routine testing of pregnant women for HIV positivity without their informed consent at certain clinics (Marte and Anastos, 1990; Chavkin, Driver, and Forman, 1989) and subsequent pressure placed on women who are positive to abort their fetuses (Selwyn et al., 1989).

Frequently it is difficult to determine whether these women are treated as less than human because of their gender or whether race and class are more significant variables. The Tuskegee Syphilis Experiment, in which the effects of untreated syphilis were studied in 399 men over a period of forty years (Jones, 1981), made it clear that poor African-American men may not receive appropriate treatment or information about the experiment in which they are participating. Feminist scholars (Dill, 1983; Ruzek, 1988) have begun to explore the extent to which gender, race, and class may become complex, interlocking political variables affecting access to and quality of health care.

Current clinical research sets up a distance between the observer and the human subject being studied. Several feminist philosophers (Keller, 1985; Hein, 1981; Haraway, 1978; Harding, 1986) have characterized this as an androcentric approach. Distance between the observer and experimental subject may be more comfortable for men, who are raised to feel more at ease with autonomy and distance (Keller, 1985), than for women, who tend to value relationships and interdependency (Gilligan, 1982).

Using only the methods traditional to a particular discipline may result in limited approaches that fail to reveal sufficient information about the problem being explored. This may be a particular difficulty for research surrounding medical problems of pregnancy, childbirth, menstruation, and menopause, for which the methods of one discipline are clearly inadequate.

Methods which cross disciplinary boundaries or include combinations of methods traditionally used in separate fields may be more appropriate. For example, if the topic of research is occupational exposures that present a risk to the pregnant woman working in a plant where toxic chemicals are manufactured, a combination of methods traditionally used in social science research with methods frequently used in biology and chemistry may be the best approach. Checking the chromosomes of any miscarried fetuses, chemical analysis of placentae after birth, Apgar scores of the babies at birth, and blood samples of the newborns to determine trace amounts of the toxic chemicals would be appropriate biological and chemical means of gathering data about the problem. In-depth interviews with women to discuss how they are feeling and any irregularities they detect during each month of the pregnancy, or weekly evaluation using written questionnaires regarding the pregnancy progress are methods more traditionally used in the social sciences for problems of this sort. Jean Hamilton has called for interactive models that draw on both the social and natural sciences to explain complex problems:

> Particularly for understanding human, gender-related health, we need more interactive and contextual models that address the actual complexity of the phenomenon that is the subject of explanation. One example is the need for more phenomenological definitions of symptoms, along with increased recognition that psychology, behavioral studies, and sociology are among the "basic sciences" for health research. Research on heart disease is one example of a field where it is recognized that both psychological stress and behaviors such as eating and cigarette smoking influence the

onset and natural course of a disease process. (1985, VI-62)

Perhaps an increase in the number of women holding decision-making positions in the design and funding of clinical research would result in more interdisciplinary research on issues of women's health care such as menstruation, pregnancy, childbirth, lactation, and menopause. Those complex phenomena fall outside the range of methods of study provided by a sole discipline. Interdisciplinary approaches developed to solve these problems might then be applied to other complex problems to benefit all health care consumers, both male and female.

Theories and Conclusions Drawn from the Research

The rationale which is traditionally presented in support of "objective" methods is that they prevent bias. Emphasis upon traditional disciplinary approaches that are quantitative and maintain the distance between observer and experimental subject supposedly eliminate bias on the part of the researcher. Ironically, to the extent that these "objective" approaches are synonymous with a masculine approach to the world, they may actually introduce bias. Specifically, androcentric bias may permeate the theories and conclusions drawn from the research in several ways.

Theories may be presented in androcentric language. Much feminist scholarship has focused on problems of sexism in language and the extent to which patriarchal language has excluded and limited women (Thorne, 1979; Lakoff, 1975; Kramarae and Treichler, 1986). Sexist language is a symptom of underlying sexism, but language also shapes our concepts and provides the framework through which we express our ideas. Being aware of sexism and the limitations of patriarchal language may allow feminist researchers to describe their observations in less gender-biased terms.

The limited research on AIDS in women has focused on women as prostitutes or mothers. Describing the woman as a vector for transmission to men (prostitute) or the fetus (mother) has produced little information on the progress of AIDS in women themselves (Rosser, 1991). Once the bias in the terminology is exposed, the next step is to ask whether that terminology leads to a constraint or bias in the theory itself.

An androcentric perspective may lead to the formulation of theories and conclusions drawn from medical research to support the status quo of inequality for women and other oppressed groups. Building upon their awareness of these biases, women scientists have critiqued studies of brain-hormone interaction (Bleier, 1984) for their biological determinism used to justify women's socially inferior position. Bleier repeatedly warned against extrapolating from one species to another in biochemical as well as behavioral traits (Bleier, 1986).

Not surprisingly, the androcentric bias in research which has led to the exclusion of women from the definitions of and approaches to research problems has resulted in differences in the management of disease and access to health care procedures based on gender. In a 1991 study in Massachusetts and Maryland, Ayanian and Epstein (1991) demonstrated that women were significantly less likely than men to undergo coronary angioplasty, angiography, or surgery when admitted to the hospital with the diagnosis of myocardial infarction, unstable angina, chronic ischemic heart disease, or chest pain. This significant difference remained even when variables such as race, age, economic status and other chronic diseases such as diabetes and heart failure were controlled for. A similar study (Steingart et al., 1991) revealed that women had angina before myocardial infarction as frequently as and with more debilitating effects than men, yet women are referred for cardiac catheterization only half as often. The 1992 *Journal of the American Medical Association* study con-

cluded that the exclusion of women from 80 percent of the trials and of the elderly from 60 percent of the trials for medication for myocardial infarction limits the ability to generalize study findings to the patient population that experiences the most morbidity and mortality from acute myocardial infarction (Gurwitz, Nananda, and Avorn, 1992). Gender bias in cardiac research has therefore been translated into bias in the management of disease, leading to inequitable treatment for life-threatening conditions in women.

Androcentric bias in AIDS research may also lead to underdiagnosis and higher death rates for women. Because the progress of AIDS in women has not been adequately studied, and since the CDC case definition for AIDS failed until very recently to include any gynecologic conditions, most health care workers are unable to diagnose AIDS in women until the disease has advanced significantly. On average, men die thirty months after diagnosis, women fifteen weeks. Theories and conclusions drawn from AIDS research should be examined to determine to what extent they represent and reinforce sexism, racism, and classism.

Recognizing the possibility of gender bias is the first step toward understanding the difference it makes. Perhaps male researchers are less likely to see flaws in and question biologically deterministic theories that provide scientific justification for men's superior status in society because they gain social power and status from such theories. Researchers from outside the mainstream (women, for example) are much more likely to be critical of such theories because they lose power from them. To eliminate bias, the community of scientists undertaking clinical research needs to include individuals from backgrounds as varied and diverse as possible with regard to race, class, gender, and sexual orientation (Rosser, 1988). Only then is it less likely that the perspective of one group will bias research design, approaches, subjects, and interpretations.

However, given that the overall agenda for research policies concerning access to health care is set in the political arena, politicians must also reflect the diversity and needs of the population. Then we can work together to overcome gender bias in health research.

References

Arditti, Rita. 1980. Feminism and science. In Rita Arditti, Pat Brennan, and Steve Cavrak (eds.), *Science and liberation.* Boston: South End Press.

Arditti, Rita; Duelli Klein, Renate; and Minden, Shelley. 1984. *Test-tube women: What future for motherhood?* London: Pandora Press.

Ayanian, J.Z., and Epstein, A. M. 1991. Differences in the use of procedures between women and men hospitalized for coronary heart disease. *New England Journal of Medicine* 325:221–225.

Bell, Nora. 1993. Board of the National Leadership Coalition on AIDS. Personal communication.

Birke, Lynda. 1986. *Women, feminism, and biology.* New York: Methuen.

Bleier, Ruth. 1984. *Science and gender: A critique of biology and its theories on women.* New York: Pergamon Press.

———. 1986. Sex differences research: Science or belief? In Ruth Bleier (ed.), *Feminist approaches to science.* New York: Pergamon Press.

Boston Women's Health Book Collective. 1984. *The new our bodies, ourselves.* New York: Simon and Schuster.

Chavkin, W.; Driver, C.; and Forman, P. 1989. The crisis in New York City's perinatal services. *New York State Journal of Medicine* 89, no. 12:658–663.

Corea, G., et al. (eds.). 1987. *Man-made women: How new reproductive technologies affect women.* Bloomington: Indiana University Press.

Corea, Gena, and Ince, S. 1987. Report of a survey of IVF clinics in the U.S. In Patricia Spallone and Deborah L. Steinberg (eds.), *Made to order: The myth of reproductive and genetic progress.* Oxford: Pergamon Press.

Cowan, Belita. 1980. Ethical problems in government-funded contraceptive research. In Helen Holmes, Betty Hoskins, and Michael Gross (eds.), *Birth control and controlling birth: Women-centered perspectives,* pp. 37–46. Clifton, N.J.: Humana Press.

Dill, Bonnie T. 1983. Race, class and gender: Prospects for an all-inclusive sisterhood. *Feminist Studies* 9:1.

Dreifus, Claudia. 1978. *Seizing our bodies.* New York: Vintage Books.

Ehrenreich, Barbara, and English, Deirdre. 1978. *For her own good.* New York: Anchor Press.

Fausto-Sterling, Anne. 1985. *Myths of gender.* New York: Basic Books.

Fee, Elizabeth. 1981. Is feminism a threat to scientific objectivity? *International Journal of Women's Studies* 4:213-233.

———. 1982. A feminist critique of scientific objectivity. *Science for the People* 14, no. 4:8.

Gilligan, Carol. 1982. *In a different voice: Psychological theory and women's development.* Cambridge, Mass.: Harvard University Press.

Goldzieher, Joseph W.; Moses, Louis; Averkin, Eugene; Scheel, Cora; and Taber, Ben. 1971a. A placebo-controlled double-blind crossover investigation of the side effects attributed to oral contraceptives. *Fertility and Sterility* 22, no. 9:609–623.

———. 1971b. Nervousness and depression attributed to oral contraceptives: A double-blind, placebo-controlled study. *American Journal of Obstetrics and Gynecology* 22:1013–1020.

Grobbee, D. E., et al. 1990. Coffee, caffeine, and cardiovascular disease in men. *New England Journal of Medicine* 321:1026–1032.

Gurwitz, Jerry H.; Nananda, F. Colonel; and Avorn, Jerry. 1992. The exclusion of the elderly and women from clinical trials in acute myocardial infarction. *Journal of the American Medical Association* 268, no. 2:1417–1422.

Hamilton, Jean. 1985. Avoiding methodological biases in gender-related research. In *Women's health report of the Public Health Service Task Force on Women's Health Issues.* Washington, D.C.: U.S. Department of Health and Human Service Public Service.

Haraway, Donna. 1978. Animal sociology and a natural economy of the body politic, Part I: A political physiology of dominance; and Animal sociology and a natural economy of the body politic, Part II: The past is the contested zone: Human nature and theories of production and reproduction in primate behavior studies. *Signs: Journal of Women in Culture and Society* 4, no. 1:21–60.

————. 1989. Monkeys, aliens, and women: Love, science, and politics at the intersection of feminist theory and colonial discourse. *Women's Studies International Forum* 12, no. 3:295–312.

Harding, Sandra. 1986. *The science question in feminism.* Ithaca, N.Y.: Cornell University Press.

Healy, Bernadine. 1991. Women's health, public welfare. *Journal of the American Medical Association* 264, no. 4:566–568.

Hein Hilde. 1981. Women and science: Fitting men to think about nature. *International Journal of Women's Studies* 4:369–377.

Hoffman, J. C. 1982. Biorhythms in human reproduction: The not-so-steady states. *Signs: Journal of Women in Culture and Society* 7, no. 4:829–844.

Holmes, Helen B. 1981. Reproductive technologies: The birth of a women-centered analysis. In Helen B. Holmes et al. (eds.), *The custommade child?* Clifton, N.J.: Humana Press.

Hubbard, Ruth. 1990. *The politics of women's biology.* New Brunswick, N.J.: Rutgers University Press.

Jaggar, Alison M. 1983. *Feminist politics and human nature.* Totowa, N.Y.: Rowman and Allanheld.

Jones, James H. 1981. *Bad blood: The Tuskegee syphilis experiment.* New York: The Free Press.

Keller, Evelyn Fox. 1982. Feminism and science. *Signs: Journal of Women in Culture and Society* 7, no. 3:589–602.

————. 1983. *A feeling for the organism: The life and work of Barbara McClintock.* New York: W. H. Freeman.

————. 1985. *Reflections on gender and science.* New Haven, Conn.: Yale University Press.

Kirschstein, Ruth L. 1985. *Women's health: Report of the Public Health Service Task Force on Women's Health Issues.* Vol. 2. Washington, D.C.: U.S. Department of Health and Human Services Public Health Service.

Klein, Renate D. 1989. *Infertility.* London: Pandora Press.

Kramarae, Cheris, and Treichler, Paula. 1986. *A feminist dictionary.* London: Pandora Press.

Kuhn, Thomas S. 1970. *The structure of scientific revolutions.* 2nd ed. Chicago: The University of Chicago Press.

Lakoff Robin. 1975. *Language and woman's place.* New York: Harper and Row Publishers, Inc.

Longino, Helen. 1990. *Science as social knowledge: Values and objectivity in scientific inquiry.* Princeton, N.J.: Princeton University Press.

Manley, Audrey; Lin-Fu, Jane; Miranda, Magdalena; Noonan, Alan; and Parker, Tanya. 1985. Special health concerns of ethnic minority women in women's health. *Report of the Public Health Service Task Force on Women's Health Issues.* Washington, D.C.: U.S. Department of Health and Human Services.

Marte, C., and Anastos, K. 1990. Women—the missing persons in the AIDS epidemic. Part II. *Health/PAC Bulletin* 20, no. 1:11–23.

McLeod, S. 1987. *Scientific colonialism: A cross-cultural comparison.* Washington, D.C.: Smithsonian Institution Press.

Money, John, and Erhardt, Anke. 1972. *Man and woman, boy and girl.* Baltimore: Johns Hopkins University Press.

Multiple Risk Factor Intervention Trial Research Group. 1990. Mortality rates after 10.5 years for participants in the Multiple Risk Factor Intervention Trial: Findings related to a prior hypothesis of the trial. *Journal of the American Medical Association* 263:1795–1801.

Narrigan, Deborah. 1991. Research to improve women's health: An agenda for equity. *The Network News: National Women's Health Network* (March/April/May):3, 9.

National Science Foundation. 1987. *Science and Engineering Indicators.* NSB-1, Appendix Table 4–10. Washington, D.C.: NSF.

Norwood, Chris. 1988. Alarming rise in deaths. *Ms.,* (July):65–7.

Pinn, Vivian, and LaRosa, Judith. 1992. Overview: Office of research on women's health. *National Institutes of Health,* pp. 1–10.

Rosser, Sue V. 1986. *Teaching science and health from a feminist perspective: A practical guide.* Elmsford, N.Y.: Pergamon Press.

————. 1988. Women in science and health care: A gender at risk. In Sue V. Rosser (ed.), *Feminism within the science of health care professions: Overcoming resistance.* Elmsford, N.Y.: Pergamon Press.

————. 1991. AIDS and women. *AIDS Education and Prevention* 3, no. 3:230–240

Ruzek, Sheryl. 1988. Women's health: Sisterhood is powerful, but so are race and class. Keynote address delivered at Southeast Women's Studies Association Annual Conference February 27, University of North Carolina–Chapel Hill.

Science and government report. 1990. Washington, D.C., March 1, 18, no. 4:1.

Selwyn, P. A., et al. 1989. Prospective study of human immunodeficiency virus infection and pregnancy outcomes in intravenous drug users. *Journal of the American Medical Association* 261:1289–1294.

Steering Committee of the Physician's Health Study Research Group. 1988. Special report: Preliminary report of findings from the aspirin component of the ongoing physician's health study. *New England Journal of Medicine* 318, no. 4:262–264.

Steering Committee of the Physician's Health Study Group. 1989. Final report on the aspirin component of the ongoing physician's health study. *New England Journal of Medicine* 321:129–135.

Steingart, R. M.; Packes M.; Hamm, P.; et al. 1991. Sex differences in the management of coronary artery disease. *New England Journal of Medicine* 325:226-230.

Thorne, Barrie. 1979. Claiming verbal space: Women, speech and language in college classrooms. Paper presented at the Research Conference on Educational Environments and the Undergraduate Women, September 13–15, Wellesley College.

Veatch, Robert M. 1971. *Experimental pregnancy.* Hastings Center Report 1:2–3.

Webster, Douglas, and Webster, Molly. 1974. *Comparative vertebrate morphology.* New York: Academic Press.

Zimmerman, B., et al. 1980. People's science. In Rita Arditti, Pat Brennan, and Steve Cavrak (eds.), *Science and liberation,* pp. 299–319. Boston: South End Press.

Man-Made Medicine and Women's Health

The Biopolitics of Sex/Gender and Race/Ethnicity

Nancy Krieger and Elizabeth Fee

Introduction

Glance at any collection of national health data for the United States—whether pertaining to health, disease, or the health care system—and several features stand out. First, notice that most reports present data in terms of race, sex, and age. Some races are clearly of more interest than others. National reports most frequently use racial groups called "white" and "black" and, increasingly, a group called "Hispanic." Occasionally, we find data on Native Americans and on Asians and Pacific Islanders. Whatever the specific categories chosen, the reports agree that white men and women, for the most part, have the best health, at all ages. They also show that men and women, across all racial groups, have different patterns of disease. Obviously, men and women differ for conditions related to reproduction (women, for example, do not get testicular cancer), but they differ for many other conditions as well—for example, men on average have higher blood pressure and develop cardiovascular disease at an earlier age. And, in the health care sector, occupations, just like diseases, are differentially distributed by race and sex.

All this seems obvious. But it isn't. We know about race and sex divisions because this is what our society considers important. This is how we classify people and collect data. This is how we organize our social life as a nation. This is therefore how we structure our knowledge about health and disease. And this is what we find important as a subject of research.

It seems so routine, so normal, to view the health of women and men as fundamentally different, to consider the root of this difference to be biological sex, and to think about race as an inherent, inherited characteristic that also affects health. The work of looking after sick people follows the same categories. Simply walk into a hospital and observe that most of the doctors are white men, most of the registered nurses are white women, most of the kitchen and laundry workers are black and Hispanic women, and most of the janitorial staff are black and Hispanic men. Among the patients, notice who has appointments with private clinicians and who is getting care in the emergency room; the color line is obvious. Notice who provides health care at home: wives, mothers, and daughters. The gender line at home and in medical institutions is equally obvious.

These contrasting patterns, by race and sex, are longstanding. How do we explain them? What kinds of explanations satisfy us? Some are comfortable with explanations that accept these patterns as natural, as the result of natural law, as part of the natural order of things. Of course, if patterns are that way by nature, they cannot be changed. Others aim to understand these patterns precisely in order to change them. They look for explanations suggesting that these patterns are structured by convention, by discrimination, by the politics of power, and by unreasonable law. These patterns, in other words, reflect the social order of people.

In this essay, we discuss how race and sex became such all-important, self-evident categories in nineteenth- and twentieth-century biomedical thought and practice. We examine the consequences of these categories for our knowledge about health and for the provision of health care. We then consider alternative approaches to studying race/ethnicity, gender, and health. And we address these issues with reference to a typically suppressed and repressed category: that of social class.

The Social Construction of "Race" and "Sex" as Key Biomedical Terms and Their Effect on Knowledge About Health

In the nineteenth century, the construction of "race" and "sex" as key biomedical categories was driven by social struggles over human inequality. Before the Civil War, the dominant understanding of race was as a natural/theological category—black/white differences were innate and reflected God's will.[1] These differences were believed to be manifest in every aspect of the body, in sickness and in health. But when abolitionists began to get the upper hand in moral and theological arguments, proponents of slavery appealed to science as the new arbiter of racial distinction.

In this period, medical men were beginning to claim the mantle of scientific knowledge and assert their right to decide controversial social issues.[2] Recognizing the need for scientific authority, the state of Louisiana, for example, commissioned one prolific proponent of slavery, Dr. Samuel Cartwright, to prove the natural inferiority of blacks, a task that led him to detail every racial difference imaginable—in texture of hair, length of bones, vulnerability to disease, and even color of the internal organs.[3] As the Civil War changed the status of blacks from legal chattel to bona fide citizens, however, medical journals began to question old verities about racial differences and, as importantly, to publish new views of racial similarities.[4] Some authors even attributed black/white differences in health to differences in socioeconomic position. But by the 1870s, with the destruction of Reconstruction, the doctrine of innate racial distinction again triumphed. The scientific community once again deemed "race" a fundamental biological category.[5]

Theories of women's inequality followed a similar pattern.[6] In the early nineteenth century, traditionalists cited scripture to prove women's inferiority. These authorities agreed that Eve had been formed out of Adam's rib and that all women had to pay the price of her sin—disobeying God's order, seeking illicit knowledge from the serpent, and tempting man with the forbidden apple. Women's pain in childbirth was clear proof of God's displeasure.

When these views were challenged in the mid-nineteenth century by advocates of women's rights and proponents of liberal political theory, conservatives likewise turned to the new arbiters of knowledge and sought to buttress their position with scientific facts and medical authority.[7] Biologists busied themselves with measuring the size of women's skulls, the length of their bones, the rate of their breathing, and the number of their blood cells. And considering all the evidence, the biologists concluded that women were indeed the weaker sex.[8]

Agreeing with this stance, medical men energetically took up the issue of women's health and equality.[9] They were convinced that the true woman was by nature sickly, her physiological systems at the mercy of her ovaries and uterus. Because all bodily organs were interconnected, they argued, a woman's monthly cycle irritated her delicate nervous system and her sensitive, small, weak brain. Physicians considered women especially vulnerable to nervous ailments such as neurasthenia and hysteria. This talk of women's delicate constitutions did not apply, of course, to slave women or to working-class women— but it was handy to refute the demands of middle-class women whenever they sought to vote or gain access to education and professional careers. At such moments, many medical men declared the doctrine of separate spheres to be the ineluctable consequence of biology.

At the same time, nineteenth-century medical authorities began to conceptualize class as a natural, biological distinction. Traditional, pre-scientific views held class hierarchies to be divinely ordained; according to the more scientific view that emerged in the early nineteenth century, class position was determined by innate, inherited ability. In both cases, class was perceived as an essentially stable, hierarchical ranking. These discussions of class usually assumed white or Western European populations and often applied only to males within those populations.

With the impact of the industrial revolution, classes took on a clearly dynamic character. As landowners invested in canals and railroads, as merchants became capitalist entrepreneurs, and as agricultural workers were transformed into an industrial proletariat, the turbulent transformation of the social order provoked new understandings of class relationships.[10] The most developed of these theories was that of Karl Marx, who emphasized the system of classes as a social and economic formation and stressed the contradictions between different class interests.[11] From this point onward, the very idea of social classes in many people's minds implied a revolutionary threat to the social order.

In opposition to Marxist analyses of class, the theory of Social Darwinism was formulated to suggest that the new social inequalities of industrial society reflected natural law.[12] This theory was developed in the midst of the economic depression of the 1870s, at a time when labor struggles, trade union organizing, and early socialist movements were challenging the political and economic order. Many scientists and medical men drew upon Darwin's idea of "the struggle for survival," first expressed in the *Origin of the Species* in 1859,[13] to justify social inequality. They argued that those on top, the social elite, must by definition be the "most fit" because they had survived so well. Social hierarchies were therefore built on and reflected real biological differences. Poor health status simultaneously was sign and proof of biological inferiority.

By the late nineteenth century, theories of race, gender, and class inequality were linked together by the theory of Social Darwinism, which promised to provide a scientific basis for social policy.[14] In the realm of race, for example, proponents of Social Darwinism blithely predicted that the "Negro Question" would soon resolve itself—the "Negro" would naturally become extinct, eliminated by the inevitable workings of "natural selection."[15] Many public health officials—particularly in the southern states—agreed that "Negroes" were an inherently degenerate, syphilitic, and tubercular race, for whom public health interventions could do little.[16] Social Darwinists also argued that natural and sexual selection would lead to increasing differentiation between the sexes.[17] With further evolution, men would become ever more masculine and women ever more feminine. As proof, they looked to the upper classes, whose masculine and feminine behavior represented the forefront of evolutionary progress.

Over time, the Social Darwinist view of class gradually merged into general American ideals of progress, meritocracy, and success through individual effort. According to the dominant American ideology, individuals were so mobile that fixed measures of social class were irrelevant. Such measures were also un-American. Since the Paris Commune, and especially since the Bolshevik revolution, discussions of social class in the United States were perceived as politically threatening. Although fierce debates about inequality continued to revolve around the axis of nature versus nurture, the notion of class as a social relationship was effectively banished from respectable discourse and policy debate.[18] Social position was once again equated only with rank, now understood as socioeconomic status.

In the early twentieth century, Social Darwinists had considerable influence in shaping public views and public policy.[19] They perceived two new threats to American superiority: the massive tide of immigration from eastern and southern Europe, and the declining birth rate—or "race suicide"—among American white women of Anglo-Saxon and Germanic descent. Looking to the fast-developing field of genetics, now bolstered by the rediscovery of Gregor Mendel's laws and by T. H. Morgan's fruit fly experiments,[20] biological determinists regrouped under the banner of eugenics. Invoking morbidity and mortality data that showed a high rate of tuberculosis and infectious disease among the immigrant poor,[21] they declared "ethnic" Europeans a naturally inferior and sickly stock and thus helped win passage of the Immigration Restriction Act in 1924.[22] This legislation required the national mix of immigrants to match that entering the United States in the early 1870s, thereby severely curtailing immigration of racial and ethnic groups deemed inferior. "Race/ethnicity," construed as a biological reality, became ever more entrenched as the *explanation* of racial/ethnic differences in disease; social explanations were seen as the province of scientifically illiterate and naive liberals, or worse, provocateurs, socialist and Bolshevik provocateurs.

Other developments in the early twentieth century encouraged biological explanations of sex differences in disease and in social roles. The discovery of the sex chromosomes in 1905 reinforced the idea that gender was a fundamental biological trait, built into the genetic constitution of the body. That same year, Ernest Starling coined the term "hormone"[23] to denote the newly characterized chemical messengers that permitted one organ to control—at a distance—the activities of another. By the mid-1920s, researchers had isolated several hormones integral to reproductive physiology and popularized the notion of "sex hormones."[24] The combination of sex chromosomes and sex hormones were imbued with almost magical powers to shape human behavior in gendered terms; women were now at the mercy of their genetic limitations and a changing brew of hormonal imperatives.[25] In the realm of medicine, researchers turned to sex chromosomes and hormones to understand cancers of the uterus and breast and a host of other sex-linked diseases;[26] they no longer saw the need to worry about environmental influences. In the workplace, of course, employers said that sex chromosomes and hormones dictated which jobs women could—and could not—perform.[27] This in turn determined the occupational hazards to which women would be exposed—once again, women's health and ill health were viewed as a matter of their biology.

Within the first few decades of the twentieth century, these views were institutionalized within scientific medicine and the new public health. At this time, the training of physicians and public health practitioners was being recast in modern, scientific terms.[28] Not surprisingly, biological determinist views of racial/ethnic and sex/gender differences became a natural and integral part of the curriculum, the research agenda, and medical and public health practice. Over time, ethnic differences in disease among white European groups were downplayed and instead, the differences between whites and blacks, whites and Mexicans, whites and Asians were emphasized. Color was now believed to define distinct biological groups.

Similarly, the sex divide marked a gulf between two completely disparate groups. Within medicine, women's health was relegated to obstetrics and gynecology, within public health, women's health needs were seen as being met by maternal and child health programs.[29] Women were perceived as wives and mothers; they were important for childbirth, child care, and domestic nutrition. Although no one denied that some women worked, women's occupational health was essentially ignored because women were, after all, only temporary workers. Outside the specialized realm of reproduction, all other health research concerned men's bodies and men's diseases. Reproduction was so central to women's biological existence that women's nonreproductive health was rendered virtually invisible.

Currently, it is popular to argue that the lack of research on white women and on men and women in nonwhite racial/ethnic groups resulted from a perception of white men as the norm.[30] This interpretation, however, is inaccurate. In fact, by the time that researchers began to standardize methods for clinical and epidemiological research, notions of difference were so firmly embedded that whites and nonwhites, women and men, were rarely studied together. Moreover, most researchers and physicians were interested only in the health status of whites and, in the case of women, only in their reproductive health. They therefore used white men as the research subjects of choice for all health conditions other than women's reproductive health and paid attention to the health status of nonwhites only to measure degrees of racial difference. For the most part, the health of women and men of color and the nonreproductive health of white women was simply ignored. It is critical to read these omissions as evidence of a logic of difference rather than as an assumption of similarity.

This framework has shaped knowledge and practice to the present. U.S. vital statistics present health information in terms of race and sex and age, conceptualized only as biological variables ignoring the social dimensions of gender and ethnicity. Data on social class are not collected. At the same time, public health professionals are unable adequately to explain or to change inequalities in health between men and women and between diverse racial/ethnic groups. We now face the question: is there any alternative way of understanding these population patterns of health and disease?

Alternative Ways of Studying Race, Gender, and Health: Social Measures for Social Categories

The first step in creating an alternative understanding is to recognize that the categories we traditionally treat as simply biological are in fact largely social. The second step is to realize that we need social concepts to understand these social categories. The third step is to develop social measures and appropriate strategies for a new kind of health research.

With regard to race/ethnicity, we need to be clear that "race" is a spurious biological concept.[31] Although historic patterns of geographic isolation and migration account for differences in the distribution of certain genes, genetic variation within so-called racial groups far exceeds that across groups. All humans share approximately 95 percent of their genetic makeup. Racial/ethnic differences in disease thus require something other than a genetic explanation.

Recognizing this problem, some people have tried to substitute the term "ethnicity" for "race."[32] In the public health literature, however, "ethnicity" is rarely defined. For some, it apparently serves as a polite way of referring to what are still conceptualized as "racial"/biological differences. For others, it expresses a new form of "cultural" determinism, in which ethnic differences in ways of living are seen as autonomous "givens" unrelated to the social status of particular ethnic groups within our society.[33] This cultural determinism makes discrimination invisible and can feed into explanations of health status that are as reductionist and individualistic as those of biological determinism.

For a different starting point, consider the diverse ways in which racism operates, at both an institutional and interpersonal level.[34] Racism is a matter of economics and it is also more than economics. It structures living and working conditions, affects daily interactions, and takes its toll on people's dignity and pride. All of this must be considered when we examine the connection between race/ethnicity and health.

To address the economic aspects of racism, we need to include economic data in all studies of health status. Currently, our national health data do not include economic information—instead, racial differences are often used as indicators of economic differences. To the extent that economics are taken into account, the standard approach assumes that differences are either economic or "genetic." So, for those conditions where racial/ethnic differences persist even within economic strata—hypertension and preterm delivery, for example—the assumption is

that something biological, something genetic, is at play. Researchers rarely consider the noneconomic aspects of racism or the ways in which racism continues to work within economic levels.

Some investigators, however, are beginning to consider how racism shapes people's environments. Several studies, for example, document the fact that toxic dumps are most likely to be located in poor neighborhoods and are disproportionately located in poor neighborhoods of color.[35] Other researchers are starting to ask how people's experience of and response to discrimination may influence their health.[36] A recent study of hypertension, for example, found that black women who responded actively to unfair treatment were less likely to report high blood pressure than women who internalized their responses. Interestingly, the black women at highest risk were those who reported *no* experiences of racial discrimination.

Countering the traditional practice of always taking whites as the standard of comparison, some researchers are beginning to focus on other racial/ethnic groups to better understand why, within each of the groups, some are at higher risk than others for particular disease outcomes.[37] They are considering whether people of color may be exposed to specific conditions that whites are not. In addition to living and working conditions, these include cultural practices that may be positive as well as negative in their effects on health. Some studies, for example, point to the importance of black churches in providing social support.[38] These new approaches break with monolithic assumptions about what it means to belong to a given racial/ethnic group and consider diversity *within* each group. To know the color of a person's skin is to know very little.

It is equally true that to know a person's sex is to know very little. Women are often discussed as a single group defined chiefly by biological sex, members of an abstract, universal (and implicitly white) category. In reality, we are a mixed lot, our gender roles and options shaped by history, culture, and deep divisions across class and color lines. Of course, it is true that women, in general, have the capacity to become pregnant, at least at some stages of their lives. Traditionally, women as a group are defined by this reproductive potential. Usually ignored are the many ways that gender as a social reality gets into the body and transforms our biology—differences in childhood expectations about exercise, for example, affect our subsequent body build.

From a health point of view, women's reproductive potential does carry the possibility of specific reproductive ills, ranging from infertility to preterm delivery to cervical and breast cancer. These reproductive ills are not simply associated with the biological category "female," but are differentially experienced according to social class and race/ethnicity. Poor women, for example, are much more likely to suffer from cervical cancer.[39] By contrast, at least among older women, breast cancer is more common among the affluent.[40] These patterns, which at times can become quite complex, illustrate the general point that, even in the case of reproductive health, more than biological sex is at issue. Explanations of women's reproductive health that ignore the social patterning of disease and focus only on endogenous factors are thus inadequate.

If we turn to those conditions that afflict both men and women—the majority of all diseases and health problems—we must keep two things simultaneously in mind. First are the differences and similarities among diverse groups of women; second are the differences and similarities between women and men.

For a glimpse of the complexity of disease patterns, consider the example of hypertension. As we mentioned, working class and poor women are at greater risk than affluent women; black women, within each income level, are more likely to be hypertensive than white women.[41] The risks of Hispanic women vary by national origin: Mexican women are at lowest risk, Central American women at

higher risk, and Puerto Rican and Cuban women at the highest risk.[42] In what is called the "Hispanic paradox," Mexican-American women have a higher risk profile than Anglo women, yet experience lower rates of hypertension.[43] To complicate the picture, the handful of studies of Japanese and Chinese women in the United States show them to have low rates, while Filipina women have high rates, almost equal those of African-Americans.[44] Rates vary across different groups of Native American women; those who live in the Northern plains have higher rates than those in the Southwest.[45] From all this, we can conclude that there is enormous variation in hypertension rates among women.

If we look at the differences between women and men, we find that men in each racial/ethnic group have higher rates of hypertension than women. Even so, the variation among women is sufficiently great that women in some racial/ethnic groups have higher rates than men in other groups. Filipina women, for example, have higher rates of hypertension than white men.[46] Obviously, the standard biomedical categories of race and sex cannot explain these patterns. If we want to understand hypertension, we will have to understand the complex distribution of disease among real women and men; these patterns are not merely distracting details but are the proper test of the plausibility of our hypotheses.

As a second example, consider the well-known phenomenon of women's longer life expectancy. This difference is common to all industrialized countries, and amounts to about seven years in the United States.[47] The higher mortality of men at younger ages is largely due to higher accident rates, and at older ages, to heart disease.

The higher accident rates of younger men are not accidental. They are due to more hazardous occupations, higher rates of illicit drug and alcohol use, firearms injuries, and motor vehicle crashes—hazards related to gender roles and expectations.[48] The fact that men die earlier of heart disease—the single most common cause of death in both sexes—may also be related to gender roles. Men have higher rates of cigarette smoking and fewer sources of social support, suggesting that the masculine ideal of the Marlboro man is not a healthy one. Some contend that women's cardiovascular advantage is mainly biological, due to the protective effect of their hormone levels.[49] Interestingly, however, a study carried out in a kibbutz in Israel, where men and women were engaged in comparable activities, found that the life expectancy gap was only four and a half years—just over half the national average.[50] While biological differences between men and women now receive much of the research attention, it is important to remember that men are gendered beings too.

Clearly, our patterns of health and disease have everything to do with how we live in the world. Nowhere is this more evident than in the strong social-class gradients apparent in almost every form of morbidity and mortality.[51] Yet here the lack of information and the conceptual confusion about the relationship between social class and women's health is a major obstacle. As previously noted, in this country we have no regular method of collecting data on socioeconomic position and health. Even if we had such data, measures of social class generally assume male heads of households and male patterns of employment.[52] This, indeed, is one of the failures of class analyses—that they do not deal adequately with women.[53]

Perhaps the easiest way to understand the problems of class measurements and women's health is to mention briefly the current debates in Britain, a country that has long collected social class data. Men and unmarried women are assigned a social class position according to their employment; married women, however, are assigned a class position according to the employment of their husbands. As British feminist researchers have argued, this traditional approach obscures the magnitude of class differences in

women's health.[54] Instead, they are proposing measures of household class that take into account the occupations of both women and their husbands, and also other household assets. Here in the United States, we have hardly any research on the diverse measures of social class in relation to women's health. Preliminary studies suggest we also would do well to distinguish between individual and household class.[55] Other research shows that we can partly overcome the absence of social class information in U.S. medical records by using census data. This method allows us to describe people in terms of the socioeconomic profile of their immediate neighborhood. When coupled with individual measures of social class, this approach reveals, for example, that working-class women who live in working-class neighborhoods are somewhat more likely to have high blood pressure than working-class women who live in more affluent neighborhoods.[56] We thus need to separate conceptually three distinct levels at which class operates—individual, household, and neighborhood.

As a final example of why women's health cannot be understood without reference to issues of sex/gender, race/ethnicity, and social class, consider the case of AIDS.[57] The definition of disease, the understanding of risk, the approach to prevention—all are shaped by our failure to grasp fully the social context of disease. For the first decade, women's unique experiences of AIDS were rendered essentially invisible. The first definition of AIDS was linked to men, because it was perceived to be a disease of gay men and those with a male sex-linked disorder, hemophilia. The very listing of HIV-related diseases taken to characterize AIDS was a listing based on male experience of infection. Only much later, after considerable protest by women activists, were female disorders—such as invasive cervical cancer—made part of the definition of the disease.[58]

Our understanding of risk is still constrained by the standard approaches. AIDS data are still reported only in terms of race, sex, and mode of transmission; there are no data on social class.[59] We know, however, that the women who have AIDS are overwhelmingly women of color. As of July 1993, of the nearly 37,000 women diagnosed with AIDS, over one half were African-American, another 20 percent were Hispanic, 25 percent were white, and about 1 percent were Asian, Pacific Islander, or Native American.[60] What puts these women at risk? It seems clear that one determinant is the missing variable: social class. Notably, the women at highest risk are injection drug users, the sexual partners of injection drug users, and sex workers.[61] The usual listing of behavioral and demographic risk factors, however, fails to capture the social context in which the AIDS epidemic has unfolded. Most of the epidemiological accounts are silent about the blight of inner cities, the decay of the urban infrastructure under the Reagan and Bush administrations, unemployment, the drug trade, prostitution, and the harsh realities of everyday racism.[62] We cannot gain an adequate understanding of risk absent a real understanding of people's lives.

Knowledge of what puts women at risk is of course critical for prevention. Yet, just as the initial definitions of AIDS reflected a male-gendered perspective, so did initial approaches to prevention.[63] The emphasis on condoms assumed that the central issue was knowledge, not male-female power relations. For women to use condoms in heterosexual sex, however, they need more than bits of plastic; they need male assent. The initial educational materials were created without addressing issues of power; they were male-oriented and obviously white—both in the mode and language of presentation. AIDS programs and services, for the most part, still do not address women's needs. Pregnant women and women with children continue to be excluded from most drug treatment programs. And when women become sick and die, we have no remotely adequate social policies for taking care of the families left behind.

In short, our society's approach to AIDS reflects the larger refusal to deal with the ways in which sex/gender, race/ethnicity, and class are inescapably intertwined with health. This refusal affects not only what we know and what we do about AIDS, but also the other issues we have mentioned—hypertension, cancer, life expectancy—and many we have not. As we have tried to argue, the issues of women's health cannot be understood in only biological terms, as simply the ills of the female of the species. Women and men are different, but we are also similar—and we both are divided by the social relations of class and race/ethnicity. To begin to understand how our social constitution affects our health, we must ask, repeatedly, what is different and what is similar across the social divides of gender, color, and class. We cannot assume that biology alone will provide the answers we need; instead, we must reframe the issues in the context of the social shaping of our human lives—as both biological creatures and historical actors. Otherwise, we will continue to mistake—as many before us have done—what is for what must be, and leave unchallenged the social forces that continue to create vast inequalities in health.

Notes

1. N. Krieger, "Shades of Difference: Theoretical Underpinnings of the Medical Controversy on Black/White Differences in the United States, 1830–1870," *International Journal of Health Services* 17(1987): 256–278; W. Stanton, *The Leopard's Spots: Scientific Attitudes Towards Race in America, 1815–59* (Chicago: University of Chicago Press, 1960); N. Stepan, *The Idea of Race in Science, Great Britain, 1800–1860* (Hamden, Conn.: Archon, 1982); W.D. Jordan, *White Over Black: American Attitudes toward the Negro, 1550–1812* (Chapel Hill: University of North Carolina Press, 1968).

2. C.E. Rosenberg, *No Other Gods: On Science and American Social Thought* (Baltimore, Md.: Johns Hopkins University Press, 1976); G.H. Daniels, "The Process of Professionalization in American Science: The Emergent Period, 1820–1860," *Isis* 58(1967): 151–166; W.G. Rothstein, *American Physicians in the 19th Century: From Sects to Science*

(Baltimore, Md.:Johns Hopkins University Press, 1972).

3. S.A. Cartwright, "Report on the Diseases and Physical Peculiarities of the Negro Race," *New Orleans Medical Surgery Journal* 7(1850): 691–715; S.A. Cartwright, "Alcohol and the Ethiopian: Or, the Moral and Physical Effects of Ardent Spirits on the Negro Race, and Some Accounts of the Peculiarities of That People," *New Orleans Medical Surgery Journal* 10(1853); 150–165; S.A. Cartwright, "Ethnology of the Negro or Prognathous Race—A Lecture Delivered November 30, 1857, before the New Orleans Academy of Science," *New Orleans Medical Surgery Journal* 15(1858): 149–163.

4. R. Reyburn, "Remarks Concerning Some of the Diseases Prevailing among the Freedpeople in the District of Columbia (Bureau of Refugees, Freedmen and Abandoned Lands)," *American Journal of Medical Science* n.s 51(1866): 364–369; J. Byron, "Negro Regiments—Department of Tennessee," *Boston Medical and Surgical Journal* 69(1863): 43–44.

5. E. Foner, *Reconstruction: America's Unfinished Revolution, 1863–1877* (New York: Harper & Row, 1988); J.S. Haller Jr., *Outcasts from Evolution: Scientific Attitudes of Racial Inferiority, 1859–1900* (Urbana: University of Illinois Press, 1971); G.W. Stocking, *Race, Culture, and Evolution: Essays in the History of Anthropology* (New York Free Press, 1968); D. Lorimer, *Colour, Class, and the Victorians* (New York: Holmes & Meier, 1978); V.N. Gamble, ed., *Germs Have No Color Line: Blacks and American Medicine, 1900–1940* (New York: Garland, 1989).

6. G.J. Barker-Benfield, *The Horrors of the Half-Known Life: Male Attitudes toward Women and Sexuality in Nineteenth-Century America* (New York: Harper & Row, 1976); E. Fee, "Science and the Woman Problem: Historical Perspectives," in *Sex Differences: Social and Biological Perspectives,* ed. M.S. Teitelbaum (New York: Anchor/Doubleday, 1976), 175–223; L. Jordanova, *Sexual Visions: Images of Gender in Science and Medicine between the Eighteenth and Twentieth Centuries* (Madison: University of Wisconsin Press, 1989); B. Ehrenreich and D. English, *Complaints and Disorders: The Sexual Politics of Sickness* (New York: Feminist Press, 1973).

7. C.E. Russett, *Sexual Science: The Victorian Construction of Womanhood* (Cambridge: Harvard University Press, 1989); R. Hubbard, *The Politics of Women's Biology* (New Brunswick, NJ.: Rutgers University Press, 1990).

8. E. Fee, "Nineteenth-Century Craniology: The Study of the Female Skull," *Bulletin of the History of Medicine* 53(1979): 415–433; C. Smith-Rosenberg and C.E. Rosenberg, "The Female Animal: Medical and Biological Views of Woman and Her Role in 19th Century America," *Journal of American History* 60(1973): 332–356; S.J. Gould, *The Mismeasure of Man* (New York: W.W. Norton, 1981).

9. C. Smith-Rosenberg, "Puberty to Menopause: The Cycle of Femininity in Nineteenth-Century America," *Feminist Studies* 1(1973): 58–72; C. Smith Rosenberg, *Disorderly Conduct: Visions of Gender in Victorian America* (New York: Knopf, 1985); J.S. Haller and R.M. Haller, *The Physician and Sexuality in Victorian America* (Urbana: University of Illinois Press, 1974); R.D. Apple, ed., *Women, Health, and Medicine in America: A Historical Handbook* (New Brunswick, NJ.: Rutgers University Press, 1990).

10. R. Williams, *Culture & Society: 1780–1950* (New York: Columbia University Press, 1958, rev. ed. 1983).

11. K. Marx, *Capital,* Vol. 1 (New York: International Publishers, 1967, orig. 1867).

12. R. Hofstadter, *Social Darwinism in American Thought* (Boston: Beacon, 1955); R.M. Young, *Darwin's Metaphor: Nature's Place in Victorian Culture* (Cambridge: Cambridge University Press, 1985); D. J. Kevles, *In the Name of Eugenics: Genetics and the Uses of Human Heredity* (New York: Knopf, 1985); A. Chase, *The Legacy of Malthus: The Social Costs of the New Scientific Racism* (New York: Knopf, 1977).

13. C. Darwin, *On the Origin of Species by Means of Natural Selection, or the Preservation of Favoured Races in the Struggle for Life* (London: Murray, 1859).

14. Hofstadter, *Social Darwinism in American Thought;* Young, *Darwin's Metaphor;* Kevles, *In the Name of Eugenics;* Chase, *The Legacy of Malthus;* all sources *supra* note 12.

15. Haller, *Outcasts from Evolution, supra* note 5; M.J. Anderson, *The American Census: A Social History* (New Haven: Yale University Press, 1988).

16. F.L. Hoffman, *Race Traits and Tendencies of the American Negro* (New York: American Economic Association, 1896); S. Harris, "Tuberculosis in the Negro," *Journal of the American Medical Association* 41(1903): 827; L.C. Allen, "The Negro

Health Problem," *American Journal of Public Health* 5(1915): 194; E.H. Beardsley, *A History of Neglect: Health Care for Blacks and Mill Workers in the Twentieth-Century South* (Knoxville: University of Tennessee Press, 1987).

17. Fee, "Science and the Woman Problem," *supra* note 6; Hofstadter, *Social Darwinism in American Thought, supra* note 12; P. Geddes and J.A. Thompson, *The Evolution of Sex* (London: Walter Scott, 1889).

18. K.M. Ludmerer, *Genetics and American Society: A Historical Appraisal* (Baltimore, Md.: Johns Hopkins University Press, 1972).

19. Hofstadter, *Social Darwinism in American Thought, supra* note 12; Ludmerer, *Genetics and American Society, supra* note 18; J. Higham, *Strangers in the Land: Patterns of American Nativism, 1860–1925,* (New Brunswick, N.J.: Rutgers University Press, 1955); M.H. Haller, *Eugenics: Hereditarian Attitudes in American Thought* (New Brunswick, N.J.: Rutgers University Press, 1963); D.K. Pickens, *Eugenics and the Progressives* (Nashville, Tenn: Vanderbilt University Press, 1968); M. King and S. Ruggles, "American Immigration, Fertility, and Race Suicide at the Turn of the Century," *Journal of Interdisciplinary History* 20(1990): 347–369; C.N. Degler, *In Search of Human Nature: The Decline and Revival of Darwinism in American Social Thought* (Oxford: Oxford University Press, 1991).

20. G.E. Allen, *Life Science in the Twentieth Century* (Cambridge: Cambridge University Press, 1978); W.E. Castle, "The Beginnings of Mendelism in America," in *Genetics in the Twentieth Century,* ed. L.C. Dunn (New York: Macmillan, 1951), 59–76; J.S. Wilkie, "Some Reasons for the Rediscovery and Appreciation of Mendel's Work in the First Years of the Present Century," *British Journal of the History of Science* 1(1962): 5–18; T. H. Morgan, *The Theory of the Gene* (New Haven: Yale University Press, 1926).

21. A.M. Kraut, *The Huddled Masses: The Immigrant in American Society, 1800–1921* (Arlington Heights: Harlan Davison, 1982); G.W. Stoner, "Insane and Mentally Defective Aliens Arriving at the Port of New York," *New York Medical Journal* 97(1913): 957–960; S.T. Solis-Cohen, "The Exclusion of Aliens from the United States for Physical Defects," *Bulletin of the History of Medicine* 21(1947): 33–50.

22. K. Ludmerer, "Genetics, Eugenics, and the Immigration Restriction Act of 1924," *Bulletin of the His-tory of Medicine* 46 (1972): 59–81; E. Barkan, "Reevaluating Progressive Eugenics: Herbert Spencer Jennings and the 1924 Immigration Legislation," *Journal of the History of Biology* 24(1991): 91–112; A.M. Kraut, "Silent Travelers: Germs, Genes, and American Efficiency, 1890–1924," *Social Science History* 12(1988): 377–393.

23. E. Starling, "The Croonian Lectures on the Chemical Correlation of the Functions of the Body," *Lancet* 2(1905): 339–341, 423-425, 501-503, 579-583.

24. J.E. Lane-Claypon and E.H. Starling, "An Experimental Enquiry into the Factors Which Determine the Growth and Activity of the Mammary Glands," *Proceedings of the Royal Society of London, Series B: Biological Sciences* 77(1906) 505–522; F.A. Marshall, *The Physiology of Reproduction* (New York: Longmans, Green, 1910); N. Oudshoorn, "Endocrinologists and the Conceptualization of Sex," *Journal of the History of Biology* 23(1990): 163-187; N. Oudshoorn, "On Measuring Sex Hormones: The Role of Biological Assays in Sexualizing Chemical Substances," *Bulletin of the History of Medicine* 64(1990): 243-261; M. Borrell, "Organotherapy and the Emergence of Reproductive Endocrinology," *Journal of the History of Biology* 18(1985): 1-30.

25. D.L. Long, "Biology, Sex Hormones and Sexism in the 1920s," *Philosophical Forum* 5(1974): 81-96; I.G. Cobb, *The Glands of Destiny (A Study of the Personality)* (New York: Macmillan, 1928).

26. E. Allen, ed., *Sex and Internal Secretions: A Survey of Recent Research* (Baltimore, Md.: Williams and Wilkins, 1939); R. Frank, *The Female Sex Hormone* (Springfield, Ill.: Charles C. Thomas, 1929); A.E.C. Lathrop and L. Loeb, "Further Investigations of the Origin of Tumors in Mice. III. On the Part Played by Internal Secretions in the Spontaneous Development of Tumors," *Journal of Cancer Research* 1(1916): 1-19; J.E. Lane-Claypon, *A Further Report on Cancer of the Breast, With Special Reference to its Associated Antecedent Conditions. Reports on Public Health and Medical Subjects, No. 32* (London: His Majesty's Stationary Office, 1926); J.M. Wainwright, "A Comparison of Conditions Associated with Breast Cancer in Great Britain and America," *American Journal of Cancer* 15(1931): 2610-2645.

27. Apple, *Women, Health, and Medicine in America, supra* note 9; W. Chavkin, ed., *Double Exposure: Women's Health Hazards on the Job and at Home* (New York: Monthly Review Press, 1984); B.

Ehrenreich and D. English, *For Her Own Good: 150 Years of the Experts' Advice to Women* (New York: Anchor, 1979).

28. P. Starr, *The Social Transformation of American Medicine* (New York: Basic, 1982); E. Fee, *Disease and Discovery: A History of the Johns Hopkins School of Hygiene and Public Health* (Baltimore, Md.: Johns Hopkins University Press, 1987); E. Fee and R.M. Acheson, eds., *A History of Education in Public Health: Health that Mocks the Doctors' Rules* (Oxford: Oxford University Press, 1991).

29. E. Fee, ed., *Women and Health: the Politics of Sex in Medicine* (Amityville, New York: Baywood, 1983); Apple, *Women, Health, and Medicine in America, supra* note 9; R. Meckel, *Save the Babies: American Public Health Reform and the Prevention of Infant Mortality, 1850-1920* (Baltimore, Md.: Johns Hopkins University Press, 1990).

30. J. Rodin and J.R. Ickovics, "Women's Health: Review and Research Agenda as We Approach the 21st Century," *American Psychologist* 45(1990): 1018-1034; B. Healy, "Women's Health, Public Welfare," *Journal of the American Medical Association* 266(1991): 566-568; R.L. Kirchstein, "Research on Women's Health," *American Journal of Public Health* 81(1991): 291-293.

31. R. Lewontin, *Human Diversity* (New York: Scientific American Books, 1982); J.C. King, *The Biology of Race* (Berkeley: University of California Press, 1981); R. Cooper and R. David, "The Biological Concept of Race and Its Application to Epidemiology," *Journal of Health Politics Policy Law* 11(1986): 97-116.

32. R. Cooper, "Celebrate Diversity—Or Should We?" *Ethnicity and Disease* 1(1991): 3-7; D.E. Crews and J.R. Bindon, "Ethnicity as a Taxonomic Tool in Biomedical and Biosocial Research," *Ethnicity and Disease* 1(1991): 42-49.

33. L. Mullings, "Ethnicity and Stratification in the Urban United States," *Annals of the New York Academy of Sciences* 318(1978): 10-22; J.R. Feagin, *Racial and Ethnic Relations*, 3rd ed. (Englewood Cliffs, NJ.: Prentice Hall, 1989).

34. J.R. Feagin, "The Continuing Significance of Race: Anti-Black Discrimination in Public Places," *American Sociology Review* 56(1991): 101-116; P. Essed, *Understanding Everyday Racism: An Interdisciplinary Theory* (Newbury Park, Calif.: Sage, 1991); N. Krieger and M. Bassett, "The Health of Black Folk: Disease, Class and Ideology in Science," *Monthly Review* 38(1986): 74-85.

35. S. Polack and J. Grozuczak, *Reagan, Toxics and Minorities: A Policy Report* (Washington, D.C.: Urban Environment Conference, 1984); Commission for Racial Justice, United Church of Christ, *Toxic Wastes and Race in the United States: A National Report on the Racial and Socioeconomic Characteristics of Communities with Hazardous Waste Sites* (New York. United Church of Christ, 1987); E. Mann, *L.A.'s Lethal Air: New Strategies for Policy, Organizing, and Action* (Los Angeles: Labor/Community Strategy Center, 1991).

36. N. Krieger, "Racial and Gender Discrimination: Risk Factors for High Blood Pressure?" *Social Science and Medicine* 30(1990): 1273-1281; C.A. Armstead, K.A. Lawler, G. Gordon, J. Cross, and J. Gibbons, "Relationship of Racial Stressors to Blood Pressure and Anger Expression in Black College Students," *Health Psychology* 8(1989): 541-556; S. James, A.Z. LaCroix, D.G. Kleinbaum, and D.S. Strogatz, "John Henryism and Blood Pressure Differences among Black Men. II. The Role of Occupational Stressors," *Journal of Behavioral Medicine* 7(1984): 259-275; W.W. Dressler, "Social Class, Skin Color, and Arterial Blood Pressure in Two Societies," *Ethnicity and Disease* 1(1991): 60-77.

37. R.G. Fruchter, K. Nayeri, J.C. Remy, C. Wright, J.G. Feldman, J.G. Boyce, and W.S. Burnett, "Cervix and Breast Cancer Incidence in Immigrant Caribbean Women," *American Journal of Public Health* 80(1990): 722-724; J.C. Kleinman, L.A. Fingerhut, and K. Prager, "Differences in Infant Mortality by Race, Nativity, and Other Maternal Characteristics," *American Journal of Diseases of Children* 145(1991): 194-199; H. Cabral, L.E. Fried, S. Levenson, H. Amaro, and B. Zuckerman, "Foreign-born and US-born Black Women: Differences in Health Behaviors and Birth Outcomes," *American Journal of Public Health* 80(1990):70-72.

38. R.J. Taylor and L.M. Chatters, "Religious Life," in *Life in Black America*, ed. J.S. Jackson (Newbury Park, Calif.: Sage, 1991): 105-123; I.L. Livingston, D.M. Levine, and R.D. Moore, "Social Integration and Black Intraracial Variation in Blood Pressure," *Ethnicity and Disease* 1(1991): 135-149; E. Eng, J. Hatch, and A. Callan, "Institutionalizing Social Support through the Church and into the Community," *Health Education Quarterly* 12(1985): 81-92.

39. Fruchter et al., "Cervix and Breast Cancer Incidence in Immigrant Caribbean Women," *supra*

note 37; S.S. Devesa and E.L. Diamond, "Association of Breast Cancer and Cervical Cancer Incidence with Income and Education among Whites and Blacks," *Journal of the National Cancer Institute* 65(1980): 515-528.

40. N. Krieger, "Social Class and the Black/White Crossover in the Age-specific Incidence of Breast Cancer: A Study Linking Census-derived Data to Population-based Registry Records," *American Journal of Epidemiology* 131(1990): 804-814; N. Krieger, "The Influence of Social Class, Race and Gender on the Etiology of Hypertension Among Women in the United States," in proceedings of the conference *Women, Behavior, and Cardiovascular Disease,* sponsored by the National Heart, Lung, and Blood Institute, Chevy Chase, Md., September 25-27, 1991.

41. U.S. Department of Health and Human Services, *Health Status of Minorities and Low-Income Groups,* 3rd ed. (Washington, D.C.: U.S. Government Printing Office, 1991).

42. M. Martinez-Maldonado, "Hypertension in Hispanics, Asians and Pacific Islanders, and Native Americans," *Circulation* 83(1991): 1467-1469; P.U. Caralis, "Hypertension in the Hispanic-American Population," *American Journal of Medicine* 88, suppl. 3b(1990): 9s-16s.

43. S.M. Haffner, B.D. Mitchell, M.P. Stern, H.P. Hazuda, and J.K. Patterson, "Decreased Prevalence of Hypertension in Mexican-Americans," *Hypertension* 16(1990): 225-232.

44. Martinez-Maldonado, "Hypertension in Hispanics," *supra* note 42; G.R. Stavig, A. Igra, and A.R. Leonard, "Hypertension and Related Health Issues among Asians and Pacific Islanders in California," *Public Health Reports* 103(1988): 28-37; A. Angel, M.A. Armstrong, and A.L. Klatsky, "Blood Pressure among Asian Americans Living in Northern California," *American Journal of Cardiology* 54(1987): 237-240.

45. J.S. Alpert, R. Goldberg, I.S. Ockene, and P. Taylor, "Heart Disease in Native Americans," *Cardiology* 78(1991): 3-12; Martinez-Maldonado, "Hypertension in Hispanics, Asians and Pacific Islanders, and Native Americans."

46. U.S. Department of Health and Human Services, *Health Status of Minorities and Low-Income Groups, supra* note 41; Stavig et al., "Hypertension and Related Health Issues Among Asians and Pacific Islanders in California," *supra* note 44.

47. I. Waldron, "Sex Differences in Illness, Incidence, Prognosis and Mortality: Issues and Evidence," *Social Science and Medicine* 17(1983): 1107-1123; D.L. Wingard, "The Sex Differential in Morbidity, Mortality, and Lifestyle," *Annual Review of Public Health* 5(1984): 433-458.

48. Ibid.

49. E. Gold, ed., *Changing Risk of Disease in Women: An Epidemiological Approach* (Lexington, Mass.: Colbamore, 1984).

50. V. Leviatan and J. Cohen, "Gender Differences in Life Expectancy among Kibbutz Members," *Social Science and Medicine* 21(1985): 545-551.

51. S.L. Syme and L. Berkman, "Social Class, Susceptibility and Sickness," *American Journal of Epidemiology* 104(1976): 1-8; A. Antonovsky, "Social Class, Life Expectancy and Overall Mortality," *Milbank Memorial Fund Quarterly* 45(1967): 31-73; P. Townsend, N. Davidson, and M. Whitehead, *Inequalities in Health: The Black Report and The Health Divide* (Harmondsworth, England: Penguin, 1988); M.G. Marmot, M. Kogevinas, and M.A Elston, "Social/economic Status and Disease," *Annual Review of Public Health* 8(1987): 111-135; V. Navarro, "Race or Class versus Race and Class: Morality Differentials in the United States," *Lancet* (1990): 1238-1240.

52. N. Krieger and E. Fee, "What's Class Got to Do with It? The State of Health Data in the United States Today," *Socialist Review* 23(1993): 59-82; H. Roberts, ed., *Women's Health Counts* (London: Routledge, 1990).

53. A. Dale, G.N. Gilbert, and S. Arber, "Integrating Women into Class Theory," *Sociology* 19(1985): 384-409; V. Duke and S. Edgell, "The Operationalisation of Class in British Sociology: Theoretical and Empirical Considerations," *British Journal of Sociology* 8(1987): 445-463; N. Charles, "Women and Class—A Problematic Relationship," *Sociology Review* 38 (1990): 43-89.

54. Roberts, *Women's Health Counts, supra* note 52.

55. N. Krieger, "Women and Social Class: A Methodological Study Comparing Individual, Household, and Census Measures as Predictors of Black/White Differences in Reproductive History," *Journal of Epidemiology and Community Health* 45(1991): 35-42; P. Ries, "Health Characteristics According to Family and Personal Income, United States," *Vital Health Statistics,* ser. 10, no. 147(1985), National Center for Health Statistics, DHHS Pub. No. (PHS) 85-1575.

56. N. Krieger, "Overcoming the Absence of Socioe-

conomic Data in Medical Records: Validation and Application of a Census-based Methodology," *American Journal of Public Health* 82(1992): 703-710.

57. K. Carovano, "More than Mothers and Whores: Redefining the AIDS Prevention Needs of Women," *International Journal of Health Services* 21(1991): 131-142; PANOS Institute, *Triple Jeopardy: Women & AIDS* (London: Panos, 1990); K. Anastos and C. Marte, "Women—The Missing Persons in the AIDS Epidemic," *HealthPAC* (winter 1989): 6-13.

58. Centers for Disease Control, "1993 Revised Classification System for HIV Infection and Expanded Surveillance Case Definition for AIDS among Adolescents and Adults," *Morbidity and Mortality Weekly Report* 41(1992): 961-962; R. Kanigel, "U.S. Broadens AIDS Definition: Ac-

tivists Spur Change by Centers for Disease Control," *Oakland Tribune,* January 1, 1993, A1.

59. Centers for Disease Control and Prevention, *HIV/AIDS Surveillance Report* 5(July 1993) 1-19.

60. Ibid.

61. PANOS Institute, *Triple Jeopardy, supra* note 57.

62. E. Drucker, "Epidemic in the War Zone: AIDS and Community Survival in New York City," *International Journal of Health Services* 20(1990): 601-616; N. Freudenberg, "AIDS Prevention in the United States: Lessons from the First Decade," *International Journal of Health Services* 20 (1990): 589-600.

63. E. Fee and N. Krieger, "Thinking and Rethinking AIDS: Implications for Health Policy," *International Journal for Health Services* 23(1993): 323-346.

The New Procreative Technologies

Ruth Hubbard

Some of the most recent research in biology is being applied in the new procreative technologies. Prenatal diagnosis and screening are becoming part of routine prenatal care, and new technical interventions can help people who are unable to beget or conceive children or to carry pregnancies to term to have children who are biologically related to at least one of the future social parents. Some of the techniques can also help people without partners of the other sex to have biological children. Why the new, or surely increased, impulse to proceed into these areas? It would be a mistake to assume that this impulse is driven mainly by the availability of new biotechnologies. Technologies can open new possibilities, but we usually do not pursue them unless there are interest groups who want, and have the power to explore and implement, them. So what are the interests?

The Meaning of Procreative Choice

The ideology of procreative choice has become important in our society. In the course of the last hundred years, we in the middle and upper-middle class, who are used to being able to plan other aspects of our lives, have come to expect that we can plan our families. We decide how many children we want and when we are ready to have them. We practice contraception and, if it fails, abortion in order to implement these decisions. Throughout we tend to assume that we will be able to have a child when we are ready. If we try and nothing happens, we feel not only distressed but wronged—and not by God or fate, as we might have in previous times, but by our bodies. In a time of artificial hearts and kidneys, we expect medical technology to be able to solve such problems. What is more, we do not want to have just any child. We want a healthy one because a child who needs more than the usual care or needs it for longer than usual will be hard to fit into our plans. Thus, prenatal diagnosis and the new technologies that let people have biological children have become part of planning our families.

Yet this kind of family planning is not a possibility for everyone. Owing largely to the work of women of color, the women's movement has begun to acknowledge that women are not a homogeneous group. Not only do we differ as individuals, but we fall into groups with common interests that may be different from those of other groups of women. We have finally realized that people who use the word *women* without qualifiers tend to focus their attention mainly on the young, white, fairly affluent women who became identified with the women's movement in the 1960s. These women have produced major changes; but if the women's movement is to continue to be a force for progressive change, it is essential that we acknowledge the differences in women's needs and interests.

It is not enough to address the issue of diversity without speaking explicitly about racism and class discrimination. And this need is nowhere more apparent than in our concerns about procreation, some of which I will discuss in the sections that follow. The way feminists have framed the important issues in this area betrays the individualistic bias of the affluent, white, American upper-middle class. Our watchwords have been "reproductive freedom" and "choice" but we have not emphasized sufficiently that access to economic and social resources is essential to freedom of choice. In the United States poor women, who because of racism are disproportionately women of color, cannot count on having adequate housing, food, healthcare, jobs, and childcare. Yet all these necessities are basic to procreative freedom and choice. The most recent report of the Washington-based Children's Defense Fund documents the dismal economic situation in which large numbers of women and children in this country are living after many years of inflation, privatization, and cuts in government expenditures for human services.

Most people take the phrase *procreative choice* to mean the choice not to have children, surely an important concern for all women who have sex with men. But procreative choice also needs to mean the choice to have children in the confidence that we will be able to care for them. And that choice is not available to many poor women and usually is not even acknowledged as part of procreative choice.

In the late nineteenth and first half of the twentieth century, a scientific and social movement developed with the aim of denying procreative choice to certain kinds of people. This eugenics movement had as its aim furthering procreation among affluent, native-born, white Americans, while discouraging poor people, immigrants, and other "undesirables" from having children by persuasion and sometimes by forcible sterilization. The birth-control movement, under the leadership of feminists like Margaret Sanger, incorporated considerable portions of this ideology.

In the sections that follow I discuss some of the ramifications of prenatal diagnosis, fetal therapy, and in vitro fertilization. But we must acknowledge from the start that these technologies are not intended for all people who might feel they need them. They are expensive and often require that clients be sophisticated in the ways they relate to the medical system. Also, the techniques designed to enable people to have children are clearly intended for those who fit the stereotypic image of "the family"—bread-winning dad, homemaking mom, and their children. They are not meant for poor people, hence not for the disproportionate number of people of color who are poor. They are not meant for lesbians or gay men. They certainly are not meant for people with disabilities. In fact, these people are high on the list of folks expected to use prenatal testing. They are supposed to avoid having children, and if they are so improvident as to want children, surely to do all they can to avoid having children who have disabilities. ...

Medical Implications of Prenatal Technologies

In the early 1950s it became possible to identify fetuses who are at risk for serious disabilities because they are Rh positive while their mothers are Rh negative. Such women produce antibodies against the Rh antigen in the fetus's blood, and, during successive pregnancies, the antibody concentration can increase sufficiently to endanger the health, or even the life, of the fetus they are carrying. This was the first instance of prenatal diagnosis. The rationale for performing the diagnosis before birth was to enable physicians to be ready to give the baby massive blood transfusions immediately after birth so as to minimize the damage. More recently, physicians have become able to transfuse such a fetus in utero. A few other prenatal diagnostic procedures were developed in the late 1960s and early 1970s.

Since 1972, when *Roe* v. *Wade* made abortion legal at least until the twenty-fourth week of pregnancy, an early diagnosis of fetal health problems has given women the option to abort a fetus that is expected to be born with a disease or disability with which they feel unable to cope. And the availability of prenatal tests has made it possible for women who have reason to believe their prospective children are at risk for a particular, serious health problem to go ahead and become pregnant knowing that they can find out whether the fetus they are carrying is affected with the disease in question. They then have the chance to decide whether to carry the pregnancy to term. Needless to say, the tests cannot guarantee that the fetus does not have some other, unanticipated, health problem. But that is true for any of us and the chance of its happening is small.

By now, quite a number of prenatal tests can be performed, and many more will become available as the project to identify and sequence the human genome gets under way. Some of them involve simply testing samples of the pregnant woman's blood; others are more invasive. Amniocentesis, one of the more usual procedures, requires that a sample of the amniotic fluid that surrounds the fetus in the womb be withdrawn by means of a hypodermic syringe and needle inserted near the pregnant woman's navel. The amniotic fluid can then be tested directly, or the fetal cells that are suspended in it can be cultured under sterile conditions and tested biochemically or examined under the microscope when a sufficient number of cells have accumulated. Amniocentesis cannot be performed until there is sufficient amniotic fluid, which usually requires waiting until about the sixteenth to eighteenth week of pregnancy.

A still experimental procedure, called chorionic villus sampling (CVS), enables physicians to collect fetal cells considerably earlier in a pregnancy than amniocentesis does. The cells are obtained by inserting a probe through the cervix into the uterus and snipping a small sample from the chorion, which is one of the membranes that surrounds the fetus. CVS must be performed during the first trimester, between the eighth and tenth weeks of pregnancy. Another procedure, called fetoscopy, is used rarely. It involves withdrawing samples of blood or other body fluids or tissues from the fetus itself.

Health Risks of Medicalizing Pregnancy and Birth

Feminist scholars have been documenting the transformation of birth and the ways this change has affected our concepts of motherhood. Birth used to be a social event, experienced at home, in which the birthing woman could get advice and support from female relatives and friends who had borne children. If a midwife was present, she usually was from the birthing woman's class and ethnic and racial group and might know her socially and have attended births by her friends and neighbors. Now childbirth takes place in a hospital, where it is made to conform to medical and hospital routines. Judith Walzer Leavitt (1987) has shown that as long as women gave birth at home, they retained considerable control, even when they were attended by male physicians. And given the risks of childbirth during the nineteenth century, many women who could afford it felt more secure in the care of physicians than they did without them. The real change, Leavitt argues, came with the move from the home, which was the birthing woman's turf, to the hospital, where physicians were in charge.

In 1900, about half of U.S. births were attended by midwives; in 1935, only about one-sixth, mostly in the rural South; and by 1972, 99 percent of births were attended by physicians. Fewer than 5 percent of women had their babies in hospitals in 1900; about half the births took place there in 1940; and essentially all of them did by 1960.

During the same period, many other changes occurred in American society and in medical knowledge and practices. New scientific ideas were formulated about the causes and proper treatment of disease. Industrialization changed patterns of transportation and urbanization, which affected the availability of food and produced changes in diet. People's ways of working and living were transformed. Maternal and infant mortality rates decreased, and life expectancies increased.

The lower rates of maternal and infant deaths and diseases cannot be attributed to any one of these changes and certainly not to the changes in birth practices. Quite the contrary. The shifts from midwives to physicians and from home to hospital births were detrimental to the health of many women and babies, particularly the poorer ones who often ended up with less individualized and expert care than before or with no care at all.

Since the beginning of medical interventions in birth, these have held some risks for women and their babies. From the eighteenth century until the discovery of antibiotics in the late 1930s, childbed fever (also called puerperal fever) took an enormous toll on women's lives and health. It was brought on by physicians with insufficient understanding of their role in spreading bacterial infections.

Similarly, artificial induction and excessive use of forceps damaged infants and their mothers. In 1920, in the first issue of the *American Journal of Obstetrics and Gynecology*, Dr. Charles B. Reed described several methods to induce birth artificially, which, he claimed, were safer than normal birth. In the same issue, Dr. Joseph DeLee advocated the prophylactic (that is, preventive) use of forceps and episiotomy (enlarging the vaginal opening by making a deep cut in the vaginal muscle). He wrote that with proper management and repair, episiotomies produced healthier babies and less debilitated women with "virginal" vaginas, which leads me to conclude that he was primarily concerned with the advantages a woman's husband would derive from the procedure. Dr. DeLee also advocated using morphine and scopolamine. He wrote that women were so frequently injured during childbirth that he "often wondered whether Nature did not deliberately intend women to be used up in the process of reproduction, in a manner analogous to that of the salmon which dies after spawning," a poetic metaphor that may have been rendered more apt by his forceps and scalpel.

By the 1940s and 1950s, hospitals were routinely using hormones to initiate and speed labor, and barbiturates and scopolamine to erase all memory of the birthing experience. Because these drugs impede the higher brain functions, they were said to induce twilight sleep, a condition in which women could "take orders" from their physicians but not "know" what was happening to them or "remember" it. Because the drugs suspended women's capacities to think rationally, they were tied down to keep them from injuring themselves as they thrashed about during labor. A labor room of the period was a superb confirmation of the cultural stereotype of women as irrational creatures who needed knowledgeable and rational men to protect them against their own unreason. There is no better place to go for a description of what this kind of birthing felt like than to Adrienne Rich's (1976) account of giving birth in Boston during the 1950s.

Twilight sleep throughout labor and birth was in wide use until the 1960s. It was discontinued partly because of the opposition of women's health advocates to the unnecessary medicalization of birth, partly because of mounting evidence that it was bad for babies. Fetuses inevitably got their share of the medication given to birthing women, so that the babies were born half-asleep, limp, and often in need of resuscitation. In the 1950s some hospitals began to depend on spinal anaesthesia, which allowed birthing women to remain conscious without feeling pain because it deprived them of all sensations below the waist. As a result, they could not push the baby out, so birthing required the use of forceps, another potential source of damage to newborns and their mothers.

The early 1960s witnessed the thalidomide disaster. Physicians prescribed this drug to allay nausea and other discomforts some women experience early in pregnancy. Before thalidomide was recalled, its use had resulted in the birth of thousands of limbless infants in Great Britain, Germany and other countries of Western Europe, and Canada. In the United States, we were spared only by the thoroughness and foresight of Dr. Frances E. Kelsey of the federal Food and Drug Administration, who refused to clear this new drug for sale because of insufficient proof of its safety.

During the 1950s and 1960s physicians prescribed the hormones progestin and diethyl stilbestrol (D.E.S.), sometimes routinely, in the mistaken belief that they prevented miscarriages early in pregnancy. Both can harm a fetus. However, because progestin induces excessive growth of the infant's clitoris so that it resembles a penis, the damage was obvious at birth and the use in pregnancy was stopped before long. Unfortunately, physicians did not realize until the late 1970s that D.E.S.

could induce a rare form of vaginal cancer and perhaps also testicular cancer and reproductive deficiencies among the daughters and sons pregnant women were carrying at the time they received the drug.

It would be a mistake to believe that all, or perhaps even most, women were unwilling victims of these medical interventions. Many women welcomed the relief offered by drugs, much as they welcomed contraception and baby bottles as respites from the stresses of motherhood. They accepted the reasons physicians gave why drugs and other interventions were necessary as well as physicians' assurances that the interventions were safe and likely to improve birth outcomes. Yet with the best will in the world, physicians cannot foresee the risks of their interventions in pregnancy and birth—risks for women and for our children. At present, physicians seem to feel that it is all right to use the new diagnostic tools and therapies as long as prospective parents have the opportunity to give their informed consent. But what does "informed" mean when applied to new procedures whose benefits and risks cannot be assessed accurately?

Most therapies become established on the basis of custom and professional consensus and are not preceded by rigorous, scientific evaluations of their outcomes. Usually, by the time therapies are tested in scientifically controlled clinical trials, they have been in use for years. Even after the trials are completed, the results are often contested. For this reason many clinicians trust their intuition and experience more than they trust scientific experiments.

Most of the information prospective parents get about the relative merits of different ways to proceed during pregnancy and birth depends on their physician's ideas about the appropriate course. Particularly with new interventions, prospective parents have access to few, if any, other sources of information. Therefore "informed consent" is better than nothing because it at least obliges physicians to try to explain what they plan to do and their reasons, but it serves mainly to provide legal protection for practitioners and hospitals. There is no way people who do not have access to a range of sources of information can make independent judgments and give truly informed consent.

That is a problem "lay" people always confront when they must make choices about technical matters, be it nuclear energy or prenatal interventions. If there is disagreement among the experts—and there often is—it usually boils down to deciding, on the basis of various criteria, which experts to trust. In the case of nuclear energy, we can gain at least some reassurance from the fact that the experts must live with the outcome. When it comes to interventions in pregnancy, only we and our families have to live with the results, not our physicians.

All tests must be as specific and accurate as possible. That means that there must be a high degree of probability that the condition one intends to test for is the only one being tested, and that the test will not indicate that the condition is present when it is not (false positives), or that it is not present when it is (false negatives). No test satisfies these criteria perfectly, but the better the test, the closer it must come to doing so.

What other risks need women consider? Tests that can be done on samples of blood drawn from the pregnant woman are not likely to impose physical risks because drawing blood is fairly routine. At present, blood samples can be used to measure the level of alpha-feto-protein (AFP), a protein secreted by the fetus at certain stages of development that enters the bloodstream of the pregnant woman. Maternal serum alpha-feto-protein (MSAFP) levels are used to indicate whether the baby is likely to have spina bifida (a malformation of the neural tube) or anencephaly (no brain), both quite rare conditions. MSAFP levels are also now being used as preliminary indications that the baby may have Down syndrome.

Because amniocentesis involves inserting a needle through a pregnant woman's abdominal wall into her uterus, it is more invasive and riskier than blood tests. This is so even when the amniocentesis is done while monitoring the position of the fetus and placenta by means of ultrasound so as not to damage them. If sufficient amniotic fluid has been collected, its AFP content and other chemical properties can be checked. The fetal cells that float in the amniotic fluid can be biochemically tested for specific diseases such as cystic fibrosis, sickle-cell anemia, or Tay-Sachs disease if there is some reason to think the baby might inherit one of them. In order to detect chromosomal abnormalities, such as are present in people who have Down syndrome, it is necessary to culture the fetal cells, which can take two weeks or more. Ultrasound by itself can reveal anatomical malformations of the fetal skeleton, nervous system, kidneys, and other organs.

Ultrasound is said to be safe because no ill effects are seen in newborns and children, but it is not clear how to evaluate this claim. There is no question that at higher levels than those ordinarily used for diagnosis ultrasound damages chromosomes and other intracellular structures and breaks up cells. And, as with other radiation, it is questionable whether there is a threshold level below which ultrasound is absolutely safe and to what extent the effects of successive exposures may be cumulative. Symposia that have reviewed the available evidence have usually ended by warning against the indiscriminate use of ultrasound, and some physicians continue to urge caution.

By now, ultrasound is used so routinely to monitor pregnancy and birth and its effects could be so varied that it will take extremely careful studies, involving large numbers of children over long periods of time, to determine whether there are risks and what they are. While such studies are in progress, prospective parents must rely on physicians' assurances not to worry. Unfortunately we were also told not to worry about x-rays, which eventually were shown to provoke an increase in the incidence of childhood cancers and leukemias. It is always a question of balancing possible risks and benefits. In some situations, the immediate benefits of ultrasound imaging clearly outweigh its possible long-term risks. At other times, the balance of benefits and risks is not so clear, and it is often hard to know where to draw the line. Unfortunately, at present many obstetricians believe that using ultrasound involves no risks.

If it is done by an experienced practitioner, amniocentesis carries a small risk of mechanical injury to the fetus or placenta and a somewhat greater risk of infection. In about one case in three or four hundred, for unknown reasons, amniocentesis results in a spontaneous abortion. CVS may involve less risk of infection than does amniocentesis but a somewhat greater risk of spontaneous abortion. There is also a greater chance of wrong diagnoses with CVS because the cells that are removed from the fetal membranes do not always have the same chromosomal constitution as the fetus itself. However, CVS has the advantage of being performed sufficiently early to permit a first-trimester abortion if the results lead the woman to decide to have one. Amniocentesis, however, necessarily involves a second-trimester abortion, which is more dangerous and psychologically stressful. Risk of spontaneous abortion from fetoscopy is much greater than from amniocentesis or CVS and so are the risks of infection and mechanical damage.

If the only alternative to prenatal testing is not to have children because one or both partners consider the risk of having a child with a particular health problem to be too high, they may be prepared to accept considerable risks from prenatal diagnosis, hoping that they will learn that the fetus does not have the disability in question. Even so, they may have difficulty accepting the possibility of injuring or losing a fetus that would have been healthy.

Because of the fear and costs of malpractice suits, physicians increasingly feel that they need to perform tests so as to be legally covered in case a baby is born with a health problem they could have detected. And because of the responsibilities and costs of raising a

child with a serious disability, prospective parents also feel pressure to use the tests. Therefore, as the number of conditions that can be diagnosed before birth increases, more women will have to decide whether to undergo testing. If they do, they will experience the uncertainty of waiting for results, which is often the most difficult part of the procedure. Reports can be slow to come, and the decision whether to abort becomes increasingly difficult as the pregnancy advances. There is no reason to doubt that this kind of stress on a pregnant woman gets communicated to her fetus. Yet threats of legal action against pregnant women as well as physicians increase the pressure to test.

If it is too soon reliably to evaluate the medical risks of prenatal diagnosis, this is even more true for fetal therapy, which is newer. At this point, fetuses are being treated mostly for hydrocephalus ("water on the brain") and for malformations or malfunctioning of the urinary tracts. These are reasonable conditions to try to remedy during pregnancy because the fetus has a better chance to develop normally if the problem is repaired. However, the risk exists that the problem will be repaired but that the baby will be born with life-threatening disabilities. To date, several fetuses who were treated in utero have been born with serious disabilities; a few have been normal; still others have died before or shortly after birth. And, of course, all the interventions are hazardous for the pregnant woman....

Prenatal Technologies and the Experience of Childbearing

I now want to explore some implications of the prenatal technologies for the experience of childbearing. Obviously, I do not mean to imply that there is just one kind of childbearing experience. I assume there are as many experiences as there are women bearing children, and that they range from bliss to agony because they depend on the social and personal circumstances of our lives. However, the new technologies raise issues that can affect all these experiences, although they may affect different ones differently.

Childbearing: A Social Construct

Before going further, I want to clear up one point: I am not trying to distinguish between "natural" and "technological" childbearing practices (and by childbearing I mean the entire range of women's activities from conception through birth and lactation). No human pregnancy is simply "natural." Societies define, order, circumscribe, and interpret all our activities and experiences. Just as our sexual practices are socially constructed and not a natural unfolding of inborn instincts, so our ways of structuring and experiencing pregnancy and birth are shaped by society.

Whether a woman goes off to give birth by herself (as !Kung women do in the Kalahari desert), calls in neighboring women and perhaps a midwife (as my grandmother did in her small town in eastern Europe), goes to a lying-in hospital (as I did in Boston around 1960), or has a lay midwife be with her and her partner at home (as several of my friends have done recently), all these are socially devised ways, approved by one's community, even if sometimes not by the medical profession or the state.

The question we feminists must ask is not which is more "natural" but to what extent different ways of giving birth empower women or, alternatively, decrease our power to structure childbearing around our own needs and those of the people with whom we live.

By now, periodic visualization of the fetus by means of ultrasound is considered routine prenatal care by many physicians in the United States and much of Europe. Indeed, in some places ultrasound visualization is mandatory at least once or twice during pregnancy. Real-time ultrasound recording allows women and their attendants to view the fetus, so to speak, in action. It also tends to reveal its sex. Most prospective parents agree that ultrasound visualization makes the fetus more real, more their baby. However, as we saw in the last section, for some women (although for which ones in the United States may depend more on their social and economic circumstances than on their health needs), ultrasound visualization is followed by amniocentesis and the possibility of a second-trimester abortion, so no baby.

These interventions, and indeed the mere fact that they may occur, affect the way we look on our pregnancies. At the very least, we must decide whether to accept the interventions and how far to take them—something we can still usually do. So you see that pregnancy has become very different from what it was as recently as the 1970s, when once women decided to become pregnant (or to accept an accidental pregnancy), they did not face further decisions about whether to carry the pregnancy to term.

Let me be clear: I completely support every woman's right to decide whether and when to bear a child. She must, therefore, have the right to abort a fetus, whatever her reasons. What is more, on the basis of my own and other people's experiences as pregnancy counselors, I know that the decision to abort need not be traumatic. Whether it is depends on the social context in which it is made and implemented. But it is one thing to terminate a pregnancy when we don't want to be pregnant and quite another to want a baby but to decide to abort the particular fetus we are carrying in the hope of coming up with a "better" one next time.

Research studies and personal accounts are beginning to document women's mixed responses to prenatal diagnosis and the necessity to decide whether to terminate a wanted pregnancy because the baby may be abnormal. The abortion itself may not be so bad once the decision is made, but some of my friends have told me how much they have hated the two or three weeks of waiting while the fetal cells were being cultured and tested, knowing that they might end up deciding not to continue the pregnancy. This state of uncertainty can last until the twentieth week—halfway through the pregnancy and several weeks after most women begin to feel the fetus move. By that time, many women look on it very much as their baby.

Ultrasound and amniocentesis confront women with a contradiction: Ultrasound makes the fetus more real and more our baby, while the possibility of following it with an abortion makes us want to keep our emotional distance in case we will not end up with a baby after all.

The specific problems are somewhat different with CVS, which is still considered experimental but is likely to be generally available soon. As we saw in the last section, CVS results somewhat more frequently in wrong diagnoses (both positive and negative) than does amniocentesis and in a slightly higher rate of spontaneous abortions. However, it lets women who have reason to fear for the health of their fetus have tests early enough to allow for a first-trimester abortion if they decide to terminate the pregnancy.

When even easier methods than we now have become available to examine a fetus early in pregnancy, the pressure to screen fetuses will increase. Once scientists develop a way to identify cells of fetal origin in the bloodstream of pregnant women, which is likely to happen before long, fetal screening could become a routine part of prenatal care.

The Question of Choice

The means to "choose" the kind of baby a parent will accept bring their own problems no matter at what point in the pregnancy they can be used. To sort these problems out, we need to put this new kind of decision into historical perspective.

In most cultures women have exercised a measure of choice about procreation by practicing some form of birth control—from contraceptive and abortifacient herbs and barrier methods to infanticide. But, until recent times, unwanted pregnancies, hazards of childbearing, and high rates of infant and early childhood mortality have made women's reproductive lives largely a matter of chance. Only during the last century have contraception and abortion gradually become sufficiently available, accepted, and reliable that socially and economically privileged women expect to be able to choose whether and when to become pregnant. At the same time, in the technologically developed, affluent countries, maternal and child health have improved sufficiently for us to be able to assume that the children we bear will become adults.

Full of this new confidence, the more privileged of us seem to have glided over into the illusion that we can control not only whether and when to have children, but the kind and quality of children we will "choose" to have. Barbara Katz Rothman (1984, 1989) points out that in this consumer society people tend to look on children as products that they can or cannot "afford." And, by that way of reckoning, it is realistic to look on the prospect of raising a child with a serious disability as beyond our means. In our economy, raising children is expensive. And in the United States, which is the only industrialized country besides South Africa without universal health insurance, the expense of bringing up a child with a disability can be overwhelming. Indeed, Americans often meet the challenge of disability with litigation as a way to increase their financial resources.

Recent medical and social practices have made it possible to commodify procreation all along the line, with eggs, sperm, embryos, "surrogate mothers," and babies available for a price. Some babies who are up for adoption are for sale outright, although this is illegal. Legal adoption agencies prohibit cash payments, but because they are at pains to establish the financial "soundness" of prospective parents, economic status is clearly important for being considered a fit adoptive parent. Once procreation is a form of commodity production, it is an easy step to require quality control. And at this point genetic screening, ultrasound visualization, and the other prenatal tests come in.

Yet all these tests carry a price tag, and many of them are scarce resources. They are not, and indeed cannot be, available to everyone. While affluent women come to view the new tests and other techniques as liberating advances that improve our lives, economically less privileged and socially more defenseless women continue to be deprived of the ability to procreate. Forced sterilizations still happen, often by means of hysterectomy. Less extreme measures also deny choice. For example, legal and financial restrictions that limit access to abortion force pregnant women who want an abortion but cannot afford it to "choose" a hysterectomy, which is covered by social insurance in all states except Arizona, which has never had Medicaid.

The consumerist way of looking at procreation creates the illusion that at least those of us who can afford prenatal tests have the choice to have healthy babies. But that choice is a mirage because it exists only in a few circumscribed situations. Each test can provide information only about a specific disability. Therefore tests help parents who have reason to worry that their child will be born with a particular disability. They cannot guarantee a healthy baby. But before I say more about the limits of our ability to predict the health of our future children, I want to raise another issue.

Trade-Offs of Scientific Progress

Feminists have often portrayed medical interventions in pregnancy as part of an attempt by men to control women's capacity to bear children. And although I agree with much in this analysis, I am bothered by the way it downgrades, and sometimes romanticizes, the pain and travail childbearing has meant for many women. Bearing and rearing children is difficult under the conditions in which most women live. Judith Walzer Leavitt (1987) amply illustrates this in her book *Brought to Bed*, in which she describes the history of childbearing in America. The literary historian Ruth Perry (1979) has calculated that in eighteenth-century England a married woman who "delivered six children (a not unusual number) ... had at least a ten percent chance of dying, and probably a much higher one." It is small wonder that women have welcomed anesthetics and the other interventions physicians introduced, hoping that these would lessen the danger and pain of pregnancy and birth.

True, the medical "improvements" took their toll. As we have seen, they brought their own dangers and gave physicians altogether too much authority and control over the ways women experience pregnancy and birth as well as over child rearing. Yet, given the limited choices most women have had and the very real risks of childbearing, it is not surprising that upper-class women in the nineteenth century opted for the benefits their physicians promised them.

Now once again we are at a point where many women believe that the new interventions in pregnancy are increasing procreative choice and improving our lives as well as those of our families. As the new technologies become part of routine pregnancy management, the experiences of past generations of women are erased, and contemporary women find it impossible to imagine how they could live without technologies that women in the past did not miss and often were better off doing without.

Take the pill as an example. Many women who became heterosexually active in the early 1960s seem to think that birth control was rare, if not unknown, for women earlier in the century. Yet in the pre-pill era, many women planned their pregnancies as successfully as women who use the newer products do now. True, condoms and diaphragms involve problems and inconveniences, but from a health viewpoint they are safer than the newer methods. And these days, when protection against AIDS should be on all our minds, a shift back to condoms, used together with spermicides, is widely recommended.

Another example is pregnancies of older women. In this context "older" denotes younger and younger women as time goes on. It used to be over forty; in this country, it is now over thirty-five; I suppose thirty-two and thirty are next. This change seems strange to me, who had my children when I was between thirty-five and forty. I did not think there was anything to worry about because my partner and I were in good health, and when I mentioned my age to the obstetrician, he agreed with this assessment.

Now women that age tell me that if it were not for prenatal diagnosis, they would not dare to have a child. Indeed, because it has been hammered into the present generation of "older" women that the risk of bearing a child with a chromosomal abnormality, such as Down syndrome, increases dramatically after the early thirties, few will just hope for the best when a test can reassure them while they are pregnant. And because all abnormalities are rare, it usually does just that. This reassuring feature is what makes for the popularity of the tests: More often than not they show that there is no problem.

But most of us would not need that reassurance if it were not for the prevalent emphasis on risks. The reasons why chromosomal abnormalities occur when they do are far from clear, and there has not been a great deal of epidemiological research on them. What are the environmental, occupational, and socioeconomic influences? How relevant are the health histories of both partners? And so forth. In the midst of such uncertainties, the prospective mother's age is the only factor we are urged to consider, even though either prospective parent can contribute the extra chromosome responsible for Down syndrome.

I have a not so sci-fi fantasy in which a woman ten years hence will tell me that she could not possibly risk having a child by "in-body fertilization." She will say that only the availability of in vitro fertilization makes childbearing possible. In my fantasy, it will by then be standard practice to fertilize eggs in vitro and allow the embryo to go through the first few cell divisions until it contains six or eight cells. At this point two of its cells will be removed, cultured, and put through a battery of tests, while the rest of the embryo will be frozen and placed in cold storage. Only if the tests are satisfactory will the embryo be thawed and implanted in the prospective mother's, or some other carrier's womb. Otherwise, it will be discarded or used for research.

How will I explain to this woman why I am troubled by this, by then routine, way of producing babies? We will live in different worlds. I in one in which I continue to look upon childbearing as a healthy, normal function that can sometimes go wrong but usually doesn't. Therefore I will want to interfere as little as possible with the delicate, complicated processes of fertilization and embryonic development. She will live in a world in which the ability to plan procreation means using all available medical techniques to try to avoid the possibility of biological malfunctioning. I will tell her that the manipulations entail unknown and unpredictable risks and that they cannot assure her of having a healthy baby. She will tell me that I am opting for ignorance and stemming progress. But what worries me most is that at that point "in-body fertilization" will not only be considered old-fashioned and quaint, but foolhardy, unhealthful, and unsafe. It will seem that way to the scientists and physicians who pioneer the "improvements" and to the women who "choose" to have their babies the new way.

Nowadays, some women over thirty-five refuse prenatal diagnosis and other, usually poor or Third World women, do not even know it exists. In reality, in this country only a minority of women are being screened. But this is because access to costly resources is uneven, not because physicians are cautious about exposing women to these techniques. In fact, to most physicians being cautious means using all available technology, however little they can yet know about its long-term consequences. By using every test they can avoid the potential legal ramifications of failing to alert future parents to the possibility of an inborn "defect."

I do not want to portray physicians as callous technocrats who think only about possible malpractice suits. Nor do I want to portray women as unwilling victims of scientists and physicians, quite a number of whom, incidentally, by now are women. When women contemplate childbearing, they try to strike the best bargain they can in a society that offers little support for this important social activity. And sometimes technological interventions seem to offer a measure of security from unexpected mishaps. The problem is not the technology itself but the fact that it generates the expectation that it is up to prospective parents, and especially mothers, to do away with disabilities by not bearing children who might have one.

Disabilities: A Social Problem

What shall be called a defect or disability and for how many and what kind shall a fetus be aborted or treated in the womb? Down syndrome? Spina bifida? Wrong sex? These questions are complicated by the fact that, for most inborn disabilities, no one can predict how serious the "defect" will be and just how it will express itself—in other words, how much of a health or social problem it will be.

To some people, and in some circumstances, the prospect of having a child with Down syndrome, no matter how mild, seems intolerable. Before there were tests, women like myself just hoped for the best when we decided to have children after thirty-five. But now that tests exist, many women who have access to them have them as a matter of course. At the same time, many people in the United States reject prenatal testing for purposes of sex selection, although it is done widely in India and China. Many feminists argue against sex selection because they expect it will most often be used to choose boys; but some feminists are for it because it makes it possible for women to choose to have only daughters if that is what they want.

I have problems with such so-called choices. Bearing and raising children is intrinsi-

cally unpredictable and knowing a person's sex tells us little about them. With all the prenatal tests in the world, we cannot know what our children will be like, whether they will be healthy and able-bodied and remain so, and what sorts of people they will be when they grow up. We have the best chance of successful parenthood if we are prepared to accept our children, whoever they are, and do the best we can to help them accept themselves and, hopefully, us too. People with disabilities have begun to speak about these issues. I agree with them when they say that all children should be welcome and that we are being short-sighted to think that we can circumvent the uncertainties of procreation by aborting "defective" or "wrong" fetuses. Sparing no expense to develop techniques for diagnosing disabilities prenatally, so as to prevent the birth of children who have them, accentuates the stigma to which people with disabilities, as well as their families, are exposed.

Another, rather different, issue we must be aware of is that the increasing emphasis on prenatal testing reinforces this society's unfortunate tendency to individualize people's problems. Yet disability cannot be dealt with properly as long as it is considered a personal problem. Parents cannot possibly provide on their own for a child who may outlive them by decades. The logical solution: Don't have one! Logical, maybe, but neither humane nor realistic. Disability-rights advocates point out that usually the disability is not the main problem. What makes it burdensome is how people are treated because they have it. And as I have said before, many (probably most) disabilities cannot be predicted unless we were to test every embryo or fetus for all conceivable disabilities—an exceedingly cumbersome and expensive process with little benefit to show for it. What is more, the incidence of disabilities resulting from accidents or exposure to chemicals or radiation is considerable and likely to increase, rather than decrease, in the future. It would be better to regard mental and physical disabilities as social, not personal, issues. Many disabilities—whether inborn or acquired later in life—are the result of social circumstances: accidents, inadequate living conditions, chronic poisoning by heavy metals or drugs, and so forth. They cannot be dealt with by victim-blaming individualizations; to prevent them requires social measures.

As the world around us becomes increasingly hazardous and threatens us and our children with social disintegration, pollution, accidents, and nuclear catastrophe, it seems as though we seek shelter among the hazards we are told lurk within us, in the illusion that we may have at least some control over them. And so we applaud the scientists and physicians who tell us that our problems lie in our genes or our womb and who propose technological solutions for them.

I remember a news story that ran in the *Boston Globe* under the headline "Some Schizophrenia Linked to Prenatal Changes in Brain Cells" (Nelson, 1983). It started with the portentous words: "The devastating mental disorder of paranoid schizophrenia seems to have roots in the womb." The rest of the story showed nothing of the sort. Rather, on the basis of the flimsiest evidence gathered by examining the brains of "10 deceased schizophrenics ages 25 to 67" and "eight nonpsychotic subjects used as controls," two researchers decided that schizophrenia has its beginnings in "the first few months of pregnancy" and suggested that visible "abnormalities [in the brain] some day may allow doctors to identify children who have a high risk of becoming paranoid schizophrenics." This is but one of many false messages women get that our children's troubles originate in our womb if not in our genes.

As I have said before, prenatal diagnosis can help the relatively small number of women who have reason to think their future children are at risk for a specific disease, but most disabilities are unexpected. Yet now that some disabilities can be detected and the fetus aborted or, in rare instances, treated in the womb, people are beginning to feel that

if parents bear a child with a disability, it is because they or their physicians were not sufficiently foresightful.

Parents are suing physicians, arguing they should have been forcefully warned about possible risks or disability and told about all available means of prenatal diagnosis. And a child who is born with a health problem that might have been detected and improved prenatally may be able to sue the mother if she refuses to be tested while pregnant. Not only that. Some attorneys have even suggested that the state should be able to mandate prenatal screening "with criminal penalties for the woman who fails to obtain it" (Robertson, 1983).

Fetal Rights

In 1971, Bentley Glass, the retiring president of the American Association for the Advancement of Science, wrote: "In a world where each pair must be limited, on the average, to two offspring and no more, the right that must become paramount is ... the right of every child to be born with a sound physical and mental constitution, based on a sound genotype. No parents will in that future time have a right to burden society with a malformed or a mentally incompetent child."

More recently, the theologian Joseph Fletcher (1980) has written that "we ought to recognize that children are often abused preconceptively and prenatally—not only by their mothers drinking alcohol, smoking, and using drugs nonmedicinally but also by their *knowingly* passing on or risking passing on genetic diseases" (original emphasis). This language of "rights" of the unborn immediately translates into obligations of the born, and especially of women.

These obligations become explicit in the writings of Margery Shaw, an attorney and physician. Reviewing what she calls "prenatal torts," Shaw (1980) argues as follows:

Once a pregnant woman has abandoned her right to abort and has decided to carry her fetus to term, she incurs a "conditional respective liability" for negligent acts toward her fetus if it should be born alive. These acts could be considered negligent fetal abuse resulting in an injured child. A decision to carry a genetically defective fetus to term would be an example. Abuse of alcohol or drugs during pregnancy could lead to fetal alcohol syndrome or drug addiction in the infant, resulting in an assertion that he [*sic*] had been harmed by his mother's acts. Withholding of necessary prenatal care, improper nutrition, exposure to mutagens and teratogens, or even exposure to the mother's defective intrauterine environment caused by her genotype ... could all result in an injured infant who might claim that his right to be born physically and mentally sound had been invaded.

What *right* to be born physically and mentally sound? Who has that kind of right and who guarantees it? Shaw goes on to urge that "courts and legislatures ... should ... take all reasonable steps to insure that fetuses destined to be born alive are not handicapped mentally and physically by the negligent acts or omissions of others."

In this argument, Shaw assumes not only that a fetus has rights (a hotly debated assumption) but that its rights are different, and indeed opposed to, those of the woman whose body keeps it alive and who will most likely to be the person who cares for it once it is born. What is more, she places the burden of implementing these so-called rights of fetuses squarely on the shoulders of individual women. Nowhere does Shaw suggest that the "reasonable steps" courts and legislatures should take include making sure that women have access to good nutrition, housing, education, and employment so that they are able to secure a fetus its "right" to proper nutrition and avoid its being exposed to mutagens and teratogens. Her language of "rights" does not advocate the kinds of improvements that would benefit women, children, and everyone. It is a language of social control.

Such control is advocated explicitly by John Robertson (1983), professor of law at the University of Texas (the same faculty on which Shaw teaches). His basic proposition is this:

The mother has, if she conceives and chooses not to abort, a legal and moral duty to bring the child into the world as healthy as is reasonably possible. She has a duty to avoid actions or omissions that will damage the fetus. ... In terms of fetal rights, a fetus has no right to be conceived-or, once conceived, to be carried to viability. But once the mother decides not to terminate the pregnancy, the viable fetus acquires rights to have the mother conduct her life in ways that will not injure it.

Because the fetus has such rights, "laws that prohibited pregnant women from obtaining or using alcohol, tobacco, or drugs likely to damage the fetus would be constitutional," and "statutes excluding pregnant women from workplaces inimical to fetal health ... would be valid." This argument leads Robertson even further:

The behavioral restrictions on pregnant women and the arguments for mandating fetal therapy and prenatal screening illustrate an important limit on a woman's freedom to control her body during pregnancy. She is free not to conceive, and free to abort after conception and before viability. But once she chooses to carry the child to term, she acquires obligations to assure its wellbeing. These obligations may require her to avoid work, recreation, and medical care choices that are hazardous to the fetus. They also obligate her to preserve her health for the fetus' sake or even allow established therapies to be performed on an affected fetus. Finally, they require that she undergo prenatal screening where there is reason to believe that this screening may identify congenital defects correctable with available therapies.

This analysis gets women into an awkward predicament, although one with a long history. While he was enunciating these legal principles, Professor Robertson was a member of a panel that proposed a model statute to guarantee a person's right to refuse treatment. The statute begins with the following proposition: "A competent person has the right to refuse any medical procedure or treatment" (Legal Advisors Committee, Concern for Dying, 1983). Yet we have just seen that Robertson argues that a woman does not have this right if she becomes pregnant and decides to carry the fetus to term. In that case, she comes entirely under the control of physicians and judges, suggesting that a willingly (or enthusiastically) pregnant woman is not a "competent person."

By defining pregnancy as a conflict of rights between a woman and her fetus, attorneys and judges have injected themselves into the experience of pregnancy, where they see themselves as advocates for the fetus. Judging by other precedents, we can see how this new mechanism of social control could be used against women not only when we are pregnant. It could be expanded to cover every woman of childbearing age by invoking "rights" not just of the fetus she is carrying but of a "potential" fetus—one she may carry at some future date. This expansion shades over into the concept of "potential" pregnancy, which has been used to bar women from more prestigious and better-paid jobs than they now have in some male-dominated industries.

To present pregnancy as a conflict of rights is even more inappropriate than to regard it as a disease. The disease metaphor is wrong because it turns the special needs of some of us into the norm for us all. The rights metaphor misrepresents most women's experience of a wanted or accepted pregnancy even more than defining pregnancy as a disability does. Yet both Shaw's and Robertson's arguments refer specifically to women who expect to carry their pregnancies to term. A wanted or accepted fetus is part of a pregnant woman's body. For this reason, contrary to

Robertson's statement, her decision to carry it to term is not binding. As long as the 1973 Supreme Court decision in *Roe* v. *Wade* stands, she can change her mind and terminate the pregnancy at any point until viability and in some states until birth.

It is in the interest of the well-being of women and children that physicians' judgments not acquire the force of law. Informed consent laws mean that a physician can suggest, advise, and urge treatment, but he or she must not be able to force treatment on unconsenting people. Fetuses cannot consent to tests or treatments. So who speaks for the fetus? Is a judge of the juvenile court, who is called in for the occasion, more appropriate than the woman whose body sustains the fetus and who will be physically emotionally, and economically affected by whatever is done? If a mother refuses to save her child's life by donating one of her kidneys, no one can force her to do it. What warped logic enables a physician, supported by a judge, to cut her open or penetrate her body with a needle or force her to take medication for the presumed benefit of the fetus she carries inside her?

Fetal Therapy

As we saw in the preceding section, the present status of fetal therapy is equivocal. After an initial rush of operations on fetuses that were hailed as breakthroughs in news and feature articles, some of the physicians who pioneered fetal interventions warned to go slow. Read cynically, the warning can be taken to mean: "We have begun to gain experience using these procedures at a few of the most prestigious teaching hospitals. Let us do them and don't get into the act!" These same physicians are far from restrained in their other writings about "the fetus." They wax eloquent, and even poetic, over the prospect of treating fetuses. For example, Michael Harrison (1982) writes in review entitled "Unborn: Historical Perspective of the Fetus as Patient":

The fetus could not be taken seriously as long as he [*sic*] remained a medical recluse in an opaque womb; and it was not until the last half of this century that the prying eye of the ultrasonogram [that is, ultrasound visualization] rendered the once opaque womb transparent, stripping the veil of mystery from the dark inner sanctum, and letting the light of scientific observation fall on the shy and secretive fetus. … Sonography can accurately delineate normal and abnormal fetal anatomy with astounding detail. It can introduce not only static images of intact fetuses, but real-time "live" moving pictures. And, unlike all previous techniques, ultrasonic imaging appears to have no harmful effects on mother or fetus. The sonographic voyeur, spying on the unwary fetus, finds him or her a surprisingly active little creature, and not at all the passive parasite we had imagined.

Who is "we"? Surely not women who have been awakened by the painful kicks of a fetus! Harrison concludes:

The fetus has come a long way—from biblical "seed" and mystical "homunculus" to an individual with medical problems that can be diagnosed and treated, that is, a patient. Although he [*sic*] cannot make an appointment and seldom even complains, this patient will at all times need a physician. … Treatment of the unborn has had a long and painstaking gestation; the date of confinement is still questionable and viability uncertain. But there is promise that the fetus may become a "born again" patient.

Frederic Frigoletto, chief of what used to be obstetrics but is now called "maternal and fetal medicine" at Boston's Brigham and Women's Hospital and another pioneer in fetal therapy, is quoted as follows in *Patient Care*, a magazine for physicians (Labson, 1983):

Real-time ultrasound—which is now widely available—allows us to develop a composite picture of [the] fetal state; it's almost like going to a nursery school to watch [the] behavior of 3-year-olds. Eventually we may be able to establish norma-

tive behavior for the fetus at various gestational stages. That will help us identify abnormal fetal development, perhaps early enough to be able to correct the environment to treat the fetus in utero.

Considering the personal and social problems that have been created when scientists have tried to establish norms, such as the IQ, for children and grownups, I shudder at the prospect of physicians coming up with norms for "fetal behavior." And remember that the "environment" to which Dr. Frigoletto refers happens to be the body of a woman.

So the fetus is on its way to being a person by virtue of becoming a patient with its own legal rights to medical treatment. As we have seen, once the fetus is considered a person, pregnant women may lose *their* right to refuse treatment by becoming no more than the maternal environment that must be manipulated for the fetus's benefit. The same Dr. Harrison, in a medical article he wrote with colleagues, described moving a pregnant woman as "transporting the fetus in situ" (Harrison, Golbus, and Filly, 1981), *in situ* being scientific parlance for "in place." It is not unusual to find pregnant women referred to as the "maternal environment," but now even that term directs too much attention to them. They are becoming "the fetus in situ" the vessel that holds the fetus, that ideal patient who does not protest or talk back.

And What About Women?

Much as this way of viewing pregnancy insults women, the issue to which I want to come back is that many—perhaps most—pregnant women will feel obligated to accept these intrusions and may even do so gratefully. As long as disability is regarded as a personal failure and parents (especially mothers) feel in some sense responsible, as well as ashamed, if their child is born with a disability, pregnant women will hail medical interventions that promise to lessen the likelihood of its happening to them. The very availability of the new techniques, however untested they may be, increases women's isolation by playing on our sense of personal responsibility to produce healthy children and on our fears and guilt if we should fail to do so.

But who is to say what "healthy" means in the face of an ever-lengthening list of diagnosable "defects" and, lately, even of "predispositions" or "tendencies" to develop them? The Human Genome Initiative will produce a raft of new diagnostic tests long before there will be relevant therapies. Add to that the fact that pharmaceutical companies always find it more profitable to market ways to diagnose and screen healthy people than to develop therapeutic measures because relatively few people need therapy. So how should we relate to the ever-increasing number of genetic and metabolic tests that will be done prenatally?

Compare the rare and almost surreal genetic threats the genome project will uncover with the starkly real threats to health reported daily in the press. For example, in July 1988 the Agency for Toxic Substances and the Disease Registry of the Department of Health and Human Services announced that in the United States an estimated four hundred thousand fetuses a year are exposed to harm because of the lead poisoning of their mothers. This is only one of many preventable risks pregnant women and fetuses run by reason of economic and social neglect.

Women are likely to accept untested (or insufficiently tested) technological interventions in their pregnancies because it is becoming more and more difficult to be a responsible childbearer and mother. We get lots of "expert" advice, but little comradely support. Unless our social supports improve, women who can afford it will feel driven to follow every new will-o'-the-wisp that promises to lessen our sense that any problems we encounter in our childbearing are our fault. Meanwhile, women who do not have the economic or social support that make it possible for them to experience a healthful pregnancy will be blamed for "their failures."

References

Fletcher, Joseph F. 1980. "Knowledge, Risk, and the Right to Reproduce: A Limiting Principle." In Aubrey Milunsky and George J. Annas, eds., *Genetics and the Law II*. New York: Plenum.

Harrison, Michael R. 1982. "Unborn: Historical Perspective of the Fetus as Patient." *Pharos*, Winter: 19–24.

Harrison, Michael R., Mitchell S. Golbus, and Roy A. Filly. 1981. "Management of the Fetus with a Correctable Congenital Defect." *Journal of the American Medical Association* 246: 744–747.

Labson, Lucy H. 1983. "Today's View in Maternal and Fetal Medicine." *Patient Care* 15 (January): 105–121.

Leavitt, Judith Walzer. 1987. *Brought to Bed: Childbearing in America, 1750–1950*. New York: Oxford University Press.

Legal Advisors Committee, Concern for Dying. 1983. "The Right to Refuse Treatment: A Model Act." *American Journal of Public Health* 73: 918–921.

Nelson, Harry. 1983. "Some Schizophrenia Linked to Prenatal Changes in Brain Cells." *Boston Globe*, June 7: 8.

Perry, Ruth. 1979. "The Veil of Chastity: Mary Astell's Feminism." *Studies in Eighteenth-Century Culture* 9: 25–45.

Rich, Adrienne. 1976. *Of Woman Born*. New York: Norton.

Robertson, John A. 1983. "Procreative Liberty and the Control of Conception, Pregnancy, and Childbirth." *Virginia Law Review* 69: 405–464.

Rothman, Barbara Katz. 1984. "The Meanings of Choice in Reproductive Technology." In Rita Arditti, Renate Duelli Klein, and Shelley Minden, eds., *Test-Tube Women*. London: Pandora Press.

Rothman, Barbara Katz. 1989. *Recreating Motherhood: Ideology and Technology in a Patriarchal Society*. New York: Norton.

Shaw, Margery W. 1980. "The Potential Plaintiff. Preconception and Prenatal Torts." In Aubrey Milunsky and George J. Annas, eds., *Genetics and the Law II*. New York: Plenum.

A Question of Genius

Are Men Really Smarter than Women?

Anne Fausto-Sterling

There is perhaps no field aspiring to be scientific where flagrant personal bias, logic martyred in the cause of supporting a prejudice, unfounded assertions and even sentimental rot and drivel have run riot to such an extent as here.

—Helen Thompson-Woolley
Psychologist, 1910

It would be difficult to find a research area more characterized by shoddy work, overgeneralization, hasty conclusions, and unsupported speculations.

—Julia Sherman
Psychologist, 1977

JOBS AND EDUCATION—that's what it's really all about. At the crux of the question "Who's smarter, men or women?" lie decisions about how to teach reading and mathematics, about whether boys and girls should attend separate schools, about job and career choices, and, as always, about money—how much employers will have to pay to whom and what salaries employees, both male and female, can command. These issues have formed an unbroken bridge spanning the length of a century. Across that passageway, year in and year out, have trucked thousands upon thousands of pages written to clarify our understanding of the intellectual abilities of men and women. Hundreds of this nation's top educators, biologists, and psychologists have done thousands of studies offering us proofs, counterproofs, confirmations, and refutations. Yet the battle rages with as much heat and as little light as ever.

Today's claims are quite specific. The science feature page of the *Boston Globe* had the following headline in an article on education:

IS MATH ABILITY AFFECTED BY HORMONES? Far more boys than girls get top scores in math test.[1]

In the same vein a mathematics teacher in a Warwick, Rhode Island, high school writes:

As a mathematics educator with over 25 years in dealing with female pupils and female mathematics teachers, I do have direct evidence ... mathematics is the water in which all intellectual creativity must mix to survive. Females, by their very nature, are oleaginous creatures in this regard. Or ... as the song says: "Girls just wanna have fun."[2]

Theories abound that there are more male than female geniuses and that boys wind up ahead of girls in the classroom and hence in the job market. Why? Because, some would hold, hormonal differences between the sexes cause differences in brain structure and function. These in turn lead to differences in cognitive ability. Boys supposedly develop greater visual-spatial acumen; girls develop better verbal and communication skills. Although many researchers take such differences for granted, my own reading of the scientific literature leaves me in grave doubt about their existence. If sex differences in cognition exist at all they are quite small, and the question of their possible origins remains unanswered. Nevertheless, the claim of difference has been and continues to be used to avoid facing up to very real problems in our educational system and has provided a rationale for discrimination against women in the workplace. The issue of cognitive differences between the sexes is not new. Scientists and educators used versions of this particular scientific tale even before the turn of the century.

In 1903 James McKeen Cattell, a professor at Columbia University and editor of *Science,* the official journal of the American Association for the Advancement of Science, noted that among his list of one thousand persons of eminence throughout the ages, only thirty-two were women. Although Cattell expressed some surprise at the dearth of eminent females, he felt that it fit with the fact that in his *American Men of Science* only a tiny number of women appeared among the top thousand scientists. From his standpoint "there [did] not appear to be any social prejudice against women engaging in scientific work," hence he found it "difficult to avoid the conclusion that there is an innate sexual disqualification."[3] Another Columbia professor, Edward L. Thorndike, an influential ed-

ucational psychologist and a pioneer in the use of statistics in educational research, also commented on the lack of intellectually gifted women. As an advocate of educational efficiency, he saw little sense in squandering social resources by trying to train so many women to join the intellectual elite. An exceptional female could become an administrator, politician, or scientist, but the vast majority were better off learning to become nurses and teachers where, as he put it, "the average level is essential."[4]

Thorndike and Cattell both thought that biological differences between the sexes explained the rarity of extremely intelligent women. Men, it seemed, were by nature more variable and this variability created more male geniuses. Since the line of reasoning may at first seem tortured, a word of explanation is in order. Researchers give

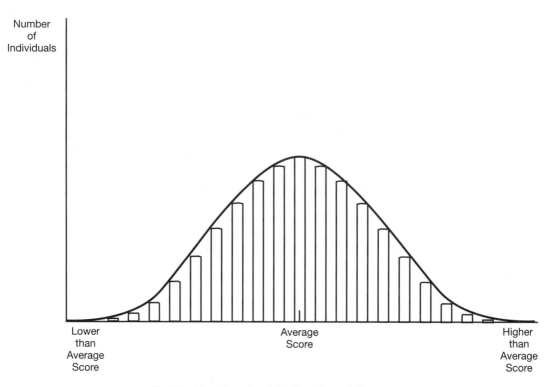

FIGURE 1   Genesis of the Bell-shaped Curve

tests to groups of individuals. If one displays the number of people with a particular test score on a graph, as shown in figure 1, the distribution of performances usually approximates a bell-shaped curve. The highest part of the curve, showing the scores most frequently attained, represents the average performance. Individuals whose scores fall to the right have performed above average while those whose scores fall to the left were below average.

There is, however, more than one way to reach an average. On a test in which the highest possible score is 100, for example, the average might be 50. If the average resulted from the fact that everyone scored very close to 50, the bell-shaped curve would be very tall and narrow. If, on the other hand, the average score of 50 resulted from a population of individuals, some of whom scored in the 90s

and some of whom scored in the teens, the shape of the bell would be low and squat (see figure 2). In the former example, where all of the individual scores hover right around the group average, the *standard deviation from the mean* is small, while in the latter case it is quite large. A population with a large standard deviation is, quite obviously, highly variable, making it harder to predict the performance of any one individual in the group.

What does all this have to do with an excess of male geniuses? Thorndike and others agreed that men and women had the same *average* level intelligence. But men were more variable; thus, their intelligence curve looked more like the short, squat one drawn in figure 2, while the women's looked more like the tall, narrow one. (I've exaggerated the effect to illustrate the point

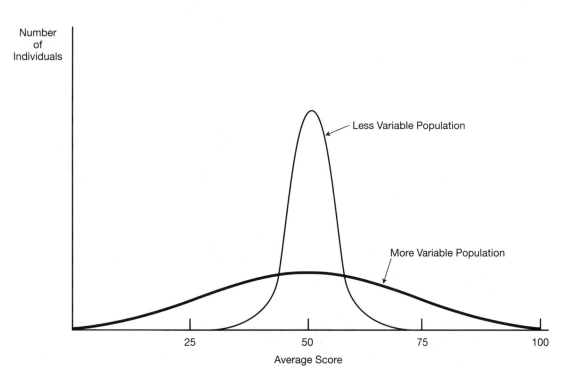

FIGURE 2 Bell-shaped Curves of Populations with the Same Average Trait but with Different Degrees of Variability

mo] clearly.) What counted for the men was he above-average tail on the bell curve, containing as it must individuals who surpassed the abilities of even the most gifted women. (The variability hypothesis also allows for the presence of a greater number of subnormal males, a fact acknowledged by both Thorndike and Cattell.)

The theme of variability is an old one. Before Darwin published his theory of evolution, Western scientists considered variability a liability to the species. They also thought that *women* constituted the more variable sex. Darwin, however, won credence for the ideas that populations with greater variability among individuals had a better chance of withstanding the evolutionary test of time, and that males were more likely to vary than were females. Thus, when high variability was considered to be a biological drawback, it was attributed to the female of the species; in its post-Darwinian status as a biological benefit, it became a male property and males remained the progressive element, the active experimenters of their race. In return for relinquishing their variability, women received the mantle of conservation, becoming the passive vessels of racial purity.[5]

A number of psychologists working in the first quarter of the twentieth century published competent scientific studies disputing the claim that men were more variable than women.[6] But the ideas of Thorndike and others that women should be educated for professions such as nursing, social work, and teaching were backed by powerful social forces. Cattell, for example, wrote at a time when women had begun to outnumber men as students in many of the large state universities—California, Iowa, Minnesota, and Texas among them.[7] The "problem of feminization" concerned educators deeply. While administrators at the University of Chicago contained the large growth in women students by placing them in a separate college within the school, other institutions responded by urging women to enter special all-female fields. Home economics, for one,

provided a new place for the increased number of women chemists.[8] The structure of the work force had also changed markedly. With job segregation a fact of life for women,[9] Thorndike and others encouraged the massing of women into certain (low-paying) occupations by urging the utility of separate vocational education for males and females. Federal aid for industrial arts programs for boys and home economics courses for girls supported this process. According to one analysis, "Hospital and school administrators welcomed these programs as a solution to their growing need for competent but inexpensive workers. Businessmen supported the growing number of secretarial and commercial courses for women for similar reasons."[10] The biological views of Cattell and Thorndike were so congenial to the economic and political establishment of the period that rational, scientific challenges to their work were studiously ignored.[11]

The debate over variability went on into the 1930s, when it finally seemed to have been laid to rest by Lewis Terman, an expert on mental testing.[12] But, like the phoenix arising fresh and beautiful from the ashes of its own cremation, the theory of variability has appeared once more on the modern scene. Curiously, its rebirth brings out few new facts, presenting only a somewhat modernized formulation of the same old idea. In 1972 the *American Journal of Mental Deficiency* published an article by Dr. Robert Lehrke entitled "A Theory of X-linkage of Major Intellectual Traits."[13] The editors were sensitive to the fact that the article would provoke controversy and took the somewhat unusual step of inviting three well-known psychologists to write critiques, which followed the original article along with a round of response from Lehrke.[14] Lehrke noted that there were more institutionalized mentally retarded males than females, an observation made by many but poorly understood.[15] Is it possible that parents keep retarded girls at home more often? Are boys more susceptible to environmental shock? Or, does the X-linkage of certain metabolic diseases* make boys more likely to be institutionalized? Lehrke's hypothesis holds that a number of genes relating to intellectual ability reside on the X-chromosome and that, because of the peculiarities of chromosomal inheritance, X-linkage means that males will exhibit greater variability in intelligence. Although he begins with the supposed excess of mental defectives, Lehrke does not shrink from the implication that there would also be more genius-level males. As he rather succinctly wrote: "It is highly probable that basic genetic factors rather than male chauvinism account for at least some of the difference in the numbers of males and females occupying positions requiring the highest levels of intellectual ability."[16]

To understand some of the details of Lehrke's argument it is worthwhile to review the idea of X-linkage. Males and females differ genetically. In addition to twenty-two pairs of chromosomes called autosomes, females have two X chromosomes. Males, on the other hand, supplement their twenty-two autosomes with one X and one Y chromosome. Because X and Y chromosomes are associated with the development of gender, they are sometimes referred to as the sex chromosomes. Hemophilia, a particularly famous X-linked disease, illustrates the process of X-linked inheritance. The hemophilia gene, which resides on the X chromosome, exists in two states—normal and mutant. The normal gene codes for a factor that helps blood to clot, while the mutant gene cannot aid in the production of the clotting factor. Since males carry only one X chromosome, and since the Y chromosome cannot counteract the effect of genes on the X chromosome, a male will suffer from hemophilia if he carries an X chromosome with the mutant state of the gene. A female must carry two abnormal

X chromosomes in order to be a bleeder, because she will be protected as long as one X chromosome carries the normal gene.

Children, however, can inherit the mother's abnormal X chromosome. Since sons derive their X chromosomes from their mothers, a mother carrying the hemophilia factor on one of her X chromosomes stands a 50 percent chance of having a hemophiliac son. On the other hand, since daughters receive one X chromosome from the mother and the other from the father, a stricken girl must have a hemophiliac father in addition to a carrier mother. In other words, if hemophilia runs in the family, sons will express the trait more frequently than will daughters.

Lehrke hypothesizes that, unlike the clotting factor gene that exists in one of two possible states, an X-linked gene for intelligence might exist in as many as six graded states—called *alleles* in the terminology of geneticists—running from lower to higher intelligence. A female would always carry two of these (one on each X chromosome), and the one evoking greater intelligence might then compromise with the one for lesser intelligence. Males, on the other hand, would only carry one allele at a time. If that one allele coded for a low state of intelligence, then the male would express that trait, while if the allele were one for the highest state, the individual would be extremely intelligent. According to Lehrke, then, one would find equal levels of retardation or genius among males and females. However, because expression of extremes of intelligence in females would require two chromosomes with the same very low or very high state of brightness, while expression in males would require the presence of only one, a larger number of males than of females would be found who were either extremely dull or incredibly brilliant. Hence, the greater male variability in intelligence.[17]

The most fundamental assumption in Lehrke's hypothesis is that intelligence is an inherited trait coded for by some finite number of factors called "intelligence genes." This

---

* Hemophilia, for example, is X-linked and therefore affects boys more frequently than girls.

claim has evoked great controversy, and many well-known biologists have argued convincingly that (1) it is impossible to define intelligence, and (2) we have no means at our disposal to measure its genetic component separately from its environmental determinants.[18] Lehrke bolsters his argument by citing the work of Arthur Jensen, who figures heavily in a long-standing debate over whether blacks are less intelligent than whites. Jensen and others believe that whites are smarter and that educational enrichment programs for underprivileged children are a waste of government money. From his comments about the lower intelligence of slum dwellers, one would suspect that Lehrke agrees with this concept.[19] Lehrke also claims that the existence of several X-linked traits that cause mental retardation proves the inherited nature of intelligence. This argument includes the hidden, circular assumption that mental deficiency results from genes specific to the development of intelligence. My point can be illustrated by looking at one often cited example, the disease called phenylketonuria (PKU).

In the very recent primary literature the simple autosomal inheritance of PKU has been called into question,[20] but virtually all genetic and medical textbooks use this disease as an example of the straightforward inheritance of a gene that "causes" mental retardation. Children born with PKU lack an enzyme called phenyl alanine hydroxylase, which converts the amino acid phenyl alanine—one of the building blocks of large protein molecules—to another amino acid, called tyrosine. Because their cells cannot make this conversion, PKU patients accumulate toxic levels of phenyl alanine—from forty to fifty times the normal amount—in the blood and brain. Since the brain continues to develop actively even after birth, its cells may be particularly sensitive to this poison. Indeed, children with PKU fed on a diet lacking in phenyl alanine develop fairly normally.

The question is whether the existence of the inherited disease phenylketonuria (or similar diseases of metabolism) provides evidence that genes govern intelligence. That normal intelligence requires normal brain development is obvious, but the existence of PKU says nothing about the presence of genes for intelligence or learning. It merely says that when the entire brain is poisoned during a critical period of development, the effects can be disastrous. From the point of view of explaining the relationship between genes and intelligence, this is no more informative than asserting, after smashing someone's head with a sledgehammer, that violence done to a person's skull causes subsequent mental dullness. The same point can be made for all of the gene and chromosome defects that severely affect normal human development. They give us a glimpse of what can go wrong, but they tell us absolutely nothing—at least in terms of intelligence—about how things work right.

Arguments against the idea of intelligence genes seem sufficient to warrant dismissal of Lehrke's hypothesis.[21] But he both resurrects old data and cites newer information purporting to show once again that males perform more variably on intelligence tests than do females, and those citations merit consideration. Investigating variability in IQ turns out to be a rather formidable task. In one recent study researchers looked for scientifically gifted children by holding math and science contests. They found a greater number of precocious boys than girls, and their top winners were all male. They noted, however, that among the precocious students the boys owned more books and equipment related to math and science, while some of the girls' parents were so uninterested in their daughters' precocity that they didn't even plan to send them to college.[22] The existence of such social differences between the boys and the girls makes the results difficult to interpret. Furthermore, a "talent search" approach looks only at a select group of students who either volunteered for the contests or were recruited by teachers or parents. Although Lehrke doesn't cite this study, he does cite an older one[23] which is subject to the same sorts of uncertainty.

The only way to get some sense of the variability of the population as a whole is to do large-scale, nonselective studies. These are expensive and difficult to design—there is only one well-done research project of this kind in the literature. Lehrke cites this project, a survey of Scottish schoolchildren, to support his view that males vary more than do females. Since the sample was very large, and since sample size is one of the components statisticians use to decide whether a particular difference is significant rather than just random, the small differences in standard deviation found among these Scottish boys and girls turned out to be statistically significant. As one of the respondents to Lehrke's 1972 paper points out, however, the male variability resulted mostly from an excess of males with very *low* scores—a result, perhaps, of physical handicaps that might have interfered with their performance on the timed tests.[24]

Lehrke's response to his critics is maddening. He concedes that "each one of the arguments for X-linkage of major intellectual traits can be interpreted to produce different emphases," but thinks that his emphasis merits attention because it is a simpler explanation.[25] In addition to this weak attempt at scientific rebuttal, and despite the fact that some of his critics are male,[26] Lehrke also directly points to what he thinks is the real source of his trouble:

> Determinants of which viewpoint a person accepts are undoubtedly highly complex, but a single, very simple one is obvious. In the small sample cited, all those accepting the hypothesis of greater male variability have been males, all those rejecting it, females.[27]

In contrast to his assessment of his female critics, however, Lehrke believes himself to be a dispassionate observer:

> I do not feel that I must apologize for the fact that certain implications of the theory may seem … to be derogatory to women. Like Topsy, the theory "just growed," its nature being determined by the data. I could not, with scientific objectivity, have changed the final result.[28]

Here, then, we have the elements of a response that … show up again and again …. In each case, the proponents of biological explanations of behavior label their attackers as biased, members of some special interest group (women, feminists, Marxists), while choosing for themselves the role of the objective, dispassionate scientist.

Before judging Lehrke's detachment, though, the reader ought to know a little something about the company he keeps. His last article, "Sex Linkage: A Biological Basis for Greater Variability in Intelligence," was published in 1978 in a book entitled *Human Variation: The Biopsychology of Age, Race, and Sex*.[29] The book is dedicated to the memory of Sir Francis Galton, founder of the eugenics movement, while its headquote comes from none other than E.L. Thorndike. Just as interesting, the volume in question is edited by Dr. R. Travis Osborn, a leader in the new eugenics movement,[30] who has received, over the years, financial support from a "philanthropic" organization called the Pioneer Fund, which promotes theories of black inferiority and has supported the work of Drs. William Shockley and Arthur Jensen. (Past members and directors include Senator James O. Eastland, the segregationist senator from Mississippi, and Representative Francis E. Walter, who chaired the House Committee on Un-American Activities during the anti-communist campaigns of the 1940s and 1950s.[31]) Are Lehrke, Osborne, and Jensen (who also has an article in the book) strange bedfellows or, as I suspect, appropriate company—each being a scientist who disclaims responsibility for the social implications of his "objective" facts?

Cattell and Thorndike formed part of the mainstream of educational psychology which to this day carries along such adherents as Lehrke. There were others in the mainstream who rejected the variability hypothesis but argued instead that innate differences between males and females are important when considering what jobs to train for and how to teach—even at the elementary level—such subjects as reading and writing. Among the most widely quoted compilations of data on sex differences is one published in 1968 by Garai and Scheinfeld. In the introduction to their book-length literature review they explicitly state that their purpose is "to make the participation of women in the labor force as efficient as their potential permits." To summarize Garai and Scheinfeld's findings in their own words:

Females, on the average, surpass males in verbal fluency, correct language usage, spelling, manual dexterity, clerical skills, and rote memory. Males, on the average, are superior to females in verbal comprehension and verbal reasoning, mathematical reasoning, spatial perception, speed and accuracy of reaction to visual and auditory stimulation, mechanical aptitude, and problem-solving ability. *These sex differences foreshadow the different occupational goals of men and women.*[32] [Emphasis added]

In a conclusion echoed in more recent writings by other psychologists, Garai and Scheinfeld infer that women's work preferences lie in the fine arts, literature, social services, secretarial jobs, and assembly-line work because these areas suit their particular aptitudes. Men, in contrast, seem drawn by their special skills to the sciences, mathematics, engineering, mechanics, and construction.

Garai and Scheinfeld call for certain educational reforms to accommodate their findings. They believe that boys are handicapped by coeducational classes because they mature more slowly, while girls are distracted, especially in more difficult subjects, by their need for approval and interaction with others. Their solution would be a return to single-sex classes, at least in high school. Garai and Scheinfeld also suggest that there are separate feminine and masculine ways of learning subjects such as mathematics and reading,

and that teaching methods for these subjects ought to be reevaluated. This thought, too, remains current. In a research paper appearing in *Science* magazine in 1976,[33] psychologist Sandra Witelson concludes that boys' and girls' brains have different physical organizations and that current methods of teaching reading (which stress phonetics rather than visual memory) may favor girls while handicapping boys. In an interview she, too, said that "separate groups or classes for the sexes would be beneficial for teaching reading."[34]

In this day of increasing coeducation, the thought of resegregating classrooms by sex carries a certain irony. At the college level there *is* evidence that coeducation as currently practiced may harm *female* students.[35] But is the solution to return to a separate but unequal form of education,[36] or to identify and remedy whatever it is about coeducation that functions to discourage female students? Of course if one believes in innate sex differences, then the latter makes no sense.

With echoes of James McKeen Cattell in our ears, we find ourselves once again in a period in which females outnumber males on the college campuses. In the current political climate the enrollment changes have led not to a move to cordon off the females as in Cattell's day, but instead to a call from students for more female faculty and better role models. Garai and Scheinfeld, however, call for the "defeminization of the elementary classroom."[37] There are, they feel, too many women teachers whose emphasis on conformity and good behavior stifles the creative expression of little boys; girls, too, need more male teachers, especially if they are to be encouraged (at least the more talented ones) to study science or to improve their creative abilities. Garai and Scheinfeld claim that "almost exclusive staffing of libraries with women and of schools with women teachers create[s] a climate which confronts the boy with hostility and lack of understanding," curiously echoing a diatribe written by Cattell in 1909 in which he, too, deplored the dominance of the female "school principal, narrow and arbitrary, and the spinster, devitalized and unsexed" over the school lives of little boys and girls.[38] Thus while feminists call for more female role models, some psychologists call for a return to the male-dominated classroom. Is there truly no scientific evidence to tell us who is right?

Male Skills/Female Skills: The Elusive Difference

The best starting point for discussing the difference between male and female skills is a book published in 1974 by two psychologists, Eleanor Maccoby and Carol Nagy Jacklin.[39] They summarize and critically evaluate a large body of work on the psychology of sex differences, concluding that at least eight different claims for sex differences (see left-hand column in table 1) were *disproved* by the results of then available scientific studies and that the findings about seven other alleged differences (see middle column) were either too skimpy or too ambiguous to warrant any conclusions at all, but that sex differences in four areas—verbal ability, visual-spatial ability, mathematical ability, and aggressive behavior—were "fairly well established" (see right-hand column). We turn our attention for the remainder of this chapter to the first three of these differences: verbal, visual-spatial, and mathematical abilities. ...

Verbal Ability

Many people believe that little girls begin to talk sooner than do little boys and that

TABLE 1   Summary of Maccoby and Jacklin's Findings on Sex Differences

Unfounded Beliefs About Sex Differences	Open Questions of Difference	Fairly Well Established Sex Differences
Girls are more social than boys	Tactile sensitivity	Girls have greater verbal ability
Girls are more suggestible than boys	Fear, timidity, and anxiety	Boys excel in visual-spatial ability
Girls have lower self-esteem than boys	Activity level	Boys excel in mathematical ability
Girls are better at rote learning and simple repetitive tasks; boys are better at higher level cognitive processing	Competitiveness	Boys are more aggressive
	Dominance	
	Compliance	
	Nurturance and "maternal" behavior	
Boys are more analytic than girls		
Girls are more affected by heredity; boys are more affected by environment		
Girls lack achievement motivation		
Girls are more inclined toward the auditory; boys are more inclined toward the visual		

Source: Eleanor Maccoby and Carol Nagy Jacklin, *The Psychology of Sex Differences* (Stanford, Calif.: Stanford University Press, 1974).

their greater speaking abilities make girls better able to cope with the word-centered system of primary education. Maccoby and Jacklin cite one summary of studies done before 1950 that points to a trend of earlier vocalization in girls. The gender differences, however, are small and often statistically insignificant, and, in fact, many of the studies show no sex-related differences at all. In their review of the literature subsequent to 1950, Maccoby and Jacklin remain skeptical about the existence of sex differences in vocalization for very young children. Although a small body of more recent work suggests that there probably is something to the idea that girls talk sooner than boys,[40] my own assessment is that the differences, if any, are so small relative to the variation among members of the same sex that it is almost impossible to demonstrate them in any consistent or statistically acceptable fashion.

The studies on early vocalization raise several interrelated issues in basic statistics that must be understood in order to delve further into the controversies surrounding verbal and spatial abilities. Among these issues are statistical significance and its relationship to sample size and the size of differences *between the sexes* compared with the size of differences *between any two individuals* of the same sex. This latter issue, of which psychologists in the field of cognitive differences have become increasingly aware, places the importance of sex differences in a whole new light.

One widely accepted scientific procedure for comparing averages obtained from individual measurements of members of a population is to apply a statistical test to the information gathered. An average difference between two groups could occur by chance and therefore would reflect no real distinction between the two test populations. A random difference is particularly likely if the individual trait under study in one or both of the groups varies a lot (that is, has a large standard deviation). Scientists have devised several methods for examining experimental information to find out if average differences

are real rather than chance. Most such statistical tests look at two things—the variability of the populations under comparison and the size of the test sample. If a test sample is very small, very variable, or both, the possibility that found differences are due to chance is great.

Suppose, for example, I suspect that more males than females have blue eyes. In order to test my idea, I look at three groups of ten students (five men and five women) borrowed from three different classrooms. In the first group it turns out that two-thirds of the men but only one-third of the women have blue eyes, in the second that two-thirds of the women but only one-third of men have blue eyes, while in the third classroom all five of the men have blue eyes, but none of the women do. Taking the average of my three samples, I see that, overall, 66 percent of the men have blue eyes compared to only 33 percent of the women.

In standard scientific convention one tries to discover the probability that a particular result can occur by accident. Because my sample in the preceding example was small and variable, this probability was 65.6 percent (calculated using a special statistical test that takes into account variance and sample size). Scientists use an agreed-upon albeit arbitrary limit, whereby a hypothesis is rejected if the probability of a found difference occurring by chance exceeds 5 percent. Thus I must reject the hypothesis that more boys than girls have blue eyes, as it is based on a poor data sample. If the probability of a difference existing by chance is 5 percent or less, then one accepts the hypothesis and calls the results *statistically significant.*

Statistical significance, however, can mislead, because its calculation comes in part from the size of the measured sample. For example, in order to show that two groups differ in performance by four IQ points, one must use a sample size of about four hundred in each test group (that is, if the sexes were compared, four hundred boys and four hundred girls). Greater differences in IQ can be shown with smaller groups, while *extremely large* samples may reveal statistically significant results, according to the convention of 5 percent probability, even though they are intellectually meaningless. Thus, in a sample of 100,000 males and 100,000 females, an IQ difference of 0.02 points would be highly significant (probability of 0.1 percent). But it doesn't actually matter if one person has an IQ of 100 and another an IQ of 100.02, because the IQ test is not designed to measure such small differences.[41]

Using a somewhat unusual statistical manipulation, Garai and Sheinfeld concluded that girls were poorer at verbal reasoning than were boys. In order to reach that conclusion, they used the following approach. They knew that boys matured physically at a slower rate than did girls. In studies done on children of the same age, then, they believed the girls to be physically more mature and thus not *really* age-matched with the boys. They reasoned, therefore, that any of the studies that showed boys and girls to perform equally actually provided proof of male superiority![42] One way to get around the problem of different maturation ages is to look carefully at the studies done on people over the age of sixteen, a point in the life cycle at which the large majority of both boys and girls have gone through puberty. Dr. Julia Sherman has done just this. Her results, reproduced in table 2, show that in forty different studies of verbal reasoning done on subjects over the age of sixteen, females did better in fifteen and males in two, while in twenty-three there were no sex-related differences.

Two observations can be made from this information. First, when there *are* sex-related differences in verbal reasoning, females usually come out ahead. Second, in the majority of cases there are no differences at all. What, then, is the take-home message? Maccoby and Jacklin chose to emphasize the female superiority in the cases where there is some difference. They are, however, perfectly aware that the frequent inability to find any difference could be quite important. Given these data, choosing to believe in sex-related differences in verbal ability is a judgment call about which knowledgeable scientists can very legitimately differ.

More recently several researchers have related the difficulty of showing differences in verbal ability to the small size of any such differences. All the papers reviewed by Maccoby and Jacklin used what is called the *hypothesis-testing approach* to the study of sex differences. Using this approach, a researcher hypothesizes

TABLE 2   Sex-related Cognitive Differences: Verbal Reasoning in Subjects over Age Sixteen

Variable	Number of Results	Female Superior	Male Superior	No Difference
Oetzel (1966)				
Vocabulary	4	2	0	2
Verbal Problem Solving	1	1	0	0
General Verbal Skill	4	1	0	3
Abstract Reasoning	4	1	1	2
Maccoby and Jacklin (1974)				
Verbal Abilities	25	8	1	16
Droege (1967)	2	2	0	0
TOTAL	40	15	2	23

Note: Julia Sherman, *Sex-related Cognitive Differences: An Essay on Theory and Evidence* (Springfield, Ill.: Charles C Thomas, 1978), 40. Courtesy of Charles C Thomas, Publisher.

the existence, for instance, of a difference in verbal ability between boys and girls. Tests are given, average scores for boys and for girls are calculated, and the means, the standard deviations, and the number of subjects used to measure the statistical significance of any difference are presented. Maccoby and Jacklin simply tabulated how frequently a particular significant difference showed up in such studies.

Since the publication of their book, however, a new approach known as *meta-analysis* has been used by Jacklin and others to reevaluate their 1974 conclusions.[43] The new approach looks at the *size* of group differences, thereby allowing questions about such matters as verbal ability to be phrased in the following way: "If all you knew about a person was his or her score on a test for verbal ability, how accurately could you guess at his/her sex?" Meta-analysis is a highly sophisticated way of evaluating the meaning of several interrelated studies. It is simple in principle, albeit statistically complex. Instead of calculating separately the averages and standard deviations of males and females, one looks at the entire population (males and females together) and estimates the variability in the population as a whole using a statistic called the *variance,* which is related to the standard deviation.[44] Like the standard deviation, the variance tells one about the appearance of the bell-shaped curve that summarizes individual scores. In meta-analysis, one calculates how much of the variance found in the mixed population can be accounted for on the basis of gender, and how much is due to variation between members of the same sex and/or experimental error. We have already seen with the hypothesis-testing approach how one can obtain a meaningless but statistically significant difference by using a very large sample size. Meta-analysis provides a way of telling how large a given statistical difference is and thus how meaningful it is in reality.

Using meta-analysis, then, what becomes of Maccoby and Jacklin's "well-established sex difference," in verbal ability (see table 1)? It teeters on the brink of oblivion. Dr. Janet Hyde, for instance, calculated that gender differences accounted for only about 1 percent of the variance in verbal ability, pointing out that the tiny size of the difference could explain why so many of the studies cited by Maccoby and Jacklin show no difference at all.[45] Two other psychologists, Drs. Robert Plomin and Terry Foch, come to the same conclusion: "If all we know about a child is the child's sex, we know very little about the child's verbal ability."[46] Clearly, it makes little sense to base educational and counseling decisions that relate to verbal ability on simple observation of a child's sex, rather than on some actual analysis of his or her particular capacities.   •

Visual-Spatial Perception

"Males," one well-known psychologist has said, "are good at maps and mazes and math. ... Females, by contrast, are sensitive to context."[47] Alliterative, yes, but is it true? Again, Maccoby and Jacklin provide the starting point. As with verbal ability, they conclude, there are no sex-related differences in visual-spatial abilities until adolescence. A summary of their findings from studies done on adolescents and adults appears in table 3. Spatial ability turns out to be somewhat elusive, but Maccoby and Jacklin have isolated two types: spatial/visual/nonanalytic and spatial/visual/analytic. Some scientists refer to this latter skill as *field articulation.*

The evidence for sex-related differences in visual-spatial ability seems a little more convincing than that for verbal differences, but the problem of "negative" data appears with both. More than half the time no sex differences show up in the visual/analytic studies, but when they do appear they always favor males. The most consistent differences materialize from the most widely used test, the rod and frame test. In this test the subject sits in a totally dark room in a chair facing a large (forty inches on a side), vertically held, luminescent frame. Bisecting the frame is a lighted rod. In one version the experimenter tilts the frame in various ways and the subject adjusts the rod to the vertical of the room, ignoring the immediate context of the tilted frame. In a different version, the subject's chair is tilted, and again he or she must make the rod inside the frame perpendicular to the floor. As seen in table 3, Maccoby and Jacklin cite twelve studies using this test. Although women never performed better than men, in five of the twelve cases there were no sex-related differences.

Dr. H.A. Witkin, the psychologist who developed and popularized the rod and frame test, dubbed those who performed them well *field independent* and those who performed them poorly *field dependent*. Field-dependent people, Witkin and his collaborators held, were less able to ignore distracting background information in order to zero in on essentials. They suggested a relationship between general intelligence, analytical ability, conformity, passivity, and visual-spatial abilities. More recently, the fact that field-dependent and field-independent personalities just happen to correlate with male/female stereotypes has led a number of investigators to drop the use of the terms. It is now clear that these two tests, at best, record some aspect of visual skill, but have nothing to do with analytical ability. Witkin himself gave a tactile version of a test designed to measure field dependence to blind men and women and, except for one case favoring females, found no sex-related differences.[48]

Some potential for sex bias is built into the rod and frame test. Picture the following: a pitch dark room, a male experimenter, a female subject. What female would not feel just a little vulnerable in that situation? Although one would expect experimenter-subject interactions to be different for males and females in such a set-up, the studies cited by Maccoby and Jacklin apparently don't take into account this possibility. In one version of the

TABLE 3 Spatial Abilities of Adolescents and Adults

Skill	Number of Studies in which Males Performed Better	Number of Studies in which Females Performed Better	Number of Studies for which No Difference Was Found	Total
Visual/Nonanalytical[a]	8	0	2	10
Visual/Analytic				
Rod and Frame or Similar Test[b]	7	0	5	12
Embedded/Hidden Figures Test	3	0	6	9
Block Design Tests	2	0	2	4
Percentage for Visual/ Nonanalytic	80%		20%	
Percentage for Visual/ Analytic	48%		52%	

Source: Eleanor Maccoby and Carol Nagy Jacklin, *The Psychology of Sex Differences* (Stanford, Calif.: Stanford University Press, 1974), tables 3.7 and 3.8.

[a] A variety of different tests involving mazes, angle matching, and 2- and 3-D visualization were used. The same test was rarely used twice.

[b] Body attitude test.

test, the subject must ask the experimenter to adjust the rod by small increments to the position he or she believes to be vertical. A less assertive person might hesitate to insist to the nth degree that the experimenter continue the adjustments. Close might seem good enough. If it is true that females are less assertive than males, then this behavioral difference, rather than differences in visual-spatial acuity, could account for their performances in the rod and frame test. At least one experiment suggests the sex bias of the rod and frame test. When, in a similar test, the rod was replaced by a human figure and the task described as one of empathy, sex-related differences in performance disappeared.[49]

The rod and frame test is probably the most suspect of the measures used to assess male/female differences in spatial visualization, but psychologists use other tools as well to measure such skills. In the embedded figures test, the experimental subject must find a hidden word or design within a larger background that camouflages it. Another measure, the Wechsler Intelligence Scales, is used to assess IQ and comprises two tests, one measuring Verbal IQ and the other measuring Performance IQ. The latter is often taken as an indication of spatial ability, although some psychologists believe it to be inadequate for that purpose.[50] Other tests, some of them components of the standard IQ test, are used to probe the ability to visualize three-dimensional figures in the mind's eye. These include the block design test, the mental rotation test, angle-matching tasks, and maze performance. Psychologists have used all of these tests with rather similar results: many times no sex difference appears but when it does, and if the subjects are in their teens or older, males outperform females. The next question is, of course, by how much?

Maccoby and Jacklin point out that, as with differences in verbal skills, differences in spatial skills are quite small—accounting for no more than 5 percent of the variance. Expressed another way, if one looks at the variation (from lowest to highest performance) of spatial ability in a mixed population of males and females, 5 percent of it at most can be accounted for on the basis of sex. The other 95 percent of the variation is due to individual differences that have nothing to do with being male or female.[51]

Despite the small size of the difference, an advocate of the idea that there are naturally more male than female geniuses would have one strong point to make. If one looks at the entire bell-shaped curve, from worst to best, a small sex difference may be of no practical interest. Suppose, though, one looks only at the upper part of the curve, the portion representing those high-level performers one would expect to become math professors, engineers, and architects. Assume for a moment that in order to become a respected engineer one must have a spatial ability in at least the ninety-fifth percentile of the population. Dr. Hyde calculates that 7.35 percent of males will be above this cutoff in comparison with only 3.22 percent of the females. Put another way, currently available information suggests that the ratio of males with an unusually high level of spatial skills to that of females with the same high level of skills might be 2:1, a much larger difference than one picks up by looking at the entire population.[52] Hyde also points out, though, that in the United States only about 1 percent of all engineers are women. If one *did* believe that the only thing standing in the way of an engineering career for women was their immutable sex-related inferior spatial ability, one would still expect to find women in about one-third of all engineering jobs. In short, the differences between men and women in this respect remain too small to account for the tiny number of women who become professional mathematicians, architects, and engineers.

What Makes a Difference?

Sex differences in spatial visualization *do* sometimes exist, even if they don't amount to much. Thus there is an obligation to look into the causes of measurable difference. Because sex-related differences in verbal or spatial abilities appear most clearly at the time of puberty, some scientists conclude that the hormonal changes associated with physical maturation must affect male and female brain development differently. Others point to the social pressures to conform to appropriate role behavior experienced so intensely by adolescents. As seems so often to be the case, the same observation can support both a hypothesis of "natural," genetically based difference and one that invokes environmental influences. Couched in these terms, however, the clash of views has all the earmarks of a sterile, even boring, debate. Without trying to resolve competing hypotheses, let's simply look at the information we have at hand about the development of verbal and spatial abilities in little boys and little girls.

To begin with, there is ample evidence that visual-spatial abilities are at least in part learned skills. As an example, consider the fact that first-grade boys do somewhat better than do first-grade girls on embedded figures and blocks tests if neither has seen such tests before. Allowed a bit of practice, however, the girls improve enough to catch up, although the boys' scores do not change much. Researchers conclude from such studies that first-grade boys have already honed these skills so that additional practice does not lead to improved performance.[53] Why boys might be more practiced is anyone's guess, but since young boys and girls have quite different play experiences, one can at least construct a plausible hypothesis. Traditional male games such as model construction, block building, and playing catch might play a key role in developing visual-spatial skills, yet the relationship between play activities and the acquisition of spatial abilities has received scant attention from the research community.

Studies done on older children also reveal that three-dimensional visual skills can be learned. In one case a researcher assessed the performance of teenage students as they began a drafting course. The expected sex differences were found, but disappeared six

weeks into the semester as the young women improved.[54] In another case teenagers showed a positive correlation between performance on tests of visual-spatial skill and the number of drafting and mechanical-drawing courses taken.[55] The sparse literature on the relationship between formal skill training (through certain types of course work) and informal (through certain types of play) suggests that girls often do not fulfill their skill potential, but that it would be relatively easy to help them do so. The hypothesis that certain kinds of play and school activities can improve girls' visual-spatial skills is eminently testable, but more research support is needed for scientists who are interested in carrying out such investigations.

It seems unlikely, however, that play and mechanical drawing are the only contributors to the development of visual-spatial skills. Some research suggests that children who experience more independence and less verbal interaction are likely to develop strong spatial skills, a result that dovetails with information obtained from anthropological studies. In a village in Kenya, children who undertook tasks that led them away from home, such as shepherding, performed better on several measures of visual-spatial ability than children remaining close to home, suggesting that children who have a wider range of environmental experiences develop richer skills.[56] Cross-cultural studies of sex-related differences in spatial functioning reveal two additional skill-learning components. Anthropologist J.W. Berry compared the abilities of Eskimos, Scots, and the Temne people of Sierra Leone, pointing out the enormous differences in visual environment they encounter. Eskimo country is open and evenly landmarked (snow covers many potential reference points), while the Temne land is covered with vegetation of various colors. The Eskimo, in order to hunt over large, relatively featureless areas, learns to be aware of minute detail. In fact, the Eskimo language is rich in words describing geometrical-spatial relationships. It is not surprising, then, that Eskimos outperform Temnes in tests of spatial ability.[57]

Child-rearing practices also differ greatly in the two cultures. Eskimos raise their children with unconditional love, only rarely resorting to physical or verbal punishment. In contrast, the Temne emphasize strict discipline, acceptance of authority, and conformity. Eskimo girls are allowed considerable autonomy, while Temne girls are raised even more strictly than the boys in this highly disciplined society. Interestingly, no sex-related differences in spatial abilities show up in the Eskimo population, although marked differences appear between Temne males and females. Berry also compared other societies, including some traditional hunting cultures, with ones undergoing Westernization.[58] In traditional cultures there were no sex differences in spatial visualization, but differences did appear in some of the transitional ones. One hypothesis that emerges from such work is that sex-related differences in visual-spatial activities are strongest in societies in which women's social (public) roles are most limited, and that these differences tend to disappear in societies in which women have a great deal of freedom. Along these lines consider that in the United States, sex-related differences in both mathematics and spatial abilities may be changing as opportunities and roles for women change. The curricula of primary and secondary schools have become less sex-segregated with the development of equal athletic facilities and both boys and girls taking shop, typing, mechanical drawing, and home economics. As these changes continue, there is no reason to believe that sex-related differences will remain constant and every reason to assume that studies done in 1955 and in 1985 will have different outcomes.

How can we sum up some of the factors influencing the acquisition of spatial skills? Early child-parent interactions may well be involved. Plenty of studies show that parents treat boys and girls differently. Mothers are more likely to repeat or imitate vocalizations from a girl baby than from a boy baby, and

they are also more likely to try to distract a male infant by dangling some object in front of him.[59] Individual personality differences also influence parent-child interactions. Preschool children have different play habits. Boys usually explore more and stay away from their parents for longer periods of time than do girls, and certainly differences in games, toys, and amount of exploration could account in part for differences in the development of spatial skills. Girls often wear physically restrictive clothing, such as frilly, starched dresses and patent leather shoes, which contributes to their more physically limited environment. As children grow older they also learn more about sex-appropriate behavior. Pressures to conform are especially strong during the teenage years, when small sex-related differences in spatial skills first consistently appear. Visual-spatial skill-dependent activities ranging from shop and mechanical drawing to mathematics and engineering are also stereotyped male strongholds, daunting to even the most talented girls. Thus the many complex components of sex-role stereotyping may be superimposed upon and may interact with earlier developmental events. In short, there is not any *one* cause of sex-related differences in visual-spatial skills. There are *many* causes. Only future research will tell which are truly significant.

The knowledge that aspects of male/female socialization very likely influence the development of male-female differences in spatial skills should not, of course, rule out the possibility that innate biological factors contribute to such differences as well. The argument I have made to this point is twofold: (1) the size of sex differences is quite small, and (2) a complex of environmental factors has *already been demonstrated* to influence the development of visual-spatial skills. Do we then even *require* the hypothesis of biologically based differences to explain our observations? I think not, although I remain open to the idea that some small fraction of an already tiny sex-related difference could result from hormonal differences between male and female.

A Plethora of Theories: Biological Storytelling

Despite the small size of sex-related differences in verbal and spatial skills, their existence has elicited numerous studies aimed at explaining them on the basis of biological differences between the sexes. Scouring the ins and outs, curves and shapes, capacities and angles of the human brain, hoping to find traits that differ in the male and female is a pastime in which scientists have engaged for more than a century. Early studies, which discovered that male brains were larger than female brains, concluded that the female's smaller size resulted in her inferior intelligence. This logic, however, ran afoul of the "elephant problem": if size were the determinant of intelligence,

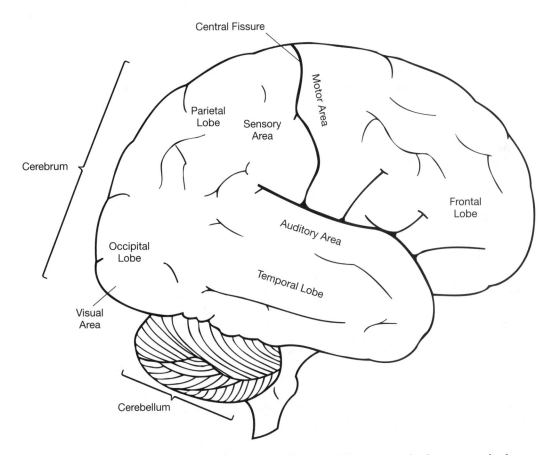

FIGURE 3 Cerebrum and Cerebellum   Localization of function in the human cerebral cortex. Only the major convolutions of the cortex are drawn. They are remarkably constant from individual to individual, and provide landmarks in the task of mapping the distribution of special functions in different parts of the cortex. Note especially the sensory area which lies posterior to the central fissure (or convolution), and the motor area which lies anterior to the central fissure.

then elephants and whales ought to be in command. Attempts to remedy this by claiming special importance for the number obtained by dividing brain size by body weight were abandoned when it was discovered that females came out "ahead" in such measurements. The great French naturalist Georges Cuvier finally decided that intellectual ability could best be estimated by the relative proportions of the cranial to the facial bones. This idea, however, ran aground on the "bird problem," since with such a measure birds, anteaters, and bear-rats turn out to be more intelligent than humans.[60] Some brain scientists believed that the frontal lobe of the cerebrum (the part that sits in the front of the head just above the eyebrows—see figure 3) was an important site of perceptive powers and was less well developed in females than in males. Others argued that even individual brain cells differed in males and females, the cerebral fibers being softer, more slender, and longer in female brains.

As neuroanatomists became more and more convinced that the frontal lobe was the repository of intelligence, an increasing number of reports appeared claiming that this lobe was visibly larger and more developed in males. One report, in 1854, concluded that Woman was *Homo parietalis* (after the parietal lobe, which lies toward the back and to the side of the head—figure 3) and Man *Homo frontalis*. In time, however, the parietal rather than the frontal lobe gained precedence as the seat of the intellect, a change accompanied by an about-face on sex differences in the brain: "The frontal region is not, as has been supposed, smaller in woman, but rather larger relatively. But the parietal lobe is somewhat smaller."[61]

Other female brain "deficiencies" found in this same period include the supposedly smaller surface area of the corpus callosum (a mass of nerve fibers that connect the left and right halves of the brain), the complexity of the convolutions of the brain, and the rate of development of the fetal cerebral cortex. These beliefs were held until 1909, when

anatomist Franklin Mall used new statistical techniques developed in the budding fields of psychology and genetics to refute the existence of such differences.[62]

From the period following the end of World War I through the first half of the 1960s, psychologists and biologists developed few additional theories. A new outbreak began in the late 1960s, and since then hypotheses have come and gone rapidly. The popular press fanfares each entry with brilliant brass, bright ribbons, and lots of column space, but fails to note when each one in its turn falls into disrepute. The number and variety of theories that have come our way in the past fifteen years are truly remarkable, and an account of their advent, an analysis of their scientific basis, and a view of their demise instructive. I've listed seven of these biological hypotheses in table 4, along with their current status and references for studying them in more detail. The pages that follow focus attention on two of the most popular and currently active ideas—the claim that spatial ability involves a pair of X-linked genes and that male and female brains have different patterns of lateralization.

Space Genes

In 1961 Dr. R. Stafford suggested that humans carry two different X-linked genetic sites, one influencing mathematical problem-solving ability and the other affecting spatial ability.[63] Similar to Lehrke's X-linked variability hypothesis, Stafford's theory proposed that males need inherit only one X chromosome in order to excel in math or spatial tasks, while females need a math and a space gene on each X chromosome, a less frequent possibility.

If his hypothesis were true, one would expect a smaller percentage of females than of males to be good at math and spatial activities. A number of studies have tested predictions about parent-child correlations in mathematical problem solving—predictions that geneticists made from Stafford's theory.

TABLE 4   Biological Theories to Explain Sex-related Cognitive Differences

Year of Initial Publication	Name of Theorist	Basic Tenet	Current Status of Theory
1961	Stafford[g]	Spatial ability is X-linked and thus males show it more frequently than do females.	Clearly disproven,[h] although still widely quoted. Current authors still feel the necessity to argue against this genetic hypothesis.
1966	Money and Lewis[c]	High levels of prenatal androgen may increase intelligence	Disproven by Baker and Ehrhardt in 1974[d].
1968	Broverman et al.[a]	Males are better at "restructuring" tasks, due to lower estrogen levels greater activity of "inhibitory" parasympathetic nervous system.	Actively, critiqued in early 1970s. Not cited in current literature.[b]
1972	Buffery and Gray[j]	Female brains are more lateralized than male brains; greater lateralization inteferes with spatial functions.	No evidence; not currently an important view.
1972	Levy[k]	Female brains are less lateralized than males brains, less lateralization inteferes with spatial funtcions	Currently in vogue; dominates the field despite a number of cogent critiques; no strong supporting evidence.
1973	Bock and Kolakowski[i]	Supplements Stafford's theory, Sex-linked spatial gene is expressed only in the presence of testosterone	Clearly disproven,[h] although still widely quoted. Current authors still feel the necessity to argue against this genetic hypothesis.
1976	Hyde and Rosenberg[e]	High blood uric-acid levels increase intelligence and ambition. Males have more uric acid than females.	Not widely cited, no supporting evidence.[f]

[a]Donald M. Broverman, Edward L. Klaiber, Yutaka Kobayashi, and William Vogel, "Roles of Activation and Inhibition in Sex Differences in Cognitive Abilities," *Psychological Review* 75(1968):23–50.   *Continued*

Table 4 *Continued*

---

[b] Julia A. Sherman, *Sex-Related Cognitive Differences: An Essay on Theory and Evidence* (Springfield, Ill.: Charles C. Thomas, 1978); Mary Parlee, "Comments on 'Roles of Activation and Inhibition in Sex Differences in Cognitive Abilities,' by Broverman et al.," *Psychological Review* 79(1972):180–84; G. Singer and R. Montgomery, "Comment on Roles of Activation and Inhibition in Sex Differences in Cognitive Abilities," *Psychological Review* 76(1969):325-27; Donald M. Broverman, Edward L. Klaiber, Yutaka Kobayashi, and William Vogel, "A reply to the 'Comment' by Singer and Montgomery on 'Roles of Activation and Inhibition in Sex Differences in Cognitive Abilities'," *Psychological Review* 76(1969):328-31.

[c] John Money and V. Lewis, "Genetics and Accelerated Growth: Adrenogenital Syndrome," *Bulletin of Johns Hopkins Hospital* 118(1966):365-73.

[d] Susan W. Baker and Anke Ehrhardt, "Prenatal Androgen, Intelligence, and Cognitive Sex Differences," in *Sex Differences in Behavior*, ed. R.C. Friedman, R.M. Richart, and R.L. Van de Wiele (New York: Wiley, 1974).

[e] J.S. Hyde and B.G. Rosenberg, *Half the Human Experience: The Psychology of Women* (Lexington, Mass.: D.C. Heath, 1976).

[f] Julia A. Sherman, *Sex-Related Cognitive Differences: An Essay on Theory and Evidence* (Springfield, Ill.: Charles C. Thomas, 1978).

[g] R.E. Stafford, "Sex Differences in Spatial Visualization as Evidence of Sex-Linked Inheritance," *Perceptual and Motor Skills* 13(1961):428.

[h] Robin P. Corley, J.C. DeFries, A.R. Kuse, and Steven G. Vandenberg, "Familial Resemblance for the Identical Blocks Test of Spatial Ability: No Evidence of X Linkage," *Behavior Genetics* 10(1980):211-15.

[i] D.R. Bock and D. Kolakowski, "Further Evidence of Sex-Linked Major-Gene Influence on Human Spatial Visualizing Ability," *American Journal of Human Genetics* 25(1973):1–14.

[j] A.W.H. Buffery and J. Gray, "Sex Differences in the Development of Spatial and Linguistic Skills," in *Gender Differences: Their Ontogeny and Significance*, ed. C. Ounsted and D.C. Taylor (London: Chirhill Livingston, 1972).

[k] Jerre Levy, "Lateral Specialization of the Human Brain: Behavioral Manifestation and Possible Evolutionary Basis," in *The Biology of Behavior*, ed. J.A. Kiger Corvalis (Eugene: University of Oregon Press, 1972).

Before 1975 some small-sized studies seemed to support Stafford's contention, although the experimental results rarely obtained statistical significance (unless, in a highly unusual procedure, groups from different studies done by different research groups were pooled to increase sample size). Large studies performed since the mid-1970s have failed to find evidence to support the X-linked hypothesis. The most recent study I found concluded that "[s]ince the previous evidence from small studies cannot be replicated, it appears that the X-linkage hypothesis is no longer tenable."[64] Even more recently, Dr. Hogben Thomas, a researcher at Pennsylvania State University, pointed out that the approach used to test Stafford's hypothesis may be fundamentally flawed and that the X-linkage theory of spatial ability may simply be untestable.[65]

Furthermore, there is a very different source of data that appears to contradict the X-linked hypothesis, one recognized some years ago by two other scientists, Drs. D.R. Bock and D. Kolakowski. Rather than discard Stafford's hypothesis, however, they modified it, turning counter-evidence into support.[66] On occasion, individuals are born with no Y chromosome. Doctors call them XOs. Since they are born with female genitalia, XO individuals are usually raised as girls, and in many respects are quite normal, although they can sometimes be recognized by their short height, webbed neck, and failure to develop fully at puberty. XO individuals, said to have Turner's Syndrome (named after the physician who first described it), have spatial abilities well below the normal range, a fact that contradicts Stafford's hypothesis. If the X-linked hypothesis were correct, Turner's Syndrome patients would not differ from XY males, expressing their spatial ability more frequently than XX females, because their single X chromosome is not "covered" by a second X. In order to get around this uncomfortable fact, Bock and Kolakowski proposed that the space gene is not only X-linked but is also sex-limited, depending for its expression on high androgen levels which circulate throughout the body in higher concentrations in men than in women. (A familiar example of a sex-limited gene is baldness, expressed only in men because it depends for its expression on higher androgen levels than are present in most females.)

The sex-limited hypothesis represents a clever stab at saving the game, but it too runs counter to the data. Psychologist Julia Sherman has offered the most succinct demolition of the theory, and table 5 represents some of her work.[67] Turner's Syndrome patients have lower than normal estrogen (a hormone found in higher concentrations in females) and androgen levels. Bock and Kolakowski argue that the gene coding for spatial ability requires a certain cellular concentration of androgen in order to function. In XO individuals, they suggest, too little androgen is present, and thus Turner's Syndrome girls have poor spatial abilities. To shore up their position, they cite another study of individuals with androgen insensitivity syndrome (AIS)—people who possess both X and Y chromosomes but who are unable to respond to androgens. AIS patients are often born with femalelike genitalia. Fifteen such persons, all raised as females, were tested and obtained an average Verbal IQ of 112 and

TABLE 5 Verbal and Performance IQ's of Individuals with Sex Chromosome and/or Hormone Abnormalities

Number of Individuals Tested	Sex of Rearing	Sex Chromosome: Constitution	Adult Hormone Levels	Average Verbal IQ Scores	Average Performance IQ Scores
45	F	XO	low estrogen low androgen	106	86
15	F	XY	intermediate estrogen, androgen-insensitivity	112	102
3	M	XY	intermediate estrogen, androgen-insensitivity	117	119
23	M	XXY	intermediate estrogen, intermediate androgens	105	88
12	M	XXY	intermediate estrogen, intermediate androgens	66	76
20	M	XYY	unknown	79	88

Note: Julia Sherman, *Sex-Related Differences: An Essay on Theory and Evidence* (Springfield, Ill.: Charles C Thomas, 1978), 84. Courtesy of Charles C Thomas, Publisher.

Performance IQ of 102.* Although both scores fit in the normal range, Bock and Kolakowski inferred from this test that inability to respond to androgen lowered spatial IQ. But who can say whether the Verbal IQ might not have been abnormally high rather than the spatial IQ being unusually low? Furthermore, Back and Kolakowski ignore additional data from the same study. Three AIS patients reared as *males* scored well above the normal range on both verbal and spatial IQ tests. If androgen really improves the expression of spatial genes, how is it that three androgen-insensitive individuals performed above average on a spatial test?[68]

Chromosomal abnormalities affect mental functioning. All people born with either one too many or one too few chromosomes show some degree of mental impairment. The information in table 5 makes this clear. Only AIS patients, who have a normal chromosome complement, score consistently in the normal range on both Verbal and Performance IQ. The data in table 5 thus suggest that good performance correlates with normal chromosome complements, *not*—as Bock and Kolakowski suggest—with hormone levels. By any scientifically acceptable standards, this attempt to save the X-linked space gene theory fails.

As a study in the sociology of science, however, the Stafford hypothesis remains interesting. From the point of view of a geneticist, the idea that two specific genes govern a complex, continuously varying trait is dubious to begin with. As we have just seen, the available data is either categorically inappropriate or lends no support to the idea. Yet since its initial publication in 1961, the X-linkage hypothesis has shown considerable tenacity, appearing as fact in some textbooks and showing up in highly political articles as part of larger arguments about the genetic incapacity of females for certain sorts of

work.[69] The real fact is that many people, both scientists and nonscientists, just plain *like* the idea and go to considerable lengths to salvage it because it fits so neatly into the entrenched stereotype of feminine inferiority. It constitutes a not uncommon example of how social views influence the progress of science.

Left versus Right: The Psychologists' Sleight of Hand

Functionally, humans have two brains. ... While the left hemisphere of the brain appears specialized to carry out analysis, computation, and sequential tasks, in the right half resides artistic abilities and an emotional, nonanalytic approach to the world. As originally developed, the idea of brain hemisphere differentiation said nothing about sex differences. But it didn't take long for scientists to suggest that left-right brain hemisphere specialization could "explain" supposed male/female differences in verbal, spatial, and mathematical ability. The development, dissemination, and widespread acceptance of such ideas provides a second and still very active example of science as social policy.

Humans, like all vertebrates, are bilaterally symmetrical. Although our left and right sides represent approximate anatomical mirror images of one another, they are not equally competent at the many daily activities in which we engage. Each of us has a particular hand and foot preference, using one side of the body more skillfully than the other to, among other things, kick a football, throw a baseball, write, or eat. Such functional asymmetry provides one tangible measure of a complex and poorly understood division of labor between the two sides of the brain. Looking down on the brain from above, one sees the convoluted folds of the right and left halves of the cerebral cortex connected by an enormous mass of nerve fibers, the corpus callosum (see figure 4). Each brain hemisphere controls movements executed by the opposite side of the body. Most people are right-sided, that is, they

---

* Performance IQ (see p. 280) is used by some scientists as a measure of spatial ability, although it is not a test designed for this use.

perform most major activities with the right side of the body, and can thus also be thought of as left-brained. The common scientific belief is that the left hemisphere controls the right side of the body's activities. The converse is probably true for many but not all left-siders.

Our understanding of how the brain mediates our behavior remains superficial, yet a few general observations are possible. For starters, we know that different portions of the cerebral cortex have primary responsibility for particular functions. For example, a region in the posterior part of the cortex (the part located at the back of the head, just above where the skull and neck hook together) enables us to see (and is thus referred to as the *visual cortex*). The region of the cortex responsible for hearing is located further forward along the left side of the head, and numerous other functions take up primary residence in other regions of the brain, as figure 4 illustrates.

A second aspect of brain function involves the notion of cerebral dominance. For many years scientists thought of the hemisphere controlling our preferred side as the major hemisphere, and the other as a minor, less competent half. During the 1950s a change in that viewpoint evolved, because discoveries made it clear that the halves of the brain were not so much dominant and dominated as they were different. Some physicians tried, with a modicum of success, to control severe cases of epilepsy by cutting the fibers of the corpus callosum, thus separating the connections between the two halves of the brain. Because patients receiving such operations appeared under most circumstances to function normally, some time passed before Dr. Roger Sperry, a well-known neurobiologist, and a number of his students designed special tests which revealed that in such "split-brain" individuals the different halves of a supposedly symmetrical brain had very different capabilities.[70] They found, for example, that if a blindfolded split-brain patient picks up a pencil in the left hand (controlled by the right brain) he or she can neither name nor

describe it, although such a patient can easily do so while holding the pencil in the right hand. Such an observation suggests that language—the ability to read and speak—is localized primarily on the left side of the brain. The fact that the same patient (still blindfolded) can use his or her sense of touch to select a pencil from among a number of other objects shows that the ability to recognize pencils remains. But when the fibers connecting the two halves of the brain are severed, there is no transfer of this recognition from the right side of the brain to the left, where the ability lies to name what the patient touches. The same is true of visual perception. With the right eye covered, these patients cannot read or copy words flashed in front of the left eye (connects to the right hemisphere), although they recognize the content. One of Sperry's patients, for example, gave an embarrassed giggle when a nude figure flashed before her left eye, but she could not explain why she had laughed.

As a result of many studies on both split-brain patients and people in whom one brain half has been damaged by a stroke, cancer, or accident, scientists now make the following generalizations about normal, *right-handed* people. (Little is yet understood about left-sidedness.) The left side of the brain has the capability for all verbal activities, and for analytical, mathematical, and sequential information processing. It is sometimes called the analytical brain. The right side specializes in spatial skills and holistic, nonverbal, Gestalt processing, including musical ability. A concert conductor who, due to a stroke, was almost completely unable to speak but could nevertheless continue to conduct his own orchestra, provides a dramatic illustration of this hemispheric specialization.

The fact that the two halves of the brain specialize for different intellectual activities is of both theoretical and practical importance. Humans are the only primates exhibiting handedness or hemispheric specialization,[71] and some speculate that the phenomenon may have evolved as part of the evolution of

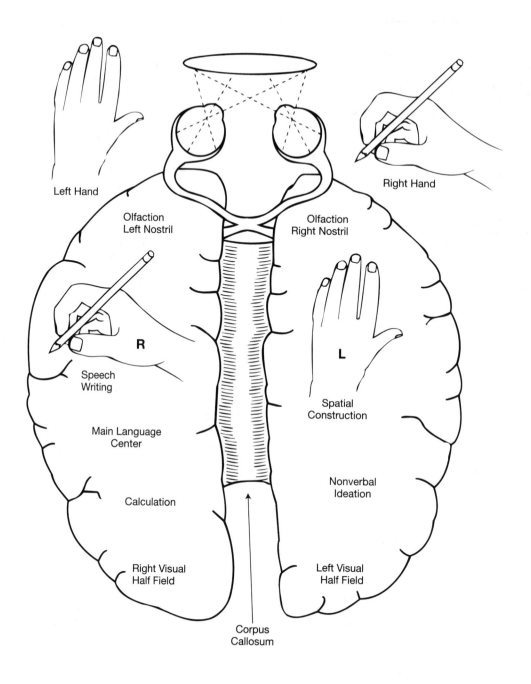

FIGURE 4 The Right and Left Hemispheres of the Brain and their Functions.
Note: Richard Restak, *The Brain, The Last Frontier* (New York: Warner, 1979), 190. Copyright © 1979 by Richard M. Restak. Reproduced by permission of Doubleday & Company, Inc.

speech and tool making. But consideration of the discoveries that have located certain functions in particular regions of the brain requires some caution. We have yet to understand how the brain thinks, and we know nothing about how, or even whether, the brains of two individuals—one skilled in mathematics and the other a talented fiction writer, for example—differ. To illustrate, fantasize for a moment about the return to earth of Benjamin Franklin, the inventor, scientist, and patriot. The year is 1985. On his return Franklin observes immediately that our roads crawl with mechanical horses (cars). Curious, he experiments to discover how they work. First he removes different parts of the car, observing that the removal of a wheel makes the ride bumpy, draining of the brake fluid makes it difficult to stop, and removal of the battery or engine prevents forward motion altogether. Although he thus localizes some functions, he uncovers little information about their mechanisms or about the natures of either batteries or internal combustion engines. Only much more painstaking analyses could reveal that. Ben Franklin reincarnate might quickly identify the seat of motive power, but he could not as easily uncover its mechanism of function.

In finding that different halves of the cerebrum specialize for different functions, we have identified a major seat of power but have learned little about how it operates. A 1980 article in *Science* magazine further illustrates how little we know. It contains a report on a British university student with an IQ of 126 who has first-class honors in math, is socially normal, yet has hardly any nerve cells in his cerebral cortex.[72] This and similar medical reports suggest that the task of understanding the mechanisms by which the brain performs intellectual functions still lies far beyond our reach.

The excitement elicited by Sperry's discoveries has led to a somewhat unbalanced view of how the brain works. As Sperry himself comments in his Nobel Laureate address: "The left-right dichotomy ... is an idea with which it is very easy to run wild."[73] He cautions that other divisions in the brain (such as front/back, up/down) may also have unrecognized importance but, most important, he stresses that the brain operates as a coherent whole, a closely integrated unit. Overemphasis on the separate abilities of particular brain regions easily leads us to neglect to inquire into the function of the integrated whole.

Sperry also suggests that each human brain may be different enough to defy generalization: "The more we learn, the more we recognize the unique complexity of any one individual intellect and the stronger the conclusion becomes that the individuality inherent in our brain networks makes that of fingerprints or facial features gross and simple by comparison."[74] Since scientists work on the assumption that they can generalize and predict, Sperry's suggestion is quite unsettling. If he is right, then entire subfields of psychology and neurobiology may have to change their approach and their focus.

One last point about hemispheric specialization: cerebral lateralization is not immutable during childhood. In children who incur brain damage on only one side, the undamaged hemisphere can carry out all of the functions of an uninjured brain, although in adults this is not the case. It seems at least plausible, then, that the developmental environment of childhood plays an important role in the attainment of adult hemispheric capacities.[75]

Not long after the discovery of hemispheric specialization, some scientists began using it to explain both the supposed female excellence in verbal tasks and the male skill in spatial visualization. In the past eight years at least four different theories on these skills have appeared, the two discussed here having received the most attention although, interestingly enough, they are mutually incompatible. The first, put forth in 1972 by two psychologists, Drs. Anthony Buffery and Jeffrey Gray,[76] now suffers disfavor. The other, elaborated by Dr. Jerre Levy[77]—who during and after her time as Sperry's student, played an important role in defining the modern concept of hemispheric specialization—is still in fashion. The pages of *Psychology Today, Quest,* and even *Mainliner* magazine (the United Airlines monthly) have all enthusiastically described her theory. Speculation also abounds that sex differences in hemispheric specialization result from different prenatal and pubertal hormonal environments.[78] Since a number of psychologists have pointed to a substantial body of experimental evidence that renders Buffery and Gray's hypothesis untenable,[79] we will consider only Levy's views.

Levy hypothesizes that the most efficiently functioning brains have the most complete hemispheric division of labor.[80] Women, she suggests, retain a capacity for verbal tasks in both hemispheres. In other words, they are less lateralized for speech than are men. When verbal tasks in women "spill over" to the right side of the brain, they interfere with the right hemisphere's ability to perform spatial tasks.* Men, in contrast, have highly specialized brain halves—the left side confining its activities solely to verbal problems, the right side solely to spatial ones.

Let's suppose for a moment that male and female brains do lateralize differently and ask what evidence exists to suggest that such differences might lead to variations in performance of spatial and verbal tasks. The answer is, quite simply, none whatsoever. Levy derives the idea not from any experimental data but from a logical supposition. In her later work[81] she takes that supposition and "reasons" that "a bilaterally symmetric brain would be limited to verbal or spatial processing. ..." Recently psychologist Meredith Kimball reviewed the small number of studies that might act as tests of Levy's logical supposition and came up

empty-handed, concluding that there is no evidence to support the key assumption on which Levy builds her hypothesis.[82]

Nevertheless, the proposal that men and women have different patterns of brain lateralization has provoked enormous interest. Scientists have published hundreds of studies, some done on normal subjects and others derived from subjects with brain damage due to stroke, surgery, or accident. The idea that verbal function might operate differently in male and female brains came in part from a long-standing observation: among stroke victims there appear to be more men than women with speech defects serious enough to warrant therapy. There may be a number of explanations for why men seek speech therapy more frequently than do women. To begin with, more males *have* strokes.[83] Also, it is possible that males seek remedial therapy after a stroke more frequently than do females. And strokes may affect speech less severely in females because females have better verbal abilities before the illness.[84]

Some researchers have attempted to sort out these possibilities, but a controlled study of stroke victims is extremely difficult. One reason is that there is no way of knowing for sure whether male and female victims under comparison experienced exactly the same type of brain damage. Even comparisons of individuals who had surgery performed on similar parts of their brains are probably quite misleading because of variation in brain morphology from individual to individual. It would be possible to ascertain the exact regions of the brain affected only by looking at microscopic sections of it, a practice that is routine in animal experiments but would of course be impossible with live human beings. Extensive reviews of clinical studies reveal a great deal of controversy about their meaning, but little in the way of strong evidence to support the idea that women have bilateralized verbal functions.[85] Consider the statement of a scientist who believes her work to *support* the differential lateralization hypothesis:

* The theory actually holds that left-handed men resemble women in this regard. The experimental support for her conclusions about left-handed men has been roundly criticized, esperically by J. Marshall (see note 79).

Neither do the data overwhelmingly confirm that male brains show greater functional asymmetry than female brains.... One must not overlook perhaps the most obvious conclusion, which is that basic patterns of male and female brain asymmetry seem to be more similar than they are different.[86]

If this is the kind of support the proponents of sex differences in laterality put forward, then it is amazing indeed that the search for sex-related differences in brain lateralization remains such a central focus of current research in sex-related cognitive differences.

In addition to looking at patients with brain damage, researchers have tested Levy's hypothesis using normal individuals. The most common way of measuring hemispheric specialization in healthy people is by the dichotic listening test. To look for language dominance, experimenters ask the subject to don a set of headphones. In one ear the subject hears a list of numbers, while in the other he or she simultaneously hears a second, different list. After hearing the two lists, the subject (if not driven nuts) must remember as many of the numbers as possible. Usually subjects can recall the numbers heard on one side better than those heard on the other. Some experimenters believe that right-ear excellence suggests left-hemisphere dominance for verbal abilities and vice versa, but this conclusion ignores other possibilities. Individuals who take the tests may develop different strategies, for instance, deciding to try to listen to both sets of numbers or to ignore one side in order to listen more closely to the other.

Some scientists have reported sex differences in performance on dichotic listening tests, but three recent reviews of the research literature indicate a lack of solid information.[87] Many studies show no sex differences and, in order to show any differences at all, large samples must be used, all of which suggests that same-sex disparities may be larger than those between the sexes. One reviewer ends her article with the following comments:

Any conclusions rest on one's choice of which studies to emphasize and which to ignore. It is very tempting to argue that there are no convincing data for sex-related differences in cognition or cerebral lateralization. ... In fact, what is required is better research.[88]

Analogous methods exist for studying visual lateralization. Tests utilize a gadget called a tachistoscope, through which a subject looks into a machine with an illuminated field. The machine flashes different items in front of either the right or the left eye, and the subject tries to identify as many as possible. Nonverbal images such as dots (as opposed to words or letters) suggest some left-field (right hemisphere) advantages for men, but here too the data vary a great deal. For example, many (but not all) studies show male left-eye advantages for perception of photographed faces, scattered dots, and line orientations, but no sex differences for the perception of schematic faces, depth, or color.[89] In addition, the fundamental question of whether such tests have anything at all to do with brain lateralization continues to cloud the picture.

Although there is no solid evidence for the idea that females are more bilateral than males in verbal functioning, there *does* seem to be evidence that females use their left hemisphere (their verbal hemisphere) more frequently to solve visual-spatial problems. As Sherman points out, this does not necessarily imply a sex-related difference in brain organization, but could instead reflect different problem-solving strategies. For whatever reasons, females may prefer to use verbal approaches to the solution of spatial problems. In fact, several studies show different *approaches* to nonverbal problem solving, but find no overall sex differences in performance. In other words, males did not have a better final outcome; they just reached the same end using a different means than did the females.[90]

As of this writing, a number of hypotheses to explain such strategic differences are actively competing with one another. Sherman, for example, suggests what she calls the "bent twig" hypothesis,[91] proposing that girls develop their language ability a bit earlier than do boys, thereby initiating a chain of reactions that give females progressively greater language skills. Because girls talk sooner, parents may talk more with and further develop their daughters' language skills. And because of their facility, little girls may choose verbal mediation over so-called "Gestalt" processes for the solution of visual-spatial problems. Sherman entertains the possibility that early verbal development in young girls is a true biological sex difference, but it is also possible that if girls learn to talk earlier than do boys it is because adults in their environment interact with them more often and intensively with the spoken word.

If there remains uncertainty about different maturation rates in early language acquisition, there is some clarity in the fact that on the average, girls reach puberty and adult size two to three years before boys. This developmental rate difference forms the basis of another hypothesis, put forth by psychologist Dr. Deborah Waber.[92] She provides evidence that late maturers, *male or female,* have more highly lateralized brains. She thus accounts for any small male/female differences in lateralization by the fact that males, on the average, grow more slowly. Not all studies, however, agree either about the correlation of maturation rate and spatial abilities or about the interpretation of any such correlation, and Waber's suggestion remains under active investigation.[93]

Finally, there is a series of suggestions, not yet in the form of full-dress hypotheses, about the ways in which physical activity might affect the development of visual-spatial skills. What kinds of cognitive capacities develop from active play—tree climbing, running, throwing, batting, and catching a ball? Virtually no information exists on this issue. Yet if scientists are truly interested in how cognitive abilities develop (in a little boy or a little girl), these questions surely require investigation.

Biological Calculus: Do the Sexes Differ in Mathematical Ability?

A few years ago, a friend phoned me for some advice. His ten-year-old daughter was upset because she had just heard on the radio about the hot new discovery that boys are genetically better at math than are girls. Girls, she had heard, would be less frustrated if they recognized their limits and stopped their fruitless struggle to exceed them.

"Daddy," she had said, "I always wanted to be a math professor like you. Does this mean I can't?"

My friend wanted to know if I had read the article. "Is it true? What can I tell my daughter?"

Just two days before, I had seen the same report in the *New York Times.*[94] One day before, the mail carrier had dropped through my mail slot the issue of *Science* magazine containing the short research article by Drs. Camilla Benbow and Julian Stanley, which I had seen summarized in the *Times.*[95] Within the week, radio advertisers hawked the latest issues of *Time* and *Newsweek,* telling me even as I sleepily brushed my teeth in the morning to buy the magazines because they contained new evidence about "male math genes."[96] And so it went. The *Time* article even had an illustration in case we couldn't get the written message. The cartoon portrayed a girl and a boy standing in front of a blackboard, with a proud, smug-looking adult—presumably a teacher—looking on. The girl frowns in puzzlement as she looks directly out at the reader. On the blackboard in front of her stands the multiplication problem 8×7, which she is clearly unable to solve. The boy looks with a toothy smile toward the adult, who gazes back at him. The cause for the satisfaction? The correct answer to the multiplication problem $7,683 \times 632$. Interpreting the image does not require a degree in art history, and the aftershocks from the *Science* article and subsequent press coverage still rumble beneath our feet.

Clearly, math and sex is a hot topic. The question is, what's all the fuss about? The issue is part of both a national and individual crisis. The 1983 report of the National Science Board's Commission on Precollege Education in Mathematics, Science and Technology puts it this way: "Our children could be stragglers in a world of technology. We must not let this happen; America must not become an industrial dinosaur. We must not provide our children a 1960s education for a twenty-first-century world."[97]

Researcher Lucy Sells labels high school mathematics achievement a "critical filter" which limits the choices of study available to women and minorities who enter college,[98] and others have pointed out how mathematics requirements restrict entry to the high-paid field of engineering.[99] A recent counseling session I had with a female student interested in biology vividly illustrates the point. The student wanted advice about choosing her major. She had taken a variety of nonscience courses during her first couple of years in college and was certain that she did not want to become a high-powered professional, preferring instead a goal of working one-on-one with people in city neighborhoods. "And," she said, "I really like biology." Fresh from reading the National Science Board's report, I cheerfully suggested that she might translate her enthusiasm for this aspect of science into becoming a science and math teacher at the primary or secondary level. It was then that her face fell. "I haven't had math since my sophomore year in high school," she confessed, "and that seems so long ago, I can't even remember whether it was a course in algebra or geometry."

That left us stuck. I urged her to take the preintroductory level course offered by our math department (pejoratively called "math for poets" by some), with the hope that she could build up enough background to enter the introductory sequence. But I realized that by the time she had done that she would be ready to graduate. The choice she had made

to stop studying math in high school now, five years later, had come back to haunt her. The damage was not irremediable but it would take time, and I would be surprised if she ended up deciding to teach math and science, badly needed though she may be.

There are very few hard facts about women and mathematics, but one thing we know for sure is that girls take fewer mathematics courses in high school than do boys.[100] Do they drop out because they are less able to achieve mathematically, or are other factors involved, such as stereotypes about math being a male field, discouragement from parents and teachers, and social pressures? Most educational researchers agree that in an unselected population, boys and girls are equally good at math until the seventh grade. Beyond that, however, the debate becomes mired in confusion. Many studies done before 1974 that claimed to find significant sex-related differences in math achievement failed to use well-matched populations. Instead the boys averaged a larger number of courses taken, and the studies really compared girls who had taken only one or two math courses with boys who had taken three or four. Later work that attempted to control for both the number of math courses and the number of related courses in areas such as mechanical drawing and drafting sometimes found only small sex-related differences favoring boys.[101] The results of studies done on large unselected samples give inconsistent results.[102]

In some of the studies for which sex-related differences in math have been found even among students with the same number of formal math courses, the role of social factors in accounting for such differences has also been measured. Differences in spatial visualization seem to play only a minor role, but other factors, such as the perceived importance of mathematics for future studies (girls less often thought it important), the perception of math as a male field (more male engineers and math professors), active discouragement of girls by teachers and parents (girls more often received negative feedback than boys), all taken together went a long way toward accounting for the small, occasional differences found in mathematics achievement between boys and girls who have taken the same number of math courses.

This being the case, how is it that the Benbow-Stanley report in *Science* provoked such widespread publicity? The authors make use of data obtained from ongoing studies of mathematically precocious youth at Johns Hopkins University. Since 1972 these researchers have run talent searches to find seventh and eighth graders who are unusually good at math, generally students found to perform in the upper 3 to 5 percent of their classes. Of the talented youth identified, 43 percent were girls. As part of their study, Benbow and Stanley gave these seventh and eighth graders the College Board Scholastic Aptitude Test in mathematics. Since such tests are designed for juniors and seniors in high school who are older and who have had more advanced math classes, Benbow and Stanley argued that the exams functioned as achievement tests in mathematical reasoning when given to much younger students. In each of the six years of the study, the results showed that on average girls obtained scores that were between 7 and 15 percent lower than the average score for boys. Furthermore, anywhere from three to ten times more boys than girls score in very high ranges, although there were usually some very high scoring girls. Such are the results; the fight, of course, is about their meaning. Benbow and Stanley point out that in the seventh and eighth grade, most children take the same math courses, so the differences cannot be due to *formal* course taking:

It, therefore, cannot be argued that these boys received substantially more formal practice in mathematics and therefore scored better. Instead, it is more likely that mathematical reasoning ability influences differential course-taking in mathematics.

After further considering their data, they end their article with the following.

We favor the hypothesis that sex differences in achievement attitude toward mathematics result from superior male mathematical ability. ... This male superiority is probably an expression of both endogenious and exogenous variables ... the hypothesis of differential course-taking was not supported. It also seems likely that putting one's faith in boy-versus-girl socialization processes as the only permissible explanation of the sex difference in mathematics is premature.[103]

In a subsequent paper, also published in *Science*, the same researchers added more subjects to their data base, a fact which they believe further substantiates their initial conclusion.[104]

Attacks on Benbow and Stanley's conclusions have been of three types: questions about the validity of the aptitude test, questions about the limitations of looking only at formal mathematical experience, and questions about whether boys and girls receive the same training even within the same math course. The debate over achievement versus aptitude tests is complex and, I feel, a little beside the point.[105] Whether one calls it aptitude, achievement, or reasoning ability, the fact remains that more very bright boys performed exceptionally on Benbow and Stanley's tests than did very bright girls. Benbow and Stanley claim they are doing nothing more than telling it like it is: "It is not the method of science ... to ignore published facts or provide a forum for subjective judgments and anecdotal evidence."[106] Since they seem willing to take on the Galilean stance of the honest but persecuted scientist in this debate, it is surprising that they fail to cite a number of studies—including both some of their own and ones by other workers in the Johns Hopkins project—that would at the very least dilute the emphasis they place on the idea of "superior male mathematical ability."

For example, they specifically attack psychologists Elizabeth Fennema and Julia Sherman's conclusion about differential course taking; yet those very same researchers in the very same articles write at length about a variety of other factors (parental attitudes, teachers' attitudes, informal mathematics experience), *all* of which contribute significantly to mathematical achievement. Another group of researchers observed thirty-three second-grade teachers as they taught reading and arithmetic in the classroom, finding that teachers spent more classroom time teaching reading to individual girls and less teaching them math. The boys received less direct instruction in reading and more in math.[107] In other words, boys and girls learning together in the same classroom did not receive the same instruction. Benbow and Stanley dismiss this study as irrelevant, saying only that it seemed inapplicable to studies of highly talented children.

Furthermore, in their most recent work they cite some of their own data[108] to support their skepticism about the inability of socialization to account for the reported achievement test differences in talented junior high school students. Surprisingly, though, they dismiss as irrelevant other information they have collected showing that (1) in high school the girls in their study get slightly better grades in math courses than do the boys,* and (2) when asked about intended college majors: "The percentage of males reporting that they intended to major in the mathematical sciences was 15%, while for females this was 17%."[110]

Dr. Helen Astin looked at the backgrounds of children in the early years of the Johns Hopkins Study and found that "parents of boys admit that they encouraged the boys more by giving them science kits, telescopes, microscopes, or other science-related gifts."[111] In addition, the parents of mathematically precocious boys had higher educational hopes for them than did the girls' parents. Finally, Lynn Fox and Sanford

Cohn, also researchers in the Johns Hopkins Study, find evidence from other aspects of the project to "support the social explanation of sex differences at higher levels of ability and achievement."[112] The evidence from these talented youngsters that boys and girls even at the seventh-grade level have had different experiences with regard to math training and have developed very different hopes for their futures makes implausible Benbow and Stanley's underlying assumption that only socialization events at puberty influence the development of mathematical skill and achievement.

In considering the debate over math ability the question foremost in my mind is, Why the rush to judgment? Benbow and Stanley, though they hedge their bets, clearly assert that boys have greater math ability than do girls. While choosing to simplify the discussion and ignore much of the literature on sex differences in both teaching and informal learning, as well as findings on career goals and hopes, they invite us all to "face facts" and accept the biological nature of sex differences in math ability if that is, indeed, what objective science proves.

We *do* know a great deal about mathematics learning and especially about why girls drop out of math classes.[113] If math and science were required for four years of high school, if girls were actively counseled to consider careers in science and warned about the ways in which dropping out of math limits their future choices, if teachers were made aware of the different ways they treat boys and girls in the classroom, and if there were many more women teaching math and science to our youngsters, the "problem" of women in math would lessen dramatically, and in all likelihood would disappear. To argue for "endogenous" differences, as Benbow and Stanley have, is to argue willy-nilly, not to bother with all of the "exogenous" changes in educational method and quality that we could make with some degree of success right now. At best their call to consider "natural" causes for the sex difference in math is premature. If, once we have reformed our informal and formal

---

* When criticized for failing to discuss the discrepancy between achievement in the classroom and scores on SAT tests, Benbow and Stanley dismissed their own finding by attributing it "to the better conduct of girls in school."[109]

systems of mathematics education and career counseling, there remain significant sex differences in mathematics ability, *then* might be the time to wonder about innate sex differences. In the meantime there are a lot of very specific changes to be made in how we educate our young people. What, then, are we waiting for?

A Question of Genius: Some Conclusions

Are men really smarter than women? The straightforward answer would have to be no. Early in this century, scientists argued that there might be more male than female geniuses because male intelligence varied to a greater extent than did female intelligence. This "fact" provided proof positive of the overall superiority of the male mind. Hypotheses in defense of this position still pop up from time to time. They consist of old ideas in modern dress and are unacceptable to most mainstream psychologists. In apparent contrast Maccoby and Jacklin believe that males and females are equally intelligent while entertaining the possibility that the two sexes have somewhat different cognitive skills; they suggest a biological origin for such differences. Although the possibility is admissible, I have tried to show both that any such differences are very small and that there is no basis for assuming a priori that these small variations have innate biological origins.

This chapter bears witness to the extensive yet futile attempts to derive biological explanations for alleged sex differences in cognition. Although these efforts all have a certain social wrong-headedness to them, they do not stand or fall on their political implications. Rather, such biological explanations fail because they base themselves on an inaccurate understanding of biology's role in human development. Sperry suggests this when he writes that each person's brain may have more physical individuality than do the person's fingerprints. His statement is radical

because it implies that attempts to lump people together according to broad categories such as sex or race are doomed to failure. They both oversimplify biological development and downplay the interactions between an organism and its environment. As a result of doing research for this book, I arrived at the same conclusion. ...

Notes

1. "Is Math Ability Affected by Hormones?," *Boston Globe*, 26 Dec. 1983, Science section.
2. Letter to the Editor, *Providence Journal*, 25 March 1984.
3. Margaret Rossiter, *Women Scientists in America: Struggles and Strategies to 1940* (Baltimore: Johns Hopkins University Press, 1982), 107.
4. Maxine Seller, "G. Stanley Hall and Edward Thorndike on "the Education of Women: Theory and Policy in the Progressive Era," *Educational Studies* 11(1981): 365–74.
5. Stephanie A. Shields, "Functionalism, Darwinism, and the Psychology of Women: A Study in Social Myth," *American Psychologist* 30(1975): 739–54.
6. Rossiter, *Women Scientists;* Seller, "G. Stanley Hall and Edward Thorndike"; and Mary Brown Parlee, "The Sexes Under Scrutiny: From Old Biases to New Theories," *Psychology Today,* (Nov. 1978), 64–69.
7. Seller, "G. Stanley Hall and Edward Thorndike."
8. Rossiter, *Women Scientists.*
9. Seller, "G. Stanley Hall and Edward Thorndike." Seller writes the following: Although the total number of women in the professions increased in the 1920s they remained clustered in "female" occupations. In New York, for example, there were 63,637 (female) teachers and about 22,000 nurses but only 60 Certified Public Accountants, 11 engineers and 8 inventors. There were fewer women in medical schools in the late 1920s than there had been at the turn of the century. [p. 371]
10. Ibid., 273.
11. Ibid.
12. Parlee, "The Sexes Under Scrutiny."

13. Robert G. Lehrke, "A Theory of X-linkage of Major Intellectual Traits," *American Journal of Mental Deficiency* 76(1972):611–19.

14. Anne Anastasi, "Four Hypotheses with a Dearth of Data: Response to Lehrke's 'A Theory of X-linkage of Major Intellectual Traits,'" *American Journal of Mental Deficiency* 76(1972):620–22; Walter E. Nance and Eric Engel, "One X and Four Hypotheses: Response to Lehrke's 'A Theory of X-linkage of Major Intellectual Traits,'" *American Journal of Mental Deficiency* 76(1972)1:623-25.

15. Nance and Engel, "One X and Four Hypotheses"; Michele A. Wittig, "Sex Differences in Intellectual Functioning: How Much of a Difference do Genes Make?," *Sex Roles* 2(1976):63–74.

16. Robert G. Lehrke, "Sex Linkage: A Biological Basis for Greater Male Variability in Intelligence," in *Human Variation: The Biopsychology of Age, Race, and Sex,* ed. R. Travis Osborne, Clyde E. Noble, and Nathaniel Weyl (New York: Academic Press, 1978), 193.

17. Lehrke makes his argument appear a little more sophisticated from the geneticist's viewpoint by including a discussion of the Lyon Hypothesis, according to which in females the paternally contributed X chromosome in some cells is genetically inactive while in other cells the maternally contributed X is inactive. According to Lehrke this would lead to an "average" expression of X-linked traits, rather than to the extreme he expects in males.

18. Stephen Jay Gould, *The Mismeasure of Man* (New York: Norton, 1981); and Richard C. Lewontin, Steven Rose, and Leon Kamin, *Not in Our Genes* (New York: Random House, 1984).

19. Lehrke, "A Theory of X-linkage."

20. Robert M. Murphy, "Phenyl Ketonuria (PKU) and the Single Gene," *Behavior Genetics* 13(1983):141–57.

21. Wittig, "Sex Differences."

22. Julia Sherman, "Effects of Biological Factors on Sex-related Differences in Mathematics Achievement," in *Women and Mathematics, Research Perspectives for Change,* no. 8, NIE Papers in Education and Work (Washington, D.C.: National Institute of Education, 1977).

23. Lehrke, "A Theory of X-linkage."

24. Anastasi, "Four Hypotheses."

25. Robert Lehrke, "Response to Dr. Anastasi and to the Drs. Nance and Engel," *American Journal of Mental Deficiency* 76(1972):630.

26. Nance and Engel, "One X and Four Hypotheses."

27. Lehrke, "Sex Linkage," 172.

28. Lehrke, "Response to Dr. Anastasi," 631.

29. Osborne, Noble, and Weyl, *Human Variation.*

30. In the epilogue to Osborne, Noble, and Weyl's *Human Variation,* noted geneticist C.D. Darlington writes the following:

> When the Negroids were taken away from Africa by slave traders they were partly ... rescued from the diseases that had infested them. But slavery did not rescue them from their genetic responses to disease, which have continued with them as an obstacle to their development individually, racially, and culturally. Nor did it rescue them from their primitive beliefs. These experiences teach us indeed that peoples cannot be separated from their history. They are bound down by their evolutionary antecedents, occupational, social and medical. ... When the Negroids were liberated from agricultural slavery, they were thrown free to shift for themselves in large urban Caucasoid societies. ... These simple unskilled rural people were suddenly offered irregular urban employment combined with the opportunities of drink and drugs, gambling and prostitution. ... The intellectually well-endowed races, classes and societies have a moral responsibility for the problems of race mixture. ... They may hope to escape from these responsibilities by claiming an intellectual and therefore moral equality between all races, classes and societies. But the chapters of this book, step by step, deprive us of the scientific and historical evidence that might support such a comfortable illusion. [pp. 383–84]

31. Barry Mehler, "The New Eugenics," *Science for the People* 15(1983):18–23.

32. Josef E. Garai and Amram Scheinfeld, "Sex Differences in Mental and Behavioral Traits," *Genetic Psychology Monographs* 77(1968):256.

33. Sandra Witelson, "Sex and the Single Hemisphere: Specialization of the Right Hemisphere for Spatial Processing," *Science* 193(1976):425-27.

34. Daniel Goleman, "Special Abilities of the Sexes: Do they Begin in the Brain?," *Psychology Today,* Nov. 1978, 59.

35. Carole Leland, ed., "Men and Women Learning Together: A Study of College Students in the Late '70s" (Report of the Brown Project, Brown University, 1980).

36. Thorough documentation of the inequality is offered by Rossiter in *Women Scientists.*

37. Garai and Scheinfeld, "Sex Differences in Mental and Behavioral Traits," 275–76.

38. Rossiter, *Women Scientists,* 106.

39. Eleanor E. Maccoby and Carol N. Jacklin, *The Psychology of Sex Differences* (Stanford, Calif.: Stanford University Press, 1974).

40. Julia A. Sherman, *Sex-related Cognitive Differences: An Essay on Theory and Evidence* (Springfield, Ill.: Charles C Thomas, 1978).

41. Anne C. Petersen and Michele A. Wittig, "Sex-related Differences in Cognitive Functioning: An Overview," in *Sex-related Differences in Cognitive Function: Developmental Issues,* ed. M. A. Wittig and A. C. Petersen (New York: Academic Press, 1979).

42. Sherman, *Cognitive Differences.*

43. Carol N. Jacklin, "Epilogue" in *Sex-related Differences in Cognitive Function,* ed. Wittig and Petersen; Janet S. Hyde, "How Large Are Cognitive Differences? A Meta-analysis Using Ω and d," *American Psychologist* 36(1981):892-901; Robert Plomin and Terryl Foch, "Sex Differences and Individual Differences," *Child Development* 52(1981):383–85.

44. Technically, one calculates the variance as the square of the standard deviation. It is a less intuitively obvious number than the standard deviation but is a direct measure of how a population varies about a particular mean. Meta-analysis is a method for analyzing the degree to which different variables in a population contribute to the overall variability of the population.

45. Hyde, "How Large Are Cognitive Differences?"

46. Plomin and Foch, "Sex Differences and Individual Differences," 384.

47. Jerre Levy, as quoted in Jo Durden-Smith, "Male and Female—Why," *Quest* 4(1980):17.

48. Maccoby and Jacklin, *The Psychology of Sex Differences.*

49. Sherman, *Sex-related Cognitive Differences.*

50. Julia Sherman, letter to author, 29 April 1981.

51. Hyde, "How Large Are Cognitive Differences?"

52. Ibid.

53. J.M. Connor, M. Schackman, and L. Serbin, "Sex-related Differences in Response to Practice on a Visual-Spatial Test and Generalization to a Related Test," *Child Development* 49(1978):24–29.

54. S. Johnson, "Effects of Practice and Training in Spatial Skills on Sex-related Differences in Performance on Embedded Figures," in Sherman, *Sex-related Cognitive Differences.*

55. E. Fennema and Julia Sherman, "Sex-related Differences in Mathematics, Achievement, Spatial Visualization and Affective Factors," *American Educational Research Journal* 14(1977):51–71.

56. S.B. Nerlove, R.H. Monroe, and R.I. Monroe, "Effect of Environmental Experience on Spatial Ability: A Replication," *Journal of Social Psychology* 84(1971):3–10.

57. J.W. Berry, "Temne and Eskimo Perceptual Skills," *International Journal of Psychology* 1(1966):207–29; and R. MacArthur, "Sex Differences in Field Independence for the Eskimo," *International Journal of Psychology* 2(1967):139-40.

58. J.W. Berry, "Ecological and Cultural Factors in Spatial Perception Development," *Canadian Journal of Behavioral Science* 3(1971):324–36.

59. H.A. Moss, "Early Sex Differences and Mother-Infant Interaction," in *Sex Differences in Behavior,* ed. R.C. Friedman, R.H. Richart, and R.L. Van de Wiele (New York: Wiley, 1974), 149–63.

60. Stephen Jay Gould, "Women's Brains," in *The Panda's Thumb* (New York: Norton, 1980), 152–59.

61. Shields, "Functionalism, Darwinism, and the Psychology of Women," 471.

62. Ibid.; G.T.W. Patrick, "The Psychology of Women," *Popular Science Monthly* 47(1895):209-25; Franklin Mall, "On several anatomical characters of the human brain said to vary according to race and sex, with especial reference to the weight of the frontal lobe," *American Journal of Anatomy* 9(1909):l–32.

63. Stafford, "Sex Differences in Spatial Visualization as Evidence of Sex-linked Inheritance," *Perceptual and Motor Skills* 13(1961):428.

64. R.P. Corley et al., "Familial Resemblance for the Identical Blocks Test of Spatial Ability: No Evidence of X Linkage," *Behavior Genetics* 10(1980):211–15.

65. Hogben Thomas, "Familial Correctional Analyses, Sex Differences and the X-linked Gene Hypothesis," *Psychological Bulletin* 93(1982):427-40.

66. D.R. Bock and D. Kolakowski, "Further Evidence of Sex-linked Major-Gene Influence on Human Spatial Visualizing Ability," *American Journal of Human Genetics* 25(1973):1–14.

67. Sherman, *Sex-related Cognitive Differences.*

68. Bock and Kolakowski, "Further Evidence of Sex-related Major-Gene Influence."

69. Michael Levin, "The Feminist Mystique," *Commentary,* Dec. 1980, 25–30.

70. Roger Sperry, "Some Effects of Disconnecting the Cerebral Hemispheres," *Science* 217(1982):1223-26.

71. S.F. Walker, "Lateralization of Functions in the Vertebrate Brain: A Review," *British Journal of Psychology* 71(1980):329–67.

72. Roger Lewin, "Is Your Brain Really Necessary?," *Science* 210(1980):1232–34.

73. Sperry, "Some Effects of Disconnecting the Cerebral Hemispheres," 1224.

74. Ibid., 1223-26.

75. Walker, "Lateralization of Functions," 1224; and R. Restak, *The Brain, the Last Frontier* (New York: Warner Books, 1979).

76. A. Buffery and J. Gray, "Sex Differences in the Development of Spatial and Linguistic Skills," in *Gender Differences: Their Ontogeny and Significance,* ed. C. Ounsted and D.C. Taylor (London: Chirhill Livingston, 1972).

77. Jerre Levy, "Lateral Specialization of the Human Brain: Behavioral Manifestation and Possible Evolutionary Basis," in *The Biology of Behavior,* ed. J. Kiger (Eugene: University of Oregon Press, 1972).

78. D. Goleman, "Special Abilities of the Sexes: Do They Begin in the Brain?," *Psychology Today,* Nov. 1978, 48–59; Tim Hackler, "Women vs. Men: Are They Born Different?," *Mainliner,* May 1980, 122–26; and Jo Durden-Smith, "Men, Women and the Brain: Are Our Brains as Different as Our Bodies?," *Quest/80* 4(1980):15–19, 93-99.

79. Sherman, *Sex-related Cognitive Differences;* J.C. Marshall, "Some Problems and Paradoxes Associated with Recent Accounts of Hemispheric Specialization," *Neuropsychologia* 11(1973):463-70.

80. Levy, "Lateral Specialization"; and Meredith Kimball, "Women and Science: A Critique of Biological Theories," *International Journal of Women's Studies* 4(1981):318-38.

81. Jerre Levy, "Possible Basis for the Evolution of Lateral Specialization of the Human Brain," *Nature* 224(1969):614–15.

82. Kimball, "Women and Science."

83. Andrew Kersetz, "Sex Distribution in Aphasia," *The Behavioral and Brain Sciences* 5(1982):310.

84. Sherman, *Sex-related Cognitive Differences.*

85. Kimball, "Women and Science"; Kersetz, "Sex Distribution and Aphasia"; and J. McGlone, "Faulty Logic Fuels Controversy," *The Brain and Behavioral Sciences* 5(1982):312–14.

86. McGlone, Jeanette, "Sex Differences in Human Brain Asymmetry: A Critical Survey," *The Behavioral and Brain Sciences* 3(1980):226.

87. Kimball, "Women and Science,"; McGlone, "Faulty Logic Fuels Controversy"; and M.P. Bryden, "Evidence of Sex-related Differences in Cerebral Organization," in *Sex-related Differences in Cognitive Functioning,* ed. Wittig and Petersen.

88. Bryden, "Evidence of Sex-related Differences," 137–38.

89. Sherman, *Sex-related Cognitive Differences;* Kersetz, "Sex Distribution in Aphasia"; McGlone, "Sex Differences in Human Brain Asymmetry"; and Bryden, "Evidence of Sex-related Differences."

90. Kimball, "Women and Science."

91. Sherman, *Sex-related Cognitive Differences.*

92. Deborah Waber, "Cognitive Abilities and Sex-related Variations in the Maturation of Cerebral Cortical Functions," in *Sex-related Differences in Cognitive Functioning,* ed. Wittig and Petersen.

93. Nora Newcombe and Mary M. Bandure, "Effect of Age at Puberty on Spatial Ability in Girls: A Question of Mechanism," *Developmental Psychology* 19(1983):215–24.

94. "Are Boys Better at Math?," *New York Times,* 7 Dec. 1980, p. 102.

95. Camilla P. Benbow and Julian C. Stanley, "Sex Differences in Mathematical Ability: Fact or Artifact?" *Science* 210(1980):1262–64.

96. "The Gender Factor in Math," *Time,* 15 Dec. 1980, p. 57; D.A. Williams and P. King, "Do Males have a Math Gene?," *Newsweek,* 15 Dec. 1980, p. 73.

97. *Chronicle of Higher Education* 27(1983):1.

98. Lucy W. Sells, "The Mathematics Filter and the Education of Women and Minorities," in *Women and the Mathematical Mystique,* ed. Lynn H. Fox, Linda Brody, and Dianne Tobin (Baltimore: Johns Hopkins University Press, 1980).

99. Elizabeth K. Stage and Robert Karplus, "Mathematical Ability: Is Sex a Factor?," *Science* 212(1981):114.

100. "The Mathematics Filter."

101. Elizabeth Fennema, "Sex-related Differences in Mathematics Achievement: Where and Why," in *Women and the Mathematical Mystique,* ed. Fox, Brody and Tobin.

102. Some people argue that it is misleading to compare boys and girls only if they have taken the same number of math courses, because the girls taking large numbers of math courses are a more highly selected sample than the boys. It might be that comparing boys and girls with the same number of math courses really means that one compares bright girls with more average boys. However, Fox, Brody, and Tobin report differential course taking even among highly mathematically gifted girls and boys, suggesting that factors other than mathematical talent are at play when girls and boys decide to proceed into upper-level math courses in high school. See Lynn H. Fox, Linda Brody, and Dianne Tobin, eds., *Women and the Mathematical Mystique* (Baltimore: Johns Hopkins University Press: 1980); see especially the chapter by Dianne Tobin and Lynn H. Fox, "Career Interests and Career Education: A Key to Change," 179-191, in *Women and the Mathematical Mystique,* ed. Fox, Brody, and Tobin.

103. Benbow and Stanley, "Sex Differences in Mathematical Ability," 1263, 1264.

104. Camilla Benbow and Julian Stanley, "Sex Differences in Mathematical Reasoning Ability: More Facts," *Science* 222(1983):1029–31.

105. A.T. Schafer and M.W. Gray, "Sex and Mathematics," *Science* 211(1981):231. Stage and Karplus, "Mathematical Ability"; Camilla P. Benbow and Julian C. Stanley, "Mathematical Ability: Is Sex a Factor?," *Science* 212(1981):118-21.

106. Benbow and Stanley, "Mathematical Ability: Is Sex a Factor?," 121.

107. Gaea Leinhardt, A.M. Seewald, and Mary Engel, "Learning What's Taught: Sex Differences in Instruction," *Journal of Educational Psychology* 71(1979):432–39.

108. Camilla Benbow and Julian Stanley, "Consequences in High School and College of Sex Differences in Mathematical Reasoning Ability: A Longitudinal Perspective," *American Educational Research Journal* 19(1982):612.

109. C. Benbow, Reply to J. Beckwith and M. Woodruff, "Achievement in Mathematics," *Science* 223(1984):1248.

110. Benbow and Stanley, "Consequences in High School and College," 612.

111. Helen Astin, "Sex Differences in Mathematical and Scientific Precocity," in *Mathematical Talent: Discovery, Description and Development,* ed. J.C. Stanley, D.P Keating, and Lynn H. Fox (Baltimore: Johns Hopkins University Press, 1974), 82.

112. Lynn Fox and Sanford J. Cohn, "Sex Differences in the Development of Precocious Mathematical Talent," in *Women and the Mathematical Mystique,* ed. Fox, Brody, and Tobin; L.H. Fox, "Sex Differences Among the Mathematically Precocious," *Science* 224(1984):1291–93.

113. Lynn Fox, "The Problem of Women and Mathematics" (Report to the Ford Foundation, New York, 1981); Jayne E. Stake and Charles R. Granger, "Same-Sex and Opposite-Sex Teacher Model Influences on Science Career Commitment among High School Students," *Journal of Educational Psychology* 70(1978):180–86; Doris R. Entwistle and David P. Baker, "Gender and Young Children's Expectations for Performance in Arithmetic," *Developmental Psychology* 19(1983):200–209; Edith H. Luchins, "Sex Differences in Mathematics: How *NOT* to deal with them," *American Mathematical Monthly* 86(1979):161–68; and Sally L. Hacker, "Mathematization of Engineering: Limits on Women and the Field," in *Machina Ex Dea,* ed. Joan Rothschild (New York: Pergamon, 1983).

PART III

WHAT KIND OF ENTERPRISE OUGHT SCIENCE TO BE?

If traditional science, the science controlled by men, has ignored or misrepresented females and things related to females, if, moreover, it has had untoward effects on women's lives, then how can it be improved? In Part II some of the readings suggested that the science done by women (or feminists, or feminist women) has been different from the men's science that preceded it, has even been better than that men's science. What implications does such a suggestion have for improving science? Must women be included in science for that science to be adequate and helpful to all in society, and if so, how (e.g., must women be included in at least sufficient numbers to have a significant voice, or must they be included in equal numbers with men, or in such a way as to control the scientific enterprise)? And how do our answers to these questions alter our traditional understanding of the scientific enterprise?

FEMINIST EMPIRICISM

According to empiricism, traditional science's house philosophy, our knowledge of the world, even the unobservable parts of the world, is based on our observations of that world. Of course, to make possible genuine knowledge of that world, our observations must not be affected by anything personal or subjective or idiosyncratic; that is, they must be observations *of the world*, and hence, be uniform among us. And our methods of inference from those observations (e.g., our methods of testing hypotheses against them) must be legitimate; that is, they must ensure that all of us come up with the same results from the same observations. To make possible genuine knowledge of the world, then, the participants in its production must be interchangeable: Each must observe and infer what every other one observes and infers and replicate every other one's results. Differences (whether of gender, race, political outlook, or the like) must be irrelevant to the knowledge-producing process. According to empiricism. But if the science done by women (or feminists, or feminist women) has been *different* from the men's science that preceded it, has yielded different, even better, results than the men's science, then gender (or political outlook, or both) *does* matter, and empiricism as a philosophy of science appears problematic.

In "Subjects, Power and Knowledge: Description and Prescription in Feminist Philosophies of Science," philosopher of science Helen Longino considers two different understandings of empiricism in response. According to the first, defined as "feminist empiricism" by Sandra Harding, empiricism specifies a scientific ideal, not a scientific reality: Though scientists *are not* interchangeable, they *ought to be.* That is to say, their (gender, race, political outlook, etc.) differences *ought to be* irrelevant, and in a sufficiently objective science, with sufficiently rigorous methods of observation and test that screen out gender and other biases, such differences *would be* irrelevant. What the readings of Part II show, accordingly, is that our science is not sufficiently objective: Its methods of observation and test are not sufficiently rigorous, or they have not been applied in a sufficiently rigorous way. (Recall, for example, that the Biology and Gender Study Group proposed feminist critique as an additional experimental control that scientists should use in their research, and Anne Fausto-Sterling criticized sex-differences researchers for failing to apply accepted methodological procedures in their research.) It follows that from an epistemological point of view women do not need to be included in science in order to avert the problems relating to science's treatment of women discussed in Part II. All that is needed is that those who do science adopt and always put to use suitable scientific methods—which, perhaps, the women scientists described in Part II did, whereas the men scientists did not.

Longino rejects this understanding of empiricism in favor of another, which has also been called "feminist empiricism." According to Longino, no scientific method, however rigorous and however rigorously applied, can screen out the various values and interests that scientists with their different genders and political outlooks and the like bring to their research. To be sure, scientists' values and interests can and do determine which questions they investigate and which they ignore, can and do motivate the background assumptions they accept and those they reject, can and do influence the observational or experimental data they select to study and the way they express those data. What can be done to ensure objectivity, however, is to limit the intrusion of such values and interests into science, and this by maximizing community criticism of each individual's scientific research. Indeed, a science will be objective, for Longino, to the degree that the community which practices it satisfies four conditions. First, the members of the community must have recognized avenues—for example, journals, conferences, and the like—for the criticism of evidence, methods, assumptions, and reasoning. Second, the members of the community must share standards—substantive principles as well as values—that critics can invoke. Third, the community as a whole must be responsive to the criticism. That is, the beliefs of the scientific community as a whole and over time—as measured by such public phenomena as the content of textbooks, the distribution of grants and awards, and the flexibility of dominant worldviews— must change in response to the critical discussion taking place within it. And fourth, intellectual authority must be shared equally among qualified members, among whom all relevant points of view which can serve as sources of criticism must be represented. A science will be objective, then, to the degree that it satisfies the above conditions—to the degree that it permits what Longino calls "transformative criticism." But, of course, Longino would add, our science has *not* satisfied these conditions: We have already seen this in the portrayals of the exclusion and marginalization of women and their points of view provided in Part I. Small wonder we have found the kinds of problems in our science reported in Part II, and the kinds of transformations, as well, when women have at least begun to be admitted to science on an equal footing with men.

Our science, even if revised in the way Longino recommends, still cannot promise another kind of objectivity, however. For, this other kind pertains not to the structure and functioning of scientific communities but to the *products* of those communities—the facts and theories and the like that those communities put forward as the results of their inquiries. In this sense a science is objective if its theories and other claims provide a true picture of the world, and in this sense Longino denies that our science can be objective. In "Epistemological Communities," philosopher of science Lynn Hankinson Nelson explains why. Considering the position taken by Nobel Prize winning physicist Sheldon Glashow that "there are eternal, objective, extrahistorical, socially neutral, external and universal truths" that "any intelligent alien anywhere would have come upon" (Nelson, p. 322), Nelson points out that the theories we have "come upon" are a response to a complicated intellectual and social context, not simply to observations of the world that both an alien and we might share. For example, "any intelligent alien anywhere" could have "come upon" our theories of proton and supernovae structure only if such an alien already shared the broad intellectual and social context that made these theories possible for us—our metaphysical views such as that macroscopic objects are "made up" of smaller, "unobservable" objects that explain events at the macroscopic level; at least extensive portions of our physics, mathematics, chemistry, and technology; our theories in which protons and supernovae already figure as well as our questions that called forth the new explanatory theories and our new methodologies that made evidence for them possible; and, of course, our generous amounts of funding and time and scientific assistance. Without all of these prerequisites and more our alien could hardly have stumbled upon our theories of proton and supernovae structure. But, of course, the same can be said of the prerequisites in turn; they, too, could not have been stumbled upon without a prior intellectual, methodological, social, and technological context like our own. Significantly change the prerequisites at any stage and it is likely that you change the product, our scientific knowledge. Indeed, as we have already seen, our science is the product of a quite narrow segment of human culture, to wit, Western, white, relatively affluent, and relatively conservative masculine culture. And as we have already seen, the addition of significant numbers of feminist women scientists have already produced changes in that science. Who is to say what further changes might come about with a further diversification of the scientific establishment, and what further changes still with an alien with an alien intellectual and social heritage.

Focusing in this way on the intellectual and social, as well as methodological and technological, context that "supports" or functions as "evidence" for scientific theories, says Nelson, helps us to better understand and assess those theories. And, of course, this holds for sexist and androcentric theories as well as other scientific theories. In this case, focusing on the intellectual and social context that supports these theories also reveals the depth, the pervasiveness, and the significance of sexism and androcentrism in science. "This makes it far less plausible for examples like man-the-hunter theory to be dismissed as 'idiosyncratic' or isolatable instances that have little import for 'science itself' . . . or as 'just models' without the potential to underwrite other theories and research or to reinforce social relations" (Nelson, p. 333). Focusing on the intellectual and social context of sexist and androcentric theories also reveals that the responsibility for such theories resides in scientific communities rather than in individual scientists. It is not the gender of individual scientists, Nelson emphasizes, or any attribute of individual scientists such as political outlook, that leads to or furthers androcentric assumptions, just as it is not the gender or political outlook of feminist scientists that leads to or furthers feminist critique of those assumptions. "The standards and knowledge that underwrite the acceptability of androcentric and feminist assumptions are communal" (Nelson, p. 334).

FEMINIST STANDPOINT THEORY

Emphasizing the communal nature of scientific objectivity and scientific knowledge does much to correct the naive individualism of traditional empiricism. But it also has its limitations. For one thing, community-wide standards and community-wide criticism can limit the intrusion of personal values and interests into science, and this surely is part of what we mean by objectivity. But only part. Indeed, as Sandra Harding points out in "'Strong Objectivity': A Response to the New Objectivity Question," "it is not individual, personal, 'subjective' error to which feminist and other social critics of science have drawn attention, but widely held androcentric, Eurocentric and bourgeois assumptions that have been virtually culture-wide across the culture of science. . . . These assumptions have constituted whole fields of study, selecting their preoccupying problems, favored concepts, hypotheses and research designs; these fields have in turn lent support to male supremacist assumptions in other fields" (Harding, p. 345). Our conception of objectivity, in short, needs to deal with the more covert cultural biases as well as the more overt individual ones. In addition, what we know and what knowledge we have individually contributed are made possible and supported by the knowledge and standards of our community. But also, the knowledge and standards of our community are made possible and supported by what we individually know and have contributed to knowledge. If we lose sight of the latter in our appreciation of the former, we lose sight of the importance of the individual in changing her community's knowledge; we lose sight even of the very possibility of change itself.

But how do we capture what is missing in feminist empiricist conceptions of scientific objectivity and knowledge? " . . . Where might one find a *method* for maximizing objectivity that has the resources to detect (a) values and interests that constitute scientific projects, (b) ones that do not vary between legitimated observers, and (c) the difference between those values and interests that enlarge and those that limit our images of nature and social relations? This is where standpoint theory has provided useful resources that are not available—or, at least, not easily available—from other epistemologies" (Harding, p. 346). Begin with androcentric values. Harding reminds us that these values directly benefit men (especially white men), whereas they oppress women. As a consequence, women are more likely than men to be critical of such values. They have less to lose by distancing themselves from the social order; thus, the perspective from their lives can more easily generate fresh and critical analyses. But similar things can be said of Eurocentric and bourgeois values. Thus, only by adopting a standpoint outside that of the most powerful groups in society—thus, inside the lives of women of different races, ethnicities, classes and sexualities—will we be provided with "a critical edge for generating theoretically and empirically more accurate and comprehensive accounts" (Harding, p. 348).

In the Introduction to her book *Tomorrow's Tomorrow: The Black Woman,* Joyce Ladner provides a concrete illustration of what Harding has in mind. Trained as a sociologist and pursuing research for her doctoral dissertation, Ladner "went into the field equipped with a set of preconceived ideas and labels" (Ladner, p. 354)—"social deviance," "social disorganization," "social pathology," and so on—that she intended to apply to the teenage Black girls she was studying. "At that time my curiosity was centered around the various activities in which the girls engaged that frequently produced harmful consequences. Specifically, I attempted to understand how such social problems as pregnancy, premarital sex, school dropout, etc. affected their life chances for success. I also felt, at the time, that a less destructible adaptation could be made to their impoverished environments" (Ladner, p. 359). But Ladner was also a Black woman, and her socialization by her family and the broader Black community equipped her with certain attitudes, values, beliefs "and in effect, a Black perspective" (Ladner, p. 354) that she also brought with her into the field. "On the one hand, I wanted to conduct a study that would allow me to fulfill certain academic requirements, i.e., a doctoral dissertation. On the other hand, I was highly influenced by my *Blackness*—by the fact that I, on many levels, was one of them and had to deal with their problems on a personal level. I was largely unable to resolve these strands, this 'double consciousness'..." (Ladner, p. 354). But what came out of this double consciousness was a quite radical reconceptualization not only of the girls' situation ["a very healthy and successful adaptation, given their limited resources, had been made by all of these girls to a set of very unhealthy environmental conditions" (Ladner, p. 359)], but also of significant parts of sociological theory and methodology.

FEMINIST POSTMODERNISM

But how can the kind of enquiry described by Harding and illustrated by Ladner—the kind of enquiry that starts from the lives of women of different races, ethnicities, classes, and sexualities—yield a more accurate and complete understanding of nature and social life? After all, the standpoints that would form our point of departure, the standpoints of these women, would be as diverse as the women themselves, and it is unclear whether such diverse standpoints could ever be made to yield a single, unified vision of the world. In "Situated Knowledges: The Science Question in Feminism and the Privilege of Partial Perspective," however, historian of science Donna Haraway asks why our goal must be a single, unified vision of the world? In the past, after all, whatever single, unified vision of the world we have had has been that of the powerful in society—that is, artificially produced. Haraway, in fact, characterizes such a goal as "the god trick of seeing everything from nowhere" (Haraway, p. 364). What Haraway suggests we strive for instead is "situated knowledges": "I would like to suggest how our insisting metaphorically on the particularity and embodiment of all vision (although not necessarily organic embodiment and including technological mediation), and not giving in to the tempting myths of vision as a route to disembodiment . . . allows us to construct a usable, but not an innocent, doctrine of objectivity.... [O]bjectivity turns out to be about particular and specific embodiment and definitely not about the false vision promising transcendence of all limits and responsibility. The moral is simple: only partial perspective promises objective vision" (Haraway, pp. 365). Haraway extends the emphasis on partiality even to the subjects of enquiry: "The knowing self is partial in all its guises, never finished, whole, simply there and original; it is always constructed and stitched together imperfectly, and *therefore* able to join with another, to see together without claiming to be another" (Haraway, p. 367). Finally, Haraway suggests that the world itself should be pictured, not as *object*, unified and unchanging, a resource to be mastered and appropriated, but as *subject*, a witty agent, even a "trickster," with whom we have the "situated conversations" that constitute our knowledge.

In "Though This Be Method, Yet There Is Madness in It: Paranoia and Liberal Epistemology," philosopher Naomi Scheman elaborates. The real world "is always slipping out from under our best attempts to pin it down. The real world is not the world of our best physics but the world that defeats any physics that would be final, that would desire to be the last word . . ." (Scheman, p. 385). What's more, the real world, in contradistinction to unreal things, looks different to those differently placed in relation to it. "(There aren't a variety of diverse takes on my hallucinations.) . . . How could there possibly be one account of a world shaped in interaction with subjects so diversely constituted and with such diverse interests in constructing and knowing it?" (Scheman, pp. 384). It has seemed otherwise, says

Scheman, only because of our ways of thinking about the self and knowledge that stem from Descartes. "The individualism of Cartesian epistemology is yoked to its universalism: Though we are each to pursue knowledge on our own, freed from the influence of any other people, what we come up with is not supposed to be our own view of the world—it is supposed to be the truth, unique and invariable. . . . Individualism is the route not to the idiosyncrasies of individuality but to the universality of reason" (Scheman, p. 377). Scheman recounts what was involved in this individualism of Cartesian epistemology—the conception of the self as a disembodied mind not located in space, the source of the epistemic authority of the self and its relation to self-discipline, on the one hand, and the body, on the other— and she spells out how this Cartesian individualism resembles the paranoia described by Freud. She also suggests how this individualism, though it was revolutionary and democratic in intent, has helped to underwrite oppression. As a result, notes Scheman, various contemporary theorists such as Haraway and Harding are articulating alternative conceptions of the self and knowledge, "conceptions that start from plurality and diversity, not just among but, crucially, within subjects. From that starting point flow radically transformed relationships between subjects and between subjects and the world they would know" (Scheman, p. 383). If our interest is in changing the world, concludes Scheman, nothing less than such radical departures from our Cartesian heritage is required.

Subjects, Power, and Knowledge

Description and Prescription in Feminist Philosophies of Science

Helen E. Longino

Prologue

Feminists, faced with traditions in philosophy and in science that are deeply hostile to women, have had practically to invent new and more appropriate ways of knowing the world. These new ways have been less invention out of whole cloth than the revival or reevaluation of alternative or suppressed traditions. They range from the celebration of insight into nature through identification with it to specific strategies of survey research in the social sciences. Natural scientists and laypersons anxious to see the sciences change have celebrated Barbara McClintock's loving identification with various aspects of the plants she studied, whether whole organism or its chromosomal structure revealed under the microscope. Social scientists from Dorothy Smith to Karen Sacks have stressed designing research for rather than merely about women, a goal that requires attending to the specificities of women's lives and consulting research subjects themselves about the process of gathering information about them. ...

[However, we cannot] simply dismiss the accumulated knowledge of the natural world produced by the traditional methods of the natural sciences. These sciences have transformed conditions of life in industrialized portions of the world, both conceptually as models of knowledge and materially through science-based technologies. Why, then, do some of us feel so uneasy not only about theories directly concerning females and gender but also about the very nature of scientific knowledge and the power it creates? After all, even feminists who wish to change the sciences are also, by that very ambition, expressing a hope for power. There are surely various sources for and locations of this uneasiness. Those of us who are feminists have been struck by the interlocking character of several aspects of knowledge and power in the sciences. Women have been excluded from the practice of science, even as scientific inquiry gets described both as a masculine activity and as demonstrating women's unsuitability to engage in it, whether because of our allegedly deficient mathematical abilities or our insufficient independence. Some of us notice the location of women in the production of the artifacts made possible by new knowledge: swift and nimble fingers on the microelectronics assembly line. Others notice the neglect of women's distinctive health issues by the biomedical sciences, even as new techniques for preserving the fetuses they carry are introduced into hospital delivery rooms. The sciences become even more suspect as analysis of their metaphors (for example, in cell biology and in microbiology) reveals an acceptance (and hence reinforcement) of the cultural identification of the male with activity and of the female with passivity. Finally, feminists have drawn a connection between the identification of nature as female and the scientific mind as male and the persistent privileging of explanatory models constructed around relations of unidirectional control over models constructed around relations of interdependence. Reflection on this connection has prompted feminist critics to question the very idea of a scientific method capable of adjudicating the truth or probability of theories in a value-neutral way.

Although the sciences have increased human power over natural processes, they have, according to this analysis, done so in a lop-sided way, systematically perpetuating women's cognitive and political disempowerment (as well as that of other groups marginalized in relation to the Euro-American drama). One obvious question, then, is whether this appropriation of power is an intrinsic feature of science or whether it is an incidental feature of the sciences as practiced in the modern period, a feature deriving from the social structures within which the sciences have developed. A second question is whether it is possible to seek and possess empowering knowledge without expropriating the power of others. Is seeking knowledge inevitably an attempt at domination? And are there criteria of knowledge other than the ability to control the phenomena about which one seeks knowledge? Feminists have answered these questions in a number of ways. I will review some of these before outlining my own answer.

Feminist Epistemological Strategies 1: Changing the Subject

Most traditional philosophy of science (with the problematic exception of Descartes's) has adopted some form of empiricism. Empiricism's silent partner has been a theory of the subject, that is, of the knower.[1] The paradigmatic knower in Western epistemology is an individual—an individual who, in several classic instances, has struggled to free himself from the distortions in understanding and perception that result from attachment. Plato, for example, maintained that knowledge of the good is possible only for those whose reason is capable of controlling their appetites and passions, some of which have their source in bodily needs and pleasures and others of which have their source in our relations with others. The struggle for epistemic autonomy is even starker for Descartes, who suspends belief in all but his own existence in order to recreate a body of knowledge cleansed of faults, impurities, and uncertainties. For Descartes, only those grounds available to a single, unattached, disembodied mind are acceptable principles for the construction of a system of beliefs. Most subsequent epistemology has granted Descartes's conditions and disputed what those grounds are and whether any proposed grounds are sufficient grounds for knowledge. Descartes's creation of the radically and in principle isolated individual as the ideal epistemic agent has for the most part gone unremarked.[2] Locke, for example, adopts the Cartesian identification of the thinking subject with the disembodied soul without even remarking upon the individualism of the conception he inherits and then struggles with the problem of personal identity. Explicitly or implicitly in modern epistemology, whether rationalist or empiricist, the individual consciousness that is the subject of knowledge is transparent to itself, operates according to principles that are independent of embodied experience, and generates knowledge in a value-neutral way.

One set of feminist epistemological strategies, sometimes described as modifications or rejections of empiricism, can also, and perhaps better, be described as changing the subject. I will review three such strategies of replacement, arguing that although they enrich our understanding of how we come to have the beliefs we have and so are more descriptively adequate than the theories they challenge, they fall short of normative adequacy. The strategies identify the problems of contemporary science as resulting from male or masculinist bias. Each strategy understands both the bias and its remedy differently. One holds out the original ideal of uncontaminated or unconditioned subjectivity. A second identifies bias as a function of social location. A third identifies bias in the emotive substructure produced by the psychodynamics of individuation.

Feminist empiricism has by now taken a number of forms. That form discussed and criticized by Sandra Harding is most concerned with those fields of scientific research that have misdescribed or mis-analyzed women's lives and bodies. It's not clear that any feminist scholars have totally conformed to the profile identified by Harding, but certain moments in the analyses offered by practicing scientists who are feminists do fit this model.[3] At any rate, feminist empiricism (*sub* Harding) identifies the problems in the scientific accounts of women and gender as the product of male bias. Typical examples of problematic views are the treatment of the male of the species as the locus of variation (and hence the basis of evolutionary change for a species), the persistent treatment of male difference as male superiority, the assumption of universal male dominance, and the treatment of sexual divisions of labor in industrialized societies as the product of biological species evolution. Each of these involves neglecting contradictory empirical information. It should be no surprise that a focus on these sorts of problems suggests their solution in replacing the androcentric subject of knowledge with an unbiased subject—one that would not ignore the empirical data already or easily available. From this perspective, certain areas of science having to do with sex and gender are deformed by gender ideology, but the methods of science are not themselves masculinist and can be used to correct the errors produced by ideology. The ideal knower is still the purified mind, and epistemic or cognitive authority inheres in this purity. This strategy, as Harding has observed, is not effective against those, research programs that feminists find troublesome but that cannot be faulted by reference to the standard methodological precepts of scientific inquiry. I have argued, for example, that a critique of research on the influence of prenatal gonadal hormones on behavioral sex differences that is limited to methodological critique of the data fails to bring out the role of the explanatory model that both generates the research and gives evidential relevance to that data.[4]

Another approach is, therefore, the standpoint approach. There is no one position from which value-free knowledge can be developed, but some positions are better than others. Standpoint epistemologies notice systematic distortions in description and analysis produced by those occupying social positions of power. Traditional Marxists identified the standpoint of the bourgeoisie as producing such distortions, whereas feminists have identified the standpoint of men (of the dominant class and race) as equally distorting. Nancy Hartsock and other feminist standpoint theorists have argued that the activities of ruling class men produce a knowledge of the world characterized by abstractness and impersonality, that their own politically structured freedom from the requirements of re/producing the necessities of daily life is reflected in the kind of understanding they produce of the social and natural world.[5] Women's work, by contrast, is characterized by greater interaction with material substances, by constant change, and by its requirement of emotional investment in the form of caring. Not only does women's characteristic activity and relation to the means of production/reproduction produce its own unique form of understanding, but also women who become self-conscious agents in this work are able to incorporate men's perspectives as well as their own and hence to develop a more accurate, more objective, set of beliefs about the world.

By valorizing the perspectives uniquely available to those who are socially disadvantaged, standpoint theorists turn the table on traditional epistemology; the ideal epistemic agent is not an unconditioned subject but the subject conditioned by the social experiences of oppression. The powerless are those with epistemic legitimacy, even if they lack the power that could turn that legitimacy into authority. One of the difficulties of the standpoint approach comes into high relief, however, when it is a women's or a feminist standpoint that is in question. Women occupy many social locations in a racially and economically stratified society. If genuine or better knowledge depends on the correct or a more correct standpoint, social theory is needed to ascertain which of these locations is the epistemologically privileged one. But in a standpoint epistemology, a standpoint is needed to justify such a theory. What is that standpoint and how do we identify *it?* If no single standpoint is privileged, then either the standpoint theorist must embrace multiple and incompatible knowledge positions or offer some means of transforming or integrating multiple perspectives into one. Both of these moves require either the abandonment or the supplementation of standpoint as an epistemic criterion.

Standpoint theory faces another problem as well. It is by now commonplace to note that standpoint theory was developed by and for social scientists. It has been difficult to see what its implications for the natural sciences might be. But another strategy has seemed more promising. Most standpoint theorists locate the epistemic advantage in the productive/reproductive experience of the oppressed whose perspective they champion. A different change of subject is proposed by those identifying the problems with science as a function of the psychodynamics of individuation. Evelyn Fox Keller has been asking, among other things, why the scientific community privileges one kind of explanation or theory over others. In particular she has asked why, when both linear reductionist and interactionist perspectives are available, the scientific community has preferred the linear or "master molecule" theory that understands a natural process as controlled by a single dominant factor. This question was made vivid by her discussion of

her own research on slime mold aggregation and the fate of Barbara McClintock's work on genetic transposition.[6]

Keller's original response, spelled out in *Reflections on Gender and Science*, involved an analysis of the traditional ideal of scientific objectivity, which she understood as the ideal of the scientist's detachment from the object of study.[7] In her view, epistemic and affective ideals are intermingled, and from the psychoanalytic perspective she adopted, distorted affective development—autonomy as exaggerated separateness—was expressed in a distorted epistemic ideal—objectivity as radical detachment. Drawing on and developing object relations theory, she attributed this "static autonomy" to the conditions under which boys develop psychologically: exaggerated separateness is a solution to the anxieties provoked by those conditions. Keller analyzed the consequent ideal of static objectivity as generating and satisfied by accounts of natural processes that foreground controlling relationships—for example, accounts of organismic development as determined by the individual's genetic program. She, therefore, proposed an alternative conceptualization of autonomy, contrasting static autonomy with what she called dynamic autonomy, an ability to move in and out of intimate connection with the world. Dynamic autonomy provides the emotional substructure for an alternative conception of objectivity: dynamic objectivity. The knower characterized by dynamic objectivity, in contrast to the knower characterized by static objectivity, does not seek power over phenomena but acknowledges instead the ways in which knower and phenomena are in relationship as well as the ways in which phenomena themselves are complexly interdependent. Barbara McClintock's work has offered one of the most striking examples of the effectiveness of such an approach, although interactionist approaches have also been applied in areas besides developmental biology. McClintock's work, long ignored, was finally vindicated by developments in molecular biology of the 1970s—the acknowledgment of genetic transposition in the prokaryotes that had been the model organisms for contemporary molecular genetics. Dynamic objectivity is not presented as a typically feminine epistemological orientation but as an alternative to an epistemological orientation associated with both masculine psychological development and masculinist gender ideology. But however much interactionist approaches might appeal to us, and however much dynamic objectivity might appeal to us, there isn't a general argument to the truth of interactionism or to the epistemological superiority of dynamic objectivity.

Both standpoint theory and the psychodynamic perspective suggest the inadequacy of an ideal of a pure transparent subjectivity that registers the world as it is in itself (or, for Kantians, as structured by universal conditions of apperception or categories of understanding). I find it most useful to read them as articulating special instances of more general descriptive claims that subjectivity is conditioned by social and historical location and that our cognitive efforts have an ineluctably affective dimension. Classical standpoint theory identifies relation to production/reproduction as the key, but there are multiple, potentially oppositional relations to production/reproduction in a complex society, and there are other kinds of social relation and location that condition subjectivity. For example, one of the structural features of a male-dominant society is asymmetry of sexual access. Men occupy a position of entitlement to women's bodies, whereas women, correspondingly, occupy the position of that to which men are entitled. Complications of the asymmetry arise in class- and race-stratified societies. There may be other structural features as well, such as those related to the institutions of heterosexuality, that condition subjectivity. Because each individual occupies a location in a multidimensional grid marked by numerous interacting structures of power asymmetry, the analytical task is not to determine which is

epistemically most adequate. Rather, the task is to understand how these complexly conditioned subjectivities are expressed in action and belief. I would expect that comparable complexity can be introduced into the psychodynamic account.

Treating subjectivity as variably conditioned and cognition as affectively modulated opens both opportunities and problems. The opportunities are the possibilities of understanding phenomena in new ways; by recognizing that mainstream accounts of natural processes have been developed from particular locations and reflect particular affective orientations, we can entertain the possibility that quite different accounts might emerge from other locations with the benefit of different emotional orientations. Although either transferring or diffusing power, the strategies discussed so far have in common a focus on the individual epistemic agent, on the autonomous subject. (The subject in the second and third approaches comes to be in a social context and as a consequence of social interactions, but its knowledge is still a matter of some relation between it and the subject matter.) The standpoint and psychodynamically based theories recommend certain new positions and orientations as superior to others but fail to explain how we are to decide or to justify decisions between what seem to be conflicting claims about the character of some set of natural processes. On what grounds can one social location or affective orientation be judged epistemically superior to another? Normative epistemology arises in the context of conflicting knowledge claims. Naturalism, or descriptivism, in epistemology presupposes that we know what we think we know and asks how. But the existence of comparably persuasive incompatible claims calls into question whether we know at all, requires that we reexamine what we take to be adequate justification, and may even call into question our very concept of knowledge.

Feminist science critics have provided analyses of the context of discovery that enable us to see how social values, including gender ideology in various guises, could be introduced into science. Some theories that have done so go on to recommend an alternate subject position as epistemically superior. But arguments are missing—and it's not clear that any particular subject position could be adequate to generate knowledge. Can a particular subject position be supported by an a priori argument? It can, but only by an argument that claims a particular structure for the world and then identifies a particular subjectivity as uniquely capable of knowing that structure. The problem with such arguments is that they beg the question. The one subject position that could be advanced as epistemically superior to others without presupposing something about the structure of the world is the unconditioned position, the position of no position that provides a view from nowhere. Attractive as this ideal might seem, arguments in the philosophy of science suggest that this is a chimera. Let me turn to them.

Feminist Epistemological Strategies 2: Multiplying Subjects

The ideal of the unconditioned (or universally conditioned) subject is the traditional proposal for escaping the particularity of subjectivity. Granting the truth of the claim that individual subjectivities are conditioned, unconditioned subjectivity is treated as an achievement rather than a natural endowment. The methods of the natural sciences constitute means to that achievement. Some well-known arguments in the philosophy of science challenge this presumption. As they have received a great deal of attention in the philosophical literature, I shall only mention them here in order to bring out their relevance to the general point. The methods of the natural sciences, in particular, have been thought to constitute the escape route from conditioned subjectivity. The difficulty just outlined for the feminist epistemological strategy of changing the subject, however, has

a parallel in developments in the philosophy of science. Both dilemmas suggest the individual knower is an inappropriate focus for the purpose of understanding (and changing) science.

In the traditional view, the natural sciences are characterized by a methodology that purifies scientific knowledge of distortions produced by scientists' social and personal allegiances. The essential features of this methodology—explored in great detail by positivist philosophers of science—are observation and logic. Much philosophy of science in the last twenty-five years has been preoccupied with two potential challenges to this picture of scientific methodology—the claim of Kuhn, Feyerabend, and Hanson that observation is theory laden and the claim of Pierre Duhem that theories are underdetermined by data. One claim challenges the stability of observations themselves, the other the stability of evidential relations. Both accounts have seemed (at least to their critics and to some of their proponents) to permit the unrestrained expression of scientists subjective preferences in the content of science. If observation is theory laden, then observation cannot serve as an independent constraint on theories, thus permitting subjective elements to constrain theory choice. Similarly, if observations acquire evidential relevance only in the context of a set of assumptions, a relevance that changes with a suitable change in assumptions, then it's not clear what protects theory choice from subjective elements hidden in background assumptions. Although empirical adequacy serves as a constraint on theory acceptance, it is not sufficient to pick out one theory from all contenders as the true theory about a domain of the natural world. These analyses of the relation between observation, data, and theory are often thought to constitute arguments against empiricism, but, like the feminist epistemological strategies, they are more effective as arguments against empiricism's silent partner, the theory of the unconditioned subject. The conclusion to be drawn from them is that what has been labeled scientific method does not succeed as a means to the attainment of unconditioned subjectivity on the part of individual knowers. And as long as the scientific knower is conceived of as an individual, knowing best when freed from external influences and attachment (that is, when detached or free from her/his context), the puzzles introduced by the theory-laden nature of observation and the dependence of evidential relations on background assumptions will remain unsolved.

It need not follow from these considerations, however, that scientific knowledge is impossible of attainment. Applying what I take to be a feminist insight—that we are all in relations of interdependence—I have suggested that scientific knowledge is constructed not by individuals applying a method to the material to be known but by individuals in interaction with one another in ways that modify their observations, theories and hypotheses, and patterns of reasoning. Thus scientific method includes more than just the complex of activities that constitutes hypothesis testing through comparison of hypothesis statements with (reports of) experiential data, in principle an activity of individuals. Hypothesis testing itself consists of more than the comparison of statements but involves equally centrally the subjection of putative data, of hypotheses, and of the background assumptions in light of which they seem to be supported by those data to varieties of conceptual and evidential scrutiny and criticisms.[8] Conceptual criticism can include investigation into the internal and external consistency of a hypothesis and investigation of the factual, moral, and social implications of background assumptions; evidential criticism includes not only investigation of the quality of the data but of its organization, structuring, and so on. Because background assumptions can be and most frequently are invisible to the members of the scientific community for which they are background and because unreflective acceptance of such assumptions can come to define what it is to

be a member of such a community (thus making criticism impossible), effective criticism of background assumptions requires the presence and expression of alternative points of view. This sort of account allows us to see how social values and interests can become enshrined in otherwise acceptable research programs (i.e., research programs that strive for empirical adequacy and engage in criticism). As long as representatives of alternative points of view are not included in the community, shared values will not be identified as shaping observation or reasoning.

Scientific knowledge, on this view, is an outcome of the critical dialogue in which individuals and groups holding different points of view engage with each other. It is constructed not by individuals but by an interactive dialogic community. A community's practice of inquiry is productive of knowledge to the extent that it facilitates transformative criticism. The constitution of the scientific community is crucial to this end as are the interrelations among its members. Community level criteria can, therefore, be invoked to discriminate among the products of scientific communities, even though context-independent standards of justification are not attainable. At least four criteria can be identified as necessary to achieve the transformative dimension of critical discourse:

1. There must be publicly recognized forums for the criticism of evidence, of methods, and of assumptions and reasoning.
2. The community must not merely tolerate dissent, but its beliefs and theories must change over time in response to the critical discourse taking place within it.
3. There must be publicly recognized standards by reference to which theories, hypotheses, and observational practices are evaluated and by appeal to which criticism is made relevant to the goals of the inquiring community. With the possible exception of empirical adequacy, there needn't be (and probably isn't) a set of standards common to all communities.

The general family of standards from which those locally adopted might be drawn would include such cognitive virtues as accuracy, coherence, and breadth of scope, and such social virtues as fulfilling technical or material needs or facilitating certain kinds of interactions between a society and its material environment or among the society's members.

4. Finally, communities must be characterized by equality of intellectual authority. What consensus exists must not be the result of the exercise of political or economic power or of the exclusion of dissenting perspectives; it must be the result of critical dialogue in which all relevant perspectives are represented.

Although requiring diversity in the community, this is not a relativist position. True relativism, as I understand it, holds that there are no legitimate constraints on what counts as reasonable to believe apart from the individual's own beliefs. Equality of intellectual authority does not mean that anything goes but that everyone is regarded as equally capable of providing arguments germane to the construction of scientific knowledge. The position outlined here holds that both nature and logic impose constraints. It fails, however, to narrow reasonable belief to a single one among all contenders, in part because it does not constrain belief in a wholly unmediated way. Nevertheless, communities are constrained by the standards operating within them, and individual members of communities are further constrained by the requirement of critical interaction relative to those standards. To say that there may be irreconcilable but coherent and empirically adequate systems for accounting for some portion of the world is not to endorse relativism but to acknowledge that cognitive needs can vary and that this variation generates cognitive diversity.

Unlike the view from nowhere achievable by unconditioned subjectivity or the view from that somewhere identified as maximizing knowledge, this notion of knowledge through interactive intersubjectivity idealizes the view from everywhere (perhaps better thought of as *views* from *many wheres*). These criteria for objective communities represent not a description of actual scientific communities but a set of prescriptions that are probably not anywhere satisfied. Nevertheless, they provide a measure against which actual communities and, indirectly, criteria for the comparison of theories can be evaluated. For example, theories accepted in different communities can be compared with respect to the conditions under which the critical dialogue concerning a given theory has occurred. Although there are any number of objections that advocates of such a notion must address, I will confine myself here to one major problem, the answer to which opens up some future directions for feminist analysis and scientific practice.

Dilemmas of Pluralism

This sort of account is subject to the following dilemma.[9] What gets produced as knowledge depends on the consensus reached in the scientific community. For knowledge to count as genuine, the community must be adequately diverse. But the development of a theoretical idea or hypothesis into something elaborate enough to be called knowledge requires a consensus. The questions must stop somewhere, at some point, so that a given theory can be developed sufficiently to be applied to concrete problems. How is scientific knowledge possible while pursuing socially constituted objectivity? That is, if objectivity requires pluralism in the community, then scientific knowledge becomes elusive, but if consensus is pursued, it will be at the cost of quieting critical oppositional positions.

My strategy for avoiding this dilemma is to detach scientific knowledge from consensus, if consensus means agreement of the entire scientific community regarding the truth or acceptability of a given theory. This strategy also means detaching knowledge from an ideal of absolute and unitary truth. I suggest that we look at the aims of inquiry (at least some) as satisfied by embracing multiple and, in some cases, incompatible theories that satisfy local standards. This detachment of knowledge from universal consensus and absolute truth can be made more palatable than it might first appear by two moves. One of these is implicit in treating science as a practice or set of practices; the other involves taking up some version of a semantic or model theoretic theory of theories.

Beginning with the second of these, let me sketch what I take to be the relevant aspects and implications of the semantic view.[10] This view is proposed as an alternative to the view of theories as sets of propositions (whether axiomatized or not). If we take the semantic view, we understand a theory as a specification of a set of relations among objects or processes characterized in a fairly abstract way. Another characterization would be that on the semantic view, a theory is the specification of a structure. The structure as specified is neither true nor false; it is just a structure. The theoretical claim is that the structure is realized in some actual system. As Mary Hesse has shown, models are proposed as models of some real world system on the basis of an analogy between the model and the system, that is, the supposition that the model and the system share some significant features in common.[11] Models often have their start as metaphors. Examples of such metaphoric models are typical philosophers' examples like the billiard ball model of particle interactions or the solar system model of the atom. What many feminists have pointed out (or can be understood as having pointed out) is the use of elements of gender ideology and social relations as metaphors for natural processes and relations. Varieties of heterosexual marriage have served as the metaphoric basis for models of the relation between nucleus and cytoplasm in the cell, for example.[12] The master molecule approach to gene action, characterized by unidirectional control exerted on organismal

processes by the gene, reflects relations of authority in the patriarchal household. Evelyn Fox Keller has recently been investigating the basis of models in molecular biology in androcentric metaphors of sexuality and procreation.[13] When Donna Haraway says that during and after the Second World War the organism changed from a factory to a cybernetic system, she can be understood as saying that the metaphor generating models of organismic structure and function shifted from a productive system organized by a hierarchical division of labor to a system for generating and processing information.[14] Alternatively put, cells, gene action, and organisms have been modelled as marriage, families, and factories and cybernetic networks, respectively. Supporting such analysis of particular theories or models requires not merely noticing the analogies of structure but also tracing the seepage of language and meaning from one domain to another as well as studying the uses to which the models are put.[15]

The adequacy of a theory conceived as a model is determined by our being able to map some subset of the relations/structures posited in the model onto some portion of the experienced world. (Now the portions of the world stand in many relations to many other portions.) Any given model or schema will necessarily select among those relations. So its adequacy is not just a function of isomorphism of one of the interpretations of the theory with a portion of the world but of the fact that the relations it picks out are ones in which we are interested. A model guides our interactions with and interventions in the world. We want models that guide the interactions and interventions we seek. Given that different subcommunities within the larger scientific community may be interested in different relations or that they may be interested in objects under different descriptions, different models (that if taken as claims about an underlying reality would be incompatible) may well be equally adequate and provide knowledge, in the sense of an ability to direct our interactions and interventions, even in the absence of a general consensus as to what's important. Knowledge is not detached from knowers in a set of propositions but consists in our ability to understand the structural features of a model and to apply it to some particular portion of the world; it is knowledge of that portion of the world through its structuring by the model we use. The notion of theories as sets of propositions requires that we view the adequacy of a theory as a matter of correspondence of the objects, processes, and relations described in the propositions of the theory with the objects, processes, and relations in the domain of the natural world that the theory purports to explain; that is, it requires that adequacy be conceptualized as truth. The model-theoretic approach allows us to evaluate theories in relation to our aims as well as in relation to the model's isomorphism with elements of the modeled domain and permits the adequacy of different and incompatible models serving different and incompatible aims. Knowledge is not contemplative but active.

The second move to escape the dilemma develops some consequences of treating science as practice. There are two worth mentioning. If we understand science as practice, then we understand inquiry as ongoing, that is, we give up the idea that there is a terminus of inquiry that just is the set of truths about the world. (What LaPlace's demon knew, for example.) Scientific knowledge from this perspective is not the static end point of inquiry but a cognitive or intellectual expression of an ongoing interaction with our natural and social environments. Indeed, when we attempt to identify the goals of inquiry that organize scientific cognitive practices, it becomes clear that there are several, not all of which can be simultaneously pursued.[16] Scientific knowledge, then, is a body of diverse theories and their articulations onto the world that changes over time in response to the changing cognitive needs of those who develop and use the theories, in response to the new questions and anomalous

empirical data revealed by applying theories, and in response to changes in associated theories. Both linear-reductionist and interactionist models reveal aspects of natural processes, some common to both and some uniquely describable with the terms proper to one but not both sorts of model. If we recognize the partiality of theories, as we can when we treat them as models, we can recognize pluralism in the community as one of the conditions for the continued development of scientific knowledge in this sense.

In particular, the models developed by feminists and others dissatisfied with the valuative and affective dimensions of models in use must at the very least (given that they meet the test of empirical adequacy) be recognized as both revealing the partiality of those models in use and as revealing some aspects of natural phenomena and processes that the latter conceal. These alternative models may have a variety of forms and a variety of motivations, and they need not repudiate the aim of control. We engage in scientific inquiry to direct our interactions with and interventions in the world. Barbara McClintock was not a feminist, but she was in part reacting against the gendered meanings in natural philosophy, meanings which shut her out of inquiry; Ruth Hubbard advocates interactionist perspectives out of more explicitly political commitments; feminists and others concerned with the environment reject the control orientation of technocrats effective in the short term for more complex models that can address long-term change and stasis in the ecosystem. If we aim for effective action in the natural world, something is to be controlled. The issue should be not whether but what and how. Rather than repudiate it, we can set the aim of control within the larger context of overall purposes and develop a more refined sense of the varieties of control made possible through scientific inquiry.

A second consequence for feminist and other oppositional scientists of adopting both the social knowledge thesis and a model-theoretic analysis of theories is that the constructive task does not consist in finding the one best or correct feminist model. Rather, the many models that can be generated from the different subject positions ought to be articulated and elaborated. Very few will be exclusively feminist if that means exclusively gender-based or developed only by feminists. Some will be more appropriate for some domains, others for others, and some for none. We can't know this unless models get sufficiently elaborated to be used as guides for interactions. Thus, this joint perspective implies the advocacy of subcommunities characterized by local standards. To the extent that they address a common domain and to the extent that they share some standards in common, these subcommunities must be in critical dialogue with each other as well as with those subcommunities identified with more mainstream science. The point of dialogue from this point of view is not to produce a general and universal consensus but to make possible the refinement, correction, rejection, and sharing of models. Alliances, mergers, and revisions of standards as well as of models are all possible consequences of this dialogic interaction.

Conclusions

Understanding scientific knowledge in this way supports at least two further reflections on knowledge and power. First of all, the need for models within which we can situate ourselves and the interactions we desire with the natural world will militate against the inclusiveness required for an adequate critical practice, if only because the elaboration of any model requires a substantial commitment of material and intellectual resources on the part of a community.[17] This means that, in a power-stratified society, the inclusion of the less powerful and hence of models that could serve as a resource for criticism of the received wisdom in the community of science will always be a matter of

conflict. At the same time, the demand for inclusiveness should not be taken to mean that every alternative view is equally deserving of attention. Discussion must be conducted in reference to public standards, standards which, as noted above, do not provide timeless criteria, but which change in response to changes in cognitive and social needs. Nevertheless, by appeal to standards adopted and legitimated through processes of public scrutiny and criticism, it is possible to set aside as irrelevant positions such as New Age "crystalology" or creationism. To the extent that these satisfy none of the central standards operative in the scientific communities of their cultures, they indeed qualify as crackpot. Programs for low-tech science appropriate to settings and problems in developing nations may, by contrast, be equally irritating to or against the grain of some of the institutionalized aspects of science in the industrialized nations, but as long as they do satisfy some of the central standards of those communities, then the perspectives they embody must be included in the critical knowledge-constructive dialogue. Although there is always a danger that the politically marginal will be conflated with the crackpot, one function of public and common standards is to remind us of that distinction and to help us draw it in particular cases. I do not know of any simple or formulaic solution to this problem.

Second, those critiques of scientific epistemology that urge a change of subject preserve the structures of cognitive authority but propose replacing those currently wielding authority with others: a genuinely unbiased subject in one case, a differently located or a differently formed subject in the other. Either no assumptions or different assumptions will be engaged in the knowledge-constructive process. In the position I am advocating, which makes salient those features of knowledge construction made invisible by more traditional accounts, the structures of cognitive authority themselves must change. No segment of the community, whether powerful or powerless, can claim epistemic privilege. If we can see our way to the dissolution of those structures, then we need not understand the appropriation of power in the form of cognitive authority as intrinsic to science. Nevertheless, the creation of cognitive democracy, of democratic science, is as much a matter of conflict and hope as is the creation of political democracy.

Notes

1. Empiricist philosophers have found themselves in great difficulty when confronting the necessity to make their theory of the knower explicit, a difficulty most eloquently expressed in David Hume's Appendix to *A Treatise of Human Nature*, ed. L. A. Selby-Bigge (Oxford, UK: Clarendon Press, 1960).

2. The later philosophy of Wittgenstein does challenge the individualist ideal. Until recently few commentators have developed the anti-individualist implications of his work. See Naomi Scheman, "Individualism and the Objects of Psychology" in *Discovering Reality*, ed. Sandra Harding and Merrill Hintikka (Boston: Reidel, 1983), 225–44.

3. Harding has treated Marcia Millman and Rosabeth Kantor's Introduction to their collection, *Another Voice* (New York: Doubleday, 1975) and my essay with Ruth Doell, "Body, Bias and Behavior," from *Signs* 9, 2 (Winter 1983) as exemplars of feminist empiricism. The latter is discussed extensively in Harding's *The Science Question in Feminism* (Ithaca: Cornell University Press, 1986). Because the article nowhere claims that masculinist bias can be corrected by application of current methodologies in the sciences, I have always found the discussion in *The Science Question* a puzzlingly perverse misreading.

4. Cf. Longino, "Can There Be A Feminist Science?" in *Hypatia* 2, 3 (Fall 1987); and chapter 7 of Longino, *Science as Social Knowledge* (Princeton: Princeton University Press, 1990).

5. Cf. Nancy Hartsock, "The Feminist Standpoint: Developing the Ground for a Specifically Feminist Historical Materialism," in Harding and Hintikka, *Discovering Reality*, 283–310.

6. Cf. Evelyn F. Keller, "The Force of the Pacemaker Concept in Theories of Slime Mold Aggregation," in *Perspectives in Biology and Medicine* 26 (1983): 515–21; and *A Feeling for the Organism* (San Francisco: W. H. Freeman, 1983).

7. Evelyn F. Keller, *Reflections on Gender and Science* (New Haven: Yale University Press, 1984).

8. For argument for and exposition of these points, see Longino, *Science as Social Knowledge*, especially chapter 4.

9. Thanks to Sandra Mitchell for this formulation.

10. My understanding of the semantic view is shaped by its presentations in Bas van Fraassen, *The Scientific Image* (New York: Oxford University Press, 1980); and Ronald Giere, *Explaining Science* (Chicago: University of Chicago Press, 1988); as well as by conversations with Richard Grandy and Elisabeth Lloyd. Nancy Cartwright's views on explanation, as developed in *How the Laws of Physics Lie*, (New York: Oxford University Press, 1983) have deeply influenced my thinking.

11. Mary Hesse, *Models and Analogies in Science* (Notre Dame: Notre Dame University Press, 1966).

12. The Gender and Biology Study Group, "The Importance of Feminist Critique for Contemporary Cell Biology," in *Hypatia* 3, 1 (1988).

13. Evelyn Fox Keller, "Making Gender Visible in the Pursuit of Nature's Secrets," in *Feminist Studies/Critical Studies*, Teresa de Lauretis, ed., (Bloomington: Indiana University Press, 1986), 67–77; and "Gender and Science," in *The Great Ideas Today* (Chicago: Encyclopedia Britannica, 1990).

14. Donna Haraway, "The Biological Enterprise: Sex, Mind, and Profit from Human Engineering to Sociobiology," in *Radical History Review* 20 (1979): 206–37.

15. This is the strategy adopted in chapter 8 of *Science as Social Knowledge*.

16. This point is developed further in *Science as Social Knowledge*, chapter 2.

17. For a somewhat different approach to a similar question, see Philip Kitcher, "The Division of Cognitive Labor," in *Journal of Philosophy* LXXXVII, 1 (January 1990): 5–23.

Epistemological Communities

Lynn Hankinson Nelson

Evidence

The conviction persists—though history shows it to be a hallucination—that all the questions that the human mind has asked are questions that can be answered in terms of the alternatives that the questions themselves present. But, in fact, intellectual progress usually occurs through sheer abandonment of questions together with both of the alternatives they assume—an abandonment that results from their decreasing vitality and a change of urgent interest. We do not solve them: we get over them. (Dewey 1910, 313)

At a recent Nobel conference, Harvard physicist Sheldon Glashow outlined his commitments as a scientist and attributed these to other scientists. I use his position as counterpoint in articulating a communal account of evidence, an account compatible with the view that knowledge is socially constructed *and* constrained by evidence ....

Glashow's self-described article of "faith" is this:

We [scientists] believe that the world is knowable, that there are simple rules governing the behavior of matter and the evolution of the universe. We affirm that there are eternal, objective, extrahistorical, socially neutral, external and universal truths, and that the assemblage of these truths is what we call physical science. Natural laws can be discovered that are universal, invariable, inviolate, genderless and verifiable.

They may be found by men or by women or by mixed collaborations of any obscene proportions. Any intelligent alien anywhere would have come upon the same logical system as we have to explain the structure of protons and the nature of supernovae.

This statement I cannot prove. This statement I cannot justify. This is my faith.[1]

But Glashow is surely being disingenuous when he says, "This statement I cannot prove. This statement I cannot justify. This is my faith." Suppose someone in the audience interrupted or followed Glashow to the podium and announced that her "faith" was that the correct (the *only* correct) understanding of the universe, the only access to the true and immutable laws of nature, is to be had through crystal ball gazing or divine revelation. What would Glashow's reaction be? Would he embrace the interloper as a "fellow" traveler who has come to Glashow's own view of proof and justification but simply come to a different though equally viable and equally reasonable view about gaining knowledge?

Of course not. It is far more likely that Glashow would be amazed and offended and that he would dismiss the interloper's claims as unworthy of response. Surely Glashow "really" believes that his own position is obviously a (or *the*) reasonable one and that the interloper's is unreasonable and not worthy of discussion. Why? Clearly because he thinks his position, his "faith," *makes sense of and explains* the success of science, whereas the interloper's position does not.

The paradox in Glashow's position is this: he clearly does not think anything goes in the realm of intellectual commitments. Yet he is locked into a view that does not give him the intellectual space within which he can defend that view. The lock is that imposed by the positivist (or perhaps more fundamentally Humean) tenet that every meaningful claim must either be derivable

322

from sense experience (or statements about sense experience) or must be a claim about the meanings of words (a matter of definition). Glashow's article of faith does not follow directly from sensory experience; nor is it (nor does he want it to be) true by definition. Hence there can be no evidence for it. Hence it is not provable (and Glashow believes proof is possible). Hence, it is "just" an article of faith....

But there is an alternative to Glashow's implicit view about evidence: a view that allows for evidence and reasonable belief without certitude, without derivability from unshakable foundations. This view allows for a discussion of Glashow's position, explains why it is *worth discussing*, and why it is more reasonable than the interloper's view. In the end, Glashow's view is less reasonable than this alternative, an alternative for which Glashow does not allow but which is needed to show that his own view is at least discussible, that it is a player in the field of epistemological theories.

The view of evidence I am alluding to is very different from Glashow's (and from any theory that places similar demands on "knowledge") in at least three ways. First, it construes evidence as communal; second, it accepts coherence (and with it explanatory power) as a measure of reasonableness; and third, it holds that communities, not individuals, are the primary loci of knowledge. I develop my arguments for this view by focusing on three assumptions implicit in Glashow's article of faith:

- There is one full and unique truth about the world.
- Our sensory organs are sufficiently refined to discriminate that truth from other candidates for truth.
- Scientific investigation is such that, at some finite point, the evidence we acquire for a view finally and decisively rules out all alternative views.

In other words, there is one world to discover, our sense organs can uniquely discriminate

that world, and science is a process which will lead, in a finite amount of time, to a single view about what that reality is.

Arguments against the third assumption are widely accepted,[2] and there have been arguments against assumptions related to the first and second. The arguments I outline here are not original. Their importance lies in the fact that they suggest that although all of the assumptions implicit in Glashow's position should be rejected, *nonetheless* the notion of a "reasonable" claim or theory makes sense and that adopting a particular view of knowledge acquisition (including science) need not be an act of faith.

There is no single way to make these points, for the threads are many and intertwined. I start with Glashow's, commitment to the view that "any intelligent being anywhere" would have "come upon" the structure of protons. The commitment presumes a universality of experience (at least the potential for such universality), which presumes, in turn, both a view of evidence and a view of knowers: specifically, that individuals have unmediated or at least unfiltered access to a reality that itself admits of only one systemization. Now, one's faith in such universality might be partly underwritten by similarities in sense organs (which might not, of course, be duplicated in an "alien" species). But it *also* requires that there is a unique, true theory of nature and that our sense organs are sufficiently refined to discover it and discriminate it from possible alternatives. Only then (in the absence of innate ideas) could it be inevitable (even possible) that any human being anywhere (let alone any "being" anywhere) would discover proton structure. The third of the assumptions I earlier attributed to Glashow is also implicit in the commitment: that scientific investigation is such that, at some finite point, we acquire evidence for a view that finally and decisively rules out all alternative views. If this were not so, Glashow's "any being" might never reach the (one) truth about protons.

I have suggested that Glashow does not really view his position as an article of faith (that he would not grant faith in, say, crystal ball gazing the status of an equally reasonable view of how to discover truths). His position is more aptly viewed as an inference to the best explanation: as the best (if not only) explanation for science's success in explaining and predicting experience and features of the world. But as an explanation, Glashow's position faces immediate problems.

Perhaps the most obvious are posed by the history of science. The problem is not (most interestingly at least) that its history includes discarded theories and abandoned projects and that we would need to find some way of accommodating these that did not undermine the position itself (we would need, perhaps, to look for some general fault in past scientific practice—although not, of course, a problem with scientists' sense organs). A deeper problem for the view that evidence is definitive and self-announcing is that many theories and assumptions eventually abandoned were, in fact, well supported within the context of then current knowledge and accepted practice.

A purported explanation either needs to be compatible with our prior understandings of what is to be explained (in this case, the history of science ...) or it should point to a reconstruction that offers a different but coherent understanding of that which is being explained. As an explanation of the history of science, Glashow's position does neither.

Using the above criteria, the three assumptions I earlier identified as implicit in Glashow's position are also deeply problematic. Many of us have come to see that we have no reason to take the third assumption I have attributed to Glashow seriously. Consider, for example, his second example of "certain" knowledge, the nature of supernovae. However much evidence we have for that account and however much we could have, we are not in a position (and never will be) to know that future experience will not cause us to abandon it or to organize things in ways that no longer include it.... There is nothing in our experience to rule out the possibility of a future theory, commensurate with all of our experiences to date but incompatible with our current theory about supernovae, for what is currently claimed about supernovae far exceeds the evidence we have or ever will have.

The point, made decades ago by Quine among others, is that our theories are and will forever remain underdetermined by all the evidence we have or ever will have for them (Quine 1960). There is, for example, nothing in our collective experience to date to preclude our abandoning our common-sense way of organizing things in terms of physical objects for a theory that makes equally good sense of our collective experience but is incompatible with physical object theory (Quine 1969).

There is also nothing in our collective experience to warrant the assumption about our sense organs implicit in Glashow's article of faith. It is commensurate with that experience that our sense organs are refined to such a degree that, so far at least, they enable us to survive by organizing and predicting relevant future experience. (Interpersonal experience figures largely in our survival. It is also, of course, dependent on our sense organs.) But there is nothing in our experience or in what we currently know about our sense organs to warrant the inference that they are able to discriminate a "best" theory of nature (if, indeed, there is such a thing) from multiple candidates. In light of current evolutionary theory, our sense organs represent a "jury rigging" of available parts, useful in the sense that they have enabled the species to survive (so far), but probably only one of the possible, functional combinations of available parts (Gould 1982). There is nothing to indicate that they are adequate to the task of encompassing all that goes on, all of the rhythms and order (or, perhaps, an inherent and even more basic disorder) of nature.[3]

This brings us to the first of the assumptions implicit in Glashow's statement: that there is one (and only one) true account of the world. It is commensurate with our collective experience, as well as developments in philosophy of science, that there are indefinitely many theories that would enable us to successfully explain and predict experience, that no single system would be better than all others and, hence, that we have no reason to think there is one unique and full account to be discovered (see, for example, Quine 1960). It is commensurate with what we know and have experienced, for example, that an alternative theory of nature that did not include "Boyle's Law" (or, for that matter, any "law"), that organized things, differently, might equally well explain and predict what we experience (Nelson 1990...). So, minimally, there is no one "most probable" account of the world. Given this, we need some further argument for the view that there is, nonetheless, one and only one *true* account. Glashow provides none, and I can provide none for him.

None of what I have said by way of criticizing the three assumptions implicit in Glashow's position suggests that any or all alternatives will do or that because we do not have evidence warranting these assumptions, all alternatives are equally viable. The bases for each of the points made so far have been our collective experience and other aspects of current knowledge (evolutionary theory, empirical psychology, and philosophy of science), and it is not, compatible with either our experience or knowledge, including feminist experience and knowledge, that any theory, any belief, or any way of organizing things will do or that all are equally warranted. That there is a world that constrains what it is reasonable to believe makes the most sense of what we experience—predictions misfire, theories fail, we can and do get things wrong—or, as Evelyn Keller makes the point, "The constraints imposed by the recalcitrance of nature are reminders ... that, despite its ultimate unrepresentability, nature does exist"

(Keller 1989, 43). What we are not warranted in assuming is that only one system could organize the world or that the world is of a determinate nature, specifiable in categories our sense organs will lead us to discover.

Now, an appeal to faith would be a reasonable resort (if not the only resort) if individuals were the primary epistemological agents, if evidence were something only individuals could gather or have. If knowledge is acquired by individuals, if all that we know, including the knowledge that emerges in our everyday interactions with nature and one another as well as in highly focused endeavors like science, has been derived from the "immediate" and unfiltered sensory experience of individuals, then, unless there is one true theory and the evidence for it is unequivocal, our allegedly individual successes in explaining and predicting experience, and the match between your experiences and theories and mine, are mysteries. That is, only a determinate reality together with fully adequate sense organs *could* explain how each individual, working on an individual basis, does (or could) come, in the end, to exactly the same theories. Hence, I am suggesting that there is a deep connection between objectivism and epistemological individualism.

The alternative account of evidence I next articulate is also compatible with our success in organizing and predicting experience and features of the world, including science's success. But it avoids the paradox inherent in Glashow's position and, unlike the latter, it is compatible with feminist experience and knowledge. I begin by telling (in very broad strokes) a different story about the discovery of proton structure. The contextual aspects of the story, the historical relativity of any such discovery and its relationship to a going context of knowledge and practices, build on the implications of feminist science criticism and epistemology. In arguing that science is an ongoing, historically relative concern, I also draw on various of Quine's arguments against positivism. My arguments relating the context for the discovery directly to evidence draw on Quine's arguments for "holism," but I extend Quine's positions in ways called for by feminist science criticism. At various points in the story, I use the insights that emerge about evidence to support the view that communities are the primary epistemological agents.

The discovery of proton structure became possible *within a going system or context* of theories and practices. That context included, minimally, a theory in which protons figured; methodologies, projects, and standards of evidence that emerged concomitantly in the process of building that theory (and possibly others); and a science community (or communities) that constructed or adopted these and rejected possible alternatives. The context permitting the discovery also included some extensive part of physics as well as knowledge and standards in other fields (mathematics, chemistry, and technology, for example) that underwrite—that is, permit and support—what is currently known about protons. The context also included some of the history of science—at least those aspects on which that current body of knowledge (including, again, physics, mathematics, and technology) builds or that led eventually to it. And it encompassed broader metaphysical commitments incorporated in theories, projects, standards of evidence, and methodologies in physics and other fields, including, for example, that macroscopic objects are "made up" of smaller, "unobservable" objects; that the actions of subatomic particles underwrite events at the macroscopic level; and perhaps even that there are laws of nature (that natural relationships are linear, hierarchical, and universal). Without something like these commitments, it is difficult to know how physicists (or anyone else) would have "stumbled upon" protons or their structure.

In fact, the story so far is too simple and, without qualification, it is deeply misleading. I have phrased the above points as if the history of science is a "history of ideas." But the history of "scientific ideas" (by which strange locution I mean the adoption and abandon-ment of theories as well as methodologies, standards of evidence, fields, research projects, models, ontologies, hypotheses, and so on), is inseparable from a social context: from a context of social relations, practices, puzzles, pressures, conflicts, and undertakings.[4] Even if we construe that history and context narrowly so as to include only the "internal" context of science communities (excluding, that is, economic, political, and other features of a broader social context that permit the existence and functioning of communities that are both self-defined and socially recognized in terms of the "pursuit of knowledge"), any such discovery occurred, and could only occur, within a context of social relations and practices.[5] Moreover, limiting the relevant social context to science communities would rely on an assumption that the directions of research and the content of science are determined solely by a logic of scientific inquiry and that such inquiry is an autonomous process, assumptions no longer plausible in light of feminist science criticism and recent historical and social studies of science.

To return to the commitment with which we began, the story I have suggests that any community with an appropriate history, knowledge base, and system of accepted practices, interests, methods, and questions (as well as the time and funding to permit such undertakings) might well have come upon protons and their structure—but this is *hardly* "any intelligent being anywhere." (Indeed, I have not mentioned an "individual" or individual "discoverer" for reasons that are probably clear by now and that I address explicitly below.) The point is in keeping with insights that have emerged in and through feminist science criticism and epistemology, but it is not itself an account of evidence—let alone a viable alternative to an objectivist account. To recognize the discovery of proton structure as relative to a particular historical, social, and scientific context is compatible with judgmental relativism, and I do not believe such a view of evidence is empirically viable any more than it is politically viable.

I now suggest that much of the "context," I have noted has a direct bearing on what constitutes the evidence for current knowledge of proton structure—more to the point, that many of the factors that I have described as "underwriting" that knowledge constitute, in fact, *part of the evidence for it.* Hence, I include as evidence for proton structure a large body of current knowledge within which protons figure directly and theories and practices in other sciences which underwrite or support these. I am using the terms "underwrite" and "support" in a strong sense, in an *evidential* sense, arguing that a body of accepted knowledge and practices (methodologies, ontologies, and so on) that includes a theory about proton structure is akin to an arch; each "piece" supports and is supported by the other pieces (Quine 1960, 11). Given this interdependence, the evidence for proton structure obviously includes theories, methodologies, and standards already noted (other aspects of physics, mathematics, and technology). And the evidence includes "common-sense" knowledge and experience of macroscopic objects and events and the standards we use to identify these, for it is terms of our experiences and knowledge of such objects and events that the evidence for—including the explanatory power of—theories in which protons figure becomes apparent and that such theories have empirical significance (Quine 1966).[6] Finally, broader metaphysical and methodological commitments incorporated in current scientific practices also constitute part of the evidence for proton structure: that there are objects and events that are not "directly" observable that explain, more systematically, what happens on the macroscopic level and that particular macroscopic events (instrument readings, for example) are evidence of these. These commitments are incorporated in theories that include protons, as well as in related methodologies and standards, and are among the things a physicist would appeal to in responding to (at least more than superficial)

queries about how and why physicists came to determine proton structure and what warrants their claims about that structure.

In short, knowledge about protons is not discrete or free floating. It is not isolatable from a larger system of theories, practices, and standards of evidence, a system that includes other aspects of scientific knowledge and practices as well as those of common sense (although, obviously, some parts of the system are more closely connected to knowledge of proton structure than others). Sentences about protons do not have empirical content—a list of sensory stimulations associated with them—in isolation from the larger system within which they figure (theoretical statements, methodologies, views about what constitutes evidence, principles for individuating objects, broader metaphysical commitments). Consequently, there is no discrete piece of evidence that warrants (or could) a claim about protons, no isolated experience against which such claims are or could be tested.

I have so far stressed a going system of knowledge and practices as evidence for particular theories and claims—a point which suggests that, in a fundamental sense, evidence is communal. No individual invented the "system" or context that underwrites knowledge of proton structure, a theoretical system the latter systematizes in turn. Moreover, without reason to think there is a unique theory of nature (and that our sensory organs could discriminate such a theory), there is no reason to assume that "any individual anywhere" *would* have recapitulated that system. But internal consistency is not the sole criterion (or an adequate one) for reasonable beliefs and explanations. Part of the evidence for protons is experience. Protons both organize and are compatible with our experiences and they have explanatory power: they allow us to explain and predict some of what happens. Here, the account of evidence I am advocating diverges from judgmental relativism (as well as coherence theories of truth), for not all theories or claims will be equally compatible with experience (as an attempt, for example, to suspend one's belief in the existence of something akin to gravity will quickly attest).

This aspect of the account of evidence also diverges from individualistic accounts. Although "experience" may seem to lend itself to an individualistic account of evidence—although it may seem (and certainly has seemed) appropriately ascribed to individuals, something individuals, as individuals, "have" (either in a phenomenological sense or in the sense of physical states)—the discussion of the discovery of proton structure suggests that experience is fundamentally social. There are no "immediate" experiences of protons, nor any determinate list of sensory stimulations from which what is known about protons is derived (or derivable). Rather, the sensory experiences currently recognized as relevant to such knowledge are themselves shaped and mediated by a larger system of historically and culturally specific theory and practice (for a historically and culturally specific community or communities), a system which not only constitutes part of the evidence for current knowledge about protons but also shapes the experiences of individuals into coherent and relevant accounts. Put another way, experiences of protons were *not possible* until relatively recently, and this did not just reflect, at least not in any simple way, a lack of technological sophistication, for the latter emerged apace with projects and knowledge. Hence, in terms of the case we are considering, the epistemological burden is appropriately attributed to communities. Individuals can in fact use such systems, but the systems themselves are communal enterprises; it is these that make possible and shape relevant experience and these by which an individual and her community will judge her claims.

To view the evidence for proton structure as relative to a larger system of theories and practices in the two ways I have outlined (and, hence, as communal) may seem unproblematic (proton structure, after all, represents

"high" theoretical ground) but not generalizable. But the view is no less appropriate for "common-sense" objects and events.[7] Our knowledge of rabbits and social movements is also not isolatable from larger systems and historical and cultural contexts and undertakings; our evidence for these is, in general terms, not different in kind from that for protons. Part of the evidence for rabbits and social movements is a larger system of organizing things (a conceptual scheme and set of practices that has long included physical objects and has, for some time, included the category "social movements" and standards for identifying them and analyzing their consequences); part of the evidence is that rabbits and social movements (or, more correctly, theories that include them) help us to organize, explain, and predict some of what happens—a point, again, about the world. (I am not endorsing a theory/world, or language/world, dichotomy here. The relationship at issue is one between *experience of* the world, experience that is shaped and made possible by communal ways of organizing things, and *systems* of connected theories, methodologies, and practices). There is no determinate list of sensory stimulations from which what we know about rabbits or social movements is derived (or derivable), nor are our abilities to recognize these different in kind from the ability of some of us to recognize protons; these, too, depend on public theories and practices that allow individuals to enjoy coherent and recoverable sensory experience and to organize the latter into coherent accounts.

Hence, an answer to the question "what is the evidence for protons?" (as well as to a question about the evidence for rabbits or social movements) has three inseparable aspects: their compatibility with other things known, their explanatory power, and their coherence with experience. On the account I have outlined, evidence for protons is neither definitive nor "self-announcing." Nor does the account (or the usefulness of positing protons) support (let alone force) the views that the theories and practices that led to the positing of protons are the only (or even best) way that things might have been organized (or will come to be organized); that the body of knowledge and practice that underwrote the discovery of proton structure could not have underwritten alternative (even incompatible) discoveries; or that different social and political relations and practices might not have resulted in different sciences in terms of interests, status, questions, and participants—differences that might well have resulted in different projects, standards, methodologies, and bodies of knowledge. Indeed, the account indicates that such possibilities are real, for it assumes no "subbasement" in terms either of "pre-social" experience or a determinate reality specifiable in only one way (or any best way); it broadens the scope of the evidence that is relevant to specific theories to include theories and practices of a broader reach than those generated in science; and it insists on a slippage between all the evidence we have and the knowledge we construct—hence, that there is "room" for alternative constructions. But the account also does not lend credence to judgmental relativism. There are two general constraints on the knowledge we construct: experience and other things known and undertaken.

This view of evidence points to communities as the primary generators and repositories of knowledge. It suggests two things of an individual who came upon the structure of protons: first, that such an individual would have been working within an ongoing context of public theory, practices, and standards that not only made it possible to discover proton structure and shaped that knowledge but constitute part of the evidence for it; second, that the standards (theoretical, practical, methodological) by which *that* person as well as her community would have determined that she *did know* proton structure would be communal standards (for some community or communities)—standards that emerged concomitantly with the

processes (intellectual, social, and political) through which a theory about protons was generated. If an individual claimed to know something that was not in keeping with the knowledge and standards of her community (or any other), it would require a change in such standards and knowledge for the individual to know—and, then, of course, some community would know. To assume an individual could know something no one else knew *or could know* would require that there is one true theory "awaiting" discovery; that our sense organs provide immediate access to a reality that is, itself, specifiable in only one way; and that our sense organs are able to discriminate a unique true theory from multiple alternatives—assumptions that are not warranted.

Recall now the hypothetical interloper who offered her or his faith in crystal ball gazing as (at least as) viable an explanation of how to get to warranted beliefs as Glashow's self-described "faith" in science. The alternative account of evidence explored here provides a way of responding to the interloper that does not involve paradox, for it allows the room and provides the grounds to say of a view that it is not warranted (or not as warranted as another) without appeal to assumptions that are themselves unwarranted. When the interloper says (as interlopers frequently do), "you cannot prove I am wrong!"—thus, however inadvertently and illogically, exposing the weakness in Glashow's present position (its reliance on assumptions that he cannot prove in the way he demands proof)—those of us who share Glashow's doubts about crystal ball gazing as a method of arriving at warranted beliefs and theories could say that the interloper's explanation is not compatible with "our" experience or current understandings of how things are (the first-person plurals here would need to be carefully and self-consciously attended to, as I address in the next section). We could go on to explain that our current understandings of how things work do not include anything to suggest (or to enable us to account for) a connection between crystal ball gazing and reasonable theories. We could not insist that no future experience will lead us to revise our views about crystal ball gazing but we could say that, by current lights, research into crystal ball gazing is not promising or warranted (and we might, if we are in the position, decline funding for such research).

What lies behind my earlier statement that "communities construct and acquire knowledge" has emerged, and with it some features of an alternative to objectivism and relativism. The term *construct* reflects the view that knowledge, standards of evidence, and methodologies, are "of our own making" rather than pieces passively discovered and added incrementally to a unique, true theory of nature and that these are constructed in the contexts of our various projects and practices and evolve in response to the latter and experience. The "social construction of knowledge" runs deep on the view, for the knowledge we build both shapes our experience as individuals into coherent and recoverable accounts and determines what we will count as evidence. Moreover, as pieces of that knowledge become more general, they bridge and systematize other knowledge and practices—hence, I have spoken of "underwriting" and of a dynamic and broad system of evidential relations. And finally, experience itself is not, on the view, unproblematic, a "natural" resting place without need of evaluation.[8] Made possible and shaped by systems of theories and standards, not all experiences will be equal, for some theories and practices will enable more veridical experience and more viable knowledge (see also Harding 1991).[9] Hence, I have spoken of reconstructing experience and knowledge on the basis of what feminists know and come to know.

But the term *acquire* is equally deliberate, reflecting the fact that there are *constraints* on knowledge. The standards of evidence, ontologies, and methodologies we adopt and the knowledge we build are communal, interconnected, interdependent, and relative to larger blocks of things known and projects undertaken: beliefs and knowledge claims are constrained by these things and experience.

It is a consequence of the arguments advanced here that communities are the primary epistemological agents. Standards of evidence and knowledge are historically relative and dynamic and of our own making. They are inherently and necessarily communal. Experience remains the heart of the matter, but it is inherently social rather than individualistic, for we experience the world through the lens of going projects, categories, theories, and standards, and all of these are generated by communities. Experience is also not the only criterion. What constitutes evidence for specific claims and theories includes the knowledge and standards constructed and adopted by epistemological communities. Based on our experiences, we can each contribute uniquely to what we know—but none of us knows what no one else could.[10]

Epistemological Communities

I stated earlier that the views of agents and evidence I would advocate are compatible with and supported by feminist experience and knowledge. To show this and to give more content to the notion of an epistemological community, I briefly consider some issues raised in and by feminist science criticism. I use one aspect of feminist criticism of "man-the-hunter theory" because the theory has received extensive attention in feminist science criticism and epistemology, and this will allow comparison between an analysis incorporating the view of evidence I have outlined and those in which evidence is construed narrowly and theories (or research programs) are considered in isolation.[11] My claim is that the reconstruction I will sketch can be generalized to other theories feminists criticize and advocate, and that such reconstructions carry significant benefits.

One aspect of the criticism feminists have offered of man-the-hunter theory is directed at an organizing principle the theory incorporates: that males are socially oriented—their activities and behaviors central to and determining of social dynamics; and that females are biologically oriented—their activities and behaviors primarily reproductive, with reproductive activities assumed to be "natural," unskilled, and without consequence for social dynamics (or culture). As evidence of the organizing principle, feminist critics point out that man-the-hunter theory credits the evolution of *Homo sapiens* to behaviors and activities its advocates attribute to our male ancestors. According to the theory, the invention of tools and the development of social organization led to the evolution of bipedalist and speaking "man," and both were the achievements of our male ancestors to facilitate the hunting of large animals (Bleier 1984; Harding 1986; Hubbard 1983).[12] Our female ancestors, on the other hand, appear to have gotten a free evolutionary ride; according to the theory, they were dependent on male providers, and their behavior and activities were primarily reproductive (again, at least by implication, "natural" and unskilled) and without consequence for human evolution. As feminist critics point out, the organizing principle has far-reaching consequences; in addition to shaping the general outlines of an androcentric reconstruction of human evolution, it shapes the interpretation of fossil and archeological data and underwrites contemporary arguments (by sociobiologists, for example) that a sexual division of labor and male dominance are genetically determined and the product of natural selection (Bleier 1984; Longino and Doell 1983).

Much of the criticism directed at the organizing principle has centered on questions of theoretical warrant. Ruth Hubbard argues, for example, that without androcentric bias there is no reason to assume a sexual division of labor in early hominid and human groups (Hubbard 1983). In her extensive and detailed criticism of the theory, Ruth Bleier argued that the theory "starts with a set of assumptions concerning the eternal nature of the characteristics … of women and men" (Bleier 1984, 123). Other feminist critics have argued similarly, citing androcentrism as shaping both the general outlines and details of the man-the-hunter account.[13]

Considered on their own terms, that is, in isolation from other theories and knowledge and, hence, in relation only to available archeological and fossil evidence, both the organizing principle and the man-the-hunter account seem without warrant. Helen Longino and Ruth Doell argue that in the case of man-the-hunter theory (and, they argue, in the case of woman-the-gatherer theory as well), the "gap" between theory and the "data" is filled in—indeed, Longino and Doell argue, given the relative lack of physical evidence, the gap could *only* be filled in—by "preconceived and culturally determined ideas"(Longino and Doell 1983, 175).

Few of us, I suspect, would deny that androcentrism and gynocentrism have been factors in the development and advocacy of the man-the-hunter and woman-the-gatherer theories or that feminist criticism of the former has been prompted and shaped by feminist politics and scholarship.[14] It seems no less clear that there is a gap between these accounts of evolution and the fossil and archeological evidence and that problems attendant to historical explanations are at work, including the role of current context in shaping these and, in the present case, the relative lack and unevenness of "data."[15]

But my arguments of the last section suggest an alternative to two assumptions at least implicit in the criticism I have summarized: one, that there was (or is) little or no theoretical warrant for the organizing principle of man-the-hunter theory; the other, that "culturally determined beliefs" (I am assuming these include androcentric and gynocentric beliefs) are either unable to function as evidence or are inappropriate when they do so function.

Consider a matter of debate between advocates of man-the-hunter theory and woman-the-gatherer theory: the significance of chipped stones found near fossil remains of *Homo erectus* (Longino and Doell 1983). Are they evidence that our male ancestors made tools to facilitate the hunting of large animals, as man-the-hunter theorists assume; evidence that women were making tools to assist them in gathering, as those advocating woman-the-gatherer theory argue; or evidence of some other activity that a future theory might posit (Longino and Doell 1983)? If we consider the stones and other artifacts to be the only relevant evidence, then any answer to the question of the stones' significance will be based, to use Longino's and Doell's phrase, on considerations other than "direct evidence" (175). Hence, on a narrow construal of evidence, any such answer will be supplied by beliefs and assumptions that are inappropriate, that cannot (at least should not) function as evidence. Our concerns about such answers would be deeper, of course, if we also assume or demand a values/science or politics/science dichotomy.

The view of evidence I have advocated suggests that the evidence we actually bring to bear, and that we should bring to bear on the question of the significance of these stones, is vast: that current work in fields related to human evolution (primate anatomy, geology, and primatology, for example) and theories that underwrite our assumptions about how such fields are relevant (or are not) will constitute part of the evidence for an explanation of the stones. And, in fact, feminist attention to man-the-hunter theory has revealed a substantial feedback system supporting the theory and the organizing principle it incorporates.

Far from being developed in isolation, man-the-hunter theory represented a synthesis of theories, models, and observations from a number of sciences. Primate anatomy, neurobiology, evolutionary biology, geology, paleontology, and population genetics were drawn on to develop and support the view

that tool use was a fundamental factor in the evolution of the brain and the move to upright posture. Connections to other current models, theories, and research are no less apparent in terms of the organizing principle feminists have criticized. Both the theory's advocates and its feminist critics note that in reconstructing the social dynamics of early hominid and human groups, man-the-hunter theorists have drawn on accounts of behavior and social dynamics in contemporary hunter-gatherer societies and models and observations in primatology and the biobehavioral sciences.[16] And in each of these fields, in anthropology, animal sociology, and the biobehavioral sciences, and specifically in terms of the observations and models drawn on by man-the-hunter theorists, feminist scientists and science critics have documented similar, androcentric methods of organizing data and observations. Finally, feminist critics of the theory have noted the deep convergence between the man-the-hunter account of early hominid social organization and behavior and contemporary Western gender relations.

When we construe evidence broadly, we are in a position to recognize that, far from being theoretically *unwarranted*, both the theory and the organizing principle enjoyed *substantial* evidential support, that the evidence for the organizing principle and the theory lay in great measure in just such connections. These points hold even if we have our doubts about, say, the relevance of primatology to a reconstruction of human evolution or to contemporary human behavior, about the extent and nature of the evidence primatology can provide, or about the models and theories that have, to date, characterized animal sociology, the biobehavioral sciences, or anthropology.

Equally important, recognizing such evidential relations is necessary to an accurate account of the evidence that supports feminist criticism of man-the-hunter theory and of that which supports woman-the-gatherer theory. In both cases, scientists and science critics are synthesizing research in primatology, anthropology, and the biobehavioral sciences—specifically, research that was not shaped by androcentric organizing principles and assumptions and, in some cases, that indicates the limits to which primate behavior or hunter/gatherer societies can provide insight into early human behavior (Longino and Doell 1983, among others). The evidence for these projects also includes knowledge of androcentrism in other sciences and of the deep relationships between gender and science that have become visible in the last three decades, as well as the more general reconstructions of women's and men's experiences that have become possible due to feminist politics.

I am not suggesting that when we construe evidence broadly, the "gap" between reconstructions of human evolution and evidence will be closed. That gap will always remain, a consequence of the more general underdetermination of theories, of the specific problems faced by historical reconstructions, and of the relative lack of artifacts in this particular case. My point has been, rather, that individual theories neither develop nor face experience in isolation, that the evidence available, relevant, and appropriate is broader than the "data," and that such evidence is not (at least when it is interesting) arbitrary or unable to be evaluated. These points are, in fact, an implication of feminist science criticism, including the three critiques I have discussed. There *is* evidence indicating that the organizing principle incorporated in man-the-hunter theory and shaping research in primatology and anthropology leads to partial and distorted accounts of social dynamics. And there *is* evidence that reproductive activities have never exhausted women's activities and that the latter are variable and integral aspects of social dynamics.

Acknowledging the evidential relations I have identified has important benefits. First, judgments of theories, research programs, methodologies, and ontologies are more sophisticated, for they are inclusive of the actual evidential support underlying these.

Hence, the judgments "good science" and "bad science" can be recognized as more complex than a focus on individual theories (or methods or ontologies) permits. In terms of the present example, it becomes apparent that far from there being "no reason" (or only "bad" reasons) for the man-the-hunter account, the evidence *was substantial* and that both those advocating and criticizing the theory need to acknowledge and evaluate more than the available data. Second, we are in a position to insist that the so-called common-sense assumptions and experiences of gender relations and dominance hierarchies that are functioning as evidence for man-the-hunter theory (and for other current theories and research) can and should be evaluated, that acknowledging these and subjecting them to evaluation is part and parcel of doing *good* science. Given the last three decades, we have perhaps never been in a better position to recognize that such beliefs can and should be evaluated. Third, without artificial boundaries, we avoid the potential paradox of arguing (or implying) that science influenced by politics and gender is, by virtue of the fact, bad science—a position which feminist science criticism undermines (or which, if we insist on it or allow it to be smuggled into our analyses of androcentric science, leads to convoluted accounts of that criticism).[17] Finally, recognizing the breadth of the evidence that supports man-the-hunter theory reveals the depth, the pervasiveness, and the significance of androcentrism in science. This makes it far less plausible for examples like man-the-hunter theory to be dismissed as "idiosyncratic" or isolatable instances that have little import for "science itself" (whatever that is, if it does not include evolutionary theory, primatology, or anthropology) or as "just models" without the potential to underwrite other theories and research or to reinforce social relations.

Philosophical legend credits Hobbes with the line, "The Inn of Evidence has no signpost." I don't know if the legend is true, but I like to cite it. Viable theories, like evidence, are not self-announcing. When we judge a theory as viable or not, when we judge a research project, a model, a methodological principle, or a theory as an example of "good" or "bad" science or judge a particular claim or belief as warranted or unwarranted, it can not be on the basis of some simple test or criterion. These judgments require attention to as much evidence as we can (or find it necessary to) accommodate. After such evaluation, we may find that rather than pointing to a theory like man-the-hunter as an example of "bad science," we will want to say that "it was once promising in the context of then current knowledge and standards, but we are now in a position—(although certainly not ever in a position to say that "all the evidence is in")—to see that it is not viable."

Our analyses would also need to focus on communities (in the present case, these include primatologists, evolutionary biologists, and feminist communities, among others). We cannot credit individual scientists with the assumptions, ontologies, organizing principles, and theories that constitute evidence for man-the-hunter theory or with choosing and synthesizing these. For one thing, the assumptions and models were common to various sciences; for another, androcentric assumptions and methodologies, like feminist assumptions and methodologies, have been generated within social experiences, relations, traditions, and historically and culturally specific ways of organizing social life. Nor, of course, can we credit any individual with the recognition that male dominance is not an inevitable feature of social groups or that organizing principles like the one at issue in man-the-hunter theory distort observations and theories. The interests, standards, and knowledge generated and shared by feminist communities made that knowledge possible. Alternatively said, it was not the *gender of* individual scientists, or any "attribute" of individual scientists, that enabled such recognition—any more than it was an "attribute" of individual scientists that led to or furthered androcentric assumptions. The

standards and knowledge that underwrite the acceptability of androcentric and feminist assumptions are communal.

There is an additional and important benefit to construing evidence broadly and focusing on communities: namely, that these preclude the claim that cases like that which we have considered are examples of incommensurability—or, in some other way, constitute "evidence for" judgmental relativism. Advocates of man-the-hunter theory and feminist critics disagree about many things, including models and observations in sciences currently viewed as relevant to human evolution (even whether some sciences are relevant) and, perhaps, so-called common-sense assumptions and knowledge about gender. But they do not disagree about everything; they share a larger body of knowledge and standards that includes physical object theory, a heliocentric view of the solar system, and the view that humans evolved and that their activities were factors in that process. Hence, members of these groups can discuss (and disagree about) the significance of "chipped stones" without any lapse in conversation and use other aspects of the knowledge and standards they share to evaluate the conflicting claims. The flip side of the point is this: although the knowledge and standards currently at issue are community specific, feminist communities and science communities both overlap (consider feminist primatologists) and are themselves subcommunities of larger communities—a fact that, along with the changing social relations that made it possible, has enabled feminist science criticism and feminist knowledge more broadly.

The discussion of this and the last section suggests that epistemological communities can be identified in terms of shared knowledge, standards, and practices. Science communities serve as obvious examples of epistemological communities, with bodies of theory, accepted procedures, questions, and projects defining such communities; and membership being a function of education in and allegiance to community-specific knowledge, standards, and practices. Moreover, science communities are both self-defined and socially recognized in terms of knowledge and, relatedly, are granted and exercise what Kathryn Pyne Addelson calls a "cognitive authority" to name and explain those features of the world that fall within their disciplinary boundaries—and, of course, beyond these (Addelson 1983).

But science communities are not the only epistemological communities, nor have they a lock on generating knowledge. In terms of their very existence and authority, and the knowledge and standards they generate, science communities are interdependent with the larger communities within which they function. More to the point, there are, in fact, *many* communities that develop and share knowledge and standards, including our larger world community and its multiple and evolving subcommunities.

As our consideration of man-the-hunter theory indicates, the boundaries of epistemological communities overlap with some aptly considered subcommunities of larger communities (e.g., part of the community of primatology falls within feminist communities), and such communities are dynamic and unstable. They evolve, disband, realign, and cohere as interests and undertakings evolve and are abandoned, as new experiences, standards, and knowledges become possible (when, for example, feminists come to be primatologists, and vice versa). There are subcommunities that have developed categories, methods, projects, knowledge, and standards in addition to those they share with larger communities (e.g., the physics community is a subcommunity of a larger community with which it shares knowledge and standards: a community on which it is, in several senses, dependent).

There are also subcommunities that have generated knowledge and standards that challenge aspects of a larger body of shared knowledge and standards. Some examples of these are the various subcommunities of feminist philosophers, communities that share some (but not all) of the knowledge and standards of the community of philosophers, an epistemological community by virtue of its "canon," professional associations, and recognition as an academic discipline. Of as much importance, feminist philosophers share knowledge and standards generated and shared by feminist communities, communities whose political goals have led, among other things, to the rethinking of the categories and assumptions of the academic disciplines (including pilosophy) and sciences, and to the development of categories and ontologies, theories, and methodologies that are enabling us to uncover women's experiences and to reconstruct and reevaluate the experiences of men and women.

There are, of course, no litmus tests for identifying epistemological communities. Not only are such communities dynamic, but there is no simple criterion for determining their boundaries. Where we recognize such communities and their parameters will be a function of the nature of our projects and purposes (e.g., in doing epistemology or in forming academic subcommunities, political action groups, or a neighborhood group to deal with local issues); of the definitions communities give to themselves and the projects they undertake; and of the importance such communities (or those engaged in epistemology or other projects) attribute to the standards and knowledge they share with larger groups and those they do not—decisions which will also be relative to specific purposes and interests. It currently seems both useful and important to recognize feminist subcommunities within the larger community of philosophy (a community within which other subcommunities can also be identified) and to recognize that these communities are subcommunities of larger feminist communities. On the other hand, it may seem appropriate to recognize a group of feminists and fundamentalists developing a policy against pornography as a coalition of communities, on the grounds that the nature and extent of the knowledge shared by the two groups is not extensive enough to outweigh the significant differences in interests, starting points, and knowledge.

There are other considerations that mitigate against the possibility and desirability of a litmus test for epistemological communities. One is that in undertaking a project focusing on community knowledge and standards, we may come to find that some of the standards of evidence or knowledge with which we begin do not withstand scrutiny (these might be our own standards or those of some community we are studying). Our community standards and knowledge will evolve in response to such results, and so, of course, might its membership. (We might, for example, decide to "throw out" the astrologers or anyone unwilling to abandon astrology.)

And, finally, epistemological communities are not monolithic. It is currently appropriate and useful to recognize feminist communities as epistemological communities, to recognize that such communities have generated bodies of knowledge, adopted standards, and developed categories of which each member of these communities accepts some—while recognizing that not all members of feminist communities agree on all things and that there may be no single belief that is held by all feminists. The point holds for any epistemological community, for we are each members of a number of such communities, a point, as I noted earlier, that is particularly relevant to feminist scholarship and politics of the last three decades, a period in which changing social relations have enabled feminists to become scientists (and vice versa) and hence have enabled experiences, knowledge, and standards that, prior to such changes, were not possible.

But although epistemological communities are not monolithic or stable, such communities also do not "dissolve" into "collections" of knowing individuals. By virtue of our membership in a number of such communities, as well as by virtue of our experiences as individuals, we can each contribute, and uniquely, to the knowledge generated by our various communities. But as I noted earlier, none of us knows (or could) what no one else could. However singular an experience may be, what we know on the basis of that experience has been made possible and is compatible with the standards and knowledge of one or more communities of which we are members: standards and knowledge that enable us to organize our experiences into coherent accounts, underwrite the specific contributions that we make as individuals, and determine what we and our communities will recognize as knowledge. It is that priority that makes it appropriate to extend the notion of an epistemological community beyond science communities—indeed, to see science communities as only special cases of a much broader category—and to recognize a multiplicity of communities as the primary knowers. This understanding of the agents of epistemology is in keeping with a long-standing feminist insight into the "collective" nature of feminist politics and knowing and the deep relationships between the latter and changing social and political relations, an insight that bridges various feminist epistemologies.

Conclusion

The unwillingness of some of us to abandon epistemology stems from considerations that are simultaneously empirical and political. Our reasons for exploring the implications of feminist knowledge for evidence and working to develop a viable account of the latter may include the view that arguments that purportedly reveal the bankruptcy or vacuousness of evidence presume, in fact, some account of evidence. Less abstractly (and without recourse to a *reductio*), we do manage to make sense of, to organize and attribute meaning to, and to predict and control events in multiple and meaningful ways and contexts, including but by no means limited to specialized contexts like science. Our successes and failures at these things indicate a reliance, and the appropriateness of that reliance, on evidence.

A second consideration underwriting such efforts is one of the central implications of feminist politics and scholarship: beliefs and knowledge claims have consequences. Although experience and evidence are inherently unstable and knowledge will never be "complete," the experiences and stories that have been the center of focus to date have been, in fact and at best, only partial; in their claims to "universality," they have simultaneously excluded and mystified other experiences and knowledges; and in their denial of their situatedness, they have been distorted.

To claim such, as well as to demand more empirically adequate knowledge, does not depend on the existence of one timeless truth in relation to which theories are partial or distorting. In reflecting the experiences of privileged men, the experiences and knowledge that have been generalized to date have been partial in terms of what it was or is possible to know in given historical, social, and cultural contexts and further qualified in terms of divisions in experience brought about by social relations (e.g., gender, race, and culture)—a point that alludes both to how things are and our ability to know them.

My arguments here indicate that identifying and explaining that partiality (and explaining why such partiality and the recognition of it are not equally warranted) require that we abandon individualism in all of its guises. They require a communal and more inclusive understanding of evidence than objectivist and relativist positions allow and, deeply related to this, the recognition of communities as the primary agents of epistemology: the primary generators and repositories of knowledge.

Notes

1. Sheldon Glashow. Quoted in *New York Times*, Sec. 4, Oct. 22, 1989, 24.

2. Ironically, given Glashow's claim to speak for scientists, arguments against the third assumption are clearly articulated in "On Being a Scientist," a booklet prepared by the Committee on the Conduct of Science of the National Academy of Sciences for students beginning graduate work in science.

3. Providing an evolutionary explanation of physical object theory in no way establishes that our sense organs are capable of discriminating a best theory or an allegedly unique, true theory of nature.

4. As I note below, I am not here assuming a theory/world or language/world dichotomy. On the view of evidence I will outline, there is no distinction to be made out between that which we talk about and organize (e.g., "a world") and our ways of organizing and attributing meaning to our experience (e.g., theories).

5. See Addelson (1983) for an important discussion of the divisions in what she calls "cognitive authority and labor" that characterize Western societies and sciences.

6. I use quotes to indicate that "common sense" cannot be granted a default status; that it, too, is dynamic, theoretical, and historically and culturally specific; and that so-called common-sense views are by no means unproblematic.

7. I have been asked if the points made about protons only obtain to "theoretical entities." As the next argument indicates, I do not believe there are any *non*-theoretical entities. See also Nelson (1990), especially chapter 3.

8. Appeals to experience can become vacuous unless the notion of what constitutes experience is further specified. As I argue in Nelson (1990), experience, at its most basic level, is the firings of sensory receptors but we do not, of course, experience such firings. We experience the world through the lens of theories generated and shared by the communities of which we are members.

9. One of the more far-reaching implications of feminism is that what Sandra Harding calls "spontaneous experience" is itself shaped and mediated by social relations and ideology (Harding 1991). In developing a feminist empiricist view of evidence, I am suggesting that such considerations do not require anti-empiricist solutions but certainly require more sophisticated accounts of evidence and experience

than traditional and foundationalist empiricist accounts were and are capable of providing. See Harding (in this volume) for a discussion of these issues from the perspective of feminist standpoint epistemology.

10. Linda Alcoff points out that, so stated, the claim is also a consequence of the repeatability criterion (private correspondence). The sense of the claim made within a framework that assumes the initial results are an individual achievement with repeatability ensuring the results because other individuals can, in fact, also (individually) achieve them, is different than the sense of my claim that even the initial results are not (in any interesting way) an individual achievement.

11. Bleier (1984), Harding (1986), Hubbard (1983), Longino and Doell (1983), and Longino (1990) include extensive analyses of man-the-hunter theory. In Nelson (1990), I use holism and an earlier version of the view of evidence I have outlined to analyze aspects of this theory, as well as feminist criticism of research in neuroendocrinology and reproductive endocrinology into sex differences, of "master molecule" theories, and commitments to linear, hierarchical models.

12. Some advocates of the theory construe the implications of hunting more broadly, arguing that what they call the "hunting adaptation" underlies human psychology, biology, emotions, and divisions of labor by sex (see the discussion in Bleier [1984]). Hence, the implications of the theory are broader than the discussion here suggests. See the works cited in note 11.

13. See works cited in note 11.

14. Those who maintain a position long described as "feminist empiricism" in Harding (1986), a position Harding and others have noted is not uncommon among scientists, may find the claim difficult as stated. But as Harding explores and I address here and in *Who Knows,* to argue that feminists are (in some straightforward way) "less biased" seems strained at the very least. I am also not convinced that androcentric and gynocentric approaches should be viewed as comparable (as equally "biased," for example). For one thing, the former were not recognized as such and viewed as "value-neutral"; the latter are often conscious and make no claim to value-neutrality. Moreover, the latter are corrective, not only in the sense that they "add to" prior knowledge but

also because they change much of what counted as knowledge and our views of epistemology and of science.

15. Bleier (1984), Harding (1986), Longino and Doell (1983), and Longino (1990) include extensive consideration of these problems.

16. See works cited in note 11.

17. In her criticism of earlier versions of "feminist empiricism" (which she distinguishes from "philosophical feminist empiricisms" currently being developed), Sandra Harding has made this point clearly. See Harding (1986, 1991), and in this volume.

References

Addelson, K.P. 1983. "The Man of Professional Wisdom." In *Discovering Reality: Feminist Perspectives on Epistemology, Metaphysics, Methodology, and Philosophy of Science.* Edited by S. Harding and M. Hintikka. Dordrecht: D. Reidel.

Bleier, R. 1984. *Science and Gender. A Critique of Biology and Its Theories on Women.* New York: Pergamon Press.

Dewey, J. 1910. "The Influence of Darwin on Philosophy." Reprinted in *Darwin: A Norton Critical Edition.* Edited by Philip Appleman. New York and London: W. W. Norton & Co., 1970, 305–314.

Gould, S.J. 1982. *The Panda's Thumb.* New York and London: W.W. Norton & Company.

Harding S. 1986. *The Science Question in Feminism.* Ithaca: Cornell University Press.

———. 1991. *Whose Science? Whose Knowledge? Thinking from Women's Lives.* Ithaca: Cornell University Press.

Hubbard, R. 1983. "Have Only Men Evolved?" In *Discovering Reality.* Edited by S. Harding and M. Hintikka.

Keller, E.F. 1989. "The Gender/Science System: or, Is Sex to Gender as Nature Is to Science." In *Feminism and Science.* Edited by N. Tuana. Bloomington and Indianapolis: Indiana University Press.

Longino, H. 1990. *Science as Social Knowledge: Values and Objectivity in Scientific Inquiry.* Princeton: Princeton University Press.

Longino, H., and R. Doell. 1983. "Body, Bias, and Behavior: A Comparative Analysis of Reasoning in Two Areas of Biological Science." *Signs* 9, no. 2: 206–227.

Nelson, L.H. 1990. *Who Knows: From Quine to a Feminist Empiricism.* Philadelphia: Temple University Press.

Quine, W.V. 1960. *Word and Object.* Cambridge, Mass.: MIT Press.

———1966. "The Scope and Language of Science." In *The Ways of Paradox and Other Essays.* New York: Random House.

———1969. "Epistemology Naturalized." In *Ontological Relativity and Other Essays.* New York: Columbia University Press.

FEMINIST STANDPOINT THEORY

"Strong Objectivity"

A Response to the New Objectivity Question

Sandra Harding

Objectivity: An Essentially Contested Concept?

Philosophers may well think that now is none too soon to define what objectivity is for the purposes of this discussion. However, I want to resist this urge. One problem is that the term has no single reference in prevailing discussions. Objectivity, or the incapacity for it, has been attributed to individuals, or groups of them, as in, "Women (or feminists, marxists, environmentalists, Blacks, welfare recipients, patients, etc.) are more emotional, less impartial, less capable of objective judgments." Second, it has been attributed to knowledge claims, where it does not seem to add anything to the assertion that a claim is better supported by evidence than its competitors. Third, objectivity is also attributed to methods or procedures that are fair: statistical, or experimental, or repeated procedures are more objective because they maximize standardization, impersonality or some other quality assumed to contribute to fairness. Fourth, objectivity is attributed to certain kinds of knowledge-seeking communities—in Kuhn's account, the kind characteristic of modern science (Kuhn 1970); in other accounts, communities of experts, or ones that include (or exclude!) members of different classes, races and/or genders, or that maximize adversarial relations of rigorous criticism of ideas and claims, or that maximize ideal speech conditions, etc. Though distinct, these different referents of 'objective' clearly are not totally independent of each other in people's thinking. Most obviously, the other three should generate results of research that are better supported by evidence; that is, that are less false.[1]

But noting these four distinct references for the term is only the beginning of mapping its convoluted outlines. I cannot take space to continue that mapping here, but refer readers instead to two recent, highly acclaimed histories of the notion. In one of them, Peter Novick shows that objectivity

> is not a single idea, but rather a sprawling collection of assumptions, attitudes, aspirations and antipathies. At best it is what the philosopher W. B. Gallie has called an "essentially contested concept," like "social justice" or "leading a Christian life," the exact meaning of which will always be in dispute. (Novick 1988, p.1)

Some elements in the notion originate in Aristotle's thought, others have arisen in the last few decades. However, "older usages remain powerful", (ibid. p. 2) and are called up today whenever people are struggling to determine the place that science, or more generally reason, should have in society. As Robert Proctor, the author of the other history, puts the point about the neutrality ideal that both he and Novick see as historically always required of anything deserving the label 'objective', "The ideal of value-neutrality is not a single notion, but has arisen in the course of protracted struggles over the place that science should have in society" (Proctor 1991, p. 262).

Both Novick and Proctor point out that asserting objectivity sometimes has been used to advance and sometimes to retard the growth of knowledge, and the same can be said of assertions of relativism. Thus neither position automatically claims the scientific or rational high-ground. Nor does either assure the political high-ground: each has been used at some times to block social justice and at other times to advance it. As Proctor puts the point, neutrality, the central requirement of the conventional notion, has been used as "myth, mask, shield and sword" (Proctor 1991, p. 262).

My concerns here are primarily with scientific methods. They arise from widespread criticisms in feminist, anti-racist, postcolonial, environmental and other movements for social justice that systematically distorted results of research in the natural and social sciences are the consequence not only of carelessness and inadequate rigor in following existing methods and norms for maximizing objectivity in research practices, but also of inadequacies in how those methods and norms are conceptualized. The prevailing standards for good procedures for maximizing objectivity are *too weak* to be able to identify such culture-wide assumptions as androcentric or Eurocentric ones.

Here I explore one line of response to the new objectivity question—the program for "strong objectivity" that draws on standpoint epistemologies to provide a kind of method for maximizing our ability to block "might makes right" in the sciences. Maximizing objectivity is not identical to maximizing neutrality, as conventional understandings have assumed. Nor, I argue, does it always require it; in a certain range of cases, maximizing neutrality is an obstacle to maximizing objectivity. Though developed as such in feminist theory, central insights of this kind of epistemology/philosophy of science have been expressed far more broadly. This is so in spite of its clear limitations, which, I shall conclude by showing, are significant, but are not those due to the misreadings of it upon which most

critics have tended to focus, and which I address in the last section.

Weak Objectivity, or When Is Neutrality an Obstacle to Maximizing Objectivity?

In some ways, the fate of science parallels that of bourgeois democracy: both were born as exuberant forces for liberation against feudalism, but their very successes have turned them into caricatures of their youth. The bold, antiauthoritarian stance of science has become docile acquiescence; the free battle of ideas has given way to a monopoly vested in those who control the resources for research and publication. Free access to scientific information has been diminished by military and commercial secrecy and by thebarriers of technical jargon; in the commoditization of science, peer review is replaced by satisfaction of the client as the test of quality. The internal mechanisms for maintaining objectivity are, at their best—in the absence of sycophancy toward those with prestige, professional jealousies, narrow cliques, and national provincialism—able to nullify individual capricious errors and biases. but they reinforce the shared biases of the scientific community. The demand for objectivity, the separation of observation and reporting from the researchers' wishes, which is so essential for the development of science, becomes the demand for separation of thinking from feeling. This promotes moral detachment in scientists which, reinforced by specialization and bureaucratization, allows them to work on all sorts of dangerous and harmful projects with indifference to the human consequences. The idealized egalitarianism of a community of scholars has shown itself to be a rigid hierarchy of scientific authorities integrated into the general class structure of the society and modeled on the corporation. And where the pursuit of truth has survived, it has become increasingly narrow, revealing a growing contradiction between the sophistication of science in the small within the laboratory and the irrationality of the scientific enterprise as a whole. (Levins and Lewontin 1993, pp. 315–316)

Two Politics of Science[2]

Has the philosophy of science conceptualized either politics or maximizing objectivity richly enough to meet the kind of widespread criticisms of contemporary sciences and their philosophy represented in this passage by two distinguished biologists? One problem is that the kinds of politics that most threaten the objectivity of science these days escape conceptualization in leading philosophies of science.

There are two kinds of politics with which the philosophies of science must be concerned. One kind is the older notion of politics as the overt actions and policies intended to advance the interests and agendas of so-called special interest groups. This kind of politics intrudes into "pure science" through consciously chosen and often clearly articulated actions and programs that shape what science gets done, how the results of research are interpreted, and, therefore, scientific as well as popular images of nature and social relations. This kind of politics is conceptualized as acting *on* the sciences from outside, as politicizing a science that was otherwise free of politics—or, at least, of that particular politics. This is the kind of relationship between politics and science against which the ideal of objectivity as neutrality—objectivism—works best, though not perfectly, as Levins and Lewontin point out. It makes sense to think of these interests and values as, paradigmatically, intruding into science from outside it and as held by less than (sometimes none of) the group of individuals who constitute legitimates member of the scientific community. In at least many cases, it also is plausible to think of these interests and values as an obstacle to the growth of knowledge. Nazi science, Lysenkoism, or creationist biology are the kinds

of examples of such threats to the neutrality of science by political "irrationalism" that the defenders of objectivism have in mind. They do not have in mind the "intrusion" into sciences of forces for maximizing objectivity and enlarging democratic tendencies; any and all "politics" are made to appear equally pernicious to the growth of scientific knowledge.

However, sciences are also always shaped by a different kind of politics. Here power is exercised less visibly, less consciously, and *not on but through* the dominant institutional structures, priorities, research strategies, technologies, and languages of the sciences—through the practice and culture that constitute a particular scientific episode (Pickering 1992; Rouse 1987; Shapin and Schaffer 1985). Paradoxically, this kind of politics functions through the depoliticization of science—through the creation of "normal" or authoritarian science. Thus a typical standard example that the neutrality enthusiasts cite to demonstrate the bad effects of politicizing science (and they are not wrong about this) can also, paradoxically, be understood as a paradigmatic example of the bad effects of depoliticizing science.

> It is certainly true that, in one important sense, the Nazis sought to politicize the sciences. ... Yet in an important sense the Nazis might indeed be said to have "depoliticized" science (and many other areas of culture). The Nazis depoliticized science by destroying the possibility of political debate and controversy. Authoritarian science based on the "Fuhrer principle" replaced what had been, in the Weimar period, a vigorous spirit of politicized debate in and around the sciences. The Nazis "depoliticized" problems of vital human interest by reducing these to scientific or medical problems, conceived in the narrow, reductionist sense of these terms. The Nazis depoliticized questions of crime, poverty, and sexual or political deviance by casting them in surgical or otherwise medical (and seemingly apolitical) terms ...

politics pursued in the name of science or health provided a powerful weapon in the Nazi ideological arsenal. (Proctor 1988, pp. 290, 293)

The institutionalized, normalized politics of male supremacy, class exploitation, racism and Eurocentrism, while only rarely initiated through the kind of violent politics practiced by the Nazis, similarly authoritarianly depoliticize Western scientific institutions and practices, thereby shaping our images of the natural and social worlds and legitimating past and future exploitative public policies. Thus feminist critics have focussed on how gender-coded concepts of the scientist, objectivity, rationality, mechanistic models, "master molecule" models, etc., escape standard procedures for producing value-neutrality because they have in the first place constituted the scientific institutions and practices which select neutrality-detecting procedures (e.g., Bordo 1987, Keller 1985; Lloyd 1984; Merchant 1980). In contrast to "intrusive politics", this kind of institutional politics does not force itself into pre-existing purportedly pure sciences; it already constitutes their natures and projects.

I have focussed here on the kinds of "normal science" authority that have especially interested feminists, but the new histories and anthropologies of science are full of examples of how state-of-the-art modern sciences draw on local cultural resources. They are all "ethnosciences" one might say after reading such accounts (e.g., Haraway 1989; Harding 1994, forthcoming; Latour 1988; Pickering 1984, 1992). This evaluation is reinforced when one notes that Joseph Needham's histories of the sciences of China (Needham 1969) have been followed by contemporary postcolonial critics who point to the constitution of European sciences through distinctively European assumptions and projects (Goonatilake 1984; Harding 1993a; Nandy 1990; Petitjean et al. 1992; Sardar 1988). Thus the feminist arguments are just one version of this now widespread analysis.

Neutrality: From Solution to Problem

In this second case, where the social *constitutes* scientific projects, the neutrality ideal provides no resistance to the production of systematically distorted results of research, as I shall shortly show in more detail. But to put the matter this way is too mild a criticism of it. It is not just useless in these circumstances; worse, it becomes part of the problem. Objectivism defends and legitimates the institutions and practices through which the distortions and their often exploitative consequences are generated. It certifies as value-neutral, normal, natural, and therefore not political at all the policies and practices through which powerful groups can gain the information and explanations that they need to advance their priorities.

Such information and explanations may well "work" in the sense of enabling prediction and control. However, this obvious fact does not end the matter. One form of explanation may at the same time obscure or draw attention away from other regularities and their causes that would suggest other possibilities for organizing nature and social relations. One can get information about nature's order that makes possible building bigger bombs or performing lobotomies, or other information that makes possible the equitable distribution of means to satisfy basic human needs for food, shelter, health, work and just social relations. Moreover, the regularities of nature that make possible healing a body, charting the stars, or mining ores may be explained in ways permitting extensive (though not identical) prediction and control within radically different and even conflicting, culturally local, explanatory models. The kinds of explanations favored by modern science have not always been the most effective ones for all projects—for example, for achieving environmental balance or preventing chronic bodily malfunctions. "It works" is no guarantee of cultural neutrality.

The neutrality ideal functions more through what its normalizing procedures and concepts implicitly prioritize than through explicit directives. This kind of politics requires no informed consent by those who exercise it, but only that scientists be "company men" (and women), following the prevailing rules of scientific institutions and their intellectual traditions. This normalizing politics frequently defines the objections of its institutions, practices, or conceptual world as agitation by special interests that threatens to damage the neutrality of science and its "civilizing mission", as an earlier generation saw the matter. Thus, when sciences are already in the service of the mighty, scientific neutrality ensures that "might makes right".

It is many decades since it has been reasonable to think of modern natural and social sciences as small-scale, weak, guerilla warriors for truth, struggling courageously against the evil empires of ignorance and superstition—Davids against the Goliaths. We need a concept of objectivity, and methods for maximizing it, that enable scientific projects to escape containment by the interests and values of the kinds of powerful social tendencies identified by Levins and Lewontin. Objectivism can't do it.

Such an analysis leads to one obvious possibility: to separate the goal of maximizing objectivity from the neutrality requirement in order to identify the knowledge-limiting values and interests that constitute projects in the first place. This possibility has been hinted at again and again in the literature without ever being formulated as a systematic program.

"Weak Objectivity" Cannot Identify Paradigms

From the perspective of this more comprehensive analysis of how politics can shape sciences, the conventional notion of objectivity that links it to the neutrality ideal appears too weak to do what it sets out to do. That it is too weak is only one thing wrong with it. But I use the term to acknowledge the usefulness of standards for objectivity-tied-to-neutrality in detecting the subset of distorting interests

and values that do differ between individuals in the scientific community.

It is method that is supposed to "operationalize" neutrality and thus achieve objectivist standards; but method is conceptualized too narrowly to permit achievement of this goal. For one thing, method—in the sense in which students take methods courses or a research report describes its methods—is conceptualized as functioning only in the context of justification.[3] It comes into play only after a problem is identified as a scientific one, after central concepts, a hypothesis and research design have already been selected. It is only after a research project is already *constituted* that methods of research, in the usual narrow sense of the term, start up. Moreover, the availability of a research technology that was itself selected in earlier contexts of discovery and found productive frequently helps select which scientific problems will be interesting to scientists and to funders.

However, as critic after critic has pointed out, it is in the context of discovery that culture-wide assumptions shape the very statement and design of the research project, and therefore select the methods. Of course in the "mangle of practice" (Pickering 1991) during scientific research, hypotheses, nature, and research technologies are adjusted to each other such that a certain element of objectivity is produced without the promise of total neutrality. Nature constrains our beliefs without uniquely confirming them. The most science can hope for is results that are *consistent* with "how nature is", not ones that are uniquely *coherent* with it, as the objectivist goal intended (Hayles 1992). Even the U.S. National Academy of Sciences certainly not a den of wild-eyed radicals—now argues that the notion of research method should be enlarged beyond its familiar meaning of techniques to

> include the judgments scientists make about interpretation or reliability of data.... the decisions scientists make about which problems to pursue or when to conclude an

investigation.... the ways scientists work with each other and exchange information. (Nat. Acad. Sci. 1989, pp. 5–6)

Thus, methods for maximizing objectivism have no way of detecting values and interests that first constitute scientific problems, and then select central concepts, hypotheses to be tested, and research designs.

Let us approach the issue another way. One point of repeating observations, through experimental or other techniques, is so that variations in the results of observations can be scrutinized for the traces of social interests and values that would distort the image of nature and social relations produced by science. Any community that *is* a community, including the community of a laboratory or discipline as well as other kinds of cultural communities, shares values and interests. But if all observers share a particular value or interest, whether this arrives from the larger society or is developed in the group of legitimated observers, how is the repetition of observations by these like-minded people supposed to reveal it? It is not individual, personal, "subjective" error to which feminist and other social critics of science have drawn attention, but widely held androcentric, Eurocentric and bourgeois assumptions that have been virtually culture-wide across the culture of science. The assumptions of Ptolemaic astronomy, Aristotelian physics, or of an organicist, world view were not fundamentally properties of individuals. Assumptions that women's biology, moral reason, intelligence, contributions to human evolution, or to history or present day social relations are inferior to men's are not idiosyncratically held beliefs of individual "subjects" but widespread assumptions of entire cultures. These assumptions have constituted whole fields of study, selecting their preoccupying problems, favored concepts, hypotheses and research designs; these fields have in turn lent support to male supremacist assumptions in other fields. The issue is not that individual men (and women) hold false beliefs, but that the conceptual structures of disciplines, their institu-tions, and related social policies make less than maximally objective assumptions.

In reflecting on how so much scientific racism and sexism could be produced by the most distinguished—and, in some cases, politically progressive—nineteenth century scientists, historian of biology Stephen Jay Gould puts the point this way:

I do not intend to contrast evil determinists who stray from the path of scientific objectivity with enlightened antideterminists who approach data with an open mind and therefore see truth. Rather I criticize the myth that science itself is an objective enterprise, done properly only when scientists can shuck the constraints of their culture and view the world as it really is.... Science, since people must do it, is a socially embedded activity. It progresses by hunch, vision, and intuition. Much of its change through time does not record a closer approach to absolute truth, but the alteration of cultural contexts that influence it so strongly. (Gould 1981, pp. 21–22)

When a scientific community shares assumptions there is little chance that more careful application of existing scientific methods will detect them.[4]

Moreover, Gould's reflection makes clear that not all cultural interests and values ("contexts") retard the growth of knowledge. Some advance it, he is saying: science has often progressed because of changes in its cultural contexts. So it is problematic that objectivism is supposed to enable the elimination of *all* social values and interests. Weak objectivity is unable to discriminate between those interests and values that enlarge our understanding and those that limit it.

Are Relative and/or Moral Exhortations the Only Alternatives?

The preceding section has identified some of the main features that make objectivism only "weak objectivity". When confronted with such issues, one apparent solution has been to turn to objectivism's other, relativism (or subjectivism), sometimes with a resignation that undermines both the critiques of objectivism and turn to relativism; at other times with the project of transforming relativism into a useful epistemological tool.[5] Excellent arguments both against objectivism and for relativism or subjectivism have been put forth by those who turn to this strategy. Without examining them further, we can nevertheless see one great disadvantage that they have: relativism is the weak term in the objective/relative pair. Since, as the historians pointed out, appeals to these epistemological notions are primarily made as part of political struggles to claim this or that position for science in society, the weak term is unlikely to be attractive for these engagements. Moreover, one cause of this weakness may well be that all alternatives to the neutrality of objectivism have been symbolized as feminine. Cultural definitions of manliness are at issue in turning away from objectivity-as-neutrality.[6]

Yet another response has been to retain the neutrality criterion for maximizing objectivity, but to settle for moral exhortations that natural and social scientists should be more critical and that they should engage in dialogue with those protesting their exclusion from scientific authority. It is better to have such moral gestures than not, but feminism and the other democracy-advancing social movements want and need more than this. Why should women feel all that optimistic that the very groups whose interests and values were constituting distorting research projects in the first place will want or know how to be more critical or engage in dialogue?

So where might one find a *method* for maximizing objectivity that has the resources to detect (a) values interests that constitute scientific projects, (b) ones that do not vary between legitimated observers, and (c) the difference between those values and interests that enlarge and those that limit our images of nature and social relations? This is where standpoint has provided useful resources that

are not available—or, at least, not easily available—from other epistemologies.

Standpoint Approaches: Systemic Procedures for Maximizing Objectivity

How could biological and social science research that clearly was guided by feminist politics manage to be producing empirically and theoretically more adequate accounts of nature and social relations? This is the question standpoint theorists set out to answer. Here I shall only review the main outlines of this theory of knowledge and philosophy of science since it has been developed, refined and critically discussed now for close to two decades.[7]

Standpoint theories argue that what we *do* in our social relations both enables and limits (it does not determine) what we can know.[8] Standpoint theories, in contrast to empiricist epistemologies, *begin* from the recognition of social inequality; their models of society are conflict models, in contrast to the consensus model of liberal political philosophy assumed by empiricists. All human thought necessarily can be only partial, it is always limited by the fact of having only a particular historical location—of not being able to be everywhere and see everything, and of being "contained" by cultural assumptions that become visible only from outside that culture (hence: "medieval thought", Renaissance thought. etc.). However, standpoint theories are concerned with a distinctive dimension of social location that is more pernicious than these kinds of "positionality", and that is difficult to grasp from within the empiricist assumptions of modern scientific rationality. In hierarchically organized societies, the daily activities of people in the ruling groups tend to set distinctive limits on their thought, limits that are not created by the activities of the subjugated groups. Administrative-managerial activities, including the work of the natural and social sciences, is the form of "ruling" in our contemporary modern societies, and the conceptual frameworks of our disciplines are shaped by administrative-managerial priorities, just as pre-scientific observations of nature are shaped by other cultural priorities. Such priorities do enable gaining the kinds of information administrators need to function effectively, but they also distort and limit our understanding of just what brings about daily social relations and interactions with nature, and they make it difficult to think possible any different kind of interactions. In order to gain a causal critical view of the interests and values that constitute the dominant conceptual projects, one must start one's thought, one's research project, from *outside* those conceptual schemes and the activities that generate them; one must start from the lives excluded as origins of their design—from "marginal lives."

The fundamental features of the standpoint proposal can be grasped most quickly by looking at *what it is not*. Those constrained by the old objectivity question will tend to distort standpoint theory by perceiving it only through the conceptual choices offered by "Objectivity or relativism: which side are you on?" They often construct it as just a variant of empiricism or, alternatively, as a kind of gynocentrism, special pleading, or unreasonably claimed privileged positionality. On such a reading, empiricism is politics-free, and standpoint theory is asserting epistemological/scientific privilege for one group at the expense of the equally valuable/distorted perceptions of other groups. Or, it is simply substituting one politics for another, and all political positions—the master's and the slave's, that of the rich and of the poor, the colonizer's and the colonized's, the rapist's and his victim's—all are equally valuable and/or distorted. This interpretation of difference as merely diversity is a serious misunderstanding of social realities, as well as of standpoint claims. Standpoint theory leads us to turn such a way of posing the alternatives into a topic for historical analysis: "What forms of social relations make *this* conceptual framework—the 'view from nowhere' versus

'special pleading'—so useful, and for what purposes?"

Not about Only Marginal Lives

First, standpoint theory is not only about how to get a less limited understanding of marginal lives—women's lives, for example. Instead, research is to *start off* from such locations (not to take as truth what people in those locations think or say) in order to explain not only those lives but also the rest of the micro and macro social order, including human interactions with nature and the philosophies that have been developed to explain sciences. The standpoint of women, as Dorothy Smith puts the point, enables us to understand women's lives, men's lives, and the relations between the two through concepts and hypotheses arising from women's lives rather than only ones arising from the lives of those assigned administrative/managerial work, a group that includes sociologists (and philosophers) (Smith 1987, 1990). The point is to produce systematic causal accounts of how the natural and social orders are organized such that the everyday lives of women and men, our activities and beliefs, end up in the forms that they do.

Grounded, but Not in the Conventional Way, in Women's Experiences

The phrase 'women's experiences' can be read in an empiricist way such that these experience are assumed to be constituted prior to the social. Standpoint theory challenges this kind of reading. For a researcher to start from women's lives is not necessarily to take one's research problems in the terms in which women perceive or articulate their problems—and this is as true for women as it is for men thinkers. The dominant ideology restricts what everyone is permitted to see and shapes everyone's consciousness. Women, like men, have had to learn to think of sexual harassment not as a matter of "boys will be boys", but as a violation of women's civil rights. Marital rape was a legal and, for most people, conceptual impossibility until collective political struggle and theorizing resulted in its articulation in the law. European American feminists, like the rest of European Americans, are only beginning to learn how to conceptualize many of our issues in anti-Eurocentric terms. Women, too, have held distorted beliefs about our bodies, our minds, nature and society, and numerous men have made important contributions to feminist analyses—John Stuart Mill, Marx, Engels, and many contemporary scholars in history, sociology, economics, philosophy, literary and art criticism, etc. Moreover, it is obvious "women's experience" does not automatically generate feminist analyses, since the former always exists but only occasionally does the latter emerge. Standpoint theorists are not making the absurd claim that feminist work simply flows from women's experiences.

Feminist knowledge is not a "neutral" elaboration of women's experiences, or what women say about their lives, but a collective political and theoretical achievement. Women's experiences and what women say are important guides to the new questions we can ask about nature, sciences, and social relations. However, the *answers* to such questions must be sought elsewhere than in women's experiences, since the latter are shaped by national and international policies and practices that are formulated and enacted far away from our daily lives—by Supreme Court decisions, international trade agreements, military policies on the other side of the world, etc. Standpoint theory is not calling for phenomenologies of women's world, or for ethnocentric (gynocentric) accounts. Nor is it arguing that only women can generate feminist knowledge; it is not an "identity politics" project. Men, too, can learn to start their thought from women's lives, as many have done. These misunderstandings come about because objectivism insists that the only alternatives, view from nowhere are special interest claims and ethno-knowledges that can be understood only within a rela-

tivist epistemology. However, institutionalized power imbalances give starting off from the lives of those who least benefit from such imbalances a critical edge for generating theoretically and empirically more accurate and comprehensive accounts. Feminist accounts of marital rape, sexual harassment, women's double-day of work or women's different and valuable forms of moral reason are capable of conceptualizing phenomena that were heretofore invisible because they start off from outside the dominant paradigms and conceptual schemes.

No Essential Woman's Life

Next, standpoint theory is not arguing that there is some kind of essential, universal woman's life from which feminists (male and female) should start their thought. In any particular research situation, one is to start off research from the lives of those who have been disadvantaged by, excluded from the benefits of, the dominant conceptual frameworks. What can we learn about that framework by starting from their lives? For example, what can we learn about biological models of the human body, or of human evolution, psychological and philosophical models of moral reasoning, historical models of social change and of progress, philosophical models of rationality, etc., by starting off thought about them from the lives of women of different races, ethnicities, classes and sexualities whose natures and activities each of these models defines as inferior in partially different ways?

The point here is that these kinds of models have also been used to define other groups—racial, ethnic, economic, etc.—as inferior. We can learn some similar and some new things about the conceptual frameworks of the disciplines by starting off thought about the latter from, for example, the lives of slaves, or "orientals", workers, etc. Moreover, "woman" and the homogeneity of "women" is an elitist fiction. These categories in everyday life are multiple and contradictory, and the theorization of this fact by women of color and others who *started off their thought from women of color's lives* is one of the great strengths of contemporary feminist thought. This "matrix theory" developed by women of color enables us to think how each of us has a determinate social location in the matrix of social relations that is constituted by gender, class, race, sexuality and whatever other macro forces shape our particular part of the social order (e.g., Collins 1991). Women are located at many positions in this matrix, and starting thought from each such group of lives can be useful for understanding social phenomena (including our relations with nature) that have effects on those lives.

Consciousness Not Determined by Social Location

For standpoint theorists, we each have a determinate location in such a social matrix, but that location does not *determine* one's consciousness. The availability of competing discourses enables men, for example, to think and act in feminist ways. They are still obviously men, who are thereby in determinate relations to women and men in every class and race, such relations cannot be changed simply by willing them. They can work to eliminate male supremacy, but no matter what they do, they will still be treated with the privilege (or suspicion!) accorded to men by students, sales people, other intellectuals, etc. A parallel account can be given about women, of course. ...

Asymmetrical Falsity and Truth in Scientific Practice

Standpoint theory claims that starting from women's lives is a way of gaining less false and distorted results of research. However, one gratuitously asks for trouble if one equates such claims with ones to truth or truth-likeness. This is a general point about scientific claims, not one peculiar to standpoint theories or to feminist philosophies of

science. The claim that a result of research is "less false" is sufficient to capture what we can establish about the processes producing such a research result, and attributions of truth or truth-likeness are too strong for scientific claims. We do not have to be claiming to approximate the one true story about nature or social relations in order for it to make sense to argue that our account is less false than some specified set of competitors to it. For one thing, all that scientific processes could in principle produce are claims less false than competing ones as a hypothesis is tested against some chosen set of rivals—the dominant hypothesis, or another new one. Moreover, as a matter of principle one is never to assume that such processes generate what one can know to be true, since empirical claims have to be held open to future revision on the basis of empirical evidence and conceptual shifts. To put the point a familiar way, our best theories are always underdetermined by the evidence. As a glance at the history of science shows, nature says "yea" to many competing and, from our perspective, quite fantastic accounts of its regularities and their underlying causal tendencies; our best theories are only consistent with nature, not uniquely coherent with natural laws that are "out there" for out detection. (Hayles 1993, Harding forthcoming.)

Standpoint approaches were developed both to explain the surprising results of feminist research and to guide future research. They show us how to detect values and interests that constitute scientific projects, ones that do not vary between legitimated observers, and the difference between those values and interests that enlarge and those that limit our descriptions, explanations and understandings of nature and social relations. Standpoint approaches provide a map, a method, for maximizing a strong objectivity that can function more effectively for knowledge projects faced with the problem of sciences that have been constituted by the values and interests of the most powerful social groups.

Standpoint theory has become a site for some of the most pressing contemporary discussions about post-foundationalism, realism versus constructivism, identity politics and epistemologies, the role of experience in producing knowledge, alternatives to both the "view from nowhere" and relativism, and other issues controversial in the philosophy and social studies of science more generally. Although it rejects and tries to move beyond many of the distorting features of modernity's conceptual framework, it also retains central commitments of that tradition. One is to the importance of the notion of objectivity.

Objectivity: An Indigenous Resource of the Modern North?

Objectivity is an important value for cultures that value sciences, and its value spreads to other cultures as they import Northern forms of democracy, their epistemologies and sciences. This is not to say that Northerners are particularly good at democracy or maximizing objectivity, or have any corner on the ideals. And, of course, Northern forms of these ideals are widely criticized by many Third World intellectuals, as they are by feminists, as ideologies that have justified excluding and exploiting the already less powerful. Nevertheless, 'objective' defines for many people today how they think of themselves; we are fair; we make decisions by principle, not by whim or fiat; we are against "might makes right"; we are rational; we can find ways to live together that value our cultural diversity … and so forth. I am not saying that everyone who claims objectivity in fact maximizes it, but that such an ideal is deeply embedded in the ethic and rhetoric of democracy at personal, communal, and institutional levels. The notion is centered in natural and many social science discourses, in jurisprudence, in public policy, in many areas where decisions about how to organize social relations are made. Thus, while the diverse arguments for abandoning the notion are illuminating and

important to keep in mind, to do so is to adopt a "bohemian" strategy; it is to do "something else" besides try to struggle on the terrain where philosophies, science projects and social policies are negotiated. Why not, instead, think of objectivity as an "indigenous resource" of the modern North? It needs updating, rehabilitation, so that it is capable of functioning effectively in the science-based society that the North has generated and that many now say is its major cultural export (cf. Harding 1994).

What of the epistemological status of this strong objectivity program itself? What limitations arise from the particular historical projects from which it started off? No doubt there are many such limitations, but four easily come to mind. First, the strong objectivity program is, indeed, a science project. It relegitimates scientific rationality (and a modern European form of it) in a world where many think the power of this rationality should be limited. Now the "context of discovery" and the values and interests shared within a research community are to be added to the phenomena to be analyzed with scientific rationality.

Second, this strong objectivity program and the standpoint theory that supports it originate in the North, and draw upon the historical and cultural legacies of those cultures—for example, European Marxian and feminist legacies. Thinkers in other cultures may well prefer to draw on the riches of their own legacies in order to develop resources for blocking "might makes right" in the realm of knowledge production. Third, one can wonder if the delinking of objectivity from the neutrality ideal can succeed eventually in bypassing the gender-coding of objectivity as inherently masculine (and European, bourgeois, etc.)? Or does the logic of discovery become feminized (no neutrality) leaving the logic of justification masculinized as usual (here seeking neutrality can be useful)?

Finally, it is hard to imagine this strong objectivity program effectively enacted right away within the present day culture and practices of sciences, which are largely resistant to the interpretive and critical skills and resources necessary to detect values and interests in the conceptual frameworks of scientific projects. Natural scientists are not trained to do this work, and they often are hostile to sharing authority about nature, let alone about how science should be done, with any individuals or groups that they conceptualize as "outside science". And yet, we should not be too pessimistic since mainstream concerns to bring science under more democratic control, the global and local social changes to which such terms as "diversity" and "multiculturalism" point, and the ever increasing adoption of feminist projects into mainstream cultures and practices (albeit without the label "feminist") offers hope that the borders of scientific culture and practice, too, can become more permeable to these tendencies.

To conclude, the strong objectivity program is one response to the new objectivity question. It is not perfect, but it does have considerable advantages over the alternatives so far in sight.

Notes

1. For reasons to be recounted below, claims to less falsity are preferable to those for truth or verisimilitude. See Megill (1991) for a related account of four senses of objectivity prevalent in the history of philosophy.
2. I have discussed these issues in a number of places. The following account most closely follows those given in Harding (1992) and (1993b).
3. This is not to say that no other good advice for successful research is given out in "methods" courses.
4. Some might think this problem can be resolved by adding members of excluded groups into the community or by seeking more criticism within scientific processes. Efforts in these directions certainly can be helpful, but reflection on the Gould discussion suggests their limitations.

Won't those "included" be only the well-socialized, least critical of the excluded? Are privileged groups likely to listen carefully to, and seriously value the distinctive perspectives of, groups that dominant institutions have devoted considerable effort to justifying as inferior? What kind of vigorous criticism should one expect to arise from a few junior (or even senior) colleagues who know well how their continued "inclusion", and the inclusion of those who follow them, depends on their "not making trouble"?

5. See, e.g., the adoption of a disabling relativism in Bloor (1977), of subjectivist epistemology in Code (1991), and the strengthening of relativist epistemologies in Feyerabend (1987).
6. I cannot take space to review these important arguments here. See Bordo (1987) and Lloyd (1984) and (1993) for important accounts of the manliness of neutrality.
7. The first essay on it is Dorothy Smith's (1974) paper, 'Women's Perspective as a Radical Critique of Sociology', reprinted in my (1987). For other important statements of this theory see Hartsock (1983), Jaggar (1983), Rose (1983), Smith (1987), (1990). See also my discussions of it in (1986b), (1991), (1993b). For two of the many innovative and clarifying recent developments of it, see Collins (1991) and Hennessy (1993).
8. This claim parallels those for experimental method where, also, what the scientist does both enables and limits (but does not determine, since our theories are always underdetermined by their evidence) what we can know.

References

Bloor, David: 1977, *Knowledge and Social Imagery*, Routledge & Kegan Paul, London.

Bordo, Susan: 1987, *The Flight to Objectivity: Essays on Cartesianism and Culture*, State University of New York Press, Albany.

Code, L.: 1991, *What Can She Know? Feminist Theory and the Construction of Knowledge*, Cornell University Press, Ithaca.

Collins, Patricia Hill: 1991, *Black Feminist Thought: Knowledge, Consciousness and the Politics of Empowerment*, Routledge, New York.

Feyerabend, P.: 1987, 'Notes on Relativism,' in *Farewell to Reason*, Verso, London.

Goonatilake, Susantha: 1984, *Aborted Discovery: Science and Creativity in the Third World*, Zed Books, London.

Gould, Stephen Jay: 1981, *The Mismeasure of Man*, W.W. Norton, New York.

Haraway, Donna: 1989, *Primate Visions: Gender, Race, and Nature in the World of Modern Science*, Routledge, New York.

Harding, Sandra: 1986, *The Science Question in Feminism*, Cornell University Press, Ithaca.

Harding, S.: (ed.): 1987, *Feminism and Methodology: Social Science Issues*, Indiana University Press, Bloomington.

Harding, S.: 1989, 'Feminist Justificatory Strategies', in A. Garry and M. Pearsall (eds.). *Women, Knowledge and Reality*, Unwin Hyman, Boston.

Harding, S.: 1991, *Whose Science? Whose Knowledge? Thinking From Women's Lives*, Cornell University Press, Ithaca.

Harding, S.: 1992, 'After the Neutrality Ideal: Science, Politics, and "Strong Objectivity"', *Social Research* 59(3), 567–87.

Harding, S.: (ed.): 1993a, *The "Racial" Economy of Science: Towards a Democratic Future*, Indiana University Press, Bloomington.

Harding, S.: 1993b, 'Rethinking Standpoint Epistemology: "What is Strong Objectivity"?' in L. Alcoff and E. Potter (eds.), *Feminist Epistemologies*, Routledge, New York.

Harding, S.: 1994, 'Is Science Multicultural? Challenges, Resources, Opportunities, Uncertainties,' in D.T. Goldberg (ed.), *Multiculturalism: A Critical Reader*, Blackwell's, London.

Harding, S.: forthcoming, 'Is Modern Science an "Ethnoscience"?', in T. Shinn, J. Spappen, R. Waast (eds.), *Sociology of the Sciences Yearbook: Science and Technology for the South*, Kluwer, Dordrecht.

Hartsock, N.: 1983, 'The Feminist Standpoint: Developing the Ground for a Specifically Feminist Historical Materialism', in S. Harding and M. Hintikka (eds.), *Discovering Reality*, D. Reidel, Dordrecht.

Hayles, N.K.: 1992, 'Gender Encoding in Fluid Mechanics: Masculine Channels and Feminine Flows', *Differences* 4(2), 16-44.

Hayles, N.K.: 1993, 'Constrained Constructivism: Locating Scientific Inquiry in the Theater of Representations', in G. Levine (ed.), *Realism and Representation*, University of Wisconsin Press, Madison.

Hennessy, Rosemary: 1993, *Materialist Feminism and the Politics of Discourse*, Routledge, New York.

Jaggar, Alison: 1983, *Feminist Politics and Human Nature*, Rowman and Allenheld, Totowa, NJ.

Keller, E. F: 1985, *Reflections on Gender and Science*, Yale University Press, New Haven.

Kuhn, T. S.: 1970, *The Structure of Scientific Revolutions*, University of Chicago Press, Chicago.

Latour, Bruno: 1988, *The Pasteurization of France*, Harvard University Press, Cambridge.

Levins, Richard and Richard Lewontin: 1993, 'Applied Biology in the Third World', in S. Harding (ed.), *The "Racial" Economy of Science: Toward a Democratic Future*, Indiana University Press, Bloomington.

Lloyd, Genevieve: 1984, *The Man of Reason: "Male" and "Female" in Western Philosophy*, University of Minnesota, Minneapolis.

Lloyd, G.: 1993, 'Maleness, Metaphor, and the "Crisis" of Reason', in L. Anthony and C. Witt (eds.), *A Mind of One's Own: Feminist Essays on Reasons and Objectivity*, Westview Press, Boulder, pp. 69-83.

Megill, A,: 1991, 'Rethinking Objectivity', in A. Megill (ed.), *Annals of Scholarship* 8(3).

Merchant, Carolyn: 1980, *The Death of Nature: Women, Ecology and the Scientific Revolution*, Harper and Row, New York.

Nandy, A. (ed.): 1990, *Science, Hegemony and Violence: A Requiem for Modernity*, Oxford University Press, New Delhi.

National Academy of Sciences: 1989, *On Being a Scientist*, National Academy Press, Washington, D.C.

Needham, Joseph: 1969, *The Grand Titration: Science and Society in East and West*, University of Toronto Press, Toronto.

Novick, Peter: 1988, *That Noble Dream: The "Objectivity Question" and the American Historical Profession*, Cambridge University Press, Cambridge, UK.

Petitjean, Patrick et al. (eds.): 1992, *Science and Empires: Historical Studies about Scientific Development and European Expansion*, Kluwer, Dordrecht.

Pickering, Andrew: 1984, *Constructing Quarks: A Sociological History of Particle Physics*, University of Chicago Press, Chicago.

Pickering, A.: 1991, 'Objectivity and the Mangle of Practice', in A. Megill (ed.), *Annals of Scholarship* 8(3).

Pickering, A. (ed.): 1992, *Science as Practice and Culture*, University of Chicago Press, Chicago.

Proctor, Robert: 1988, *Racial Hygiene: Medicine under the Nazis*, Harvard University Press, Cambridge, MA.

Proctor, R.: 1991, *Value-Free Science? Purity and Power in Modern Knowledge*, Harvard University Press, Cambridge, MA.

Rose, H.: 1983, 'Hand, Brain and Heart: A Feminist Epistemology for the Natural Sciences', *Signs* 9, 73–90.

Rouse, Joseph: 1987, *Knowledge and Power: Toward a Political Philosophy of Science*, Cornell University Press, Ithaca, NY.

Sardar, Z. (ed.): 1988, *The Revenge of Athena: Science, Exploitation and the Third World*, Mansell, London.

Shapin, Steven and Simon Schaffer: 1985, *Leviathan and the Air Pump: Hobbes, Boyle, and the Experimental Life*, Princeton University Press, Princeton.

Smith, Dorothy: 1974, 'Woman's Perspective as a Radical Critique of Sociology', *Sociological Inquiry* 44(1), 7–13.

Smith, Dorothy: 1987, *The Everyday World as Problematic: A Feminist Sociology*, Northeastern University Press, Boston.

Smith, D.: 1990, *The Conceptual Practices of Power: A Feminist Sociology of Knowledge*, Northeastern University Press, Boston.

Introduction to *Tomorrow's Tomorrow: The Black Woman*

Joyce A. Ladner

It is very difficult to determine whether this work had its beginnings when I was growing up in rural Mississippi and experiencing, all the tensions, conflicts, joys, sorrows, warmth, compassion, and cruelty that was associated with *becoming a Black woman*; or whether it originated with my graduate school career when I became engaged in research for a doctoral dissertation. I *am* sure that the twenty years I spent being socialized by my family and the broader Black community prior to entering graduate school shaped my perception of life, defined my emotive responses to the world and enhanced my ability to survive in a society that has not made survival for Blacks easy. Therefore, when I decided to engage in research on what approaching womanhood meant to poor Black girls in the city, I brought with me these attitudes, values, beliefs and in effect, a Black perspective. Because of this cultural sensitivity I had to the life-styles of the over one hundred adolescent, preadolescent and adult females I "studied," I had to mediate tensions that existed from day to day between the *reality* and *validity* of their lives *and* the tendency to view it from the *deviant perspective* in accordance with my academic training.

Deviance is the invention of a group that uses its own standards as the ideal by which others are to be judged. Howard Becker states that

> Social groups create deviance by making the rules whose infraction constitutes deviance, and by applying these rules to particular people and labeling them as outsiders. From this point of view, de-

viance is *not* a quality of the act the person commits, but rather a consequence of the application by others of rules and sanctions to an "offender." The deviant is one to whom that label has successfully been applied; deviant behavior is behavior that people so label.[1]

Other students of social problems have adhered to the same position.[2] Placing Black people in the context of the deviant perspective has been possible because Blacks have not had the necessary power to resist the labels. This power could have come only from the ability to provide the *definitions* of one's past, present and future. Since Blacks have always, until recently, been defined by the majority group, that group's characterization was the one that was predominant.

The preoccupation with *deviancy*, as opposed to *normalcy*, encourages the researcher to limit his scope and ignore some of the most vital elements of the lives of the people he is studying. It has been noted by one sociologist that:

It is probably a fact and one of which some contemporary students of deviance have been cognizant—that the greater portion of the lives of deviant persons or groups is spent in normal, mundane, day-to-day living. In the researcher's focus on deviance and this acquisition of the deviant perspective, not only is he likely to overlook these more conventional phenomena, and thus become insensitive to them, but he may in the process overlook that very data which helps to explain that deviance he studies.[3]

Having been equipped with the *deviant perspective* in my academic training, yet lacking strong commitment to it because it conflicted with my objective knowledge and responses to the Black women I was studying, I went into the field equipped with a set of preconceived ideas and labels that I intended to apply to these women. This, of course, meant that I had gone there only to validate and

elaborate on what was *alleged to exist*. If I had continued within this context, I would have concluded the same thing that most social scientists who study Black people conclude: that they are pathology-ridden.

However, this role was difficult, if not impossible, for me to play because all of my life experiences invalidated the deviant perspective. As I became more involved with the subjects of this research, I knew that I would not be able to play the role of the dispassionate scientist, whose major objective was to extract certain data from them that would simply be used to *describe* and *theorize* about their conditions. I began to perceive my role as a Black person, with empathy and attachment, and, to a great extent, their day-to-day lives and future destinies became intricately interwoven with my own. This did not occur without a considerable amount of agonizing self-evaluation and conflict over "whose side I was on." On the one hand, I wanted to conduct a study that would allow me to fulfill certain academic requirements, i.e., a doctoral dissertation. On the other hand, I was highly influenced by my *Blackness*—by the fact that I, on many levels, was one of them and had to deal with their problems on a personal level. I was largely unable to resolve these strands, this "double consciousness," to which W. E. B. DuBois refers.[4] It is important to understand that Blacks are at a juncture in history that has been unprecedented for its necessity to grope with and clarify and *define* the status of our existence in American society. Thus, I was unable to resolve the dilemmas I faced as a Black social scientist because they only symbolized the larger questions, issues and dilemmas of our times.

Many books have been written about the Black community[5] but very few have really dealt with the intricate lives of the people who live there. By and large, they have attempted to analyze and describe the pathology which allegedly characterizes the lives of its inhabitants while at the same time making its residents responsible for its creation. The unhealthy conditions of the community such as drug addiction, poverty, crime, dilapidated housing, unemployment, and the multitude of problems which characterize it have caused social analysts to see these conditions as producing millions of "sick" people, many of whom are given few chances ever to overcome the wretchedness which clouds their existence. Few authorities on the Black community have written about the vast amount of strength and adaptability of the people. They have ignored the fact that this community is a force which not only acts upon its residents but which is also acted upon. Black people are involved in a dynamic relationship with their physical and cultural environment in that they both influence and are influenced by it. This reciprocal relationship allows them to exercise a considerable amount of power over their environs. This also means that they are able to exercise control over their futures, whereas writers have tended to view the low-income Black community as an all-pervasive force which is so devastating as to compel its powerless residents to succumb to its pressures. Their power to cope and adapt to a set of unhealthy conditions—not as stereotyped sick people but as normal ones—is a factor which few people seem to accept or even realize. The ways Blacks have adapted to poverty and racism, and yet emerged relatively unscarred, are a peculiar quality which Americans should commend.

The concept of social deviance is quite frequently applied to the values and behavior of Blacks because they represent a departure from the traditional white middle-class norm, along with criminals, homosexuals, and prostitutes.

But these middle-class standards should not have been imposed because of the distinctiveness that characterizes the Black lifestyle, particularly that of the masses.

Most scholars have taken a dim view of any set of distinct life-styles shared by Blacks, and where they were acknowledged to exist, have of course maintained that these forces were negative adaptations to the larger society. There has never been an admission that the

Black community is a product of American social policy, *not* the cause of it—the structure of the American social system, through its practices of institutional racism, is designed to create the alleged "pathology" of the community, to perpetuate "the social disorganization" model of Black life. Recently, the Black culture thesis has been granted some legitimization as an explanatory variable for much of the distinctiveness of Black life. As a result of this more positive attitude toward understanding the strengths of life in the Black community, many scholars, policy makers et al. are refocusing their attention and reinterpreting the many aspects of life that comprise the complex existence of American Blacks.

There must be a strong concern with redefining the problem. Instead of future studies being conducted on *problems* of the Black community as represented by the *deviant perspective,* there must be a redefinition of the *problem as being that of institutional racism.* If the social system is viewed as the *source* of the deviant perspective, then future research must begin to analyze the nature of oppression and the mechanisms by which institutionalized forms of subjugation are initiated and act to maintain the system intact. Thus, studies which have as their focal point the alleged deviant *attitudes* and *behavior* of Blacks are grounded within the racist assumptions and principles that only render Blacks open to further exploitation.

The challenge to social scientists for a redefinition of the basic *problem* has been raised in terms of the "colonial analogy." It has been argued that the relationship between the *researcher* and his *subjects,* by definition, resembles that of the oppressor and the oppressed, because it is the oppressor who defines the problem, the nature of the research, and, to some extent, the quality of interaction between him and his subjects. This inability to understand and research the fundamental problem—*neo-colonialism*—prevents most social researchers from being able accurately to observe and analyze Black life and culture and the impact racism and oppression have upon Blacks. Their inability to understand the nature and effects of neo-colonialism in the same manner as Black people is rooted in the inherent bias of the social sciences. The basic concepts and tools of white Western society are permeated by this partiality to the conceptual framework of the oppressor. It is simple enough to say that the difference between the two groups—the oppressor and the oppressed—prevents the former from adequately comprehending the essence of Black life and culture because of a fundamental difference in perceptions, based upon separate histories, life-styles, and purposes for being. Simply put, the slave and his master do not view and respond to the world in the same way. The historian Lerone Bennett addresses this problem below:

> George Washington and George Washington's slaves lived different realities. And if we extend that insight to all the dimensions of white American history we will realize that blacks lived at a different time and a different reality in this country. And the terrifying implications of all this is that there is another time, another reality, another America....

Bennett states further that:

> It is necessary for us to develop a new frame of reference which transcends the limits of white concepts. It is necessary for us to develop a total intellectual offensive against the false universality of white concepts whether they are expressed by William Styron or Daniel Patrick Moynihan. By and large, reality has been conceptualized in terms of the narrow point of view of the small minority of white men who live in Europe and North America. We must abandon the partial frame of reference of our oppressors and create new concepts which will release our reality, which is also the reality of the overwhelming majority of men and women on this globe. We must say to the white world that

> there are things in the world that are not dreamt of in your history and your sociology and your philosophy.[6]

Currently there are efforts underway to "decolonize" social research on the *conceptual* and *methodological* levels.[7]

Although I attempted to maintain some degree of objectivity, I soon began to minimize and, very often, negate the importance of being "value-free," because the very selection of the topic itself reflected a bias, i.e., I studied Black women because of my strong interest in the subject.

I decided whose side I was on and resolved within myself that as a Black social scientist I must take a stand and that there could be no value-free sanctuary for me. The controversy over the question of values in social research is addressed by Gouldner:

> If sociologists ought not express their personal values in the academic setting, how then are students to be safeguarded against the unwitting influence of these values which shape the sociologist's selection of problems, his preferences for certain hypotheses or conceptual schemes, and his neglect of others? For these are unavoidable and, in this sense, there is and can be no value-free sociology. The only choice is between an expression of one's values as open and honest as it can be, this side of the psychoanalytic couch, and a vain ritual of moral neutrality which, because it invites men to ignore the vulnerability of reason to bias, leaves it at the mercy of irrationality.[8]

I accepted this position as a guiding premise and proceeded to conduct my research with the full knowledge that I could not divorce myself from the problems of these women, nor should I become so engrossed in them that I would lose my original purpose for being in the community.

The words of Kenneth Clark, as he describes the tensions and conflicts he experienced while conducting the research for his classic study of Harlem, *Dark Ghetto,* typify the problems I faced:

> I could never be fully detached as a scholar or participant. More than forty years of my life had been lived in Harlem. I started school in Harlem public schools. I first learned about people, about love, about cruelty, about sacrifice, about cowardice, about courage, about bombast in Harlem. For many years before I returned as an "involved observer," Harlem had been my home. My family moved from house to house, and from neighborhood to neighborhood within the walls of the ghetto in a desperate attempt to escape its creeping blight. In a very real sense, therefore, *Dark Ghetto* is a summation of my personal and lifelong experiences and observations as a prisoner within the ghetto long before I was aware that I was really a prisoner.[9]

The inability to be *objective* about analyzing poverty, racism, disease, self-destruction, and the gamut of problems which faced these females only mirrored a broader problem in social research. That is, to what extent should any scientist—white or Black—consider it his duty to be a dispassionate observer and not intervene, when possible, to ameliorate many of the destructive conditions he studies. On many occasions I found myself acting as a counselor, big sister, etc. Certainly the question can be raised as to whether researchers can continue to gather data on impoverished Black communities without addressing these findings to the area of social policy.

This raises another important question, to which I will address myself. That is, many people will read my work because they are seeking answers to the dilemmas and problems facing Black people in general and Black women in particular. A great number of young Black women will expect to find forever-sought formulas to give them a new sense of direction as *Black women.* Some Black men will read this work because they are con-

cerned about this new direction and want to become involved in the shaping of this process. Others, of course, will simply be curious to find out what a Black woman has to say about her peers. I expect traditional-type scholars to take great issue with my thesis and many of my formulations because I am consciously attempting to break away from the traditional way in which social science research has analyzed the attitudes and behavior patterns of Blacks. Finally, a small but growing group of scholars will find it refreshing to read a work on Black women which does not indict them for all kinds of alleged social problems, which, if they exist, they did not create.

All of these are problems and questions which I view as inescapable for one who decides to attempt to break that new ground and write about areas of human life in ways in which they are not ordinarily approached.

There are no standard answers for the dilemmas I faced, for they are simply microcosms of the larger Black community. Therefore, this work is not attempting to resolve the problems of Black womanhood but to shed light on them. More than anything else, I feel that it is attempting to depict what the Black woman's life has been like in the past, and what barriers she has had to overcome in order to survive, and how she is coping today under the most strenuous circumstances. Thus, I am simply saying, "This is what the Black woman was, this is how she has been solving her problems, and these are ways in which she is seeking to alter her roles." I am not trying to chart a course of action for her to follow. This will, in large measure, be dictated by, and interwoven with, the trends set in that vast Black American community. My primary concern here is with depicting the strength of the Black family and Black girls within the family structure. I will seek to depict the lives of Black people I knew who were utilizing their scant resources for survival purposes, but who on the whole were quite successful with making the necessary adaptive and creative responses to their oppressed circumstances. I am also dealing with the somewhat abstract white middle-class system of values as it affects Blacks. It is hoped that the problems I encountered with conducting such a study, as well as the positive approach I was eventually able to take toward this work, will enable others to be equally as effective in breaking away from an intellectual tradition which has existed far too long.

One of the primary preoccupations of every American adolescent girl, regardless of race and social class background, is that of eventually becoming a woman. Every girl looks forward to the time when she will discard the status of child and take on the role of adult, wife and possibly mother.

The official entry into womanhood is usually regarded as that time when she reaches the prescribed legal age (eighteen and sometimes twenty-one), when for the first time she is granted certain legal and other rights and privileges. These rights, such as being allowed to vote, to go to certain "for adults only" events, to join certain social clubs and to obtain certain types of employment, are accompanied by a type of informal understanding that very few privileges, either formal or informal, are to be denied her where age is the primary prerequisite for participation. Entry into womanhood is the point at which she is considered by older adults to be ready to join their ranks because she has gone through the necessary apprenticeship program—the period of adolescence. We can observe differences between racial and social class groups regarding, for instance, the time at which the female is considered to be ready to assume the duties and obligations of womanhood. Becoming a woman in the low-income Black community is somewhat different from the routes followed by the white middle-class girl. The poor Black girl reaches her status of womanhood at an earlier age because of the different prescriptions and expectations of her culture. There is no single set of criteria for becoming a woman in the Black community; each girl is conditioned by a diversity of factors depend-

ing primarily upon her opportunities, role models, psychological disposition, and the influence of the values, customs and traditions of the Black community. It will be demonstrated that the resources which adolescent girls have at their disposal, combined with the cultural heritage of their communities, are crucial factors in determining what kind of women they become. Structural *and* psychological variables are important as focal points because neither alone is sufficient to explain the many factors involved with psychosocial development. Therefore, the concepts of motivation, roles and role model, identity, and socialization, as well as family income, education, kin, and peer group relations are important to consider in the analysis. These diverse factors have rarely been considered as crucial to an analysis of Black womanhood. This situation exists because previous studies have substituted simplistic notions for rigorous multivariate analysis. Here, however, these multiple factors and influences will be analyzed as a "Black cultural" framework which has its own autonomous systems of values, behavior, attitudes, sentiments, and beliefs.

Another significant dimension to be considered will be the extent to which Black girls are influenced by the distinct culture of their community. Certain historical as well as contemporary variables are very important when describing the young Black woman. Her cultural heritage, I feel, has played a stronger role than has previously been stated by most writers in shaping her into the entity she has become.

Life in the Black community has been conditioned by poverty, discrimination, and institutional subordination. It has also been shaped by African cultural survivals. From slavery until the present, many of the African cultural survivals influenced the way Blacks lived, responded to others, and, in general, related to their environment. Even after slavery many of these survivals have remained and act to forge a distinct and viable set of cultural adaptive mechanisms because discrimination acted as an agent to perpetuate instead of to destroy the culture.

I will illustrate, through depicting the lives of Black pre-adolescent and adolescent girls in a big-city slum, how distinct sociohistorical forces have shaped a very positive and practical way of dealing and coping with the world. The values, attitudes, beliefs, and behavior emerge from a long tradition, much of which has characterized the Black community from its earliest beginnings in this country.

What is life like in the urban Black community for the "average" girl? How does she define her roles, behaviors, and from whom does she acquire her models for fulfilling what is expected of her? Is there any significant disparity between the resources she has with which to accomplish her goals in life and the stated aspirations? Is the typical world of the teenager in American society shared by the Black girl or does she stand somewhat alone in much of her day-to-day existence?

In an attempt to answer these and other questions, I went to such a community and sought out teenagers whom I felt could provide me with some insights. I was a research assistant in 1964 on a study of an all-Black low-income housing project of over ten thousand residents in a slum area of St. Louis. (This study was supported by a grant from the National Institute of Mental Health, Grant No. MH-9189, "Social and Community Problems in Public Housing Areas.") It was geographically located near the downtown section of St. Louis, Missouri, and within one of the oldest slum areas of the city. The majority of the females were drawn from the Pruitt-Igoe housing project, although many resided outside the public housing project in substandard private housing.

At that time my curiosity was centered around the various activities in which the girls engaged that frequently produced harmful consequences. Specifically, I attempted to understand how such social problems as pregnancy, premarital sex, school dropout, etc. affected their life chances for success. I also felt, at the time,

that a less destructible adaptation could be made to their impoverished environments. However, I was to understand later that perhaps a very healthy and successful adaptation, given their limited resources, had been made by all of these girls to a set of very unhealthy environmental conditions. Therefore, I soon changed my focus and attempted to apply a different perspective to the data.

I spent almost four years interviewing, testing (Thematic Apperception Test), observing, and, in general, "hanging out" with these girls. I attempted to establish a strong rapport with all of them by spending a considerable amount of time in their homes with them and their families, at church, parties, dances, in the homes of their friends, shopping, at my apartment, and in a variety of other situations. The sample consisted of several peer groups which over the years changed in number and composition. I always endeavored to interview their parents, and in some cases became close friends of their mothers. The field work carried me into the community at very unregulated hours—weekends, occasional evenings, and during school hours (when I usually talked to their mothers). Although a great portion of the data collected is exploratory in nature, the majority of it is based on systematic open-ended interviews that related to (1) life histories and (2) attitudes and behavior that reflected approaching womanhood. During the last year and a half I randomly selected thirty girls between the ages of thirteen and eighteen and conducted a systematic investigation that was designed to test many of my preliminary conclusions drawn from the exploratory research. All of the interviews and observations were taped and transcribed. The great majority of the interviews were taped live, and appear as direct quotations throughout my book. (All of the girls have been given pseudonyms.)

I feel that the data are broad in scope and are applicable to almost any group of low-income Black teenage girls growing up in any American city. The economic, political, social and racial factors which have produced neo-colonialism on a national scale operate in Chicago, Roxbury, Detroit, Watts, Atlanta—and everywhere else.

The total misrepresentation of the Black community and the various myths which surround it can be seen in microcosm in the Black female adolescent. Her growing-up years reflect the basic quality and character of life in this environment, as well as anticipations for the future. Because she is in perhaps the most crucial stage of psychosocial development, one can capture these crucial forces—external and internal—which are acting upon her, and which, more than any other impact, will shape her life-long adult role. Thus, by understanding the nature and processes of her development, we can also comprehend the more intricate elements that characterize the day-to-day lives of the Black masses.

Notes

1. Howard S. Becker, *The Outsiders*, New York: Free Press, 1963, p.9.

2. See the works of Edwin Lemert, *Social Pathology*, New York, McGraw-Hill, 1951; John Kituse, "Societal Reaction to Deviance: Problems of Theory and Method," *Social Problems*, Winter 1962, pp. 247–56; and Frank Tannenbaum, *Crime and Community*, New York, Columbia University Press, 1938.

3. See Ethel Sawyer, "Methodological Problems in Studying Socially Deviant Communities," in Joyce A. Ladner, ed., *The Death of White Sociology*, New York, Random House, 1973.

4. W.E.B. DuBois, *Souls of Black Folk*, New York, Fawcett World Library, 1961.

5. I am using the term "Black community" to refer to what is traditionally called the "ghetto." I am speaking largely of the low-income and working-class masses, who comprise the majority of the Black population in this country.

6. Lerone Bennett, *The Challenge of Blackness*, Chicago: Johnson Publishing Co., 1972.

7. Refer to Robert Blauner, "Internal Colonialism and Ghetto Revolt," *Social Problems*, Vol. 16, No. 4, Spring 1969, pp. 393–408; and see Robert Blauner and David Wellman, "Toward the Decolonization of Social Research," in Ladner, *The Death of White Sociology*.

8. Alvin W. Gouldner, "Anti-Minotaur: The Myth of a Value-Free Sociology," *Social Problems*, Winter 1962, pp. 199–213.

9. Kenneth Clark, *Dark Ghetto*, New York, Harper & Row, 1965, p. xv.

FEMINIST POSTMODERNISM

 ## Situated Knowledges

The Science Question in Feminism and the Privilege of Partial Perspective

Donna Haraway

Academic and activist feminist inquiry has repeatedly tried to come to terms with the question of what *we* might mean by the curious and inescapable term "objectivity." We have used a lot of toxic ink and trees processed into paper decrying what *they* have meant and how it hurts *us.* The imagined "they" constitute a kind of invisible conspiracy of masculinist scientists and philosophers replete with grants and laboratories. The imagined "we" are the embodied others, who are not allowed *not* to have a body, a finite point of view, and so an inevitably disqualifying and polluting bias in any discussion of consequence outside our own little circles, where a "mass"-subscription journal might reach a few thousand readers composed mostly of science haters. At least, I confess to these paranoid fantasies and academic resentments lurking underneath some convoluted reflections in print under my name in the feminist literature in the history and philosophy of science. We, the feminists in the debates about science and technology, are the Reagan era's "special-interest groups" in the rarified realm of epistemology, where traditionally what can count as knowledge is policed by philosophers codifying cognitive canon law. Of course, a special-interest group is, by Reaganoid definition, any collective historical subject that dares to resist the stripped-down atomism of Star Wars, hypermarket, postmodern, media-simulated citizenship. Max Headroom doesn't have a body; therefore, he alone *sees* everything in the great communicator's empire of the Global Network. No wonder Max gets to have a naive sense of humor and a kind of happily regressive, preoedipal sexuality, a sexuality that we ambivalently—with dangerous incorrectness—had imagined to be reserved for lifetime inmates of female and colonized bodies and maybe also white male computer hackers in solitary electronic confinement.

It has seemed to me that feminists have both selectively and flexibly used and been trapped by two poles of a tempting dichotomy on the question of objectivity. Certainly I speak for myself here, and I offer the speculation that there is a collective discourse on these matters. Recent social studies of science and technology, for example, have made available a very strong social constructionist argument for *all* forms of knowledge, most certainly and especially scientific ones.[1] According to these tempting views, no insider's perspective is privileged, because all drawings of inside-outside boundaries in knowledge are theorized as power moves, not moves toward truth. So, from the strong social constructionist perspective, why should we be cowed by scientists' descriptions of their activity and accomplishments; they and their patrons have stakes in throwing sand in our eyes. They tell parables about objectivity and scientific method to students in the first years of their initiation, but no practitioner of the high scientific arts would be caught dead *acting on* the textbook versions. Social constructionists make clear that official ideologies about objectivity and scientific method are particularly bad guides to how scientific knowledge is actually *made*. Just as for the rest of us, what scientists believe or say they do and what they really do have a very loose fit.

The only people who end up actually *believing* and, goddess forbid, acting on the ideological doctrines of disembodied scientific objectivity—enshrined in elementary textbooks and technoscience booster literature—are nonscientists, including a few very trusting philosophers....

In any case, social constructionists might maintain that the ideological doctrine of scientific method and all the philosophical verbiage about epistemology were cooked up to distract our attention from getting to know the world *effectively* by practicing the sciences. From this point of view, science—the real game in town—is rhetoric, a series of efforts to persuade relevant social actors that one's manufactured knowledge is a route to a desired form of very objective power. Such persuasions must take account of the structure of facts and artifacts, as well as of language-mediated actors in the knowledge game. Here, artifacts and facts are parts of the powerful art of rhetoric. Practice is persuasion, and the focus is very much on practice. All knowledge is a condensed node in an agonistic power field. The strong program in the sociology of knowledge joins with the lovely and nasty tools of semiology and deconstruction to insist on the rhetorical nature of truth, including scientific truth. History is a story Western culture buffs tell each other; science is a contestable text and a power field; the content is the form.[2] Period.

So much for those of us who would still like to talk about *reality* with more confidence than we allow to the Christian Right when they discuss the Second Coming and their being raptured out of the final destruction of the world. We would like to think our appeals to real worlds are more than a desperate lurch away from cynicism and an act of faith like any other cult's, no matter how much space we generously give to all the rich and always historically specific mediations through which we and everybody else must

know the world. But the further I get in describing the radical social constructionist program and a particular version of postmodernism, coupled with the acid tools of critical discourse in the human sciences, the more nervous I get. The imagery of force fields, of moves in a fully textualized and coded world, which is the working metaphor in many arguments about socially negotiated reality for the postmodern subject, is, just for starters, an imagery of high-tech military fields, of automated academic battlefields, where blips of light called players disintegrate (what a metaphor!) each other in order to stay in the knowledge and power game. Technoscience and science fiction collapse into the sun of their radiant (ir)reality—war. It shouldn't take decades of feminist theory to sense the enemy here. Nancy Hartsock got all this crystal clear in her concept of abstract masculinity.[3]

I, and others, started out wanting a strong tool for deconstructing the truth claims of hostile science by showing the radical historical specificity, and so contestability, of *every* layer of the onion of scientific and technological constructions, and we end up with a kind of epistemological electroshock therapy, which far from ushering us into the high stakes tables of the game of contesting public truths, lays us out on the table with self-induced multiple personality disorder. We wanted a way to go beyond showing bias in science (that proved too easy anyhow) and beyond separating the good scientific sheep from the bad goats of bias and misuse. It seemed promising to do this by the strongest possible constructionist argument that left no cracks for reducing the issues to bias versus objectivity, use versus misuse, science versus pseudo-science. We unmasked the doctrines of objectivity because they threatened our budding sense of collective historical subjectivity and agency and our "embodied" accounts of the truth, and we ended up with one more excuse for not learning any post-Newtonian physics and one more reason to drop the old feminist self-help practices of repairing our own cars. They're just texts anyway, so let the boys have them back. ...

Another approach, "feminist empiricism," also converges with feminist uses of Marxian resources to get a theory of science which continues to insist on legitimate meanings of objectivity and which remains leery of a radical constructivism. ... Feminists have to insist on a better account of the world; it is not enough to show radical historical contingency and modes of construction for everything. Here, we, as feminists, find ourselves perversely conjoined with the discourse of many practicing scientists, who, when all is said and done, mostly believe they are describing and discovering things *by means of* all their constructing and arguing. Evelyn Fox Keller has been particularly insistent on this fundamental matter, and Sandra Harding calls the goal of these approaches a "successor science." Feminists have stakes in a successor science project that offers a more adequate, richer, better account of a world, in order to live in it well and in critical, reflexive relation to our own as well as others' practices of domination and the unequal parts of privilege and oppression that make up all positions. In traditional philosophical categories, the issue is ethics and politics perhaps more than epistemology.

So, I think my problem, and "our" problem, is how to have *simultaneously* an account of radical historical contingency for all knowledge claims and knowing subjects, a critical practice for recognizing our own "semiotic technologies" for making meanings, *and* a no-nonsense commitment to faithful accounts of a "real" world, one that can be partially shared and that is friendly to earthwide projects of finite freedom, adequate material abundance, modest meaning in suffering, and limited happiness. ...

Natural, social, and human sciences have always been implicated in hopes like these. Science has been about a search for translation, convertibility, mobility of meanings, and universality—which I call reductionism only when one language (guess whose?) must be enforced as the standard for all the translations and conversions. What money does in the exchange orders of capitalism, reductionism does in the powerful mental orders of global sciences. There is, finally, only one equation. That is the deadly fantasy that feminists and others have identified in some versions of objectivity, those in the service of hierarchical and positivist orderings of what can count as knowledge. That is one of the reasons the debates about objectivity matter, metaphorically and otherwise. Immortality and omnipotence are not our goals. But we could use some enforceable, reliable accounts of things not reducible to power moves and agonistic, high-status games of rhetoric or to scientistic, positivist arrogance. This point applies whether we are talking about genes, social classes, elementary particles, genders, races, or texts; the point applies to the exact, natural, social, and human sciences, despite the slippery ambiguities of the words "objectivity" and "science" as we slide around the discursive terrain. In our efforts to climb the greased pole leading to usable doctrine of objectivity, I and most other feminists in the objectivity debates have alternatively, or even simultaneously, held on to both ends of the dichotomy, a dichotomy which Harding describes in terms of successor science projects versus postmodernist accounts of difference and which I have sketched in this essay as radical constructivism versus feminist critical empiricism. It is, of course, hard to climb when you are holding on to both ends of a pole, simultaneously or alternatively. It is, therefore, time to switch metaphors.

The Persistence of Vision

I would like to proceed by placing metaphorical reliance on a much maligned sensory system in feminist discourse: vision. Vision can be good for avoiding binary oppositions. I would like to insist on the embodied nature of all vision and so reclaim the sensory system that has been used to signify a leap out of the marked body and into a conquering gaze from nowhere. This is the gaze that mythically inscribes all the marked bodies, that makes the unmarked category claim the power to see and not be seen, to represent while escaping representation. This gaze signifies the unmarked positions of Man and White, one of the many nasty tones of the word "objectivity" to feminist ears in scientific and technological, late-industrial, militarized, racist, and male-dominant societies, that is, here, in the belly of the monster, in the United States in the late 1980s. I would like a doctrine of embodied objectivity that accommodates paradoxical and critical feminist science projects: Feminist objectivity means quite simply *situated knowledges*.

The eyes have been used to signify a perverse capacity—honed to perfection in the history of science tied to militarism, capitalism, colonialism, and male supremacy—to distance the knowing subject from everybody and everything in the interests of unfettered power. The instruments of visualization in multinationalist, postmodernist culture have compounded these meanings of disembodiment. The visualizing technologies are without apparent limit. The eye of any ordinary primate like us can be endlessly enhanced by sonography systems, magnetic reasonance imaging, artificial intelligence-linked graphic manipulation systems, scanning electron microscopes, computed tomography scanners, color-enhancement techniques, satellite surveillance systems, home and office video display terminals, cameras for every purpose from filming the mucous membrane lining the gut cavity of a marine worm living in the vent gases on a fault between continental plates to mapping a planetary hemisphere elsewhere in the solar system. Vision in this technological feast becomes unregulated gluttony; all seems not just mythically about the god trick of seeing everything from nowhere, but to have put the myth into ordinary practice....

A tribute to this ideology of direct, devouring, generative, and unrestricted vision, whose technological mediations are simultaneously celebrated and presented as utterly transparent, can be found in the volume celebrating the 100th anniversary of the National Geographic Society. The volume closes its survey of the magazine's quest literature, effected through its amazing photography, with two juxtaposed chapters. The first is on "Space," introduced by the epigraph, "The choice is the universe—or nothing."[4] This chapter recounts the exploits of the space race and displays the color-enhanced "snapshots" of the outer planets reassembled from digitalized signals transmitted across vast space to let the viewer "experience" the moment of discovery in immediate vision of the "object."[5] These fabulous objects come to us simultaneously as indubitable recordings of what is simply there and as heroic feats of technoscientific production. The next chapter is the twin of outer space: "Inner Space," introduced by the epigraph, "The stuff of stars has come alive."[6] Here, the reader is brought into the realm of the infinitesimal, objectified by means of radiation outside the wave lengths that are "normally" perceived by hominid primates, that is, the beams of lasers and scanning electron microscopes, whose signals are processed into the wonderful full-color snapshots of defending T cells and invading viruses.

But, of course, that view of infinite vision is an illusion, a god trick. I would like to suggest how our insisting metaphorically on the particularity and embodiment of all vision (although not necessarily organic embodiment and including technological mediation), and not giving in to the tempting myths of vision as a route to disembodiment and second-birthing allows us to construct a usable, but not an innocent, doctrine of objectivity. I want a feminist writing of the body that metaphorically emphasizes vision again, because we need to reclaim that sense to find our way through all the visualizing tricks and powers of modern sciences and technologies that have transformed the objectivity debates.

We need to learn in our bodies, endowed with primate color and stereoscopic vision, how to attach the objective to our theoretical and political scanners in order to name where we are and are not, in dimensions of mental and physical space we hardly know how to name. So, not so perversely, objectivity turns out to be about particular and specific embodiment and definitely not about the false vision promising transcendence of all limits and responsibility. The moral is simple: only partial perspective promises objective vision. All Western cultural narratives about objectivity are allegories of the ideologies governing the relations of what we call mind and body, distance and responsibility. Feminist objectivity is about limited location and situated knowledge, not about transcendence and splitting of subject and object. It allows us to become answerable for what we learn how to see.

These are lessons that I learned in part walking with my dogs and wondering how the world looks without a fovea and very few retinal cells for color vision but with a huge neural processing and sensory area for smells. It is a lesson available from photographs of how the world looks to the compound eyes of an insect or even from the camera eye of a spy satellite or the digitally transmitted signals of space probe-perceived differences "near" Jupiter that have been transformed into coffee table color photographs. The "eyes" made available in modern technological sciences shatter any idea of passive vision; these prosthetic devices show us that all eyes, including our own organic ones, are active perceptual systems, building on translations and specific *ways* of seeing, that is, ways of life. There is no unmediated photograph or passive camera obscura in scientific accounts of bodies and machines; there are only highly specific visual possibilities, each with a wonderfully detailed, active, partial way of organizing worlds. All these pictures of the world should not be allegories of infinite mobility and interchangeability but of elaborate specificity and difference and the loving care people might take to learn how to see faithfully from an-

other's point of view, even when the other is our own machine. That's not alienating distance; that's a *possible* allegory for feminist versions of objectivity. Understanding how these visual systems work, technically, socially, and psychically, ought to be a way of embodying feminist objectivity.

Many currents in feminism attempt to theorize grounds for trusting especially the vantage points of the subjugated; there is good reason to believe vision is better from below the brilliant space platforms of the powerful.[7] Building on that suspicion, this essay is an argument for situated and embodied knowledges and an argument against various forms of unlocatable, and so irresponsible, knowledge claims. Irresponsible means unable to be called into account. There is a premium on establishing the capacity to see from the peripheries and the depths. But here there also lies a serious danger of romanticizing and/or appropriating the vision of the less powerful while claiming to see from their positions. To see from below is neither easily learned nor unproblematic, even if "we" "naturally" inhabit the great underground terrain of subjugated knowledges. The positionings of the subjugated are not exempt from critical reexamination, decoding, deconstruction, and interpretation; that is, from both semiological and hermeneutic modes of critical inquiry. The standpoints of the subjugated are not "innocent" positions. On the contrary, they are preferred because in principle they are least likely to allow denial of the critical and interpretive core of all knowledge. They are knowledgeable of modes of denial through repression, forgetting, and disappearing acts—ways of being nowhere while claiming to see comprehensively. The subjugated have a decent chance to be on to the god trick and all its dazzling—and, therefore, blinding—illuminations. "Subjugated" standpoints are preferred because they seem to promise more adequate, sustained, objective, transforming accounts of the world. But *how* to see from below is a problem requiring at least as much skill with bodies and language, with the mediations of vision, as the "highest" technoscientific visualizations.

Such preferred positioning is as hostile to various forms of relativism as to the most explicitly totalizing versions of claims to scientific authority. But the alternative to relativism is not totalization and single vision, which is always finally the unmarked category whose power depends on systematic narrowing and obscuring. The alternative to relativism is partial, locatable, critical knowledges sustaining the possibility of webs of connections called solidarity in politics and shared conversations in epistemology. Relativism is a way of being nowhere while claiming to be everywhere equally. The "equality" of positioning is a denial of responsibility and critical inquiry. Relativism is the perfect mirror twin of totalization in the ideologies of objectivity; both deny the stakes in location, embodiment, and partial perspective; both make it impossible to see well. Relativism and totalization are both "god tricks" promising vision from everywhere and nowhere equally and fully, common myths in rhetorics surrounding Science. But it is precisely in the politics and epistemology of partial perspectives that the possibility of sustained, rational, objective inquiry rests.

So, with many other feminists, I want to argue for a doctrine and practice of objectivity that privileges contestation, deconstruction, passionate construction, webbed connections, and hope for transformation of systems of knowledge and ways of seeing. But not just any partial perspective will do; we must be hostile to easy relativisms and holisms built out of summing and subsuming parts. "Passionate detachment"[8] requires more than acknowledged and self-critical partiality. We are also bound to seek perspective from those points of view, which can never be known in advance, that promise something quite extraordinary, that is, knowledge potent for constructing worlds less organized by axes of domination. From such a viewpoint, the unmarked category would *really* disappear— quite a difference from simply repeating a

disappearing act. The imaginary and the rational—the visionary and objective vision— hover close together. I think Harding's plea for a successor science and for postmodern sensibilities must be read as an argument for the idea that the fantastic element of hope for transformative knowledge and the severe check and stimulus of sustained critical inquiry are jointly the ground of any believable claim to objectivity or rationality not riddled with breathtaking denials and repressions. It is even possible to read the record of scientific revolutions in terms of this feminist doctrine of rationality and objectivity. Science has been utopian and visionary from the start; that is one reason "we" need it.

A commitment to mobile positioning and to passionate detachment is dependent on the impossibility of entertaining innocent "identity" politics and epistemologies as strategies for seeing from the standpoints of the subjugated in order to see well. One cannot "be" either a cell or molecule—or a woman, colonized person, laborer, and so on—if one intends to see and see from these positions critically. "Being" is much more problematic and contingent. Also, one cannot relocate in any possible vantage point without being accountable for that movement. Vision is *always* a question of the power to see—and perhaps of the violence implicit in our visualizing practices. With whose blood were my eyes crafted? These points also apply to testimony from the position of "oneself." We are not immediately present to ourselves. Self-knowledge requires a semiotic-material technology to link meanings and bodies. Self-identity is a bad visual system. Fusion is a bad strategy of positioning. The boys in the human sciences have called this doubt about self-presence the "death of the subject" defined as a single ordering point of will and consciousness. That judgment seems bizarre to me. I prefer to call this doubt the opening of nonisomorphic subjects, agents, and territories of stories unimaginable from the vantage point of the cyclopean, self-satiated eye of the master subject. The Western eye has fundamentally been a wandering eye, a traveling lens. These peregrinations have often been violent and insistent on having mirrors for a conquering self—but not always. Western feminists also *inherit* some skill in learning to participate in revisualizing worlds turned upside down in earth-transforming challenges to the views of the masters. All is not to be done from scratch.

The split and contradictory self is the one who can interrogate positionings and be accountable, the one who can construct and join rational conversations and fantastic imaginings that change history.[9] Splitting, not being, is the privileged image for feminist epistemologies of scientific knowledge. "Splitting" in this context should be about heterogeneous multiplicities that are simultaneously salient and incapable of being squashed into isomorphic slots or cumulative lists. This geometry pertains within and among subjects. Subjectivity is multidimensional; so, therefore, is vision. The knowing self is partial in all its guises, never finished, whole, simply there and original; it is always constructed and stitched together imperfectly, and *therefore* able to join with another, to see together without claiming to be another. Here is the promise of objectivity: a scientific knower seeks the subject position, not of identity, but of objectivity, that is, partial connection. There is no way to "be" simultaneously in all, or wholly in any, of the privileged (i.e., subjugated) positions structured by gender, race, nation, and class. And that is a short list of critical positions. The search for such a "full" and total position is the search for the fetishized perfect subject of oppositional history, sometimes appearing in feminist theory as the essentialized Third World Woman.[10] Subjugation is not grounds for an ontology; it might be a visual clue. Vision requires instruments of vision; an optics is a politics of positioning. Instruments of vision mediate standpoints; there is no immediate vision from the standpoints of the subjugated. Identity, including self-identity, does not produce science; critical positioning does, that is, ob-

jectivity. Only those occupying the positions of the dominators are self-identical, unmarked, disembodied, unmediated, transcendent, born again. It is unfortunately possible for the subjugated to lust for and even scramble into that subject position—and then disappear from view. Knowledge from the point of view of the unmarked is truly fantastic, distorted, and irrational. The only position from which objectivity could not possibly be practiced and honored is the standpoint of the master, the Man, the One God, whose Eye produces, appropriates, and orders all difference. No one ever accused the God of monotheism of objectivity, only of indifference. The god trick is self-identical, and we have mistaken that for creativity and knowledge, omniscience even. ...

I am arguing for politics and epistemologies of location, positioning, and situating, where partiality and not universality is the condition of being heard to make rational knowledge claims. These are claims on people's lives. I am arguing for the view from a body, always a complex, contradictory, structuring, and structured body, versus the view from above, from nowhere, from simplicity. Only the god trick is forbidden. ...

There is no single feminist standpoint because our maps require too many dimensions for that metaphor to ground our visions. But the feminist standpoint theorists' goal of an epistemology and politics of engaged, accountable positioning remains eminently potent. The goal is better accounts of the world, that is, "science."

Above all, rational knowledge does not pretend to disengagement: to be from everywhere and so nowhere, to be free from interpretation, from being represented, to be fully self-contained or fully formalizable. Rational knowledge is a process of ongoing critical interpretation among "fields" of interpreters and decoders. Rational knowledge is power-sensitive conversation.[11] Decoding and transcoding plus translation and criticism; all are necessary. So science becomes the paradigmatic model, not of closure, but of that which is contestable and contested. Science becomes the myth, not of what escapes human agency and responsibility in a realm above the fray, but, rather, of accountability and responsibility for translations and solidarities linking the cacophonous visions and visionary voices that characterize the knowledges of the subjugated. A splitting of senses, a confusion of voice and sight, rather than clear and distinct ideas, becomes the metaphor for the ground of the rational. We seek not the knowledges ruled by phallogocentrism (nostalgia for the presence of the one true Word) and disembodied vision. We seek those ruled by partial sight and limited voice—not partiality for its own sake but, rather, for the sake of the connections and unexpected openings situated knowledges make possible. Situated knowledges are about communities, not about isolated individuals. The only way to find a larger vision is to be somewhere in particular. The science question in feminism is about objectivity as positioned rationality. Its images are not the products of escape and transcendence of limits (the view from above) but the joining of partial views and halting voices into a collective subject position that promises a vision of the means of ongoing finite embodiment, of living within limits and contradictions—of views from somewhere.

Objects as Actors: The Apparatus of Bodily Production

Throughout this reflection on "objectivity," I have refused to resolve the ambiguities built into referring to science without differentiating its extraordinary range of contexts. Through the insistent ambiguity, I have foregrounded a field of commonalities binding exact, physical, natural, social, political, biological, and human sciences; and I have tied this whole heterogeneous field of academically (and industrially, e.g., in publishing, the weapons trade, and pharmaceuticals) institu-

tionalized knowledge production to a meaning of science that insists on its potency in ideological struggles. But, partly in order to give play to both the specificities and the highly permeable boundaries of meanings in discourse on science, I would like to suggest a resolution to one ambiguity. Throughout the field of meanings constituting science, one of the commonalities concerns the status of any object of knowledge and of related claims about the faithfulness of our accounts to a "real world," no matter how mediated for us and no matter how complex and contradictory these worlds may be. Feminists, and others who have been most active as critics of the sciences and their claims or associated ideologies, have shied away from doctrines of scientific objectivity in part because of the suspicion that an "object" of knowledge is a passive and inert thing. Accounts of such objects can seem to be either appropriations of a fixed and determined world reduced to resource for instrumentalist projects of destructive Western societies, or they can be seen as masks for interests, usually dominating interests. ...

It seems clear that feminist accounts of objectivity and embodiment—that is, of a world—of the kind sketched in this essay require a deceptively simple maneuver within inherited Western analytical traditions, a maneuver begun in dialectics but stopping short of the needed revisions. Situated knowledges require that the object of knowledge be pictured as an actor and agent, not as a screen or a ground or a resource, never finally as slave to the master that closes off the dialectic in his unique agency and his authorship of "objective" knowledge. The point is paradigmatically clear in critical approaches to the social and human sciences, where the agency of people studied itself transforms the entire project of producing social theory. Indeed, coming to terms with the agency of the "objects" studied is the only way to avoid gross error and false knowledge of many kinds in these sciences. But the same point must apply to the other knowledge projects called sciences. A corollary of the insistence that ethics and politics covertly or overtly provide the bases for objectivity in the sciences as a heterogeneous whole, and not just in the social sciences, is granting the status of agent/actor to the "objects" of the world. Actors come in many and wonderful forms. Accounts of a "real" world do not, then, depend on a logic of "discovery" but on a power-charged social relation of "conversation." The world neither speaks itself nor disappears in favor of a master decoder. The codes of the world are not still, waiting only to be read. The world is not raw material for the thorough attacks on humanism, another branch of "death of the subject" discourse, have made this point quite clear. In some critical sense that is crudely hinted at by the clumsy category of the social or of agency, the world encountered in knowledge projects is an active entity. Insofar as a scientific account has been able to engage this dimension of the world as object of knowledge, faithful knowledge can be imagined and can make claims on us. But no particular doctrine of representation or decoding or discovery guarantees anything. The approach I am recommending is not a version of "realism," which has proved a rather poor way of engaging with the world's active agency.

My simple, perhaps simple-minded, maneuver is obviously not new in Western philosophy, but it has a special feminist edge to it in relation to the science question in feminism and to the linked question of gender as situated difference and the question of female embodiment. Ecofeminists have perhaps been most insistent on some version of the world as active subject, not as resource to be mapped and appropriated in bourgeois, Marxist, or masculinist projects. Acknowledging the agency of the world in knowledge makes room for some unsettling possibilities, including a sense of the world's independent sense of humor. Such a sense of humor is not comfortable for humanists and others committed to the world as resource. There are, however, richly evocative figures to promote feminist visualizations of the world as witty agent. We need not lapse into appeals to a primal mother resisting her translation into resource. The Coyote or Trickster, as embodied in Southwest native American accounts, suggests the situation we are in when we give up mastery but keep searching for fidelity, knowing all the while that we will be hoodwinked. I think these are useful myths for scientists who might be our allies. Feminist objectivity makes room for surprises and ironies at the heart of all knowledge production; we are not in charge of the world. We just live here and try to strike up noninnocent conversations by means of our prosthetic devices, including our visualization technologies. No wonder science fiction has been such a rich writing practice in recent feminist theory. I like to see feminist theory as a reinvented coyote discourse obligated to its sources in many heterogeneous accounts of the world.

Another rich feminist practice in science in the last couple of decades illustrates particularly well the "activation" of the previously passive categories of objects of knowledge. This activation permanently problematizes binary distinctions like sex and gender, without eliminating their strategic utility. I refer to the reconstructions in primatology (especially, but not only, in women's practice as primatologists, evolutionary biologists, and behavioral ecologists) of what may count as sex, especially as female sex, in scientific accounts.[12] The *body*, the object of biological discourse, becomes a most engaging being. Claims of biological determinism can never be the same again. When female "sex" has been so thoroughly retheorized and revisualized that it emerges as practically indistinguishable from "mind," something basic has happened to the categories of biology. The biological female peopling current biological behavioral accounts has almost no passive properties left. She is structuring and active in every respect; the "body" is an agent, not a resource. Difference is theorized *biologically* as situational, not intrinsic, at every level from gene to foraging pattern, thereby fundamentally changing the biological politics of the body. The relations between sex and gender need to be categorically reworked within these frames of knowledge. I would like to suggest that this trend in explanatory strategies in biology is an allegory for interventions faithful to projects of feminist objectivity. The point is not that these new pictures of the biological female are simply true or not open to contestation and conversation—quite the opposite. But these pictures foreground knowledge as situated conversation at every level of its articulation. The boundary between animal and human is one of the stakes in this allegory, as is the boundary between machine and organism....

Objectivity is not about disengagement but about mutual *and* usually unequal structuring, about taking risks in a world where "we" are permanently mortal, that is, not in "final" control. We have, finally, no clear and distinct ideas. The various contending biological bodies emerge at the intersection of biological research and writing, medical and other business practices, and technology, such as the visualization technologies enlisted as metaphors in this essay. But also invited into that node of intersection is the analogue to the lively languages that actively intertwine in the production of literary value: the coyote and the protean embodiments of the world as witty agent and actor. Perhaps the world resists being reduced to mere resource because it is—not mother/matter/mutter—but coyote, a figure of the always problematic, always potent tie between meaning and bodies. Feminist embodiment, feminist hopes for partiality, objectivity, and situated knowledges, turn on conversations and codes at this potent node in fields of possible bodies and meanings. Here is where science, science fantasy and science fiction converge in the objectivity question in feminism. Perhaps our hopes for accountability, for politics, for ecofeminism, turn on revisioning the world as coding trickster with whom we must learn to converse.

Notes

1. For example, see Karin Knorr-Cetina and Michael Mulkay, eds., *Science Observed: Perspectives on the Social Study of Science* (London: Sage, 1983); Wiebe E. Bijker, Thomas P. Hughes, and Trevor Pinch, eds., *The Social Construction of Technological Systems* (Cambridge: MIT Press, 1987); and esp. Bruno Latour's *Les microbes, guerre et paix, suivi de irréductions* (Paris: Métailié, 1984) and *The Pasteurization of France, Followed by Irreductions: A Politico-Scientific Essay* (Cambridge: Harvard University Press, 1988).

2. For an elegant and very helpful elucidation of a noncartoon version of this argument, see Hayden White, *The Content of the Form: Narrative Discourse and Historical Representation* (Baltimore: Johns Hopkins University Press, 1987). I still want more; and unfulfilled desire can be a powerful seed for changing the stories.

3. Nancy Hartsock, *Money, Sex, and Power: An Essay on Domination and Community* (Boston: Northeastern University Press, 1984).

4. C.D.B Bryan, *The National Geographic Society: 100 Years of Adventure and Discovery* (New York: Harry N. Abrams, 1987), 352.

5. I owe my understanding of the experience of these photographs to Jim Clifford, University of California at Santa Cruz, who identified their "land ho!" effect on the reader.

6. Bryan, 454.

7. See Hartsock, "The Feminist Standpoint: Developing the Ground for a Specifically Feminist Historical Materialism"; and Chela Sandoral, *Yours in Struggle: Women Respond to Racism* (Oakland: Center for Third World Organizing, n.d.); Harding; and Gloria Anzaldua, *Borderlands/La Frontera* (San Francisco: Spinsters/Aunt Lute, 1987).

8. Annette Kuhn, *Women's Pictures: Feminism and Cinema* (London: Routledge & Kegan Paul, 1982), 3-18.

9. Joan Scott reminded me that Teresa de Lauretis put it like this:

   Differences among women may be better understood as differences within women. ... But once understood in their constitutive power—once it is understood, that is, that these differences not only constitute each woman's consciousness and subjective limits but all together define the *female subject of feminism* in its very specificity, is inherent and at least for now irreconcilable contradiction—these differences, then, cannot be again collapsed into a fixed identity, a sameness of all women as Woman, or a representation of Feminism as a coherent and available image.

See Theresa de Lauretis, "Feminist Studies/Critical Studies: Issues, Terms, and Contexts," in her *Feminist Studies/Critical Studies*

(Bloomington: Indiana University Press, 1986), 14–15.

10. Chandra Mohanty, "Under Western Eyes," *Boundary* 2 and 3 (1984): 333–58.

11. Katie King, "Canons without Innocence" (Ph.D. diss., University of California at Santa Cruz, 1987).

12. Donna Haraway, *Primate Visions: Gender, Race, and Nature in the World of Modern Science* (New York: Routledge & Kegan Paul), 1989.

Though This Be Method, Yet There Is Madness in It

Paranoia and Liberal Epistemology

Naomi Scheman

When you do not see plurality in the very structure of a theory, what do you see?
—Maria Lugones,
"On the Logic of
Pluralist Feminism"

Somewhere every culture has an imaginary zone for what it excludes, and it is that zone we must try to remember today.
—Catherine Clément,
The Newly Born Woman

In an article entitled "The Politics of Epistemology," Morton White argues that it is not in general possible to ascribe a unique political character to a theory of knowledge.[1] In particular, he explores what he takes to be the irony that the epistemologies developed by John Locke and John Stuart Mill for explicitly progressive and democratic ends have loopholes that allow for undemocratic interpretation and application. The loopholes White identifies concern in each case the methods by which authority is granted or recognized.

Neither Locke nor Mill acknowledges any higher epistemic authority than human reason, which they take (however differently they define it) as generic to the human species and not the possession of some favored few. But for both of them, as for most other democratically minded philosophers (White discusses also John Dewey and Charles Sanders Peirce), there needs to be some way of distinguishing between the exercise of reason and the workings of something else, variously characterized as degeneracy, madness, immaturity, backwardness, ignorance, passion, prejudice, or some other state of mind that permanently or temporarily impairs the development or proper use of reason. That is, democracy is seen as needing to be defended against "the excesses of unbridled relativism and subjectivism" ("Politics," 90).

The success of such a defense depends on the assumption that if we eliminate the voices of those lacking in the proper use of reason, we will be eliminating (or at least substantially "bridling") relativism. This, I take it, can only mean that those whose voices are listened to will (substantially) agree, at least about those things that are thought to be matters of knowledge, whether they be scientific or common-sense statements of fact or fundamental moral and political principles or specific judgments of right or wrong. To some extent this assumption is tautological: It is frequently by "disagreeing" about things the rest of us take for granted that one is counted as mad, ignorant, or otherwise not possessed of reason. But precisely that tautologousness is at the root of what White identifies as the loophole through which the antidemocratic can pass: Moral, political, and epistemological elitism is most attractive (to the elite) and most objectionable (to others) when the nonelite would say something different from what gets said on their behalf, allegedly in the name of their own more enlightened selves....

A striking feature of the advance of liberal political and epistemological theory and practice over the past three hundred years has been the increase in the ranks of the politically and epistemically enfranchised. It would seem, that is, that the loopholes have been successively narrowed, that fewer and fewer are being relegated to the hinterlands of incompetence or unreliability. In one sense, of course, this is true: Race, sex, and property ownership are no longer explicit requirements for voting, officeholding, or access to education in most countries. But just as exclusionary gestures can operate to separate groups of people, so similar gestures can operate intrapsychically to separate those aspects of people that, if acknowledged, would disqualify them from full enfranchisement. We can understand the advance of liberalism as the progressive internalization—through regimes of socialization and pedagogy—of norms of self-constitution that (oxymoronically) "democratize privilege."

Thus various civil rights agendas in the United States have proceeded by promulgating the idea that underneath the superficial differences of skin color, genitalia, or behavior in the bedroom, Blacks, women, and gays and lesbians are really just like straight white men. Not, of course, the other way around: Difference and similarity are only apparently symmetrical terms. In the logic of political identity, to be among the privileged is to be among the same, and for the different to join those ranks has demanded the willingness to separate the difference-bearing aspects of their identity, to demonstrate what increasingly liberal regimes were increasingly willing to acknowledge: that one didn't need, for example, to be a man to embrace the deep structure of misogyny. It is one of my aims to argue that the norms that have structured modern epistemic authority have required the internalization of such exclusionary gestures, the splitting off and denial of (or control over) aspects of the self that have been associated with the lives of the disenfranchised, and that those gestures exhibit the logic of paranoia....

Part of my aim is to provide an account of what I think underlies this shift in mainstream Anglo-American epistemology and philosophy of science, to place that shift in social and historical context. But I am also concerned with the extent to which much work is still captive to older pictures, notably in the continuing dominance of individualism in the philosophy of psychology. A fully social conception of knowledge that embraces diversity among knowers requires a corresponding conception of persons as irreducibly diverse and essentially interconnected. The individualism of modern personhood entails a denial both of connection and of individuality: Modern subjects are distinct but not distinctive. Philosophers have taken this subject as theirs: It is his (*sic*) problems that have defined the field, the problems of anyone who takes on the tasks of internalizing the norms of privilege. As these norms change, so must the corresponding conceptions of personhood.

It is in this light that I want to examine the influence of Descartes's writings, works of intentionally democratic epistemology that explicitly include women in the scope of those they enfranchise. I have argued elsewhere, as have many others,[2] for the undemocratic nature of the influence of Cartesian epistemology, an influence that extends even to those epistemologies standardly treated as most antithetical to it (notably, empiricism). In particular, I want to argue that the structures of characteristically modern epistemic authority (with science as the central paradigm) normalized strategies of self-constitution drawn from Cartesian Method. The discipline that is meant to ensure that proper use of the Method will not lead to "unbridled relativism and subjectivism," although intended by Descartes to be both liberatory and democratic, has come to mirror the repressions that mark the achievement of privilege. Those strategies find, I believe, a peculiarly revelatory echo in the autobiographical writings of Daniel Paul Schreber and in their use in Freud's theory of paranoia.[3] Ironically, by the very moves that were meant to ensure universal enfranchisement, the epistemology that has grounded modern science and liberal politics not only has provided the means for excluding, for most of its history, most of the human race but also has constructed, for those it authorizes, a normative paranoia.

Schreber

The pedagogical conviction that one must bring a child into line ... has its origin in the need to split off the disquieting parts of the inner self and project them onto an available object.... The enemy within can at last be hunted down on the outside.[4]

[Anti-Semites] are people who are afraid. Not of the Jews, to be sure, but of themselves, of their own consciousness, of their instincts, of their responsibilities, of solitariness, of change, of society, and of the world—of everything except the Jews. ... Anti-Semitism, in short, is fear of the human condition. The Anti-Semite is a person who wishes to be a pitiless stone, a furious torrent, a devastating thunderbolt—anything except a human being.[5]

Daniel Paul Schreber, a German judge, was thrice hospitalized for mental illness. After a brief confinement in a Leipzig clinic in 1884–1885, he recovered sufficiently to serve as *Senatspräsident* (head of a panel of judges) in Dresden. He was rehospitalized in 1893 until 1903, when he left the asylum after succeeding in a legal suit for his release from "tutelage" (that is, involuntary state guardianship). He returned to the asylum in 1907 and remained there until his death in 1911, the same year Freud published the case history based on the *Memoirs of My Nervous Illness*, which Schreber published in 1903 to draw attention to what he took to be happening to him.

Subsequent discussions of Schreber's case and of the *Memoirs* have taken issue with Freud's account. Sam Weber, in his introduction to recent publications (in German and English) of the *Memoirs*, gives a Lacanian reading of the text; and Morton Schatzman, in *Soul Murder: Persecution in the Family*,[6] takes Schreber's account as a transformed but intelligible description of what was done to him as a child by his father, Daniel Gottlieb Moritz Schreber. The elder Schreber was a renowned doctor whose theories of child rearing were exceedingly influential in the development of some of the more extreme forms of what Alice Miller describes as "poisonous pedagogy,"[7] by which she means the accepted, even normative, use of coercion and violence against children supposedly "for their own good." I find helpful correctives to Freud both in Weber's Lacanian remarks and, especially, in Schatzman's antipsychoanalytic analysis[8] (to which I will return); but I want to start with Freud's account, in part because its logical structure mirrors that of the *Meditations* and the *Discourse on Method*.

Freud suggests that central to symptom-formation in paranoia is the process of projection, but that this process can't be definitive of paranoia, in part because it appears elsewhere—for example, "when we refer the causes of certain sensations to the external world, instead of looking for them (as we do in the case of others) inside ourselves" (*SE*, 12:66). He expresses the intention of returning to a general theory of (nonpathological as well as pathological) projection, but he never does. I want to suggest that the account he does give—of projection as a mechanism of paranoia—is closer to such a general theory than he thought it to be, because the relationship to the external world that was epistemically normative in his time and in ours is, by that account, paranoid.

Paranoia, for Freud, starts with the repression of a homosexual wishful fantasy—that is, for a man, sexual desire for another man.[9] In paranoia, as in all cases of repression more generally, there is a detachment of the libido: What is previously cathected becomes "indifferent and irrelevant" (*SE*, 12:70). In paranoia this decathexis spreads from its original object to the external world as a whole, and the detached libido attaches itself to the ego, resulting in megalomania. It is the subsequently megalomaniacally re-created world that is permanently hostile to the paranoid: "The human subject has recaptured a relation, and often a very intense one, to the people and things in the world, even though the relation is a hostile one now, where formerly it was hopefully affectionate" (*SE*, 12:71).

The hostility of the re-created world is a function of the mechanism of projection. The repression of the fantasy of loving a man takes the form of its contradiction, I *hate* him," which is transformed by projection into "*he* hates—and persecutes—*me*, which justifies my hating him." Freud says only that the "mechanism of symptom-formation in paranoia requires that internal perceptions—feelings—shall be replaced by external perceptions" (*SE*, 12:63). Presumably an account of just why such replacement should be required was to await the never-delivered general account of projection, but the mechanism isn't very mysterious: Placing all the initiating feeling out there, on what had been its object, is a far more effective way of shielding the ego from the acknowledgment of its own forbidden desires than would be a simple transformation of love into (inexplicable) hate.

The hostile forces in Schreber's world—God and his "rays"—are unequivocally male, and he believes that part of their plan is to transform him into a woman. The meaning of the transformation is twofold. Men, according to Schreber, have "nerves of voluptuousness" only in and immediately around their penises, whereas women's entire bodies are suffused with such nerves. (*Memoirs*, p. 204). God is directing toward Schreber, who has captured all of God's attention, rays that stimulate these nerves, requiring Schreber to "strive to give divine rays the impression of a woman in the height of sexual delight" by imagining himself "as man and woman in one person having intercourse with myself," an activity that Schreber insists, obviously protesting too much, "has nothing whatever to do with any idea of masturbation or anything like it" *Memoirs*, p. 208). The rays also impose demands, in the form of compulsive thinking, on Schreber's "nerves of intellect," and he is forced to strike a balance between intellectual thought and sensual ecstasy. But, most important, he must attempt always to be engaged in one or the other.

As soon as I allow a pause in my thinking without devoting myself to the cultivation of voluptuousness—which is unavoidable as nobody can either think all the time or always cultivate voluptousness—the following unpleasant consequences ... occur: attacks of bellowing and bodily pain; vulgar noises from the madmen around me, and cries of "help" from God. Mere common sense therefore commands that as far as humanly possible I fill every pause in my thinking—in other words the periods of rest from intellectual activity—with the cultivation of voluptuousness. (*Memoirs*, pp. 210–211)

In addition to being provided with soul-voluptuousness, God's other aim in "un-manning" him was eventual "fertilization with divine rays for the purpose of creating new human beings." Schreber was cognizant of the humiliating aspects of his position: The rays themselves taunted him, saying such things as, "Fancy a person who was a *Senatspräsident* allowing himself to be f … d." He initially entered into complicity with his transformation into a woman at a time when he believed that he was the only real person existing: "All the human shapes I saw were only 'fleeting and improvised,' so that there could be no question of any ignominy being attached to unmanning" (*Memoirs*, p. 148). He subsequently defends the essential honor of his position as an accommodation with necessity and with God's will: "Since then I have wholeheartedly inscribed the cultivation of femininity on my banner.... I would like to meet the man who, faced with the choice of either becoming a demented human being in male habitus or a spirited woman, would not prefer the latter" (*Memoirs*, p. 149).

The logic of Schreber's madness seems to me not that of homosexuality, repressed or otherwise. His delusions mirrored his treatment as a boy at the hands of his father, and his madness indicts that treatment even while preserving the idealization of the powerful father who administered it. What that combination of terror and enthralled submission in the face of remembered or imagined male power does reflect is the logic of male homophobia. 'Homophobia' is often used as though it meant the same thing for women as for men; but, given the very different social constructions of female and male sexuality, there is no reason to think this should be so.

In particular, male homophobia attaches with greatest force not to the general idea of sexual desire for another man but to the specific idea of being in the receptive position sexually. Given a culturally normative definition of sexuality in terms of male domination and female subordination, there is an understandable anxiety attached to a man's imagining another man's doing to him what men are expected to do to women: Real men, *Senatspräsidenten* or not, are not supposed to allow themselves to be fucked. (Thus in men's prisons, the stigma attaches not to rapists but to their victims.)

Male homophobia combines this anxiety with its corresponding desire, that of being, as we might say, ravished or swept away. It's notoriously difficult to speak—or think—clearly about such desires or pleasures, a difficulty made apparent by the intertwinings of rape and rapture (which themselves share a common Latin root) in the *Oxford English Dictionary*'s definition of 'ravish.' The story seems to be the bad old one of the woman falling in love with the man who rapes her, a staple of pornography and Gothic romance and barely veiled in Freudian accounts of normative femininity and in fairy tales. (Did Sleeping Beauty consent to the Prince's kiss?) Part of what is so insidious about these stories is that they link violence and domination to the pleasures of release—for example, the pleasure that sneezing can be, the sudden unwilled flood of sensation. Not, that is, *against* our will, inflicted upon us and a threat to our integrity, but *un*willed, a respite from will, a momentary reprieve from the exigencies of bodily discipline, an affront not to our humanity but to our solemnity, not to our self-respect but to our self-conceit. (The unlinking of such pleasure from the sado-masochistic structure of normative sexuality—the uncoupling of rape from rapture—is a fairy tale worth believing in, even if we can't quite tell it clearly.)

Schreber enacts both the anxiety and the desire: His body and mind are wracked by the struggle to resist what he ultimately succumbs to—being "unmanned" in the name of perpetual feminine "voluptuousness." His compensation for being subjected to such humiliating pleasure is the knowledge both that God has singled him out to receive it and that from his feminized loins will issue a new race of humans to re-create the world. Homophobia thus gets joined to another venerable fantasy structure: the usurpation by men of women's reproductive power. At least as far back as Socrates, men have taken the imagery of childbirth to describe their allegedly nobler, sublimated creative activities. Schreber's fantasies expose the homophobic anxieties that underlie the use of this imagery. You can't give birth without being fucked.

Descartes

They are, in essence, captives of a peculiar arrogance, the arrogance of not knowing that they do not know what it is that they do not know, yet they speak as if they know what all of us need to know.[10]

Cartesian philosophy is a paradigmatic example of White's thesis about the subversion of the democratic intent of an epistemology, although not because of Descartes's own views about who it authorized. Descartes's explicit intent was the epistemic authorization of individuals as such—not as occupiers of particular social locations, including the social location of gender.[11] Most important, Descartes wanted to secure epistemic authority for individual knowers, who would depend on their own resources and not on the imprimatur of those in high places, and, he argues, those resources could only be those of mathematized reason, not those of the senses. Only such a use of reason could ensure the sort of stability that distinguishes knowledge from mere opinion. Descartes's Method was designed to allow anyone who used it to place him- or herself beyond the influence of anything that could induce error. Human beings,

he argues, were not created as naturally and inevitably subject to error: God wouldn't have done that. What we are is finite, hence neither omniscient nor infallible. But if we recognize our limits and shield ourselves from the influence of what we cannot control, we can be assured that what we take ourselves to know is, in fact, true.

The Method is a form of discipline requiring acts of will to patrol a perimeter around our minds, allowing in only what can be determined to be trustworthy and controlling the influence of the vicissitudes of our bodies and of other people. Purged of bad influences, we will be struck by the "clarity and distinctness" of truths like the cogito. We will have no real choice but to acknowledge their truth, but we ought not to find in such lack of choice any diminution of our freedom. Because the perception of truth comes from within us, not "determined by any external force," we are free in assenting to it, just as we are free when we choose what we fully and unambivalently want, even though it makes no sense to imagine that, given our desire, we might just as well have chosen otherwise.[12]

Freedom from determination by any external force requires, for Descartes, freedom from determination by the body, which is, with respect to the mind, an external force. Thus, when Descartes invokes the malicious demon at the end of the First Meditation to help steel him against lazily slipping back into credulity,[13] his efforts are of a piece with his presentation at the end of *The Passions of the Soul* of "a general remedy against the passions."[14] Passions are no more to be dispensed with entirely than are perceptions (or, strictly speaking, *other* perceptions, given that passions are for Descartes a species of perception). But no more than other perceptions are passions to be taken at face value: They can be deceptive and misleading. Still less are they to be taken uncritically as motives to act, whether the action in question be running in fear from the dagger I perceive before me or assenting to its real existence. In both cases, I (my mind) need to exercise control over my perceptions or, at least, over what I choose to do in the face of them. Seeing ought *not* to be believing in the case of literal, embodied vision, but when ideas are seen by the light of reason in the mind's eye, assent does and should follow freely.

The individualism of Cartesian epistemology is yoked to its universalism: Though we are each to pursue knowledge on our own, freed from the influence of any other people, what we come up with is not supposed to be our own view of the world—it is supposed to be the truth, unique and invariable. When Descartes extols, in *Discourse*,[15] the greater perfection of buildings or whole towns that are the work of a single planner over those that sprang up in an uncoordinated way, he may seem to be extolling the virtues of individuality. But what he finds pleasing are not the signs of individual style; it is the determining influence of reason as opposed to chance. Individualism is the route not to the idiosyncrasies of individuality but to the universality of reason.

This consequence is hardly accidental. Scepticism, which was a tool for Descartes, was for some of his contemporaries the ultimate, inevitable consequence of ceding epistemic authority to individual reason. If epistemic democratization was not to lead to the nihilism of the Pyrrhonists or the modesty of Montaigne, Descartes needed to demonstrate that what his Method produced was knowledge, not a cacophony of opinion.[16] It could not turn out to be the case that the world appeared quite different when viewed by people differently placed in it. More precisely, everyone had to be persuaded that if it *did* appear different from where they stood, the remedy was to move to the Archimedean point defined by the discipline of Cartesian Method. Those who could not so move were, in the manner of White's discussion, relegated to the ranks of the epistemically disenfranchised....

It is central to Descartes's project, as it is to the social and political significance of that project, that no one and nothing other than

agents themselves can confer or confirm epistemic authority (despite God's being its ultimate guarantor: His guarantee consists precisely in our each individually possessing such authority). Epistemic authority resides in the exercise of will that disciplines one's acts of assent—principally to refrain from assenting to whatever is not perceived clearly and distinctly.[17] And the will, for Descartes, is not only equally distributed among all people but is also, in each of us, literally infinite: What is required is not the acquisition of some capacity the exercise of which might be thought to be unequally available to all; rather, it is the curbing of a too-ready willingness to believe.

Of course, such restraint will lead only to the avoidance of error; in order actually to acquire knowledge, one has also to clearly and distinctly perceive ideas to which one will, freely and inevitably, assent. But even such acquisition is, for Descartes, not reserved for the few, and even it is more a matter of disciplining the interference of distracting and misleading influences from the body, and from the external world through the body, than it is a positive matter of access to recondite truths....

But, as I argued above, there is no reason why philosophers' own views about who can and cannot fully exemplify their requirements of epistemic enfranchisement should carry any special weight when the question concerns the democratic or antidemocratic effect of their theories, especially as those theories have been influential far beyond those philosophers' lifetimes. Descartes is a paradigmatic case in point.

The Cartesian subject was revolutionary. The individual bearer of modern epistemic authority became, through variations on the originating theme of self-constitution, the bourgeois bearer of rights, the self-made capitalist, the citizen of the nation-state, and the Protestant bound by conscience and a personal relationship to God. In Descartes's writings we find the lineaments of the construction of that new subject, and we see the centrality of discipline to its constitution. Such discipline is supposed in theory to be available to all, not only to those whose birth gave them a privileged place in the world. If one was placed where one could not see the truth, or obtain riches, or exercise political or religious freedom, the solution was to move to some more privileged and privileging place. The "New World" was precisely constituted by the self-defining gestures of those who moved there from Europe and who subsequently got to determine who among those who followed would be allowed to take a stand on the common ground. (That constitution of the "New World" is one reason why the people who already lived there merited so little consideration in the eyes of those who invaded their home. The relationship the Indians took—and take—themselves to have to the land, a relationship grounded in their unchosen, unquestionable ties to it, was precisely the wrong relationship from the perspective of those who came to that land in order to define themselves anew by willfully claiming it, unfettered by history.)

With the success of the revolutions prefigured in the Cartesian texts, it became clear that the theoretical universalism that was their underpinning existed in problematic tension with actual oppression. Those who succeeded in embodying the ideals of subjecthood oppressed those whose places in the world (from which, for various reasons, they could not move) were (often) to perform the labor on which the existence and well-being of the enfranchised depended and (always) to represent the aspects of embodied humanness that the more privileged denied in themselves.

The 'often' and 'always' in the preceding sentence reflect differences in the form taken by the oppression of various groups and the concomitant applicability of various methods for explaining that oppression. With respect to certain groups, most clearly the working class but also many women and people of color, oppression has been in large measure a matter of exploitation. Members of privileged groups benefit directly from the labor done by the exploited, whose oppression is a function both of the theft of their labor and of the ideological representation of that labor as disenfranchising. Such labor is disenfranchising either positively, in that its nature (for example, the bearing and rearing of children) is taken to be incompatible with intellection, or negatively, in that it doesn't allow for the leisure to cultivate the "higher" capacities that authorize the enfranchised.

For other oppressed groups, notably gay men, lesbians, and the disabled, the element of exploitation is either missing or at least far less evident, and an economic analysis of why they are oppressed is less evidently promising. It is striking, however, that such groups share with the others the representation of their supposed natures as incompatible with full social, political, and epistemic authority. For various reasons they are portrayed in hegemonic discourses as incapable of full participation in public life: They are put into one or more of the categories of disenfranchisement that White discusses. All the oppressed—the obviously exploited and the others—share in the minds of the privileged a defining connection to the body—whether it is seen primarily as the laboring body, the sexual body, the body insufficiently under the control of the rational will, or some combination of these. The privileged are precisely those who are defined not by the meanings and uses of their bodies for others but by their ability either to control their bodies for their own ends or to seem to exist virtually bodilessly. They are those who have conquered the sexual, dependent, mortal, and messy parts of themselves—in part by projecting all those qualities onto others, whom they thereby earn the right to dominate and, if the occasion arises, to exploit....

Privilege, as it has historically belonged to propertied, heterosexual, able-bodied, white men, and as it has been claimed in liberal terms by those who are variously different, has rested on the successful disciplining of one's mind and its relation to one's body and to the bodies and minds of others. The discourses of gender, race, class, and physical and cognitive abilities have set up dichotomies that, in each case, have normalized one side as the essentially human and stigmatized the other, usually in terms that stress the need for control and the inability of the stigmatized to control themselves. Acts of violence directed against oppressed groups typically are presented by their oppressors as preemptive strikes, justified by the dangers posed by the supposedly less-civilized, less-disciplined natures of those being suppressed. Workplace surveillance through lie detectors and drug testing (procedures in which subjects' bodies are made to testify to the inadequacies of their minds and wills), programs of social control to police the sexual behavior of homosexuals, the paternalistic disempowerment of the disabled, increasing levels of verbal and physical attacks on students of color by other students, and the pervasive terrorism of random violence against women all bespeak the need on the part of the privileged to control the bodies and behavior of those who are "different," a need that both in its targets and in its gratuitous fierceness goes beyond securing the advantages of exploitation.

Cartesian strategies of epistemic authorization, viewed through the lens of Schreber's paranoia, are illuminating here. As the authorized subject constitutes himself by contrast with the disenfranchised others, so he constitutes himself by contrast with the world that is the object of his knowledge. He also, by the same gestures, reciprocally constitutes that world. Freud, in his discussion of Schreber, quotes Goethe's *Faust*:

> Woe! Woe!
> Thou hast it destroyed,
> The beautiful world,
> With powerful fist!
> In ruins 'tis hurled,
> By the blow of a demigod shattered!
> . . . .

> Mightier
> For the children of men,
> More splendid
> Build it again,
> In thine own bosom build it anew![18]

The gesture is not only Schreber's; it is, of course, Descartes's. Like Schreber, Descartes imaginatively destroys the world through the withdrawal of his attachment to it (he becomes agnostic about its very existence), and like Schreber, his ego is thereby aggrandized and goes about the task of reconstituting the world, or a semblance of it, under the problematic aegis of an all-powerful father. This reconstituted world is perceived as hostile—made up as it is of everything the ego has split off—and as permanently in need of vigilant control. It is also perceived, and needs to be perceived, as independent of the self as the self needs to be perceived as independent of it. There can be no acknowledgment of the self's complicity in the constitution of the world as an object of knowledge: "Indeed," as Paul Smith puts it "it is the desired fate of both paranoia and classical realism to be construed as interrelations of an already existing world, even though the world they both create is their own."[19]

Smith notes the need of the paranoiac (or that of the humanist intellectual—he has in mind, in particular, heremeneutically inclined anthropologists such as Clifford Geertz) "to objectify or *realize* a reality and yet to proclaim the 'subject's' innocence of its formation" (*Discerning the Subject*, p. 87; emphasis in original). Not only as hostile—or exotic—but as *real*, the world has to be regarded as wholly independent of the self. And the very activity of securing that independence has to be repressed; the subject and the world have to be innocent of each other, unimplicated in each other's identity.[20]

Despite Descartes's genuinely democratic intentions, as his epistemology was taken up by those who followed him, it authorized those—and only those—whose subject positions were constituted equally by their relationship to a purportedly objective world and by their relationship to the disenfranchised Others, defined by their inescapable, undisciplined bodies.

Paranoia, Discipline, and Modesty

Whatever we seek in philosophy, or whatever leads us to ask philosophical questions at all, must be something pretty deep in human nature, and what leads us to ask just the questions we do in the particular ways we now ask them must be something pretty deep in our tradition.[21]

The most influential theorist of surveillance, discipline, and control is Michel Foucault. His *Discipline and Punish: The Birth of the Prison* traces the development and deployment of characteristically modern systems of power as pervasively applied to the bodies of the subjugated; his *The History of Sexuality*, volume 1, looks at those systems largely as they shape subjectivity, desire, and knowledge. In both cases power is not the simple possession of certain individuals or groups; rather, it is omnipresent, constitutive as much as constraining, expressed through the tissue of our personal and institutional lives. But whereas the forms of administrative power discussed in *Discipline and Punish* construct individuals as objects, the discursive constructions of sex construct us as subjects in what we take to be our freedom, the expression of our desire. As we struggle against what we have learned to call repression, we speak our desire in terms that construct it—and us—according to a distinctively modern regime, even as we take ourselves to be striving toward the liberation of timelessly human wants and needs.

I want to use Foucault to bring together Descartes and Schreber. With the success of the economic, social, cultural, and political revolutions that empowered the Cartesian subject,[22] the discipline Descartes called for moved from being the self-conscious work of

self-constituting radicals to finding expression in the pedagogy of the privileged.[23] The soul-shaping regimes of the elder Schreber are a particularly stark version of that pedagogy, which finds coded expression in the *Memoirs* of Freud's Schreber and a chilling critique in the works of Alice Miller.

Morton Schatzman's *Soul Murder* is a detailed argument for the thesis that Schreber's *Memoirs* recount in coded form what his father did to him when he was a child. Daniel Gottlieb Moritz Schreber wrote prolifically about child-rearing regimes aimed at suppressing a child's will and replacing it with automatic obedience to the will of the parent while simultaneously inculcating in the child enormous powers of self-control, which the child was to exercise over his or her own body and desires. That is, the goal was not an attitude of subservient obedience, such that children would have no idea of what they were to do until commanded by their parents. Rather, the child's will was to be replaced by the will of the parent in such a way that the child would not notice (or, at least, would not remember[24]) that this was done and would henceforth act "autonomously," as though the now-internalized commands came from her or his own true self. And that commanding self needs precisely not to be weak and unassertive, charged as it is with keeping under control the child's unruly body, emotions, and desires.

Not surprisingly, prominent among the desires and unruly impulses that need to be kept under control are those connected with masturbation and sexual curiosity. Foucault's characterization of modern Europe as hardly silent about sexuality is borne out by Miller's examples of instructional techniques for extracting from children confessions of masturbation (*For Your Own Good*, pp. 18–21) and of arguments that sexual curiosity needs to be (albeit perhaps fraudulently) satisfied, lest it grow obsessive. One recommended means is to have children view naked corpses, because "the sight of a corpse evokes solemnity and reflection, and this is the most appropriate mood for a child under such circumstances" (*For Your Own Good*, p. 46). J. Oest, whose advice this was in 1787, also advised "that children be cleansed from head to foot every two to four weeks by an old, dirty, and ugly woman, without anyone else being present; still, parents should make sure that even this old woman doesn't linger unnecessarily over any part of the body. This task should be depicted to the children as disgusting, and they should be told that the old woman must be paid to undertake a task that, although necessary for purposes of health and cleanliness, is yet so disgusting that no other person can bring himself to do it" (*For Your Own Good*, pp. 46–47).

Miller quotes extensively from the elder Schreber as well as from these and other, similar eighteenth- and nineteenth-century pedagogues who counseled parents on how, for example, "exercises can aid in the complete suppression of affect" (*For Your Own Good*, p. 25; the counsel comes from J. Sulzer, whose *Essay on the Education and Instruction of Children* was published in German in 1748). The same theorist made it clear that such suppression of autonomy was not intended only or even primarily for those whose place in society was subordinate: "Obedience is so important that all education is actually nothing other than learning how to obey. It is a generally recognized principle that persons of high estate who are destined to rule whole nations must learn the art of governance by way of first learning obedience.... [T]he reason for this is that obedience teaches a person to be zealous in observing the law, which is the first quality of the ruler" (*For Your Own Good*, pp. 13–14).

The choreography of will breaking and will strengthening has one additional turn: The shaping fiction of the enterprise is that the unruliness of children, however omnipresent, is nonetheless unnatural. In Schreber's words: "The noble seeds of human nature sprout upwards in their purity almost of their own accord if the ignoble ones, the weeds, are sought out and destroyed in time."[25] Thus the parental will that replaces the child's is in fact more truly expressive of the child's true nature than was the "bad" will the child took to be her or his own. It is not just that children should come to think so.

All this is, of course, much more reminiscent of Kant than of Descartes. It is Kant who argued that our passions[26] are not expressive of our true, autonomous selves and, hence, that acting on them is neither morally right nor autonomous, and that those categories—the lawbound and the free—are actually identical. It is Kant who most clearly taught us to control our passions and to identify with a self that we experience not as idiosyncratic but as speaking in the voice of impartial reason. Descartes, on the other hand, seems far more human, more playful, more respectful of the body and the emotions, more intrigued by the diversity in the world around him, more—and this is the crucial difference—antiauthoritarian than Kant.

As, of course, he was. He was in the midst of making the revolution that the pedagogues and Kant inherited, and it was a revolution precisely against entrenched authority, a revolution waged in the name of the individual. There is an exhilaration that even today's undergraduates can find in reading Descartes; he can speak, for example, to the woman student who is in the midst of discovering for herself that she has been systematically lied to about the world and her place in it, that authorities she had trusted disagree with each other and that none of them seems to have it right, and that even her own body can be untrustworthy: She may, for example, find food repulsive because even as she becomes emaciated she sees herself as hideously fat, or she may have learned from a sexual abuser to desire her own humiliation.

But, I want to argue, the Descartes we have inherited (and, more broadly, the liberal politics his epistemology partially grounds) is a problematic ally for this young woman, as he is for the other women and men who have been the excluded Others.

Though he is not Kant, let alone Schreber (either the paranoid son or the "paranoidogenic"[27] father), the discipline of the Method that lies at the heart of Descartes's constitution of himself as epistemically authoritative bears the seeds of paranoia, seeds that germinated as the revolution he helped to inaugurate moved from marginality to hegemony.

As Freud argues, the central mechanism of paranoia is projection, that process by which something that had been recognized as a part of the self is detached from it (a process called "splitting") and reattached onto something or someone other than the self. An underlying motivation for such splitting is narcissism: What is split off is incompatible with the developing ego. But it is significant to note that one obvious effect is the diminution of the self—it no longer contains something it once did. One consequence of that recognition is that it provides a motivation for thinking of that which is split off as wholly bad, perhaps even worse than it was thought to be when it was first split off. It has to be clear that the self really is better off without it.

This is one way of thinking about the fate of the body in Cartesian and post-Cartesian epistemology. The self of the cogito establishes its claim to authority precisely by its separation from the body, a separation that is simultaneously liberating and totally isolating. Although Descartes goes on, under the protection of God, to reclaim his body and to place himself in intimate and friendly relation to it, the loss to the self remains: René Descartes, along with all those who would follow his Method, really is a *res cogitans*, not a sensual, bodily person. One can glimpse the magnitude of the loss in Descartes's attempts to theorize his relationship to the body he calls his own, an attempt he ultimately abandons,[28] but the full force of it is found elsewhere, when the demand that one separate from and control one's body is joined both to Christian associations of the body with sin and to the pedagogical practices that replaced Descartes's self-conscious self-constitution.

It became impossible to empower the mind without disempowering and stigmatizing the body, or, in Foucauldian terms, anatomizing, administering, scrutinizing, and disciplining it. The body Descartes regains and bequeaths to his heirs is mechanical, not the lived body but the object of scientific practices, a body best known by being, after its death, dissected. It became the paradigmatic object in an epistemology founded on a firm and unbridgeable subject-object distinction....[29]

The Cartesian God—the poisonously pedagogical parent, seen by the successfully reared child as wholly benevolent—conscripts the infinite will of the privileged son and sets it the task of "autonomously" disciplining the body, the perceptions, and the passions, with the promised reward being the revelation of guaranteed truths and the power that goes with knowledge. ...

Such a self, privileged by its estrangement from its own body, from the "external" world, and from other people, will, in a culture that defines such estrangements as normal, express the paranoia of such a stance not only through oppression but, more benignly, through the problems that are taken as the most fundamental, even if not the most practically pressing: the problems of philosophy. Those problems—notably, the mind-body problem, problems of reference and truth, the problem of other minds, and scepticism about knowledge of the external world—all concern the subject's ability or inability to connect with the split-off parts of itself—its physicality, its sociability. Such problems are literally and unsurprisingly unsolvable so long as the subject's very identity is constituted by those estrangements. A subject whose authority is defined by his location on one side of a gulf cannot authoritatively theorize that gulf away. Philosophers' problems are the neuroses of privilege; discipline makes the difference between such problems and the psychosis of full-blown paranoia.

Beyond Madness and Method

The new *mestiza* copes by developing a tolerance for ambiguity. ... She has a plural personality, she operates in a pluralistic mode—nothing is thrust out, the good, the bad and the ugly, nothing rejected, nothing abandoned.[30]

The alternative to relativism is partial, locatable, critical knowledges sustaining the possibility of webs of connections called solidarity in politics and shared conversations in epistemology.[31]

The authorized subject thus achieves and maintains his authority by his ability to keep his body and the rest of the world radically separated from his ego, marked off from it by policed boundaries.[32] Within those boundaries, the self is supposed to be unitary and seamless, characterized by the doxastic virtue of noncontradiction and the moral virtue of integrity. The social mechanisms of privilege aid in the achievement of those virtues by facilitating splitting and projection: the unity of the privileged self is maintained by the dumping out of the self—onto the object world or onto the different, the stigmatized Others—everything that would disturb its pristine wholeness.

Various contemporary theorists are articulating alternative conceptions of subjectivity, conceptions that start from plurality and diversity, not just among but, crucially, within subjects.[33] From that starting point flow radically transformed relationships between subjects and between subjects and the world they would know.

One way to approach these discussions is to return to Freud. Mental health for Freud consisted in part in the acknowledgment by the ego of the impulses of the id: "Where id was, there ego shall be."[34] The German is more striking than the English: The German words for 'ego' and 'id' are 'ich' and 'es';[35] the sense is "Where *it* was, there *I* shall be." One can take this in two ways. Under the sorts of disciplinary regimes that constitute epistemic privilege, the exhortation has a colonizing ring to it. The not-I needs to be brought under the civilizing control of the ego; the aim is not to split it off but to tame it. Splitting represents the failure of colonization, the loss of will for the task of domestication. The healthy ego is unified not because it has cast out parts of itself, but because it has effectively administered even the formerly unruly outposts of its dominion. Or so goes the story one is supposed to tell. (Any splitting goes unacknowledged.)

There is another way to take Freud's exhortation. The aim might be not to colonize the "it" but to break down the distinction between "it" and "I," between object and subject. "Where it was, there I shall be," not because I am colonizing it, but because where I am is always shifting. As Nancy Chodorow puts it, in giving an object-relational alternative to the classical Freudian account, "Where fragmented internal objects were, there shall harmoniously related objects be."[36] Moving becomes not the installment of oneself astride the Archimedean point, the self-made man taming the frontier of the "New World," but the sort of "World" travel María Lugones discusses as the ground of what she calls, following Marilyn Frye, "loving perception."[37] By putting ourselves in settings in which we are perceived as—and hence are able (or unable not) to be—different people from who we are at home, we learn about ourselves, each other, and the world. And part of what we learn is that the unity of the self is an illusion of privilege, as when, to use Lugones's example (from a talk she gave at the University of Minnesota), we think there is a natural, unmediated connection between intention, will, and action, because if we are privileged, the world collaborates with us, making it all work, apparently seamlessly, and giving us the credit. As Frye puts it, we are trained not to notice the stagehands, all those whose labor enables the play to proceed smoothly.[38]

What is problematic about Descartes's Faustian gesture is not the idea that the world is in some sense our creation. Rather, it is on the one hand the individualism of the construction (or, what comes to the same thing, the unitary construction by all and only those who count as the same, the not-different) and on the other the need to deny any construction, to maintain the mutual independence of the self and the world. Realism ought not to require such independence on the side of the world, any more than rationality ought to require it on the side of the knowing subject, if by realism we mean the recognition that the world may not be the way anyone (or any group, however powerful) thinks it is and if by rationality we mean ways of learning and teaching that are reliably useful in collective endeavors.

Philosophical realism has typically stressed the independence of the world from those who would know it, a formulation that, at least since Kant, has been linked with the intractability of scepticism. But it's hard to see exactly why independence should be what is required. A world that exists in complex interdependence with those who know it (who are, of course, also part of it) is nonetheless real. Lots of real things are not independent of what we think about them, without being just what anyone or any group takes them to be—the economy, to take just one obvious example. The interdependencies are real, as are the entities and structures shaped by them. One way we know they are real is precisely that they look different to those differently placed in relation to them. (There aren't a variety of diverse takes on my hallucinations.) The only way to take diversity of perspectives seriously is to be robustly realistic, both about the world viewed and about the material locations of those doing the viewing. Archimedean, difference-denying epistemology ought to be seen as incompatible with such a robust realism: How could there possibly be one account of a world shaped in interaction with subjects so diversely constituted and with such diverse interests in constructing and knowing it?

A specifically Cartesian feature of the conception of the world as independent is the world as inanimate, and consequently not reciprocally engaged in the activities through which it comes to be known. Thus, for example, the social sciences, which take as their objects bearers of subjectivity and the entities and structures they create, have been seen as scientifically deficient precisely because of the insufficiently independent status of what they study. (The remedy for such deficiency has typically been the dehumanizing objectification of the "subjects" of the social sciences, an objectification especially damaging when those subjects have been otherwise oppressed.) But it's far from obvious that being inert should make something more knowable: Why not take 'subject' and 'object' to name not ontological categories but reciprocal, shifting positions? Why not think of knowledge emerging paradigmatically in mutual interaction, so that what puzzles us is how to account not for the objectivity of the social sciences but for the intersubjectivity of the natural sciences?[39]

In a discussion of the problems from an African-American perspective, with the critical legal theorists' rejection of rights, Patricia Williams suggests that rather than discarding rights,

> society must *give* them away. Unlock them from reification by giving them to slaves. Give them to trees. Give them to cows. Give them to history. Give them to rivers and rocks. Give to all of society's objects and untouchables the rights of privacy, integrity, and self-assertion; give them distance and respect. Flood them with the animating spirit that rights mythology fires in this country's most oppressed psyches, and wash away the shrouds of inanimate-object status.[40]

One might respond similarly to the suggestion from postmodernist quarters that we discard subjectivity and agency; rather, we should profligately give them away and invest the things of the world with subjectivity, with the ability and interest to return our gaze.[41] Realism can mean that we see ourselves as inhabiting a world in which the likes of us (whoever we may be) are not the only sources of meaning, that we see ourselves as implicated in, reciprocated by, the world.

The world as real is the world as precisely not dead or mechanistic; the world as trickster, as protean, is always slipping out from under our best attempts to pin it down.[42] The real world is not the world of our best physics but the world that defeats any physics that would be final, that would desire to be the last word, "the end of the story, the horizon of interpretation, the end of 'the puzzlement,'" a desire Paul Smith calls "claustrophilic."[43] Donna Haraway imaginatively sketches an epistemology for the explicitly partial, fragmentary, ununified knowers we are and need to be if we are to move within and learn from the complexities of the world and the complexities of how we are constructed in it. As she puts it, "Splitting, not being, is the privileged image for feminist epistemologies of scientific knowledge" ("Situated Knowledges," p. 586).

A trickster reality is thus matched by a trickster subjectivity, a subjectivity that finds expression in African and Afro-American oral and written traditions. In *The Signifying Monkey*, Henry Louis Gates, Jr., builds "a theory of African-American literary criticism" (the book's subtitle) on the ground of Afro-American vernacular traditions.[44] Literature, the written word, was the privileged site for the attainment and display of Enlightenment rationality, the place for former slaves and the descendants of slaves to stake a claim to full membership in the human community. The signifying monkey and other traditional African trickster figures from oral traditions are for Gates a way of exploring the simultaneous appropriations and subversions of the site of writing, the attempts of Afro-American writers not to mimic the texts of the masters but to write themselves and their communities into history and culture by transforming the nature of writing itself, by giving voice to the written word. Gates's central trope of "Signifyin(g)" complexly spins a story about the multivocality of Afro-American texts, the weaving of vernacular voices into literature, and the subversions, parodies, and appropriations of earlier texts. Even when the singular voice is seen as a desirable ideal, its achievement is never a simple matter, never seen as a birthright; there are always other voices playing around the edges of the text.

The unity of privileged subjectivity is mirrored in the demand that language be transparent, a demand most explicit in the now-discredited ideal languages of the logical positivists but lingering in the demands of present-day analytic philosophers for (a certain picture of) clarity, as though the point of language was to be seen through. When June Jordan writes of Black English that one of its hallmarks is "clarity: If the sentence is not clear it's not Black English," she might seem to be endorsing such a demand, but the clarity she extols is contextual and "person-centered": "If your idea, your sentence, assumes the presence of at least two living and active people, you will make it understandable because the motivation behind every sentence is the wish to say something real to somebody real."[45] The clarity of analytic philosophy, by contrast, is best exhibited in argumentative contexts, detached from the specificities of anyone's voice, in avoidance of ad hominem and other genetic fallacies. The clarity of Black English, Jordan explains, is grounded in the rhythms and intonations of speech, in the immediacy of the present indicative, and in an abhorrence of abstraction and the eschewal of the passive (non)voice: It is the clarity of illumination, not of the transparent medium. In contrast to the language of philosophy, which assumes its adequacy as a vessel for fully translatable meaning, Black English does not take its authority for granted. It is a language "constructed by people constantly needing to insist that we exist, that we are present."[46] It aims not at transparent representation but at subversive transformation; it is an act of intervention, used by communities of resistance and used within those communities for collective self-constitution.

There are many other theorists of trickster subjectivity. Gloria Anzaldúa, for example, in *Borderlands/La Frontera* writes in a combination of English and Spanish, refusing the demand to choose one or another "pure" language, as she moves along and across the borders that are supposed to define and separate, finding/creating herself by refusing the definitions and separations.

Teresa de Lauretis finds in some women's films a challenge to the unity of the subject. For example, Lizzie Borden's *Born in Flames* discomfits some privileged women viewers precisely in its not addressing them alone, in its not (re)presenting the women of color in the film *to* them but, rather, addressing an audience of women as diverse as the women on the screen. There is no unitary viewer for the film, a move that de Lauretis takes to express the feminist understanding "that the female subject is engendered, constructed and defined in gender across multiple representations of class, race, language, and social relations; and that, therefore, differences among women are differences *within* women."[47]

In *The American Evasion of Philosophy,* Cornel West finds in pragmatism a challenge to the Enlightenment that can make room for a historical subject constituted otherwise than by the norms of European epistemology.[48] He sees what he calls "prophetic pragmatism" as an intellectual stance for liberationist struggles, in part because of its inheritance from earlier pragmatists, notably Dewey, of a rejection of foundationalism and individualism and an openness to the "fluidity, plurality, and diversity of experience" (*American Evasion*, p. 91). Knowledge and the knowing subject emerge together from continuous engagement with the world; such engagement (with our actual lives at stake) and not the abstractions of epistemology ought to be the stuff of our reflection.[49]

There is, however, an obvious problem with taking splitting and internal multiplicity as the hallmarks of liberatory subjectivity. The most striking and clear-cut cases of internal multiplicity are cases of multiple personality, a pathological condition typically caused by severe childhood abuse, that is, by the most poisonous of pedagogies.[50] Recent clinical work with people with multiple personalities suggests such multiplicity is a means of coping with the terror and pain of the child's situation.[51] Part of that coping consists in a protective amnesia of what the child can neither stop nor understand nor tell anyone about. Consequently the lines of communication between the different selves become blocked, and some of the relations between them become antagonistic as some of the selves adopt coping strategies that are at odds with those of others. Multiple personality, on such a view, is a comprehensible, perhaps even rational, response to an intolerable situation, a way of maintaining some degree of agency in the face of profoundly soul-destroying attacks on one's ability to construct a sense of self. Such construction, throughout life, but especially when one is a child, proceeds interactively. We all are, to use Annette Baier's term "second persons,"[52] and when those we most trust to mirror us abuse that trust, the conditions for wholeness are shattered.

In reflecting on the experiences of "multiples," Claudia Card (to whom I owe much of this discussion) suggests that we can see the main difference between them and the rest of us as lying not in their internal multiplicity but in the amnesia that both guards it and keeps it at odds. Therapy can succeed not by integrating all the personalities into one, or by making all but one go away, but by creating the possibility for respectful conversation among them, facilitating their mutual recognition and acceptance. Analogously with oppressed communities, Card argues, multiples are internally in strife, unable to confront those who have damaged them, needing not seamless unity but effective alliance building.[53] They need from trusted others a mirror of themselves not as unitary but as united, which requires, in part, that those others be committed to the joint survival of all the selves they are and to at least some of the projects in which those selves might engage, either jointly or individually, with mutual respect.

Such an account parallels María Lugones's account of her experiences as a "multiplicitous being," a U.S. Latina lesbian who could not be unitary without killing off a crucial part of who she is, without betraying both herself and others with whom she identifies and for whom she cares.[54] Without identification with and engagement in struggle within *la cultura hispana Nuevomejicana*, the imperiled community in which she "has found her grounding," she risks becoming "culturally obsolete," but as a lesbian within that culture, she is not a lover of women—she is an "abomination." Needing to be both of the very different people she is in the *Nuevomejicana* and lesbian cultures, she works not for unity but for connection, for the not-to-be-taken-for-granted understanding of each of her selves by the other, understanding that is cultivated by work in the "borderlands," "the understanding of liminals." Victoria Davion contends that it is such connection that can ground a conception of integrity that does justice—as she argues any usable feminist notion of integrity must—to the experiences of multiplicitous beings,[55] and it is just that connection that it would seem multiple personalities need to acquire within/among themselves.

Thus we can see the splitting characteristic of multiple personality as a response to oppression that needs resolution by the achievement not of unity but of mutual respect, an achievement that requires the loving collaboration of others. On this view, such splitting is the most striking example of a far more common phenomenon, seen also in experiences such as those María Lugones theorizes. I want to suggest that, without blurring the specificities of such experiences, we can recognize that the experiences even of those who identify with dominant cultures can lead, in different ways, to multiplicitous identities. Gloria Anzaldúa, for example, stresses the importance for *mestizas* of the acceptance of all of who they are, "the white parts, the male parts, the queer parts, the vulnerable parts."[56] But she equally calls for such self-acceptance on the part of the privileged, as the only alternative to the splitting and projection, that underwrite domination: "Admit that Mexico is your double, that we are irrevocably tied to her. Gringo, accept the doppelganger in your psyche. By taking back your collective shadow the intracultural split will heal" (*Borderlands/La Frontera*, p. 86).

Erica Sherover-Marcuse suggests that all children are subject to what she calls 'adultism,' a form of mistreatment which targets all young people who are born into an oppressive society.[57] Such mistreatment, she argues, is "the 'training ground' for other forms of oppression," a crucial part of the socialization of some as oppressor, some as oppressed, and most of us into complex combinations of both. Central to such socialization is its normalization, the denial of its traumatic nature, the forgetting of the pain; and central to emancipation is "a labor of *affective remembrance*."[58] Alice Miller argues similarly in *For Your Own Good* that those who have been abused become abusers, and her account focuses on the mechanisms of splitting and projection: "Children who have grown up being assailed for qualities the parents hate in themselves can hardly wait to assign those qualities to someone else so they can once again regard themselves as good, 'moral,' noble, and altruistic" (p.91).

The abuse of which Alice Miller writes, which ranges from the normative to the horrific, shares the requirement of amnesia, which means that the split-off parts of the self, whether they be the survival-ensuring "alters" of the multiple or the stigmatized Others of the privileged, are empathically inaccessible. What Sherover-Marcuse calls "an emancipatory practice of subjectivity" (*Emancipation and*

Consciousness, p. 140) requires memory, connection, and the learning of respect for the Others that we are and for the Others outside of us. Schreber, as privileged jurist and as incarcerated madman, emblematizes the victimized child who grows up to become the dominating adult, the possessor of power—power that is real enough (as is the privilege it secures) but that rests on a history of abuse. As long as we hold on to the ideal of the self as a seamless unity, we will not only be marginalizing the experiences of those like Maria Lugones and Gloria Anzaldúa, for whom such unity could only be bought at the price of self-betrayal, but we will be fundamentally misrepresenting the experiences of even the most privileged among us, whose apparent unity was bought at the price of the projection onto stigmatized Others of the split-off parts of themselves that they were taught to despise.

As Quine has persuasively argued,[59] epistemology cannot come from thin air: To naturalize epistemology is to acknowledge that we need to study how actual people actually know. But one thing we ought to know about actual people is that they inhabit a world of systematic inequality, in which authority—centrally including epistemic authority—is systematically given to some and withheld from others. If our interest is in changing that world, we need to look critically at the terms of epistemic authority. Certainly there is no reason why those who have historically been dominated by the epistemology of modernity—the objects to its subjects—should accept the terms of that epistemology as the only route to empowerment.

That epistemology presents itself as universal, a universal defined by precisely that which is not different in the ways that some are defined as different: women (not men), people of color (not white people), the disabled (not the able-bodied), gays and lesbians (not heterosexuals). To again echo Foucault, none of these categories is natural or ahistorical, and they all came into existence as strategies of regimentation and containment. They all represent aspects of the multiple, shifting, unstable ways that people can be, aspects that have been split off from the psyches from the psyches of the privileged, projected onto the bodies of others, and concretized as identities. The privileged, in turn, having shucked off what would threaten their sense of control, theorize their own subjectivity (which they name generically human) as unitary and transparent to consciousness and characterized by integrity and consistency. Not only is such subjectivity a myth; its logic is that of paranoia.[60]

Notes

1. Morton White, "The Politics of Epistemology," *Ethics* 100 (October 1989): 77–92.

2. See Genevieve Lloyd, *The Man of Reason* (Minneapolis: University of Minnesota Press, 1984); Susan Bordo, *The Flight to Objectivity: Essays on Cartesianism and Culture* (Albany: SUNY Press, 1987); my "Othello's Doubt/Desdemona's Death: The Engendering of Scepticism," in *Power, Gender, Values,* ed. Judith Genova (Edmonton, Alberta: Academic Printing and Publishing, 1987); and Jacquelyn Zita, "Transsexualized Origins: Reflections on Descartes's *Meditations,*" *Genders* 5 (Summer 1989): 86–105.

3. Daniel Paul Schreber, *Memoirs of My Nervous Illness,* tr. and ed. Ida Macalpine and Richard A. Hunter (Cambridge, Mass.: Harvard University Press, 1988); Sigmund Freud, "Psycho-Analytic Notes upon an Autobiographical Account of a Case of Paranoia (Dementia Paranoides)," *Standard Edition* , (hereafter *SE*), 12:9–82 (London: Hogarth Press, 1958).

4. Alice Miller, *For Your Own Good: Hidden Cruelty in Child-Rearing and the Roots of Violence,* tr. Hildegarde Hannum and Hunter Hannum (New York: Farrar, Straus, and Giroux, 1984), P.91.

5. Jean-Paul Sartre, *Anti-Semite and Jew,* quoted in Erica Sherover-Marcuse, *Emancipation and Consciousness: Dogmatic and Dialectical Perspectives in the Early Marx* (Oxford: Basil Blackwell, 1986), p. 158.

6. Morton Schatzman, *Soul Murder: Persecution in the Family* (New York: Random House, 1973).

7. Miller, *For Your Own Good*.

8. It is antipsychoanalytic in the manner of Jeffrey Moussaieff Masson's later but better known work, *The Assault on Truth: Freud's Suppression of the Seduction Theory* (New York: Faffar, Straus, and Giroux, 1984), i.e., in reading patients' reports and symptoms as expressions not of fantasies but of what was actually done to them as children.

9. Freud's account is almost entirely in masculine terms, but here, as elsewhere, he took his analysis to apply also to women, *mutatis mutandis*. As I will go on to argue, the phenomena he describes are, in fact, wholly gender inflected and are grounded in distinctively masculine experiences.

10. Molefi Kete Asante, *The Afrocentric Idea* (Philadelphia: Temple University Press, 1987) p.4.

11. Cartesian philosophy was, in fact, influential on and in some ways empowering for contemporary feminists. See Ruth Perry, "Radical Doubt and the Liberation of Women," *Eighteenth-Century Studies* 18 (1985): 472–493.

12. Descartes, Meditation 4, in *The Philosophical Writings of Descartes*, 2 vols. tr. John Cottingham and Dugald Murdoch (Cambridge: Cambridge University Press, 1985), p. 40 (hereafter C&M).

13. Meditation 1, C&M, 2:15.

14. Descartes, *The Passions of the Soul*, pt. III, sec. 211, C&M, 1:403.

15. Descartes, *Discourse on the Method*, pt. II, C&M, 1:116–117.

16. On Pyrrhonist and Montaignean skepticism, see Richard Popkin, *The History of Scepticism from Erasmus to Descartes* (New York: Humanities Press, 1960).

17. See Margaret Dauler Wilson, *Descartes* (London: Routledge and Kegan Paul, 1978), pp. 17–31.

18. Freud, "Notes on a Case of Paranoia," *SE*, 12:70. The quote is from Part 1, Scene 4 of *Faust*.

19. Paul Smith, *Discerning the Subject* (Minneapolis: University of Minnesota Press, 1988), p. 98. Smith's parallels between paranoia and what he calls "humanist epistemology," which I came across in the final stages of writing this paper, are very similar to mine, as is his aim to articulate a conception of human subjectivity and agency that is politically and socially usable.

20. See my "From Hamlet to Maggie Verver: The History and Politics of the Knowing Subject," *Poetics* 18 (1989): 449–469 and "Missing Mothers/Desiring Daughters: Framing the Sight of Women," *Critical Inquiry* 15 (1988): 62–89.

21. Barry Stroud, *The Significance of Philosophical Scepticism* (New York: Oxford University Press, 1984), p.x.

22. See, e.g., Francis Barker, *The Tremulous Private Body: Essays on Subjection* (London: Methuen, 1984), for an account of the emergence of the distinctively modern subject.

23. The echo of Paulo Freire's *Pedagogy of the Oppressed* is intentional. Freire's aim is to develop an explicit pedagogy that will be empowering to those who are currently oppressed; I want to examine the implicit pedagogy that actually empowers the currently privileged.

24. Alice Miller stresses the importance for the success of "poisonous pedagogy" that its victims not have any memory of what was done to them, that they never see their parents as anything other than good and loving. My discussion draws heavily on her *For Your Own Good*.

25. Quoted in Miller, *For Your Own Good*, p. 90; from Schatzman, *Soul Murder*, p. 19, quoting Schreber.

26. But we should not obliterate them. Kant suggests, for example, that we should visit places that house the poor and the ill to reinvigorate in ourselves sympathetic feelings that can be enlisted on the side of motivating us to do what duty commands. Immanuel Kant, *The Doctrine of Virtue: Part II of the Metaphysics of Morals*, tr. Mary J. Gregor (Philadelphia: University of Pennsylvania Press, 1964), sec. 35, p. 126.

27. The term is Schatzman's, *Soul Murder*, p, 137.

28. For the attempt, see Descartes, Meditation 6, C&M, 1: 56–57; the Fourth Set of Replies (to Arnauld), C&M, 2:60; Sixth Set of Replies (to Mersenne), C&M, 2:297–299. For further attempts and, in the face of Princess Elizabeth's persistent questioning, his abandonment of the possibility of getting a rationally grounded theoretical account of the union of mind and body, see Deseartes's Letters IX (a and b) and X (a and b) to Princess Elizabeth, in *Descartes: Philosophical Writings*, ed. Elizabeth Anscombe and Peter Thomas Geach (Indianapolis: Bobbs Merrill, 1954).

29. Barker, *Tremulous Private Body*. See also my "From Hamlet to Maggie Verver."

30. Gloria Anzaldúa, *Borderlands/La Frontera: The New Mestiza* (San Francisco: Spinsters/ Aunt Lute, 1987), p.79.

31. Donna Haraway, "Situated Knowledges: The Science Question in Feminism and the Privilege of Partial Perspective," *Feminist Studies* 14, 3 (Fall 1988): 584.

32. Firm ego boundaries are typically taken as a measure of mental health: One is supposed to be clear about where one's self leaves off and the rest of the world begins. An alternative view—that part of mental health, or of an adequate epistemology, consists in the acceptance of a sizable intermediate domain—has been developed by the object relations theorist D. W. Winnicott. For a discussion of the relevance of his work to feminist theory, see Keller, *Reflections on Gender and Science*, pp. 83, 99–102; and Jane Flax, *Thinking Fragments: Psychoanalysis, Feminism, and Postmodernism in the Contemporary West* (Berkeley/Los Angeles: University of California Press, 1990), pp. 116–132.

33. Sandra Harding and Donna Haraway are two such theorists, who also give excellent overviews of work in this area. See, especially, Haraway, "Situated Knowledges," 575–599; and Harding, "Reinventing Ourselves as Other: More New Agents of History and Knowledge," in Harding, *Whose Science? Whose Knowledge? Thinking from Women's Lives* (Ithaca, N.Y.: Cornell University Press, 1991), pp. 268–295. See also three papers in which Maria Lugones develops a pluralistic theory of identity: "Playfulness, 'World'-Traveling, and Loving Perception," *Hypatia* 2, 2 (Summer 1987): 3–19; "Hispaneando y Lesbiando: On Sarah Hoagland's *Lesbian Ethics*," *Hypatia* 5, 3 (Fall 1990): 138–146; and "On the Logic of Pluralist Feminism," in *Feminist Ethics*, ed. Claudia Card (Lawrence: University Press of Kansas, 1991), pp. 35–44.

34. Freud, *New Introductory Lectures on Psychoanalysis*, SE, 22: 80.

35. See Bruno Bettelheim, *Freud and Man's Soul* (New York: A. A. Knopf, 1983). The *New Introductory Lectures* were originally written in English, but the point still holds: Freud used the English of his translators.

36. Nancy Chodorow, "Toward a Relational Individualism: The Mediation of Self Through Psychoanalysis," in *Reconstructing Individualism: Autonomy, Individuality, and the Self in Western*

Thought ed. Thomas C. Heller, Morton Sosna, and David E. Wellbey (Stanford, Calif.: Stanford University Press, 1986), pp. 197–207.

37. Lugones, "Playfulness, 'World'-Traveling, and Loving Perception"; Frye, "In and Out of Harm's Way."

38. Frye, "To Be and Be Seen," *Politics of Reality*, pp. 167–173.

39. For a start on such an account, as well as an argument for why we should seek one, see Lorraine Code, W*hat Can She Know? Feminist Theory and the Construction of Knowledge* (Ithaca, N.Y.: Cornell University Press, 1991), esp. chs. 3 and 4; and Sandra Harding, *Whose Science? Whose Knowledge?* Esp. ch. 4.

40. Patricia J. Williams, *The Alchemy of Race and Rights: Diary of a Law Professor* (Cambridge, Mass.: Harvard University Press, 1991), p. 165.

41. See Rainer Maria Rilke's "Archaic Torso of Apollo": "There Is no place / that does not see you. You must change your life." *Translations from the Poetry of Rainer Maria Rilke*, tr. M. D. Herter Norton (New York: W. W. Norton, 1938).

42. Haraway, "Situated Knowledges," p. 596.

43. Smith, *Discerning the Subject* p. 98.

44. Henry Louis Gates, Jr., *The Signifying Monkey: A Theory of African-American Literary Criticism* (New York/Oxford: Oxford University Press, 1988).

45. June Jordan, "Nobody Mean More to Me than You/And the Future Life of Willie Jordan," in *On Call: Political Essays* (Boston: South End Press, 1985), pp. 129–130. Such accounts make evident the Eurocentrism of deconstructive sorties against such notions as presence, voice, and authorship. See, for example, Jacques Derrida, "Plato's Pharmacy," in his *Dissemination*, tr. Barbara Johnson (Chicago: University of Chicago Press, 1981).

46. Jordan, "Nobody Mean More to Me than You," p. 129.

47. Teresa de Lauretis, "Rethinking Women's Cinema: Aesthetics and Feminist Theory," in *Technologies of Gender: Essays on Theory, Film, and Fiction* (Bloomington: Indiana University Press, 1987), p. 139.

48. West, *American Evasion of Philosophy.*

49. George Herbert Mead has also inspired theorists of subjectivity concerned with sociality and internal diversity. See, in particular, Karen

Hanson, *The Self Imagined: Philosophical Reflections on the Social Character of Psyche* (New York: Routledge and Kegan Paul, 1986); and Catherine Keller, *From a Broken Web: Separation, Sexism, and Self* (Boston: Beacon Press, 1986).

50. Thanks to Louise Antony for stressing the importance of dealing with these issues.

51. "Dissociative Disorder," *Diagnostic and Statistical Manual of Mental Disorders,* 3d ed., rev. (Washington, D.C.: American Psychiatric Association, 1987), 269–279.

52. Annette Baier, "Cartesian Persons," in *Postures of the Mind: Essays on Mind and Morals* (Minneapolis: University of Minnesota Press, 1985), pp. 74–92. See also the chapter on "Second Persons" in Code, *What Can She Know?* pp. 71–109.

53. Claudia Card, "Responsibility and Moral Luck: Resisting Oppression and Abuse," manuscript, 1989.

54. Lugones, "Hispaneando y Lesbiando."

55. Victoria M. Davion, "Integrity and Radical Change," in Card, ed., *Feminist Ethics,* pp. 180–192.

56. Anzaldúa, *Borderlands/La Frontera,* p. 88.

57. Sherover-Marcuse, *Emancipation and Consciousness,* p. 139.

58. Ibid., p. 140. Emphasis in original.

59. W. V. Quine, "Epistemology Naturalized," *Ontological Relativity and Other Essays* (New York: Columbia University Press, 1969).

60. Louise Antony's detailed and erudite response to an earlier draft was a model of friendly, feminist criticism: It is a rare thing to have one's writing so thoroughly disagreed with and at the same time taken so seriously and with so much care. Ruth Wood was, as usual, of enormous help in clarifying the convolutions.